MADNESS
IN CIVILIZATION

Praise for *Madness in Civilization*

'Andrew Scull's fluent mastery of the history of madness has long been established. In this engrossing volume, he gives us the long view of how reason has understood and treated unreason. Aided by a telling and sumptuous array of images, he takes us from ancient Greece, early Christianity and Islam through science, secularization and Freud, to the brain sciences and pharmacopoeias of the present. It's a story filled with good intentions and punctuated by greed. Flashes of wisdom war with cures that are far madder than patients. Some two thousand years of journeying and it's unclear whether the chemical asylum we've arrived at is any better than its bricks and mortar precedent. This is history at its best, scintillating in its detail and passionate about a subject that concerns us all.'

Lisa Appignanesi, author of *Mad, Bad and Sad: A History of Women and the Mind Doctors from 1800 to the Present* and *Trials of Passion: Crimes in the Name of Love and Madness*

'A wonderful book, fascinating and beautifully written, with Scull's usual verve and erudition. *Madness in Civilization* explores how ancient and medieval societies coped with psychosis and shows that, brain imaging and psychotropic drugs notwithstanding, modern psychiatry has much to learn from them.'

Sylvia Nasar, author of *A Beautiful Mind*

'An engaging, learned and wonderfully thought-provoking history of human efforts to understand and manage those behaviours we call mad. An uncommon combination of learning and accessible writing, I would recommend Scull's admirable book to anyone interested in this "most solitary of afflictions".'

Charles Rosenberg, Professor of the History of Science, Harvard University, author of *Our Present Complaint: American Medicine, Then and Now*

'Andrew Scull is probably our most knowledgeable and certainly most readable historian of madness. In his new book, the magisterial *Madness in Civilization*, he presents a panoramic view of the subject that's both clear-eyed and critical. Crisply written, and furnished with a wealth of cultural and clinical reference, this is a great, tragic story.'

Patrick McGrath, author of *Asylum*

'Andrew Scull is the premier historian of psychiatry in the Anglophone world, and this book triumphantly demonstrates this. Taking a broad canvas, from antiquity to modernity, Scull dissects what madness has meant to societies throughout history and throughout the world. He writes with passion but humour, has a brilliant eye for a pungent quotation or a telling story, and holds the reader spellbound. This is a compelling book from a master of his craft.'

William Bynum, Professor Emeritus of the History of Medicine, University College London, editor of *Companion Encyclopedia of the History of Medicine*

'A work of heroic scholarship, an eloquent overview of the changing theories and treatments of madness from ancient religion, medicine and myth to contemporary neuroscience and psychopharmacology. Scull shows not only how writers, artists and composers have taken madness as a muse, but also how the shifting symbolic forms of unreason are truly part of its history. Compendious and compassionate.'

Elaine Showalter, Professor Emeritus, Princeton University, author of *The Female Malady*

'Dr Scull is one of the pre-eminent historians of psychiatry in the world today. There is almost no one else who could write a volume of this kind with the panache he brings to it, the ability to hold both a lay and an academic readership in thrall at the same time and the sense of balance and proportion that comes to some with experience but to others not at all. There is no other volume comparable to this in scope and this is a once in a generation effort.'

David Healy, Professor of Psychiatry, Bangor University, author of *Pharmageddon*

'*Madness in Civilization* is a brilliant, provocative and hugely entertaining history of the treatment and mistreatment of the mentally ill. Packed with bizarre details and disturbing facts, Andrew Scull's book offers fresh and compelling insights on the way medicine's inability to solve the mystery of madness has both haunted and shaped two thousand years of culture. Required reading for anyone who has ever gone to a shrink!'

Dirk Wittenborn, author of *Pharmakon*

Andrew Scull

MADNESS
IN CIVILIZATION

A Cultural History of Insanity
from the Bible to Freud,
from the Madhouse to Modern Medicine

With 128 illustrations,
44 in color

Princeton University Press
Princeton and Oxford

For Nancy, and for our grandchildren
born, and yet to be born

Comme quelqu'un pourrait dire de moi que j'ai seulement fait ici un amas
de fleurs étrangères, n'y ayant fourni du mien que le filet à les lier.

[As one might rightly say of me, in this book I have just created
a bouquet of other people's flowers, providing myself only
the thread that holds them together.]

Montaigne

Text on the front of the jacket: excerpt from pp. 224–26.

Frontispiece:
'Madness', from *The Anatomy and Philosophy of Expression,*
as Connected with the Fine Arts, by Sir Charles Bell (1844).

Published in the United States and Canada in 2015 by Princeton University Press,
41 William Street, Princeton, New Jersey 08540
press.princeton.edu

First published in the United Kingdom in 2015 by Thames & Hudson Ltd,
181A High Holborn, London WC1V 7QX
thamesandhudson.com

Madness in Civilization © 2015 Andrew Scull

Designed by Karolina Prymaka

Library of Congress Control Number 2014956046

ISBN 978-0-691-16615-5

Printed and bound in China by Everbest Printing Co. Ltd

10 9 8 7 6 5 4 3 2 1

CONTENTS

Acknowledgments 8

Chapter One
CONFRONTING MADNESS 10

Chapter Two
MADNESS IN THE ANCIENT WORLD 16

Chapter Three
THE DARKNESS AND THE DAWN 48

Chapter Four
MELANCHOLIE AND MADNESSE 86

Chapter Five
MADHOUSES AND MAD-DOCTORS 122

Chapter Six
NERVES AND NERVOUSNESS 162

Chapter Seven
THE GREAT CONFINEMENT 188

Chapter Eight
DEGENERATION AND DESPAIR 224

Chapter Nine
THE DEMI-FOUS 268

Chapter Ten
DESPERATE REMEDIES 290

Chapter Eleven
A MEANINGFUL INTERLUDE 322

Chapter Twelve
A PSYCHIATRIC REVOLUTION? 358

Notes 412
Bibliography 428
Sources of Illustrations 440
Index 441

Acknowledgments

Madness in Civilization is in many ways the product of my more than forty years of work in the history of madness. During that time, I have accumulated more debts to more people than I can possibly list here. Moreover, in this book, I attempt a task of surpassing chutzpah, and in doing so, I am inevitably indebted to the work of countless other scholars – a debt that is partially, though inadequately, acknowledged in the notes and bibliography that accompany my text.

However, a number of people have been so extraordinarily kind and generous in helping me during the course of writing this particular book that I am delighted to have the chance to thank them here. Though it is but poor recompense for all they have done for me, I would first like to thank five people who have been so gracious as to read the entire text, and to send me detailed comments and suggestions for improvement: William Bynum's knowledge of the history of medicine has few equals, and he has saved me from a multitude of sins, as well as providing much-needed encouragement along the way. My friends Stephen Cox and Amy Forrest have given every chapter close and sympathetic readings. They made numerous penetrating suggestions on matters of style and substance, and did not hesitate to point out where my writing stumbled, or my arguments seemed to be going astray. I cannot thank them enough. Every writer should be lucky enough to have such generous friends. My wonderful editor at Thames & Hudson, Colin Ridler, has been the sort of publisher every author dreams of: responsive, endlessly helpful and full of enthusiasm for the project. His colleague Sarah Vernon-Hunt likewise edited my final draft with exceptional care and attention. In countless ways I have benefited from her marvellous skills as an editor. As all these readers can attest, I can be stubborn, and though in many cases I listened to their sage advice, I sometimes refused to do so. Thus none of them can in any way be held responsible for the errors of commission and omission that remain. They do, however, bear a large measure of credit for whatever virtues my text may possess.

Others have read substantial portions of various chapters, or have responded to importunate queries of various sorts. I would particularly like to thank my brother-in-law, Michael Andrews, and my colleagues and friends Emily Baum, Joel Braslow, Helen Bynum, Colin Gale, Gerald Grob, Miriam Gross, David Healy, John Marino and Akihito Suzuki. I am grateful as well to various organizations that have helped to make this book possible. The Academic Senate of the University of California has on many occasions provided the funds that enabled me to spend time in distant archives. That assistance has been invaluable for someone concerned with madness's past, for the primary sources I have needed to consult are but seldom available in southern California, its current reputation as the home for the kooky notwithstanding. Over the years, fellowships and support from the Guggenheim Foundation, the American Council of Learned Societies, the American Philosophical Society, the Commonwealth Fund, the Shelby Cullom Davis Center for Historical Studies at Princeton University, and two University of California Presidential Humanities fellowships have underwritten major portions of my research. I am most grateful to them all, since all that prior labour in the archives has contributed in ways both large and small to the synthetic work this volume represents.

At my British publisher Thames & Hudson a whole team of people besides the above-mentioned have provided invaluable assistance with the preparation of this book, including the design, production and marketing staff who have transformed my raw text and images into such a handsome volume. I would like to thank them all. I owe an especial debt of gratitude to my picture editor Pauline Hubner. Pauline helped me to locate and obtain permission to use the images that do so much to enhance and enrich the text and analysis that follow. It is a great pleasure, too, on the North American side, to have the estimable Peter Dougherty and Princeton University Press publish another of my books. Peter is a model director of a scholarly press, and has taken a deep personal interest in the book's success. I would also like to thank *History of Psychiatry* and its long-time editor, German Berrios, for permission to reprint some text that first appeared in that journal's 25th anniversary issue, and that now forms a part of Chapter Eleven.

I love to write, and the dedication of this book reflects how much I owe to my wife Nancy for all she has done to create the conditions that have made it possible for me to do so over the years. More importantly, I owe her more than is in my power to express for her love and companionship over many decades. Those who have grandchildren will know what joy they bring, and this book is also dedicated to those Nancy and I are already fortunate enough to have, and to those we hope to welcome and treasure in years to come.

Andrew Scull

La Jolla, California

Chapter One

CONFRONTING
MADNESS

Madness *in* civilization? Surely madness is the very negation of civilization? Enlightenment thinkers, after all, used to argue that Reason is the faculty that distinguishes human beings from beasts. If that is so, then surely Unreason is what lies beyond the pale, corresponding in some sense to the point at which the civilized becomes the savage. Madness is not *in* civilization, but something wholly outside it and alien to it.

On reflection, however, matters are not quite so simple. Paradoxically, madness exists not just in opposition to civilization, or solely on its margins. On the contrary, it has been a central topic of concern for artists, for dramatists, novelists, composers, divines, and physicians and scientists, not to mention how closely it affects almost all of us – either through our own encounters with disturbances of reason and emotion, or through those of family members and friends. In important ways, that is, madness is indelibly part of civilization, not located outside it. It is a problem that insistently invades our consciousness and our daily lives. It is thus at once liminal and anything but.

Madness is a disturbing subject, one whose mysteries puzzle us still. The loss of reason, the sense of alienation from the common-sense world the rest of us imagine we inhabit,[1] the shattering emotional turmoil that seizes hold of some of us and will not let go: these are a part of our shared human experience down through the centuries and in every culture. Insanity haunts the human imagination. It fascinates and frightens all at once. Few are immune to its terrors. It reminds insistently of how tenuous our own hold on reality may sometimes be. It challenges our sense of the very limits of what it is to be human.

My subject is madness in civilization. Their relationship, and their complex and multi-vocal interactions are what I mean to explore and make sense of here. Why *madness*? That is a term that has overtones of anachronism, even of a callous disregard for the sufferings of those we have learned to call the mentally ill, an ill-mannered, or worse, resort to a vocabulary at once stigmatizing and offensive. Heaping more miseries on the mad, adding to the stigma that has enveloped them through the ages, could not be further from my intent. The pain and misery that losing one's mind entails for its victims, for their loved ones and for society at large is something no one who encounters this subject can or should ignore, nor minimize. Here lie some of the most profound forms of human suffering – sadness, isolation, alienation, misery and the death of reason and of consciousness. So once more, and more insistently this time, why do I not opt for some softer term – mental illness or mental disturbance, let us say – rather than deliberately employ what we have come to view as the harsher word, madness?

For psychiatrists, our designated authority these days on the mysteries of mental pathologies, the use of such terms is often seen as a provocation, a rejection of science and its blessings, which they claim to exemplify. (Oddly enough, precisely for that reason, madness is a word defiantly embraced by those who vociferously reject psychiatry's claims and resist the label of psychiatric patient, preferring to refer to themselves as psychiatric survivors.) So is my choice of title and terminology perverse, or a sign that, like some influential writers – the late Thomas Szasz, for example – I consider mental illness a myth? Not at all.

In my view, madness – massive and lasting disturbances of reason, intellect and emotions – is a phenomenon to be found in all known societies, one that poses profound challenges of both a practical and symbolic sort to the social fabric, and to the very notion of a stable social order. The claim that it is all a matter of social constructions or labels is to my mind so much romantic nonsense, or a useless tautology. Those who lose control of their emotions, whether melancholic or manic; those who do not share the common-sense reality most of us perceive and the mental universe we inhabit, who hallucinate or make claims about their existence that people around them conclude are delusions; those who act in ways that are profoundly at variance with the conventions and expectations of their culture, and are heedless of the ordinary corrective measures their community mobilizes to induce them to desist; those who manifest extremes of extravagance and incoherence, or who exhibit the grotesquely denuded mental life of the demented: these form the core of those we look upon as irrational, and are the population that for millennia was regarded as mad, or referred to by some analogous term.

Why am I writing a history of 'madness' or 'mental illness'? Why not call it a history of psychiatry? To such questions I have a simple answer. That kind of 'history' wouldn't be a history at all. I plan to discuss the encounter between madness and civilization over more than two millennia. For the great majority of that time, madness and its cognates – insanity, lunacy, frenzy, mania, melancholia, hysteria and the like – were the terms in general usage, not just among the masses or even the educated classes, but universally. Indisputably, 'madness' was not only the everyday term employed to come to terms with Unreason, but a terminology embraced by those medical men who sought to account for its depredations in naturalistic terms, and at times to treat the alienated. Even the first mad-doctors (for such they called themselves, and were known as by their contemporaries) did not hesitate to use the word, and it persisted in polite discourse, alongside other terms including lunacy and insanity, almost all the way through the nineteenth century, only gradually becoming linguistically taboo.

As for 'psychiatry', it is a word that did not begin to emerge until the nineteenth century in Germany. It was fiercely rejected by the French (who preferred their own term *aliénisme*), and by the English-speaking world, which began, as I alluded to in the previous paragraph, by calling medical men who specialized in the management of the mad 'mad-doctors'. Only later, when the ambiguities and implied contempt – the slur embodied in that term – came to seem too much, did the proto-profession embrace without a clear preference a whole array of alternatives: 'asylum superintendent', 'medical psychologist' or (in a nod to the French) 'alienist'. The one label English-speaking specialists in mental disorders could not abide, and fought against using into the early years of the twentieth century (when it finally began to be the preferred term), was 'psychiatrist'.

More broadly, the emergence of a self-conscious and organized group of professionals who laid claim to jurisdiction over mental disturbance, and who obtained a measure of social warrant for their claims, is largely a phenomenon of the period from the nineteenth century onwards. Madness is now mostly viewed through a medical lens, and the language preferred by psychiatrists has become the officially approved medium through which most (though not all) speak of these matters. But this is the result of historical

TYPES OF INSANITY,

FROM PHOTOGRAPHS TAKEN IN THE DEVON COUNTY LUNATIC ASYLUM.

For description see the first seven cases in the Appendix.

'Types of Insanity', the frontispiece to John Charles Bucknill and Daniel Hack Tuke's A Manual of Psychological Medicine *(1858)*, *one of the first widely used textbooks on the diagnosis and treatment of insanity. Like other alienists, Bucknill and Tuke believed that madness took different forms, and that those distinct types of insanity could be read on the countenances of their patients.*

change, and in a wider view, quite a recent development. The creation of such professionals, their language and their chosen interventions, are phenomena that we shall discuss and try to comprehend. But they are not, and ought not to be, our starting place.

So madness it is, a term that even now few people have difficulty in understanding. Using that age-old word has the further advantage that it throws into relief another highly significant feature of our subject that a purely medical focus neglects. Madness has much broader salience for the social order and the cultures we form part of, and has resonance in the world of literature and art and of religious belief, as well as in the scientific domain. And it implies stigma, and stigma has been and continues to be a lamentable aspect of what it means to be mad.

Even in our own time, definitive answers about the condition remain almost as elusive as ever. The very boundaries that separate the mad from the sane are a matter of dispute. The American Psychiatric Association, whose *Diagnostic and Statistical Manual* (DSM) has achieved global influence, not least because of its linkages to the psychopharmacological revolution, has subjected its bible to seemingly endless iteration and revision. Yet despite these various efforts to achieve resolution, the DSM remains enmeshed in controversy, even at the highest reaches of the profession itself. Depending upon how one counts, it is now on its fifth or its seventh revision, and the publication of its latest incarnation has been delayed by years of wrangling and public controversy over its contents. As its lists of diagnoses and 'diseases' proliferate, the frantic efforts to distinguish ever-larger numbers of types and sub-types of mental disorder come to seem like an elaborately disguised game of make-believe. After all, despite the plethora of claims that mental illness is rooted in faulty brain biochemistry, deficiencies or surpluses of this or that neurotransmitter, the product of genetics and one day perhaps traceable to biological markers, the aetiology of most mental illness remains obscure, and its treatments are largely symptomatic and generally of dubious efficacy. Those who suffer from serious psychoses make up one of the few segments of our societies whose life expectancy has declined over the past quarter of a century[2] – one telling measure of the gap between psychiatry's pretensions and its performance. In this arena, at least, we have not yet learned how to cut nature at the joints.

The wager that handing madness over to the ministrations of medics will have a practical payoff has had some successes – most notably with respect to tertiary syphilis, a terrible disorder that accounted for perhaps 20 per cent of male admissions to asylums in the early twentieth century. For the most part, however, it is a bet we have yet to collect on. Notwithstanding periodic breathless proclamations to the contrary, the roots of schizophrenia or of major depression remain wrapped in mystery and confusion. And with no X-rays, no MRIs, no PET scans, no laboratory tests that allow us to proclaim unambiguously that this person is mad, that person sane, the boundaries between Reason and Unreason remain shifting and uncertain, contested and controversial.

We run enormous risks of misconstruing history when we project contemporary diagnostic categories and psychiatric understandings back on to the past. We cannot safely engage in retrospective diagnosis even in the case of diseases whose contemporary reality and identities seem far more securely established than schizophrenia or bipolar disorder – not to mention a host of other, more controversial psychiatric diagnoses. Observers in earlier times recorded what *they* saw as relevant, not what *we* might like to know. Besides, the manifestations of madness, its meanings, its consequences, where one draws the boundary between sanity and insanity – then and now – these are matters that are deeply affected by the social context within which Unreason surfaces and is contained. Context matters, and we cannot attain an Archimedean view from nowhere, beyond the partialities of the present, from which we might survey in a neutral and unbiased fashion the complexities of history.

Madness extends beyond the medical grasp in other ways. It remains a source of recurrent fascination for writers and artists, and for their audiences. Novels, biographies, autobiographies, plays, films, paintings, sculpture – in all these realms and more, Unreason continues to haunt the imagination and to surface in powerful and unpredictable ways. All attempts to corral and contain it, to reduce it to some single essence seem doomed to disappointment. Madness continues to tease and to puzzle us, to frighten and to fascinate, to challenge us to probe its ambiguities and its depredations. Mine will be an account that seeks to give psychological medicine its due, but no more than its due; one that stresses how far we remain from any adequate understanding of the roots of madness, let alone from effective responses to the miseries it entails; and one that recognizes that madness has a social and cultural salience and importance that dwarf any single set of meanings and practices.

So let us begin.

Chapter Two

MADNESS IN THE ANCIENT WORLD

Madness and the Israelites

No one should underestimate the dangers of courting the displeasure of a savage and jealous God. Consider the Hebrew tradition. Saul, the first king of the Israelites, and Nebuchadnezzar, the mighty king of Babylon, both offended Yahweh, and both received a terrible punishment for their *lèse-majesté*. They were made mad.

What was Saul's offence? He was, after all, in many ways a heroic figure. He had been chosen by Yahweh to be the first king of the Jews, and went on to defeat all the Israelites' enemies with the exception of the Philistines. Moreover, when David, his successor, overcame that final powerful adversary, it was largely thanks to the army Saul had created. Yet on a single occasion, Saul disobeyed his God and, when he did so, his punishment was swift and severe.

In ancient Palestine, enmity between the Israelites and the nomadic tribe of the Amalekites dated back to the time of the Exodus from captivity in Egypt. As the Hebrews fled, they crossed the Red Sea and travelled through the Sinai Peninsula, where they came under attack. The Amalekites 'smote the hindmost...all that were feeble behind'.[1] Nor was that the last occasion on which the Amalekites assailed the Jews. Indeed, in Jewish tradition the Amalekites came to represent their archetypical enemy. Finally, Yahweh, their God, had had enough. His orders to his chosen people were straightforward: 'go and smite Amalek, and utterly destroy all that they have, and spare them not, but slay both man and woman, infant and suckling, ox and sheep, camel and ass'.[2] Kill them all.

In the first book of Samuel, we see Saul failing to carry out his Lord's barbaric instructions to the letter. To be sure, Saul and his army 'utterly destroyed all the people with the edge of the sword. But Saul and the people spared Agag [the Amalekites' king], and the best of the sheep, and of the oxen, and of the fatlings, and the lambs, and all that was good, and would not utterly destroy them.'[3] What were the consequences? The prophet Samuel, who had anointed Saul as king of Israel, berates him. He has disobeyed the Lord, for which there can be no forgiveness, and repentance comes too late.[4]

Shortly thereafter, the Lord deserted Saul and sent an evil spirit to torment him. The torments would persist until the end of his reign. By turns fearful, raging, homicidal and depressed, Saul was intermittently the victim of intense mental turmoil for the rest of his time on the throne. In battle against the Philistines, the last remaining enemy of the Israelites, Saul was deserted by his God. Three of his sons were slaughtered, he was badly wounded, and as his uncircumcised enemies closed in for the kill, he fell on his own sword. The evil spirit sent by the Lord had destroyed him.[5]

Faced with the puzzle that was madness, the Hebrews, like many in the ancient world, turned to the notion of possession by evil spirits to explain the frightening depredations visited upon the insane. The vengeful God they worshipped was never slow to visit such horrors on those who displeased Him or challenged His majesty. Indeed, the Israelites had only been able to make their exodus from slavery in Egypt after Yahweh had rained down ten plagues on the Pharaoh and his people. Moses, the leader of the Israelites, and the Egyptian sorcerers had faced off in a contest about the respective powers of their gods: plagues of blood, frogs, lice, flies, the mass death of livestock, boils that refused to heal, hail, locusts and darkness all failed to sway the Pharaoh, until at length Yahweh arranged for the death of the first-born of all Egyptian humans and animals, and Moses was finally allowed to lead his people out of bondage. Even then, the Lord had not finished with the Egyptians: having parted the Red Sea to allow the Israelites to cross, He caused the waters to rush back to drown the pursuing Egyptian army (PL. 5).

That the Jews believed Saul's madness was a curse from God is made clear in the verses of the book of Samuel. The precise nature of his madness is less clear, though we know something about its external manifestations. Some sources speak of him being 'choked', and Samuel's account describes rapid shifts in mood, from a depressed and withdrawn state to rampant pathological suspiciousness, raving and episodic violence,[6] including a murderous assault on his own son, Jonathan.[7] Josephus (AD 37–c. 100), the Roman-Jewish historian, writing on the basis of oral tradition, tells us that Saul 'was beset by strange disorders and evil spirits which caused him such suffocating and strangling that physicians could devise no other remedy save to order search be made for one with power to charm away spirits'.[8]

It is the shepherd boy David who succeeds from time to time in charming the evil spirit with which God has cursed Saul. He does so, of course, with music, plucking his harp and temporarily appeasing the evil spirit, though never managing to remove the source of Saul's anguish completely.[9] And his efforts were not always effective. Once, 'the evil spirit from God came upon Saul, and he prophesied in the midst of the house: and David played with his hand, as at other times: and there was a javelin in Saul's hand. And Saul cast the javelin; for he said, I will smite David even to the wall with it. And David avoided out of his presence twice'[10] – rather advisable, under the circumstances.

Samuel was, of course, but one of a long line of Jewish prophets, men who acted as emissaries of the divine. Such figures were scarcely without their analogues in other times and places, including among the tribes in Palestine with whom the Israelites were so often at war. But figures like Samuel played a large role in Jewish history over a span of many centuries. When Samuel speaks of Saul 'prophesying', the word is used in a loose sense, for as the medical historian George Rosen has reminded us, the Hebrew for 'to behave like a prophet' can also be rendered as 'to rave', 'to act like one beside himself', or 'to behave in an uncontrolled manner'.[11] On another occasion, for example, we hear of Saul acting as a prophet for a day, travelling to Ramah, where 'he stripped off his clothes also, and prophesied before Samuel...and lay down naked all that day and all that night. Wherefore they say, Is Saul also among the prophets?'[12]

An Isaiah, a Jeremiah, an Elijah or an Ezekiel: these were men of disproportionate influence on the Israelites, and people whose behaviour often seemed to invite confusion between the inspired and the mad, the merely eccentric and the thoroughly crazy. Ecstatic, erratic, often seen to possess and exercise magical powers (Joshua, for example, stops the sun in its tracks), prophets could divine the future, and, if true prophets, they spoke the words of the Lord. They also hallucinated, went into trances, reported seeing visions and had periods of frenzied behaviour when they claimed to be seized by the spirit of the Lord.[13]

Their words and actions courted peril, as well as predicting it. Mockery and isolation were commonly their fate, but much worse might befall them. When Jeremiah pronounced the imminent destruction of Jerusalem, he was scorned as a traitor, beaten and placed in the stocks.[14] Later, efforts were made to kill him by tossing him into a dungeon where he might starve, and he was then locked up, a captivity from which he was released only after the Babylonian conquest of Jerusalem that he had prophesied had come to pass.[15] Uriah was even less fortunate. King Jehoiakim denounced him for having 'prophesied against this city and against this land' and Uriah fled to Egypt, but was handed back to the king of Judah and put to the sword.[16] That God spoke to man through his prophets was not a proposition the Israelites doubted. Their very identity as a chosen people stemmed from such beliefs, and from a special covenant with God, a distinctiveness the prophets played a large role in interpreting. But false prophets abounded, and the reproaches and jeremiads of those laying claim to prophetic status were never likely to bring popularity in their train.

Some prophets may well have been seen as mad (and certainly some twentieth-century psychiatrists were tempted to dismiss them as examples of psychopathology).[17] Yet for their contemporaries, believing as they did in a jealous and all-powerful God who spoke routinely through human instruments and who was inclined to visit the most severe penalties on those who defied Him, there must always have been reasons for doubt. Madness they recognized, but prophets who exhibited some of the attributes of insanity might well instead be divinely inspired.

The Egyptian Pharaoh was not the last foreign ruler to challenge the power of Yahweh and, according to Jewish tradition, to pay a heavy price. Centuries later, in 587 BC, Nebuchadnezzar, king of Babylon, captured Jerusalem, destroyed its Temple, and took the Jews into exile, all apparently without provoking divine wrath. His immunity did not last. Swollen with pride at his conquests he boasts of 'the might of my power', only for a voice from heaven to denounce his impiety. Driven mad, he 'did eat grass as oxen, and his body was wet with the dew of heaven, until his hairs were grown like eagles' feathers, and his nails like birds' claws' (PL. 2).[18] According to the Bible, seven years later, the curse was removed. His reason returned. His kingship was restored, and he regained his former power and glory.

In a divinely ordered world where the vagaries of nature, the misfortunes of the polity and the perils of daily life were invested with religious or supernatural meaning, the transformations madness wrought upon the sane were readily attributed to divine displeasure, to the casting of spells or possession by evil spirits. Such perceptions were long-lasting. Nearly six centuries after Nebuchadnezzar's death, the risen Christ appears first to Mary Magdalene, 'out of whom', we are told, 'He had cast out seven devils'[19] – an action his disciples had witnessed him performing at other times. Recall, for example, the occasion when Jesus visited the country of the Gadarenes, where he was immediately confronted by 'a man with an unclean spirit' who was so unmanageable that even chains and fetters could not restrain him. The frightened villagers had left him to roam a graveyard, to scream and self-mutilate, but seeing Jesus, the wretched man ran to worship him. Jesus asked,

> 'What is thy name?' And he answered, saying, 'My name is Legion: for we are many.... Now there was there nigh unto the mountains a great herd of swine feeding. And all the devils besought him, saying, 'Send us into the swine, that we may enter into them.' And forthwith Jesus gave them leave. And the unclean spirits went out, and entered into the swine: and the herd ran violently down a steep place into the sea, (they were about two thousand) and were choked in the sea.[20]

The story of the Gadarene swine casts light on other aspects of the treatment of the mad in ancient Palestine. The possessed man had been inhabited by devils for a long time. He lived in the open, without shelter or clothing. His fearful neighbours tried restraining him with chains and fetters. In his mad fury he tore them asunder, and the Devil drove him into the wilderness. Yet though the villagers greatly feared him, they nonetheless continued to feed him.[21] It would scarcely be the last occasion when insanity was seen as an affront to civilized existence and associated with nakedness, with chains and fetters, and with the movement of the madman to the very margins of society. Such indeed would continue to be the fate of many of the deranged for centuries.

The Hellenic World

Among the ancient Greeks, judging from an abundance of literary sources, the notion of the divine origin of human mental suffering was also widely accepted.[22] Their gods were never averse to meddling in human affairs, and religious causes of mental illness were a prominent part of Classical culture[23] – an interpretation that gained added strength once Christianity became the official religion of the Roman empire. The links between madness and the machinations of the gods are likewise a staple of Greek drama and poetry, so much so that millennia later, Sigmund Freud would call upon Greek myth when he named the psychological trauma he claimed indelibly marked the whole human race the Oedipus complex. Panic, too, is a word that derives from Greek: *panikon*, of or pertaining to Pan, a god notorious for spreading terror.

The *Iliad* and the *Odyssey*, the oldest surviving works of Western literature, were initially handed down via an extended oral tradition, and in that sense pre-date the civilization that was Classical Greece. The epics, most scholars now believe, were fashioned out of the great store of pre-existing Greek myths in the eighth century BC, and passed on orally until the invention of the Greek alphabet. They formed the basis, the foundation of Greek culture, narratives familiar to every educated citizen in Classical Greece and beyond, and the inspiration for a number of the plays of Aeschylus, Sophocles and Euripides, the great dramatists of the Classical age (and many others whose work has not survived) in the fifth century BC. And running through all this work is a literary and artistic fascination with madness that will persist throughout Western civilization ever afterwards.

The suitors who lay siege to Penelope in the years of Odysseus' absence (whom Odysseus will slay to a man on his return) gather for a feast. Athena (the goddess of wisdom) intervenes to arouse mirth and tears, and soon their behaviour so exceeds the bounds of propriety that the participants seem to lose themselves in madness. She produces 'unquenchable laughter in the suitors and deranged their minds. Now they laughed with jaws not their own, and ate meat dripping with blood, and their eyes were filled with tears, and their minds were impelled to lamentation.'[24] Lament they might. Their doom is foreshadowed.

Perhaps the most common situation in which we encounter madness in Homer is in the heat of battle, where men become frenzied, lose control over themselves, rave, behave like men possessed. Diomedes, Patroclus, Hector, Achilles, all are shown falling prey to a temporary madness in the midst of the fight. Hector strips the armour from Patroclus after killing him, and puts it on himself. At once, 'terrible Ares the god of war entered him, and he was filled inside his limbs with force and strength'.[25] Grief and a desire for vengeance against Hector drives Achilles mad, the rampaging frenzy of battle being followed by a duel to the death between the two men. Even as he stands over his defeated enemy, Achilles' consuming rage is not assuaged. Hector begs, not for his life, but for his body to be treated respectfully after his death, only to be rebuffed by a maddened Achilles: 'my rage, my fury would drive me now to hack your flesh away and eat you raw – such agonies you have caused me'. And indeed, having dragged it behind his chariot, 'he treated the body of noble Hector with contumely, laying it at full length in the dust beside the bier of Patroclus'.[26]

The people who populate the *Iliad* are frequently, though not always, at the mercy of the gods and the fates. Supernatural forces are everywhere. Gods, Sirens, the Furies lie in wait, destroying, avenging, punishing, toying with mere humans. Divine anger is ubiquitous, and Homer's characters are often its victims. In the dramas of Athens, some centuries later, a richer psychological world emerges and, alongside the machinations of the gods, the agonies of guilt and responsibility, the conflicts thrown up by duty and desire, the unshakeable effects of grief and shame, the demands of honour and the disastrous impact of hubris all complicate the picture. But the supernatural accounts of the origins of unreason, seemingly adopted by non-literate peoples everywhere, continue to hold sway.

Half-man and half-god, the offspring of Zeus' adulterous affair with Alcmene,[27] Heracles is inevitably the object of the goddess Hera's hate, for his very existence is proof of her husband's infidelity. Homer speaks of the dangers and sufferings she rains down on his head, and such is the power of the story that later authors, Greek and Roman alike, return to it again and again, elaborating upon it as they proceed. In later accounts, such as those in Euripides, Hera drives Heracles mad: 'Send madness on this man, confound his mind, and make him kill his sons. Madden his feet; drive him, goad him, and shake out the sails of death.'[28] In his frenzy, Heracles attacks what he thinks are the children of his mortal enemy, Eurystheus. Foaming at the mouth, his eyes rolling in their sockets, veins gorged with blood and laughing like a maniac, he slaughters them all, only to discover when the madness passes that those he has killed are his own offspring (PL. 4). Hence the twelve labours of Heracles (or Hercules, as the Romans preferred), from slaying the lion of Nemea to retrieving the monster Cerberus from the Underworld, that he is forced to undertake to atone for his actions.

In Euripides' play of that name, Medea, arch-victim and villain both, is driven out of her senses by Jason's desertion and betrayal. Spurning her as a barbarian after she has helped him to win the Golden Fleece and borne him two children, Jason has chosen instead to marry Glauce, daughter of King Creon. Medea takes her revenge. First she murders the woman who has replaced her in Jason's affections, sending Glauce a poisoned golden cloak that, once put on, causes her rival to die in agony; and then she dispatches her own sons, revelling in Jason's grief. Elsewhere, Orestes, Pentheus, Agave, Oedipus, Phaedra and Philoctetes all are shown as out of their minds – visually hallucinating, mistaking one object for another, violent and murderous by turns.[29]

Can we assume a simple correspondence between representations of madness in poetry and drama and the nature of popular beliefs? Of course not. To embrace such a homology without further ado would be remarkably naïve. Myths and metaphors bear some relation to 'reality', but by their very nature are not the same thing. The melodramatic demands of the stage and plot inevitably drive the choices of authors, and though the works must resonate with and be comprehensible to the audience, they may be far from being a reflection of the man in the street's beliefs and attitudes. Tragedy is about things going wrong, and madness is most certainly one of those things, so perhaps it should occasion no surprise that it plays so central a role in these literary forms – that and the dramatic possibilities such departures from convention provide. We need to remember, though, how central tragedy was to Athenian life and culture, in a way that has no modern parallel. Life stopped for the play, quite literally. The audience shut up shop, and did so for days at a time, to view, in conditions that themselves imposed considerable physical discomfort, representations of pain and trouble, and of the precariousness of human existence – and its condition as merely the plaything of the gods.[30]

Storytelling bound the community together, both the elite, who were by now fully literate, and *hoi polloi*, among whom even the male grasp of reading and writing was less certain and less practised. It is no exaggeration to speak of tragedy as one of the most pervasive tropes in Athenian, and more generally in Greek culture of this period, when Hellas stretched from Spain to the shores of the Black Sea.[31] So while caution is in order before we extrapolate from literary sources to claims about popular beliefs, what we learn from them about how the Greeks looked at human beings and conceptualized their relations with the world undoubtedly reveals some things of importance about the inner life of the citizenry.[32]

Besides, there is much in the surviving historical record, though some of it is of an indirect sort, that suggests that at a fundamental level the belief that the depredations of madness had preternatural origins was one that was widely held – in Greece, Rome and beyond their borders, both temporally and geographically. The gods were everywhere for the Greeks, from the shrines to Apollo, Hecate and Hermes that greeted everyone arriving at the threshold of the dwelling, to the acknowledgment of a multitude of other deities scattered throughout the house. All aspects of the natural world and its functioning were linked to the realm of the gods, and their all-pervading influence was inescapable. The strangeness, the otherness, the fearsomeness of madness – where else was that rooted but in the unseen universe populated by the divine and the diabolical?

Like bodily pathologies that wrenched lives from their customary course, mental disturbances were profoundly disruptive in their effects, both for those experiencing the illness and for those around them. On one level they might be a solitary affliction – indeed, in some instances the sufferer withdrew from contact with fellow humans – but in their ramifications they had the most powerful and unsettling effects, and in that sense were the most social of maladies. Uncontrollable, inexplicable, threatening to self and others, these frightening and hateful conditions could not (and cannot) be ignored, calling into question the sense of a common, shared reality (common sense in the literal meaning of the term), and threatening, both symbolically and practically, the very foundations of social order.

If madness is seen to be random, that only adds to its terrors, so it is little wonder that efforts were made to contain it, conceptually as well as practically, to provide some account of how it came to possess its victims and to hold them in its thrall so that they were heedless of the lessons from experience that usually save us from error. Evidence from a multitude of sources suggests that, as held true for the invented characters who stalked the stage, Greeks and Romans often embraced the notion that the mad among them had the gods or demons to blame for their madness. Granted, our knowledge of popular beliefs and practices is fragmentary and we know little, for example, about the subjective experience of the mad and the sorts of treatment meted out to them, but the thrust of the evidence we do have is clear.

Herodotus (c. 484–425 BC), who was writing his *Histories* in the same period that the Classical dramatists created their plays, announces that his researches 'are here set down to preserve the memory of the past', and treats of the madness of at least two of the monarchs whose reigns he records: Cleomenes, king of Sparta (r. 520–490 BC), and the Persian king Cambyses II

(r. 530–522 BC). Though Herodotus was notoriously prone to fanciful statements, much of his account accords with what later scholarship has uncovered, and while there may be room for scepticism about some of the details of these episodes of monarchical madness, his discussion of what had driven them mad surely has its roots in contemporary beliefs among his audience, and indeed he explicitly claims to be reporting on the beliefs prevalent in Greek society.[33] These narratives likewise make clear the sorts of behaviours that led contemporary observers to conclude that certain people had lost their wits, and had moved from the world of the sane to that of the mad.

Book 3 provides us with an extensive narrative of Cambyses II's attacks on Egypt and the kingdom of Kush (in modern Sudan), and his subsequent descent into insanity. Retreating from a failed campaign in the south, Cambyses returns to Memphis, where he finds the Egyptians celebrating the birth of a calf born with peculiar markings: 'black, with a white diamond on its forehead, the image of an eagle on its back, the hairs on its tail double, and a scarab under its tongue'. The Egyptians regard the animal as an incarnation of the bull-god Apis. Cambyses orders the priests to bring the sacred beast to him, then 'drew his dagger, aimed a blow at its belly, but missed and struck its thigh'. He ridicules the credulity of the Egyptians, mocks the priests and orders them beaten, and breaks up the festival. And the injured animal, 'which lay in the temple wasting away from the wound in his thigh, finally died'. Cambyses then suffers what observers see as 'the complete loss of his reason'. He behaves ever more extravagantly, and eventually kicks his pregnant sister (whom he had married) in the belly, causing her to miscarry. 'These', Herodotus comments, 'were the acts of a madman, whether or not his madness was due to his treatment of Apis' – the favoured conclusion, with which many Greeks concurred.[34]

Then there was the case of Cleomenes, king of Athens' great rival, Sparta. Always somewhat erratic and unscrupulous, he had bribed the priestess of the oracle at Delphi to support his claim that his co-king and enemy, Demaratus, was not the son of Ariston (the king who had ruled Sparta before them for nearly half a century) so he could depose him. Fearing his corruption of the priestess had become known, Cleomenes fled. A shift in his political fortunes would later see him restored to the throne, but his triumph was brief. He

> began poking his staff in the face of everyone he met. As a result of
> this lunatic behaviour his relatives put him in the stocks.

As he was lying there, fast bound, he noticed that all his guards had left him except one. He asked this man, who was a serf, to give him a knife. At first the fellow refused, but Cleomenes, by threats of what he would do to him when he recovered his liberty, so frightened him that he at last consented. As soon as the knife was in his hands, Cleomenes began to mutilate himself, beginning on his shins. He sliced his flesh into strips, working upwards to his thighs, and from them to his hips and sides, until he reached his belly, which he chopped into mincemeat. This finished him.[35]

What was one to make of his madness and his savage end? Most Greeks (Herodotus tells us) believed that his unpleasant death was due to the fact that he corrupted the priestess at Delphi; the Athenians, however, put it down to his destruction of the sacred precinct of Demeter and Persephone; while the Argives maintained that it was a punishment for the acts of treachery and sacrilege he committed when, after a battle, he fetched the Argive fugitives from the Temple of Argos, where they were taking shelter, and cut them into pieces, and then showed such contempt for the grove where the temple stood that he burned it down.

Given such a record of impiety, who could doubt that divine anger had brought about his madness and his demise? The Spartans. They argued that Cleomenes had gone mad because he had spent too much time with the Scythians, where he had acquired the barbarous 'habit of taking wine without water'. Strong drink, they believed, was the root of his troubles. But while Herodotus records their account, he immediately dismisses it: 'my own opinion is that Cleomenes came to grief as a punishment for what he did to Demaratus'.[36] Earlier, he had not been so certain in the case of Cambyses. 'There is a story', Herodotus acknowledged, 'that he had suffered from childbirth from the serious disease that some call sacred. There would then be nothing strange in the fact that since a serious disease affected his body, so too he was not well in his mind.'[37]

Greek and Roman Physick

Such naturalistic accounts of epilepsy – the so-called sacred disease – and of mania, melancholia and other forms of mental disturbance, were increasingly being put forward by Greek physicians, who sought to root them in the body and not in some supernatural intervention by the gods. With the advent of literacy, Greek medical ideas were being written down for the first time, most systematically in a group of texts once referred to as the writings of Hippocrates of Kos (*c.* 460–357 BC). These writings have only survived in fragmentary form, and we now know that they were the work of multiple hands, though deriving from the teachings of Hippocrates. Significantly, one of these essays directly confronts the question of the origins of epilepsy and its associated mental disturbances (see below).

Presumably building upon and further developing ideas about disease and its treatment that had a more ancient, pre-literate lineage, the Hippocratic corpus attempted to provide a wholly naturalistic account of diseases of all types, resisting the temptation to call upon the divine or the demonic as explanatory factors. Its central speculations about illness and its treatment would exercise an enormous influence, not just in Greece, but also in the Roman empire; and after a period when most such ideas were largely lost in western Europe in the aftermath of the fall of Rome, they would be

Hippocrates of Kos, a fanciful depiction as an antique bust in an engraving of 1638 by the Flemish master Paulus Pontius, after an original by Peter Paul Rubens.

re-imported from the Arab world in the tenth and eleventh centuries. From then onwards, so-called humoral medicine would reign almost unchallenged as the standard naturalistic account of illness for many centuries, extending (albeit in somewhat modified form) even into the early nineteenth century. What, then, were Hippocratic medicine's distinguishing features, and what did its practitioners have to say about the source (and perhaps treatment) of mental disorder?

While there are considerable variations and nuances to be seen in the surviving texts, which are far from homogeneous (and Galen and other physicians at work in the Roman empire some centuries later would further modify the initial ideas contained in the fifth-century BC documents), at Hippocratic medicine's core was the claim that the body was a system of interrelated elements that were in constant interaction with its environment. Moreover, the system was tightly linked together, so that local lesions could have generalized effects on the health of the whole. According to this theory, each of us is composed of four basic elements which contend for superiority: blood (which makes the body hot and wet); phlegm (which makes the body cold and wet, and is composed of colourless secretions such as sweat and tears); yellow bile or gastric juice (which makes the body hot and dry); and black bile (which makes the body cold and dry, and originates in the spleen, darkening the blood and stool). The varying proportions of these humours with which an individual is naturally endowed give rise to different tempera-ments: sanguine if generously supplied with blood; pale and phlegmatic where phlegm predominates; choleric if possessed of too much bile (PL. 6).

Humoral balance was susceptible to being thrown into disarray by a variety of influences including seasonal variation and developmental changes over the course of the life cycle, but also by a host of other poten-tial sources of disturbance coming from without. Bodies assimilated and excreted, and thus were affected by such things as diet, exercise and sleeping patterns, and by emotional upsets and turmoil. If these external intrusions threatened the balance of the system, a skilful physician might be able to regulate it once more by drawing unwanted matter out, via bleedings, purges, vomits and the like, and by adjustments to aspects of lifestyle.

Gender differences too were rooted in the moister, laxer state of women's bodies, which in turn had effects on their characteristic tempera-ment and behaviour. Such notions led to separate treatises on female diseases and reproductive problems, including a disorder often, but not always in its long and tortured history, seen as quintessentially belonging to the female of the species – hysteria. In women, so one Hippocratic text read, 'the womb is the origin of all diseases'. It was not just that the female of the species was differently constituted from the male. Her body was more readily deranged, for example by puberty, pregnancy or parturition, by menopause or by suppressed menstruation, all of which could impose profound shocks on her internal equilibrium (for her wetter constitution produced an excess of blood, which regularly needed to be drained from her system); or by the womb wandering about internally in search of moisture (or, later, sending forth vapours that rose through the body), disturbances that were held to be the source of a great variety of organic complaints.

It was from these notions, reworked by Galen (c. AD 129–216) and other Roman commentators, and for the most part later re-entering the West from Arabic medicine, along with other Hippocratic ideas, that the Classical accounts of hysteria were constructed. For example, the Roman Celsus (c. 25 BC–AD 50) and the Greek Aretaeus (first century AD), both closely associated with the Hippocratic tradition, adopted the notion of the womb wandering about the abdomen, stirring up all manner of troubles. If it migrated upwards it compressed other bodily organs, producing a sense of choking, even a loss of speech. 'Sometimes', Celsus claimed, 'this affection deprives the patient of all sensibility, in the same manner as if she had fallen in epilepsia. Yet with this difference, that neither the eyes are turned, nor does foam flow from the mouth, nor are there any convulsions: there is only a profound sleep.'[38] Both Soranus (first/second century AD) and Galen, by contrast, disputed the notion that the womb could wander, though they did accept that it was the organ from which hysterical symptoms derived. These manifestations of the disease could take a multitude of forms, including extreme emotionality, and also a variety of physical disturbances, ranging from simple dizziness, through paralyses and respiratory distress. Then there was the commonly reported sensation of a ball in the throat, constricting breathing and creating a sense of suffocation, the so-called *globus hystericus*.[39]

There was a clear recognition at the heart of this whole intellectual edifice that upset bodies could produce upset minds, and vice versa. The key to good health was keeping the humours in equilibrium, and when the patient fell ill, the physician's task was to deduce what had become unbalanced and to use the therapies at his disposal to readjust the patient's internal state. Body and environment; the local and the systemic; *soma* (body) and

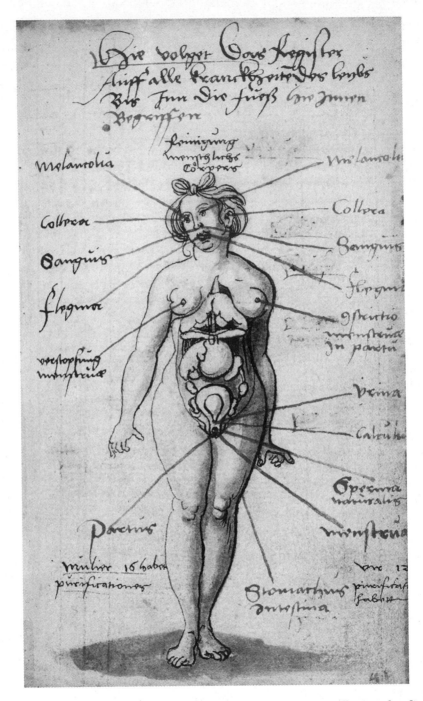

A diagram of female anatomy from a sixteenth-century manuscript collection of medical 'receipts' kept by an anonymous German physician, with notes for instance on blood-letting and astrology. It was amended and added to by several contemporary hands.

psyche (soul): each element of these dyads was capable of influencing the other, and of throwing the individual into a state of dis-ease. Hippocratic medicine was a holistic system, one that paid close attention to every aspect of the individual patient, and tailored therapeutic regimes to each specific case. And, most importantly, it was a view of human health that emphasized the natural, rather than the supernatural causes of disease.

In taking this stance, the Hippocratics were attempting to differentiate themselves from a rival school of healers, the practitioners of temple medicine. Shrines to local healing gods were found across Greece, and the faithful came to them to be made well (as well as to improve their fortunes more generally). Claims of miraculous cures were widespread; but at least as important, the temples offered forecasts of the likely outcome of the patient's complaint. The cult of Asclepius enjoyed particular popularity, and spells, charms and incantations were resorted to, along with purification rites, to induce divine intervention and produce a cure. If these methods did not bring about the desired result, failure could always be explained away. The gods were still displeased, the prayers insufficiently fervent.[40]

Perhaps unsurprisingly, the clash between temple medicine (and folk beliefs) and the insistence of the Hippocratics on locating the sources of pathology in bodies, not as perturbations visited by the gods, was especially fierce in the case of madness and kindred disorders. The position taken by one side in this battle is preserved in the Hippocratic treatise, dating from around 400 BC, with the misleading title *On the Sacred Disease* – misleading because the whole thrust of its argument is to refute the claim that the disorders it discusses (which most likely encompass cases of hysteria as well as what we now recognize as the various forms of epilepsy) were 'sacred' or visited upon their victims by the gods, but were, on the contrary, the product of bodies gone wrong. Extending its arguments in places to encompass manic and melancholic disturbances of the spirit, the text constitutes a full-blooded assault on attempts to invoke magical and religious explanations of these phenomena. In so doing, it provides us with an unparalleled (if tendentious) insight into the kinds of religious and folk beliefs surrounding madness that were prevalent in Classical Greece, and persisted for many centuries thereafter.

Altered mental states, followed by such dramatic symptoms as fits, foaming at the mouth, grinding of teeth and biting of tongues, loss of control of bladder and bowels, and the descent into unconsciousness, all were readily interpreted as signs of possession. We learn that the uneducated, and the priests who ministered to their gullibility, saw such events as not merely amazing or frightening, but as sent by a deity, or the result of a demon entering the sufferer, or a punishment for offending Selene, the goddess of the moon. And if the cause be supernatural, surely so too was the cure. Epileptics, like madmen, were unclean, and their malign influence was to be warded off by spitting and isolation, lest contamination of those around them occurred. Horror and disgust, fear and disdain, these were the emotions such sights provoked, and for many observers disturbances of this sort were best met by magical and religious forms of intervention.[41]

The Hippocratics would have none of it. They poked fun at such accounts: 'If a patient imitate a goat, if he roar, or suffer convulsions on the right side, they say that the Mother of the Gods is to blame. If he utter a piercing and loud cry, they liken him to a horse and blame Poseidon...' or they summon Apollo, Ares, Hecate, the Heroes – a whole list of menacing figures.[42] All such invocations of the gods, and any suggestion that they might be capable of bringing about a cure, are firmly rejected: 'It is thus with regard to the disease called Sacred: it appears to me to be nowise more divine nor more sacred than other diseases, but has a natural cause [blocked phlegm] from which it originates like other affections. Men regard its nature and cause as divine from ignorance and wonder, because it is not at all like to other diseases.'[43] The ignorance and credulity of the masses are to blame, along with the cynical preachers who exploit their gullibility:

> My own view is that those who first attributed a sacred character
> to this malady were like the mages, purifiers, charlatans and
> quacks of our own day, men who claim great piety and superior
> knowledge. Being at a loss, and having no treatment that would
> help, they concealed and sheltered themselves behind the divine,
> and called this illness sacred, in order that their utter ignorance
> might not be manifest. They added a plausible story, and
> established a method of treatment that secured their own position.
> They used purifications and incantations; they forbade the use
> of baths, and of many foods that are unsuitable for sick folk....
> These observances they impose because of the divine origin of
> the disease...so that, should the patient recover, the reputation for
> cleverness may be theirs; but should he die, they may have a sure
> fund of excuses...[44]

In contrast, as an intellectual construct the humoral theory of disease was immensely powerful, making sense of symptoms and pointing the way towards remedies for what had gone wrong. It simultaneously provided reassurance to the patient and an elaborate rationale for the interventions of the physician. The Hippocratics did not emphasize human anatomy, save for their close attention to the external appearance of the body, and they actively avoided dissecting corpses, something that was almost taboo within Greek culture. Even the physician to successive Roman emperors, Galen, relied upon dissecting animals for his view of the way bodies were put together (the Romans had forbidden human dissection from around 150 BC), so that mistaken views of human anatomy persisted in medical circles well into the Renaissance. But the Hippocratics' rejection of the notion that either magic or divine displeasure played any role in the causation of disease was fierce and unambiguous, and their holism, and stress on the role of the psychosocial as well as the physical in bringing about ill-health, encouraged them to proffer thoroughly naturalistic accounts of madness, alongside their explanations of other forms of sickness – indeed to draw no sharp distinctions between them.

There was much else to encourage a common approach to madness and more clearly physical diseases. Distortions of perception, hallucinations, emotional upset and turmoil often accompany serious illness. 'Fevers', which we regard as symptoms but which for centuries were seen as the disorder itself, could have a multitude of sources, particularly in an era when infectious and parasitic diseases were rife, and contamination and decay of food common. The delirium and altered consciousness, the raving and the agitation that were fever's frequent concomitants often resembled the disordered thinking of the mad. Many people had also encountered (or deliberately sought) the cognitive and emotional disturbances that ingesting too much alcohol or partaking of other mind-altering substances bring in their train. And virtually everyone, then as now, had experienced moments of extreme psychological anguish, suffering and pain. Emotional and cognitive dysfunctions were (as they remain) a familiar part of human existence, though for most of us, mercifully, they are a transient one. The analogies to madness were hard to miss, and the Hippocratics insisted that both types of illness had their origins in the underlying make-up of the human frame.

Where Aristotle had seen the heart as the seat of the emotions and of mental activity, Hippocratic texts saw the brain as their centre: 'Men ought to know that from nothing else but the brain come joys, delights, laughter and sports and sorrows, griefs, despondency and lamentations. And by this, in an especial manner, we acquire wisdom and knowledge, and see and hear, and know what are foul and what are fair, what are bad and what are good, what are sweet and what unsavoury.'[45] If it was the head, not the heart which ruled, this was also where madness lurked:

> It is the brain too which is the seat of madness and delirium, of the fears and frights which assail us, often by night, but sometimes even by day; it is there where lies the cause of insomnia and sleepwalking, of thoughts that will not come, forgotten duties and eccentricities. All such things result from an unhealthy condition of the brain...when the brain is abnormally moist it is necessarily agitated.[46]

Madness could assume different forms, each the outward manifestation of deeper but differing disturbances of the system. As with other kinds of ill-health, the problem lay in an imbalance of the humours: too much blood led to warming of the brain, and hence to nightmares and terrors; too much phlegm might produce a mania whose victims 'are quiet and neither shout nor make a disturbance...[while] those whose madness results from bile shout, play tricks and will not keep still but are always up to some mischief.'[47] The very term 'melancholy' derives from the Greek word for black (*melan*) and that for bile (*chole*). Hence depression as a black mood.

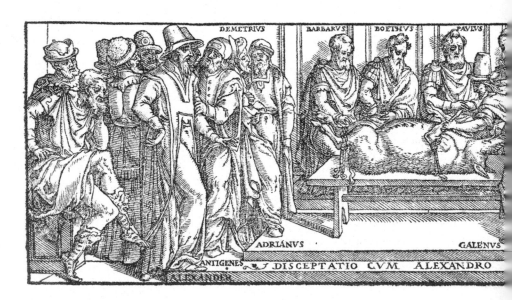

The Greeks and the Romans thus bequeathed both natural and supernatural accounts of the ravages of madness to subsequent generations. Doctors and priests offered comfort and solace in different ways. Both had their successes and failures, and both had ready explanations for why they sometimes proved powerless. Among medical men, those who wrote on the subject had already set out a number of different varieties of the disorder, rather than a single undifferentiated condition. Whether these were distinct from one another or merely phases through which distraction might pass was the source of some debate, but a broad differentiation between mania and melancholia had been established. And there was an acknowledgment, too, that there were still other forms of madness that existed on the borderlands of insanity, including epilepsy, hysteria and phrenitis (mental confusion with fever).

Religious and secular, supernatural and what purported to be naturalistic explanations of all these myriad phenomena would persist alongside one another down the centuries. Both might be invoked when the occasion demanded it, and religious and spiritual interventions might be tried alongside the heroic remedies of the anti-phlogistic physicians.[48] Desperate disorders called for desperate remedies, and if the price of trying an eclectic array of approaches to their solution was to court charges of intellectual inconsistency and incoherence, it was a price few were disinclined to pay. And speaking of pay: for most, of course, the services of the physician were simply out of reach, meaning that folk remedies of whatever sort were widely employed, though the poverty of the masses, and the illiteracy of most of them, leaves us bereft of reliable information about how they coped.

Finally, Greek epistemology provided one last and potentially more positive interpretation of madness, one that is found in Plato and in Socrates, and that in some

Galen gained his knowledge of anatomy from dissecting animals, in this case a pig; from an edition of his Opera Omnia, *published in Venice in 1565.*

ways echoed the Hebrew idea of the inspired prophet. Madness might represent another possible way of 'seeing': bacchic, erotic, creative, prophetic, transformational. For many, reason seemed to provide the royal road to knowledge. Others insisted, however, that there was another, concealed kind of knowledge – intuitive, visionary and transformative knowledge or mysticism (a word that etymologically derives from the Greek word *mystikos*, or 'secret') – and that madness might provide the keys to this mystical kingdom. The idea of non-rational means of knowing and the notion that madness might sometimes be a means to truth (divine madness, as some would have it) would resurface repeatedly, in medieval Christianity, in the ecstasies and raptures of Christian visionaries and saints, in Erasmus's *The Praise of Folly*, in Shakespeare's mad lovers, in Cervantes, in Dostoevsky's and Tolstoy's representations of the holy fool, and even in the late twentieth century in the work of psychiatrists such as R. D. Laing.

If the influence of the Greeks had spread across an immense territory, not just the Mediterranean but also, thanks to the conquests of Alexander the Great and continued trading contacts, through modern Iran and Afghanistan, and even into parts of India, the Roman empire at its zenith was even more extensive. Romans with wealth and those practising professions that benefited from Greek learning were attracted to Greek culture and philosophy, and a knowledge of Greek became a mark of superior status. Like leisured classes everywhere, these Roman citizens sought emblems of their greater taste and discernment, and in such circles, in the words of the eminent historian of Classical medicine Vivian Nutton, 'Greek physicians were necessary, as much for ostentation as for practical value.... Some Greeks came of their own volition [like Galen], but others came as prisoners of war or slaves.'[49] They were useful ornaments, but the ornaments brought with them their perspectives on disease, including madness. Rome's doctors, by the time of the first century AD, came overwhelmingly from the Hellenized East, as continued to be the case in subsequent centuries.[50]

Greece and Rome and Imperial China: Worlds Compared

Further East, another great empire was forming, and from its consolidation under the Qin (221–206 BC) and Han (206 BC–AD 220) dynasties would constitute a polity and a civilization in many ways more durable than Classical Greece and Rome – despite intermittent periods of political disunity and fragmentation, which saw the temporary rise of warlords and multiple king-doms. Those disruptions, as we may in retrospect choose to define them, were often long and serious. About half the Chinese dynasties were run by various outsiders from the north, and for much of the time, more than one kingdom existed within the huge region we now think of as China, as the Han fled south in the face of northern incursions. Those northern kingdoms in some cases persisted for centuries, so they can scarcely be regarded as temporary. Still, imperial China in various guises survived as a vast, inde-pendent, civilizing project (not without some outside influences via trade along the ancient Silk Road) for more than a millennium and a half, until it finally fell prey to European guns, trade and Western imperial ambitions in the nineteenth century, existing in a semi-dependent state until 1911. A substantial literate class (though probably no more than 1–2 per cent of the total population until the Ming dynasty, 1368–1644) occupied a key place in the administration of immense territories, and it was this bureaucracy that enabled the emperor of China to control these lands and a population that dwarfed that of the Roman empire, and even more so the Greek city-states.

The demographic differences are most obvious, of course, when one compares Classical Greece and China. The autonomous Greek city-states were tiny when compared with the Chinese imperial state: the largest and most prestigious, Athens, had a population in the fifth century BC of perhaps a quarter of a million, counting citizens, foreign residents and slaves, compared with the nearly 60 million inhabitants recorded in the Chinese census of AD 1–2 – and that was the low point for China, for during the Song economic revolution (960–1279), its population rose to perhaps double that. More importantly, Athens, Sparta and the other city-states that made up Hellenic civilization were characterized by remarkably diverse political arrangements: tyrannies, monarchies, oligarchies, even participatory democracies. Nor did the later political hegemony of the Romans put an end to the cultural plu-ralism that was the natural consequence of these variations. Indeed, as the career of Galen, one of those who made the journey to Rome, demonstrates, it led to the spread of this intellectual diversity westwards. Born in Pergamum, in modern Turkey, Galen had absorbed a variety of medical teachings across the Hellenic East, visiting both Athens and Alexandria before moving, like many ambitious Greeks, to Rome in AD 162. Here, he eventually became a court physician to successive emperors, beginning with Marcus Aurelius (r. AD 161–80). Even in the following century, traditional governing elites of the old Greek city-states clung to a sense of the particularities of place. The oligarchs, still in control of local power, saw themselves as part of a complex mosaic of cities and tribes, whose distinctive qualities had not been reduced to a homogeneous Roman world.[51] In this they were not mistaken, and it was in sharp contrast to imperial China, in later periods at least.

All sorts of consequences flowed from the immense differences between East and West. Physicians in the Greco-Roman world were much less tightly bound to the political elites than their Chinese equivalents during the Han dynasty, and mostly depended upon finding custom in the marketplace, rather than political patronage, for their livelihoods.[52] Such competition could produce fierce conflicts (apprehensive of the jealousy of fellow-physicians in Rome to the extent that he was frightened of being poisoned, Galen, for example, briefly left Rome, before being summoned back to the imperial court by Marcus Aurelius),[53] not to mention separate schools of doctrine as practitioners sought to build reputations, to distinguish themselves from one another and to lay claim to superior expertise.

To be sure, the much-belittled 'country doctors' in China who sought patients among the masses sold their skills (such as they were) in an open marketplace. And in later imperial China, as elite physicians could invoke their links to an unbroken medical lineage, they too developed a degree of autonomy; by that period they could draw upon the custom of a vast array of merchants and literati, and thus became substantially independent of the state. What was true under the Han emperors, in other words, became steadily less so in later centuries.

But at elite levels in China during the Han dynasty in particular, ties to the imperial court were all-important. Intellectuals could and did secure a measure of security by obtaining positions in the imperial civil service.[54] Such security, however, came at the price of circumspection and a compelling need to maintain the goodwill of their patrons, the loss of which could prove quite literally fatal. The requirement to stay within the conventional bounds defined by tradition, or at the very least represent innovations as modifications of what had gone before, and to remain part of the consensus, lest apostasy in intellectual matters be seen as a harbinger of disloyalty in the political sphere, these were among the defining features of elite Chinese medical thinking during the Han era, as they were of Chinese attempts at understanding the cosmos more broadly at this time. Not surprisingly, 'The principal (though not the sole) Chinese approach [in these centuries] was to find and explore correspondences, resonances, interconnections. Such an approach favoured the formation of syntheses unifying widely divergent fields of inquiry. Conversely, it inspired a reluctance to confront established positions with radical alternatives.'[55]

In that sense, medical conservatism was as one with the broader intellectual consensus that marked the so-called Han synthesis. That synthesis began to dissolve across a whole social spectrum after the Han dynasty collapsed in AD 220. In medicine, as family lineages consolidated their individual authority, each tended to protect its own methods and secrets, so that in reality over time a vast array of ideas, methods, theories and even medical compounds resulted – though each lineage proclaimed it adhered to 'true' tradition. Within this growing heterogeneity, however, the idea of correspondences remained central to elite Chinese medicine, re-emerging as one of its organizing and distinctive principles in the alternative medicine of the twentieth century.

Our knowledge of how the Chinese responded to illness, both mental and physical, is – even more than for ancient Greece and Rome – very partial and incomplete. Classical Chinese medicine was developed (like contemporary efforts in the West) among educated males, whose knowledge and practices were directed towards a literate elite. Madness drew less attention among these Chinese medical men than it received from the Hippocratics, and of the effects of its depredations on the masses, and how they responded to the trials and tribulations it brought in its wake, we know little.

The general problems that frustrate any attempt to describe societal responses to madness in the millennia that precede the age of mass literacy, and that persist in many respects even then – the bias of sources towards the elite; the silence that characterizes these materials on many key issues; the merely indirect and extremely fragmentary information that we have about ordinary people, let alone the sufferers themselves – all these are felt with particular force with respect to Chinese society, and the literature on these subjects is sparse, if gradually increasing.[56] Without question, though, one thing we do know is that, as in the West, the elaborated medical system which the written record concentrates upon persisted alongside folk medicine and religious and supernatural accounts of mental and physical disease. It was religious medicine (Buddhist or Taoist), along with a folk medicine that explained much illness (illness that in the West might be somewhat separated into mental or physical) through the actions of evil spirits or demons, to which the great bulk of the population seems to have had recourse. Patients – or more accurately patients' families and the surrounding community – often resorted to an eclectic mix of these various elements, in a desperate search for meaning and efficacy.[57]

Past life indiscretions, fate, demonic possession, ghosts or disruptions of the cosmic order were as likely to be invoked as internal disorders of the body or the intrusion of external pathogens when coming to terms with all forms of pathology. Miasmas, excessive heat or cold, dampness and dryness, and wind – all these were forces that might be cited to explain illness, though Han scholarly medicine 'made the harmfulness of these elements contingent on internal weakness.... In a body brimming with vitality, there simply wasn't room for noxious elements to enter.'[58] For the majority of the populace, shamans or faith healers were as likely to be consulted as medical men. The particular elements that made up the popular medical systems clearly varied a great deal over time, and were not without influence on the kinds of medicine practised on and among the elite, just as elements of the intellectual system that underpinned the latter might influence popular medical systems. Then, too, resort might be made to prayer and advice from religious figures. Faced with all kinds of disease and debility, it made sense to try everything, and most people, in any event, felt that the anger of the gods, fate or misdeeds in a past life were of great general significance.

Ancient Chinese elite medicine, particularly during the Han dynasty, shared with the Hippocratic tradition a holistic approach to the understanding of health and illness. As in Classical Greece, disease was often conceived of as a form of invasion (though for Chinese physicians internal disruptions were often at fault): a hostile attack on the body that hindered and blocked the flow of vital fluids and of *qi*, not a word that can readily be translated, but one that may roughly be thought of as breath or energy. In the face of such blockages, sickness was the inevitable result. There are apparent structural resemblances between ideas of this sort and Hippocratic notions of the balance and imbalance of the humours, the interpenetration of mind and body, and disease as disequilibrium. But the conception of the relationship between the individual and the cosmos, of how bodies were put together, the descriptions of the forces that were at work, and the means that the two groups of practitioners developed to intervene in cases of pathology, were radically different. The Hippocratics placed much emphasis on the physical imbalance of the humours, but the elite Chinese medicine of correspondences (and even the medicine that derived from Taoist ideas) saw *yin* and *yang* as apparently contrary forces that were in fact interconnected and interdependent, with good health dependent upon the balance between the two.

The earliest compilation of medical knowledge, though far from the only text that was seen as authoritative, was the *Yellow Emperor's Inner Canon*, considered to be the revelation of the wisdom of ancient sages. Like the Hippocratic texts, it had many anonymous authors, and scholars debate when it was first composed, with informed guesses ranging from 400 BC to 100 BC. It would remain a fundamental intellectual foundation of elite Chinese medicine for over two millennia, and acquired the status of a sacred text. In principle, human beings might mistake its meanings – the language of the various ancient texts was terse and often inscrutable. Hence there was an immense literature devoted to its explication and exegesis, which certainly allowed for the incorporation of new ideas under the guise of improved reading of the early texts. Those committed to these traditions acknowledged that they could not hope to surpass the wisdom the *Inner Canon* encompassed and argued that human knowledge derived from experience was inevitably, by contrast, prone to error and subject to revision. That stance suggested that at the core of the strand of Chinese medicine that mattered most to the elite was a rejection of the notion of the historical 'progress' of knowledge, and a commitment to the preservation of a classical tradition.

Much was open to debate, however, and those disputes, and the ongoing theoretical and philological deliberations among scholars, allowed for considerable alterations in the original meanings of the texts. Then, too, the various elements of the traditional system – the so-called Five Phases, and *yin-yang* theory – could be employed in very different ways by those who could still present themselves as adhering to ancient tradition. Symptomatic of the instabilities that existed despite the emphasis on continuities was the fact that the *Inner Canon* was originally not a single, unified text, and it was not until the eleventh century that an authoritative version was agreed upon. In the preceding centuries, scholars had vied with one another to rearrange the texts, to amend them and to extend them with added critical commentary of their own. Moreover, medical knowledge was not systematized in universities (as eventually came to be true of the West), but instead passed down via family lineage or training under a master-doctor, which meant that there was inevitably great variation from one practitioner to another.[59]

Thus in reality there were important changes within a larger frame-work that remained notionally the same, even when we ignore the other kinds of quite different medicine that were available to and embraced by the lower orders. Over time, for example, elite Chinese physicians, who had originally been inclined to attribute insanity to the intrusion of Wind and to demons, increasingly from the twelfth century AD onwards came to stress the action of inner Fire, and of mucus obstructing the system.[60] Yet if the medical understanding of the roots of psychological and behavioural dis-turbances in China underwent some crucial modifications, it remained an understanding that linked those pathologies to imbalances of the sort that explained other kinds of illness as well.

When the Chinese of all ranks of society spoke of possession, of mental confusion, of fits of fury, they used a variety of terms: *kuang*, but also *feng* and *dian* most notably among them.[61] There were not, of course, any more than in the West, clear-cut boundaries between madness and other forms of distress, but in large degree this terminology was used to refer to disruptive behaviours and chaotic disturbances of perception, speech and affect – very much the sorts of commotions, disorders, dislocations and loss of emotional and rational control that make up the common-sense understanding of 'madness'.[62] Chinese physicians on occasion broached the subject of madness, and articulated some notions of whence it came. But where Western doctors eventually constructed a specialized literature concerning the origins and treatment of madness, no comparable body of doctrine and set of proposed therapies emerged in China. Until the twentieth century, even within the elaborated medicine resorted to by the Chinese elite, madness was never interpreted as a distinct illness, but was instead, like other forms of ill-health, seen as deriving from a more comprehensive corporeal and cosmological imbalance. Consequently, no attempt was made to modify or extend what little traditional texts had to say about madness, and it seldom seems to have become the focus of sustained medical attention or reflection – all of which creates enormous difficulties when one attempts to study how Chinese perceptions of madness may have evolved over time.

For nearly two millennia, however, such descriptions on the subject as were offered by elite practitioners depended upon ancient texts,[63] most notably the *Yellow Emperor's Inner Canon*, but also the *Treatise on Cold Damage Disorders* (dating to somewhere between AD 196 and 220). Since it was not anatomical structures but bodily functions that lay at the centre of

Chinese models of health and illness, it was the interruption of such things as breathing, digestion and temperature regulation that underlay all sorts of pathology. Disease was disharmony, and the presumed sources of that disharmony in turn suggested how therapy, or the re-establishment of harmony, should proceed. And as with other forms of disharmony, the troubles that revealed themselves in psychological and behavioural disturbances could be addressed by mobilizing a wide variety of treatments, adjusted to the requirements of the individual case: a broad array of drugs and decoctions; the use of needles in the form of acupuncture; diet and exercise; and a variety of other techniques designed to break up the obstacles to the circulation of *qi*, or drive out its pathological forms. And that is not mention exorcism and faith healing, popular among the masses (who relied upon common healers who had little or no grounding in scholarly texts) and often resorted to by desperate members of the elite.

Even physicians, wedded as they were to organic accounts of mental disturbance, could not at times escape recognizing that madness was defined socially, and was more than simply a bodily condition. For both families and for the imperial authorities it was those social implications of mental disturbance that generally loomed largest. Thus there emerged practical attempts to cope with its depredations, and eventually a codified body of legal doctrines that set out to advise officials on how to handle mad acts and to direct families to undertake the preventative confinement of their mad relations.

Murder by madmen, for example, seems to have drawn increasing attention by the seventeenth century. Such killings were likened to accidental homicides since they were void of intention. If they sometimes provoked punishment, and virtually always the payment of compensation to the victim's family along with some form of confinement for the perpetrator, they often did not lead to executions (though that began to change from the mid-eighteenth century). Soon, by extension, all cases of mental disturbance began to attract the notice of the authorities and to be subject to various forms of confinement, as the law began treating even non-criminal madmen as presumptively dangerous.[64] Relatives were held responsible if they neglected to take necessary precautions, and punishments for failing to do so were periodically made more severe, an indication that official injunctions were being ignored.

But if mad murderers were on occasion spared the full force of sanguinary imperial law – which included sentences that varied from dismemberment through decapitation to death by strangulation – the same

*Instruction in acupuncture: the master and one of the pupils are holding acupuncture
needles, and the second pupil a text, signifying the combination of theory and practice.
The frontispiece to* Xu Shi's Great Compendium of Acupuncture and Moxibustion.

cannot be said of other madmen, particularly those whose ravings and behaviours might be interpreted as having seditious overtones. It was one thing
when unpredictable mad behaviour led to fatal violence, but something far
more sinister and threatening when the lunatic's actions seemed to call into
question imperial authority. Take the case of Lin Shiyuan, who in 1763 hurled
a roof tile, to which he had attached slips of paper on which were written
crazy and nonsensical words that are difficult to understand, in the general
direction of the governor of Fujian, Dingzhang. He was seized by the guards
and interrogated to see whether his intent was treasonous. Lin's relatives
insisted he was mad, and had been so for months. Investigators were sent
to investigate whether he was faking or really mad. Mad, they concluded, he

Dhanvantari, the physician of the gods and the god of Ayurvedic medicine, an ancient medical tradition in South Asia and one that is still practised today.

was. All the testimony they uncovered pointed in that direction. The governor agreed. Nonetheless, Lin was sentenced to immediate decapitation. His offence? 'Blithely circulating devious words, writing placards and rousing and confusing people's hearts.'[65] While certain kinds of madness might prove legally exculpatory, others, as Lin Shiyuan's fate makes emphatically clear, most certainly were not.

East and West

Imperial China survived in its various guises, as we have noted, very many centuries longer than imperial Rome. In the West, wrenching political and social disruptions were the order of the day. For a time, and it stretched for centuries, the collapse of the Roman empire led to the loss of the Classical legacy, including the Hippocratic tradition in medicine, a loss that might well have proved irretrievable. In an age before print, the transmission of Classical culture was dependent upon the preservation and laborious transcription of fragile manuscript materials, and the continuity of an urban leisured class that simply disappeared. Peter Brown, the great historian of Classical antiquity, has spoken of how in the West, as ancient institutions were irrevocably lost, 'Classical culture went by default'.

There was every possibility, save for fortuitous events elsewhere – the tenuous survival of a Classical elite in medieval Constantinople, and the echoes of Greek culture in the world that Islam made, as described in the following chapter – that we might now live in a world that knew nothing of Plato or Thucydides, Euclid or Sophocles, 'except', as Brown reminds us, 'from fragments of papyrus'.[66] We may add Hippocrates and Galen to that list. China, for all its periods of political turmoil, experienced no such caesura and, among many consequences that flowed from this, in the medical arena the wisdom codified in the ancient texts exercised a major continuing influence on the way the literate Chinese classes viewed madness.

In South Asia another long-standing medical tradition had evolved, one that, like its Chinese equivalent, still enjoys a following today, and which is not limited to its ancient heartlands. Born initially from Hindu traditions, Ayurvedic medicine was not static or uniform across the whole of South Asia and it absorbed other elements syncretically over time, but its classical texts, composed in Sanskrit between the third century BC and the seventh century AD, embody a common set of understandings of the make-up of the human body and the sources of ill-health, physical and mental. (As in Chinese traditional medicine, there is no real separation between the two.) Like humoral and Chinese medicine, Ayurveda emphasizes the holistic and the systematic. Fluids in the body – *doshas* – mediate between the individual and the world, and are of three basic types: *vata* is cold, dry and light; pitta is hot, sour and pungent; and *kapha* is cold, heavy and sweet.

Disease arises from the misalignment or imbalance of these *doshas*, and the job of the Ayurvedic physician is to detect the reasons for the underlying loss of equilibrium and find ways to restore it – ways that might involve massage, drugs derived from vegetable and mineral and more rarely animal sources (especially opium and mercury), diet, exercise, changes of regimen and so forth, but that could also call upon ritual therapies involving invocations directed at supernatural demons and gods.

The twelfth century AD saw the establishment of the first Islamic states in the Indian subcontinent, a set of incursions that ultimately resulted in the gradual conquest of most of South Asia. The Muslim rulers brought with them another medical system, a tradition whose name, Yunani, at once reveals its origins, since the word is Arabic for Greek. It was the ideas of Galen and other Greek physicians that were the basis for the authority and the substance of Yunani medicine, or Unani Tibb as it was also known, though those Greek ideas were frequently refracted through the work of great Persian physicians such as al-Majusi or Haly Abbas (d. 994), al-Razi or Rhazes (854–925), and above all Ibn Sina or Avicenna (980–1037)[67] – whose influence on the West would also prove to be enormous, as we shall see.

Yunani was not just court medicine, and enjoyed considerable success across a broader swathe of society, but it did not displace Ayurveda among the masses.[68] Both systems, in any event, saw physical and mental existence as one, with each possessing the capacity to influence the other. Digestion and excretion, intake and outflow, were vital for the maintenance of health, as was good hygiene. But so too were herbal remedies (often in doses modern Western medicine would regard as toxic), and mineral therapies that involved the ingestion of toxic heavy metals: lead, mercury and arsenic notable among them. If modern Western medicine sees these remedies as potentially triggering mental symptoms as brains become poisoned, traditional Indian healers were convinced, on the contrary, that they could cure disordered minds as well as disordered bodies. Devotees of alternative medicine embrace such notions even today.[69]

Chapter Three

THE DARKNESS
AND THE *DAWN*

Successor States

Even at the height of the Roman *imperium*, a rival on the empire's eastern frontier posed a constant military threat. Persia, initially under the rule of the Parthians (247 BC–AD 224) and then under the Sasanian dynasty (AD 244–651), first fought the Romans at the battle of Carrhae in 53 BC, and by 39 BC had captured virtually all of the Levant. Rome periodically counter-attacked, sometimes with success, sometimes not. Though the two empires managed a long period of relative peace between the late fourth century and the early sixth century, it did not last. The Eastern Roman (Byzantine) Empire in Constantinople, which had been established in the fourth century, was at war with the Persians once more by AD 525. Though 'eternal peace' was pledged in 532, made possible in part by a bribe of 440,000 pieces of gold from the Byzantine emperor Justinian I, the Persians invaded Syria only eight years later. Back and forth battles raged for nearly a century.

Both sides were severely weakened by the effects of so much war, and the need to levy oppressive taxes to support military adventures, a problem exacerbated for the Byzantine empire by also having to fend off attacks from the Avars and Bulgars from the north and the west. By 622 the Persians appeared to have achieved remarkable military and political success, but the cost was an exhausted treasury and an even more exhausted army. Briefly, a counter-offensive by the Byzantine emperor Heraclius between 627 and 629 led to the recovery of Syria and the Levant, and the restoration of the True Cross to Jerusalem. But it left both warring parties vulnerable to assaults from without. When the Persians were attacked from the south by the newly expansive Arabs, their empire rapidly collapsed. And while the Byzantine empire initially at least avoided that fate, after the battle of Yarmouk in 636, Syria, the Levant, Egypt and portions of North Africa were lost to the Arabs – and with the exception of Syria for a comparatively brief period beginning in the late tenth century, irretrievably so.

From Constantinople's dedication as the new capital of the Roman empire in 330, it had grown into a rich and powerful city, and after the fall of Rome to the barbarians in the fifth century it was the largest and wealthiest in Europe, becoming the capital of Christian civilization. In the ninth and tenth centuries, its population has been variously estimated as between 500,000 and 800,000. The city's rulers surrounded it with massive defences, built a series of architectural masterpieces and for centuries could draw upon much of the wealth of the eastern Mediterranean. Its libraries preserved large numbers of Greek and Latin manuscripts, a cultural inheritance which thereby escaped the mass destruction that overtook such materials in western Europe during the instability and disorder that marked the fifth and sixth centuries with the disintegration of the Roman empire there. Some of these cultural treasures would make their way west in the hands of Christian refugees later, when Constantinople finally fell to the Ottoman Turks in 1453. Both indirectly and then more directly, therefore, Constantinople contributed extensively to the revival of Hellenic and Roman culture, independent of the influence of Arab civilization, and thus ultimately played a vital role in the transformation in western Europe that we know as the Renaissance.

The collapse of the Eastern Roman Empire in many ways can be traced back to the sack of Constantinople in 1204 – a historically unprecedented orgy of destruction visited on the city by crusading Christians. Works of art and manuscripts that had survived from ancient Greece, and centuries of other treasures were now wantonly destroyed. For three days the crusaders

> rushed in a howling mob down the streets and through the houses, snatching up everything that glittered and destroying whatever they could not carry, pausing only to murder or to rape, or to break open the wine cellars.... Neither monasteries nor libraries were spared...sacred books and icons were trampled under foot.... Nuns were ravished in their convents. Palaces and hovels alike were entered and wrecked. Wounded women and children lay dying in the streets.[1]

Constantinople and the Eastern Roman Empire never really recovered. By the time the city fell in 1453, its population numbered no more than 50,000 people. Immediately after the successful Turkish siege, the main orthodox cathedral, the Hagia Sophia, was transformed into a mosque – a gesture of enormous symbolic significance – and work began on rebuilding the city and its population, this time as a centre of Islamic culture.

What have all these momentous political events to do with madness? A great deal. The Eastern Roman Empire had formally adopted Greek in place of Latin as the language of administration early in the seventh century, and Greek Classical philosophy and medicine endured and prospered there. Likewise, particularly during the period of Sasanian rule, Persian civilization had been heavily influenced by Greek culture. Kavadh I (r. 488–531) had encouraged the translation of Plato and Aristotle, and subsequently the Academy of Gundishapur near the Persian capital became a major seat of learning. Greek medical texts were translated into Syriac, and local physicians drew upon that tradition, mingled with influences from Persia and even northwest India (into which the empire had penetrated). Pre-Islamic Persia had in any event been in near-continuous contact with the world of Classical Greece and then Byzantium, not only through its own wars and attempted territorial expansion, but also during the conquest of Persia in 334 BC by Alexander the Great, who for a time made Greek the imperial language there.[2] Thus the writings and teachings of the Hippocratic circle and of Galen, largely lost in western Europe by this time, continued to exercise a profound influence on medical practices in the Near East. That influence would grow stronger yet with the triumph of the Arabs and of Islam, though as this complex genealogy shows, much of what we think of as Arab medicine, and Arab innovations in the delivery of medical care, actually had their origins in Persian society and in Byzantium, and in the incorporation of Hippocratic and Galenic medical traditions.

The Arabs who smashed the institutions of the Sasanian empire and seized control of large portions of the Near East would, by 750, expand their own empire. It extended to northern India in the east, all across North Africa and encompassed most of Spain. These conquests were undertaken in the name of the monotheistic religion that had united the Arabian peninsula by the time of the Prophet Muhammad's death in 632. Islam's spread had proceeded so rapidly in part because the Arabs were welcomed by local Christian and Jewish inhabitants who had been persecuted and heavily taxed by previous rulers. The conquerors offered, by contrast, protection and toleration, provided Christians and Jews paid a fixed tribute, and though the Muslim armies moved with amazing swiftness on their camels, and fought fiercely and extremely effectively when they had to, as often as not the Arabs used diplomacy rather than military force to attain their ends.[3] They assimilated the more valuable elements of the cultures of those who submitted to their rule, soon creating a rich synthetic Muslim culture with Arabic at its core, engulfing and building upon existing intellectual centres. Through an extensive and active trading network that spanned the Mediterranean, they then spread the achievements of that civilization across great distances.[4] The new culture evolved over nearly two centuries, and was the product in part of military conquest, but also of imperial measures that spread knowledge and ideas westwards.

The Muslim conquest of Iberia had begun in 711, and by 718, Moorish control extended over the Iberian Peninsula and into southern France. But that would prove to be the high point of their advance in the region. Slowly, the Christian *Reconquista* began. By 1236, the northern half of modern Spain had been claimed for Catholicism, and further skirmishes over the next 250 years slowly shrank the remaining territory under Muslim rule. Finally, during the reign of King Ferdinand of Aragon and Queen Isabella of Castile – two of the more powerful of the feuding Christian kingdoms that had emerged in the north of the peninsula – a war was launched in 1482 to drive the Muslims from their last remaining territory, the Emirate of Granada, then as thoroughly Arab a city as Cairo or Baghdad. After Granada itself fell in 1492, Muslims and Jews were killed, forcibly converted to Catholicism or expelled, their wealth and property conveniently appropriated. A century later, Philip III of Spain (r. 1598–1621), continuing to suspect that conversions compelled by the Inquisition might be less than genuine, and needing to divert attention from his decision to sign an armistice with the rebellious Low Countries[5] – modern Belgium and the Netherlands – drove out the last remnants of the Muslim and Jewish population. While Constantinople was captured by the Turks in 1453, and much of the Balkans and Greece were falling under Islamic control, politically and culturally Islamic influence in the West was receding by the second half of the fifteenth century.

In the intervening centuries, Islamic culture had exercised an enormous influence, in ways both large and small. The Arabs were great traders and sailors. From them, western Europeans adopted advances in such areas as the technology of sails and the development of nautical charts that would prove vital when the Portuguese, then the Spanish, the English and the Dutch began to voyage across the Atlantic and beyond. The Arabs also brought with them a new culture of luxurious living, architectural marvels that survive to this day, irrigation systems that turned arid Spain into a place capable of producing new crops such as oranges, lemons, artichokes, apricots, aubergines and more. Paper and printing – Chinese inventions – also came with the Arabs to the West, along with books and learning. (Johannes Gutenberg's development and use of movable metal type in the mid-fifteenth century was not original – both the Chinese and the Koreans had previously developed such systems, but movable type was more readily adapted to the alphabetic Western languages, and Gutenberg's invention of a system of mass-producing metal type and combining it with oil-based ink and wooden presses was genuinely revolutionary.) The Arabs had built a paper-mill in Baghdad in 800, and brought the technology with them to Spain. French pilgrims to Compostela thought paper a great curiosity when they first encountered it in the twelfth century, and paper-mills were not established in Germany and Italy until the fourteenth century. Of great importance, too, the Arabs introduced to the region a new and much more useful numerical system, this time of Indian rather than Chinese origins. That change proved enormously consequential once Arabic numerals replaced the clumsy Roman system previously in use, because the new way of writing numbers transformed accounting and business practices.

Arab civilization in Spain – and in Sicily, which the Arabs had conquered and controlled until the very late eleventh century – was an urban civilization richer (in more than one sense) and more complex than anything to be found in most of western Europe in this period, more tolerant, more ecumenical. Faced with Arab achievements in the twelfth century, Europeans reacted with a mixture of fear, admiration and justified feelings of inferiority. And intellectually, in fields including mathematics, science and medicine, the indebtedness of the West to Islamic civilization would increase for centuries more.[6]

Islam and Madness

The Arabs also carried with them as they consolidated their political rule a belief in spirits and spells, incantations and charms designed to placate and manipulate the *jinn* (demons) whom they held responsible for disease and disorder.[7] The animistic traditions from which these practices were derived and that were characteristic of tribal society did not vanish immediately with the adoption of Islam – not least because the Qu'ran is essentially silent on questions of health and disease[8] and thus provided little guidance to the faithful, or encouragement, at least initially, to break with older traditions. Indeed, with its explicit acknowledgment of the existence and powers of malevolent *jinn*, the Islamic order co-existed quite comfortably for a time with supernatural accounts of various forms of misfortune, madness notable among them. Even as high culture absorbed Hellenistic elements, and Greek medicine became the foundation for an Islamic medical tradition, supernatural explanations for madness continued to survive alongside accounts couched in naturalistic terms, and religious solutions were sought when medical interventions proved unavailing, as they frequently did.

Though Islam had no rites of exorcism paralleling those that spread through Christianized Europe, its followers sought religious consolation and divine intervention in the face of the threats and disturbances insanity brought in its train. The evidence we possess of popular beliefs and practices is fragmentary at best, but it strongly suggests a frequent resort to supernatural healing and demonic explanations of insanity. There are frequent references to *jinn* and to *jinn-gir* (a demon catcher), and even today, in some areas around the Persian Gulf there is a rite of passage to puberty, known as the *zar* ceremony, in which demons are extracted from the person. (*Zar* refers to a harmful wind associated with spirit possession, and the ceremonies are designed to placate it and reduce its dangerous influence.) Michael Dols, a noted historian of madness in medieval Islam, aptly captures how broadly religious interpretations of madness were almost everywhere in this period when he speaks of 'a freemasonry of preternatural beliefs.... For pagans as well as Jews and Christians in the early Christian era, the cause and possibly the cure for mental disorders were supernatural.... Muslims were heirs to a rich legacy of spiritual healing...and...there is a striking continuity of Christian healing in Muslim society.'[9]

The earlier Arab promises of toleration for Jews and Christians – whom the conquerors saw as followers of other, albeit corrupted, Abrahamic religions – were also mostly kept by the later Ottomans. In return for tribute – both protection money and a fine for failing to embrace Islam – they were freed from their traditional obligation to send tributes of grain to Constantinople, and allowed to live their lives largely free of interference from the state. Trade and commerce flourished. Irrigation works were repaired, great buildings erected and a rich intellectual and cultural life materialized throughout the conquered territories. And under the Ottomans, the control of territory became primarily a political rather than a religious project: not a *jihad*, designed to convert polytheists, but more a *ghaza*, an attempt to consolidate territory by military means – hence the title of Ottoman sultans, *ghazi*.

While literacy survived in the West in only the most tenuous and attenuated fashion in the Catholic church, and the Classical legacy in the Eastern Empire – initially extensive – eventually shrank to little more than what remained within the walls enclosing Constantinople, Islamic civilization, and with it Islamic medicine, went from strength to strength. An educated, urban and urbane elite conversing in the lingua franca of classical Arabic shared a literate culture that extended from Cordoba to Samarkand. And since all Muslims were considered equal in the sight of God, Syrians and Persians soon rivalled and then largely replaced those who had originally sought to rule them. The accession of the Abbasids, unseating the Umayyad caliphate from Damascus and establishing the new capital of Baghdad in 762, was the culmination of trends that had been under way for more than a century. Persians from the northeastern region of Khorasan played a major part in this revolution and Persian cultural influences grew thereafter. The spread of Islam westwards, across North Africa and into the Iberian Peninsula, brought further cultural influences to bear. In many ways, the Islamic civilization of the medieval period was not exclusively Arab, but the creation of Muslims and even other religious communities within the larger mosaic of Muslim lands.[10]

For much though not all of the time, Arabic medicine in particular was the creation of non-Muslims. It is not just that the medicine that was practised was firmly rooted in the Galenic system of pagan antiquity. Rather, as medicine developed in succeeding centuries, many of its leading practitioners were Jews and Christians. Perhaps the most famous physician within this tradition was Ibn Sina or Avicenna, a Persian polymath, whose *Canon of Medicine* (PL. 7) would become the single most influential medical compilation within the Arabic tradition – indeed, many consider it the single most important medical text ever published.[11] Completed in 1025, the *Canon* constituted the summation of existing medical knowledge in five books, its encyclopedic reach extending to all forms of illness and debility. It would eventually be translated into Persian, Greek, Latin, Hebrew, French, German and English, and even into Chinese. In Europe, it continued to be used as a textbook into the eighteenth century, though by then Greek and Latin authorities were largely preferred. The *Canon* opens with the claim that: 'Medicine is the science by which we learn about the conditions of the human body in health and in the absence of health in order to maintain health or to restore it.' Avicenna's is a work of magisterial synthesis rather than presenting original new perspectives of his own, and he largely followed in the footsteps of Hippocrates and Galen, though he also drew to a much more limited extent on Persian, Hindu and Chinese medical teachings.

More than a century and a half before Avicenna's birth, efforts had begun to translate key Classical texts – medical and otherwise – into Arabic.[12] This work of translation was stimulated in part by the decline of Greek as a lingua franca in some of the regions that were later included in the Muslim dominion. Its replacement by Arabic[13] was principally the work of Christian scholars, who already possessed a knowledge of Syriac and Greek, and were experienced translators.[14] Hunayn ibn Ishaq (d. 873) boasted that he and his circle had translated 129 Galenic texts – in part a work of preservation, and one that contributed greatly to the survival and later dissemination of Galen's work, for Hunayn elsewhere asserts that Greek medical works were extremely rare, and had to be searched for diligently.[15] A number of consequences flowed from this surge of translations, an activity that largely subsided in the following century. First, hundreds of ancient texts were saved for posterity (and would later be re-introduced to western Europe); secondly, the pronounced tendency to favour the work of Galen above all others meant that his was the system that spread throughout the Arab lands; and thirdly, the need to translate Greek medical terminology into Arabic created, for the first time, a systematic language in which Islamic physicians could discuss disease and its treatment.[16] Few passages in Galen offended Islamic sensibilities, and those could easily be excised with no loss of coherence. And the Galenic emphasis on health as the product of harmony, order and equilibrium could be seen as implicitly endorsing the Muslim conception of God in terms of the existence of a supreme being who provided them.[17]

Islamic medicine was not entirely static. On the contrary, in certain directions it made continuing efforts to pursue original research. New advances were made in the understanding of diseases as different as smallpox and ocular disorders, and in drawing upon the cornucopia of plants, animals and minerals to find novel substances that medicine might find useful. Still, that work rested firmly on the Galenic foundations that had been established in the ninth century. It systematized knowledge in vast compendia, and because medical texts were copied and re-copied at a furious pace – no small feat in an era before print technology – it spread formal medical ideas across the vast territory over which Islam held sway, and helped make possible the European re-appropriation at a later date of its own intellectual heritage. But whereas Galen's ideas, and the broader Greek tradition his work in some sense summarized, would face increasing criticism in Europe from the Renaissance onwards, and would be largely abandoned as the basis for medical understanding in the nineteenth century, in the Islamic world no comparable break occurred. Ancient medical traditions persisted, and remained largely unchanged well into the nineteenth century, then only giving way reluctantly under the pressures brought to bear by Western imperialism. As Classical teachings were reproduced, however, they were also simplified and adulterated, losing much of their intellectual force in later versions.[18]

The various incarnations of madness were scarcely one of Galen's primary concerns, but he did recognize and discuss the major distinctions that had emerged in ancient medicine between mania and melancholia, epilepsy, hysteria and phrenitis (mental confusion with fever), all attributable to imbalances in the humours. His explanations, and those of other Greek authors such as Rufus of Ephesus (first century AD, whose work has survived in only small fragments), were widely influential among Islamic physicians,[19] who therefore shared the conviction that alterations in the equilibrium of the body were fundamentally what lay behind disturbances of mental stability. Ishaq ibn Imran (d. 908), for example, who wrote a substantial treatise on melancholy, attributed that 'feeling of dejection and isolation which forms in the soul because of something which the patients think is real but which is in fact unreal' to the vapours rising from black bile – dimming and destroying reason and apprehension.[20] Some were predisposed to its ravages from birth, cursed with a melancholic temperament; others, through immoderate eating and drinking, too much or too little exercise, or the failure to evacuate their bowels regularly (which allowed waste to rot and turn into black bile), brought the illness upon themselves. Ishaq acknowledged that fear, anger or loss could also precipitate this form of madness, but here, too, the breakdown was exacerbated when excessive black bile was accumulated;

1 PREVIOUS PAGE
The Fairy Feller's Master-Stroke *(1855–64) by Richard Dadd. Dadd was a promising young artist confined in Bedlam after he murdered his father. The microscopic attention to detail and the surreal qualities are typical of much of Dadd's work.*

2 BELOW *Nebuchadnezzar as a wild animal, his hair grown long and his nails like claws. This striking image of the biblical story of the Babylonian king's madness is a detail from a manuscript painted by an unknown artist in Regensburg, Germany (c. 1400–10).*

3 OPPOSITE ABOVE LEFT
Hieronymus Bosch, The Ship of Fools *(c. 1510–15). Plato compared democracy to a ship of fools and in 1494, Sebastian Brant, a German theologian, used the same allegory to satirize his contemporaries' sins. Bosch's painting shows a ship laden with all manner of fools, drifting aimlessly.*

4 OPPOSITE ABOVE RIGHT
On this red-figure krater from c. 340 BC by the Asteas Painter, Heracles is shown in his maddened rage about to throw one of his children on to a pile of smashed household goods. His wife watches on in horror, powerless to prevent him.

5 OPPOSITE BELOW
God intervenes to protect his chosen people: the hands of Yahweh reach down from the heavens to part the Red Sea to let the Jews pass, while their pursuers are drowned, in this wall painting from the third-century AD Dura-Europos synagogue in Syria.

6 ABOVE *The theory of the Four Humours – Phlegmatic, Sanguine, Choleric and Melancholic – formed the basis of Galenic medicine and is here illustrated by a medieval artist. Imbalance created ill-health, bodily and mental.*

7 ABOVE *An illuminated manuscript page from the* Canon of Medicine *by Ibn Sina (Avicenna), painted in Isfahan, Persia, 1632. Completed in 1025, the* Canon *was a highly influential compilation of existing medical knowledge, extending to all forms of illness and debility.*

8 ABOVE *In this scene from Nizami's tale of the star-crossed lovers Layla and Majnun painted in Tabriz (1539–43), the mad Majnun is brought in chains to Layla's tent. Children throw stones at him and he is set upon by a dog, for most Muslims a ritually unclean animal.*

9 LEFT *A vivid portrayal of the murder of Thomas à Becket, from a mid-thirteenth century codex. The saint's blood was thought to cure insanity, blindness, leprosy and deafness, not to mention a host of other ailments.*

10 BELOW LEFT *In medieval Europe there was a great belief in the efficacy of the relics of saints. The skull of St Foy, reputed to have miraculous powers, was housed in an elaborate reliquary in the abbey of Conques, France.*

11 BELOW *Christ blessing a possessed youth, the demon fleeing as he does so, from the Très riches heures du duc de Berry (c. 1412–16).*

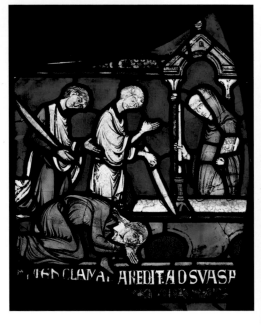

12–14 ABOVE *Three stained glass windows from Trinity Chapel, Canterbury Cathedral, telling the story of Mad Matilda of Cologne, who had murdered her own baby.* *She was one of many pilgrims brought, or dragged, to Canterbury to seek a miracle cure. By the third panel (bottom right), the poor woman has been restored to her senses.*

this then 'sympathetically' affected the brain. Though it was written towards the very end of Ishaq's career, his treatise is based entirely on book-learning, not clinical experience.[21] In this he was a thoroughly representative figure.

Early Hospitals

Hospitals for the sick and infirm as charitable foundations had first been founded in the Byzantine empire (if we disregard the military hospitals the Western Roman Empire had occasionally created),[22] but the idea was quickly adopted by Christians elsewhere in the Near East well before the rise of Islam. Under Islamic rule, however, hospitals proliferated, with the first appearing in the late eighth century; and among the patients for whom they made systematic provision were the insane.[23] As with Christianity, Islam emphasized the obligations of the rich to the poor, and once Islamic physicians had begun to emerge in numbers, a rivalry with their Christian counterparts naturally ensued. Muslims most certainly could not be seen to be less charitable than their *dhimmis* (protected non-Muslims). Thus by the twelfth century, no large Islamic town was without a hospital.[24]

Evidence of the treatment meted out to the mad confined in the wards set aside for them in these hospitals is fugitive and fragmentary. Surviving floor plans suggest combinations of individual cells and open wards were common, an impression reinforced by comments from travellers who visited these monuments to Islamic charity. There are many reports of iron windows, and of patients in chains,[25] which should scarcely occasion surprise, for even though hospitals spread all across the Arab lands, as far as Spain (where a hospital was built in Granada between 1365 and 1367), there was room for only small numbers of the insane, and it is likely that many of them were the dangerous and furiously mad – those whom communities would otherwise have had great difficulty containing and controlling. Perhaps the largest hospital was the Mansuri Hospital in Cairo, founded in 1284. At most it housed a few dozen lunatics at a time.[26] Others must have contained many fewer.

Besides being chained to the walls, patients were often beaten, something even Avicenna considered to be therapeutic as it provided a means of beating sense into the wildly irrational. But inmates were also treated, as Galen had recommended, with a diet designed to cool and moisten their bodies, to counter the heating and drying effects of the burnt black or yellow bile that was held to have driven them mad, and given baths to produce

The Arab hospital in Granada, Spain: many hospitals were built across the Islamic world, and included some provision for the treatment of the insane.

similar effects. Blood-letting, cupping, vomits and purges were employed to evacuate the noxious humours, along with opium and other more compli-cated drugs designed to calm or to stimulate, depending upon whether the patient was frantic or withdrawn. Lavender, thyme, pomegranate or pear juice, chamomile and black hellebore (**PL. 26**) were among the substances Avicenna listed as possibly helpful, along with milk applied to the head, and a variety of oils and ointments. Centuries later, these and similar approaches would be recommended by the first Western mad-doctors.

That separate spaces were set aside for mad women indicates that some of them, too, proved too difficult to handle in domestic settings, for Muslim men were extremely reluctant to expose their women-folk in this fashion. But male and female alike, most of the mad were dealt with at home by their families, an obligation much easier to fulfil for the rich, of course, because they could more readily mobilize the required resources and if necessary make provision for informal confinement. For the bulk of the population of the Islamic empire, who lived far from urban centres, such relief as the hospitals provided was obviously unavailable, and besides, for most people, the ministrations of one versed in formal medicine were financially out of reach. For a variety of reasons, therefore, as long as they were generally perceived to be harmless and unthreatening, the mad were left at large, 'free' to wander and to beg, at the mercy of a community that might respond with taunts and jeers, not to mention violence.

Demonic Possession and Spiritual Healing

Prior to the Arab conquests, many in the Near East had converted to Christianity, particularly from the fourth century, when it was made the state religion of the Roman empire. As early as 300, Christianity had become a force to be reckoned with in the major cities of the eastern Mediterranean, from Antioch to Alexandria, and by century's end it could count itself the majority religion of the Roman empire, a new mass religion.[27] Miraculous healing, and especially the casting out of demons through rites of exorcism, had an important place among the new community of believers. In the third century, when adult baptism was common, 'drastic' exorcism of the healthy was part of the preliminaries to that rite.[28] More broadly, Christian missionaries, from the religion's earliest years, had used the exorcism of demons and the healing of the possessed as proof of the power of the word of Christ over the invisible enemies faced by humans.[29] Such claims had broad scriptural authority, for Jesus had (as we saw in the previous chapter) on many occasions cast out demons and cured the blind, the lame and the sick. Some Christian clerics claimed to have inherited the same powers, as did those holy men who came to be seen as saints.

Thus in the Byzantine empire, the notion of spiritual healing and demonic possession came to be firmly established, and widely accepted. Some have suggested that this development was brought about by the penetration of pagan thinking into Christianity, following the mass conversions of the fourth century.[30] The existence of demons and the power of religious healing were widely canvassed, and by no means were these beliefs only to be found among ordinary folk – even the powerful and the relatively well-educated embraced them.[31] Unseen demons were everywhere, and everywhere were responsible for havoc and misfortune.[32] With ample biblical precedent, madness was especially easily understood through the lens of demonic possession, and patients flocked, or were dragged, to healing shrines and monasteries.

Nor did such practices disappear in the aftermath of the Arab conquests. The majority of the population in the Near East remained Christian for at least two or three centuries more (and a substantial minority even after that). In such circles, attempts to heal the mad through a variety of religiously based interventions persisted. Meanwhile, among Muslims, with the Qu'ran largely silent on these matters, Islam could boast of no comparable tradition of religious healing.[33]

Muhammad, as Allah's prophet, received the text of the Qu'ran from God, but unlike Jesus, he is not portrayed as possessing divine powers. God's messenger, he does not heal the sick, nor cast out demons, nor raise the dead. Yet after his death, it gradually came to be believed that he had performed miracles. *Hadith*, or religious traditions – compiled, so it was said, from the first-hand testimony of the faithful about the Prophet's actions and words – were mobilized to create a basis for prophetic healing,[34] one of the objects of which was to explain and offer remedies for madness. Besides prayers and incantations, these remedies included more robustly physical treatments not dissimilar from those proposed by physicians: the opening of veins to draw off blood, purges and cauterization of the head with hot irons – *jinn* were popularly believed to shy away from iron, which may explain the popularity of the last technique.

Reinterpretations of *hadith* led gradually to a change. By the later Middle Ages, Muhammad too was seen as a miracle worker, and Islamic 'saints' appeared who could perform lesser feats of divine grace.[35] The Arabs certainly believed in spirits and demons.[36] Indeed *jinn* are often invoked in the early portions of the Qu'ran and are a frequent subject in Islamic art, and stories about them proliferate in popular literature and in religious tracts.[37] The notion that the mad were bedevilled or possessed followed from this as the explanation for their behaviour and strange notions.

To borrow an Arabic phrase, '*al-junun funun*' – madness is of many kinds. In a literary or mystical sense *junun* could even be used as a form of praise, denoting an alternative to narrow calculative reason. In Persian, too, the term for a mad person, *divaneh* (derived from *div* and *aneh* – demon-like or possessed by demons) encompassed both kinds of meaning (and *div* itself had deep roots in Persian and Indian mythologies). But Arabic-speakers could also refer more narrowly to madness in its medical and juridical forms by making use of the term *majnun*, often used for 'lunatic', with particularly negative connotations. And it was this term '*Majnun*', most literally meaning 'possessed by *jinn*', that was given eponymously to one of the great romantic heroes of Islamic literature, Qays, whose obsessive love for Layla ends in tragedy (PL. 8).

Many versions of the story of Layla and Majnun exist. Its tale of star-crossed lovers prompts comparisons with Shakespeare's much later tragedy, *Romeo and Juliet*, and its cultural resonance is even greater. Perhaps the most famous version was the long narrative poem by the late twelfth-century Persian poet Nizami,[38] but the tale was endlessly retold, in musical form and in paintings, as well as in poetry and prose. The standard elements are always present: Layla and Majnun fall in love. The latter becomes obsessed with the object of his affections, and loses all sense of perspective and propriety (hence the renaming of Qays as Majnun). And ironically his very obsession leads him to give up his selfhood to the beloved, and to extreme actions that result in the rejection by Layla's family of his attempts to marry her. For to marry a madman is to bring dishonour on the house. Majnun retreats to the desert and communes with the animals, periodically making desperate efforts to contact his beloved, to whom he writes endless poems. He is rebuffed, and eventually the two parted lovers die, but not before Majnun has descended into ever more overt madness. In some versions he is shackled, only to break loose from his chains. He lives like a hermit in the desert, emaciated, incoherent, hair long and unkempt, nails like the claws of one of the beasts with whom he associates, his skin blackened by the sun, crawling on all fours, hallucinating and staring into space, and at other times lapsing into a frenzy; and naked – a shocking violation of social norms for a Muslim. In a moment of lucidity, he acknowledges, 'I am a thorn in the flesh of my people, and even my name brings shame upon my friends. Anyone may shed my blood; I am outlawed, and who kills me is not guilty of murder.'[39] Here are classic stereotypes of madness – asocial, estranged from reality and the norms of conventional morality, reduced to the level of a beast, a fearsome outcast, unpredictable – and possessed, in many versions of the story, by a malicious *jinn*.

Christian Europe

In Europe, medieval societies in the centuries that followed the breakdown of the Roman *imperium* were riven by the twin scourges of poverty and disease, their depredations exacerbated by endemic violence and insecurity.

This was a world of malnutrition and famine, with mass starvation an ever-present possibility and often a reality.[40] So, too, with disease, whose ravages are most visible in the brute demographic fact of low life expectancy: the medieval man who reached the age of forty-five was the exception, and given the perils of childbirth, his female counterpart was generally even shorter-lived. In the immediate aftermath of the advent of the Black Death in 1348, mortality rates were yet higher, as outbreaks of plague continued throughout the fourteenth century, reducing European population by perhaps a third. Many people lived on the very margins of subsistence, with diets lacking in basic nutrients, especially in the winter months, and unable to understand let alone control raging infections, or the multitude of parasitic and insect-borne pathogens (not to mention society's failure to deal with the routine contamination of both food and water by excrement, human and animal). It is thus no surprise to learn that the burden of sickness was staggering.[41] As were the numbers of maimed and crippled people – deaf, blind, deprived of the use of one or more limbs, afflicted with rickets, infected with leprosy, sufferers from all manner of defects and deformities. And to those largely helpless and dependent victims of misfortune, we may add the mad – epileptic, frenzied, melancholic, hallucinating, demented.

Our knowledge of the fate of the multitudes in the period between the seventh and the thirteenth centuries is scanty at best. We can offer no secure generalizations grounded in detailed evidence about individual sufferers. The loss of literacy that had accompanied the collapse of the Western Empire was severe and long-lasting, exacerbating the always difficult task of recovering the experience of suffering among the lower orders, the less fortunate who made up all but a tiny fraction of medieval society. Only in the monasteries and the Church did much semblance of literacy survive, and for the most part the focus was on religious texts, not the pagan legacy of Rome. The medicine of the Greeks and the Romans was but one of the casualties of this cultural neglect, but its decline had important implications for medieval understanding of and responses to madness.

The Roman Church (it began to be referred to as the Catholic Church following the Reformation of the sixteenth century) was the only major institution to survive and ultimately thrive in the aftermath of the collapse of the Roman empire. The earliest Christians had been subjected to periodic torture, repression and martyrdom at the hands of their Roman rulers, who found their stiff-necked refusal to pay tribute and to sacrifice to the traditional

Roman gods an insult verging on sacrilege. Public religious practice was considered to be vital to the stability and success of the empire. Persecution that began under Nero in AD 64 and reached its peak during the third century created numerous martyrs and saints (though even in the third century there were periodic lulls in the repression). The official toleration of Christianity announced by the emperor Constantine in the Edict of Milan of AD 313 and his own adoption of the Christ-cult marked a decisive shift, reinforced by his death-bed conversion to Christianity in AD 337. Only one of Constantine's successors, the emperor Julian in the AD 360s, made any sustained effort to turn back to the pagan gods, and with official approval (or perhaps without official repression), Christianity steadily, indeed dramatically, increased in strength over the next two centuries.[42] It became 'an established church that absorbed men and wealth like a sponge'.[43] Ironically, too, it was an organization that ultimately brought about a new intolerance and hatred, terror and prejudice.

Between 375 and 800, Christians undertook a remarkably effective programme of evangelization directed towards the barbarian societies to the north and west. The tribal character of these societies made it easier to spread Christianity, for it meant that the conversion of a chief or key elder was often rapidly followed by mass conversion of the rest of the tribe. A crucial element in the process was the use of miracles and wonders to demonstrate the power of the Christian God, including the smashing of shrines, the destruction of pagan temples, the exorcism of demons, and the accomplishment of magical cures of the crippled and the crazed.[44] My God is more powerful than your gods was the message. See us destroy your sacred objects without retribution. Witness our miracles, our ability to cure your sick and tortured souls. St Martin of Tours (316–97), for example, made a practice of burning pagan temples, thereby convincing the barbarians that his God should be venerated and the pagan idols cast aside, since they could not even save themselves.[45]

Miracles were interwoven with Christianity from the very beginning. Officially, the early church vehemently opposed magic, though in practice the distinction between magic and miracle was often hard to draw, an ambiguity that was not without its dangers. Pagans and Christians alike blamed demons for their misfortunes, and these suprahuman creatures were, for the Christian faithful, ultimately the agents of the Evil One, Satan himself.[46] Jesus had demonstrated his ability to cast them out, to revive the dead, heal the sick, dismiss demons from the bodies of the possessed, and his powers had been passed down to his apostles: 'when he had called unto him his twelve disciples, he gave them power against unclean spirits, to cast them out, and to heal all manner of sickness and all manner of disease.... Heal the sick, cleanse the lepers, raise the dead, cast out devils: freely ye have received, freely give.'[47] These powers were believed to have then passed to the saints and the bishops. At every mass, a sacrament was enacted. Through the miraculous mystery of divine intervention, bread and wine became Christ's body and blood. And yet, somewhat surprisingly, early Christians shied away from using miracles as propaganda.[48]

Saints and Miracles

Not so in later centuries. All those martyrs and saints from the period of early Christian persecution rematerialized (or more accurately their material remains were given new spiritual efficacy) to help to underpin a set of potent beliefs and practices centred upon the notion of saintly powers, often through the medium of relics, to cure the afflicted and perform posthumous miracles. Tombs were powerful; bones even more so. 'Although pagan temples and altars were closed down, converted or destroyed, the old cures, visions and miracles of the healing god Aesculapius [Asclepius] or Apollonius, still occurred at Christian shrines under the patronage of a new spiritual hierarchy, the martyred saints.'[49] As early as 386, the still pagan St Augustine of Hippo (354–430) recorded witnessing such miracles at a recently opened tomb outside Milan: two saints' bones gave new sight to a blind man and chased demons out of another who was possessed. And Pope Gregory I (c. 540–604), who sent St Augustine of Canterbury on a mission to convert the Anglo-Saxons of England, published a whole collection of miracles, signs, wonders and healings in his *Dialogues*.[50] In this he was very much within the medieval mainstream. His was a devotion broadly shared by his flock, and one that won him instant sainthood by popular acclaim on his death.

By the end of the sixth century, few could doubt the centrality of saints' graves to the power and reach of the Church.[51] In later centuries, as pilgrims sought the intercession of the saints, burials were opened and remains removed – sometimes parcelled out so that more than one site could proclaim its possession of the miraculous healing powers, and benefit from the donations thus attracted. The distances relics travelled might be short or long: the monks of Pontigny in central France, for instance, where a Cistercian abbey was founded in 1114, opened up the tomb of St Edmund Rich of Abingdon who was buried there and cut off one of his arms before closing it again.[52] That way they could set up a second place in the monastery for the pilgrims to worship and seek cures (and leave offerings). At the much older (675) Benedictine monastery in Abingdon in Oxfordshire, by contrast, a mass of holy relics was gathered together over the years from great distances. As listed in 1116, these included 'five relics of Christ, pieces of six apostles, bits of thirty-one martyrs, assorted remains of thirty-nine confessors, and particles of sixteen virgins' – a massive collection of miracle-working substances that attracted hordes of the faithful.[53] And after the soldiers of the Fourth Crusade diverted their attentions to Constantinople, besieging and sacking it in 1204, an orgy of theft and destruction ensued: churches 'were ransacked and crate upon rattling crate of bones was sent to the West'.[54] Such remains were so valuable that thefts, deceptions, forgeries, battles over ownership were regularly recorded.

St Catherine of Siena was widely venerated after her death in Rome in 1380. In life, she proclaimed that she had undergone a mystical marriage with Christ in 1368, at the age of twenty-one. Later she stated she no longer needed earthly food, subsisting mostly on communion wafers, before ceasing to take either food or water. In a matter of weeks she was dead. The Sienese wanted to retrieve her body, but to smuggle it out of Rome intact was impossible, so they settled for her head and one of her thumbs, which supposedly remained incorruptible.[55] Stories proliferated of saints whose bodies had remained intact, or whose coffins, once opened, perfumed the air rather than stank – the mysterious 'odour of sanctity' that gave further proof to the credulous of the divine blessings saints' relics could bestow.

Centuries later, the English poet Andrew Marvell would proclaim that the grave is 'a fine and private place'.[56] For some perhaps, but not for the beatified. Saints' graves might be elaborate – some came to be loaded with gold and ornamentation – but they were scarcely private places. Remains were often transferred to reliquaries, highly elaborate containers that pilgrims came to kiss and worship. The abbey at Conques in the Languedoc, France, for example, contained the skull of St Foy, who was said to have been tortured to death by the Romans in the late third century by being cooked atop a red-hot brazier when she refused to abjure her Christian faith. (The relic had been stolen by a monk in the ninth century from its original resting place in Agen.) Some time between 983 and 1013, the skull, reputed to have extraordinary miraculous powers, was placed inside a statue, resting inside a silver lining that was then covered with gold plates and inlaid with precious stones (PL. 10) – so gaudy that priests visiting from Chartres claimed that it resembled a pagan idol, as indeed it did (not that that inhibited its appeal to the peasantry). Similarly, the bones of Thomas à Becket, murdered by four knights in his cathedral in 1170 after tussling with Henry II over the rights and privileges of the Church (PL. 9), were placed in a gold and bejewelled shrine in Canterbury Cathedral in 1220.

All through the Middle Ages, large numbers of the crippled, the sick and the mad sought solace and cure at these shrines (PLS 12–14). Many would have tried folk remedies – herbs, ointments, amulets, the ministrations of local healers. And from the eleventh century onwards, as Hippocratic and Galenic medicine began to re-enter western Europe from the East, others would have been subjected to its bleedings and its purges, its cupping and its vomits, not to mention changes of diet and regimen. But chronic disorders, in particular, led to efforts to enlist the healing powers of the saints and martyrs. Various fragmentary accounts survive. At the tomb of St Wulfstan (1008–95) in Worcester Cathedral, for example, one insane girl lay raging for fifteen days.[57] We do not know her fate. But when 'miracles' did occur, shrines were quick to record them, so the inference must be that she remained mad. Clearly, the presence of people behaving in this fashion could disrupt church routines, lying there as they did for days or even weeks at a time. At Norwich, on another occasion, 'a girl was rapt into a frenzy and brought bound to Hugh's tomb; she remained there until the feast of All Souls, and that night her screaming was more violent than usual, disturbing the choir and the whole church, so that they would not celebrate mass at the altar of St John the Baptist, near the tomb. Finally she fell asleep; when a crowd of worshippers woke her up she was well again.'[58] Partial cures and later recoveries were credited to the power of the saint and, of course, mental troubles of psychogenic origin (even those that involved blindness or paralysis and were not seen as mental troubles at the time) may well have responded to the powerful suggestive effects of a visit to such a sacred place.

Many shrines were thought to cure a multitude of ills. The blood of St Thomas à Becket was reckoned to cure blindness, insanity, leprosy and deafness, not to mention a host of other ailments, so Canterbury drew pilgrims from all over Europe as well as England, until 1538, when Henry VIII ordered that the saint's shrine be dismantled and the bones destroyed, and that the renegade priest should never be spoken of again. Chaucer's *Canterbury Tales* recounts the lives of a company of pilgrims on their way from London to worship at Becket's shrine.[59]

The tombs of other saints developed a more specialized reputation. Martyrs who had been beheaded seem to have been popular choices for those seeking relief from mental distress. One of the most important of these places – a site that attracted mad pilgrims and their escorts for centuries – was the shrine of St Dymphna at Gheel, in what is now Belgium. The legend of St Dymphna incorporated a variety of elements found widely scattered in European folklore, here brought together to create a compelling narrative of attempted incest, madness and murder. According to the saint's

The beheading of St Margaret of Antioch, twelfth century, a painting from the Catalan church in Vilaseca, Spain. Margaret was executed for refusing to renounce Christianity.

A bronze panel on the right door of the Basilica di San Zeno Maggiore, Verona, Italy (twelfth century), showing St Zeno performing an exorcism. Commanded by the saint, a devil exits from the mouth of the emperor Gallienus's daughter. There are forty-eight such panels, illustrating biblical themes and the lives of St Michael and St Zeno.

vita, which was not compiled until the mid-thirteenth century by Pierre, a canon of Cambrai, the young Irish maiden was born to a pagan king and his Christian wife early in the seventh century. When she was fourteen, her mother died, and her grief-stricken father, Damon, later conceived the idea of marrying the person who most closely resembled his dead wife, his own daughter. With her priest in tow, Dymphna fled across the seas and settled in the small village of Gheel. But her father pursued them, and on finding the two had the priest beheaded; when his daughter persisted in defying him, he cut off her head too in a fit of frenzy. Dymphna and her martyred companion Gerebernus were subsequently buried in a cave, but their remains were later exhumed – his transported to Sonsbeck, Germany (by some accounts his head was left behind),[60] and hers placed in an urn and moved to a chapel, where pilgrims bringing with them their mad relations began to flock in search of miraculous cures.

Some of the insane slept in the church awaiting their restoration to sanity. When the original church was burned down by fire in 1489, a new and more elaborate replacement was erected. By 1532, it was overseen by ten clerics, later joined by ten canons, who supervised an elaborate ritual of prayers, penances and ceremonial offerings, all seeking the intercession of the martyred virgin. Lunatics were placed in the church and chained by the ankle, and for eighteen days efforts were made to exorcize the evil demons who had possessed them. If madness still persisted, many of the afflicted moved in to live with a local peasant family, and in this way, Gheel and its environs for centuries constituted a curious sort of lunatic colony, the whole economy being based on the donations made by the relations of the mad.[61] Similar shrines specializing in miracles for the mad emerged at the tomb of St Maturinus (Mathurin) in Larchant, and of St Acharius (Achaire) at Haspres, both in France,

It may well be that the cures of the mad exercised a particular hold on the faithful because they so often involved the casting out of demons. Here was perhaps the most powerful and unanswerable demonstration of God's omnipotence. The drama of an exorcism was unmatched. Preceded by a struggle and often accompanied by fits and screams, the Devil's minions were driven forth.[62] Hence the popularity of vivid portrayals in the Middle Ages and even into the Reformation of demons being driven forth, images that appear in both paintings and sculpture. One panel of the great bronze doors of the basilica at Verona, for example, dating to around 1100, shows the local bishop, Zeno, expelling a devil from the mouth of the emperor's daughter. Giotto's fresco in the Upper Church in Assisi completed in 1299 shows St Francis casting out a host of demons from the city of Arezzo. And the *Très riches heures du duc de Berry*, created between 1412 and 1416 as a devotional book for John, Duke of Berry, and perhaps the best surviving example of a French illuminated manuscript of the period, likewise contains a striking image of the exorcism of a demon (PL. 11). But exorcism didn't always work. Indeed, more often than not it failed. Fortunately, those failures could always be explained away, leaving religious faith mostly intact.

Literature and Madness

One striking feature of medieval culture was the emergence of a popular form of religious drama, the so-called mystery and miracle plays. (Mysteries were another name for miracles, and the two terms were used largely interchangeably at the time.) The various cycles of miracle plays were a medium for biblical stories to be told and retold, and moral messages to be brought to the masses, for usually there was a whole series of performances over a period of days. Originally these were religious pageants performed in church, with many devoted to Christ's Passion and others to such popular subjects as Adam and Eve and the Last Judgment. During the course of the thirteenth century they spread across Europe and were increasingly performed in the vernacular and produced by guilds.

Representations of the miracles accomplished by the Virgin Mary or a panoply of saints were popular parts of the repertory. Madness and possession were recurrent themes, offering the audience graphic and educational demonstrations of how sinking into sin allowed the Devil to possess the sinner, and then to render him mad. Saul and Nebuchadnezzar were particular favourites, both for the entertainment they offered and the moral lessons their lives contained, as also were stories about the demoniacs of the New Testament. One of two fates beckoned these characters: either to be hurried off to hell, or to be saved by the grace of Our Lady or one of her saints.

Miracle plays were often elaborate occasions and were performed by a mixture of travelling professionals and locals on festival days. The spectacles were staged from Spain to the Netherlands, from France to Germany, and in many of England's largest cities (though there, after the Reformation, they would be suppressed by Henry VIII as vehicles for the transmission of Papist superstition).[63] Freed from direct ecclesiastical supervision, the plays in their later incarnations often diverged from the Scriptures, incorporating popular beliefs and exaggerating the lessons of biblical stories for dramatic effect. Herod, who owed his position as king of Judea to the Romans, and who in Christian tradition was the man who slaughtered the innocents as he sought to eliminate the infant Jesus, was another popular subject. The story of an immoral madman bent on killing God grew steadily more embroidered and extreme as the early Latin versions were reworked in the vernacular, until Herod became the very embodiment of the blasphemous and mad sinner, punished by God the Father with the loss of his reason and the most painful of deaths.[64] Here is madness as violence, frenzy, anger without limit – and a punishment from God. The Chester Cycle follows Herod's fate in a series of plays to the bitter end:

> My legges rotten and my armes;
> I haue done so many harmes,
> that now I see of feends swarms
> from hell cominge for me.
> (My legs and arms are rotten; I have done so much harm,
> that now I see swarms of fiends coming from hell for me.)[65]

Hell was a destination made vivid in the greatest of medieval literary works, Dante's *Divine Comedy*, and here, too, the medieval reader encountered madness as divine punishment. After meeting his guide, the poet Virgil (condemned to the outer circle of hell because he was not a Christian), Dante begins his tour of the Inferno, a region filled with perpetual lamentations, a universe of miserable souls enduring unending and exquisitely refined tortures. Here are the sinners who have given way to passion, 'those who make reason slave to appetite'. There at the edge of the Wood of Suicides is the river of boiling blood, Phlegethon, and the burning sands. The gluttonous and the greedy, the deceitful and the depraved, the heretic and the blasphemer, the thieves and the murderers, the priests violating their vows: all have their place and pass in review. And in the tenth and last ditch of the eighth circle of hell, just one remove from Satan himself, are the falsifiers, the quacks and the counterfeiters, the liars and the impersonators, whose fate is to be afflicted with leprosy, dropsy – and madness. There the Trojan queen Hecuba, wife of Priam, afflicted with the sight of her two dead children,

> forsennata latrò si comme cane;
> tanto il dolor le fé la mente torta.
> (barked, out of her senses, like a dog – her agony had so deformed
> her mind.)[66]

A few steps further on, Dante and Virgil encounter madness in its most violent form:

> Ma né di Tebe furie né troiane
> si vider mäi in alcun tanto crude,
> non punger bestie, nonché membra umane,

> Quant'io vidi in due ombre smorte e nude,
> che mordendo correvan di quel modo
> che 'l porco quando del porcil si schiude.
> (But neither fury – Theban, Trojan – ever was seen to be so cruel
> against another, in rending beasts and even human limbs. As
> were these two shades I saw, both pale and naked, who, biting, ran
> berserk in just the way a hog does when it's let loose from its sty.)[67]

And then Dante recoils, as the indecent Myrrha, who seduced her father into committing incest by changing her form, hurries by, raging, threatening, frightful to behold. Madness is nakedness, violence, animality, and above all the wages of sin. In all these ways, it is the very negation of civilization.

This strong sense of madness as the consequence of sin was echoed by many medieval writers.[68] But one could just as well invert the equation: sin itself was madness. Indeed it was the very worst sort of madness, for to violate God's laws was to put oneself at risk of eternal damnation, of being thrust into the unending horrors of the netherworld that Dante so vividly invited his audience to contemplate: people with limbs pierced or hacked off; a man ripped open from stem to stern, 'his bowels hung between his legs, one saw his vitals and the miserable sack that makes of what we swallow excrement'; a crowd circling endlessly before a devil who slices them with his sword, then lets them shuffle round 'the road of pain' until back they come, 'wounds closed again…to meet his blade once more'; still another of the perpetually condemned, throat slit, nose hacked off, one ear remaining, 'his windpipe on the outside, all bloodred';[69] and on and on, a catalogue of the most ingenious and frightful tortures. Who but a madman would allow passion and temptation to overthrow his reason, when the price of doing so was such barely imaginable and unmitigated suffering? In the words of John Mirk, the late fourteenth-century prior of the abbey of Lilleshall in Shropshire, 'he who so lyueth a fowle lyfe, he may be sure of a foule ende' ('he who lives a foul life, may be sure of a foul end').[70]

Medicine and Madness

For the medieval mind, all forms of illness, mental and physical alike, were the consequences of the Fall. Eve's fatal temptation of Adam thrust mankind out of Paradise into a world of corruption, disorder and decay. In this world, illness was one of God's punishments for sinners, a torment they deserved, and a warning of what might well await them in the hereafter. Disturbances of mind and body might prompt them to repent, or else hurry them off to hell – of which mortification of the flesh and the anguish of minds diseased were but a foretaste. In the words of Rabanus Maurus Magnentius (c. 780–856), archbishop of Mainz in Germany and a prolific commentator on Holy Scripture, 'Sickness is a disease caused by vice.... Fever is a fleshly desire, burning insatiably.... Swelling leprosy is puffed-up pride.... He has scabs on his body whose mind is ruined by the lusts of the flesh.'[71]

It was through this lens of Christian belief that ruined minds were most often interpreted and attitudes to the mad were formed. But from the eleventh century onwards there had been renewed interest in an alternative approach to explain madness and treat its ravages, one that involved a reincarnation of pre-Christian traditions. That revival emerged from broader economic and political changes that began to mark medieval Europe and to transform its culture.

As migrating peoples came to rest, political institutions stabilized and eventually the socio-economic improvements bequeathed by the new feudal system took hold, so Christian Europe became a little more prosperous, a little more urban, a little more secure. One symptom and demonstration of this growing power and self-confidence in the Christian world was the *Reconquista* in the Iberian Peninsula (see p. 51). In 1064, Pope Alexander II (d. 1073) issued a thirty-year indulgence for those who sought to reclaim Aragon for Christianity. Pope Urban II (1042–99) then sought to persuade the fighters to stay on and add to their conquests, and later still, military orders such as the Knights Templar joined the fight. Gradually the Moors were pushed back, though the last remnants of Islamic authority were not expelled from Spain until the fall of Granada in 1492.

One of the effects of the efforts to expel the Moors was a more intimate encounter with Arabic-speaking culture and civilization, even if the rulers of Christian Spain persecuted, killed and forced out its exponents. Another was the launch of a series of Crusades to the Holy Land, which also inevitably brought a closer acquaintance with the achievements of Muslim civilization. As mentioned at the beginning of this chapter, such fundamental changes as a shift from Roman to Arabic numbering systems, paving the way for mathematical advances, can be traced to these heightened cultural contacts. So, too, can the re-importation to the West of Greek medicine, either directly, via the acquisition of Galenic and other texts that had largely vanished when Roman rule collapsed, or indirectly through the glosses and compilations of the great Muslim physicians such as Avicenna. Fragmentary Latin texts had survived in some monasteries, and been consulted by monks who served their communities (and sometimes neighbouring villages) as healers. But such texts as survived were few and far between. Even the richest monasteries seldom possessed more than eight or ten medical manuscripts. Most could at best lay claim to one.[72] But now larger numbers and a much broader array of medical treatises reached the West.

The contemporary rise of the university did much to forward this process, as did the formation of guilds, including medical guilds, in the newly emerging urban spaces. At Salerno, Naples, Bologna, Padua, Montpellier, Paris, Oxford and Cambridge, medical teaching developed informally and then in more organized fashion. And the Classical texts, and their Arabic successors, were translated from Syriac, Persian and Arabic into Greek and Latin, the lingua franca of the emerging educated class. Academic medicine began to find its feet, and through their guilds, newly learned doctors sought to ratify their superior status and to gain some degree of control and dominance over the medical marketplace. In the latter respect they were conspicuously unsuccessful, and a broad spectrum of healers continued to peddle their services for centuries to come. But their medical theories gained increasing influence among the elite, giving them access to an expanding market for their skills.

As literate men of learning they more readily created a common medical culture, and they were possessed of a complex intellectual system that allowed them to diagnose and prescribe in systematic ways. The invention of the printing press made the mass production of books possible for the first time, allowing the rapid spread of texts across a broad geographical area, and breaking the connection to the old scribal tradition, predominantly the preserve of the monasteries. Physicians could exchange ideas and develop a common consciousness across broad swathes of geographical territory, and could also appropriate the cultural authority that came with their knowledge of the ancients.

What purported to be a complete edition of Galen in Greek was published in Venice in 1525, and became the basis for Latin translations. Portions of the Hippocratic corpus also appeared in that year. By the close of the century, almost six hundred editions of Galen had been printed across

The title-page of an early edition of Avicenna's text, the influential Canon of Medicine, *translated into Latin and printed in Venice, 1595.*

western Europe. Even earlier, printed editions of the great Muslim physicians had appeared, symptomatic of how much the revival of Classical medicine depended upon the Arabs. Avicenna's *Canon of Medicine* was printed in 1473 and reprinted two years later. Its third edition came out before the first printed version of any of Galen's work, and by 1500, it had already gone through sixteen editions. Other medical works soon followed, including books by Rhazes (al-Razi), Averroes (Ibn Rushd), Hunayn ibn Ishaq, Issac Israeli and Haly Abbas (al-Majusi).[73] Though the connection would later be repressed and forgotten, well into the sixteenth century, learned medicine in Europe was in many ways an extension of the medicine nurtured and developed in the Arabic-speaking world. Its practitioners found that they now commanded an immensely powerful intellectual construct, one that made sense of symptoms, and pointed the way towards remedies for what had gone wrong. Simultaneously, it offered reassurance to the patient that someone understood what had brought about their suffering, and what might relieve it.

Nor were texts the only innovations imported from the Islamic world. Both the crusaders in the East and the Spanish armies in the West had encountered Islamic hospitals (see p. 65), and these institutions now began to appear in western Europe. Many were initially attached to monasteries, and almost all were religious rather than medical institutions. They took in travellers and pilgrims, for example, as well as orphans and the elderly. But they also provided succour to the sick, and over time, they grew larger and began to move beyond their religious origins and acquire a more distinctly medical identity. Some were tiny, but others – in Paris, Florence, Milan and Siena – grew to contain some hundreds of patients.

Some began to specialize in the management of the mad. Bethlehem Hospital would eventually become the most famous such institution in the English-speaking world. More usually referred to as Bedlam (the name that will be used generally here), its evolution towards becoming a madhouse was gradual. Founded in 1247 at the Priory of St Mary of Bethlehem, Bishopsgate, just outside the walls of the City of London, in its early years it took in the usual heterogeneous collection of the helpless and dependent, the stranger and the pilgrim, that were the stock-in-trade of the first hospitals. But some time in the late fourteenth century it began to acquire a reputation for caring for the mad, though the numbers it took in were tiny. A visitation in 1403 recorded the presence of six inmates who were *menti capti*, deprived of their wits. Only in the late seventeenth century would the numbers of patients rise above a hundred. Slightly earlier, in 1632, the clergyman Donald Lupton (d. 1676) had written that the hospital 'would bee too little, if all that are besides themselves should be put in here'.[74]

In Spain, following Arab precedent, a whole series of asylums – seven by the fifteenth century, in Valencia, Zaragoza, Seville, Valladolid, Palma de Mallorca, Toledo and Barcelona – specialized in the institutional confinement and care of the insane. What sorts of treatment were meted out in these places in medieval times remains conjectural. Though the segregation of the mad from society would become routine some centuries later, it is vital to remember that these establishments were the exception, not the rule, in the medieval and early modern period, when most of the mad were still the responsibility of their families and remained in the community, either locked up via a variety of ad hoc expedients if deemed dangerous, or left to roam (and to rot) if not.

Armed with humoral medicine, some physicians sought, like Galen and the Hippocratics before them, to make sense of madness, and to apply their repertoire of cure-alls to the treatment of the insane. Theirs was an intellectual system that rooted madness in the body, and saw it as a naturalistic, not a supernatural, event. But doctors were prudent enough – and not yet sufficiently sure of their status – also to acknowledge cases of possession, and deferred, some of the time, to their clerical brethren. A conflict between these two contrasting interpretations of madness would eventually emerge, but for the moment, much like everyone else, physicians embraced a whole range of explanations and approaches to the mentally disturbed. In situations so desperate and distressing, why not try anything that might offer a chance of relief? If such beliefs and practices strike us as contradictory, perhaps they were. But madness bore no single meaning, and answered to no single approach. The religious who ran the shrines gloated on occasion when madmen who had not been cured by the doctors were brought to them for relief, particularly in the handful of cases where recovery ensued. Often, they sneered about how foolish it was to seek the help of human doctors in the first place.[75] But ultimately many of them, too, were willing to concede that on occasion, madness was the product of psychological stress or catastrophe, of physical trauma or of a body otherwise thrown violently out of equilibrium. God's mysteries were many.

Chapter Four

MELANCHOLIE
AND MADNESSE

Fairies, Ghosts, Goblins and Witches

Historians like to speak of the period in Europe from the late fifteenth to the dawn of the eighteenth century as the early modern era. This was an age of great religious, political, cultural and economic transformations. It saw the withering of the feudal system and the rise of the nation state, the extension of trade and markets in Europe, the circumnavigation of the globe and the growing power of absolute monarchs. It saw the Catholic Church lose its hold on portions of Europe as the various manifestations of the Protestant Reformation took hold and mostly succeed in repelling the efforts at Counter-Reformation, in northern Europe at least. And it saw the massive cultural transformations we over-schematically refer to as the Renaissance: the revival of Classical learning; the spread of print culture; ferment in art, architecture, music, literature, drama and knowledge-making; and the birth of the Scientific Revolution. Not to mention something that seemingly sits incongruously amid this list, except when one recalls the century of religious wars and blood-letting that accompanied the Reformation: witch-hunts all across Europe, a veritable epidemic of trials, tortures and executions – agonizing deaths most often inflicted by being burned alive, though other witches were hanged or drowned, dismembered or crushed to death under piles of rocks.

The European witch craze was so dramatic, and in many areas so long-lived,[1] that it has attracted enormous attention. The *bien-pensants* of the eighteenth-century Enlightenment dismissed it as false and foolish, a product of popular ignorance and superstition, aided and abetted by the exploitation of the credulity of the lower orders by the Christian churches

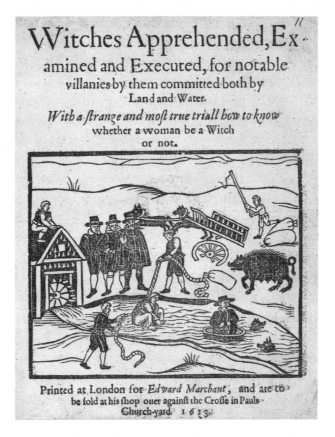

Witches Apprehended *(1613), an account of the 'several and damnable practises of Mother Sutton and Mary Sutton her daughter' from Bedford, England. The woodcut shows Mary being dunked in a river – 'a strange and most true triall how to know whether a woman be a Witch or not'. The two women were subsequently convicted of witchcraft and executed.*

– most notably, so far as figures including the French *philosophe* Voltaire (1694–1778) were concerned, the Church of Rome. (Witch-hunts, in reality, were as prevalent in Protestant territories as in Catholic, and just as deadly.) Witches were commonly seen as in league with the Devil, indeed many were alleged to have copulated with him. (They confessed as much under torture – which led to the infliction of still more frightful tortures designed to kill them.) They were themselves possessed by demons and caused their victims to be possessed. They were responsible for all manner of misfortunes, some of which befell individuals, while others (such as crop failures, epidemics of disease and destructive weather) afflicted whole communities. Somewhere between 50,000 and 100,000 witches are estimated to have perished at the hands of their persecutors before the craze for killing them (though not always the belief in their existence) finally subsided.

Most moderns share with Voltaire and with the philosopher David Hume (1711–76) a scepticism about such supernaturalism, a rational contempt for the notions of demons and magic that underpin the world of the witches. Possession, as we have seen, had been a staple explanation for some kinds of madness for centuries before the early modern era, and when earlier historians of psychiatry looked with puzzlement at a spirit-drenched world whose assumptions they did not share, they were sorely tempted to amalgamate the persecution of the witches and the mad. Witches (and the bewitched), they concluded, were really the mentally ill in another guise: deluded folk who fell victim to the demonology of the age.

This simply won't do, and not just because a majority (though by no means all) of those accused of being witches were old women, while the mad, then as now, were found in all ranks of society, old and young, male and female alike. Some witches were people we would now consider to be mad, and some of the mad continued to be seen as possessed by devils or punished by God. But if the two categories overlapped, they were seen by contemporaries as quite distinct from each other; and so for the most part they were. In the sixteenth and seventeenth centuries, both the educated and uneducated believed that Satan was active in daily life and that the world was filled with spirits and ghosts – beliefs they defended as being founded in divine Scripture and in the evidence of their own eyes. Theirs was a world where death was omnipresent, but then so too was Satan. Both were equally real. And Satan was always on the lookout for souls to seduce and sinners he could co-opt to his cause, driving out their resistance to his schemes and turning them into instruments of evil.

Catholic apologists saw Protestant reformers as agents of Satan, heretics in league with the forces of darkness. Men such as Martin Luther (1483–1548) returned the charge with interest. The Pope was the 'Anti-Christ', 'and', claimed the English divine George Gifford (c. 1548–1600), 'his false religion was set up…by the efficacie of [Satan's] power'.[2] The rites of exorcism for most Protestants were a ruse, in which the Devil pretended to leave the bodies of the possessed in order to strengthen the beliefs of deluded onlookers in the superstitions and idolatry pushed by the Papists. Luther himself fiercely denounced these priestly pretensions:

Who could list all the knavery done in the name of Christ or Mary
to drive out devilish spirits!... Such spirits arise now and confirm
purgatory, Masses for the dead, the service of all the saints,
pilgrimage, monasteries, churches and chapels.... But all of this
comes from the devil in order to maintain his abomination and
lies and to hold people charmed and caught in error.... It is a
small matter for the devil that he allows himself to be expelled,
if he wants, by an evil villain; and yet he remains really unexpelled
for he thereby possesses people all the more firmly, trapped in
his shameful deceit.[3]

Thomas Hobbes (1588–1679), the English philosopher, might anathematize 'the opinion that rude people have of fairies, ghosts and goblins
and the power of witches',[4] but his was the deviant view. To reject the ideas
of witchcraft and possession was to threaten the truths of Christianity and
the prospects of man's salvation, even to embrace atheism. It meant, in the
words of Joseph Glanvill (1636–80), a clergyman and Fellow of the Royal
Society, 'Denial of Spirits, a Life to come, and all other Principles of Religion.'[5]
It was only a 'fool', he added, 'who swaggers and huffs, and swears there are
no WITCHES'. Glanvill was not a natural philosopher (this was not yet the
age of the 'scientist', a term that would not be coined until the nineteenth
century), though he was perhaps the foremost apologist for the new virtuosi,
the leading natural philosophers of the age, and on this point, as on so many
others, he gave voice to their views.

Few among Glanvill's educated contemporaries doubted that devils
and witches were real, or that they acted in accordance with natural law.[6]
That last point was important: Satan lacked the divine power to overturn the
laws of nature. He and his minions performed wonders, not miracles. The
latter were reserved for God, and so a great deal of attention was devoted
to distinguishing 'Mirum' from 'Miraculum'. 'Sathan can doo nothing', as
Lambert Daneau (1530–95), the French Calvinist theologian, articulated the
consensus, 'but by naturall meanes and causes.... As for any other thing, or
that is of more force hee, cannot doe it.'[7]

Practitioners of Physick (as well as of Physics) granted a place in their
world for evil spirits, and their arguments with the clerics were not over the
issue of the natural versus the supernatural, but where to draw boundaries. In
medicine, this meant decoding which cases should be explained in humoral

The Possessed Woman, or Exorcism *(c. 1618), by Jacques Callot. A barefoot, obviously distracted and frantic woman, arms outstretched, arches back as she is restrained by two men while the priest on the left calls on the Virgin Mary to expel the demon who has possessed her.*

terms, and which were to be attributed to the effects of the divine or the diabolical. It was a nice question, on which the learned disagreed among themselves, and disagreements about particular cases did not necessarily neatly map on to the distinctions between the theological and the medical. On the contrary, academic medical writers discoursed on the demonic as a source of pathology as often as their theological contemporaries, and the medically orthodox differed little, if at all, on these matters, from those who specialized in writing about witchcraft. In studies of the diabolical, the Catholic exorcist Francesco Maria Guazzo (b. 1570), author of the authoritative *Compendium Maleficarum* (1608) or *Book of Witches*, relied heavily on the published writings of 'other most learned physicians'.[8] Doctors and divines – both Protestant and Catholic – were convinced that some forms of madness were a spiritual affliction, the product of possession or divine punishment for sin; but equally they were ready to concede that others were a kind of illness, brought about by traumatic injury, or by physical disorders that had mental effects.[9]

Melancholie Madnesse

One of the more notable features of the sixteenth- and seventeenth-century discourse on madness was a pronounced intellectual vogue for melancholia, and many Renaissance figures wrote on the subject in the vernacular all across Europe.[10] Interpretations of the affliction owed much to the newly circulating texts of Avicenna and, more remotely, Rufus of Ephesus and Galen, and gave prominence to the notion of what the English physician and divine Andrew Boorde (*c.* 1490–1549) called 'an evyl melancholy humour'. 'They the which be infested with this madnesse', he wrote, 'be ever in feare and drede, and doth thynke they shall never do well, but ever be in parell either of soule or body or both, wherefore they do fle from one place to another, and can nat tel where to be except they be kept in safegarde.'[11] The darkness and clouding of their minds were, for the most part, to be attributed to dark humours – black bile, or roasted, burned and acrid yellow bile, whose residues corrupted the body.

In keeping with ancient tradition, melancholy was seen to arise in diverse ways. Some cases, according to Andreas Laurentius (1560?–1609), professor of anatomy at Montpellier (and a man who conformed closely to Galenic orthodoxy in all things medical), 'cometh of the onely and sole fault of the braine'. But melancholy could also be a more systemic disorder, 'when…the whole temperature and constitution of the bodie is melancolick', or in still another form, 'the flatuous or windie melancholie…ariseth from amongst the bowels, but especially from the spleene, liver and the membrane called mesenterium' – 'a drie and hote distemperature' that he elsewhere called 'the Hypochondriake disease'.[12]

Melancholy's diverse origins were matched by its protean symptomatology. 'All melancholike persons', said Laurentius, 'have their imagination
troubled', but in many cases also 'their reason corrupted.'[13] His contemporary, the English physician Timothie Bright (1551?–1615), concurred.
Melancholics, as the word still suggests, displayed 'feare, sadnes, desperation, teares, weeping, sobbing, sighing...' and 'without cause...they can
neither receive consolation, nor hope of assurance, notwithstanding ther
be neither matter of feare, or discontentment, nor yet cause of danger'. But
the disturbances of the humours, whence the disorder arose, are responsible
for 'polluting both the substance, and the spirits of the brayne', and thus
'counterfetteth terible objectes to the fantasie...[and] causeth it without
externall occasion, to forge monstrous fictions', so that 'the hart, which hath
no judgement of discretion in it self, but giving credit to the mistaken report
of the braine, breaketh out into that inordinate passion, against reason'.[14]
Melancholics thus might suffer from hallucinations and delusions, on top of
the disturbances of mood and affect that were obvious to those around them.

Few would envy those suffering from such a catalogue of afflictions. To
make matters worse, it was widely recognized that 'all melancholike diseases
are rebellious, long and very hard to cure' – and thus 'the very scourge and
torment of Phisitions'.[15] Close attention to diet, exercise, the provision of
fresh air and a healthy environment, warm baths, soothing music and sleep
were essential to any hope of progress, as were the traditional weapons of
the well-trained physician – bleeding, cupping, scarification, vomits and
purges – all utilized carefully in a sustained attempt to bring the body back
into balance, and thus relieve the disturbances of reason, the passions and
the imagination.

Yet in this same period, melancholia also became something of a
fashionable disorder among the cultivated classes, an affliction to which it
appeared that the scholar and the man of genius were particularly prone.
Once again, this was a conceit with Classical origins. Aristotelian natural
philosophy had revived with the renewed access to Classical learning, and
within that philosophical tradition, the idea that melancholia and outstanding accomplishment were closely connected had long been canvassed – by
some of Aristotle's most devoted pupils, if not by the great man himself.
Both intellect and the imagination were stimulated, it seemed, by the possession of the melancholic humour, a connection celebrated in the poet John
Dryden's famous couplet that 'Great wits are sure to madness near allied, And

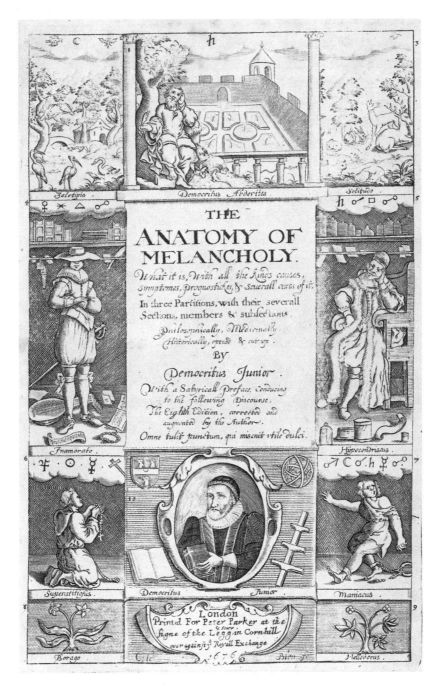

The Anatomy of Melancholy: *this frontispiece appeared for the first time in the third edition of Robert Burton's famous book. It depicts various forms of melancholy madness as well as animals, herbs and astrological signs associated with insanity, including a picture of a raving maniac, straining against his chains, his face contorted with rage.*

thin partitions do their bounds divide.'[16] Raphael thus places the brooding Michelangelo as Heraclitus in his fresco in the Vatican, the *School of Athens* (1509/10), and Dürer's famous engraving *Melancholia I* (1514) has the winged creative genius in the grip of melancholic madness.

Such notions were expounded upon at length in the greatest compilation of Renaissance thinking on melancholy, *The Anatomy of Melancholy*, published in 1621 pseudonymously by Democritus Junior, in reality the Oxford academic and divine Robert Burton (1577–1640). By the time its final, posthumous edition appeared in 1660, Burton's tome consisted of nearly 1,500 pages, a compilation and synthesis of Western lore and learning on the subject that incorporated the work of his predecessors, and put them in his shade. Perhaps Burton's own melancholic temperament encouraged him to laud melancholia's connections to creativity, though he was certainly intimately familiar with the paralysing depression the black humour could bring in its train. As he affirms, '*that which others hear or reade of, I felt and practised my selfe*', and while '*they get their knowledge by books*' he commented wryly, '*I mine by melancholizing*'. For him, as for most of his predecessors, '*Fear & Sorrow* are the true Characters and inseparable companions of most *Melancholy*' – emotions that struck down the sufferer '*without any apparent occasion*' and that served to distinguish melancholia from the other major form of madness, mania.[17]

Like his medical forebears (from whom he quoted extensively), Burton viewed melancholia as generally the product of an imbalance of the humours, and especially a superfluity of black bile. He rejected the tendency to turn to 'Sorcerers, Witches, Magicians, etc.' in search of cures (or, as he preferred to put it, 'unlawful cures'), commending instead those 'which God has appointed' – predominantly the anti-phlogisitic or reducing remedies proffered by 'God's intermediate Ministers', the physicians. Thus bleeding and medicines for 'purging upwards or downward', leeches and lancings, blisters and cuppings, but also the other stock-in-trade of the doctors, attention to the so-called non-naturals: 'diet, retention and evacuation, fresh air, exercise of both body and mind, sleeping and waking, and the passions or perturbations of the mind'.[18] Above all, Burton counselled those who would avoid melancholy's toils and troubles, '*Be not solitary, be not idle.*'[19]

However, and it is a very important qualification, not all cases of melancholia could be explained or treated in this way. Even while recommending medical interventions, Burton had enjoined his readers who suffered from melancholy to 'first begin with prayer, and then use physick; not one without the other, but both together'.[20] But prayer first. And that was in cases where the melancholy originated in the body. However, it might also issue from other sources, and then the relevance of medicine was less clear-cut. Burton wrote at length on religious melancholy, and like almost all educated men of his era, had a lively sense of Satan's active presence in the world, his ability to materialize in people's lives, and to tempt and torture them. 'How farre the power of Spirits and Devils doth extend,' he wrote, 'and whether they can cause this, or any other Disease, is a serious question, and worthy to be considered.' Further 'Many thinke he can work upon the body, but not upon the minde. But experience pronounceth otherwise, that he can worke both upon body and minde.' 'Hee begins first with the phantasie, and moves that so strongly that no reason is able to resist...of all other, melancholy persons are most subject to diabolicall temptations, and illusions, and most apt to entertain them, and the Devill best able to worke upon them' – though 'whether by obsession, or possession, or otherwise, I will not determine, 'tis a difficult question.'[21]

Here, too, Burton did not fundamentally disagree with his medical contemporaries and near-contemporaries, who agreed that mind, body and soul were closely conjoined. Timothie Bright, for example, who practised as a physician but later took holy orders, thought spiritual consolation the only effective response for those who suffered from 'the affliction of soule through the consciousness of sinne'. Such tormented creatures were not afflicted with 'natural melancholie', no matter how similar 'the infirmities of the mind', and medical care in cases like these would prove of no avail.[22] Andrew Boorde had argued that, alongside madness rooted in the body, there was 'another kinde of madnesse. And they the which be in this madness be ever possessed of the devyl, and be develyshe persons.'[23] Felix Platter (1536–1614), who taught medicine at the University of Basle, encountered melancholics who 'persuade themselves that they are damned, abandoned by God, and...fear the last judgment and eternal punishment'. Like other forms of 'Alienation of Mind', these disturbances were often 'Natural, a certain affect so affecting the Brain the seat of Reason'. But equally, they might prove to be 'Preternatural proceeding from an evil Spirit'. And where the disorder depended upon a '*preternatural Cause* proceeding from *the Divil*', the means to its cure in 'no waies belong to the Physitian'. Rather than by medicine, '*the Divil* is forcibly expel'd by the Prayers of Divines and godly people in the Name of Jesus'.[24]

Not uncommonly, clerics who ministered to people's souls also took an interest in the disorders of their bodies. Across western Europe, no effective licensing system existed to keep healing in the hands of a defined group of professionals, and if clergymen were called upon to treat their flock's physical ailments, it comes as no surprise to learn that they also sought to succour those troubled in mind. Thanks to the accidental survival of the notebooks of one such provincial practitioner, the Anglican divine Richard Napier (1559–1634) (PL. 15), and their careful excavation by the modern historian of psychiatry Michael MacDonald, we know a great deal about his patients, their ailments and the kinds of treatment they received at Napier's hands. Perhaps 5 per cent of his patients consulted him for mental troubles: mad, mopish, melancholic, distracted and despairing, they came, sometimes from considerable distances, to seek his advice, as did both ordinary folk and the more well-to-do from the region around his north Buckinghamshire parish in the hope of remedies for a whole range of physical ailments. As an orthodox, Oxford-educated clergyman with the security of an Anglican 'living', Napier responded eclectically to their needs.

Like his contemporary, Galileo (1564–1642), Napier was an astrologer, and like Isaac Newton (1642–1727), he dabbled extensively in alchemy, a reminder of how different the mental world of even the most educated inhabitants of the seventeenth century was from that we now live in, and how readily they reconciled what we take to be contradictory mental universes within a common frame.[25] Napier employed these occult practices in his treatment of his patients, keeping careful note of their symptoms, and using astrology, for example, to help him divine their prognosis. Simultaneously, he bled, purged and vomited them, and gave them magical amulets engraved with astral symbols to wear. Confronted by 'anyone that is mopish and distempered in brain or else [harmed by] any witchery, sorcery or inchantment', he advised 'First let them blood...then say "Lord, I beseech Thee, let the corruption of Satan come out of this man or woman or child that doth so trouble or vex her or him".'[26] It was an eclectic mix of magic, religion, supernaturalism and medicine that seems to have matched the beliefs of both the learned and *hoi polloi*, who thought that these realms could and indeed must be reconciled by those who sought to influence the course of a variety of disorders. It brought Napier thousands of patients over the course of the period between 1597 and 1634 for which his notebooks have survived, and brought him as well a considerable fortune.

Richard Napier treated a wide variety of mental ills, some of them quite minor, others evidently very serious. More of his patients were women than were men: he treated 1,286 cases of mental disorder among females and only 748 among males, and this despite his open contempt for women and their intellectual capacities. It is difficult to know how to interpret these gendered differences. Did they reflect an imbalance in the sex ratio of the local population; the greater tendency of women to confide in their physicians; the abundance of protracted gynaecological troubles that made many women's lives a misery; or some greater vulnerability of women in this era to psychiatric disorders? Even MacDonald, who spent years trying to unravel the mystery, confesses he has to remain agnostic. Patients were both rich and poor, but mostly from the middle ranks – farmers and artisans and their spouses – though from the mid-1610s, as Napier's reputation grew, members of the nobility also sought his services – Earls and Countesses, even the brother of a Duke. Many were miserable and despairing, often in the aftermath of grief and loss. Others displayed disorders of perception and were actively hallucinating or delusional. Napier tended to refer to such people as 'light-headed' or 'distracted'. Cases of grave behavioural disturbance, those prone to wild ravings and unpredictable actions, those who threatened or committed actual violence, menacing and perhaps destroying people or property, or others apparently on the brink of self-destruction: for these people, perhaps one in every twenty of the mentally disturbed that came to his attention, he reserved the words 'mad' or 'lunatic'. These were, for both him and their families, the worst, the most distressing forms of mental disorder, and at once the most difficult and the most urgent cases he came into contact with: oblivious to the normal constraints governing behaviour, heedless of social niceties and social hierarchies, terrifyingly unpredictable, disgusting and beyond all control. If lunatics like these were chained up, it was more because of the fear they engendered than because their captors were cruel.[27] These madmen threatened, after all, to turn the world upside-down.

Drawing Boundaries

Of course, the question of where to draw the line between cases of mental disturbance that were the province of medicine and those that belonged to the divine was a complex one, and an issue that naturally not infrequently provoked professional jealousy and disputes. John Cotta (1575–1650), who practised in Northampton, not far from Napier, insisted on 'the necessitie of consulting with the Physition…in all diseases supposed to be inflicted by the Divell'.[28] He was scornful of the 'ignorant practisers' who meddled in medical matters, most particularly 'ecclesiastical persons, vicars, and parsons, who now overflow this kingdom with this alienation of their own proper office and duties and usurpation of others'.[29] Perhaps his near-neighbour Napier was one of his targets, though we have no way of knowing. The underlying professional tensions are clear, however, even though Cotta did not dispute that 'many things of great power and wonder, above reason and beyond the power of nature, have bene effected through…a true worke of the Divell'.[30]

On the surface, at least, a particularly fraught example of this sort of conflict played itself out in London, beginning in the last year of Queen Elizabeth's reign, in April 1602. A young girl, Mary Glover, was tasked with delivering a message to an old crone who lived nearby, Elizabeth Jackson. But Jackson had a grudge against Mary and, cornering her, shouted abuse and imprecations and wished her an 'evill death'. The fourteen-year-old eventually escaped her clutches, only to fall into fits. By turns choking, speechless and blind, and often unable to eat, her body at one time contorted into almost impossible poses, at another seemingly paralysed, Glover (whose parents were strict Puritans) drew crowds who witnessed her behaviours and concluded that she was possessed. In short order, Dame Jackson was arrested, tried and convicted of being a witch. She escaped the death penalty only because the witchcraft statutes had temporarily fallen into abeyance. At Jackson's trial, a London physician named Edward Jorden (1569–1633) had appeared as a witness for the defence. Mary Glover, he insisted, was not bewitched but sick, a victim of 'suffocation of the mother', or hysteria (from the Greek *hystera* = womb, uterus) – the belief that the womb could wander, causing a sense of suffocation, choking fits or difficulty in swallowing – another form of madness with ancient roots, as we have seen.

Here, it would seem, is a clash between the world of superstition and the world of science, between those who clung to a belief in the occult and those who saw the world in purely naturalistic terms. Jorden wrote a pamphlet after the trial, insisting that Mary Glover needed medicines, not the interventions of divines: 'why', he asked, 'should we not prefer the judgments of Phisitions in a question concerning the actions and passions of mans [sic] body (the proper subject of that profession) before our owne conceites; as we do the opinion of Divines, Lawyers, Artificers, &c. in their proper Elements?'[31] Surely science and divinity are squarely at odds on how to account for Mary Glover's actions, science invoking the natural world, and religion the supernatural?

Except that it turns out that Jorden's intervention had been solicited by the Bishop of London, Richard Bancroft (1544–1610), and was first and foremost a piece of religious propaganda, designed to discredit Puritans and Papists alike, who attributed Glover's behaviour to possession, and sought to cast the Devil out by rites of exorcism or the power of prayer and fasting. Most of Jorden's colleagues in the College of Physicians were convinced that Glover had indeed been bewitched, and Bishop Bancroft's machinations proved ineffectual on two levels: first because Jackson was convicted of being a witch; and then as Mary Glover's Puritan friends and relations gathered around her bedside after the trial. A titanic struggle ensued. The Puritans prayed. The young girl convulsed. Her body contorted into a circle, the back of her head touching her heels. Her symptoms intensified. Then all at once she cried out that God had come and the Lord had delivered her. She was cured – or the Devil departed, as her audience believed. The Puritans circulated her story for the rest of the seventeenth century. What better proof could there be of the truth of their religious convictions?[32]

Hysteria was, as it would remain, a highly controversial diagnosis even among medical men. All save the wilfully blind, who dismiss mental illness as a myth, have little trouble recognizing a case of Bedlam madness – someone so out of touch with our common-sense reality that we no longer seem to share the same mental universe – even though fierce debates still rage about what causes such conditions and how to respond to them. But hysteria is different, a chameleon-like disease that, alongside the emotional turmoil that engulfed sufferers and those who witnessed it alike, could apparently mimic the symptoms of almost any other illness, and that seemed somehow to mould itself to the culture in which it appeared. Real or fictitious, it attracted (and continued to attract down the centuries) controversy about its status and its causes. It was a label often rejected by many who received the diagnosis, and a state that to many seemed closer to malingering and deceit than to genuine pathology. Alternatively, of course, as we have just seen, its peculiar manifestations in a spirit-drenched world were easily viewed through the lens of possession. Its victims would persist, however, sometimes on the periphery, at other times seemingly nearer the centre of the kingdom of the mad, now ignored, now seen as paradigmatic of what ailed the mentally disturbed.

The Puritan exploitation of Mary Glover's 'dispossession' to promote their form of Christian belief is likewise a standard trope. Early Christians had used miracles as a valuable weapon to advance their cause. In the age of the Renaissance (which was also the age of the Reformation and the Counter-Reformation), curing the mad by expelling the demons who had trapped them in a universe of the irrational and the crazed became the occasion for competing claims by Protestants and Catholics. Puritans overwhelmingly rejected Popish rituals, including the Catholic rite of exorcism, but they substituted sessions of prolonged prayer and fasting by the bedside of the afflicted, and boasted whenever these had the desired effect (as of course did the Catholics when the rites of exorcism drove forth the Devil) that the cured madman or madwoman was testimony of divine favour and proof of the truth of their teachings. Anglicans who sought a middle way between these two extremes poured scorn on both sets of claims. Samuel Harsnett (1561–1631), for example, who would go on to become successively Bishop of Chichester and then of Norwich, and subsequently Archbishop of York, first railed against the Puritan exorcist, John Darrell,[33] and then against his Catholic counterparts,[34] in the process casting doubt on the existence of both demons and witchcraft and proffering naturalistic accounts of supposedly supernatural phenomena. For Harsnett, the scenes of exorcisms were elaborately staged 'impostures'. Those commanding these occasions proceeded to 'open the curtaine, and see their Puppettes play' – a 'play of sacred miracles', that was at once a 'wonderful pageant' and 'holy ledgerdemaine', the whole making up a 'tragicall comedie' wherein both Catholic priests and Puritan divines deceived their equally credulous audiences. With wonderful irony, in England at least, religious politics thus contributed on this and on subsequent occasions to changed views about the origins of distraction and to the rise of a more secular perspective on madness.

And it did so in unexpected and wholly unintended ways. For Harsnett's diatribe against exorcism was read by Shakespeare, and it influenced in multiple aspects his presentation of madness in *King Lear*, first performed in 1606. When Edgar pretends to be mad, for instance, he claims to be possessed by devils – 'Poor Tom' is haunted by 'the foul fiend Flibbertigibbet', and by Obdicut, Hoppedance, Mahu and Modo. The names are striking, and all were borrowed directly from Harsnett's account of fake Jesuit exorcisms. Edgar's feigned madness thus mirrors and parodies the false possessions Catholics used to deceive the gullible, even down to some of the images – the strange voices, the numbness, the cursing – and the very language Shakespeare employs.[35] The feigned madness also recalls the well-known case of the prolific Calabrian philosopher and Dominican friar Tommaso Campanella (1568–1639), who avoided execution for heresy and rebellion in 1599 by pretending to be insane.[36] But where madness as possession is presented by Shakespeare in one case, Edgar, as a sham – a disguise adopted by a desperate character in fear of his life, hunted by his bastard brother – Lear's own distraction is explicitly given a very different gloss: not supernatural, but all too human in its origins. Madness is naturalized. It emerges gradually, as the King is buffeted by cold and by storms, but more importantly by the hammer blows of a series of overwhelming psychological onslaughts: betrayal by two of his daughters; the dawning realization of his own foolishness and guilt; the death of Cordelia. 'O, let me not be mad, not mad, sweet Heaven!' Lear implores, 'Keep me in temper, I would not be mad!' But mad he is, as the audience well knows – as is, perhaps, the Fool, whose mental state licenses him to tell truths other mortals dare not utter.

Dramatic Possibilities

Madness is a theme that runs through many of Shakespeare's plays, tragedies and comedies alike. It occupies a very different place and is presented in a very different register in the two genres, but in his repeated use of it as a dramatic device, he is at one with his contemporaries and near contemporaries. For when the commercial theatre emerged late in Elizabeth's reign, the first dramatists often had recourse to madness as an element in their plots. Before Shakespeare presented his first play, others had demonstrated the appeal of mad scenes to the audience that the theatrical companies sought to attract. Shakespeare employed this plot device to greater effect than his predecessors usually did, and presents us with a far richer series of observations about madness and human nature. But he was working in a time when the fascination with the problem that was madness was clearly preoccupying writers and artists to an unprecedented extent.

A generation and more before Shakespeare's plays, the revival of Classical learning across Europe had brought with it a new acquaintance with an ever-broader array of Greek and Roman literature. That revival served, of course, as both cause and consequence of the admiration of and enthusiasm for Classical antiquity that characterized the Renaissance – indeed gave it its very name. In Italy, in France, in Spain, as well as in England, the most important Classical influences on drama were the comedies of Plautus of the end of the third and the early second centuries BC, and the tragedies of Seneca, written in the first century AD. It was this Roman drama, not the earlier plays of the Greeks, that sixteenth-century writers became acquainted with, trans- lated into the vernacular, and used as their model – all too rigidly at first in Italy and France, more freely (and more successfully) in Spain and England.[37]

Based on Greek models, Plautus employed his comedies as political satire and social commentary at the time of republican Rome's conflicts against Carthage and Hannibal at the end of the Second Punic War, and against Greece at the beginning of the Second Macedonian War. Plautus revels in stock plots and stock characters, such as the braggart soldier, clever slave and lusty old man, to poke fun at the pretensions and inversions of authority and power.[38] As the titles of Seneca's plays make clear – *Agamemnon, Oedipus, Medea, Hercules Furens*, and the rest – his source of inspiration was also the Greeks. But his were tragedies adapted to the culture of imperial Rome, most notably the rules of Caligula and of Nero as emperors: a world of radical evil, of torture, incest, intrigue and violent death, which in barely disguised form surfaces repeatedly in his versions of these tales of tragedy.

It was the violence, the fury, the uncontrolled and uncontrollable rage of maniacal madness that we encounter in Seneca's tragedies, and that constitute the forms of insanity most strikingly portrayed on the sixteenth- century English stage, to the audience's apparent delight. Seneca's *Phaedra*, although based on Euripides' play *Hippolytus*, was notable for its far more lurid and unrestrained depictions of inflamed passions, incestuous desires, frenzied emotion and gore-spattered death. Or consider the actions of Atreus in Seneca's *Thyestes*. Borrowing from Classical myth, Atreus catches, murders and cooks his brother's sons, and serves the flesh to their father, taking voyeuristic pleasure in watching Thyestes as he enjoys his meal, then belches. The sheer horror, the moral monstrosity of the behaviours that were por- trayed on stage, the sadism that assaulted the audience's sensibilities, are quite remarkable. They are exceeded, if anything, in *Hercules Furens*, where on-stage not off, the maddened hero shoots one son with an arrow through the neck, and corners another as

Madly whirling him again and yet again, has
Hurled him; his head crashed loudly against
stones; the room is drenched with scattered brains.

As for his wife, he beats her savagely with a club, until

Her bones are crushed,
Her head is gone from her mangled body,
Gone, utterly.[39]

In late sixteenth-century England, similar themes make their appearance in the genre of revenge tragedies that soon began to supplement, then supplant, their Roman inspiration, of which one of the earliest and most influential was Thomas Kyd's *The Spanish Tragedy, or Hieronimo is Mad Again*, written some time between 1584 and 1589. Its blood-drenched plot sees a whole series of hangings, stabbings and suicides, not to mention a character biting his own tongue out to preclude any chance of his talking under torture, all orchestrated around the descent of several of the protagonists into madness.

Whatever Kyd could do, Shakespeare could do much better. *Titus Andronicus* (performed in 1594) was a play so riddled with violence and horror that in the centuries after Shakespeare's death, it was often considered un-stageable, and his authorship even brought into question – though there seems little doubt that it is his, in whole or in part. The action begins with Titus, returned to Rome in triumph, ordering two of his sons to kill the oldest son of the captured Queen of the Goths, Tamora, as revenge for the loss of several of his own sons in battle. With relish, they proceed to do so, lopping off Alarbus's limbs, disembowelling him and burning his remains. Next, Titus stabs to death one of his own sons, who dares to question his father's whims; and then in short order, Tamora's surviving sons (their mother having married the emperor whom Titus has put on the throne) arrange to kill the emperor's brother, rape Titus's daughter Lavinia (cutting out her tongue and chopping off her hands to silence her), and to frame Titus's two remaining sons for the murder they have just committed. Titus is tricked into having his own left hand cut off to send to the emperor, on the promise that by so doing, he will secure pardons for his doomed sons – only to receive in return both his own severed hand and the severed heads of his offspring. Perhaps mad, perhaps feigning madness (a device Shakespeare will later re-use in *Hamlet*),

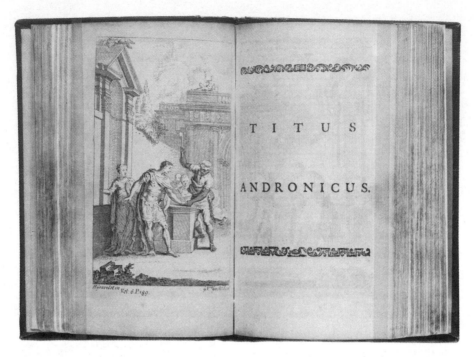

The madness of a world unhinged: Titus Andronicus having his hand cut off, just one of a relentless series of acts of seeming unreason in Shakespeare's play of that name.

Titus is shortly thereafter, at his own instigation, left under the supervision of Lavinia's two sons. He promptly cuts their throats, and drains their blood into a basin – held out between her stumps by his mutilated daughter.

For the feast that follows, he invites Tamora and the emperor to join him. Immediately after he has killed his own raped and mutilated daughter before the assembled company (she who was 'enforced, stain'd, and deflower'd', and thus must die, supposedly to save her further shame), Titus takes his final twisted revenge:

'Why, there they are both,' he tells the emperor, who inquires after Tamora's children, 'baked in that pie,

> Whereof their mother daintily hath fed,
> Eating the flesh that she herself hath bred.

Having revealed that Tamora has eaten her sons, Titus pauses just long enough for her to register the horror of the scene, then stabs her in the heart. When the emperor Saturninus stabs him in turn, Lucius, one of Titus's two surviving sons, brings the tumultuous action to a climax, dispatching the emperor with his dagger. The whole gory tale now lurches to its conclusion (and this is only a fraction of its parade of horrors). Lucius, who had helped to mutilate and kill Tamora's eldest son in the play's first scene, ascends the imperial throne and takes one last act of revenge: Tamora's secret lover, Aaron, an evil *éminence grise* throughout the action, is brought before him to hear his fate:

> Set him breast-deep in earth, and famish him;
> There let him stand, and rave, and cry for food;
> If anyone relieves or pities him,
> For the offence he dies.

To which Aaron responds with scorn:

> I am no baby, I, that with base prayers
> I should repent the evils I have done:
> Ten thousand worse than ever yet I did
> Would I perform, if I might have my will;
> If one good deed in all my life I did,
> I do repent it from my very soul.

Amid this catalogue of gore, the 'crimson river of warm blood',[40] the piling up of corpses, the parade of rape, mutilation and feeding on human flesh, the charnel house that results as revenge piles on revenge, madness stalks the stage: not madness in its less demonstrative, more introverted form, but rather, as the slaughter, violence and depravity go on and on, the madness of a world unhinged. It is a vision of moral codes dissolved, of humanity torn to shreds – like more than one of the characters who suffer for the audience's entertainment.

Immensely popular, the play proved a great commercial success. The masses who stood before the stage for a penny a time enjoyed its action, and the better classes who occupied the tiers above pretended they were there to listen to its poetry. Only half a century later did critics draw back and audiences decide its serial horrors were too strong for their stomachs – a revulsion that would persist, with only a few exceptions, until the closing decades of the bloody century we recently left behind, when once more its hellish scenes were revived, seemingly regarded as acceptable entertainment once more.

A whole series of commercial theatres sprang up in late sixteenth-century London, mostly on the margins of the settled city, and revenge tragedies like *The Spanish Tragedy* and *Titus Andronicus* made regular appearances on their stages. But soon a broader array of plays materialized, and madness on the stage began to assume a new and more variegated guise. Shakespeare and his contemporaries produced a host of entertainments: comedies, historical plays, dramas of an infinitely variable sort for an audience that began to appreciate more sophisticated forms of entertainment.

Madness in Its Infinite Variety

As they did so, madness became part of the dramatist's stock-in-trade: not just in the older manner of frenzied characters, their insanity signified by raving, foaming at the mouth, rolling of the eyes, and violence of language and action; but also a different and much broader range of mad creatures, who served as a source of entertainment or of comedy, and as a plot device that might provide a means to release tension, or perhaps to create it. In the real world, few Jacobean lunatics were locked up in madhouses – indeed, other than the small and increasingly dilapidated charitable hospital, Bedlam (taking in but a handful of patients), there is no surviving evidence at all of specialized facilities to confine the mad. Yet despite that, madhouse scenes, and more particularly scenes set in Bedlam or revolving around Bedlamites, were ten a penny in the plays written in the early decades of the seventeenth century.

Sometimes they had a very artificial air, bearing little relationship to the underlying plot. Thomas Middleton's *The Changeling* (1622), for example, presents an entire subplot that revolves around mad folk locked up in Alibius's madhouse, an establishment clearly modelled on Bedlam. The mad scenes are a diversion, an interlude with few connections to the main tragic story, but one that provides the occasion for an extravagant and crowd-pleasing dance of the lunatics. By contrast, John Fletcher's *The Pilgrim* (1621) sends both its heroine and her father into confinement in the madhouse and makes the mad scenes less peripheral, though no less a source of mirth and diversion. The mad characters there encountered include a woman 'as lecherous...as a she-ferret', and a serious young scholar who at first appears quite sane. He is on the brink of being discharged when someone casually alludes to the weather. At once, his madness reappears: 'Upon a dolphin's back', he assures the assembled company, 'I'll make all tremble, for I am Neptune'; and a little later he commands, 'My sea-horses! I'll charge the northern wind, and break his bladder.'

The audience's response to these sallies encouraged the proliferation of such scenes. But madness had also begun to be used for more serious purposes. Lending themselves as they did to satire, the mad became a vehicle for pricking pretensions and for voicing uncomfortable reflections about society. Puritans were an obvious target – killjoys who loathed the theatre and all it stood for: the Sweeper in Thomas Dekker's *The Honest Whore* (1604) may be the first but is hardly the last to take a swipe in this direction. The Puritan? – 'there's no hope of him, unless he may pull down the steeple, and hang himself i' the bell-ropes'.[41] And, hinting at how nice the boundary might prove between the mad and the sane, he demanded to know 'How all? … Why if all the mad folk…should come hither, there would not be left any ten men in the city' – a recycling of a pointed joke from Shakespeare, who has Hamlet ask of the Clown, who has no inkling of whom he is speaking to (and who assures Hamlet the mad Prince has been sent away): 'Ay marry, why was he sent into England?' To which the Clown ripostes, 'Why, because he was mad. He shall recover his wits there; or if he do not, it is no great matter there.' 'Why?' asks Hamlet. 'Twill not be seen in him,' says the Clown, 'there the men are as mad as he.'

Shakespeare was as capable as any of his contemporaries of sprinkling his tragedies with scenes intended as comic relief, and playing with allusions to madness in his comedies, making jokes that sometimes had a serious point. Here too one sees imagery that plays off (and spreads) the stereotypes of madness and its treatment. 'Love is merely a madness,' he tells us in *As You Like It* (1599/1600), 'and, I tell you, deserves as well a dark house and a whip as madmen do; and the reason why they are not so punished and cured is, that the lunacy is so ordinary that the whippers are in love too.' (James Shirley in *The Bird in a Cage* (1633) speaks of the madhouse as 'a house of correction to whip us into our senses'; and John Marston in *What You Will* (1601) orders 'Shut the windows, darken the room, fetch whips: the fellow is mad, he raves – talks idly – lunatic.')

But in Shakespeare, in particular, one sees a richer portrait of madness and its putative origins emerging, with a stress on a natural rather than a supernatural aetiology that both draws upon and helps to further the break now being made with accounts pitched in terms of magic or divine displeasure. Disruptions of the natural order, and most especially the rousing of the passions, were seen as profoundly dangerous to the body, and to mental as well as physical health. Take the scene of Lady Macbeth sleepwalking, reliving the nightmare of stabbing Duncan to death:

> Out, damned spot! Out, I say...who would have thought the
> old man to have had so much blood in him?...Here's the
> smell of the blood still; all the perfumes of Arabia will not
> sweeten this little hand.

Steadfast in her vaulting ambition at first, more so than her hesitant husband, her mind at last gives way, and is unhinged by the memory of the horror she has witnessed. 'This disease is beyond my practice', says the doctor hiding in the shadows. 'More needs she the divine than the physician.'

Still another, more pitiable creature is Ophelia, driven to distraction by the cruelties visited upon her by Hamlet – bullying and betraying her; pretending to love her, then scorning her; killing her father. Her wits falter and fail. Mistreatment and loss have left her 'Divided from herself and her fair judgment, without which we are pictures [i.e., external facsimiles of human beings] or mere beasts.' How do we learn of her descent into madness? The formerly chaste maiden reappears on stage singing bawdy songs. She speaks incoherently and in riddles. Then she disappears, and the audience learns she has wandered down by the river bank, and clambered out on a branch of a willow tree, whence she

> Fell in the weeping brook. Her clothes spread wide;
> And, mermaid-like, awhile they bore her up; ...
> Till that her garments, heavy with their drink,
> Pull'd the poor wretch from her melodious lay
> To muddy death.

In madness, she has broken with the submission she has previously shown to the men around her, flaunted her body (at least in her words), and in the end she escapes the limits of her life, but only at the cost of her life (PL. 17).

As for Hamlet himself, for contemporaries he was the chief protagonist in a familiar genre now given a distinctive twist. Hesitant, irresolute, unstable, he is the very model of ambiguity, unable to choose 'to be, or not to be', to act or refrain from acting; and for generations to come, he is a vivid embodiment of an issue that continues to vex: where to draw the line between sanity and madness. Is Hamlet mad, or merely feigning distraction? 'I am', he tells us himself, 'but mad north-north-west: when the wind is southerly, I know a hawk from a handsaw.' And yet there is much that points in another direction: his introspective melancholy; his meditations on suicide; his inappropriate and blunted emotional responses – to Ophelia's death and much else besides.

One of the most notable features of all these literary images of madness as they appeared on the stage, of course, was that in principle they were available to everyone. As the debates about Hamlet's mental status remind us, the 'same' spectacles might be understood in very different ways by different segments of the audience, and by audiences who brought different sets of cultural expectations to bear. Such portraits of the mad were something that could be appropriated by the literate and the illiterate alike. And we do well to remember that the theatre in these years commanded a remarkably large and diverse audience. In some London theatres, as many as 3,000 people assembled to watch the action, drawn from all social classes, and though certain companies performed in private for a purely aristocratic clientele, many more did so at theatres just outside the city limits – places like the Curtain, the Globe, the Rose and the Swan. Hence the demand for a large and varied repertoire, the emergence of stable professional companies such as the Lord Chamberlain's Men (Shakespeare's company), and the multiple opportunities for commoners and their betters alike to view representations of madness on the stage.

Fictions and Fables

But drama was not the only fictional vehicle in which representations and discussions of madness increasingly proceeded. Besides ballads and broadsides sung and distributed on the streets, in which mad themes often surfaced from the sixteenth century, there were other increasingly elaborate literary forms which entertained and enlightened the literate, and offered portraits of minds unhinged. Throughout sixteenth-century Europe, versions of Ludovico Ariosto's epic poem on the madness of Roland, *Orlando furioso*, circulated in both the original Italian and then in translations, and it had an extraordinary influence on other writers. Originally published in Ferrara in 1516, it cleverly combined elements drawn from the chivalric romances of Roland, the Arthurian legends and the Classical tales of Hercules and his furious madness.

Orlando's temporary madness is but one of several elements in a sprawling romance, but Ariosto's portrait of his character's manic response to his unrequited love for the pagan princess Angelica not only gives the poem its title and frames its central episode, but also provides some of the poem's most vivid passages. *Furioso* in Italian means frenzied, raging and mad, not to mention its evocation of fury and the mythological Furies, the Greek Avengers who punished human crimes.[42] Driven out of his wits by Angelica's flight, Orlando 'wandered all unarmed and naked'. Yet such was the threat his madness posed, that 'at his presence all the countrie quaked'. People fled as he approached.

> For those he caught he did this lesson teach,
> To keep aloof from out a madman's reach...
> Among the rest he takes one by his heele
> And with his head knocks out an others braine.

Cutting a swathe of wild and indiscriminate violence, his mad rampages have obvious parallels with the manic ferocity of revenge tragedies – and indeed the English dramatist Robert Greene (1558–92) transformed the poem into a play that was staged in London in 1591 and again the following year. *Orlando furioso* also made an appearance in a still more influential portrait of madness that began to appear in the early seventeenth century, Cervantes' *Don Quixote*. For not only is Cervantes' tale another one that harks back to Roland and the age of chivalry – it is, after all, Alonso Quijano's obsessional and excessive devotion to books of chivalry that drives him to distraction and transforms him into the knight errant, Don Quixote – but it is also one that explicitly references elements of *Orlando furioso* at various points in the hero's picaresque wanderings.

But Quixote's madness assumes a very different form from the catastrophically violent rampages of Orlando, though it is not without its fights and injuries. Quixote's follies are first and foremost hilarious, not frightening. There is no question but that the man is mad. He hallucinates, he is someone helplessly trapped in the web of his own obsessions, and he manifestly fails to share the common-sense reality of all around him. His very first sally, clad in a rusty old suit of armour, takes him to an inn that he mistakes for a castle, where he begs the inn-keeper he assumes is its lord to knight him. The man demurs, but when Quixote provokes a fight next morning with a bunch of muleteers, he relents, and dubs Quixote a knight to be rid of him.

Orlando's unrequited love for Princess Angelica has driven him mad. He rampages through the countryside destroying everyone and everything he comes across. Naked, he uses a corpse as a club with which to brain those who flee from his fury.

From then on, our knight-errant is as a man possessed. Those he encounters in his mock-heroic rounds respond by mocking him, accusing him of being crazy, assaulting him. Notoriously, he tilts at windmills that he mistakes for giants, and fights and slaughters sheep, which he thinks are an army of his enemies: 'he rode into the army of sheep and began to spear them with as much fury and determination as if he really were attacking mortal enemies.'

The shepherds whose flock he assaulted, however, are not surprisingly outraged by his actions and disinclined to sit idly by. They pelt him with rocks. They tumble him, bleeding, from the saddle of his horse. Perhaps this restores him to sanity? On the contrary, when the faithful Sancho Panza remonstrates with him for assaulting the poor beasts, and points out that the corpses that litter the battlefield are sheep not men, Quixote meets the objection with the unassailable logic of the madman. Appearances are deceptive: they had indeed been soldiers, against whom Quixote had valiantly fought, but 'this villain who is persecuting me, envious of the glory he saw I was about to conquer in this battle, turned the armies of enemy forces into flocks of sheep'.[43]

The mad, we thus are instructed, are impervious to reason and to experience, and so Quixote remains, through endless trials and tribulations, at once tragic and a figure of fun. His life is inseparable from his illusions and delusions, so much so that when Quixote finally recovers his sanity (at the very end of Part Two of the novel, which was published ten years after the first series of sallies appeared in print), he promptly dies.

The novel, of course, most certainly did not. Part One appeared in English translation as early as 1611, and versions swiftly materialized all across Europe. If it founded a whole new literary genre, as it certainly did, it was a genre rooted in madness, one that meditated on appearance and reality in a world turned chaotic. Such was its power that it stimulated artists then, and for centuries afterwards, to translate its arresting verbal imagery into the very different languages of drawing and painting. At first, these were line drawings that appeared in illustrated editions of the book. But in later centuries, artists including Doré and Daumier (**PL. 16**), Dalí and Picasso would manifest an endless fascination with trying to translate Cervantes' prose into a whole series of memorable images.

Madness and Art

From the palaces of the Italian Renaissance to (somewhat later) their counterparts all across Europe, royal and aristocratic patrons funded a great flowering of art, and the fifteenth to the seventeenth centuries saw rapid and extraordinary advances in artistic innovation. Churches, too (in Catholic countries), sought new altarpieces, and were powerful patrons of the visual arts. And advances in printing technology, particularly in the techniques of engraving, allowed multiple copies of artworks to be produced and disseminated to a wide audience. Unlike architects and sculptors, painters could not imitate the Classical era so directly, not least because Roman paintings weren't rediscovered before the eighteenth century. Roman mosaics were known, and exercised considerable influence as sources of images of mythological subjects, but could not serve as direct models for artists committed to the use of very different media. So if themes from Classical mythology were popular subjects, they were painted in quite novel ways, and the artists who claimed to be returning to Classical roots were in reality doing nothing of the sort. They took inspiration from Greek and Roman literature, but what that meant in terms of artistic styles depended upon leaps of imagination and a whole variety of technical innovations that accompanied the transition from the conventions of the late medieval period to those of the Renaissance.[44]

A variety of visual signs and symbols were used to signal madness. Some of these were adapted from medieval depictions of Hell and the Last Judgment, the despairing scenes of sinners about to be cast into the pit now adapted to depict others suffering from indescribable loss. Cases of Bedlam madness featured biting, bestial characters, with tensed, contorted limbs and staring eyes. Maniacs regularly appeared, their clothing torn and tattered, or in states of shameless nakedness, the lack of civilized attire a marker of their distance from polite society, and of their insanity. The Flemish sculptor Pieter Xavery's intertwined terracotta figures of *Two Madmen* (1673) (PL. 20) are a striking example: the chained erect figure chews on his own beard and tears at his clothing, while a half-hidden figure lies contorted at his feet, eyes rolling, mouth shouting imprecations, muscles bulging, hair matted, and naked as the day he was born. Sufferers were painted as the very embodiment of fury: eyes rolled back in their sockets, dishevelled, pulling their hair, straining at their chains, a gallery of turbulent, writhing, gesticulating bodies, visibly out of control. Often they appeared on the brink of violence, faces swollen with rage, brandishing weapons and full of menace. Bruegel the Elder's *Dulle Griet* (*Mad Meg*), a c. 1562 oil on panel, portrays a madwoman armed with a sword, rushing across a hellish landscape (perhaps the very gates of Hell, or perhaps an allegorical scene portraying the consequences of rage, gluttony, avarice, lust, all the deadly sins), mouth agape, clothing dishevelled, hair tangled in knots, shovelling random loot into her basket, oblivious of all around her: a veritable vision of the Apocalypse or of a world gone surreally mad (see p. 411).[45]

Other paintings and drawings exhibited those who put on display a preternatural contempt for decorum, spitting, vomiting and urinating in public,

Bernard Lens created this scene in Bedlam for Jonathan Swift's A Tale of a Tub *in 1710. As visitors peer in at the lunatics for amusement, the naked and chained inmate in the foreground hurls the contents of his chamber-pot directly in the face of the voyeur – you.*

their faces glaring, tongues protruding, with heads shorn or hair standing on end. One of the most famous and widely circulated of these portraits appeared in the very early years of the eighteenth century to accompany Jonathan Swift's *A Tale of a Tub*. Gazing on Bernard Lens's 1710 engraving of the interior of a straw-strewn Bedlam cell, barred windows and all, the viewer involuntarily recoils, for in the foreground a near-naked lunatic hurls the contents of his chamber-pot in the voyeur's face. As for the less overtly violent mad, the melancholic were seen to be worn-out, passive, withdrawn, often seated, with near-demented expressions, their complexions dark (a covert reference to the black bile that coursed beneath their skin, and a feature that is clearly visible in the representation of the face in Dürer's 1514 engraving of *Melancholia I*), their heads downcast and their bodies almost wilting in the extremity of their dolour and distress.

Some scenes also recreated in novel visual form mad characters from the Classical age. Peter Paul Rubens, for example, painted the scene from Sophocles' *Tereus* in which the Thracian king, having already unknowingly consumed the flesh of his son, Itys, is then presented by his vengeful wife with the boy's severed head. Other artists produced allegorical images which captured the sense of the mad as liminal figures, haunting the imagination, lurking half-seen on the very margins of civilized existence. One especially powerful set of images from the late medieval and early Renaissance period cast the mad as some sort of crazed human cargo, cut loose from their moorings in society, crammed together on a boat. Away they float on the *Narrenschiff* or Ships of Fools (PL. 3), down the Rhine or on storm-tossed seas, deluded pilgrims voyaging in perpetual search of their lost reason, as satirically narrated in 1494 by the German humanist Sebastian Brant (1457–1521) in a text illustrated with numerous woodcuts, two-thirds of them by Albrecht Dürer, his first major commission.[46] All of which made for such striking compositions, recycled by numerous artists, that, six centuries later, they would tempt the famous French philosopher and historian Michel Foucault (1926–84) into embracing the wholly mistaken notion that these powerful paintings were representations of something real, instead of merely an artistic conceit. Foucault acknowledges that these paintings had their origins in an early series of literary inventions: Ships of Virtuous Ladies, of Princes and Nobles, and Ships of Health, as well as Ships of Fools. But he insists that only the last were 'real', and indeed 'quite a common sight' in the great cities of Europe.[47] Except in artists' works, they most certainly were not.

Fools and Folly

The omnipresence of fools, from popes and princes to paupers and peasants was, however, the central theme of *The Praise of Folly* (1509) by Erasmus (1466–1536), an encomium delivered by a female dressed as a jester, and one of the major documents of Renaissance humanism. Its title notwithstanding, Erasmus's central purpose was not to provide a discourse on madness in its many various forms. Rather, folly was mobilized to hold up a mirror to the moral failings of all humanity, not those the sane dismissed as insane. And yet Erasmus did also suggest that insanity might not be the wholly negative phenomenon many of his contemporaries took it to be, turning the meaning of the fool upside-down. The best and true fools, he proclaimed, are fools for Christ. In that sense, some forms of Christian humanism sought to connect folly and madness to the mystical, and to suggest that some 'fools' at least ought to be viewed in a very different light.

Perhaps the most famous portrait of Erasmus was painted by Hans Holbein the Younger, who became the most celebrated artist at the court of Henry VIII and left us iconic portraits of the monarch himself and those who surrounded him: Thomas More and Thomas Cromwell most notable among them. Less noted, a dozen years or so after Erasmus produced his *The Praise of Folly*, Holbein had created his own image of the fool, part of a series of ninety-four woodcuts, the *Icones Historiarum Veteris Testamenti*, that he produced during a decade of violent religious controversy and were his attempt to illustrate Old Testament themes. Intended to accompany Psalm 52, the picture of the fool incorporates a number of stereotypical elements. The fool or madman is being followed and mocked by children, and amid their scorn, his tattered clothing barely covers his nakedness. Missing a shoe and with a cape of feathers in place of the foolscap preferred by Erasmus's counterpart, Holbein's figure clutches two wooden staffs or cudgels, one under each arm. Such an accoutrement had become a stock image that other artists employed to signal the presence of madness. On and on Holbein's fool marches, going who knows where, gaping vacantly at the world he passes through.

Erasmus's essay was mostly written in a matter of days while he was a guest of his friend Thomas More in England in 1509, waiting on the arrival of his books. It appeared in print in Paris in 1511, though its first 'authorized' edition was not published until the following year. During Erasmus's lifetime, there were thirty-six editions, and the text had been translated into both German and French from its original Latin. Its first English translation appeared in 1549, and it exercised an enormous influence for centuries thereafter, something which, one suspects, would have surprised its author, who originally conceived of it as an amusement for More and other friends. (Its Latin title *Moriae Encomium*, a pun on More's name, hints at the humorous cloak within which Erasmus hid his serious intent.)

One of the great humanist thinkers of the early Renaissance, Erasmus devoted much of his life to editing authoritative Greek and Latin texts of the New Testament in an effort to correct the inadequacies of earlier Latin versions; to the exegesis of Christian doctrine; and to the cultivation of Classical erudition and literary taste. A fierce critic of abuses within the Catholic Church, he nonetheless remained faithful to it, and was sharply disapproving of Protestant reformers like his contemporary Martin Luther, both over matters of theology and over their break with Rome – an apostasy he thought threatened to unleash disorder and violence, and to smash traditions he venerated. Often seen as an early advocate of religious tolerance, Erasmus succeeded in arousing both Luther's anger and (after his death) his own condemnation by the Church he strove at once to reform and to remain devoted to. Pope Paul IV placed all his works on the *Index of Prohibited Books*, and leading figures of the Counter-Reformation denounced him as one of the architects of the 'tragedy' that was the rise of Protestantism, because he failed to anathematize Luther in sufficiently strong terms, and because his scriptural criticism weakened the Church's authority.

Yet in the long run, Erasmus's influence survived criticism from both quarters. His learning, his subtlety, his wit, his stress on the value of reason and moderation and his humane outlook on life ultimately brought him many admirers. The very things that provoked enmity from many of his contemporaries and the admiration of later generations are fully on display in *The Praise of Folly*. The rich and the powerful, religious and secular alike, are attacked in a prose dripping with irony and paradox, and satire sharpened so as to wound. Princes and Popes, monks and theologians, the follies of superstition ('absurdities so foolish that even I [says Folly] am almost ashamed of them'),[48] the pretensions of the learned and the irrationality of the ignorant – all are lampooned, sometimes gently, sometimes savagely. People's moral failings are mordantly mocked, their foolishness exposed, whatever and whoever they

Hans Holbein the Younger's portrait of Erasmus of Rotterdam (1523) shows him as a scholar, his hands resting on a book and with other volumes on a shelf behind him.

may be. For laughter at the foibles of others soon turns rueful when Folly's gaze shifts to subjects that strike nearer to home. Illusions, self-deceptions, the human susceptibility to flattery, all pass under review. Erasmus scorned superstitions and decried both attempts to purchase salvation and those churchmen who purported to sell indulgences.[49] He was scathing about the worship of saints and stories of miraculous cures at their tombs.[50] Repeatedly he used the trope of madness to remind his readers of their moral failings.

No one, not even Erasmus himself, seems to escape unscathed. (As he wrote to Thomas More, replying in advance to 'the false charge that the work is too biting.... Surely it should be taken as judicious and instructive satire. Besides, I beg you to notice on how many counts I indict my own self.')[51] Folly is, after all, the illusions the world has to embrace to make this vale of tears a happy one, as well as to allow corrupt and vicious leaders to deceive themselves about their behaviours. It is an essential thing for the 'businessman or soldier or judge who thinks that if he throws into the collection basket one coin from all his plunder, the whole cesspool of his sinful life will be immediately wiped out. He thinks all his acts of perjury, lust, drunkenness, quarrelling, murder, deception, dishonesty, betrayal are paid off like a mortgage, and paid off in such a way that he can start off once more on a whole new round of sinful pleasures.'[52]

In the end, the Christian is paraded as the greatest of all fools.[53] It is folly that allows the believer to renounce the pleasures of this world, and to embrace visions of the hereafter. Here he echoes the apostle Paul, who proclaimed 'we are fools for the sake of Christ', and even the Redeemer himself. For did not 'even Christ, though he was the wisdom of the Father, [become] somehow foolish in order to relieve the folly of mortals when he took on human nature and appeared in the form of a man? Just as he became sin in order to heal sins. Nor did he choose any other way to heal them but through the folly of the cross....'[54] And 'to put it in a nutshell', Folly concludes, 'it seems to me that the Christian religion taken all together has a certain affinity with some sort of folly and has little or nothing to do with wisdom.'[55] Perhaps there was not so much, after all, that separated the pious from the mad – a theme reminiscent, as Erasmus was well aware, of the more positive interpretations of some forms of madness put forward by Plato and Socrates.[56]

Indeed, Platonic philosophy features in many places in Erasmus's essay. He draws, for instance, on Alcibiades' comparison of the inner and outer Socrates to a Silenos, a little statuette that was all ugliness and deformity on the outside, but turned inside out, proved to be the very image of a god.[57] Thus Folly tells us, to quote the first English translation of *The Praise of Folly*, that

> what outwardly seemed death, yet lokyng within ye shulde
> fynde it lyfe; and on the other side what seemed life, to be death:
> what fayre, to be foule: what riche, beggarly: what cunnyng, rude:
> what stronge, feable: what noble, vile: what gladsome, sadde:
> what happie, unlucky: what friendly, unfriendly: what healthsome,
> noysome. Briefely the Silene ones beyng undone and disclosed,
> ye shall fynde all thyngs tourned unto a new semblance.[58]

Elsewhere, Plato's myth of the cave is the basis for a passage praising fools who live a happy life, content to believe in shadows and rejecting the wise person who looks to the reality that lies outside. But Folly turns paradoxical once more when discussing the Christian 'fool' in the essay's closing section: here it is those who reject the temptations and vanities of this world for the enduring delights of the hereafter who are the wise, scorned as they are by those who cling to the delights of the material world. What appears on the surface, Folly now suggests, may mask the deeper truth to which the wise aspire. As always in *The Praise of Folly*, irony competes with irony.

Reformation and Counter-Reformation

In the years following Erasmus's death, in the midst of fierce contests between militant Protestants and Counter-Reformation Catholics, burning of books and burning of heretics, his even-handed criticisms and his gestures towards toleration of competing views stood little chance of being heard. Indeed, even in his lifetime Erasmus had found himself condemned by both sides, his refusal to endorse extremes being interpreted as a sign of intellectual cowardice on his part. And certainly his strictures about superstition, exorcism, the misplaced worship of saints' tombs and demonic possession appear to have had limited traction until more than a century later. The appeal of these long-held beliefs surfaced repeatedly in the visual arts after his passing, and continued to find expression in some of the great paintings of the sixteenth and early seventeenth centuries.

Among the most powerful examples of the latter were the series of paintings Rubens undertook between 1618 and 1630. These commissions were intended to serve as altarpieces, and to deploy the new aesthetic of the

Baroque as a weapon in the Counter-Reformation struggle against Calvinists and other heretics. Through them, the Church militant sought to reinforce its legitimacy against the burgeoning challenges to its authority, and to do so by reminding those who worshipped within its walls of its powerful links to established tradition. Huge, extravagantly sensual and colourful images, Rubens's altarpieces invited the viewer to serve as an eyewitness to the power of a saint (or candidate for sainthood) to cast out the Devil and his minions. His painting of *The Miracles of St Ignatius of Loyola*, for example, was undertaken in 1617–18, when Ignatius had been beatified, but not yet elevated to sainthood (his canonization would take place four years later in 1622). Two possessed figures are being restrained as Ignatius stands on the high altar, his arm raised in a gesture of benediction, as small devils stream from them, desperate to escape the saintly presence (PL. 18).

Not that nothing had changed. One of the many departures from medieval depictions of the casting out of devils was the shift from biblical literalism. For instead of the earlier tradition in which Christ himself was shown healing the possessed, such miracles were now performed by his divinely inspired followers. It was a claim fiercely resisted, of course, by Rubens's Protestant contemporaries, just to the north of the Spanish Netherlands in the Calvinist United Provinces, who would have no truck with such Catholic propaganda. In any event, their literal acceptance of the Old Testament injunction against graven images meant that paintings hung behind an elaborate altar were anathema to them. (One of the defining moments of their revolt against Philip II of Spain had been the so-called Beeldenstorm, or 'Iconoclastic Fury' of 1566, when churches by the hundreds were stripped of religious statues and decoration.) The Dutch made an exception, however, for painted organ covers portraying biblical scenes, one of the few visual ornamentations in their otherwise rigidly plain buildings. Perhaps David Colijns's organ cover, painted some time between 1635 and 1640 for the Nieuwezijds Kapel in Amsterdam, had a contemporary political subtext, a warning against the dangers posed by the irrational ruler (a subject of more than passing interest to the Dutch, whose struggle for independence from Catholic Spain lasted intermittently for eighty years). In any event, it vividly recreates the scene in the first Book of Samuel, when the maddened 'Saul cast the javelin; for, he said, I will smite David even to the wall with it.' David's futile attempt on this occasion to use music to soothe the savage breast must have made it a particularly apposite image with which to screen an organ (PL. 19).

Music was scarcely the only form of therapy for madness that made its way into the artistic repertoire of the Renaissance. Given the increasing salience of medical perspectives on madness, this development should perhaps occasion no surprise, and the figure of the doctor often features prominently. Perhaps the single most popular subject of such paintings was cutting for stone, an ancient notion that embodied the idea that madness had physical roots. From Hieronymus Bosch's painting of *c.* 1490 (also known as *The Cure of Folly*; PL. 21) to Pieter Huys' mid-sixteenth century version of a surgeon extracting the stone of madness and beyond, images of this sort were legion. The funnel hat resembling a dunce's cap on the doctor in Bosch's picture perhaps hints at a satirical gloss on medical hubris, though other versions seem to lack this dimension. In reality what is being referred to in such paintings is possibly the relatively common practice of trepanation, scraping or drilling a hole in the skull to relieve headaches or pressure, or cauterization of the skull, as forms of treatment.

Puzzles and Complexities

The place of madness in European civilization in the years before the dawn of the long eighteenth century is thus a complex one. A source of growing fascination in the arts and literature, insanity was still viewed in many quarters as a consequence of supernatural forces – though such views faced increasing challenges, not least because the invention of printing and the rediscovery of Greek and Roman medical ideas about mental illness gave new life to theories that implicated bodily upset in disturbances of the mind. Most mad folk still remained at large, a charge and a burden on their blood relatives. Only a very small fraction indeed were to be found locked up, mostly those who were without friends and relations, or who were so threatening that confinement seemed the only answer to the problems they posed. But the tiny numbers to be found in places like Bedlam sufficed to capture the imagination of playwrights and their public. Soon enough, madhouses would begin to proliferate, as life imitated art; and naturalistic accounts of madness would come to be embraced among a widening circle of the literate. But change was slow and halting. Old traditions and beliefs still retained much of their power, and their hold over the human imagination.

Chapter Five

MADHOUSES AND MAD-DOCTORS

Changing Responses to Madness

The images are arresting: three faces at the windows of their cells, staring, agitated, dishevelled; a young man, a simpering fool, peering from his hiding place behind one of two massive figures in the foreground, furious maniacs, one of whom is busy gnawing on his own flesh, while both are evidently oblivious of the other and of the world in front of them. The panel was carved by Peter van Coeverden in 1686, and erected in front of the *dolhuis* (madhouse) that had been constructed to contain half a dozen lunatics in the Dutch town of 's-Hertogenbosch more than two centuries earlier. Across the North Sea, Robert Hooke's grand design for a palatial new Bedlam (the original now decayed and inadequate) had been completed in 1676 in Restoration London, constructed on a suitably liminal site in Moorfields, just beyond the old city wall (PL. 22). Over its gates were erected two even more impressive and enormous sculptures, by the Danish artist Caius Gabriel Cibber. To the left, near-recumbent on a bed of straw, face vacant, sprawled the figure of a melancholic. On the opposite side lay a menacing, chained figure of a maniac, fists clenched, muscles tensed, agitated, writhing, with his head tilted back and his face deformed into a near bestial look. Asylums in the late seventeenth century thus began to advertise their presence in novel ways, as institutions to confine the mad and the morally disreputable assumed a more prominent place in many European societies.

To be mad is to be idle, or at least generally incapable of productive labour. Until the modern age, that meant that those who had lost their wits formed a part of the much larger group of the poor, the morally disreputable, the crippled, the orphaned, the aged and the maimed. All manner of

A relief panel depicting inmates of the 's-Hertogenbosch lunatic asylum, carved by Peter van Coeverden (1686). Three mad faces peer out through openings to their cells, while two other madmen and a young boy grimace and posture in front of us.

dependent folk were lumped together, and seldom carefully distinguished from one another. Of course, on some levels, no one confused the blind and the mad, the young and the old, the dissolute and the depraved. But socially speaking, it was mostly their shared incapacity and poverty that mattered, not the disparate sources of their dependency.

In the seventeenth century, things began to change. The impetus for this varied. In northern Europe, the revival of trade, the expansion of towns and the spread of market relations seem to have prompted a more secular and sceptical attitude towards the poor, especially the idle and the vagabond. In the United Provinces (the area we now know as the Netherlands), in Britain and in other parts of the region, there were intermittent attempts to confine people of this sort in a new kind of institution, a bridewell or house of correction, where it was hoped they might be disciplined and taught to labour. The first Dutch madhouses, or *dolhuizen*, had begun to appear as early as the fifteenth century. They were tiny affairs, with room for fewer than a dozen patients, but by the late sixteenth and early seventeenth centuries, several were experiencing pressure to expand, as families and communities sought ways to dispose of threatening madmen. In a move characteristic of the entrepreneurial Dutch, their expansion was often funded not through

Melancholy and raving madness (c. 1676): these two massive figures by Cibber loomed over the entrance to Bedlam. John Keats, who grew up in their shadow, surely had them in mind when describing the 'bruis'd Titans' in his epic poem 'Hyperion'.

charitable giving but by setting up lotteries, with attractive prizes, to extract the necessary sums from the burghers. In Amsterdam, tickets were sold for a year prior to the grand drawing in 1592, and so numerous were the prizes that it took sixty-eight days and nights to complete the process. (The Amsterdam Dolhuis had been founded in 1562 in a bequest from Hendrick van Gisp, whose pregnant wife had been attacked by a madwoman.) The proceeds of the lottery funded an impressive expansion of the building that was completed in 1617. Leiden (1596) and Haarlem (1606–07) soon followed suit, though their prize-drawings lasted a mere fifty-two days and nights each.

The absolutist monarchies of Catholic Europe, disinclined to such commercial expedients, nonetheless viewed the idle and social misfits as a political threat and a potential source of tumult and disorder. Here, too, efforts were under way, using taxes extracted from the peasantry, to sweep up the poor from the streets and neutralize the danger they represented. Beggars, vagrants and prostitutes found themselves incarcerated, along with others whose connections to the stable world of work and employment were suspect. Large numbers of them were thrust into new institutions, the most famous being the *Hôpitaux généraux* and *dépôts de mendicité* that pock-marked seventeenth- and eighteenth-century France. Neglected no

more, the idle and dependent poor were to be forced to work – or at least that was the theory.

Even in medieval times, a variety of expedients had been employed to remove the most violent and menacing of the mad, locking them up and chaining them to mitigate the threat they represented. It would be surprising, therefore, if some of the insane were not now to be found amid the licentious and the lazy newly subject to discipline and constraint. But the mad were not the primary target of those bent on building the new houses of correction. Indeed, in the Netherlands in particular, efforts were made to exclude the sick and the crazed from such establishments. Their presence was scarcely compatible, after all, with a stress on hard labour, discipline and order. Hence Dutch preference, where the threat was severe enough, for putting the mad in institutions of their own, the *dolhuizen*, of which the institution at 's-Hertogenbosch had been the very first.

The Salpêtrière, the first and grandest of the French general hospitals, founded in 1656 by royal decree and built on the site of an old gunpowder factory in Paris, did house a number of lunatics – perhaps a hundred or so at first, rising to ten times that number by the outbreak of the French Revolution, though by then it had for many years confined mostly women. But the insane were always a small fraction of the whole. In 1790, for example, they made up no more than a tenth of the total number confined there, which then exceeded ten thousand souls. All sorts of socially disruptive and troublesome people crowded the vast establishment's halls (PL. 23). When the French surgeon Jacques Tenon (1669–1760) issued his critical report on Paris hospitals in 1788, he provided a concise summary of its heterogeneous demography:

> The Salpêtrière is the largest hospital in Paris and possibly in Europe: this hospital is both a house for women and a prison. It received pregnant women and girls, wet nurses and their nurslings; male children from the age of seven or eight months to four and five years of age; young girls of all ages; aged married men and women; raving lunatics, imbeciles, epileptics, paralytics, blind persons, cripples, people suffering from ringworm, incurables of all sorts, children afflicted with scrofula, and so on and so forth. At the centre of this hospital is a house of detention for women, comprising four different prisons: *le comun*, for the most dissolute girls; *la correction*, for those who are not considered hopelessly depraved; *la prison*, reserved for persons held by order of the king; and *la grande force*, for women branded by order of the courts.[1]

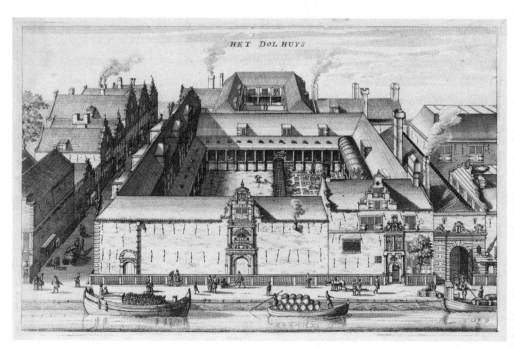

The Amsterdam Dolhuis or madhouse after the completion of its renovation and extension in 1617. The engraving is possibly by J. van Meurs, and appeared in 1663.

As this recital suggests (lunatics being relegated to the status of an after-thought), the notion once propagated by Michel Foucault that the seventeenth and eighteenth centuries saw a 'Great Confinement' of the insane vastly overstates the true state of affairs – something that becomes even clearer when one looks beyond the crowded French capital.

In Montpellier in the south of France, for example, an *Hôpital général* had been built by the provincial authorities in the last decades of the seventeenth century, which did not stop complaints in the early eighteenth century about 'des gens qui roulent la ville et commettent plusieurs désordres se trouvant déporvus de raison et du bon sens' ('people who rove through town deprived of reason and common sense, committing a whole series of outrages'). Eventually, one of these incidents, in which a madman first killed his wife and then burned down his own and his neighbours' houses, forced the authorities to act: the town's officers arranged with the local hospital for the construction of twelve cells, or *loges*, in which the violently mad could be safely confined. Over the course of the century, a handful more cells were added under various auspices, until by the outbreak of the Revolution there were twenty-five, together containing barely twenty mad folk – this in a city of some 30,000 people.[2]

Montpellier was a major centre of medical learning; its medical faculty ranked only behind that in Paris in prestige and renown.[3] But the fact that these cells were located on the grounds of the hospital should not mislead us: there was little or no medical involvement or interest in the treatment of the insane.[4] The handful of patients locked up in the cells for lunatics seem to have been those who posed an obvious threat to the community – a man who ran about at night trying to set fire to the neighbourhood, another who attacked and injured numerous people, a third who entered the local church and began smashing religious images and ornaments – or whose actions threatened embarrassment or scandal to a family, a pretext also used to confine 'dissolute' young women whose sexual proclivities (and perhaps prostitution) placed family honour in jeopardy. Their care, such as it was (inmates were locked up in small barred cells that measured about eight feet square), was delivered by the Catholic sisters, Les Filles de la Charité, a reflection of the fact that their problems were seen as being social rather than medical.[5]

As the small number of lunatics locked up at the local hospital makes clear, most of the mad were dealt with elsewhere. As in centuries past, the primary burden fell upon families, and given the poverty and poor living conditions of the lower orders the expedients employed were rough and ready. Chained in attics or cellars, or in outbuildings, the lot of these sufferers was still less enviable. If family could not be found, some of the insane poor might be locked up in a jail or placed in the local *dépôt de mendicité* or poor-house, alongside other members of the disreputable classes. For the better-off, an alternative to the strains of managing lunacy in the home was provided by placing their relatives in religious institutions, a form of confinement often officially licensed by a royal *lettre de cachet*, or warrant bearing the king's signature, which authorized the indefinite detention of the individual it named. Perhaps the most famous figure locked up in this fashion was the Marquis de Sade (1740–1814). *Lettres de cachet* closed off all access to the courts or grounds of appeal, and Sade's repeated sexual escapades had prompted his mother-in-law, Madame de Montreuil, to obtain the warrant. She may have been driven to this expedient by Sade's affair with a second daughter of hers, not to mention his frequent recourse to prostitutes of both sexes and seductions of all and sundry around him. If so, she did so against the wishes of Sade's wife, long his accomplice. But having lured him to Paris on a pretext, she secured his imprisonment, first in the Château de Vincennes, and then in the Bastille, from which he was removed to the insane asylum at Charenton just ten days before the revolutionary mob stormed the Parisian prison and released its inmates.[6] After a period of liberty Sade was returned to Charenton in 1803 and remained there until his death in 1814.

France also had its private madhouses by the early eighteenth century, euphemistically called *Maisons de santé*.[7] A formal (and expensive) legal process existed to legitimize the dispatch of lunatics to such places. A hearing before a magistrate, the *interdiction*, was usually initiated by the family, though occasionally by the royal authorities. The magistrate heard evidence and often spoke to the insane person before deciding whether to authorize his or her incarceration. Such proceedings were also designed to protect the individual's property. But besides their considerable expense, these occasions were seen as a threat to 'family honour' and reputation, so many shied away from using them. More frequently, the all-purpose *lettres de cachet* were used to license consigning the mad relation to these establishments. That approach, too, was not without its drawbacks. In particular, the looseness of the criteria on the basis of which these warrants were granted helped to immerse the reputation of the *Maisons de santé* in scandal and fear.[8] That these instruments were simultaneously being used to silence the king's political adversaries and critics, and to shut up (in multiple senses) the high-born whose antics caused disquiet among their relations, did not go unnoticed. Not for the last time, stigmatizing an inconvenient person as mad had obvious attractions, but falling prey to the temptation to do so tainted the confinement of the mentally ill with the odour of tyranny. Under Louis XVI, the suppressed but simmering discontent with this arbitrary means of silencing and imprisoning people spilled out into the open, and from the 1770s protests against the practice were repeatedly voiced by the *parlement* of Paris, its provincial counterparts and eventually by the Estates-General. This led to its abolition in the immediate aftermath of the Revolution by the Constituent Assembly on 27 March 1790 – a decision which complicated the problem of how to dispose of threatening madmen, and produced difficulties that would not be fully resolved until the passage of a new law regulating the confinement of the mad in 1838.

Representations of Madness

If suspicions about false confinement in French madhouses were closely bound up with a broader fear of royal tyranny and arbitrariness, across the English Channel they were linked to quite another set of fears. Private, profit-making madhouses had begun to emerge in England perhaps as early as the late seventeenth century, as the wealthier sought a means to relieve themselves of the burdens and troubles associated with managing the lunatic in domestic surroundings. The eighteenth century witnessed the birth of a consumer society, as the market and trade grew apace, and a growing middle class began to enjoy a measure of affluence.[9] More and more goods and services became objects of commerce, from which the entrepreneurial classes might seek to earn a living. Etiquette and dancing classes, music lessons and instruction in how to paint provided opportunities for many as a source of income.

As literacy spread, the market for pulp fiction grew, and the hacks of Grub Street (a London street famous for such writers) provided titillating tales for the masses, even as at the upper end of the literary marketplace more ambitious writers found a larger audience for their wares. So too in art, with astute practitioners such as William Hogarth (1697–1764) exploiting the new commercial opportunities by selling expensive paintings to an aristocratic clientele, and mass-produced engravings of the same images to parvenus seeking to emulate their betters. Among Hogarth's subjects, along-side the usual portraits of the rich and consequential, were novel sorts of social commentary: a picture of a starving writer in a Grub Street garret, and a whole series of satirical images lambasting the sins of eighteenth-century London – 'modern moral subjects' as Hogarth called them – that included such topics as *Marriage à-la-mode*; *Industry and Idleness*; the *Four Stages of Cruelty*; *Gin Lane*; and *A Harlot's Progress*.

Arguably, the most famous of them all was *A Rake's Progress*, eight paintings depicting the downfall of young Tom Rakewell, who inherits a fortune from his rich and miserly merchant father and proceeds to squander it on riotous living, drink, gambling and whores. In the final scene, near-naked and chained, Tom lies on the floor of Bedlam, driven mad by his life of excess, and surrounded by a cast of the crazy, all under the inspection of two finely dressed fashionable women – either aristocratic voyeurs or tarts, we are left to wonder which. Bars, chains, nakedness – the stereotypical accompaniments of lunacy – and a ward crowded with such figures as a mad Papist with mitre and Trinitarian staff, a crazed astronomer, a love-sick melancholic, a deluded snake-charmer, a deranged musician and a would-be king, naked save for his mock-crown and urinating on to the straw: here is a pathetic parade of irrationality in a multitude of guises, madness as the wages of sin. The paintings were completed in 1733, and Hogarth began to accept subscriptions for the engraved versions towards the end of the year. Prudently, however, he delayed publication until 25 June 1735, the day the new Engravers' Copyright Act became law: Hogarth was thus able to charge two guineas per set, and when that market was exhausted, he produced a smaller and cheaper line that he sold for a mere 2s. 6d.

The same mix of aristocratic patrons and members of the aspiring merchant class who were the primary consumers of Hogarth's work also formed the bulk of the audience for another form of artistic endeavour. Opera, combining poetry, dance, drama and music, is conventionally held to have originated in Renaissance Florence at the very end of the sixteenth century, and represented an effort to revive Greek drama. Originally mostly staged for audiences at court (where extravagance of all sorts was seen as a positive virtue, for it provided a suitable occasion for the untrammelled display of wealth and power), operas subsequently began to be performed for a paying, if still well-to-do, audience – first in Venice (with works by Monteverdi), and soon all over Italy, before spreading to the rest of Europe.

The final scene of A Rake's Progress *shows Tom's fate: the wages of sin and dissipation are madness and confinement in Bedlam; an engraving after the original painting.*

By Hogarth's time, it was a genre attracting major composers and its appeal to the affluent was increasingly established, an association that would persist all the way down to the present, to both its advantage and its detriment.

Opera involved spectacle, on-stage drama and plots that deliberately employed exaggeration almost to the point of the excessive and the absurd, involving heightened emotions, love, betrayal, grief, vengeance, violence and death. As such, its composers and audiences were almost immediately attracted to the melodramatic possibilities madness presented, and the way the passions, aroused to fever pitch, might border upon and then tip over into insanity. If operatic performers could sing long arias while confronting grief, suffering agonies, dying, then assuredly they could also give voice to madness.[10] In its ability to make use of poetry's potential to bend and stretch the limits of language and to combine those attributes with expressive dramatic action, scenery and costumes, opera had enormous advantages as a form with which to capture Unreason – to display it, to place it under a magnifying glass, perhaps even to domesticate it in some senses, and most certainly to illuminate the breakdown and fragmentation of the world through the contrivances of art. And that leaves aside one even more salient aspect. Opera had a second 'language', one that could amplify, illustrate and even act as a counterpoint to the verbal and visual: the musical idioms and sounds that could be exploited by a composer of sufficient skill to delineate character, mood and situation.

Handel's *Orlando* (a reworking of *Orlando furioso*) had first been performed in London on 27 January 1733, while Hogarth was at work on *A Rake's Progress*. Working within the usually stately and ordered musical idioms of the Baroque period, Handel nonetheless took full advantage of the opportunity to bring together acting, words and music to render Orlando's disintegration and madness in the long scene that ends Act Two. He makes use of a variety of clever musical devices to signal the outbreak of disorder and the loss of Orlando's hold on reality. What begins as a simple, rhythm-based orchestration becomes more frenzied as the scene develops. While the string section begins by playing together, the violins subsequently take a higher-pitched, melodic line, as the underlying rhythm increases. Chords are played in an increasingly frantic fashion. Recorders and violas d'amore provide unusual colours, signalling Orlando's flight from reality. Seven different tempi and five shifts in time signature add to the musical twists and turns. The most fraught thematic element is repeated several times, and eventually returns again, underpinned at the last by a much more frenzied and complex instrumental accompaniment. Here is music gone awry, symbolizing a world that has lost its compass. (Handel even resorts to a few bars in 5/8 time in the accompanied recitative that precedes the aria, a rarity in Baroque music, and one that must have added to the contemporary audience's sense of unease.)[11] Finally, the demented Orlando thinks he has boarded the boat of Charon, the ferryman across the Styx, launching him on a journey to the underworld. 'Già solco l'onde nere' ('Already I am cleaving the black waves') sings Orlando, descending into madness.

Handel's was only the first of many borrowings from literary forms by other composers of opera.[12] Almost a half a century later, in 1781, in the Classical period, Mozart's *Idomeneo*, set in Crete in the aftermath of the Trojan Wars, combines orchestral colour, libretto and dramatic action more richly still. Mozart's music differs markedly from Handel's, its rhythms more complex, its dynamic range greater, its instrumentation more varied, its orchestration strikingly different, as is Mozart's use of multiple melodic lines. The opening overture already heralds the menace that is to come, the swirling sea, the sense of an angry god, of forces threatening to break order down. As the drama unfolds, we witness Elettra, racked with jealousy towards her rival for Prince Idamente's hand, the captured Trojan Princess Ilia, calling on the Furies to take revenge on her rival and then, when thwarted, slowly dissolving into the raging madness of her final aria. The music acquires a furious intensity. Elettra gives expression to her despair and her anger, her voice soaring, then dissolving into fragmentary hysterical cries, while the agitated orchestral accompaniment mixes syncopation and harmonically unstable elements with dissonance, an explosive combination that evokes her raging, tormented soul.[13] Handel had used repetition in *Orlando*, perhaps to suggest the compulsions of madness, and Elettra's aria is notable too, as Daniel Heartz has emphasized, both for stammering repetitions in Elettra's singing, and for 'a turning figure, repeated incessantly in the strings like a haunting obsession'.[14] Like *sommeil* or sleep scenes (and the links between the world of dreams, with its loosened restraints and grasp on reality, and the dislocations of madness scarcely need labouring here), the madness scene would become a recognized set piece, a familiar part of the opera-going experience for those who regularly made up the audience.[15]

Shutting People Up

If art and writing now began to offer new ways to earn a living – perhaps even a fortune – from a wider clientele than the traditional patrons among church and aristocracy, more mundane matters could also be turned into sources of profit. Dealing with life's less agreeable aspects was assuredly one of those. Corpses, for example, were increasingly handed over to a new group of specialists, the undertakers, who took an unpleasant task traditionally handled domestically, elaborated upon it, and sold their services to the bereaved.

So too with madness, a sort of legal and moral death-in-life, whose depredations and disturbances laid waste to private life. The presence of a disturbed relation threatened the social fabric and domestic peace. The manic and the moping provoked upheaval and uncertainty at every turn; they created a host of practical problems, and all sorts of commotion and disarray. Neither property nor persons seemed safe in their presence. Social embarrassment and scandal were an ever-present danger, as was the looming financial disaster that might result from the unwise expenditure of material resources and the dissipation of the family's wealth. Often themselves in great distress, the mad simultaneously inflicted great stress on those who surrounded them, and for relief from these travails, many respectable citizens were increasingly willing and able to pay.

Here was the structural underpinning of the new trade in lunacy, as eighteenth-century Englishmen increasingly came to call it. As an ever-larger segment of the population was in a position to pay handsomely for discreet aid, advice and reassurance, and for a practical solution to the problems that the presence of a lunatic posed, so an informal network of madhouses arose to cope with the most severely disturbed. These places of confinement provided families with a mechanism for removing their mad relatives from the prying eyes of others, and thus also a measure of insulation from the shame and stigma that threatened their social standing. The most severe forms of mental alienation were a human catastrophe, and for a (still relatively small) fraction of the mentally ill, being shut up in one of the new madhouses was the answer.

Neither licensed nor regulated to any significant degree throughout the century, and in the business of purveying tactful silences, madhouses were often isolated and sinister spaces. Those speculating in this particular variety of human misery were a motley crew, drawn from a wide variety of social backgrounds – a reflection of the extraordinarily fluid and innovative society from whose ranks they came. Clergymen, both orthodox and non-conformist, saw part of their task as ministering to sick and troubled souls, and a number of them began to take an interest in managing the mad. Joseph Mason, for example, a Gloucestershire Baptist preacher, established a small madhouse in Stapleton, near Bristol, in 1738 (it later moved to Fishponds, a village nearby), that remained in the family for generations. (His grandson, Joseph Mason Cox, see below, would obtain a medical degree from Leiden in 1788, and was the third of five generations of family members to own the business.) But businessmen and speculators, widows seeking to supplement their meagre incomes, and those with a variety of claims to medical knowledge, from illiterate self-taught apothecaries to classically trained physicians such as Anthony Addington (1713–90) of Reading, all made their living in this fashion.

And sometimes it was a very good living indeed. The pioneering (and appropriately named) Sir William Battie (1703–76), author of *A Treatise on Madness* (1758), grew rich and prominent enough to earn a knighthood, become president of the Royal College of Physicians and rise from

Whitmore House in Hoxton: a watercolour of one of London's largest private madhouses in the eighteenth and early nineteenth century. It was acquired in 1800 by Thomas Warburton, a former butcher's apprentice who had served as a keeper there, by the shrewd, if unoriginal, ploy of marrying the previous owner's widow.

near-poverty to leave a fortune of between £100,000 and £200,000 – tens of millions in modern money. Addington's wealth from his establishment launched his son Henry's political career, which culminated in three years as Prime Minister (1801–04) and elevation to the peerage. Not all fared anything like so well, of course. Most eked out a far more modest living, and perhaps handed over their business to the next generation. Inheritance, keeping the lucrative trade and its secrets within the family, was early on established as a feature of the mad-doctoring trade.

Businessmen know to go where the money is, and so for the most part the entrepreneurs entering the trade in lunacy sought patients from the wealthier classes. But some of the poorer sort also found themselves for the first time in these more specialized surroundings. Parish authorities occasionally concluded that the particularly troublesome who were without family to keep them confined and controlled might best be disposed of by being removed to one of the new establishments. With the rise of wage labour, increased geographical mobility and the separation of work from household, working-class families were finding it increasingly difficult to cope with the mad at home, a problem felt with particular acuteness among those drawn to London, who were highly vulnerable to economic misfortune. The rise of a market-orientated society may well also have effected a subtle change in world view. As more calculative attitudes to existence took hold, so kinship and family solidarities may have weakened, augmenting the number of lunatics thrown on the public charge. Certainly, while most provincial madhouses remained small affairs, taking in perhaps a dozen or so patients at most, in London their counterparts sometimes swelled to a quite remarkable size. By 1815, the two madhouses owned by Thomas Warburton in Bethnal Green, the White House and the Red House, contained 635 patients between them, and Sir Jonathan Miles' establishment at Hoxton as many as 486. (Miles had secured lucrative contracts with the Admiralty to confine sailors who had gone mad during the war against Napoleon.)

A few hundred lunatics of the poor and middling sort also found themselves confined in the growing number of charity asylums that materialized from the mid-eighteenth century onwards. The new Bedlam (completed in 1676) had added more accommodation for chronic patients in 1728, and acquired a competitor in 1751, when St Luke's Hospital opened its doors on the other side of Moorfields. Plain where Bedlam was ornate, it soon gave birth to provincial imitators, often constructed – as at Leicester or Manchester – as part of, or alongside the new general hospitals that the charitably inclined began to underwrite in the eighteenth century.

Built as part of the reconstruction of London after the great fire of 1666 that had consumed so much of the city's fabric (though its existing building had not been destroyed in the conflagration), Bedlam had also been a celebration of the Restoration of the monarchy, a delivery of the English from the madness of Cromwell's Commonwealth, with its assaults on hierarchy and the divinely ordained social order. But the new Bedlam's ostentatious exterior and its opulent ornamentation that had once served to advertise the benevolence of the London rich were in many quarters by the mid-eighteenth century seen as useless vanity and extravagance. Its ostensible grandeur was somewhat undercut by its insalubrious location, for Cripplegate and Moorfields, the neighbourhoods it abutted, were marshy and unhealthy slums, the haunt of the idle, the outcast, criminals and miscellaneous vagrants – and ironically the site also of gibbets from which the corpses of those hanged dangled and rotted.

The promoters of St Luke's had insisted by contrast that 'Plainness and simplicity are [to be] commended in buildings intended for charitable purposes.'[16] It was a sentiment echoed by their contemporaries across Europe. The Austrian physician Johann Peter Frank (1745–1821), for example, proclaimed that a healthy, airy site and efficiency were the 'best and only ornaments' of a hospital; while in Paris, the scientist Jean-Baptiste Le Roy (1720–1800) complained that 'People always prefer things that are flashy and frivolous to those that offer only miserable utility' and contended that 'great, extreme cleanliness, as pure an air as possible – one cannot say it too often: this is the true, the only magnificence that one seeks in these buildings'.[17]

Whether their exteriors were plain or decorated, however, and even though they were newly built to contain small numbers of the lunatic, these charitable asylums paid little attention to the special needs of the mad they shut up. Patients were indiscriminately mixed together. Even the sexes were not necessarily separated. Accommodation was in large galleries as well as individual cells, where the more obstreperous were unceremoniously chained to the walls. The lack of a distinctive architecture was even more marked in the profit-making trade in lunacy, whose entrepreneurial owners disdained the expense of building from scratch – to what purpose? – and instead crudely adapted and renovated existing buildings, often decaying mansions

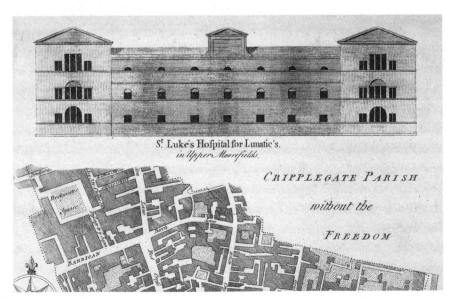

St Luke's Hospital for Lunatics, founded in 1751. In sharp contrast to the ornamental exterior of Bedlam, just across Moorfields, St Luke's was deliberately plain.

Thomas Rowlandson's acquatint of the interior of St Luke's Hospital (1809) exaggerates the height of the women's ward, but contains a host of mad figures, hair and clothing askew, in largely bare surroundings.

in once-fashionable areas that could be cheaply fitted up to contain their charges. A century later, enthusiasts for the reformed asylum would come to consider a moralized, purpose-built architecture to be a vital component of their schemes to manage those in the grip of Unreason and return them to the ranks of the sane. But the first madhouses embodied no such conceits, even as their invention marked the dawning acceptance of the notion that lunacy was a condition perhaps best treated away from the home. So it was that a new geography of madness first began to emerge.

If security and isolation from society were among the central advantages the madhouse offered its clientele – for patients' families and perhaps the local community more broadly, if not the patients themselves – the need to adapt old spaces for new purposes for which they were ill-suited led to a variety of expedients that emphasized their custodial function: high walls and bars on the windows to guard against escape; and often chains and manacles to facilitate the task of the daily management of people who by definition were generally disinclined or unable to adhere to the norms of polite social intercourse. Asylums and madhouses were in the business of offering discretion, and their overtly prison-like features, plus the separation these created between the world of the mad and the sane, helped to spawn and exacerbate the fears and rumours that soon swirled around them.

Bitter complaints began to emerge from patients that they had been confined by family members in league with corrupt keepers. If the French worried about the abuses of royal power associated with the infamous *lettres de cachet*, their British counterparts spoke scathingly of the trampling on the rights of free-born citizens. Alexander Cruden (1699–1770), mainly remembered these days as the author of the first Concordance (1737) to the King James edition of the Bible (a book still in print and in use), spoke bitterly of his confinement in a madhouse, one that had left this 'London citizen exceedingly injured'. It was, he averred (and for a devout Calvinist like Cruden, the image was particularly awful) nothing less than a 'British Inquisition'.[18] Daniel Defoe (1660?–1731), always alive to new ways of producing prose for profit, authored a pamphlet condemning

> the vile Practice now so in vogue among the better Sort, as they
> are called, but the worst sort in fact, namely, the sending their
> Wives to Mad-Houses at every Whim or Dislike, that they may
> be more secure and undisturb'd in their Debaucheries...Ladies
> and Gentlewomen are hurried away to these Houses...[and]
> if they are not mad when they go into these cursed Houses, they
> are soon made so by the barbarous Usage they there suffer.[19]

And a variety of lawsuits, a number of them successful, suggest that these claims had some substance. Men as well as women could find themselves locked away in this fashion. William Belcher, who had been confined for seventeen years (1778–95) in a Hackney madhouse from which he was eventually liberated with the assistance of one of London's most famous mad-doctors (Thomas Monro, the physician to Bedlam), spoke publicly of being 'bound and tortured in a strait-waistcoat, fettered, crammed with physic with a bullock's horn, and knocked down, and declared a lunatic by a Jury that never saw me....' Locked up in 'that premature coffin of the mind' he had long despaired of his freedom.[20] The trade in lunacy thus always operated under a cloud. The eighteenth-century physician William Pargeter (1760–1810), who wrote on madness but did not own a madhouse of his own, was scathing about the reputation of such places:

The idea of a *mad-house* is apt to excite, in the breasts of most people, the strongest emotions of horror and alarm; upon a supposition, not altogether ill-founded, that when once a patient is doomed to take up his abode in these places, he will not only be exposed to very great cruelty; but it is a great chance, whether he recovers or not, if he ever more sees the outside of the walls.[21]

Novel Predicaments

Writers of fiction, for whose wares a burgeoning market was now emerging, were not slow to seize upon the dramatic possibilities the madhouse presented. As respectable a writer as Tobias Smollett arranged for the eponymous hero of his *The Life and Adventures of Sir Launcelot Greaves* (1760), a mock-heroic English Quixote, to be seized and carried off to a madhouse run by the villainous Bernard Shackle. Further down-market (and often finding a secretive and unacknowledged following among those protesting their disdain for this low-class stuff) madness was exploited in a cruder fashion. The frisson that could be aroused by wild imaginings about life amid the lunatic proved irresistible to hack writers. The setting provided salacious entertainment as well as a pleasing sort of terror for their readers. The pages of the gothic and sensational novels were soon replete with madhouse scenes – titillating episodes in which helpless heroines found themselves shut up and cut off from civilized society, their chastity and their very sanity threatened by the pitiless ruffians who held them captive. A few whippings and some chains added a little sado-masochistic colour.

There was perhaps a touch of irony in the fact that Grub Street, synonymous with this sort of sensationalist writing, lay almost in the shadow of Bedlam.[22] Far from that hospital's walls, however, the French developed their own novels of horror, diabolism and debauchery, the genre known there as *romans noirs* (black novels); while the Germans, not to be outdone, created something they called *Schauerroman* (shudder novels).

Eliza Haywood provided an early example of the genre. She originally published her novella *The Distress'd Orphan, or Love in a Mad-house* anonymously in 1726. So popular was her tale of the virtuous Annilia, nefariously confined by her scheming uncle Giraldo and then spirited off to a madhouse, that it stayed continuously in print throughout the century, in both authorized and pirated editions. The orphaned girl, made the ward of her uncle, has

'Annilia at the dead of Night hurried away to a Mad-house by the orders of her Great Uncle.' The frontispiece to the 1790 edition of Eliza Haywood's The Distress'd Orphan.

inherited a fortune, and Giraldo decides to seize it by forcing her to marry his son. She demurs. He locks her up until she changes her mind, then arranges for her to be carried off in a hackney coach, in the dead of night, 'under the Guard of two or three Men belonging to the Keeper of the Lunaticks', her protests silenced by 'stopping her mouth'. Readers were titillated by the image of a confinement so harsh as to threaten the heroine's sanity: 'The rattling of Chains, the Shrieks of those severely treated by their barbarous Keepers, mingled with Curses, Oaths, and the most blasphemous Imprecations, did from one quarter of the House shock her tormented Ears; while from another, Howlings like that of Dogs, Shoutings, Roarings, Prayers, Preaching, Curses,

Singing, Crying, promiscuously join'd to make a Chaos of the most horrible Confusion' – a confusion from which she is providentially rescued by the man with whom she has previously secretly fallen in love, Colonel Marathon, who steals upon her disguised as a melancholy country gentleman named 'Lovemore', and scales the high walls of the madhouse with his 'trembling' sweetheart over his shoulder. In the end, love receives its just reward, and the perpetrators of Annilia's false confinement are punished by banishment and premature death.[23]

It was a plot-line that would be endlessly recycled through the century, all the way down to Mary Wollstonecraft's *Maria: or, the Wrongs of Woman* (1798).[24] Indeed, it would find its echoes as late as the early Victorian age (albeit in a scene of domestic confinement) in Charlotte Brontë's *Jane Eyre* (1847). Madhouses and mad-doctors were absent here, but ancient stereotypes about madness and animality most certainly were not. Mad Bertha Mason lurks in the attic, while the oblivious Jane Eyre, in another wing of the mansion, seeks to keep her erotic longings for the handsome Mr Rochester in check. But Jane's blissful ignorance does not last. Abruptly, she is introduced to the sequestered Mrs Rochester, a woman of untamed appetites:

> In the deep shade, at the farther end of the room, a figure ran
> backwards and forwards. What it was, whether beast or human
> being, one could not, at first sight tell: it grovelled, seemingly,
> on all fours; it snatched and growled like some strange wild
> animal; but it was covered with clothing, and a quantity of dark,
> grizzled hair, wild as a mane, hid its head and face.

Here was madness, shrieking, violent, dangerous and destructive. Here was the madwoman as fiend.

Sir Walter Scott's *The Bride of Lammermoor* (1819) had provided an earlier nineteenth-century portrait of a violent madwoman, Lucy Ashton. Pushed by her scheming mother into an unwanted marriage (having been wrongly persuaded that her betrothed has jilted her), she learns the truth on her wedding night, stabs her new husband, descends into madness and kills herself. Scott's novel in turn was the inspiration for Donizetti's opera, *Lucia di Lammermoor* (1835), which alters the plot in a variety of ways, but keeps the central elements of betrayal, madness and murder. After stabbing her husband to death, in the climactic scene the crazed Lucia emerges on stage in her blood-stained wedding dress, sings one last vocally demanding aria

In this scene from a production of Donizetti's opera Lucia di Lammermoor *the maddened Lucia, having killed her husband Arturo on their wedding night, enters in blood-stained white dress to sing the aria 'Il dolce suono', in which she imagines her forthcoming marriage to her real love, Edgardo.*

and dies. The story has all the dramatic elements opera feasts upon, and Donizetti has the distinct advantage of being able to combine acting, singing and his instrumentation of the score to heighten the tension, the violence and the horror of the madness around which the plot ultimately turns. Perhaps not surprisingly, the opera has outlived the novel. It remains a standard part of the operatic repertoire, and the title part was performed on multiple occasions by the great twentieth-century divas, Maria Callas and Joan Sutherland. As Donizetti's example shows (and mad scenes of a less violent sort are a feature of several of his other operas), gothic novelists were not alone in exploiting madness; nor, as we shall see, did tales of false confinement vanish in the nineteenth century, as the asylum became a brooding, unmistakable presence.[25]

Another group of eighteenth-century writers, the so-called sentimental novelists, aimed their work squarely at those who sought to be seen (and to see themselves) as the genteel. Particularly in a fluid society such as Britain, where social status no longer seemed immutable, differences of taste and sensibility provided an invaluable opportunity to mark status boundaries and to create distinction. Here was a chance for a certain class of readers to emphasize the distance between polite and popular culture and to put on display through their literary choices their superior refinement, rationality and sensitivity. For these were the qualities that served to distinguish people like themselves from the unwashed masses, those inferior beings who continued to wallow in mindless superstition, depraved attitudes and moral coarseness.[26]

Among the most successful at exploiting this mawkish but lucrative sector of the literary marketplace was Henry Mackenzie, whose *The Man of Feeling* is a classic example of the genre. Published in April 1771, it had sold out by June, and a sixth edition was printed in 1791. In one of the key episodes in the novel, the hero, Harley, visits Bedlam, where, so he is assured, he will be mightily entertained by the antics of the patients. To the contrary, the sight and sounds – 'the clanking of chains, the wildness of their cries, and the imprecations which some of them uttered, formed a scene inexpressibly shocking'. The sight of the mad kept as 'wild beasts for show' provokes a flood of crocodile tears and a rapid exit. The masses might react with mirth and mockery; the man of feeling knew better: 'I think it an inhuman practice to expose the greatest misery with which our nature is afflicted to every idle visitant who can afford a trifling perquisite to the [Bedlam] keeper; especially as it is a distress which the humane must see, with the painful reflection, that it is not in their power to alleviate it.'[27]

Melodramas of these various sorts should not be taken as balanced or accurate representations of the fate of the mad in confinement. Global indictments of the trade in lunacy would be used by nineteenth-century lunacy reformers, for whom painting the *ancien régime* madhouse in the darkest of hues would prove a vital weapon in stirring the moral consciences of their contemporaries and persuading them of the need for change. Horrors certainly existed, and the reformers would delight in rehearsing them. But from another perspective, the unregulated state of the mad-business did at least allow for the growth of experience in the handling of the insane in an institutional setting, and for experimental approaches to their treatment.

15 ABOVE *Portrait of Richard Napier (1559–1634) by an unknown artist. Napier was the Rector of Great Linwood in Buckinghamshire, England, and an astrologer, alchemist, magician and mad-doctor. Nervous and distracted patients came from great distances to be treated by him with priest craft and physick administered at astrologically propitious moments.*

16 TOP *Don Quixote, lance lowered, charges a flock of sheep he believes in his delusional state to be a troop of his enemies, as Sancho Panza sits on his weary donkey; an oil sketch by Daumier (1855).*

17 ABOVE Ophelia *(1851–52), by John Everett Millais. The meticulously recorded background for the tragic figure of Ophelia, driven out of her mind, cost Millais endless hours of work and observation.*

18 ABOVE The Miracles of St Ignatius (c. *1617–18*), *by Peter Paul Rubens. Its huge scale and rich detail were designed to impress the devout with the powers of the saintly in the service of the Counter-Reformation. In the foreground lies a near-naked possessed man. Other sufferers crowd the picture, and above them stream small airborne devils, fleeing to escape from Ignatius's exhortations.*

19 ABOVE *Organ cover painted by David Colijns in c. 1635–40, originally for the Nieuwezijds Kapel in Amsterdam, showing David playing his harp in an attempt to sooth the troubled soul of King Saul – on this occasion without success, as Saul throws a spear at him. Dutch Calvinists were deeply hostile to anything that smacked of idolatry so this painted screen was an unusual object.*

20 RIGHT *Hieronymus Bosch's* The Cure of Folly: The Extraction of the Stone of Madness *(c. 1494). A doctor, or possibly a quack, uses a scalpel to remove the supposed cause of madness from the head of a patient. The popular belief in 'the stone of madness' was widespread.*

21 BELOW Two Madmen (Twee kranksinnigen), *a terracotta statue of 1673 by Pieter Xavery, probably designed for a madhouse. Like many of Xavery's works, this is a small piece, but filled with telling detail and movement.*

I. Maurer Delin.

Publish'd accorde

The Hospital of Bethlehem

— *Printed for John Bou*

22 ABOVE *An engraving of* The Hospital of Bethlehem. *Bedlam, as it is usually known, was rebuilt in 1675–76, its opulence designed to show off London's charity, and to advertise the restoration of the monarchy and the rule of reason after the turmoil of the English Revolution and the Commonwealth.*

L'Hospital de Fou

Horse in Cornhil.

T. Bowles sculp.

23 TOP La Conduite des filles de joie à la Salpêtrière, *or* Transporting Prostitutes to the Salpêtrière *(1755), by Étienne Jeaurat. Many kinds of morally suspect and disruptive people were deposited in this enormous establishment, which housed mostly women.*

24 ABOVE *Philippe Pinel releasing lunatics from their chains in the Salpêtrière in 1795, by Tony Robert-Fleury (1876) – a famous event though in fact a myth created decades later.*

Disciplining the Unruly

In many quarters, the overthrow of Reason, 'the sovereign power of the soul',[28] is seen as unleashing the appetites and the passions in their full fury: 'Fancy gets the ascendant,' said John Brydall (*c.* 1635–1705?), author of the first English treatise on the jurisprudence of insanity, published in 1700, 'and Phaeton-like, drives on furiously',[29] stripping away the veneer of civilization, effacing all that is distinctively human. Pascal (1623–62), the French philosopher and mathematician, had spoken of what it meant to lose one's reason:

> I can easily conceive of a man without hands, feet, head (for it is
> only experience which teaches us that the head is more necessary
> than the feet). But I cannot conceive of a man without thought;
> that would be a stone or a brute.[30]

And that, for those who thought about the ontological status of the mad, seemed to be the inescapable conclusion. Preaching a Spital sermon in 1718 – an annual appeal for charity for London's poor – on behalf of 'those unhappy People, who are bereft of the dearest Light, the Light of Reason', the cleric Andrew Snape (1675–1742) spoke of how

> Distraction...divests the rational soul of all its noble and
> distinguishing Endowments, and sinks unhappy Man below the
> mute and senseless part of Creation: even brutal Instinct being
> a surer and safer guide than disturb'd Reason, and every tame
> Species of Animals more sociable and less hurtful than humanity
> thus unmann'd.[31]

For those who accepted this portrait, madness required a firm hand. Discipline should therefore accompany the traditional medical remedies of depletion, evacuation and bleeding. So far as we know, Thomas Willis (1621–75), who pioneered research into the anatomy of the brain and nervous system (and coined the term 'neurologie'), had no clinical contact with the mad during his years at Oxford, but he was emphatic about what treatment of their condition required:

> To correct or allay the furies and exorbitancies of the Animal
> Spirits...requires threatenings, bonds, or strokes as well as Physick.
> For the *Mad-man* being placed in a House convenient for the
> business must be so handled by the *Physician*, and also by the

Servants that are prudent, that he may be in some manner kept in, either by warnings, chidings, or punishments inflicted upon him, to his duty, or his behaviour, or manners. And indeed for the curing of Mad people, there is nothing more effectual or necessary than their reverence or standing in awe of such as they think their Tormentors…. Furious Mad-men are sooner and more certainly cured by punishments and hard usage, in a strait-room, than by *Physick*, or Medicines.[32]

Willis's work and the implication of the nervous system and the brain in the aetiology of madness marked the beginnings of a move away from the humoral explanations of madness that medical men had embraced since Hippocrates and Galen, and his views would be promulgated and elaborated by those who followed after him in the early eighteenth century. His ideas were widely embraced by the society physicians who sought a lucrative new market in the treatment of 'nervous' patients, those whose uncertain mental states others were tempted to dismiss as *maladies imaginaires*[33] – and though these men too seem to have had little interest in treating the Bedlam mad, they confidently repeated their master's injunctions about what ought to be done for and to them:

It is Cruelty in the highest Degree [the prominent physician and governor of Bedlam Nicholas Robinson assured his readers], not to be bold in the Administration of Medicine. [Only] a Course of Medicines of the most violent Operation [would suffice] to bring down the Spirit of Stubborn Persons [and] reduce their artificial Strength by compulsive Methods.[34]

Such thinking was not without its influence on those who actually *did* take charge of the crazed. Madhouse keepers were not keen to advertise their skills as whip-masters; it was scarcely an attractive way to drum up custom. But harsh treatment was commonly meted out in many a madhouse, and even so august a personage as the English king George III (1738–1820) was subjected to beatings and intimidation. Francis Willis (1718–1807), who kept a madhouse in Lincolnshire, was summoned to treat the monarch in 1788, when the royal physicians despaired of curing his lunacy. Willis was clear about how he intended to proceed:

> As death makes no distinction in his visits between the poor
> man's hut and the prince's palace, so insanity is equally impartial
> in her dealings with her subjects. For that reason, I made no
> distinction in my treatment of persons submitted to my charge.
> When, therefore, my gracious sovereign became violent, I felt it
> my duty to subject him to the same system of restraint as I should
> have adopted with one of his own gardeners at Kew: in plain
> words, I put a strait waistcoat on him.[35]

Willis was dissembling somewhat. His treatment went much further than the application of a strait-jacket. He boasted elsewhere that

> The emotion of fear is the first and often the only one by which
> they can be governed. By working on it one removes their thoughts
> from the phantasms occupying them and brings them back to
> reality, even if this entails pain and suffering.[36]

And he suited his actions to his words. The Countess Harcourt, who served as Lady of the Bedchamber to the Queen, gave a fuller account of the King's treatment:

> The unhappy patient...was no longer treated as a human being.
> His body was immediately encased in a machine which left no
> liberty of motion. He was sometimes chained to a stake. He was
> frequently beaten and starved, and at best was kept in subjection
> by menacing and violent language.[37]

The king duly recovered (only temporarily, as we shall see in Chapter Seven), and Willis was rewarded with a substantial pension for his troubles.

To some extent, Francis Willis's interventions were idiosyncratic, but the underlying logic of his approach to the problems of managing and curing mad patients – he sought to break them in, like 'Horses in a ménage' as one close observer put it[38] – was one broadly shared among many in his trade, and not just in England. New machinery was invented to stimulate fear and shock patients back to reality. One of the most formidable examples was presented by Joseph Guislain (1797–1860), who ran an asylum at Ghent. His *Traité sur l'aliénation mentale*, published in Amsterdam in 1826, included detailed drawings of a device he dubbed 'The Chinese Temple'. The famous Dutch physician Herman Boerhaave (1668–1738) had suggested that the

sensation of near-drowning might have therapeutic uses in recalling the
mad from their distraction. Guislain proudly put on display his improved
method for achieving this effect:

> It consists of a little Chinese temple, the interior of which consists
> of a movable iron cage, of lightweight construction, which plunges
> down into the water descending in rails, of its own weight, by
> means of pulleys and ropes. To expose the madman to the action
> of this device, he is led into the interior of this cage, one servant
> shuts the door from the outside, while the other releases a brake
> which, by this manoeuvre, causes the patient to sink down, shut
> up in the cage, under the water. Having produced the desired
> effect, one raises the machine again.

Somewhat superfluously, he commented: 'Toute fois ce moyen sera plus ou
moins dangereux' ('this is always a more or less dangerous procedure').[39]

Perhaps marginally less terrifying was the machine invented by the
American mad-doctor, Benjamin Rush (1746–1813), who dubbed his contrap-
tion 'The Tranquillizer', and promised similarly salutary effects:

> I have contrived a chair and introduced it into our [Pennsylvania]
> Hospital to assist in curing madness. It binds and confines every
> part of the body. By keeping the trunk erect, it lessens the impulse
> of blood toward the brain. By preventing the muscles from acting,
> it reduces the force and frequency of the pulse, and the position
> of the head and feet favors the easy application of cold water
> or ice to the former and warm water to the latter. Its effects have
> been truly delightful to me. It acts as a sedative to the tongue and
> temper as well as to the blood vessels. In 24, 12, 6, and in some
> cases in 4 hours, the most refractory patients have been composed.
> I have called it a *Tranquillizer*.[40]

Erasmus Darwin (1731–1802), Charles Darwin's grandfather, had suggested a slightly different approach, drawing upon some hints from Classical
antiquity: perhaps a swinging motion might break through the barriers put
up by the mad and bring them back into contact with the world of common
sense. The suggestion was enthusiastically taken up in both England and
Ireland, and soon spread to the rest of Europe. Joseph Mason Cox (1763–
1813), proprietor of a madhouse near Bristol, was first with a workable

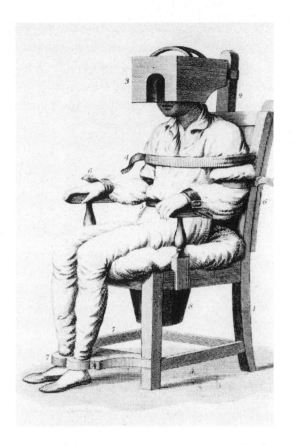

'The Tranquillizer', 1811. Its inventor Benjamin Rush boasted that: 'Its effects have been truly delightful to me.' His patients' reactions are not recorded.

design. He proudly promoted the remarkable ability to bring both moral and physiological pressures to bear on those strapped into his swinging chair. It provided a clever way of exploiting 'the sympathy or reciprocity of action that subsists between mind and body'. Each of these acted 'in its turn [as] the agent, and the subject acted on, as when fear, terror, anger, and other passions, excited by the action of the swing, produce various alterations in the body, and where the revolving motion, occasioning fatigue, exhaustion, pallor, horripilatio [the hairs of the body standing up on end], vertigo, etc., effect new associations and trains of thought.' Everything could be varied with extraordinary precision. Acting on the stomach, one could produce 'either temporary or continued nausea, partial or full vomiting'. Pressing matters further still could induce 'the most violent convulsions...the agitation and concussion of every part of the animal frame'. For those who still remained obstinate, the swinging chair could be 'employed in the dark, where, from unusual noises, smells, or other powerful agents, acting forcibly on the senses, its efficacy might be amazingly increased'.[41] More ingeniously still, by 'increasing the velocity of the swing, the motion be[ing] suddenly reversed every six or eight minutes, pausing occasionally, and stopping its circulation suddenly: the consequence is, an instant discharge of the stomach, bowels, and bladder, in quick succession'.[42]

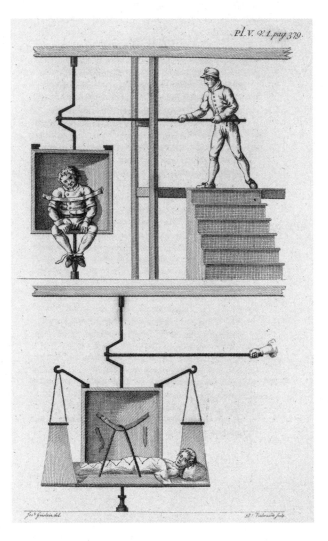

More elaborate versions of Joseph Mason Cox's original swinging chair were soon developed. The first one above provided better support for the patient's spinal column while he was whirled about; the second allowed the treatment of a recumbent patient.

What greater refinement could possibly be added to such a marvellous device? The Dublin mad-doctor William Saunders Hallaran (*c.* 1765–1825) almost immediately devised one: he designed a safer version, the seat that 'supports the cervical column better, and guards against the possibility of the head in the vertiginous state from hanging over the side'.[43] He could personally testify to the powers of the device: 'since the commencement of its use, I have never been at a loss for a direct mode of establishing a supreme authority over the most turbulent and unruly'.[44]

Notwithstanding such encomiums, and the rapid initial spread of these curative machines across Europe and North America, they enjoyed only a brief period of popularity. The Berlin Charité hospital, for example, which had quickly imported Cox's swing, had banned its use by the 1820s. Public and professional opinion had swung in a contrary direction almost as violently as Cox's device, and what had once seemed a logical and sensible set of interventions to treat the mad was now viewed by many with incomprehension and outrage.

For if some of those dealing with the small fraction of the mad now confined in asylums and madhouses sought to control them through fear and intimidation, others had drawn different lessons from a closer encounter with the problems of managing the mad. Not for them the external imposition of order on the disorderly, if necessary by force. These men (and the occasional woman) learned through trial and error to regard their charges as not necessarily completely deprived of their reason. On the contrary, those who adopted this alternative viewpoint saw not creatures but fellow creatures, people who, if dealt with in a more nuanced, skilful fashion, could be induced to behave, to curb their madness, to resume a life that had some semblance of normality.

Kindness and Humanity?

Significantly, the central features of this new approach emerged independently and almost simultaneously in various settings, and eventually also found a receptive audience among the public – in Italy, France, Britain, the Netherlands and North America. Living in a world seemingly being transformed before their eyes by human action – canals cut, rivers straightened, whole new towns conjured out of the ground almost overnight, new breeds of animals and plants created by selective breeding on an unprecedented scale – old notions of an immutable nature, even an immutable human nature, were coming to be questioned. If Enlightenment thinkers saw man as born a tabula rasa, on whom experience then imprinted its lessons, what might not be achieved by the rational application of human skill? In the classic dictum of the eighteenth-century philosopher Helvétius, 'l'education peut tout'.

Child-rearing, initially among the upper classes, had begun to break away from an older notion that it consisted primarily in 'the suppression of evil, or the breaking of the will'.[45] The Enlightenment thinker John Locke had formulated the rationale for the change in 1693:

> Beating is the worst, and therefore the last Means to be used in
> the Correction of Children.... The Rewards and Punishments then,
> whereby we should keep Children in order are of quite another
> kind.... Esteem and Disgrace are, of all others, the most powerful
> incentives to the Mind, when once it is brought to relish them.
> If you can once get into Children a Love of Credit, and an
> Apprehension of Shame and Disgrace, you have put into them
> the true principle.[46]

Little more than a century later, in 1795, this was almost precisely the language and approach the proponents of what came to be called 'moral treatment' began to use. 'The first salutary operation on the mind of a lunatic', said John Ferriar (1761–1815), the physician to the Manchester Asylum, lay in 'creating a habit of self-restraint', something that required 'the management of hope and apprehension.... Small favours, the show of confidence, and apparent distinction' rather than the use of coercion.[47] Thomas Bakewell (1761–1835), keeper of a provincial madhouse in Staffordshire, likewise stressed the need to rouse the madman's 'moral feelings' and use them as a sort of 'moral discipline':

> Certainly, authority and order must be maintained, but these
> are better maintained by kindness, condescension, and indulgent
> attention, than by any severities whatsoever. Lunatics are not
> devoid of understanding, nor should they be treated as if they
> were; on the contrary, they should be treated as rational beings.[48]

As for the fiercer approaches in vogue elsewhere:

> [by terror lunatics] may be made to obey their keepers, with the
> greatest promptitude; to rise, to sit, to stand, to walk, or run at their

pleasure; though only expressed by a look. Such an obedience, and even the appearance of affection, we not infrequently see in the poor animals who are exhibited to gratify our curiosity in natural history; but, who can avoid reflecting, in observing such spectacles, that the readiness with which the savage tiger obeys his master, is the result of treatment at which humanity would shudder.[49]

The two men most commonly associated with the new approach were the Quaker tea and coffee merchant William Tuke (1732–1822) – whose grandson Samuel is quoted above – who founded a madhouse called the York Retreat in 1792; and the physician Philippe Pinel (1745–1826), who supposedly liberated the insane in 1795 at the Salpêtrière (PL. 24) and the Bicêtre, respectively the main receptacles for female and male pauper lunatics in Revolutionary Paris – developments we shall return to in Chapter Seven. But Tuke was only one of a number of figures arguing for a new way of handling the insane: John Ferriar, the Manchester physician, and Edward Long Fox (1761–1835), proprietor of the private madhouse Brislington House, near Bristol, were urging a similar set of ideas – and indeed Tuke recruited the matron for the York Retreat, Katherine Allen, from Fox's establishment.

As for Pinel, whose unchaining of the insane was a myth created decades after the event – what some have called a 'fairy tale'[50] – his version of moral treatment was learned at the feet of the lay administrators of the wards for the insane at the Bicêtre and the Salpêtrière, Jean-Baptiste Pussin (1746–1811) and his wife Marguerite Pussin (1754–?), who had the extensive practical experience of managing the insane that Pinel at first lacked.[51] Nevertheless, it was Pinel who 'theorized' the changes, and provided the first systematic published account of the French version of moral treatment, and in the process helped to institutionalize the new approach. And it was the utopian optimism that moral treatment gave rise to – the sense that a new, more humane and effective form of therapy had been found, one inextricably linked to a reformed version of the madhouse – that gave birth to the age of asylumdom. Here was the true Great Confinement of the insane, one that materialized in the nineteenth century all across Europe and the North American continent, and eventually spread, through the imperial efforts of the European powers, to other countries and continents as well. We shall return to the rise of the empire of asylumdom in Chapter Seven.

Chapter Six

NERVES AND NERVOUSNESS

Owning a Disease

There are some diseases no one wants to own, and for which everyone immediately wants to blame someone else. Syphilis (PL. 25), for example, was brought back to Europe at the very end of the fifteenth century by Columbus's crew and later would contribute mightily to the population of asylums in the nineteenth and twentieth centuries. When it arrived in Europe, the English promptly dubbed it the French disease. The French, whose army had contracted the disease in great numbers while laying siege to Naples (and whose mercenaries then helped to spread the pox all across Europe), preferred to call it the Neapolitan disease. The Neapolitans in turn tried to disclaim the title and called it the Spanish disease, while the Portuguese, aiming to be more precise, referred to it as the Castillian disease. The Turks, not to be outdone, just blamed the whole lot of them and spoke of the Christian disease.

In the early eighteenth century, however, another disease came to be eagerly embraced by the English, who had hitherto shied away from the diagnosis in question. An odd sort of reaction, one might think. What was alleged to be the heightened national sensitivity to this disorder was worn as a badge of pride. Why, one might reasonably ask, did the term 'the English malady' appeal so powerfully to 'the quality' in England when a transplanted Scottish diet doctor, George Cheyne (1671–1743), coined it in 1733 in the title of his book on the subject? Why the rush to embrace it? Who would want to be labelled as sick? How did Cheyne manage to transform a reproach into a sign of superior sensibility? And what precisely was this malady anyway?

Treatments for syphilis (1690): such a desperate disease invited a variety of desperate remedies, often dispensed by quacks, including sweating and cautery.

The subtitle of Cheyne's book provides a preliminary answer to the last of these questions. It was, he announced, 'a treatise of Nervous Diseases of all Kinds, as Spleen, Vapours, Lowness of Spirits, Hypochondriacal and Hysterical Distempers' – quite a mouthful, but eighteenth-century authors were in love with lengthy titles for their books. And in addressing this complicated array of disorders, he acknowledged that it was 'a Reproach universally thrown on this Island by Foreigners, and all our Neighbours on the Continent, by whom Nervous Distempers, Spleen, Vapours, and Lowness of Spirits, are, in Derision, call'd the ENGLISH MALADY'. The English, it would seem, were a peculiarly nervous lot, prone to all sorts of hysterical breakdowns and attacks of hypochondria or the Hyp – a word then not given its modern sense (Molière's *Le Malade imaginaire* notwithstanding), but instead referring to disorders thought to have their origins in the hypochondrium, or the upper abdomen.

For many at the time, hysteria and the Hyp (and their various cognates) were two sides of the same coin. In the view of the prominent society physician Sir Richard Blackmore (1654–1729), who held the title of Royal Physician successively to King William and Queen Anne, they were different manifestations of the same malady.

> It is true, that the convulsive Disorders and Agitations in the
> various Parts of the Body, as well as the Confusion and Dissipation
> of the animal Spirits, are more conspicuous and violent in the
> Female Sex, than in Men; the Reason of which is, a more volatile,
> dissipable, and weak Constitution of the Spirits, and a more
> soft, tender, and delicate Texture of the Nerves [among women];
> but this proves no Difference in their Nature and essential
> Properties, but only a higher or lower Degree of the Symptoms
> common to both.[1]

But Blackmore also commented ruefully that 'this Disease called Vapours in Woman and the Spleen in Men is what neither Sex are pleased to own', and furthermore that any physician who ventured such a diagnosis was putting his future employment at risk. A doctor, he claimed, 'cannot ordinarily make his Court [his chances of obtaining fees from moneyed patients] worse, than by suggesting to such Patients the true Nature and Name of their Distemper'.[2] And Blackmore knew whereof he spoke: when his colleague John Radcliffe (c. 1650–1714) had ventured to suggest to the then Princess (later Queen) Anne that her symptoms had a hysterical origin, he had been abruptly dismissed.

Given the general popular sentiment about those who attracted such a diagnosis, Radcliffe ought surely to have anticipated her Royal Highness's reaction. Molière's satirical humour had directed much of its irreverent mockery towards a critique of physicians as pompous know-nothings who used execrable Latin to cover up their ignorance while they ushered their

patients to an early grave – a conceit that William Hogarth would caricature in his portrait of London's medical elite that rendered them as 'The
Company of Undertakers' (or 'Quacks in Consultation'). But the French
dramatist had been equally scathing about the foibles of the idle rich, with
their propensity to imagine themselves ill and their capacity to be gulled by
their medical attendants. The main character Argan's false conviction that
he is an invalid on the brink of death is the central element in the plot of
Le Malade imaginaire (*The Imaginary Invalid*; 1673), and it is an irony that
necessarily escaped its author that he himself expired from a massive pul-
monary haemorrhage while playing the role – his own death brought on by
his all-too-real tuberculosis.

Molière was scarcely the last literary figure to pour scorn on those who
put on display the sorts of mysterious and protean symptoms that some now
sought to relabel nervous illness. The English poet Alexander Pope (1688–
1744), for example, delighted in making fun of ladies affecting the 'Vapours'.
Umbriel in 'The Rape of the Lock' openly mocks those 'superior' sorts who
worship the Queen of Spleen:

> ... Hail, wayward Queen!
> Who rule the sex to fifty from fifteen:
> Parent of Vapours and of female wit,
> Who give th'hysteric, or poetic fit,
> On various tempers act by various ways,
> Make some take physic, others scribble plays.

Pope himself suffered from a variety of ailments – he famously spoke of the
'long Disease, my Life'[3] – but he was at pains to distinguish his genuine sufferings from these sorts of modish pretence: on his deathbed, he peevishly
insisted, 'I was never Hyppish in my life'.[4] And his friend and fellow satirist
Jonathan Swift (1667–1745), who would end his days demented, left part of
his fortune to found an asylum for Dublin's mad folk – in his own words,

> He gave the little Wealth he had
> To build a House for Fools and Mad;
> And Shew'd by one satiric Touch,
> No Nation wanted it so much.

but was equally keen to make everyone aware that he was and always had
been 'a stranger to the spleen'.[5]

It was easy to poke fun at the fashionable folk who complained of lassitude and of a whole litany of disagreeable but not life-threatening symptoms, which cruel bystanders were apt to dismiss as malingering. Plenty of literary sorts joined in the sport. It thus comes as no surprise to learn that, like Queen Anne before them, and in the face of a barrage of derision and contempt, few who complained of mysterious pains and lowness of spirits seemed keen to embrace the label of hysteric or hypochondriac. Who could blame them, when the 'Vulgar and Unlearned' were so prone to place 'nervous Distempers...under some kind of Disgrace': either pronouncing them 'a lower Degree of Lunacy, and the first Step towards a distemper'd Brain'; or else, and more commonly, as purely imaginary, nothing else than 'Whim, Ill-Humour, Peevishness or Particularity; and in the [female] sex, Daintiness, Fantasticalness, or Coquetry.'[6] Which once again raises the awkward question: how was it that George Cheyne transformed what many regarded as a standing reproach into a badge of honour?

Disordered Nerves

First, and most importantly, Cheyne insisted that Vapours and the Spleen, Hysteria and the Hyp, were not imaginary disorders at all, but real diseases, rooted in what he and the most modern doctors, advancing at last beyond the humoral medicine of the Hippocratics and Galen, had come to see as the new animating principle of the human body, the nerves. No longer could these sufferers be dismissed as conniving malingerers. Their complaints were 'as much a bodily Distemper...as the Small-Pox or a Fever'.[7] So far from being trivial or imaginary, they were 'a Class and Set of Distempers, with atrocious and frightful Symptoms, scarce known to our Ancestors' – and so common that they now accounted for 'almost one third of the Complaints' of the age.[8]

Cheyne's views largely echoed an emerging medical consensus that had its origins in the preceding century with Thomas Willis's anatomizing of the human brain and nervous system, and with the clinical practice of Thomas Sydenham (1624–89), who was so widely worshipped by his medical brethren that he had been dubbed 'the English Hippocrates'. Based upon an unprecedented series of experiments and observations, dependent in their turn on advances in the preservation of brains and nervous tissue that allowed him to see what none of his predecessors had available to them, Willis had claimed that

the anatomy of the nerves [nervous system]...[had] revealed
the true and genuine reasons for very many of the actions and
passions that take place in our body, which otherwise seem most
difficult to explain: and from this fountain, no less than the
hidden causes of diseases and symptoms, which are commonly
ascribed to the incantation of witches, may be discovered and
satisfactorily explained.[9]

No longer was the explanation of pathology to be couched solely in
terms of the derangement of the humours. The 'animal spirits' that chased
around the body, ferrying messages to and from the brain, were what animated the human frame, and their derangement was the secret source of
all manner of illness and pathology. Here was a radical reconceptualization
of the role of 'the Brain and the Nervous Stock'.[10] It was one, of course, that
was of particular relevance to the possible aetiology of mental illnesses, both
major and minor. Bedlam madness, and the milder forms of melancholy,
hysteria and the like, were symptomatic of disorders of the brain or the
jangling of the nerves.

The French philosopher René Descartes (1596–1650) had done much a
few decades earlier to encourage the view of the body as a mechanism, and
the new ideas about the nervous system provided a means of understanding
what animated the corporeal machine and made it work. For succeeding generations, the attractions of this novel perspective were all the greater because
it appeared to bring medicine into closer alignment with the mechanical
philosophy of Galileo and Newton. And it did so while leaving traditional
therapeutics largely undisturbed, neither calling into question the wisdom
of the Ancients, nor destabilizing a congeries of remedies that were as deeply
embedded in folk beliefs as in medical dogma. It was at once both entirely
modern and up-to-date, and could also be comfortably aligned with the
familiar interventions at the bedside that were hallowed by tradition and
the authority of the great men of the past. It thus comes as no surprise that
a goodly number of medical men who speculated about madness, or even
dabbled in its treatment and possible cure, were inclined to speak the language of the nerves.

Willis's researches and publications had provided the first detailed
mapping of the brain and the nervous system. He had identified a variety
of distinctive features of the brain: the brain stem, the pons, the medulla,

and the circle of arteries at the base of the brain still known as the 'circle of Willis'; the in-folding of the cerebellum and the cerebral cortex; and the structure of the mid-brain. Taken together, these amounted to a remarkable reconstruction of the understanding of the physical reality of the brain, and a re-imagining of its role as the organ of thought. Taking these anatomical discoveries a step further, in crucial ways that nonetheless remained opaque to Willis (and to his followers in succeeding generations), the nervous system could be, and was increasingly, thought of as the interface between the nervous and the psychic realms.

Thomas Sydenham, Willis's contemporary, had disdained his rival's anatomical researches, seeing them as having little clinical relevance. But he too recognized the importance of nervous disorders, even asserting that 'no chronic disease occurs as frequently as this'. That did not mean that Sydenham embraced the sorts of reductionist physiology Willis had put forward to explain the origins of nervous illnesses. He preferred to emphasize 'disturbances of the mind, which are the usual causes of this disease'.[11] Still, the great authority of both men formed the foundation on which Cheyne and his contemporaries constructed their claims about nervous illness, and legitimated their assertion that they were treating something real.

But syphilis was without question all too real, and nobody wanted to own that. Why was 'the English malady' different? Because, Cheyne proclaimed, it was a disease of civilization. There was an implicit if unacknowledged contrast here: syphilis was associated with unbridled lust and with the animal passions overturning the rule of reason. Emblematic of sin, it was an affliction that could scarcely be further removed from the polish and *politesse* that were the mark of a civilized being. In contradistinction, on Cheyne's account, the more civilized and refined the society (and the individual), the more prone to outbreaks of nervous illness. Foreigners thought they were indicting the English by asserting their susceptibility to nervous prostration. Nothing could be further from the truth. The epidemic of these illnesses among the most exalted ranks of English society was instead incontrovertible evidence of superior refinement and national pre-eminence.

Primitive peoples were essentially exempt from the ravages of this new class of disorders, for 'Temperance, Exercise, Hunting, Labour, and Industry kept the Juices sweet, and the Solids brac'd'. Where all was 'simple, plain, honest, and frugal, there were few or no Diseases'.[12] Modern life, by contrast, was filled with excitement, artifice and stress. The prospect of riches and the search for success necessarily brought in their train heightened 'Anxiety and Concern'. Moreover, in the process of becoming the wealthiest and most successful commercial society on the planet, the English had 'ransack'd all parts of the Globe to bring together its whole Stock of Materials for Riot, Luxury, and to provoke Excess...sufficient to provoke, and even gorge, the most large and voluptuous Appetite'.[13] And then there was the superiority of the English climate, the stimulating effects of 'the Moisture of our Air, the Variableness of our Weather' – not to mention 'the Rankness and Fertility of our Soil, the Richness and Heaviness of our Food, the Wealth and Abundance of the Inhabitants (from their universal Trade), the Inactivity and sedentary Occupations of the better Sort (among whom this Evil mostly rages), and the Humour of living in great, populous and consequently unhealthy Towns....'[14]

If these remarks were calculated to appeal to national pride, Cheyne's further observations on the social location of nervous disorders were cleverly

This 1732 engraving of George Cheyne only hints at his corpulence. He could barely totter a few steps before having to rest, or was carried around in a sedan chair.

designed to appeal to the snobbery of the successful. By his account, nervous illnesses were at once the product and the proof of social superiority. 'Fools, weak or stupid Persons, heavy and dull Souls, are seldom much troubled with Vapours or Lowness of Spirits' – any more than is 'a heavy, dull, earthy, clod-pated Clown'.[15] The lower orders were thus largely exempt from their ravages. It was quite otherwise among 'the People of Condition in England'. Their more sophisticated and civilized lives led them to develop more refined and delicate nervous systems. So it was that nervous complaints were mostly to be found amoung those 'of the liveliest and quickest natural Parts, whose Faculties are the most bright and spiritual, whose Genius is most keen and penetrating, and particularly where there is the most delicate Sensation and Taste'.[16]

Even that great sceptic David Hume proved susceptible to such flatteries, acknowledging when he wrote of human nature that 'the skin, pores, muscles, and nerves of a day-labourer are different from those of a man of quality [and] so are his sentiments, actions and manners'. And James Boswell (1740–95) was stimulated to acknowledge his own membership in this superior class by penning a whole series of autobiographical essays (albeit under the pseudonym 'The Hypochondriack'). 'We Hypochondriacks may', he boasted, swallowing Cheyne's bait whole, 'console ourselves in the hour of gloomy distress, by thinking that our sufferings mark our superiority.'[17]

Verbal testimonies to the appeal of Cheyne's conceit were one thing, but actions that cost hard cash were perhaps a more tangible proof of its attractions. *The English Malady* went through six editions in the space of two years, and continued to sell steadily thereafter. More revealingly, its appearance brought the good doctor a vast increase in his practice and his income. In the last ten years of his life, as he reported with much satisfaction to his friend and publisher, the novelist Samuel Richardson, Cheyne's income tripled. Moreover, while Richardson was a man of roughly similar social standing, others of Cheyne's new-found clientele came from the very highest ranks of English society: a Duke, a Bishop, the Canon of Christ Church and a host of aristocrats, from Lord Chesterfield to the Countess of Huntingdon. Even the most fashionable of society physicians would have been proud of such a roster of patients, and the enormous financial and social success that followed the publication of Cheyne's book are irrefutable evidence of the appeal of the ideas it contained. Not for the last time, those whose physical and mental symptoms were regarded with suspicion by those around them embraced with enthusiasm doctors who would certify that they were indeed ill, that their pains and suffering were not 'all in their minds', and that they deserved the dignity of the sick role, not the opprobrium meted out to counterfeiters and frauds. That they could also proclaim that their nervous complaints elevated them into the ranks of the most refined and civilized of souls was perhaps an unlooked for bonus, and one most patients were delighted to receive.

Prominent physicians such as Bernard de Mandeville (1670–1733), Nicholas Robinson (1697–1775) and Sir Richard Blackmore, who shared Cheyne's conviction that the nervous system presented a new key to understanding the workings of the body, broadly adopted the same approach to this array of 'diseases'. But their use of novel words to describe what they thought was happening disguised a profound therapeutic conservativism. The language of nerves might be new; the treatments it licensed were the old familiar 'anti-phlogistic' remedies Western medicine had been employing for millennia – bleedings, purges, vomits and the like, along with attention to diet and regimen.

Not that the consensus was complete. Nicholas Robinson, who served as a governor of Bedlam, was perhaps the most crudely reductionist of them all:

It clearly appears [he proclaimed] that whenever the Mind
perceives itself uneasy, low-spirited, or dejected, it is as full
a Demonstration, as the Nature of the Thing will admit, that
the Instruments, by which the Mind directs the Powers of its
Operations, are affected.... While the Nerves...are in good Plight,
the Ideas they convey through any of the Senses will be regular,
just, and clear; upon which the Understanding will judge
and determine of Objects, as they are, by the Laws of Nature....
But if the Structure or Mechanism of these Organs happen to
be disorder'd, and the Springs of the Machine out of Tune; no
Wonder the Mind perceives the Alteration, and is affected with
the Change.... [All forms of mental alienation] from the slightest
Symptoms of the Spleen and Vapours, to the most confirm'd
Affections of Melancholy Madness and Lunacy...are no imaginary
Whims or Fancies, but real Affections of the Mind, arising from
the real, mechanical Affections of Matter and Motion, whenever
the Constitution of the Brain warps from its natural Standard.[18]

He was equally blunt about how the treatment of the 'Machine out of Tune' ought to proceed. Physicians must not hesitate, but should employ 'the most violent Vomits, the strongest purging Medicines, and large Bleeding...often repeated'.[19] After all, he insisted,

> it is Cruelty in the highest Degree, not to be bold in the
> Administration of Medicines, when the Nature of the Disease
> absolutely demands the Assistance of a powerful Remedy, and
> more especially in Cases where there can be no Relief without it.[20]

Many of his fellow nerve-doctors shied away from such extreme views, though they shared the same understandings of disease, and accepted that bringing the body back into equilibrium sometimes required drastic measures. And admittedly, eighteenth-century patients were used to the heroic remedies their medical men often prescribed. But many society physicians, contemplating their prospects of attracting the custom of swooning ladies and depressed gentlemen, must have paused to wonder whether such refined and civilized creatures would submit their tender nerves to such rough treatment. For anxious and despondent patients, Sir Richard Blackmore insisted, soothing and calming remedies were much more likely to prove successful than fearsome and painful ones, interventions that threatened to produce a further shock to the already shaky nerves, and might even 'demolish' the patient rather than effect a cure. So far as Blackmore and his allies were concerned, Robinson could reserve his rough remedies for Bedlam. The sensitive souls of the fashionable, who they hoped would crowd their waiting rooms, blessed as these patients were with ultra-refined sensibilities, would fare much better under a milder regimen, perhaps with the prescription of a little opium to help matters along.

It was a position for which they could cite the authority of the great Thomas Willis himself. For while Willis had urged that Bedlam madness required the most forceful and violent of interventions (after all, madmen were caught up in 'the raging of the Spirits and the lifting up of the Soul' and thus could only be dealt with by inducing a 'reverence or standing in awe of such as they think their Tormentors'), he had simultaneously recognized that milder nervous disorders 'are healed more often with flatteries, and with more gentle Physick'.[21] Flattery was what the aristocracy was used to and what it liked from its servants, among whom physicians most assuredly still ranked.

Nervous disorders were, of course, no more the exclusive province of the English upper classes than syphilis was the exclusive province of the French or the Neapolitans. Once Willis's theories began to spread (and he had written about them in the Latin that was still the lingua franca of the European educated classes), it was not long before others took them up and developed them. The Dutch physician Herman Boerhaave, professor of medicine at the University of Leiden and the most famous medical teacher of the eighteenth century, was an intellectual eclectic, a synthesizer rather than an original scholar. But he was an enormously influential figure, and though he continued to pay obeisance to Hippocrates and the Classical authors (for like most physicians of his age, he felt that the principal source of medical authority lay in books), he could not ignore the growing consensus about the importance of the nerves, and particularly their relevance to the problems of psychopathology.

Between September 1730 and July 1735 (three years before his death), Boerhaave delivered over two hundred lectures on nervous diseases, their contents only partially reprised in a posthumous two-volume compilation by his pupil Jakob Van Eems.[22] Boerhaave's influence spread far and wide. The Russian tsar Peter the Great came to hear him; princes of Europe sent their personal physicians to learn from him; and his fellow-physician Albrecht von Haller dubbed him *communis europae praeceptor* ('the instructor of all Europe'). A letter even arrived from China, addressed only to 'the illustrious Boerhaave, physician in Europe'. Like Willis, Boerhaave thought milder cases of nervous prostration could be treated with persuasion, or by influencing the brain by rousing the opposite emotions to the ones presumed to have provoked the disorder. A change of scene might also be useful, and travel would become a remedy commonly suggested for richer folk who felt out of sorts, sometimes with the addition of visits to spa towns where they could take the tonic waters. But, also like Willis, Boerhaave recommended stronger treatment in cases of outright madness, where the *sensorium commune*, as he termed it, had been captured and needed to be shocked out of its disordered state.

Ancient medical remedies including poisonous hellebore (PL. 26) and doses of mercury and copper were suggested, and where these did not suffice he speculated that more drastic interventions might be in order: near drowning, or spinning the madman through the air, impaled like a cockchafer.[23] In Boerhaave's hands, these remained hypothetical means of cure, but as we have already seen, later in the eighteenth century others gave them practical effect. Meanwhile, there was much squabbling about whether the nervous system was a set of hollow tubes through which the animal spirits or nervous fluid found their way; or whether, on the contrary, it was a matter of nervous fibres, tense or lax, which provided the means by which the brain communicated with the other parts of its dominion.

The lesser nervous disorders that had attracted such attention from English society physicians, and brought them a torrent of high-paying patients desperate to obtain the imprimatur of the medical profession for a litany of ailments others were disposed to view with amusement and disdain, proved common enough also in places where neither the moistness and other delights of the British climate, nor the stimulation its commercial society was now wont to provide, could be invoked to explain its depredations. Strangely enough, Germans, Austrians, French, all seemed prone to suffer from similar complaints. What to make of them? And how to treat them?

Enthusiasm and Spiritual Agony

Religious explanations and therapies for such troubles had not vanished from the scene. In England, the evangelical revival led by John Wesley (1703–91) and George Whitefield (1714–70) drew legions of followers. If the disciples of Newton and the Scientific Revolution seemed wedded to the material-istic, mechanistic foundations of the new philosophy and sought a form of Christianity rooted in rational principles, with a God who ruled from a distance – a divine architect who simply contemplated the wonders He had wrought – the enthusiasts who swelled the crowds at the outdoor Methodist meetings exhibited extremes of religious conviction and emotional agoniz-ing. Their preachers were inspired and inspiring, and while men such as Wesley were not averse to popularizing humoral medicine for the masses (his *Primitive Physick* was a bestseller), he and Whitefield were keener still to offer spiritual consolation, and to seek out individuals who were troubled in mind, to pray over and to succour. Their revival meetings in the fields were the occasion for scenes of emotional and religious transport, and for prayer and the comfort of souls directed towards the sick, the distressed and the distracted. For the Methodists, mental turmoil was invested with profound spiritual significance, and their kinds of passionate religious commitment, which vividly made manifest the tortures of guilt and sin, and set the horrors of damnation against the promise of salvation, kept alive an older mix of

Credulity, Superstition and Fanaticism: A Medley *(1762), by William Hogarth,*
a satire on the folly and perils of enthusiastic religion. The thermometer at the front
registers lust, rapidly rising towards madness and raving, and the cross-eyed preacher
at the lectern is George Whitefield, one of the founders of Methodism, whose doctrines,
so mad-doctors alleged, sent legions of the credulous to the madhouse.

religious and magical causation of madness, alongside the now more respectable naturalistic forms of explanation. Divine retribution and demoniacal possession remained for the Methodists entirely plausible accounts of human distraction. Wesley himself was a firm believer in demonomania, and a forceful advocate of spiritual healing of the mentally disturbed through communal rituals of fasting and prayer.[24]

But the British ruling classes had seen in their Civil War in the 1640s where such 'enthusiastic' religion could lead – straight to excess, danger and irrationality, the overthrow of established order and social hierarchies, and a state that literally lost its head – and they wanted nothing to do with any of it. With sectarian divisions and social unrest still fresh in their minds, the aristocracy and the propertied classes plumped for a rational, reserved religion, one that embodied polite restraint and moral sobriety. If that made them allies of the natural philosophers and medical men, and by extension of mad-doctors, so be it.

The upshot was a discourse of ridicule, parody and satirical abuse aimed squarely at the 'Enthusiasts', a campaign that was as evident in the caricatures of Hogarth as in the sarcastic comments of Horace Walpole, youngest son of Sir Robert Walpole, the longest-serving Prime Minister in British history, not to mention the satires of Swift and Pope. Rather than curing madness, the Methodists were accused of fomenting it. They were full of vapours, wind and afflatus, their preachers creating and simultaneously exhibiting infected imaginations, irrational fancies, fanaticism and folly. The Methodists' 'unseemly' forms of worship, their transports of fear and enthusiasm, their melodramatic invocations of hellfire and damnation: who of a more sober mien could view such spectacles and not immediately grasp how closely allied they were to the world of irrationality and madness, and how likely such rituals were to tip the credulous and the superstitious into the ranks of the crazed? Many a mad-doctor opined that the activities of Wesley and Whitefield were of inestimable value in creating customers for the trade in lunacy.[25] Poor, emotional and intellectually frail members of the weaker sex were particularly prone to be driven mad, though men too could fall under the spell.

Hogarth took a special delight in his 1762 depiction of *Credulity, Superstition and Fanaticism: A Medley* (a reworking of the previous year's *Enthusiasm Delineated*) in skewering the follies of these mountebanks. We see the preacher's vociferations rousing the congregation to a fever pitch. Many are falling into hysterical ecstasies, even cataleptic trances. Some members of the audience gnaw on icons of the body of Christ, suggesting a link between another form of religion Hogarth loathed, Catholicism, and cannibalism, bestiality and madness. The fanatical preacher in the pulpit has chosen an appropriate biblical text (from 2 Corinthians, 11: 23) – 'I speak as a fool' – and as he preys upon popular gullibility a thermometer in the foreground registers the emotional temperature of the audience, climbing inexorably from lust (a randy aristocrat next to a swooning servant girl is thrusting a religious icon down her dress) towards raving madness. The globe dangling from the ceiling registers the regions of hell, and two figures towards the front represent some of the pious frauds the enthusiastic preachers have perpetrated on their followers: Mary Toft, who is giving birth to rabbits and a cat; and the Boy of Bilston, whose false miracle involved him vomiting nails and staples. The notoriously cross-eyed George Whitefield presides, with his suggestion that his Tabernacle would serve as a 'soul trap' parodied by a cherub above who holds a sign reading 'Money Trap'. A Jew from Malta stares through the window at this vision of Christian madness. With their melodramatic rants about the dangers of hellfire and damnation, preachers like these preyed on the credulity of people bereft of much money or intellect, frightening and maddening them to extract from them what little cash they had.

Exorcizing Demons

The British elite wanted a polite religion, one devoid of excitement and excess. The situation was rather different in rural southwestern Germany, a region of baroque Catholicism where Wesley and Whitefield's contemporary, an obscure priest of Austrian origin, Johann Joseph Gassner (1727–79), began performing rites of exorcism in Ellwangen in the 1760s and 1770s. Gassner drew crowds of the faithful afflicted with all manner of ills: blindness, manic propensities to dance (the so-called St Vitus's dance), the epileptic, the lame, the halt, the hysteric and the crazed. Belief in the Devil, and in the possibility of demoniacal possession, had not, it would seem, simply vanished with the dawn of the Enlightenment and the so-called Age of Reason. On the contrary, it continued to exercise a powerful hold on the popular imagination. A noisy scandal ensued.[26]

The sick came to seek Gassner's blessings and departed well – or so it seemed. Freed of the unclean spirits and demons that had possessed and

Johann Joseph Gassner expelling a demon. The Swabian priest is shown exorcizing a patient, the demon flying from his mouth, as seen in so many Renaissance images of the treatment of the possessed. Belief in demonic possession obviously survived untouched among many people in the so-called Age of Reason.

haunted them, they had, through the ministrations of a holy man, been restored to their senses. Word spread. Crowds gathered. Father Gassner took his show on the road. Protestants to the north hurled abuse about Catholic superstition and folly. Cures mounted. What did it all mean? And how were the authorities to cope with the public tumult that threatened to erupt? Unrest and religious excitement, coupled with the movement of potentially thousands of peasants in search of cures, were an obvious threat to order, and one neither secular nor ecclesiastical authority could take lightly. And in the complicated political geography of South Germany, these two domains intersected, overlapped and often coincided.

Most of those seeking Gassner's ministrations were not, after all, the effete and refined ladies and gentlemen who required the attendance of a Cheyne or a Blackmore, though Gassner did attract (and apparently cure) the occasional Countess, in this case Countess Maria Bernardina Truchsess von Wolfegg und Friedberg, and we know that the mother of the depressed Prince Karl of Saxony at least contemplated consulting Gassner to see if he could intervene successfully. Some nobles and their ladies appeared, but most of the thousands the good Father treated were more akin to the common folk who flocked to Methodist sermons. In South Germany, though, instead of Protestant prayer and watching, those in attendance were subjected to ancient rituals of exorcism that conjured the evil one from their bodies and miraculously banished their aches and pains, their paralyses and their despondency. Or they were if Father Gassner decided they were suitable cases for treatment, for he was quite selective about whom he was prepared to treat.

A fierce pamphlet war erupted all across Germany, spilling over into parts of France. Faint echoes of ancient religious wars could be heard. Gassner had his supporters among the Church hierarchy, and he took care to conduct his exorcisms in their principalities. Elsewhere, however, prudent Catholic churchmen counselled caution. The Protestant ridicule of Catholic superstition had been relentless, and stung. Besides, these churchmen had their temporal responsibilities to consider, for in much of southern Germany, bishops were also secular rulers, though their dioceses and their principalities might not overlap. And in cases where they were not both prelate and prince, the churchmen were the scions of noble families, whose interests they were keen to care for. Secular concerns about the social order and the potentially destabilizing effects of Gassner's ministry were never far from their thoughts. After all, the witch craze was far from being a distant memory, and if Gassner's casting out of devils revived popular fears, a new epidemic of religious excitement and enthusiasm for witch-burning might erupt, with unpredictable consequences.

Jealous of one another, the Catholic prelates were for the most part incapable of acting in unison. When early reports of Gassner's exorcisms surfaced, the Bishop of Constance immediately sought to curb and cast doubt on the enterprise, and the Bavarian ecclesiastical council and the church authorities in Augsburg soon followed suit, banning Gassner from their territories. But elsewhere, secular and church authorities took a more benign view. In Regensburg, for instance, the prince-bishop, Anton Ignaz von Fugger, extended his support and protection, as did his counterparts in Freising and Eichstätt. In the end, however, higher levels of secular and ecclesiastical powers felt compelled to intervene. The Empress Maria Theresa of Austria, who had earlier moved to forbid further prosecutions of witches, had no time for Gassner's activities, and in the summer of 1775 she sent two imperial physicians whom she knew shared her scepticism to investigate the contentious priest. Shortly thereafter, the Emperor Joseph, the nominal head of the Holy Roman Empire, ordered Gassner to leave Regensburg. Papal intervention was slower, but Rome eventually concluded that the whole affair had to stop. At the instigation of Gassner's enemies within the church, Pope Pius VI finally issued his judgment: deploring the sensationalism that had surrounded the priest's activities, and attacking him for promulgating the 'false' idea that most illnesses were induced or exacerbated by the Devil, the Pope moved to silence him. Gassner was told to cease his exorcisms, and to return to being a simple parish priest in the tiny hamlet of Pondorf. Three years later, reduced to obscurity, he was dead.

The silencing of Gassner at the behest of 'enlightened' rulers and the Pope himself surely did not kill off popular beliefs in the Devil and possession, but it did indicate the degree to which polite society was distancing itself from older religious accounts of illness and suffering, and of madness in particular. Driven beneath the surface, the belief in evil spirits no doubt persisted in popular consciousness. It had biblical warrant as well as the force of tradition, and for those who retained their faith in the older cosmology, it seemed to explain much of their daily experience. Pilgrimages and the veneration of saints and shrines, so popular in earlier times, did not simply disappear at the behest of the authorities. But in educated circles, they became the mark of ignorance and superstition. The literate knew better, or thought that they did.

Invisible Forces

If traditional Catholics had their invisible Devil and demons (for Gassner never claimed to have observed the creatures he had evicted from his possessed patients, contemporary images notwithstanding), Enlightenment thinkers had their own invisible forces that moved the world of the senses: to Newton's gravity, they had added electricity and magnets, and now perhaps another invisible influence had been uncovered. For in Vienna, in the very years Gassner had been honing his skills and reputation as an exorcist, a Viennese physician who had married extraordinarily well, Franz Anton Mesmer (1734–1815), announced that he had discovered a new vital force, animal magnetism, a powerful fluidum that coursed through every human being. Furthermore, he possessed the power to manipulate this fluid, and to use it to effect cures. No God, no Devil, no religious rite of exorcism, but supposedly remarkable results – ones that brought the rich and fashionable of the imperial capital to his door, and promised him wealth and fame beyond those his wife had already brought him.

Mesmer travelled to Bavaria in 1775 to give a demonstration of his system before the Academy of Sciences. The members were so impressed – Mesmer treated one of their number in front of them and performed a variety of dramatic feats when he mesmerized other patients – that they voted to make Mesmer a member. And he in turn assured them that Gassner's successful treatments – if successful they were – reflected the fact that his touching of those who came in search of cures had actually constituted an inadvertent use of the power of animal magnetism.

Moving gratefully back from the rural periphery that was Bavaria to his preferred residence amid the glories of the seat of Hapsburg power, Mesmer resumed his treatment of the imperial elite. His wife's fortune had bought him a splendid estate in Vienna, to which *tout le monde* (or all the *monde* who counted) could be invited to share his elevated artistic tastes and partake of the new wondrous therapy he had discovered. Joseph Haydn was a frequent guest, as were the Mozart family. Indeed, young Wolfgang's first opera, *Bastien und Bastiene*, received its premiere in the grounds of Mesmer's mansion (and mesmerism itself would later make an appearance in the composer's *Così fan tutte*). Leopold Mozart proclaimed his admiration of the setting: 'The garden is incomparable, with its avenues and statues, a theatre, a birdhouse, a dovecot, and a belvedere on the summit.'[27] As a demonstration of his own musical tastes and talents, Mesmer himself became an expert performer on the glass harmonica, an instrument perfected by the American polymath, Benjamin Franklin (1706–90). The good doctor subsequently embellished his mesmeric séances by playing soft and soothing airs to his patients.

In the beginning, Mesmer had employed special magnets to amplify his efforts to alter the flow of animal magnetism in his patients, but these were now abandoned. What he had discovered, Mesmer claimed, was that sickness resulted from the development of blockages or obstacles to the flow of animal magnetism around the body. His skill, which resided in both his gaze and his finger-tips, was in the detection of these obstacles, and his ability to redirect the flow of the fluid. Holding a patient's knees between his own, Mesmer probed for the sources of the patient's difficulties, running his fingers all over the body, and through a procedure similar to a massage, bringing about a trance or a crisis, a fit resembling epilepsy. This marked the breaking down of interior obstacles to the free flow of animal magnetism, particularly between the twin poles of the head, prone to receive mesmeric fluid from the heavens, and the feet, whose contact with the earth provided an alternative source of magnetism. (As Mesmer himself put it in the first of the twenty-seven propositions in which he summarized his discovery: 'There exists a mutual influence between the heavenly bodies, the earth and living organisms.') At times, the power of his personal touch and gaze was augmented by the use of iron bars, brought into contact with the particular regions where the patient complained of aches and pains.

The sexual overtones of this process were all too transparent, and provoked much mirth and crude commentary among those opposed to the new doctrines. Mesmer concentrated on the body's meridian, staying away from the magnetic poles, and he seemed to focus much of his attention on the upper abdomen and the chest, the region of the hypochondrium according to traditional medical theory. Such attention, he announced in the twenty-third of his propositions, 'could immediately cure nervous maladies, and alleviate others'.

Perhaps his most famous Viennese patient was a young blind girl, Maria Theresia Paradis (1759–1824). Eighteen years of age, she had mysteriously gone blind at the age of three and a half. Doting parents had mobilized all the resources of Vienna in an effort to cure her, and to educate her to cope with her disability. She had, by the time she encountered Mesmer, been

Though mesmerism enjoyed considerable popularity, it also had many detractors, and was often the butt of humour that had strong sexual overtones. Here the mesmerist, caricatured as an ass, uses his 'magic finger' to cure a female patient.

subjected to thousands of electrical charges in the hope of stimulating her sight, but to no avail. Meanwhile, her wealthy parents had employed a host of tutors to devise ways of teaching their daughter the ornamental accomplishments to be expected of a young woman of her station. Not least, she had received extensive instruction in playing the harpsichord and piano, an activity for which she apparently possessed considerable talent.[28] The spectacle of a blind girl performing at the keyboard won her a host of admirers, including the Empress Maria Theresa herself.

Mesmer treated her. She proclaimed that she had recovered her sight. Rumours at once began to swirl that their relationship had gone beyond the therapeutic. Mesmer's rivals, perhaps jealous of the host of high-paying nervous patients he was now attracting, spread gossip that Maria Theresia had become his mistress. As for the young lady herself, she discovered that her talents at the keyboard were now less appreciated. A blind young woman who could play the piano was one thing; a sighted one – well, there were hundreds of well-brought-up women who were better than she.

There may well have been substance to the salacious stories. At all events, within weeks Mesmer abruptly left Vienna for Paris, sans his wife, with whom he severed all ties. Miss Paradis sadly lost her sight again, but soon regained her popularity as a blind keyboardist, and once more enjoyed the patronage of the Empress Maria Theresa. Meanwhile, Viennese society doctors did not seem to lament their colleague's departure.

By February 1778, Mesmer had arrived in Paris, where he set about establishing himself and attracting an aristocratic clientele. Within weeks, he had moved to the Place Vendôme and thereafter he enjoyed a growing

The fashionable crowd around Mesmer's tub filled with iron filings. Music plays, and Dr Mesmer stands to one side, 'seeming always to be absorbed in profound reflection... the patients, especially women, have fits, which bring about their recovery.'

success. His fees were large, but nobody blinked, not when he promised relief from the chronic ills that had ailed his rich clients for so long, the reality of which so many others had doubted. The nervous, the hysterical and the disturbed flocked to receive his ministrations. A year later, Mesmer published his *Mémoire sur la découverte du magnétisme animal*, which gave further publicity to his grand discovery, and he now introduced various technical advances designed to make its remarkable effects more broadly available.

The most notable of these was the *baquet*, a table or tub filled with iron filings from which protruded iron rods that could be inserted at various heights, so that those sitting round the apparatus could direct the effects to particular regions of their anatomy – the stomach, the spleen or the liver, or less mentionable parts – that required special attention. Patients sat around the table, linked together by a rope that formed a mesmeric circle (rather on the analogy of an electric circuit), and waited for the therapy to take effect. Mesmer alternately engaged in the laying on of hands and the playing of his glass harmonica to augment the effects of the apparatus, and soon, on most occasions, nervous patients were swooning and falling unconscious, or having seizures, some of them so violent that one of Mesmer's assistants scooped them up and conducted them to an antechamber lined with mattresses, designed to prevent the patients from injuring themselves as they thrashed about. Differences of social status were provided for: in an adjacent room, Mesmer set up a 'tub for the poor'. Soft carpets, mirrors, heavy curtains and astrological portraits were all mobilized to heighten the atmosphere. As one contemporary described the scene:

> M. Mesmer's house is like a divine temple upon which all the
> social orders converge: abbés, marquises, grisettes, soldiers,
> doctors, young girls, accoucheurs, the dying, as well as the strong
> and vigorous – all drawn by an unknown power. There are
> magnetizing bars, closed tubs, wands, ropes, flowering shrubs,
> and musical instruments including the harmonica, whose piping
> excites laughter, tears, and transports of joy.[29]

Mesmer was keen to secure official recognition of his great discovery. He lobbied the French Royal Society of Medicine and the Academy of Sciences in Paris for their approval, but it was not forthcoming. Meanwhile, he had begun to magnetize trees, so that even more of the poor could benefit from his therapy. It can only have added to the air of a charlatan that had now begun to surround him, and to the criticisms he received from professional rivals. But such criticisms seemed to have little effect. A veritable who's who of the aristocracy joined together to raise funds to pay Mesmer to establish a network of mesmeric clinics in the provinces. He amassed a great fortune. The French, it seemed, were as prone to nervous maladies as the perfidious English, and people afflicted with these milder forms of mental disorder flocked to a treatment that promised to alleviate their sufferings, and without the pain and unpleasantness associated with traditional bleedings, purges and vomits.

And then abruptly in 1784, when mesmerism seemed to be at the height of its success, things went wrong. Mesmer's rivals bitterly resented the fact that he had succeeded in attracting so many lucrative clients. They spoke with disdain about the quackish nature of his cures, and the dangerous, erotically charged character of his séances. Beautiful women fell under his power. Their passions aroused, they swooned and convulsed, gazing adoringly into the eyes of the man who placed them in a trance, and then were led obediently to the 'crisis room', where mattresses lined the floor. The danger to public morals could scarcely be clearer, and yet even the most refined aristocratic ladies seemed vulnerable to Mesmer's charms. Cloaking themselves in self-righteousness, his critics manoeuvred to put a stop to the challenge he represented.

Pressed by Mesmer's jealous competitors, the French king, Louis XVI, appointed a commission to examine his claims. Its members included some of the most eminent scholars of the age: the chemist Antoine Lavoisier; the astronomer Jean Sylvain Bailly; Joseph Guillotin, who would subsequently invent an apparatus with which the king would enjoy an all-too-intimate acquaintance; and Benjamin Franklin, American ambassador to France, known widely for his experiments with lightning and electricity. It was a formidable group, and though they actually investigated the work of an estranged former assistant, Charles D'Eslon, rather than Mesmer himself, and ignored the question of mesmerism's therapeutic efficacy – the subject of most interest to Mesmer's clientele – on the crucial issue of whether there was such a fluid as 'animal magnetism' their conclusion was unambiguous: no physical evidence could be found to confirm its existence. And a whole series of ingenious experiments was cited in support of their verdict.

In respectable intellectual quarters, the commission's report inflicted considerable damage, and it was fatal for the official recognition of his discovery that Mesmer had hoped for. But on a practical level, it seems not to have dissuaded many of those tempted by its charms as a therapy. Abstruse debates among scientists, whose own work rested on claims about the existence and power of other sorts of invisible forces, were of little moment to those attracted by the possibility of a cure for their nervous complaints. Mesmer's disciples dismissed the report as the predictable product of a group of self-interested academicians.

Soon, however, a reminder of past scandals surfaced: on Good Friday, 16 April 1784, the Concert Spirituel for Lent was attended by the cream of Paris society and the monarch. The artist playing the harpsichord was a blind musician from Vienna, Maria Theresia Paradis herself. Old stories about her purported affair with Mesmer resurfaced.[30] The gossip grew when Miss Paradis elected to extend her stay in Paris for six months. Meanwhile, Mesmer had been invited to Lyon to provide a public demonstration of the value of his technique to the younger brother of King Frederick II of Prussia. It was a catastrophic failure. Humiliated, Mesmer fled Paris, and was scarcely heard from again, though he lived for another two decades.

Certainly, in the aftermath of Mesmer's abrupt departure from the Parisian scene, mesmerism lost some of the extraordinary popularity it had achieved at its height in the mid-1780s. But general interest in it remained strong, and in the following century, mesmeric séances would attract a steadily growing audience. Charles Dickens dabbled repeatedly in mesmerism, and his was anything but an eccentric interest. His friend the novelist Wilkie Collins often wove mesmerism into his plots.[31] By now, however, mesmerism was less a therapeutic procedure and more a sort of entertainment. And increasingly it had fallen under the influence of spiritualists and those dabbling in the paranormal, not a shift likely to heighten its credibility among doctors or most scientists. Though it still bore his name, mesmerism had escaped its discoverer's control. Only decades after Mesmer's death would the technique he had pioneered undergo a revival – albeit under a different name, and resting whatever authority it could muster on something very different than a mysterious magnetic fluid.

Chapter Seven

THE GREAT
CONFINEMENT

Nervous or Mad?

The language of nerves was a seductive way of accounting for the depredations of madness, and not just for medical men. Certainly, for the medical elite, the exploration of the complexities of the brain and nervous system was a source of growing fascination, and for ordinary practitioners claims about the nervous origins of madness provided an account of disturbed mental states that rooted them firmly in the body. Simultaneously, for an educated lay public increasingly inclined to view the world in naturalistic terms and to shy away from the 'superstitions' that the uneducated still clung to, embracing accounts pitched in these terms allowed them to put on display their superior sophistication, and provided a reassuring sense that the deeply distressing and frightening excesses of madness could be rationally understood. For the wealthy, and especially the idle rich, prone to bouts of depression or of ennui, or afflicted with a whole array of mysterious mental and physical troubles, the language of nerves was doubly attractive. For it made legitimate what cruel observers were inclined to dismiss as malingering, or *maladies imaginaires*.

It was not clear, however, that nervous invalids were quite as keen for their troubles to be seen as simply a lesser form of madness, for the temptation remained strong to cast the lunatic into an outer darkness. Deprived of the most crucial of human qualities – reason – it was all too easy to see the mentally ill as creatures of a different ontological order. In the early seventeenth century, Shakespeare had suggested that, divided from their truer selves and from their judgment, the mad were no more than 'pictures'

– external facsimiles of human beings – 'or mere beasts'.[1] Eighteenth-century writers embraced an even more extreme view. Preaching a sermon on behalf of 'those unhappy People, who are bereft of the dearest light, the Light of Reason', the clergyman Andrew Snape spoke of 'distraction' as sinking 'unhappy Man below the mute and senseless part of creation'.[2] The thought was echoed by an anonymous contributor to *The World* (possibly Samuel Richardson), who wrote that madness brought 'the mighty reasoners of the earth, below even the insects that crawl upon it'.[3] Small wonder that successive generations of commentators repeated, almost by rote, the cliché that 'There is no disease more to be dreaded than madness.'[4]

So it was that when the last king of North America, George III, sensed that he was losing his reason, he insisted to anyone who would listen that 'I am nervous...I am not ill, but I am nervous; if you would know what is the matter with me, I am nervous.'[5] But he wasn't. He was mad. Talking incessantly until he foamed at the mouth, his agitation and delirium grew steadily more marked, till the king's physician Richard Warren (1731–97) was heard to observe that 'the seizure upon the brain was so violent, that, if he did live, there was little reason to hope that his intellects would be restored'.[6] George became violent and delusional, unpredictable and increasingly unmanageable, sleepless and frequently obscene. And so he continued from October 1788 to March of the following year, when miraculously he appeared to recover. A dozen years later, he relapsed, then got better, a pattern repeated in 1804. But when the madness descended again in 1810, it was permanent. For the last decade of his life, George was out of his mind – first incoherent and rambling, then demented and blind.

The king's illness provoked a constitutional crisis each time it recurred, and in 1810, this was resolved with the accession of his son George as Prince Regent. The secrecy surrounding the king's madness encouraged gossip and rumour. It also made manifest the vast gulf between the milder forms of nervous disorder and more deeply rooted and extreme forms of madness. By coincidence – and for the most part it was no more than that, for the developments in question can be traced all across Europe and North America – the English king's recurrent descent into madness corresponded remarkably closely with crucial developments in perceptions of how mental illness could and should be managed, and the nascent shift towards an embrace of the asylum as the preferred solution to the problems the lunatic posed for families and for society at large.

The Rise of the Empire of Asylumdom

Soon, the presumed need to segregate the mad from society, and the decision to construct an ever-larger network of new institutions to accomplish this task, would launch that great confinement of the insane that remained so notable a feature of the Western response to mental disorder until the last decades of the twentieth century. Nervous prostration might continue to be managed informally, and those experiencing its pains still left at large, but it was very different for the manic and the melancholic, the deranged and the demented. For them, a new geography of suffering rapidly emerged. The asylum everywhere became the chosen solution to the problems posed by the Bedlam mad. And from the new concentration of the mad in social space, a new breed of experts in asylum medicine also materialized, increasingly organized and self-conscious, their identity as specialists intimately linked to the existence and expansion of asylumdom. That expansion, in its turn, soon was everywhere rooted in a growing role for the state in funding and administering the institutions that sprang forth all across Europe and North America: an unsurprising development, perhaps, in France and the Austrian empire, where few checks existed on central authority; but it was as evident in Britain and the United States, where suspicion of centralization and state action was deeply ingrained in the culture and the body politic.

A paradox lay at the heart of this embrace of the institution. Much of the moral fervour and enthusiasm that drove what was widely hailed as a scientific and humanitarian advance in the treatment of the mentally ill derived from the exposure of the horrors of the *ancien régime* madhouse. In France, the ambitious Jean-Étienne Dominique Esquirol (1772–1840), who had come to Paris to work under the eminent Revolutionary-era physician Philippe Pinel, had, with the help of his patron, opened his own *maison de santé* or private madhouse in 1802, and then secured a post in 1811 as *médecin ordinaire* at the Salpêtrière Hospital. Seeking to ingratiate himself with the restored Bourbon monarchy, he had begun lecturing on mental diseases in 1817, and the following year secured a commission from the minister of internal affairs to travel the country and provide an assessment of the status of the insane. His report was a catalogue of horrors:

> I have seen them naked, clad in rags, having but straw to shield them from the cold humidity of the pavement where they lie.

I have seen them coarsely fed, lacking air to breathe, water to
quench their thirst, wanting the basic necessities of life. I have
seen them at the mercy of veritable jailers, victims of their brutal
supervision. I have seen them in narrow, dirty, infested dungeons
without air or light, chained in caverns, where one would fear
to lock up the wild beasts that luxury-loving governments keep
at great expense in their capitals.[7]

The images would have been familiar to Englishmen who paid attention
to the stream of parliamentary inquiries into the state of madhouses that
punctuated the first decades of the nineteenth century. Magistrates and
self-described philanthropists vied with one another to produce the most
lurid exemplary tales of the horrors that faced the institutionalized lunatic.
The banker Henry Alexander, who made it his practice to tour the places
where the mad were confined as he travelled round the countryside, testified
that he had visited the lunatic ward at the Tavistock workhouse in Devon,
though he had secured admittance only over the strenuous objections of
the workhouse master:

I have never smelt such a stench in my life, and it was so bad, that
a friend who went with me [into the first cell] said he could not
enter the other. After having entered one, I said I would go into the
other; that if they could survive the night through, I could at least
inspect them…. The stench was so great I felt almost suffocated;
and for hours after, if I ate anything, I still retained the same smell;
I could not get rid of it; and it should be remembered that these
cells had been washed out that morning, and the doors had been
opened some hours previous.[8]

Conditions were if anything still worse in institutions that specialized
in the confinement of the mad. John Rogers, who had worked as an apothecary at Thomas Warburton's Red and White Houses, two of the largest private,
profit-making madhouses in London, testified that they were infested with
fleas and rats and were so cold and damp that many patients suffered from
gangrene and tuberculosis; patients were also grossly abused by the attendants. Beating and whipping were widely employed, and female patients were
frequently raped. As for incontinent patients, they were regularly dragged
out into the courtyard and mopped down under a stream of cold water from

a pump. At Bedlam, witnesses testified to the presence of naked women chained haphazardly to the walls, men too: 'Their nakedness and their mode of confinement gave...the complete appearance of a dog kennel.'[9] Even then, they may have been better off than their counterparts at the York Asylum, where patients were raped and murdered, and most were kept in filth and neglect.[10] One set of cells that had been carefully hidden from sight was, according to the Yorkshire magistrate Godfrey Higgins,

> in a very horrid and filthy condition...the walls were daubed
> with excrement; the airholes, of which there was one in each cell,
> were partly filled with it.... I then went upstairs...into a room...
> twelve feet by seven feet ten inches, in which there were thirteen
> women who...had come out of those cells that morning....
> I became very sick, and could not remain any longer in the room.
> I vomited.[11]

In what turned out to be a futile effort to disguise the enormity of what had been going on there, the asylum's physician set fire to the building, succeeding in destroying one wing and burning several patients to death, but failing to erase yet more evidence of malfeasance. A nationwide inspection nearly three decades later suggested that not much had changed across wide swathes of the country.[12]

In France, Esquirol had devised a scheme for a national system of asylums as early as 1819, but it was not until nearly two decades later, in 1838, that the National Assembly passed a law directing every department in the country to build an asylum at public expense to house the insane, or to make alternative arrangements for their treatment.[13] In addition, the law laid down that 'No person may direct or start a private institution for the insane without the authorization of the government.' In practice, its provisions came into force but slowly. Two years later, there were seven such asylums; by 1852, only seven more had been built, and four of these were annexes to general hospitals. Private, religiously run establishments still existed in numbers in the provinces, legally required now to have a medical director but in reality clinging to their clerical identity and to a model based on Christian charity. Their Catholic supporters suggested that if moral means were the royal road to curing the insane, their religious sisters were well qualified to dispense the necessary firmness and gentleness, a proposition met with scepticism and fierce resistance among the ranks of the new *médecins aliénistes*. Over time, the movement towards a secularized, publicly run system would prove all but irresistible, but for some decades, religious and medical approaches to the management of the mad co-existed uneasily, and tensions between the two sometimes spilled out into open conflict.[14] Nonetheless, it was to asylums rather than the older system of family care that the French now looked when confronted with the problems of mental disorder.

The English, too, passed legislation in 1845 mandating the construction of asylums at public expense by counties and boroughs, and requiring the licensing of all private asylums for the well-to-do by a new body, the Commissioners in Lunacy, who were also given general supervisory authority over the emerging empire of asylumdom. As in France, reformers had initially promoted such a plan much earlier, in 1816, and had to overcome considerable opposition to achieve their goals – opposition that was based upon both the costs of the new asylums and the expansion of centralization they embodied. Even after the legislation reached the statute book, there continued to be some dragging of feet, motivated by the usual mix of penny-pinching and resistance by local authorities to impositions from Westminster. But by 1860, the asylum revolution was essentially complete. All across the country, new county asylums had been built and now became the preferred solution to the problems posed by the mad. And those running profit-orientated, private asylums for paying patients had accustomed themselves to oversight by the Lunacy Commissioners from Whitehall.

The German-speaking lands present an altogether more complicated picture. In Austria, the imperial authorities had constructed a *Narrenturm*, or Fools' Tower, in the grounds of the huge Vienna General Hospital in 1784, a gloomy building with barred cells within which lunatics were confined and chained. It had nothing in common with the sorts of places the nineteenth-century reformers had in mind, and though Bruno Görgen (1777–1842) opened a small private facility in Vienna in 1819 that resembled the new asylums being constructed in other parts of Europe, the imperial authorities remained indifferent to developments elsewhere, and it was not until 1853 that they created the first new public asylum.[15]

Germany's political fragmentation and the depredations of Napoleon's armies in the early years of the nineteenth century both contributed to a patchwork and heterogeneous set of outcomes. As Napoleon retreated, the German princes west of the Rhine seized the opportunity to take over church property, and a number of castles and monasteries would be transformed into places to house lunatics. Elsewhere, entirely new asylums were constructed, beginning with Sonnenstein in Saxony in 1811, Siegburg in the Rhineland in 1825, then Sachsenburg in 1830 and Illenau in 1842, so that by mid-century, across the complicated political landscape of the old Holy Roman Empire, there were perhaps fifty asylums, as many as twenty of which were privately run (though all of these were very small). Though far from a monolithic set of institutions, many of these asylums nonetheless claimed to be part of a modern approach to madness, and to embody the techniques of treatment that were being embraced elsewhere.[16]

Italy too had been badly disrupted by Napoleon's military adventures. But following Napoleon's final defeat and exile in 1815, Italy returned, in the Austrian diplomat Prince Metternich's famous phrase, to its status as no more than 'a geographical expression'. The Congress of Vienna of 1815 reconstituted the patchwork of independent polities descended from the medieval city-states that had divided the country politically, restoring among much else Austrian rule in the northeast and papal authority in Rome and the Papal States. As late as 1860, four states still divided up the territory that now constitutes the great majority of present-day Italy, and Rome and the Pope's territories were not absorbed into the kingdom until the end of 1870.

As with Germany, therefore, no single pattern of asylum provision emerged. There were old custodial institutions dating back to the Middle Ages in Rome (c. 1300), Bergamo (1352) and Florence (1377), religious foundations that served largely as places of confinement. Venice had set up a religiously run 'Island of the Mad' on San Servolo in 1725, originally for men only (Shelley, who visited it with Byron called it 'a windowless, deformed and dreary pile'),[17] and in 1844, an old monastery on another island, San Clemente, began to take mad female patients (see p. 358). Adapting monks' cells to house mental patients was an easy task. In Tuscany, the Florentine authorities had authorized the detention of the mentally ill in 1774, and a decade and a half later, Vincenzo Chiarugi (1759–1820), a Florentine physician had sought to outlaw the use of chains and introduce a version of moral treatment in the Santa Dorotea Hospital (which housed insane patients alongside others), and later at the ancient San Bonifacio Hospital (PL. 28). Chiarugi's attempted reforms collapsed, however, on his death in 1820.

To these more or less ancient religious foundations, a handful of new asylums were added in the first half of the nineteenth century. They included, among others, Aversa in 1813, Bologna in 1818, Palermo in 1827 and Genoa in 1841. More were added in the second half of the nineteenth century, particularly in northern and central Italy, and some of these were directly established by the provincial authorities. The Italian alienist Carlo Livi (1823–77) complained bitterly in 1864 that asylum provision in Italy was the most backward in Europe, attributing it to 'the indolence and neglect of the governments',[18] and as late as 1890 only seventeen of Italy's provinces made public provision for the mad. In much of the country, religiously based charities provided what little institutional care existed. Only thirty-nine of a total of eighty-three Italian asylums were supported by the state. Together, near the end of the century, all these establishments housed barely 22,000 patients (fewer than 4,000 of them in southern Italy and the islands of Sicily and Sardinia, even though the south contained more people) – far fewer, proportionately, than in other western European countries.[19]

Tsarist Russia was even slower to embrace the asylum. After the Crimean War (1853–56), the Russian authorities sought a reform of medical education in the empire, and for the first time made plans to institutionalize the mad. A training school was set up at the prestigious Military-Medical

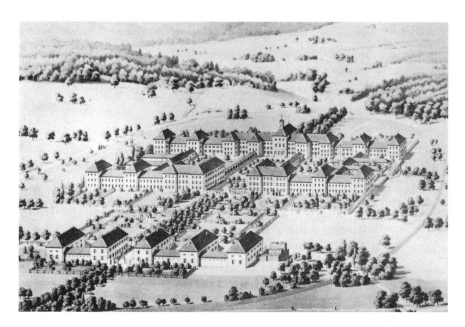

Illenau asylum, in Baden, Germany, 1865. Originally built in 1842 for 400 patients, it soon grew to contain many more. Politically fragmented, Germany built no rationalized, centralized asylum system and most German asylums, like Illenau, were constructed in isolated rural locations.

Academy in St Petersburg, and the training of a handful of asylum doctors began. Simultaneously, the tsarist regime began to urge provincial governments to construct a network of asylums all across the empire. These *zemstvo* (local government) asylums were to be built to plans rigidly dictated from the capital, generating complaints that local conditions were being ignored. The programme moved slowly in any event. Moscow dragged its feet, and provision for the insane in the city long remained among the most primitive and inadequate in the empire.[20] Even more than was the case in other countries, Russian psychiatry remained a creature of the state.

Perhaps because of their status as a frontier society, with few concentrations of people in urban centres, England's American colonies had largely managed their lunatics in the time-honoured fashion, in their families or in ad hoc arrangements elsewhere in the community. In the years following the Declaration of Independence in 1776, change came gradually. Workhouses and almshouses began to take in some of the poor; jails and penitentiaries began to be employed as means of punishing the vagrant and the criminal classes, as was happening in Europe as well. And a handful of small, charitable asylums were created, heavily influenced by parallel developments in Europe, particularly in England, where the moral treatment practised by the Quakers at the York Retreat had begun to attract international attention. These handful of so-called corporate asylums provided no scandals to match those uncovered by the European reformers, but that did not stop their most notable North American counterpart, the remarkable moral entrepreneur Dorothea Dix (1802–87), from creating a parallel set of exemplary tales of horror to advance her chosen cause of lunacy reform.

Following a sojourn in England that had been prompted by her own unstable mental state, Dix returned to her native Boston, where she encountered a number of lunatics confined amid the criminals in the Cambridge jail. In short order, her career as a reformer was launched. Her first Memorial was sent to the legislators of her own state, Massachusetts, in 1843, and in both its tone and its content it resembled the complaints that had been voiced in Europe: 'I proceed, Gentlemen, briefly to call your attention to the present state of insane persons confined within this Commonwealth, in cages, closets, stalls, pens! Chained, naked, beaten with rods, and lashed into obedience!'[21] At the Newburyport almshouse, for example, she reported that she had found a madman hidden away in a dilapidated shed, which opened, not on the yard, but on the deadhouse, 'affording in lieu of companionship

Dorothea Dix: a moral entrepreneur who crusaded relentlessly to bring the asylum to every American state.

with the living, a contemplation of corpses'. Nearby was still another inmate, this one a woman, hidden away 'in a cellar', padlocked and left in the dark, where she had wailed without surcease 'for years'.[22]

In the years that followed, travelling alone from state to state, penetrating into the American wilderness and fording the Mississippi in flood, invading the South as a Yankee reformer, Dix bludgeoned male politicians everywhere she went with the horrors the insane faced in confinement. She scoured each state for local examples, and where they were scarce or hard to come by, she did not scruple to invent and to embroider. Only occasionally did her economical relationship with the truth catch up with her. For the most part, despite the resolute exclusion of women from politics and public life, her determination, her single-mindedness, her willingness to lobby and to embarrass, broke down all barriers. Again and again she brought politicians to heel, and forced them somehow to embrace her recommendations. In the South, her success owed much to her complete blindness to the evils of slavery. The mentally ill were members of an oppressed and unfortunate class, fellow-creatures whose suffering cried out for legislative intervention and relief. Slaves were somehow invisible to her, or beneath her notice.

The federalism of the United States meant that asylum provision proceeded somewhat spasmodically there too, for legislation had to be procured on a state-by-state basis. But Miss Dix was indefatigable, and one by one the states fell in line. When the last hold-outs succumbed, she briefly transferred her energies to reforming the Scots. Protective of the last remnants of their political autonomy, the Scottish authorities had left their mad folk in the hands of their families and to the vagaries of private charity. They wanted no part in the demoralizing effects of state compulsion, or the English Poor Law. Dix would have none of it, and soon proved her powers of persuasion were not lost on British politicians. In the teeth of local opposition to the interference of a foreigner (and a woman!), she pressured Westminster to impose the English model of tax-supported asylums and a supervisory Lunacy Commission on the Calvinists to the north. A whirlwind campaign completed, and legislation successfully passed, she retreated back to the United States, eventually spending her declining years in a room at the New Jersey State Lunatic Asylum at Trenton, an institution she liked to refer to as her first-born child.[23]

The asylum, Dix had argued, was a symbol of civilization, and has 'become so general among all civilized and christianized nations, that the neglect of this duty seems to involve aggravated culpability'.[24] It was sentiment later echoed by Queen Victoria's physician Sir James Paget (1814–99), who called the modern lunatic asylum 'the most blessed manifestation of true civilization that the world can present'.[25] The mid-nineteenth century was proud of its asylums, symbols of the triumph of humanity and science. An almost utopian set of hopes surrounded the birth of these new institutions, and contributed mightily to their appeal.

Remarkable as it may now seem, therefore, for Dix, as for her European counterparts, the solution to the horrors of the madhouse (PL. 29) and the other institutions that locked up the insane was the construction of asylums. Asylums organized of course on a very different model from those their investigations had pilloried. But asylums nonetheless. And with remarkable rapidity, this profound alteration in the place of insanity had taken hold, creating a great confinement of the mad that would last for well over a century, and eventually spread to a degree across the rest of the world through the reach of Western imperialism.

Imperial Psychiatry

In Britain's settler colonies – Canada, Australia, New Zealand – where indigenous populations had been partially exterminated or otherwise marginalized, asylums modelled on the institutions being built in Britain were created relatively rapidly.[26] The predominance of men among the early settlers was mirrored in the early excess of male patients who found their way to the asylum, and it appears that the violent formed a larger proportion of those confined than was true in Europe. In the Cape Colony in South Africa, institutionalization was slower to arrive. Robben Island (later notorious as the prison colony where Nelson Mandela and other African nationalists were confined under apartheid), began as a 'general infirmary' – for which one should read 'dumping ground' – for a heterogeneous mass of troublesome sorts, lepers, the chronically ill, the insane, beginning in 1846; but it was not until the 1890s that even two hundred mental patients were confined there at any given time.[27]

Asylums generally arrived on the scene even later in colonies where there was just a tiny white administrative class. In Nigeria, for example, the first asylums were not established until the early twentieth century, and even then they were purely custodial places. Gestures towards establishing a curative regime were not made until the mid-1930s, and in reality nothing substantial changed.[28] Most 'natives' continued to be managed and dealt with by their families, with some assistance from traditional Yoruba healers, who sometimes had recourse to a form of herbal treatment derived from a species of the plant rauvolfia. Ironically, Western psychiatrists would experiment with using an alkaloid derived from rauvolfia (reserpine) in treating their patients in the 1950s (PL. 27) – it had also been used in Indian folk medicine for its calming effects as a remedy for madness – though they rapidly came to prefer psychotropic medications of their own devising.[29]

In India, the British East India company mostly solved the problem of its mad employees by packing them off back to London, but this expedient began to fail as the numbers of white mad folk increased. The presence of crazed Europeans was an obvious threat to the ideology of white superiority, and provided an important motivation for the establishment of places where the insane representatives of the Raj could be safely hidden from public scrutiny.[30] Only later did the colonial authorities seek to make some limited provision for 'natives' who went mad, and only slowly did these establishments begin to import Western models of treatment and Western therapeutic techniques.[31]

France, too, had its colonial asylums, in the Maghreb, Indo-China and elsewhere, co-existing uneasily almost entirely outside the societies they nominally served.[32] One such asylum, the Blida-Joinville Hospital in Algeria, in 1953 took on as the head of its psychiatric staff a young black man from Martinique, Frantz Fanon (1925–61). Fanon had already produced one scathing critique of the place of the black intellectual in a whitened world, *Black Skin, White Masks* (published as *Peau noire, masques blancs* in 1952), and he promptly undertook the desegregation of the asylum under his control. But with the outbreak of the Algerian war for independence, he learned of the French resort to torture – both torturers and the tortured became his patients – and he promptly resigned his post, throwing in his lot with the Algerian National Liberation Front. In the final months of his short life, he published *Les Damnés de la terre* (*The Wretched of the Earth*), a book that advocated violence as the only language the colonial oppressor understood. It was an international bestseller that for a time had an extraordinary influence among those struggling to secure independence, and that prompted many in the metropole to rethink the psychological consequences of racial domination. If colonial psychiatry often served the interests of the imperial powers, in this instance at least, it emphatically did not.

Even in countries that did not directly succumb to Western imperialism, such as China and Japan, or that early threw off the colonial yoke, Argentina for instance, the asylum model eventually took root. Proponents argued that it was a mark of a civilized society. Argentina secured its independence from Spain in 1810, but national consolidation did not begin to take place until mid-century. Once the civil and international wars subsided, however, it began to receive floods of immigrants from Europe. Its newly emerging Porteño elite in Buenos Aires, aspiring to be seen as members of a civilized nation and to win European approval, quickly embraced the asylum. An institution for women opened in 1854, even in the era of the Rosa dictatorship, a period educated Argentinians viewed as an interlude of barbarism, and charitable institutions for men and women in Buenos Aires soon followed.[33]

China's first asylum of a Western sort was opened by an American missionary, John G. Kerr (1824–1901), in 1898 in Canton (now Guangzhou). A Beijing municipal asylum followed in 1912, though in its early years it was run by the police along traditional lines rather than on the model of a Western asylum. It was simply a way to dispose of the public nuisance some of the mad represented. Subsequent attempts in the 1920s and 1930s, fuelled in part by Rockefeller money (see p. 323), to 'reform' the municipal asylum and bring the dubious benefits of Western psychiatry to a largely uncomprehending Chinese population, enjoyed only a limited and extremely brief existence. Modernizing elites saw Western medicine as a crucial component of Republican China's attempt to strengthen the country and help it compete successfully with the predatory Western powers, but made little headway, not least because the effort smacked of cultural imperialism.[34]

Japan adopted the Western model of the asylum about a century after Europe and North America. This photograph of a patient under home confinement in 1910 mirrors descriptions we have from nineteenth-century reformers about the ways European and American families coped with an insane relative.

Much the same pattern can be observed in Japan. Not until 1919 did the Meiji regime pass a Mental Hospitals Act promoting institutional treatment of the mad, nearly a century after similar efforts had materialized in Europe and North America. At that point, it appears that perhaps 3,000 of Japan's mentally ill were already confined in some sort of institution. The new legislation prompted a sharp increase in the numbers under confinement, with the asylum census reaching 22,000 in 1940. But even at that, in a society of 55 million people, Japan institutionalized but a small fraction of the mad when compared to Britain or the United States, where hospitalization rates were considerably more than ten times higher.[35] In 1940, many of the mad in Japan remained the responsibility of their families and were kept in close confinement if they constituted a nuisance, and especially if they were unruly and violent. And they were likely to be treated, if at all, with traditional folk remedies and religiously based interventions, rather than in accordance with the tenets of Western psychiatry.

Imperialism, whether political or cultural, spread the notion of institutionalizing the mad all over the globe, but in few places, save the settler states that most closely resembled and aped the mother country, did it succeed in exporting a psychiatric great confinement. Without question, Western physicians looked with condescension on indigenous beliefs and practices. And wherever there were strong and established traditions about mental disturbance and its treatment, the local populace returned the favour. Imperial psychiatry in such settings almost universally experienced enormous difficulty in transforming popular local customs. Try as its practitioners might to ignore, suppress and invalidate native attitudes, they were doomed to frustration.

Moral Treatment

In the English-speaking world, the York Retreat, a small institution founded in 1792 (mentioned briefly in Chapter Five), exercised an extraordinary influence. Though the management techniques it pioneered were simultaneously being discovered elsewhere, both in England and abroad, it was the version propounded by the Tuke family, Quaker tea and coffee merchants, that served as the inspiration and the model for reformers elsewhere. In the York Retreat chains were dispensed with and all forms of physical violence and coercion forbidden. Others, too, facing the task of managing maniacs collected under one roof had begun to break with an earlier consensus, and were emphasizing the importance of 'creating a habit of self-restraint', something their experience had suggested might be managed by making use of small rewards, actions which implied trust that patients could control themselves and approbation when they did so, rather than by coercion.[36] William Tuke and his grandson Samuel systematized these observations and publicized them.[37]

The mad, it seemed, might be sensitive to the same inducements and emotions as the sane. Some remnants of reason remained in almost anyone, and could be made use of through skilful manipulation of their environment to encourage them to suppress their wayward propensities. Indeed, it was only by 'treating the patient as much in the manner of a rational being, as the state of mind will possibly allow' that one could hope to educate him to discipline himself. By walking, talking, working, taking teas with their superintendent, all within the confines of a carefully constructed therapeutic environment, patients could be taught to restrain themselves. 'Morbid propensities' were not to be reasoned with or refuted. 'The very opposite method is pursued. Every means is taken to seduce the mind from its favourite but unhappy musings.'[38]

Even the name William Tuke chose for his new institution, the Retreat, suggested its role: to provide a humane and caring environment, where those who could not cope with the world could find respite. That environment included, very importantly, the physical architecture of the building within which the lunatic found himself, for the insane were very sensitive to their surroundings, and anything that conjured up the air of a prison was to be avoided at all costs. Hence the domestic appearance of the Retreat; the disguising of the bars on its windows to make them look like wood; the substitution of a 'ha-ha' – a hidden ditch – for a high, forbidding wall round the perimeter of the grounds. Work was important, not, as it would later become,

The York Retreat, the model institution for English-speaking lunacy reformers, with no high walls or bars dividing the building from the world at large.

as a way of cutting costs, but because 'of all the modes by which the patients may be induced to restrain themselves, regular employment is perhaps the most generally efficacious'.[39] Instrumentally speaking,

> whatever tends to promote the happiness of the patient, is found
> to increase his desire to restrain himself, by exciting the wish
> not to forfeit his enjoyments; and lessening the irritation of
> mind which too frequently accompanies mental derangement....
> The comfort of the patients is therefore considered of the highest
> importance, in a curative point of view.[40]

It was the experience of the Retreat that guided English lunacy reformers and generated their enthusiasm for the asylum. Skilled publicists including the Scottish alienist William Alexander Francis Browne (1805–85) endorsed such moral treatment as the foundation of the asylum of the future, the 'moral machinery' that would return the mad to sanity.[41] And it was Tuke's establishment that the first American reformed asylums modelled themselves on, right down to its external appearance. Quakers in Philadelphia and New York corresponded directly with the family and published the advice they received. Their institutions, the Frankford Retreat and the Bloomingdale Asylum, were then emulated at the Hartford Retreat and the McLean Asylum in Connecticut and Boston respectively.[42] In turn, it was the existence of these new reformed asylums that Dorothea Dix pointed to (and whose statistics she employed) in her campaign to spread the benefits of asylumdom everywhere.

Philippe Pinel had discovered closely analogous principles in the unpropitious atmosphere of post-Revolutionary Paris. His *traitement moral* drew heavily on the experiences of the lay governor of the Bicêtre, Jean-Baptiste Pussin, and his wife Marguerite (see Chapter Five), who had independently come to many of the same conclusions as Tuke about the management of the mad, albeit in much larger and more anonymous surroundings.[43] Guided by them, Pinel acknowledged that he had

> very carefully examined the effects which the use of iron chains
> had on psychiatric patients, compared with the results of their
> abolition, and I can no longer entertain any doubts about wiser
> and gentler restraint. The very patients, confined to chains for long
> stretches of years, who had remained in a constant state of rage,

thereupon walked about calmly in a simple straitjacket, conversing with everybody, whereas previously nobody could go near them without being in great danger. There was no more menacing yelling or shouted threats, and their agitated state progressively passed away.[44]

Like his English counterparts, Pinel insisted that 'deranged patients can hardly ever be cured in the bosom of their family...the patients whose isolation is the most complete are cured the most easily'. The presence of near-relations 'always increase[s] their agitation and untamable character', whereas in the hands of the skilled staff of an asylum, they 'become docile and calm'.[45] In assisting this process, the internal arrangement of the asylum was of great importance. From the most disturbed, through the stage where madness was declining, and culminating in wards for the convalescent, physical divisions reinforced moral boundaries, and coupled with increased freedoms and opportunity for work and amusement, this system provided further ways of inducing patients to bring their deranged faculties and feelings under control. At intermediate stages in this process, for example, patients are

> unconstrained and with complete freedom of movement barring some transient agitation from an incidental cause. They walk about under the trees or in an adjacent spacious enclosure and some, getting closer to the convalescent stage, share in the work of the servant girls, busying themselves in drawing water, removing dirt from the lodges, washing the cobblestones and carrying out other more or less energetic heavy tasks.[46]

All the various proponents of moral treatment were united in emphasizing the importance of a single director of the whole enterprise – knowledgeable about the peculiarities of each of his charges, swift to modify treatment according to the specific characteristics of the individual case, and providing a constant check against any disposition on the part of the asylum's staff to mistreat their charges. Pinel's chief assistant, Esquirol, who became the most influential French alienist on his master's death, articulated the consensus: 'The doctor has to be, in some way, the principle of the life of a hospital for the alienated. It is by him that everything has to start its movement. He has to regulate all actions as he is called to be the regulator of all thoughts.'[47]

Just as reformed asylums run on moral treatment principles were nothing like the madhouses and jails in which the mentally ill had previously languished, so too the new generation of superintendents were necessarily quite unlike their predecessors. Previously, 'the care of the insane was monopolized by medical and other adventurers [creating] a ridiculous stigma [which] deterred regular and well-educated practitioners from attempting to compete, and even from qualifying themselves to do so'. Finally such mountebanks were giving way to the professional man of 'high integrity and honour', possessed of

> that moral and physical courage and firmness which confer
> calmness and decision in the midst of danger...and imbues the
> whole character with that controlling influence, which...governs
> the turbulent while it appears to guide, and commands the most
> wild and ferocious by the sternness and at the same time by the
> serenity of its orders.[48]

In such hands, humanity and cures were all but guaranteed.

If one were to accept at face value the claims of its proponents, the new institutions were 'miniature worlds, whence all the disagreeable alloys of modern life are as much as possible excluded'.[49] They were, in the words of John Conolly (1794–1866), who had become the most prominent English alienist of the mid-Victorian age, the place where

> calmness will come; hope will revive; satisfaction will prevail...
> almost all disposition to meditate mischievous or fatal revenge,
> or self-destruction, will disappear...cleanliness and decency will
> be maintained or restored; and despair itself will sometimes be
> found to give way to cheerfulness or secure tranquillity. [This is]
> where humanity, if anywhere on earth, shall reign supreme.[50]

The embrace of asylumdom was virtually everywhere accompanied by such Utopian expectations. It was in the New World, however, that the sense of what could now be accomplished soared to the greatest heights. The first American asylum superintendents were swept up in a wave of enthusiasm and optimism for what moral treatment could achieve. They reported cure rates of 70, 80, 90 per cent of recent cases, and Dr William Awl (1799–1876) of Virginia then trumped them all, claiming he had cured 100 per cent of his recent cases over the preceding twelve months, earning himself the moniker

Nineteenth-century reformers were adamant about separating the sexes in asylums. Carefully choreographed lunatic balls, such as this one of 1848, however, demonstrated the power of the new moral treatment regime to domesticate the mad.

'Dr Cure-Awl'. It was the statistics produced by this 'cult of curability' that Dorothea Dix drew upon with great effect when she lobbied state legislatures. 'All experience', she told them, 'showed that insanity reasonably treated is as curable as a cold or a fever.' Asylums were thus in the long run a true economy, as well as a great humanitarian advance.[51]

Few would dispute the claim that asylums operated along moral treatment lines provided a more humane environment than the worst of the traditional madhouses. Well, actually the French philosopher Michel Foucault and his followers would. Foucault famously dismissed 'moral treatment' as a form of 'gigantic moral imprisonment', and however exaggerated the sentiment, it contains at least a kernel of truth. The Scottish alienist and propagandist W. A. F. Browne bluntly acknowledged that: 'There is a fallacy even in conceiving that Moral Treatment consists in being kind and humane to the insane.'[52] The new approach sought to transform the asylum into a 'great moral machine', whose goal was to ensure that 'the impress of authority is never withdrawn, but is stamped upon every transaction'.[53] In his own practice, Browne boasted, he sought to continue 'the discipline and inspection exercised during active pursuits into the night, and during silence and sleep. Control may thus penetrate into the very dreams of the insane.'[54] The imagination run riot must be brought to heel, domesticated and civilized even in those who had lapsed into a state of deep unconsciousness.

Though he did not resort to such hyperbolic claims, Philippe Pinel was equally clear about the Janus-faced nature of moral treatment: *douceur*, or kindness, must always be backed by 'an imposing apparatus [*appareil*] of repression', a willingness if 'necessary to subjugate [lunatics] first and encourage them afterwards'.[55] As with Tuke's version, Pinelian moral treatment was a superior method of managing madness, and over time it was its usefulness in controlling the otherwise uncontrollable without overt violence that gave it its lasting appeal.

From Madness to Mental Illness

Both ideologically and practically, in other words, moral treatment had many virtues. For the medical men who increasingly sought to transform the treatment of mental illness into a medical monopoly, however, it had one serious drawback: it was not clear why physicians were best placed to administer it. In France, the persistent presence of religiously staffed asylums made this problem a particularly salient one, but it was forcibly felt almost everywhere as the new asylums were built.

Pinel, after all, had absorbed his practical lessons about how to manage the insane from two lay persons who had learned from direct experience. Their long years of service had placed before them 'the continuing spectacle of all the phenomena of insanity', giving them a 'multifarious and detailed knowledge that is lacking in the physician' whose interactions with the patients were fleeting, 'most often limited to...transitory visits'.[56] More than that, Pinel had been quite sceptical of most medical treatments for madness, from bloodletting to what he scornfully called the 'large inventory of powders, extracts, juleps, syrups, potions, topicals, etc. designed to overcome mental alienation', lamenting the many instances of patients forced to endure 'the harsh ordeals of confused polypharmacy managed in an empirical manner'.[57] Medical men needed to abandon 'their blind faith in a sumptuous array of medicaments' and to recognize that 'medication comes into the general plan as a secondary means and it is only then that they are opportune, which is something quite rare'.[58]

Besides the establishments with which Pinel was connected, Parisian lunatics might find themselves confined in the asylum at Charenton (including the Marquis de Sade, as already mentioned). Originally founded by the Frères de la Charité in 1641, Charenton had acquired an evil reputation under the *ancien régime* for confining the king's enemies seized by *lettres de cachet* alongside its lunatic and incapacitated population, so much so that the revolutionaries had ordered its closure. Within two years, however, the problem of what to do with the discharged madmen forced its re-opening, this time as a fully secular establishment. Here much of the day-to-day supervision of the inmates was conducted by a medically unqualified priest, François Simonet de Coulmier (1741–1818), and though the Directory appointed a physician to Charenton, it was Coulmier who dispensed the *moyens moraux* that were the principal means of managing the patients, and a 'lay-medical battle continued to smoulder inconclusively at Charenton' for years.[59]

Across the Channel, Samuel Tuke, the grandson of William, almost simultaneously pointed out that 'the experience of the Retreat...will not add much to the honour or extent of medical science. I regret...to relate the pharmaceutic[al] means which have failed, rather than those which have succeeded.'[60] His discussion of the therapeutic regime at York sharply distinguished between moral and medical treatment, separating them from one another, and emphasizing that even the medical men who had been invited in to treat the patients had ended up agreeing that 'medicine, as yet, possesses very inadequate means to relieve the most grievous of human diseases'.[61] It was the lay-authored and lay-administered moral treatment that had brought about the institution's enviable record of recoveries, and that principle of placing the superintendency in lay hands would be emulated in the United States at the Bloomingdale Asylum in New York and the Frankford Retreat in Philadelphia.

For medical men now interesting themselves in ever greater numbers in the treatment of the insane as the spread of the asylum opened up new career opportunities, the threat this situation posed was obvious: if all medical men could do was to treat bodily afflictions, then why did they deserve any privileged place in the treatment of *mental* illness. Their prestige, their elaborate theories, their very livelihood were all under threat.[62] That some of the most lurid scandals exposed by the British parliament had occurred at medically run institutions scarcely helped matters, and the laymen who were more closely involved in developing proposals for a new state asylum system were among those voicing great scepticism about the relevance of medicine to the treatment of the mentally ill.

Yet within a matter of a quarter of a century, medicine's pre-eminence in the treatment of mental illness was almost complete. Granted, the persistence of clerical asylums in France provided an institutional base for ongoing criticisms of French alienists. But the York Retreat had acquired a medical superintendent by 1837, and in North America the Bloomingdale Asylum in 1831 and the Frankford Retreat in 1850 did the same. Statutes in France, England and the United States required that asylums appoint medical men to their staffs. Symbolically and practically, these changes marked the hugely significant moment when the multiple meanings that had for so long attached themselves to madness were supplanted by the dominance of a medical perspective. 'Madness', indeed, like the word 'mad-doctor' before it, began to seem an objectionable term, a slur on the sick.

Though some medical men had responded to moral treatment with hostility and disdain, that strategy had little chance of success. Instead, most interested in the problem of insanity came to embrace the new approach, but to argue that a judicious combination of medical and moral treatment was likely to be attended with far greater success than either one employed in isolation. Men such as Pinel and John Haslam (1764–1844), the apothecary at Bedlam from 1795 to 1816, had publicly acknowledged that the sorts of post-mortem examinations that had begun to unravel the pathology of diseases including tuberculosis and pneumonia had had no comparable successes when it came to cases of insanity. The brains of most madmen could not be distinguished from their sane brethren, so the presumed biological basis of mental illness remained a hypothesis unsupported by any unimpeachable anatomical findings. Indeed, Pinel went further, explicitly questioning the organic basis of most madness:

> One of the most fatal prejudices for humanity, one which is
> perhaps the deplorable cause of the state of abandonment in
> which almost all the insane are left, is to look upon their sickness
> as incurable, and to relate it to an organic lesion within the brain
> or in some other part of the head. I can assure you that, in most
> of the facts I have gathered concerning delirious mania that

has become incurable or has ended up in another fatal illness,
all the results discovered by opening up the body, compared to the
symptoms that have been manifested, demonstrate that this form
of insanity has generally a purely nervous character, and that it is
not the outcome of any organic defect in the substance of the brain.[63]

But that way lay danger. If madness lacked a physical basis, if both its
origins and its treatment lay in the realm of the social and the psychological, what warrant was there for handing over cases of mental derangement
to medical men? Was there, indeed, any reason to believe that doctors were
uniquely qualified to distinguish the mad from the sane?

Some medical reductionists such as William Lawrence (1783–1865),
surgeon to Bedlam, insisted that medical science had established that 'physi-
ologically speaking...the mind, the grand prerogative of man' was simply
a function of the brain. The separation of the physical and the mental was
a myth, a category mistake. In reality, the symptoms of insanity possessed
'the same relation to the brain, as vomiting, indigestion, heartburn to the
stomach; cough, asthma to the lungs; or any other deranged functions to
their corresponding organs'.[64] Or, as the eighteenth-century French physician
and *philosophe* Pierre Cabanis (1757–1808) put it more pithily, the brain
secretes thought as the liver secretes bile.[65] But the explicit materialism, and
in Britain the association of such views with the bloody excesses of the French
Revolution, made these assertions anathema to most respectable citizens.
Lest others were tempted to adopt them, the response of the medical establishment was swift and merciless. Lawrence, for example, was attacked as
an atheist and a menace to the moral order, someone who implicitly denied
the existence of the immortal, immaterial soul. Threatened with professional
ruin, he agreed to recall all remaining copies of the book in which the offending sentiments appeared, and destroy them. The retraction was a success:
he subsequently became surgeon to Queen Victoria, and a baronet, but the
lesson had been driven home.

Ironically, medical men on both sides of the Atlantic then developed
a compelling argument that purported to demonstrate beyond all doubt the
physical origins of mental disorders, an argument that rested precisely on
the Cartesian distinction between mind and brain. In French, the term for
'mind' and 'soul' is one and the same: *l'âme*. To argue that the mind or soul
was prone to disease, or in the case of idiotism or dementia, to death, was

therefore to call into question the very foundation of Christianity, and thus of civilized morality. By contrast, locating madness in the body caused no such problems. As W. A. F. Browne wrote in 1837: 'From the admission of this principle, derangement is no longer considered a disease of the understanding, but of the centre of the nervous system, upon the unimpaired condition of which the exercise of the understanding depends. The brain is at fault and not the mind.'[66] The immortal and immaterial on this side of the grave was utterly and intimately dependent on the material and thus corrupt sensory apparatus. Indeed, as John Conolly wrote in 1830, while still professor of medicine at University College London:

> Nay, so dependent is the immaterial soul upon the material
> organs, both for what it receives and what it transmits, that a slight
> disorder in the circulation of the blood through different portions
> of the nervous substance, can disturb all sensation, all emotion,
> all relation with the external and living world.[67]

That also helped to explain, Browne suggested, how medical treatment might produce cures, for by relieving the irritation of the brain, the 'calm, uninjured, immutable, immortal' mind could once again exercise its dominion over daily life.[68]

It was a wonderfully appealing syllogism, one the theologians rushed to embrace. Writing in the *Christian Observer*, the medical practitioner William Newnham (1790–1865) warmly welcomed this resolution of the problem of mental disorder:

> A great error has arisen, and has been perpetuated even to the
> present day, in considering cerebral disorder as mental; requiring,
> and indeed admitting, only of moral remedies...whereas the
> brain is the mere organ of mind, not the mind itself; and its
> disorder of function arises from its ceasing to be a proper medium
> for the manifestation of the varied action and passion of the
> presiding spirit.[69]

John Gray (1825–86), the American alienist, was still employing virtually identical arguments to those developed by his colleagues in the 1820s half a century later, a sign of how important this metaphysical embrace of the body was to alienists' jurisdictional claims.[70]

Lumps and Bumps, or Mental Cures for Bodily Afflictions

But if insanity was at root a medical illness, how might one explain the success of the social and psychological weapons that made up moral treatment? How could mental therapies cure a physical disease? For many, the solution to these difficulties lay in doctrines developed by the Viennese physician and brain anatomist Franz Joseph Gall (1758–1828) and his collaborator Johann Spurzheim (1776–1832) during the first decade of the nineteenth century. Phrenology is now mostly remembered as the pseudoscience of 'lumps and bumps', the attempt to relate character and behaviour to the shape of the skull, which was presumed to map the underlying structures of the brain. But before it became a fairground entertainment and the butt of ridicule, many saw phrenology as a serious intellectual endeavour. Leading figures across Europe and North America were drawn to its doctrines and attested to its value in understanding human behaviour and psychology.

Gall's investigations had convinced him that the brain was a collection of organs, and that individual mental functions were localized in particular regions of the brain. He and Spurzheim conducted careful and technically innovative dissections of brains, which formed the empirical foundation for their claims about the brain's anatomical and functional diversification. They concluded that the relative size of a particular organ was indicative of the strength of the associated mental function, and that its size could be increased or decreased to the extent that a given function of mind was exercised or neglected, rather as muscles can be developed or atrophy. Acquisitiveness, spitefulness, cautiousness, combativeness – a whole host of psychological propensities were located in particular regions of the brain, as were the ability to see, to hear and so forth. As the brain developed in infancy, Gall believed, the cranial bones conformed to the underlying comparative development of its different parts. In turn, that meant that one could deduce the person's character and mental capacities from the conformation of the head (PL. 30). The enigma of mind could now be solved. If the various organs making up the brain became unbalanced, character, thoughts and emotions would be affected. And ultimately, in extreme cases, the imbalance in the mind could become a form of insanity.

At first blush, here was a set of doctrines that licensed a thoroughgoing materialism, with all the socially and morally destabilizing implications conservative thinkers believed that position implied. Unsurprisingly, when Gall and Spurzheim began to promulgate their findings, the Viennese authorities took umbrage, and they were forced to leave for Paris after the government forbade Gall from teaching about his theory 'due to the peril it represented for religion and good morals'.[71] In the French capital they encountered resistance from those on the right, but encouragement among the anti-clerical left. They found a receptive audience that soon extended across Europe and North America, thanks in large part to the lecture tours undertaken by Spurzheim and the energetic efforts of popularizers such as the Scotsman George Combe (1788–1858; whose *On the Constitution of Man and Its Relationship to External Objects*, first published in 1828, sold more than 200,000 copies and ran to nine editions) and the Italian Luigi Ferranese (1795–1855).

Gall and Spurzheim were all too aware, given their experiences, of the danger they courted were their doctrines to be labelled materialistic. They carefully sought to deflect the charge. The various organs that made up the brain provided 'the material condition which makes possible the manifestation of the faculty'. But that faculty itself, they insisted, was a 'property of the soul [*l'âme*]'[72] (though how precisely they knew that, or how the soul and body co-existed, was left diplomatically and purposely vague). A year later, writing specifically on insanity, Spurzheim was more direct: 'I have no idea of any disease, or of any derangement of an immaterial being itself, such as the mind or soul is. The soul cannot fall sick, any more than it can die.'[73]

Not everyone was convinced by these disclaimers, and not every alienist was brave enough to embrace the new doctrine, but for most the attractions were overwhelming. While the majority of French academics remained sceptical, a legion of prominent French alienists took up the ideas enthusiastically. In England and Scotland, phrenology made even greater inroads, and the same was true in the United States, where both the asylum superintendents and leading lay reformers became vocal proponents of its truth and usefulness. Esquirol in France, Conolly and Browne in Britain, and Amariah Brigham (1798–1849) and Samuel B. Woodward (1790–1838) in the United States – a galaxy of prominent asylum doctors espoused the concept of phrenology.

After all, if insanity was a physical disorder of the brain, it was unambiguously a medical matter. And Spurzheim's modifications of the original doctrine, in particular, helped explain why moral treatment could affect the course of mental disease, by exercising and strengthening dormant and underdeveloped parts of the brain. But equally, phrenology left room for

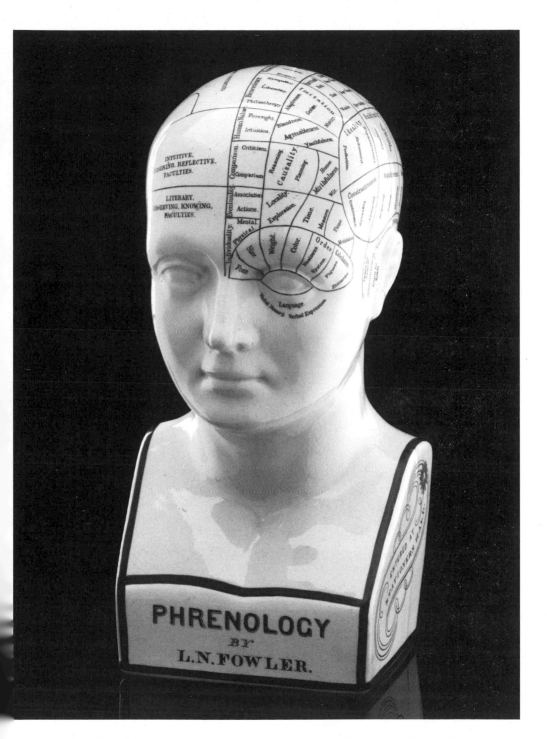

A phrenological head by L. N. Fowler, whose firm specialized in mass-producing them.

more conventionally medical treatments directed at the body. Theoretically, phrenology provided a clear physiological explanation of the operations of the brain, one that permitted a unified account of normal as well as abnormal mental functioning. Its grounding in the most advanced brain anatomy of the era, at a time when medicine as a whole was re-orientating its theories of disease around the findings of pathological anatomists in the morgue, promised to link members of the marginal specialty descended from mad-doctoring firmly to the most recent developments in scientific medicine. It also explained why recently arising cases of insanity were more curable than those that were chronic, because the functional changes of the former had become the structural changes of the latter, and beyond a certain point, defects of cerebral organization were beyond help. And it helped to legitimize notions that were gaining ground among many of the medical men who concerned themselves with insanity and its treatment: that insanity could be partial, not total, and could affect some aspects of mental life while leaving others untouched; and that mania might manifest itself as monomania, a single pathological preoccupation rather than total derangement. For the rise of the asylum, and with it the creation of a large number of stable positions for those specializing in the treatment of insanity, was leaving its mark on the way lunacy was understood, as well as transforming the geography of madness in striking ways.

The duration of phrenology as a serious science was short, barely four decades long. Craniology always lent itself to satire, and its exploitation by charlatans in the fairgrounds reflected its popularity among the public, but undermined phrenology's claims in more sober quarters. The materialism that many of phrenology's adherents tried hard to finesse or deny had always limited its appeal to religious and political conservatives. Now an increasing volume of new research on the physiology of the brain and the nervous system by William Carpenter (1813–85), François Magendie (1783–1855), Jean Pierre Flourens (1794–1867) and others made its specific claims seem increasingly implausible and then untenable, and attitudes to it hardened. Fatally, its doctrines came to seem ridiculous (PL. 31).

Mark Twain had encountered itinerant phrenologists during his youth in Hannibal, Missouri, greeting their performances with his characteristic scepticism, and when, later in life, the opportunity presented itself to expose phrenological readings as a snare and a delusion, he couldn't resist. Presenting himself anonymously at the London office of the transplanted

American phrenologist, Lorenzo Fowler (a man who had made a fortune from mass-producing china phrenological heads), Twain had his lumps and bumps scrutinized and read. 'Fowler received me with indifference, fingered my head in an uninterested way, and named and estimated my qualities in a bored and monotonous voice.' Twain, it seemed, had a variety of excellent qualities, but 'each of the hundred was coupled up with an opposing defect which took the effectiveness all out of it.' Then Fowler announced he had found a cavity in a particular region of Twain's skull that had no compensating bump. It was something he had never encountered before, in all his tens of thousands of readings: 'that cavity represented the total absence of the sense of humor!' Twain retreated, and bided his time. Three months later, he showed up under his own name. All was transformed: 'the cavity was gone, and in its place was a Mount Everest – figuratively speaking – 31,000 feet high, the loftiest bump of humor he had ever encountered....'[74]

Madness and the Morgue

For alienists, this trajectory from serious science to target of satirical jokes scarcely seems to have mattered. By the time phrenology lost its credibility, its doctrines had already been used to see off the challenge to medical authority that moral treatment might have represented. Medical men had secured a control over asylumdom that was written into law and enshrined in custom and in day-to-day authority over the ever-expanding numbers of institutionalized lunatics. Few doubted the proposition that madness was rooted in the pathologies of the brain and the nervous system, and of those few none were to be found in the ranks of those specializing in the treatment of mental disease. If a minority of alienists began to dissent from this orthodoxy late in the nineteenth century, that apostasy came only after a long period when biological accounts of madness ruled virtually unchallenged.

And yet, of course, the confidence manifested by many alienists in the early decades of the nineteenth century that the morgue would disclose the secrets of madness was mostly misplaced. There was an exception, however, and it was an important one: in 1822, Antoine Bayle (1799–1858), a young assistant physician at Charenton, had conducted autopsies on some 200 corpses of mental patients (Paris's huge public hospitals provided a never-ending supply of dead patients in these years). Some of these had suffered from a collection of symptoms that Bayle dubbed *paralysie générale*

– impairments of speech, loss of control of their arms and legs, progressive loss of sensation, accompanied by sometimes dramatic psychiatric symptoms, with delirium giving way to dementia, followed by death, usually brought on by choking, as the swallowing reflex became paralysed. In half a dozen of these cases, in particular, post-mortem examination of the brain revealed characteristic lesions: inflammation of the meninges and cerebral atrophy.

Paralysie générale, or General Paralysis of the Insane (GPI) as it became known in the English-speaking world, was scarcely a rare condition. By the end of the nineteenth century, it would account for 20 per cent or more of the male admissions to asylums in both Europe and North America. Many initially thought it might represent the end condition of most or perhaps all states of lunacy, but increasingly it was regarded as a distinct species of insanity, with its own, still unknown, pathology. Its ravages were implacable, and though its course might be erratic, it was invariably attended with a dreadful end. Bayle's discovery in the long run did much to reinforce the sense that mental illness was rooted in the brain,[75] though it did not do him much good personally: his mentor at Charenton, Antoine-Athanase Royer-Collard, died in 1825, and lacking any ties to his great rival Esquirol, Bayle found himself ostracized and completely unable to obtain an appointment as an asylum physician. He found work instead as a medical librarian.

Alienists became very skilled at detecting the early symptoms of GPI – minor speech difficulties, small changes in gait, differences in the reactions of the pupils of the eyes to light – though the aetiology of the disorder would remain a matter of debate into the early twentieth century (as discussed in Chapter Eight). By the 1840s, however, they had to confess that no other forms of insanity could be read in the brains of the mad. All such efforts had proved fruitless. Not that these failures caused any widespread questioning of the assertion that insanity was a somatic disorder. Why should they? The truculent assertion that '[i]nsanity is purely a disease of the brain' had as its corollary that 'The physician is now the responsible guardian of the lunatic and must remain so.'[76]

Responsible Guardians

Those 'responsible guardians' had become steadily more numerous in the first half of the nineteenth century, and by the 1840s they were forming professional associations and beginning to publish journals devoted to

A woman suffering from General Paralysis of the Insane (though men far outnumbered women among those afflicted with GPI), 1869, at the West Riding Lunatic Asylum in Yorkshire. When this photograph was taken it was not yet realized that the condition had its remote origins in infection with syphilis.

exchanging information about asylum management, developing a specialized literature on the pathology and treatment of madness, and, not coincidentally, building a sense of collective identity.

In Britain, they met for the first time in 1841 and called themselves the Association of Medical Officers of Asylums and Hospitals for the Insane, a mouthful that became the Medico-Psychological Association a quarter of a century later. No one could at first be found to take on the task of founding and editing a professional journal, but in 1848 Forbes Winslow (1810–74), proprietor of one of the somewhat suspect private asylums for the rich, launched the *Journal of Psychological Medicine and Mental Pathology* as a personal speculation. A split already existed to some degree between those who ran small, profit-orientated asylums for the rich (a lucrative, if stigmatized part of the mad-business, since it involved semi-surreptitious advertising and made money from something that looked more like trade than the provision of professional services), and those who now ran the much larger and rapidly proliferating network of public asylums, where the great bulk of patients were housed. And despite Winslow's protests, within five years that rival group had started its own journal. First called the *Asylum Journal* and then the *Asylum Journal of Mental Science*, in 1858 the word '*Asylum*' disappeared from the title entirely. As elsewhere, the name of the professional association and the original title of its journal make clear how closely the emergence of the new profession was bound up with the creation of the new network of 'reformed' asylums.

In the United States, thirteen heads of asylums gathered in Philadelphia in 1844 and formed their own Association of Medical Superintendents of American Institutions for the Insane. At once, one of their number, Amariah Brigham, who ran the New York State Lunatic Asylum at Utica, launched an American journal, the wonderfully titled *American Journal of Insanity*, whose typesetting and printing were undertaken by some of the patients at his asylum. (Not until 1921 would the *American Journal of Insanity* be renamed the by-then more respectable *American Journal of Psychiatry*.)

The French fashioned things backwards: their alienists waited until 1852 to found the Société médico-psychologique, but the *Annales médico-psychologiques* had been launched nearly a decade earlier, in 1843. In Germany, political fragmentation created considerable obstacles to any project to create a single organization linking together asylum doctors, who necessarily practised in a diverse array of political environments, and though an attempt had been made as early as 1827 to create a society to improve the practical treatment of the insane, and there was a feeble effort to form a sub-section of the broader Association of German Natural Scientists and Physicians devoted to psychiatry, a separate Verein der Deutschen Irrenärtze (Society of German Doctors of the Insane) met for the first time only in 1864, some twenty years after the first issue of the *Allgemeinen Zeitschrift für Psychiatrie und psychisch-gerichtliche Medicin* (*General Journal for Psychiatry and Mental-Forensic Medicine*) had first appeared. (In 1903, it changed its name to the Deutscher Verein für Psychiatrie, the German Society for Psychiatry.)

Everywhere, these societies and journals served similar functions. The annual meetings of the professional associations were one of the few occasions when asylum superintendents left their institutions behind. For whatever salary, security and local authority they possessed as heads of these establishments were purchased at a heavy price. It is true that they were not forced to compete in what all across Europe was an over-crowded, under-remunerated and often tenuously respectable medical profession. But the reality was, they were trapped and isolated in their asylums almost as surely as the patients whose lives they supervised. Meanwhile, the journals provided an ongoing means of communication about administrative matters – how to heat huge buildings, run the asylum farm on which many patients worked, deal with problems of water supply and the disposal of sewage and the like – and the occasion for more elevated speculations on the pathology and treatment of insanity, its classification, and the political issues confronting the profession. In an era when medical journals of all sorts were proliferating, it signalled, as well, alienism's ambition to be thought of as part of the broader medical enterprise, and provided ammunition for the claim that the science of dealing with madness was alive, well and ever-expanding. Individually and collectively, the emerging specialty could promote itself through print. And the journals could also help alienists to distinguish themselves from the older kind of mad-doctor. In the past it had not been uncommon to find many a madhouse proprietor, like many a quack, boasting that he possessed secret remedies for the cure of lunacy. In contrast, publication of and debate about one's theories cultivated an image of open and disinterested inquiry.

The term 'psychiatry' had been coined by the German physician Johann Christian Reil (1759–1813) in 1808 from the combination of the Greek words for soul (*psykhe*) and for medical treatment (*tekhne iatrike*), but outside the German-speaking world it gained little traction until the very end of the nineteenth century. Instead, those specializing in the treatment of the mad preferred to call themselves asylum superintendents, medico-psychologists or alienists (the latter term of course a French invention).[77] Italian specialists in mental medicine, disdaining the term 'psyche', with its connotations of soul, spirit and religion, created their own neologism, *freniatra*, and their professional society, formed in 1873, clung to the name Società Italiana di Freniatria as a symbol of their secular, scientific identity for nearly sixty years, finally adopting 'psychiatry' in 1932. But whatever they called themselves, these doctors' identity and authority, such as it was, derived in the last instance from the institutions they ran. There was a near-universal insistence on 'the improbability...of an insane person's regaining the use of his reason, except...with a mode of treatment...which can be fully adopted only in a Building constructed for the purpose.'[78] The modern asylum, they agreed, was 'a special apparatus [designed] for the cure of lunacy'.[79] In the words of Luther Bell (1806–76), a leading American member of the fraternity: 'An Asylum or more properly a Hospital for the insane, may justly be considered an architectural contrivance as peculiar and characteristic to carry out its designs, as is any edifice for manufacturing purposes to meet its specific end. It is emphatically an instrument of treatment.'[80]

If one were to measure the effectiveness of these new 'instruments of treatment' by the numbers they attracted and housed, they would everywhere seem to have been an enormous success. Like giant magnets, more powerful by far than Mesmer's *baquets*, asylums drew legions of the lunatic into their ambit. No matter how many new asylums were built, more and more lunatics materialized to fill them. That pattern persisted year on year. *The Times* reported the waspish observation in 1877 that 'if the lunacy continued to increase as at present the insane would be in the majority, and, freeing themselves, would put the sane in the asylums.'[81] North of the border, *The Scotsman* complained that 'build as we may, in every succeeding year we find the same demand for further accommodation...a work which shows as little promise of coming to an end as that of filling a bottomless pitcher.... Instead of finding that the great outlay which has been incurred in building asylums has led to the decrease in insanity, we find, on the contrary, an enormous and continuous development.'[82] Three decades later, in 1908, the German psychiatrist Paul Schröder (1873–1941) was still complaining of the 'unsettling' growth in the number of 'patients needing institutional care', an increase 'that bears no relationship to the increase in population'.[83]

But as patient numbers remorselessly rose, the cures the asylum super-intendents had promised failed to materialize, at least in anything like the proportions they had proclaimed they could provide. Relentlessly, not just the number of asylums, but also their average size, began to increase. In sub-stantial measure, this was a matter of simple arithmetic: if only one-third or two-fifths of each year's intake left 'improved' or 'cured', and only 10 per cent died (and these became the common sort of statistics at most institutions), then over time, cases inevitably accumulated, and the chronic formed a larger and larger portion of the asylum population. But the availability of the alternative of confining awkward, inconvenient and even impossible people in an institution, instead of having somehow, desperately, to cope with and contain them in a domestic setting, provided another unexpected source of inmates. How disturbed someone needed to be before institutionalization seemed warranted was not measured by some immutable, unchanging stand-ard, and over time the boundaries of what constituted 'Bedlam madness' widened, and more and more distracted souls were deemed in need of con-finement. The small, intimate asylum that William Tuke had presided over, or that Esquirol had provided for his private patients, was largely superseded, save for the very rich, by asylums of three and four hundred, and then of a thousand and more.

These developments had ominous implications for the alienists, for their inability to produce the cures they had promised created an inevita-ble backlash, and eventually a growing unwillingness on the part of public authorities to expend 'extravagant' sums of money on those who seemed destined forever to remain a drain on the public purse. The very legitimacy of the alienists' claims to expertise and to the status of a healing profession came under threat. From another quarter, these unwelcome developments produced a sharp drop in professional morale; a casting about for explanations for the collapse of the promise that had accompanied the birth of the asylum; and a new rationale for the perpetuation of the museums of madness that had multiplied and now formed such an unmistakable feature of the nineteenth-century landscape. Once more, what had purported to be humane institutions, places of respite and recovery, were degenerating in the public mind into places 'providing convenient storage of heaps of social debris',[84] warehouses for the unwanted, the 'Bluebeard's cupboard of the neighbourhood'.[85]

Chapter Eight

DEGENERATION
AND DESPAIR

The Disorders of Civilized Existence

From the early eighteenth century onwards, it had become commonplace to see nervous illnesses of a milder sort as part of the price one paid for civilization, indeed as afflictions to which the most refined and civilized were particularly prone. A century later, these ideas began to be extended to encompass the most severe and frightening forms of Bedlam madness. Insanity, alienists and their allies argued, was a disease of civilization and of the civilized. By contrast, the condition was all-but-unknown among 'savages' and primitive peoples. Those Rousseauean Noble Savages were apparently immune to the ravages of insanity.

As civilization advanced, life became more complex, more 'unnatural', faster-paced, more unsettled, more stressful, less stable. Political upheavals, of which the French and American revolutions were merely the most obvious, stirred passions and ambitions, as did the roiling economic changes of the new, market-based economic order. Ancient beliefs and status hierarchies were cast aside. Minds were disturbed by the headlong pursuit of wealth, and ambitions soared out of control. Agitation of the body politic reverberated in the bodies and minds of the citizenry. The older restraints which had kept people's appetites and expectations within bounds – church, family, lack of mobility both geographical and social, the sheer weight of tradition – were stripped away. Luxurious living and excess of every kind weakened moral and mental fibre, or so it was thought, and helped to explain the rapid rise in the number of the mad, who were most likely to be found, like their nervous counterparts, among the most ambitious, the most elevated, the

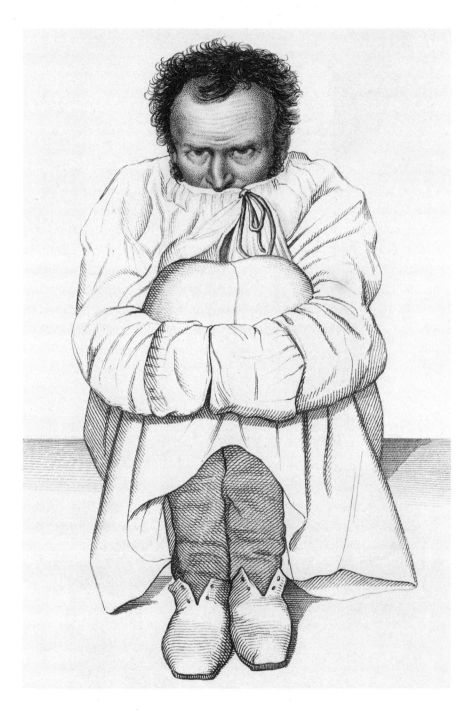

The French alienist J.-É. D. Esquirol included many drawings of insane patients in the throes of their madness, such as this one, in his treatise Des Maladies mentales, *published in 1838.*

most cultivated men and women of the age. It was the subject of much anxious contemporary commentary.

Philippe Pinel and his favourite pupil, Esquirol, had briefly suggested that the sweeping away of the *ancien régime* might have salutary effects on the mental health of their fellow-citizens. After all, that had been a social order 'ready to expire', its most privileged elements 'mired in softness and luxury'. Surely the liberty ushered in by the Revolution could not fail to have salutary effects, replacing ennui and idleness with 'vigour and energy'.[1] But the Terror swiftly disabused them of such conceits. Pinel recast his thinking: the passions unleashed by the Revolution had frightful implications for the stability, not just of the state, but of its citizens.[2] Esquirol spoke of 'our revolutionary torment' as the most powerful cause of the rapid rise in the number of the mad.[3] Time drove home this lesson for him, and reinforced his belief that: 'Madness is the product of society and of moral and intellectual influences.'[4] Henri Girard de Cailleux (1814–84), director of the asylum at Auxerre, voiced in 1846 what rapidly became the consensus:

> The movement of ideas and political institutions has rendered
> once immovable and stable occupations subject to change....
> Many minds, over-stimulated by a headlong and unlimited
> ambition, having worn themselves out, perverted in a struggle
> beyond their strength [end] up in madness.... [For] others...
> discouragement and misery have led them to stray from the
> light of reason.[5]

Curiously, the musings of the leading American physician of *its* revolutionary age, Benjamin Rush of Philadelphia, had already followed a trajectory similar to that of Pinel and Esquirol. For him, independence meant that his fellow-citizens

> are constantly under the invigorating influence of liberty. There
> is an indissoluble union between moral, political, and physical
> happiness; and if it be true, that elective and representative
> governments are most favourable to individual as well as national
> prosperity, it follows of course, that they are most favourable to
> animal life.[6]

Such benefits accrued only to the patriots who had supported independence. Those who had mistakenly remained loyal to the British crown suffered from

'*Revolutiana*', and were cursed with weakened bodily and mental health. Soon, however, Rush, like Pinel and Esquirol, was singing from a different hymn sheet. It turned out that

> The excess of the passion for liberty, inflamed by the successful
> issue of the war, produced, in many people, opinions and
> conduct which could not be removed by reason nor restrained
> by government...[and] constituted a species of insanity, which
> I shall take the liberty of distinguishing by the name of *Anarchia*.[7]

Rush's neologisms did not command universal assent – indeed they were simply ignored – but the basic thrust of his later position became the orthodoxy among the next generation of American alienists. Samuel B. Woodward, the first superintendent of the Worcester State asylum in Massachusetts, which opened in 1833, saw peril everywhere:

> Political strife, religious vagaries, over-trading, debt, bankruptcy,
> sudden reverses, disappointed hopes...all seem to have
> clustered together in these times, and are generally influential
> in producing insanity.[8]

Isaac Ray (1807–81), another of the thirteen alienists who gathered in Philadelphia in 1844 to form a new professional association (p. 220), insisted that 'insanity is now increasing in most, if not all, civilized communities',[9] and his colleague Pliny Earle (1809–92), noting the 'constant parallelism between the progress of society and the increase of mental disorders', openly raised the question of 'whether the condition of highest culture in society is worth the penalties which it costs'.[10] It was the hardest-working, the most ambitious, the most successful who were most at risk:

> Insanity is rare in a savage state of society. One reason for
> this disparity, undoubtedly, is the substitution of the luxurious
> and artificial, for the more simple and natural modes of life.
> Another and more important one is, that among the ignorant
> and uncultivated, the mental faculties lie dormant, and hence
> are less liable to derangement.[11]

The British saw Revolutionary France as an object lesson in the perils of political instability (the less said about their former colonists across the Atlantic the better), but British alienists joined happily in the opinions voiced on the continent of Europe and in North America. Thomas Beddoes (1760–1808) spoke of nations 'civilized enough to be capable of insanity',[12] and Alexander Morison (1779–1866) (PL. 32) reported that madness appeared to be 'very small in South America, and among the Indian tribes, etc'. 'It is probable', he gravely concluded, 'that the increasing civilization and luxury of this country, co-operating with hereditary disposition, tends to increase ... numbers in proportion to the population.'[13] So, far from wealth providing protection against the inroads of insanity, it was the agricultural population, and particularly the rural poor, that 'is to great degree exempt from insanity', while the bourgeoisie and the plutocrats enjoyed no such immunity, exposed as they were 'to excitement...and...to the formation of habits of thought and action inimical to the preservation of mental serenity and health'.[14]

To the extent that these assertions about the social geography of madness secured public acceptance, they provided yet another set of reasons for the elite to support the construction of asylums. It was those who competed hardest in the race of life and who were most constantly and directly exposed to the noxious effects of heightened competition, speculation and ambition, who were, it appeared, those who had most to fear from the spectre of madness. The upwardly mobile incurred the greatest risks of all:

> Pianos, parasols, Edinburgh Reviews, and Paris-going desires, are now found among a class of persons who formerly thought these things belonged to a different race; these are the true source of nervousness and mental ailments.[15]

But everywhere, these predictions about the social location of madness turned out to be mistaken. It was from among the poor and the middling sort that the overwhelming bulk of the rapidly expanding numbers of certified lunatics immediately came. The designation of the mass of patients who crowded into public asylums as pauper lunatics was to a degree misleading – by no means were all drawn from the *lumpenproletariat*. But to rely to any extent on the public purse was to be designated a pauper, and madness made making a living virtually impossible. Its ravages meant that all but the wealthiest were soon threatened with poverty, a circumstance compounded by the strains insanity's presence placed on family life. Even those who began with some measure of economic security and independence soon found themselves impoverished and forced to rely upon public subsidy. As a result, they acquired a title that ordinarily made the 'respectable' classes recoil, but in these circumstances they had little choice. Desperation made them swallow their pride. But recognizing that the label 'pauper insane' masks a fair amount of social heterogeneity does not change the fundamental reality. By the 1850s, few could doubt that the bulk of those officially identified as insane were drawn from the lower orders, those who had to work to earn a living.

Waning Confidence

By this time, as well, pessimism about the fate of the mad was growing once more. Alienists proved incapable of delivering the high proportion of cures that they had promised, and the accumulation of chronic patients inevitably began to clutter up the asylum. These hordes of the hopeless and the spectre of chronicity came to haunt psychiatry in the last third of the nineteenth century, and to influence the wider culture's view of the nature of madness. Addressing the nation's assembled alienists on the fiftieth anniversary of the formation of their professional society, the forerunner of today's American Psychiatric Association, the eminent Philadelphia neurologist Silas Weir Mitchell (1829–1914) chided the psychiatrists, complaining that they presided over a collection of 'living corpses', pathetic patients 'who have lost even the memory of hope, [and] sit in rows, too dull to know despair,

These images of mania and melancholia served as the frontispiece to Alexander Morison's Outlines of Lectures on Mental Diseases *for 1826, a series he repeated annually for many years to advance both his own career, and medical claims to expertise in the management of lunacy.*

watched by attendants: silent, grewsome [sic] machines which eat and sleep, sleep and eat'.[16] Madness, it seemed, experts notwithstanding, was not something that could be cured by moral treatment (or even a judicious mixture of moral and medical treatment); but rather was a crushing, cruel life sentence.

The waning confidence of the alienists in the remedies they had to offer manifested itself everywhere. Those whose careers had begun in the midst of great optimism had somehow to cope with the reality of sharply constrained professional horizons. W. A. F. Browne, for instance, had been among the most prominent and effective proselytizers for the reformed asylum. He was a dedicated and talented administrator, who had the good fortune to run one of the most richly endowed asylums in Europe, in Dumfries, in southwestern Scotland. He devoted enormous energy to the treatment of his charges, providing language classes in Arabic, Hebrew, Greek, French and Latin; setting up a theatre and a literary magazine to which his patients contributed; providing concerts, dances, public readings and lectures, and a host of other activities designed to ward off boredom and stimulate them; and pioneering the use of gas to light the long Scottish winter evenings. (When he turned the gas lights on, the townspeople gathered at the asylum gates, expecting to view the spectacle of the asylum blowing up.) Despite his best efforts, within five years, his reported cure rate had fallen to little more than a third of his patients. Before the decade was out, he was lamenting that, utopian expectations aside,

> All men entrusted with the care of the insane must be conscious
> of how infinitely inferior the actual benefit conferred is to the
> standards originally formed of the efficacy of medicine, or of the
> powers of the calm and healthy over the agitated and perverted
> mind...how intractable the disease is found to be and how indelible
> its ravages are even where reason appears to be restored.[17]

'Appears to be restored': a telling phrase. Matters only got worse with time. By 1852, Browne spoke despairingly of 'how little can be done to restore health, to re-establish order and tranquillity', and that the results of all his efforts 'are so barren and incommensurate, that in defiance of sympathy and solicitude, misery and violence, and vindictiveness should predominate'.[18] Five years later, as he finally left behind the suffocating atmosphere of the asylum for a well-paid sinecure overseeing Scotland's asylums as a lunacy commissioner, he was blunter still:

> It has been customary to draw a veil over the degradation of
> nature, which is so often a symptom of insanity. But it is right
> that the real difficulties of the management of large bodies of

the insane should be disclosed: it is salutary that the involuntary debasements, the animalism, the horrors, which so many voluntary acts tend to, should be laid bare. No representation of blind frenzy, or of vindictive ferocity, so perfectly realizes, so apparently justifies, the ancient theory of metempsychosis, or the belief in demoniacal possession, as the manic glorying in obscenity and filth; devouring garbage or ordure, surpassing those brutalities which may to the savage be a heritage and a superstition.... These practices are not engrafted upon disease by vulgar customs, by vicious or neglected training, or by original elements of character. They are encountered in the most refined and polished portions of society, of the purest life, the most exquisite sensibility. Females of birth drink their urine.... Outlines of high artistic pretensions have been painted in excrement; poetry has been written in blood, or more revolting media.... Patients are met with...who daub and drench the walls as hideously as their disturbed fancy suggests; who wash or plaster their bodies, fill every crevice in the room, their ears, noses, hair, with ordure; who conceal these precious pigments in their mattresses, gloves, shoes, and who will wage battle to defend their property.[19]

Small wonder that one of Browne's counterparts south of the border, John Charles Bucknill (1817–97), who headed the Devon County Asylum at Exeter, and edited the *Journal of Mental Science*, complained that alienists 'spend our lives in a morbid mental atmosphere' and of 'the number of mental physicians who have suffered more or less from the seeming contagion of mental disease'[20] – in other words, went mad themselves.

There is something distinctly odd in this confession that an institution still publicly presented as curative for patients could prove so toxic for those supervising it. Not just in England and Scotland, but everywhere the asylum solution had spread, the problems were similar. The wretchedness, the monotony, the scarcely contained violence, the overcrowding and the misery were inescapable, and were compounded by the difficulties of supervising a motley crew of attendants (who rarely shared the alienists' perspective on their charges), and by the stubborn, if often mute, resistance of the patients, who had been brought there involuntarily and fought, often literally, against the constraints and boredom of hospital life.

Shutting Up the Mad: Pictorial and Literary Protests

Asylumdom shut up mental patients in a double sense. It separated them from society, and by and large it stifled and silenced their voices – assuming, that is, that they were not already silenced for posterity by their lack of literacy, or by the depths of their mental decline. Although one of the features of the new network of asylums was the plethora of statistics it spawned, those statistics tell us more about the confiners than the confined. Case notes reveal a little more about those who were incarcerated: how they came to be confined; something about their symptoms and behaviour both before and after they were certified as lunatics; and a little about their reactions to the asylum regime. Except in very occasional circumstances, however, our knowledge of how patients responded to asylumdom is almost always filtered through the eyes and ears of their doctors.

The accounts of what brought patients to the asylum, recorded in the certificates of insanity that legitimized their confinement, were usually copied into bound ledgers, where they were amplified occasionally by details supplied by the patient's family. Thereafter, entries were added periodically, either as a matter of routine, or when something out of the ordinary occurred. Over time, with chronic patients, records ceased or were at best formulaic. In

Ebenezer Haskell was one of many patients to claim he had been forced into an asylum while perfectly sane, and then horribly mistreated. He self-published a pamphlet recording his experience – here he is being punished in the guise of treatment.

increasingly huge asylums, patients became part of an anonymous crowd. The records of long-stay patients were often separated in multiple volumes, making it difficult to trace the arc of their asylum careers. Only much later were case records kept on single sheets of paper and inserted into files.

But driven in part by the phrenological notion that the shape of the skull might reveal something about the underlying insanity, recordings were made of patients' appearance and expressions, first via drawings and engravings. Once the daguerreotype and the technology of photography advanced, patients found themselves placed before the lens of the camera. Early glass plate negatives still may be found in the Bethlem Hospital archives and elsewhere, sometimes devoted to recording the patient's expression on admission, and then when 'cured'. Later in the nineteenth century, when Darwin became interested in the question of *The Expression of the Emotions in Man and Animals* (1872) he conducted an extended correspondence with James Crichton-Browne (1840–1938), superintendent of the West Riding Lunatic Asylum in Yorkshire, between May 1869 and December 1875, receiving multiple photographs of patients apparently in the grip of strong emotions.

Occasionally, very occasionally, the tables were turned, and patients recorded their impressions of their doctors, their fellow patients and the asylums that confined them. Sometimes these were set down on paper. One Ticehurst patient recorded her sense of herself as 'a human football' kicked around by all and sundry.[21] Ebenezer Haskell, who escaped the Pennsylvania Hospital for the Insane in 1868 and sued the institution he had been confined in, denounced his captivity in a self-published pamphlet, and drew a graphic scene of a patient stripped, spread-eagled and abused by attendants on the Fourth of July holiday. He followed it with a picture of himself jumping down from the high wall that surrounded the establishment, top hat lodged firmly on his head.[22] There cannot be much doubt about his view of his confinement, or that of some other protesting patients discussed below.

Other patients produced drawings that gave some shape to their delusions, crude and clumsy in many cases, striking and powerful in others. Sometimes, patients drew or painted their surroundings, and perhaps even the asylum superintendent who ruled over them. Much of this sort of material has simply vanished, though odd examples survive buried in asylum archives. Where professionally trained artists of some standing came to be confined, however, they sometimes produced quite remarkable and moving work that was preserved and occasionally made available to a wider public.

Richard Dadd (1817–86) had been seen as a highly promising artist in the early 1840s, till one day he cut off his father's head, and then fled to Paris, where he was finally detained by the French authorities. Confined to Bedlam (and later to the specialized hospital for the criminally insane at Broadmoor, which opened in 1863), Dadd was allowed to continue to paint, and alongside sketches of those in the throes of madness and fantastical scenes of dream worlds crammed with meticulous details (PL. 1), he produced a particularly haunting portrait of a careworn Sir Alexander Morison in 1852, then the visiting physician to Bedlam, and presumably the man who arranged for him to continue to paint (PL. 32). Reciprocally, it turns out, the asylum authorities had him photographed, so we can see him at work, painting *Contradiction: Oberon and Titania* (1854–58).

Some four decades later, Vincent van Gogh (1853–90) would paint his own portraits: of the alienist who treated him at Arles, Félix Rey (PL. 33), and of Dr Paul Gachet, the man who sought to care for him on his release from the private asylum at Saint-Rémy. Rey's portrait was one of a number of paintings van Gogh completed during his confinement at Arles. Others provide a view of the asylum garden, a picture of ward life that accentuates the isolation and self-absorption of those who inhabit it (PL. 35), and a moving portrait of a depressed inmate. Van Gogh worried that his mental condition might be affecting his work, and wrote to his brother imploring him 'not to exhibit anything too mad'.[23] But if we did not know of his confinement, and his often anguished mental state, there is little here that would suggest them. To the contrary, Otto Dix's portrait of the German nerve doctor Heinrich Stadelmann, painted in 1922 by someone who had never spent time in an asylum is a far more disturbed and disturbing image: with his hands clenched tightly, the hypnotist stares out at the viewer (PL. 34). A mad-doctor indeed.

Even where fugitive bits and pieces written or drawn by patients have survived, they are those their captors kept, and are scarcely a representative basis on which to surmise how the patients thought about and reacted to asylum life. By their very nature, these sorts of records are biased and partial. Biased by class, because rich patients were confined in small institutions with large numbers of staff to dance attendance on them and minister to their needs (though no more able to make them better); and because the much higher doctor–patient ratio, if it could not buy more cures, brought more attention, and more disposition to record what was going on. And of course, these patients were literate, as many of their poorer counterparts were not.

Richard Dadd painting Contradiction: Oberon and Titania, *a typically intricate image of the argument between Oberon and Titania over an Indian boy. This early photograph is an astonishing picture both of Dadd himself and of a work-in-progress.*

Of the great mass of mad folk locked up in warehouses with thousands of their fellow lunatics we know much less.

But less is not nothing. Some letters survive from patients expressing gratitude for their restoration to sanity. More common, however, is a literature of protest, for not all patients suffered in silence. Some gave voice to their torments, in paint or in print, and some spoke of their months and years confined in the asylum – though these were without question a biased sample, since most who did so complained that they had no business being locked up with the lunatic, and even those who conceded that some measure of madness had been their lot were scathing about the treatment they received.

For a rare insight into what it must have been like to be a patient wrestling with the demons of madness while confined in an asylum, consider the writings of the peasant poet of Northamptonshire, John Clare (1793–1864). Clare spent all but a few months of the last twenty-seven years of his life in two asylums: first, in Matthew Allen's private asylum, High Beach, in Essex, between 1837 and early 1841, and then, after a few months of stolen freedom, from the end of that year till his death in the Northampton General Lunatic Asylum. With but little formal education,[24] and forced to earn much of his living as an agricultural labourer, Clare had succeeded in attracting a publisher and some patrons for his poetry in the 1820s. But partly because of his propensity to drink, and partly because of the impact of the economic troubles of the 1830s, his cares mounted. With a wife and seven children to feed, his work as a haymaker, a bird-scarer, a fiddler and jack-of-all trades was becoming insufficient to make ends meet, even with the help of a small annuity from his literary sponsors. More and more frequently, he suffered from depression and panic attacks, and became dejected, delusional and alienated from those around him, and eventually his increasingly agitated mental state led to his voluntary admission to a madhouse. Locked up, he continued to write, though not overtly to protest his confinement. His most famous poems of this era are nonetheless haunting and disturbing by turns, and it seems perverse not to see in them both his struggles to sustain his sense of self, and some meditations on what it meant to be locked up and designated a lunatic.

Consider his *Invitation to Eternity*. Nominally an entreaty to an anonymous maiden to come and share his life, it eerily conjures up images of lingering social death, of being trapped in a world from which there is no escape – just as, in fact, Clare could not escape the claustrophobic world of the asylum. How else to read the following lines?

> ...wilt thou go with me
> In this strange death-in-life to be,
> To live in death and be the same,
> Without this life or home or name,
> At once to be, and not to be...

Consigned to 'night and dark obscurity', Clare here presents us with a life of everlasting, never changing

...sad non-identity,
Where parents live and are forgot,
And sisters live and know us not?

The sense of loss – loss of identity, loss of contact with the world, with family, with friends, with any larger community, the strange fate that leaves one 'to be, and not to be' – looms even larger in his slightly earlier poem, *I Am!* Its title seems to promise something truculent, a vigorous assertion of personal autonomy and individuality. What follows is anything but. It is instead a lament, marked by a keening sense of abandonment and helplessness:

I AM: yet what I am none cares or knows,
My friends forsake me like a memory lost;
I am the self-consumer of my woes,
They rise and vanish in oblivious host,
Like shades in love and death's oblivion lost;
And yet I am, and live, with shadows tost

Into the nothingness of scorn and noise,
Into the living sea of waking dreams,
Where there is neither sense of life nor joys,
But the vast shipwreck of my life's esteems;
And e'en the dearest – that I loved the best –
Are strange – nay, rather stranger than the rest.[25]

Many an inmate consigned to an asylum, though quite incapable of giving such powerful voice to their feelings, must have shared a sense of being scorned and abandoned, of living in a world of 'waking dreams' and woe, forsaken and forgotten, their hopes wrecked and their existence permanently cast into shadow.

Gothic Tales

To be certified as mad was to lose one's civil rights and one's liberty. But for the families, one of the key benefits madhouses could potentially offer was the capacity to draw a veil of silence over the existence of a mad relation in their midst. That was a major reason why England's growing prosperity in the eighteenth century had given birth to such establishments, allowing families to rid themselves of the insufferable and impossible people who put their lives, their property, their peace of mind and their reputations at risk. But this shutting up of the mad in what purported to be a therapeutic isolation could easily be cast in a more sinister light. Many patients likened the experience to being confined in a living tomb, a cemetery for the still breathing. Madhouses at this time, moreover, with their barred windows, high perimeter walls, isolation from the community and enforced secrecy, invited gothic imaginings among the public at large about what might transpire hidden from view. Circulation of these gothic tales had begun in the eighteenth century, as soon as such establishments appeared, and showed no signs of slackening as the numbers of the mad in confinement surged in the nineteenth century.

Some stories were avowedly fictional. Charles Reade (1814–84), in his day almost as popular a novelist as Dickens, created a scandalous and hugely successful melodrama, *Hard Cash* (1863), which stitched together reworked versions of horrors that had surfaced in parliamentary inquiries and in the press to present an indictment of asylums and those who ran them. John Conolly, the most famous English alienist of the age, appears in thinly disguised form as the bumbling Dr Wycherly, who stands accused of conniving in the confinement of the perfectly sane hero of Reade's tale, Alfred Hardie. Wycherly, Hardie sardonically records, 'is the very soul of humanity', in whose asylum there are 'no tortures, no handcuffs, nor leg-locks, no brutality'. But his 'vast benevolence of manner' and the 'oleaginous periphrasis' of his conversation concealed a second-rate mind 'blinded by self-interest' and apt 'to perceive insanity wherever he looked'. In Reade's savage satire, the not-so-good doctor's pretensions to gentlemanly status are mocked, and his vaunted psychological acumen exposed as a pious fraud. 'Bland and bald', this psychocerebral expert was 'a man of large reading and the tact to make it subserve his interests' and 'a voluminous writer on certain medical subjects'. As 'a collector of mad people...[whose] turn of mind, co-operating with his interests, led him to put down any man a lunatic, whose intellect was manifestly superior to his own', he is easily duped into diagnosing a sane man as a lunatic, and thereafter persists stubbornly in his opinion till the unfortunate inmate is willing to grant that 'Hamlet was mad'.[26]

But other stories about the horrors of being captured by the trade in lunacy were real enough, or so their authors alleged. For almost as soon as the madhouse appeared, a literature of patient protest materialized. In the nineteenth century, as lunacy reformers brought about the real Great Confinement of the insane, and thousands upon thousands of patients flooded into the expanding empire of asylumdom, protests of this sort multiplied apace. All the efforts of those who now sought to re-label themselves as alienists or medical psychologists ('mad-doctor' was too ambiguous and perhaps too apposite a term) proved fruitless. They could neither persuade the public that they possessed infallible talents as diagnosticians, nor succeed in discrediting the claims of rogue ex-patients that they were an unscrupulous and mercenary lot, all-too-willing to connive with malevolent relations to violate the rights of free-born Englishmen (and women). In pamphlets, in the courtroom, in the pages of both the popular and serious press, alienists found themselves traduced, their skills and their motives held up to ridicule, and their livelihoods threatened.

Victorians developed an insatiable appetite for these tales of the sane cast among the lunatic. Almost without exception, the complaining parties were rich, and often socially prominent. Most wrote voluminously of their confinement, to their families' dismay, or else were the subject of one of the wonderfully named Inquisitions in Lunacy undertaken by the Court of Chancery when propertied people were accused of being mad. Not only did these trials produce the sorts of ruinous legal bills so memorably satirized by Charles Dickens in *Bleak House* (1853),[27] but they also took place in open court – and not just in front of a crowd of titillated onlookers, but before tens of thousands of virtual witnesses when the proceedings were mined by journalists for *The Times* and the *Daily Telegraph* (not to mention the gutter press) for juicy bits for gentlemen (and even ladies) to peruse over breakfast.

Perhaps the most socially prominent contributor to this literature was John Perceval (1803–76), son of the only British Prime Minister to be assassinated, Spencer Perceval. The younger Perceval patronized a prostitute while a student at Oxford in 1830. A pious Evangelical Christian, he feared he had contracted syphilis, dosed himself with mercury and soon lapsed into a delusory religious state, leading his family to lock him up, first in Edward Long Fox's madhouse near Bristol, Brislington House, and then in what became the favourite asylum for the English upper classes, Ticehurst House in Sussex. Elaborate as these establishments were, they could not provide accommodations that matched Perceval's expectations. He complained of violence from his attendants, and their failure to display sufficient deference to their distinguished, gentlemanly patient. He was treated, he asserted, as if I were a piece of furniture, an image of wood, incapable of desire or will as well as judgment...men acted as though my body, soul and spirit were fairly given up to their control, to work their mischief and folly upon.... I was fastened down in bed; a meagre diet was ordered for me; this and medicine forced down my throat or in the contrary direction; my will, my wishes, my repugnances, my habits, my delicacy, my inclinations, my necessities, were not once consulted, I may say, thought of. I did not find the respect usually paid even to a child.

Once he had secured his release, to his family's horror, he wrote two accounts of his treatment, only one of them anonymous, and joined with other disaffected former inmates and their relations to form the Alleged Lunatics' Friend Society.[28]

Many of the most prominent complainers were women. In the United States, Elizabeth Packard (1816–97) had been committed to the Illinois State Asylum in Jacksonville by her clergyman-husband in 1860. Illinois law at the time permitted the confinement of married women by their husbands without the independent evidence of insanity required in other cases. Mrs Packard bitterly asserted that she was sane and had simply been confined for holding unorthodox spiritualist views, and on securing her release, launched a multi-state campaign to reform commitment laws, succeeding in persuading several states to pass laws entitling prospective patients to a jury trial. Alienists argued in vain that the result was to equate the mentally ill with accused criminals, and asylums with prisons. The analogies were too close for comfort.

The Reverend Packard was not the only man to live to regret his efforts to shut up a disorderly and assertive female by confining her in a madhouse. The novelist and politician, Sir Edward Bulwer Lytton (1803–73; he of the infamous 'It was a dark and stormy night' opening line), had a strong-willed and spendthrift wife, Lady Rosina (1802–82), of whom he eventually tired. His novels having proved hugely successful, he set up a stable of mistresses. The married couple's domestic bliss was by now over. Bulwer Lytton on occasion beat Rosina, and perhaps sodomized her. They officially separated in 1836, nine years after their marriage. Lady Lytton then began her own career as a writer, much of what she wrote consisting of barely veiled criticism of her estranged husband, and full of her sense of rage and betrayal. He threatened

A portrait of Lady Rosina Bulwer Lytton (unknown artist, Irish School). The demure look was deceptive.

to ruin her if she kept it up. An affair in Dublin cost her custody of her children, and the whole sorry business of a broken Victorian marriage took a further turn for the worse when Lady Lytton discovered that her daughter, dying of typhoid, had been exiled to a down-at-heel boarding house.

Rosina now began to bombard her well-connected husband and his powerful friends with letters filled with obscenities and libels: allegations of adultery and illegitimate offspring, of incest and of cant, and unspecified villainies. She threatened to attend the opening night of Bulwer Lytton's play, *Not So Bad As We Seem*, and pelt the Queen – or the person she referred to as 'the little sensual, Pigheaded Queen' – with rotten eggs. And eventually, in 1858, when Bulwer Lytton stood for re-election as a Member of Parliament at

Hertford, she showed up and denounced him before the electors, haranguing them for nearly an hour.

The response from her angry spouse was immediate: he cut off her allowance (which in any event he had paid only intermittently and with great reluctance) and he denied her access to their son. But then he took a further step, which he would live to regret: obtaining lunacy certificates from two compliant doctors, he had Rosina scooped up in a carriage and carted off to a madhouse run by Robert Gardiner Hill (1811–78), the alienist who ought to have received the credit for abolishing mechanical restraint that instead went to John Conolly, another of Bulwer Lytton's friends.[29] (Lady Rosina tartly commented that Conolly 'would sell his mother for money'.)

If shutting up Rosina was intended to silence her, it had the opposite effect. Bulwer Lytton evidently thought that his many connections – his close friendship with one of the Lunacy Commissioners, John Forster (1812–76), for example, and with the editor of *The Times* (who indeed tried to protect him by suppressing all mention of the scandal) – would keep the whole thing quiet. But *The Times*' great rival, the *Daily Telegraph* (whose very existence, ironically enough, owed much to Bulwer Lytton's efforts to reduce the stamp tax newspapers had to pay), took great delight in pursuing the salacious scandal. Within weeks, Bulwer Lytton, facing an avalanche of bad publicity, had capitulated, releasing his wife on condition that she relocate abroad – something she briefly did, only to return and spend the rest of her life blackening his name, not desisting even after his death from complications following ear surgery.[30]

Degenerates

In France, the crisis of psychiatric legitimacy that flowed both from the failure to cure and from the litany of complaining patients was felt particularly acutely. Through the 1860s and into the 1870s, anti-psychiatric sentiments increased, surfacing in both the liberal and conservative popular press, newly freed from state censorship, in a series of books assaulting alienists' competence and alleged disposition to confine the sane as mad, and in pressure from politicians. In 1864, the prominent alienist Jules Falret (1824–1902) complained that 'the law of 1838 and the asylums for the insane are being attacked on all sides. It is proposed to overturn everything, destroy everything....'[31] Many in the medical profession, doubtful of psychiatric claims to expertise, seemed disposed to join in the chorus of disapproval. Though alienists emphasized that the insane were unpredictably violent, and posed a major threat to society, they were clearly on the defensive.

It was French alienists who found a way forward – a means to reinforce the claim that madness was a medical problem and simultaneously a new justification for confining the mad in asylums. Such was the ideological appeal of these notions that they quickly spread throughout Europe and North America, and influenced public policy and perceptions for generations. In 1857, Bénédict-Augustin Morel (1809–73) published a *Treatise on the Intellectual, Moral, and Physical Degeneracy of the Human Race*. Within a decade or a decade and a half, Morel's ideas were received wisdom. Madness – like other forms of social pathology – was now seen as the product of degeneration and decay. So, far from being the victims of civilization and its stresses, the mad were instead its antithesis, the dregs of society who were a biologically inferior lot. And their inferiority was written clearly in many, if not all cases, on their physiognomy. In the words of Daniel Hack Tuke (1827–95), great-grandson of the founder of the York Retreat, the insane were 'an infirm type of humanity.... On admission "no good" is plainly inscribed on their foreheads.'[32]

Darwin's *On the Origin of Species* appeared in 1859, two years after Morel's *Treatise*. However, it was not to the Darwinian notion of natural selection that the alienists appealed, but to the alternative theory, championed by the Frenchman Jean-Baptiste Lamarck (1744–1829), which stressed the inheritance of acquired characteristics. Adopting this view, madness could be seen as the price of sin – a price sometimes paid not by the original sinner for fornication, excessive drinking or other violations of conventional morality (or 'natural law', as its defenders preferred to see it), but by his or her children, grandchildren or great-grandchildren. It is customary to think of evolution as a progressive force, but this was its supposed darker side: once launched, degeneration would proceed rapidly from generation to generation. Madness, then idiocy, then sterility were the steps on the pathway to the final extinction of these inferior beings, and were the ultimate penalty paid for vice and immorality, because, as Henry Maudsley (1835–1918) wrote in the *Journal of Mental Science* in 1871, 'the so-called moral laws are laws of nature which [men] cannot break, any more than they can break physical laws, without avenging consequences.... As surely as the raindrop is formed and falls in obedience to physical law, so surely do causality and law reign in the production and distribution of morality and immorality [not to mention, I might add, sanity and madness] on earth.'[33]

The received wisdom of an earlier generation about the linkage between civilization and insanity was thus abruptly turned on its head: 'there is most madness where there are the fewest ideas, the simplest feelings, the coarsest desires and ways.'[34] But as ideology, the new theory of degeneration had surpassing virtues for alienists, which perhaps helps to account for the rapidity with which such notions spread and were endorsed. For the profession, these accounts of insanity were couched in terms of physical pathology. Instead of the symptom-based interpretations of madness as melancholia, mania, dementia, and the assorted mono-manias (nymphomania, kleptomania and the like), which an earlier generation of alienists had sought to legitimize, here was a protean explanation of all forms of madness, from its mildest to its most dismal forms, that traced it to defective brains. That those defective brains could not be observed in nature scarcely mattered. That minor problem was the product of what were surely the temporary technical limits of microscopy. The physically deteriorated external appearance of many of those confined in asylums testified eloquently to the forces at work, and was now 'documented' using modern photography. What mattered for alienists was that they had an explanation for madness that corresponded with contemporary developments in medical theory more generally, and that unambiguously rooted lunacy in the body.

More than that, the theory of degeneracy provided a new justification for the isolation of the mad in asylums, and an explanation for psychiatry's apparent therapeutic failings. The problem did not lie in the impotency of the profession, but in the very nature of mental illness itself. Indeed, psychiatry's 'failings' were actually a blessing in disguise, a demonstration that Nature herself embraced Hegel's cunning of reason. Difficult as it might be to confront the harsh realities, psychiatric science had now discovered that

> The subversion of reason involves not only present incompetency,
> but a prospective susceptibility of disease, a proclivity to relapse....
> The mind does not pass out of the ordeal unchanged.... Recovery...
> may be little more than the exercise of great cunning, or self-
> control, in concealing the signs of error and extravagance.[35]

And, once released, worse would surely follow. The mad were, after all, 'tainted creatures', who by definition lacked willpower and self-control. Cast

Hugh W. Diamond (1809–86), superintendent of the Brookwood County Asylum, Surrey, was an early proponent of the use of photography in the treatment of mental disorders. This is one of a series of images he took of patients between 1850 and 1858. The idea that madness might show itself on the countenance had a long history, and photographs of psychiatric patients were a source of great fascination to Darwin.

loose upon an unsuspecting society, they were liable to 'attend upon the calls of their instincts and passions as does the unreasoning beast' and 'to act as parents to the next generation...centres of infection deliberately laid down, and yet we marvel that nervous disease increases'.[36]

Degeneration was invoked to explain far more than insanity alone. All the pathologies of modern life were laid at its door: prostitution, crime, delinquency, alcoholism, suicide, epilepsy, hysteria, feeble-mindedness, the physical deformation of many of the lower classes (in reality a result of want and malnutrition) – what could not be attributed to its ravages?

It was a narrative that fed into fin-de-siècle fears of national decay and decline that were particularly potent in France after the humiliation of its defeat by the Prussians in 1870–71, but felt everywhere, even in Germany itself, as Max Nordau's book *Entartung* (*Degeneration*; 1892), vividly reflects and illustrates.[37] (The book provoked much controversy – it was mocked by the Harvard philosopher and psychologist William James – and ironically, since Nordau was a Jew and a Zionist, its ideas were later borrowed by the Nazis.) But nowhere was the theory of degeneration more powerful than in the realm of madness, where 'psychiatric science' was mobilized to lend it seeming substance.

Artistic Licence

In spreading these notions of a biologically rooted social menace, whose most extreme manifestations were uncontrollable passions, violence and madness, nothing was more influential than the fiction of Émile Zola, and more particularly his twenty-novel cycle, *Les Rougon-Macquart*. Though it has obvious echoes on one level of Balzac's *La Comédie humaine*, Zola's focus was much narrower: not the grand sweep of contemporary society, but the history of a single family, and a family, as he put it in the preface to *La Fortune des Rougon* (1871), marked and marred by 'their ravenous appetite', and one whose physically rooted fate he plans to trace 'through the slow succession of accidents pertaining to the nerves or the blood, which befall a race after the first organic [hysterical] lesion', leading irrevocably on to sexual depravity, incest, murder and madness. Excess and decay are everywhere, in the drunkenness of *L'Assommoir* (1877), the prostitution and debauchery of *Nana* (1880), the murder and madness that inhabit the pages of *Thérèse Raquin*. Primitive, uncontrolled passion overwhelms conscience and rational constraint, and, like puppets, Zola's characters act out their biologically based destiny.

Thérèse Raquin is one of the first novels in the series, published in 1867, just a decade after Morel's *Treatise* on degeneration. Thérèse's marriage to a cousin, Camille, whom she has grown up alongside, is near-incestuous and forced by her aunt. Soon she embarks on a torrid affair with one of her husband's childhood friends, and when their trysts are threatened, the two take Camille out on a boat trip and drown him, passing his death off as an accident. Nightmares and hallucinations about Camille and his death struggles threaten to drive the two lovers insane. Meantime, Camille's mother, with whom they live, has suffered a succession of strokes, the second of which leaves all but her eyes paralysed. The lovers quarrel in front of her and reveal their guilt, about which the wretched mother can do little save spit hate through her gaze. Ultimately, however, racked with remorse, the two murderers plot each other's death, realize what each has in mind, and end their torment by both taking poison, dying in front of the implacable Madame Raquin, who has her revenge at last.

The violence, sexual passion and madness that haunt the pages of this novel are a recurrent feature of the *Rougon-Macquart* series, and the explicitness of Zola's prose provoked much controversy at the time. It scarcely hurt sales, however, and Zola's fiction thus did much to articulate the abstractions of the theory of degeneration for a wider audience. All the travails of his characters, their descent into madness and suicide, can ultimately be traced back to the seemingly trivial mental flaws of an eighteenth-century ancestor, Adelaide Fouque. Down through the generations, that original deficiency produces, as Morel had argued it would, ever-greater levels of pathology. The surfacing of primitive instincts, passions and physical aggression fills the pages of the novels, with the inevitable accompaniments of alcoholism, epileptic seizures, hysteria, idiocy, madness and death.

The very title of *La Bête humaine* (1890) signals what is to come. Tics and convulsions, the involuntary spasms of the body, have their psychological counterparts in instinctive and impulsive actions, driven by passions that escape the control of reason. Of one of the anti-heroes, Jacques Lantier, we learn that: 'Toujours le désir l'avait rendu fou, il voyait rouge.' ('Desire had always driven him mad, he saw red.') Attacking the object of his desire, he tears her blouse open. 'Then, gasping for breath, he stopped, looked at her instead of possessing her. A fury seemed to take hold of him.' But on this occasion, he flees. His constitution is such that he can't help himself: 'c'étaient dans son être, de subites pertes d'équilibre, comme des cassures, des trous par lesquels son moi lui échappait au milieu d'une sorte de grande fumée qui déformait tout. Il ne s'appartenait plus, il obéissait à ses muscles, à la bête enragée.' ('[I]t was in his being, sudden losses of equilibrium, like cracks, holes through which his true self escaped from him in the midst of a sort of thick smoke that deformed everything. He no longer belonged to himself, he obeyed his muscles, the enraged beast.') Ultimately, Lantier murders one of the objects of his desire, but his is scarcely the only such crime. On the contrary, the debauched and degenerate characters that populate the tale lay waste around them, with jealousy, lust, greed and drink leading inexorably to violence, murder, suicide, the death of innocents.

Though no other novelist explored these degenerationist ideas with the same intensity and sustained attention as Zola, they surfaced in fiction and drama all across Europe. Gerhart Hauptmann's *Vor Sonnenaufgang* (*Before Sunrise*; 1889) put the degeneration of a peasant family, fuelled by alcohol, on stage, and launched a career that would bring its author a Nobel Prize in Literature. More explicit still was Arthur Schnitzler's *Reigen* (1900), best known to English-speaking audiences by its French title, *La Ronde*, which presents life in turn-of-the-century Vienna through a series of sexual encounters: prostitute and soldier; soldier and parlour maid; parlour maid and young gentleman; young gentleman and young wife; husband and little miss; little miss and poet; poet and actress; actress and count; and the count back in bed with the prostitute – the sub-text being the spread of syphilis one to another. Though the play sold briskly in print, the Viennese censors promptly banned it from the stage, and it was not performed in public until December 1920 in Berlin, and the following February in Vienna. Even at that later date, its sardonic view of the human condition drew violent reactions, and its author was attacked as a Jewish pornographer. Schnitzler felt compelled to withdraw permission for further performances in German-speaking countries, though the gesture did not stop him becoming a major target for Austrian anti-Semites. (Hitler would later hold his work up as a prime example of 'Jewish filth' masquerading as art.)

British sensationalist fiction of the same era drew heavily on similar examples of 'shocking subject matter – mental instability, moral insanity, venereal disease, and their threat to the sanctity and purity of marriage and family'.[38] But the contaminating effects of defective heredity and their dire consequences on human fates surface in more serious literary work, too, and nowhere more so than in Thomas Hardy's novels. In *Tess of the d'Urbervilles* (1891), Tess's connections to the degenerate d'Urbervilles, for example, drive her on, helplessly, into the abyss, towards murder and her ruin. 'I can't help it', she cries, and indeed she cannot. When Tess's father, John Durbeyfield, learns that he is descended from Sir John d'Urberville, the foolish man takes it as a mark of distinction. In fact, his lowly status embodies the very notion of degeneration, the irresistible decline from wealth, status and power to a place among the peasantry.

5 ABOVE *In one of his earliest woodcuts, and the oldest surviving image of the disease, Albrecht Dürer depicts a syphilitic man (1496). The orb above the man's head hints at an astrological cause of the affliction, and it was only centuries later that syphilis was connected with certain mental disorders.*

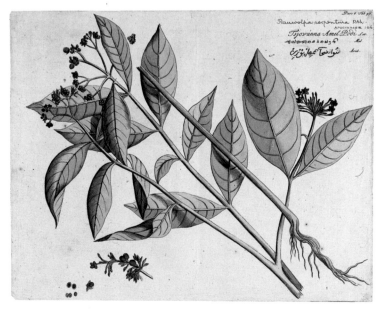

Helleborus niger humilifolius.

26 OPPOSITE ABOVE
A *poisonous plant in the buttercup family, black hellebore* (Helleborus niger) *was reputed to have anti-maniacal properties, and was employed from ancient Greek times by both physicians and folk healers as a cure for madness.*

27 OPPOSITE BELOW
Rauvolfia serpentina, *or Indian Snakeroot, was used as a remedy for insanity (among other illnesses) in Indian medicine. An alkaloid isolated from it was introduced to Western psychiatry as reserpine in the 1950s, but was soon superseded by other drugs.*

28 ABOVE Ward of the Madwomen at San Bonifacio's Hospital, Florence *(1865), by Telemaco Signorini. San Bonifacio's Hospital was founded in Florence in 1377, becoming an asylum for the insane in the eighteenth century under the rule of Grand Duke Pietro Leopoldo I.*

29 ABOVE Corral de locos *or* The Yard of a Madhouse *(1793–94), by Francisco Goya. Goya painted this scene when he feared he was going mad. A bleak and disturbing vision, it depicts two naked inmates fighting, while their keeper beats them – a pitiless picture, full of suffering and redolent of the hopelessness of lost reason.*

30 RIGHT *Phrenological busts belonging to Jean-Martin Charcot, the French neurologist who specialized in the treatment of hysteria. The idea of the localization of brain function, central to the phrenological theories of Franz Joseph Gall and Johann Spurzheim, exercised a continuing hold on the neurological imagination.*

31 BELOW *Franz Joseph Gall examines the head of an attractive young woman, while three gentlemen wait their turn to have their own characters read, in a satirical image published in 1825.*

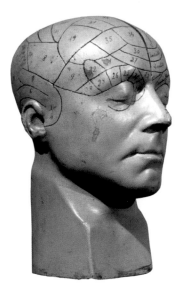

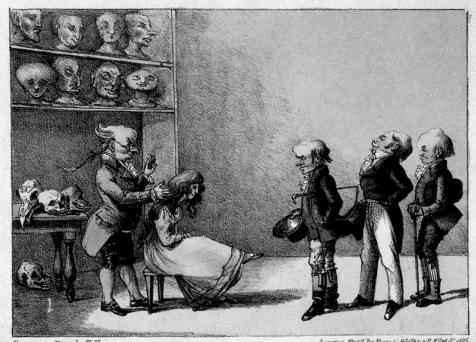

Drawn on Stone by E.H.

London Pub.d by Rowe & Waller 49 Fleet St. 1825.

THE PHRENOLOGIST.

32 ABOVE *Richard Dadd's portrait of Sir Alexander Morison (1852) shows the careworn physician to Bedlam in the countryside outside his Scottish estate, a landscape Dadd knew only from sketches.*

33 RIGHT *Dr Félix Rey treated Vincent van Gogh when he was confined for madness in the hospital in Arles, and the artist painted his portrait (1889) as an act of gratitude, though Rey pronounced himself 'simply horrified' by it.*

34 OPPOSITE *Portrait of Dr Heinrich Stadelmann (1922), by Otto Dix. Stadelmann was a psychiatrist, hypnotist and specialist in the treatment of nervous disorders.*

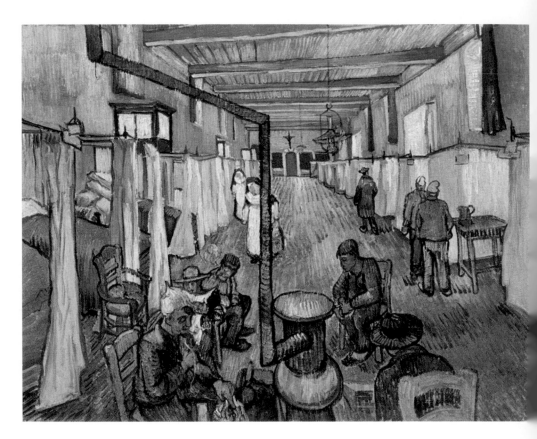

35 ABOVE The Ward in the Hospital at Arles *(1889)*, *by Vincent van Gogh. Van Gogh first stayed here briefly following the episode in December 1888 when he cut off part of his left ear, and was then hospitalized again in February 1889. He painted the ward scene in April, while living in rooms owned by his doctor, Félix Rey.*

The d'Urbervilles are nearly extinct. Tess and her father are the last of the breed, just as the theory of biological decline requires. Tess resembles the portraits of aristocratic d'Urberville women, but in her the resemblance is full of foreboding, for it masks a fatal flaw. On the night of her wedding to a clergyman's son-turned-farmer, Angel Clare, he confesses to a prior affair, and she in turn reveals that she is not a virgin, not from any prior indiscretion but because she was raped by Alec, the libertine son of the man who purchased the right to the d'Urberville name. Angel cannot forgive her for this 'sin', and soon abandons her, leaving on an ill-fated journey to Brazil.

Hardy undoubtedly intended a damning criticism of sexual double-standards in this portion of his plot. But the theme of degeneration nonetheless runs all through the novel. As Angel bitterly informs Tess, in his eyes her problems stem ultimately from her family. 'Decrepit families imply decrepit wills, decrepit conduct.... Here was I thinking you a new-sprung child of nature; there were you, the belated seedling of an effete aristocracy.' And an aristocratic family with murder in its past: Angel is aware that one of her ancestors 'committed a dreadful crime in his family coach', and her rapist, Alec d'Urberville, later informs Tess that the man 'is said to have abducted some beautiful young woman, who tried to escape from the coach in which he was carrying her off, and in the struggle he killed her – or she killed him – I forget which'. Tess eventually gives in to Alec's importunings and his assurances that her husband is gone forever, and becomes his mistress, only for a chastened Angel to return.

The doomed woman 'can't help it'. To free herself, she plunges a knife into Alec, and flees to her husband, and the ill-assorted couple manage a few days of bliss. Then, however, desperate and forced from their temporary hiding place, they take refuge overnight at Stonehenge. Like a sacrificial victim, Tess lies down to sleep on a stone altar. Next morning, it is over. In the high-priced lodgings where she murdered Alec d'Urberville, the evidence of her crime has swiftly manifested itself: 'The oblong white ceiling, with this scarlet blot in the midst, had the appearance of a gigantic ace of hearts.' The landlady discovers the corpse. Tracked and surrounded by the police, Tess wakens to face her fate: confinement in Wintoncester (Winchester) prison, and death on the gallows. Her execution is announced to the world, and to her husband, when a black flag is raised to symbolize her successful hanging. Her death extinguishes the degenerate d'Urberville lineage. Its decline and fall are now complete.

Then there is Ibsen's *Ghosts* (1882), with its unblinking focus on drunkenness, incest, congenital syphilis and madness. It shocked the sensibilities of its bourgeois audience, even as it laid bare their hypocrisies. The Alvings are a rich and respectable family. Captain Alving, though a brutal philanderer, is a man his wife cannot leave, as the local clergyman tells her, on pain of social disgrace. On the captain's death, she resolves to build an orphanage. Ostensibly the extravagant act of charity is to honour her husband's memory, but in reality she aims to deplete his estate, for she wishes their son, Oswald, to inherit as little as possible, financially and otherwise, from his degenerate father. But Oswald has already inherited something else: congenital syphilis. Moreover, he has fallen in love with the family maid, Regina Engstrand, who is in reality his half-sister, the product of one of his father's many affairs. Rotten to the core, physically and morally, Oswald Alving is the living embodiment of degeneracy, and his mother, more concerned with appearances and upholding conventional morality than with truth, is finally forced to confront what her devotion to 'duty' has wrought.

Deliberately offensive, Ibsen's drama drew the heated response he must have expected. At a reception in his honour, the scandalized King of Sweden told him to his face that it was a very bad play. Ibsen was unabashed. When it was produced in translation, the critic at the *Daily Chronicle* denounced it as 'revoltingly suggestive and blasphemous'; his counterpart at the *Era* thought it 'as foul and filthy a concoction as has ever been allowed to disgrace the boards of an English theatre'. Not to be outdone, the *Daily Telegraph*, ever the bellwether of bourgeois sensibilities, duly pronounced itself outraged. *Ghosts* was a 'disgusting representation...of an open drain, of a loathsome sore unbandaged, of a dirty act done publicly...gross, and almost putrid indecorum...literary carrion'. The theory of degeneration was wonderful, it seems, so long as it was used to explain lower-class pathology and madness – but not so wonderful when it trained its sights on the moral middle classes.

Ironically, given his own embrace of degenerationist ideas, Zola found himself one of a panoply of literary figures traduced by Nordau as degenerate artists. Some chose to glory in the label. Perversity, the unclean and the unnatural are embraced, and convention flouted: consider the cases of Baudelaire, Rimbaud or Oscar Wilde, or Toulouse-Lautrec's evocations of the decadent Parisian demi-monde. Many lived the part. Baudelaire and his mistress, the Haitian Jeanne Duval, both died of syphilis, as did Maupassant and Nietzsche, who ended their days mad besides.[39] Then there was 'le fou roux', the red-headed madman, Vincent van Gogh, whose paintings of alienists, patients and asylums we have already encountered. Alcoholism, epilepsy, recurrent venereal infections, serial involvement with prostitutes and brothels, madness, confinement in an asylum, self-mutilation and suicide – a poster boy for degenerationists, his art appreciated only after his premature death.

Of course, the idea of modern art and artists as degenerate lived on into the twentieth century. Hitler hated Expressionist art and its offspring, denouncing them as the product of the racially impure and a betrayal of the 'Greco-Nordic' tradition. In 1937, on Hitler's orders, *entartete Kunst*, 'degenerate art', both painting and sculpture, was seized and brought to Munich. In all, 15,997 pieces were assembled, from which the works of 112 artists were selected and shown in an 'Exhibition of Degenerate Art', arranged as a demonstration of the perfidious impact of Bolsheviks and Jews on the creative arts. Thousands of the confiscated art works, by Picasso, Braque, Kandinsky, Gauguin, Mondrian and others, were subsequently burned – though others were sold off for profit.

Dealing with the Depraved

For the fate of the insane, the message of the shift towards degenerationist ideas was clear. William Booth (1829–1912), the first General of the Salvation Army, announced it in suitably apocalyptic tones. Once it has been

> recognized that he has become a lunatic, morally demented,
> incapable of self-government...upon him, therefore, must be
> passed the sentence of permanent seclusion from a world
> in which he is not fit to be at large.... It is a crime against the
> race to allow those who are so inveterately depraved the freedom
> to wander abroad, infect their fellows, prey upon Society and
> to multiply their kind.[40]

The construction of massive museums of madness had not waited upon the theory of degeneration, but in the aftermath of the spread of these notions, asylums began to burst their previous bounds. The London authorities built asylums for 2,000 patients and more at Caterham and Leavesden, at Darenth, Sutton and Tooting, to augment the huge asylums they were already responsible for at Hanwell, Colney Hatch, Banstead and Cane Hill. When that did not suffice, they built another vast constellation of buildings at Claybury in Essex, and another at Bexley. Still it did not seem to meet the demand. A thousand-acre site near Epsom was purchased, and no fewer than five barracks-asylums built to contain upwards of 12,000 patients.

Such mammoth asylums, with their own water-supply, police force, fire brigade, electric generators, graveyards and the like – everything required to serve the needs of patients from admission to the grave – were scarcely a British monopoly. In Vienna, for example, the Austrian authorities opened a new asylum, Am Steinhof, in 1907, with sixty 'pavilions' spread over a vast site, laid out for 2,200 patients and soon housing more. In Germany, asylums were often larger still. Bielefeld in North-Rhine Westphalia, for example, housed more than 5,000 patients – inmates might be a more accurate term. In the United States, Milledgeville in Georgia resembled a not-so-small town, with upwards of 14,000 residents. But even this was dwarfed by developments on Long Island, New York, where a cluster of asylums (or mental hospitals, as their rulers now preferred to call them) was constructed: Central Islip, Kings Park and Pilgrim housed more than 30,000 of New York's mad.

On one level, psychiatrists (a label we can now use without anachronism) were autocratic masters of these self-contained worlds. On another level, however, psychiatrists soon found that their apparent therapeutic impotence and their embrace of degenerationist ideas, coupled with popular scepticism about their ability to distinguish the mad from the sane in a reliable fashion, placed them in a highly precarious position. Mainstream medicine, with the advent of germ theory, aseptic surgery and the laboratory, saw its prestige and prospects improve by leaps and bounds. In the first part of the nineteenth century, amid the optimism of the early years and the security the superintendency of an asylum had provided, ministering to the mentally ill had seemed an attractive career. By the last third of the century, it was anything but.

In many ways, psychiatrists were trapped in their custodial institutions every bit as much as their patients, and they also shared in the stigma heaped upon the mentally ill (a stigma that their own insistence that most mental illness was a biologically rooted social menace helped, of course, to reinforce). With the sole exception of Germany, where a different model prevailed (discussed below), the insularity of the profession was reflected in the absence of any substantial connection to medical schools or the potent symbols of modern scientific medicine. Recruitment was by means of an apprenticeship as a poorly paid assistant physician (one of a whole hierarchy of assistants as asylums grew in size), an induction into a dull administrative specialty that to many contemporary critics seemed more concerned with such matters as running the asylum farm and the disposal of sewage than with investigating and treating mental illness.

Psychiatrists were, sneered the New York neurologist Edward Spitzka (1852–1914) in 1878, 'experts at everything but the diagnosis, pathology, and treatment of insanity'.[41] In unguarded moments, the profession's leaders confessed as much. Bedford Pierce (1861–1932), superintendent of the York Retreat, spoke of the 'humiliating reflection' that '[i]t is not possible as yet to make a scientific classification of mental disorders.'[42] David Ferrier (1843–1928), among the most distinguished of Victorian students of the physiology of the brain, who had spent his early years at the West Riding Lunatic Asylum in Yorkshire, noted sombrely that

> Much has been written on the symptomology and classification
> of the various forms of insanity, but I think we really know
> nothing with regard to the physical conditions underlying those
> manifestations…we cannot be said to possess any real knowledge…[43]

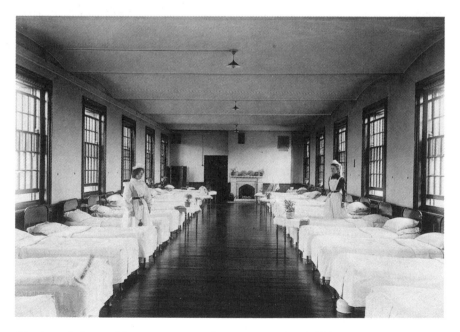

Claybury Asylum in Essex was a vast colony for more than 2,000 lunatics, with several hundred staff. Here (1893) we see a typical dormitory, with beds along both walls and starched nurses standing rigidly to attention; patients are conspicuously absent.

A decade and a half later, in 1907, when he rose to address America's assembled psychiatrists as their president, Charles Hill was still more succinct: 'our therapeutics', he acknowledged, 'are simply a pile of rubbish'.[44]

The Roots of Madness

Only in Germany had there been some serious attempt to elaborate an alternative pathway for the profession, and to conduct determined and sustained research on the aetiology of insanity. German psychiatry had, during the second half of the nineteenth century, sought to emulate the approach that had served to vault German general medicine to the forefront of the world. German unification had remained incomplete until 1870, and in the middle years of the nineteenth century, many principalities had chosen to compete for visibility and prestige through underwriting universities, the advance of science conferring lustre on those who served as its patrons. Exploiting this largesse, their academic institutes had become knowledge-factories, propelling German science and medicine into the lead internationally. University-based clinics and institutes brought together teaching and research in novel ways, and created a culture that did much to revolutionize the understanding of disease and to establish the centrality of the laboratory and the microscope in the generation of new knowledge.

It was this model that German psychiatry adopted. The Germans had the same barracks-asylums as everyone else, but beginning with the appointment of Wilhelm Griesinger (1817–68) as professor of psychiatry in Berlin in 1865, they also had smaller clinics attached to universities, where intensive research could proceed. Most of Griesinger's career had been devoted to internal medicine, though he had authored an influential textbook of psychiatry as early as 1845. A revised edition appeared in 1861, to great acclaim, and Griesinger's insistence that 'patients with so-called "mental illnesses" are really individuals with illnesses of the nerves and brain'[45] became the guiding principle for the next generation. Griesinger's death from a ruptured appendix, aged only fifty-one, did nothing to derail the spread of the approach he had pioneered.

In the decades that followed, German psychiatrists seemed to be engaging in the same sorts of research as their colleagues in general medicine, and in certain respects their results were impressive, helping perhaps to persuade alienists elsewhere to adopt the German term for their specialty. Detailed studies were conducted on the anatomy of the brain and the spinal cord. New techniques for fixing and staining cells for microscopic examination were pioneered. At times, these led to discoveries that demonstrated that some of the inhabitants of the vast asylums were indeed suffering from illnesses rooted in their brains. In 1906 in Germany, Alois Alzheimer (1864–1915) detected the plaques and neurofibrillary tangles that were associated with the form of dementia that now bears his name, and in 1913 in the United States, Hideyo Noguchi (1876–1928) and J. W. Moore definitively demonstrated what had been suspected for two decades and more, that General Paralysis of the Insane (GPI) was in fact a tertiary stage of syphilis. The identification of the syphilitic spirochetes in the brains of paretics, as those suffering from GPI were often called, removed all reasonable doubt.[46]

These linkages between mental symptoms and underlying tissue pathology served to reinforce the sense that biological researches might help to uncover the aetiology of madness, but for the overwhelming bulk of mental illness, the hypothesized brain lesions remained as elusive as ever. Worse still, the discovery of Alzheimer's disease and of the syphilitic origins of GPI tended to reinforce rather than alleviate the pessimism and despondency that enveloped the psychiatric profession. Like the pathologists who had pioneered hospital medicine in early nineteenth-century Paris, and helped to bring the West's long infatuation with humoral medicine to a close, these German clinicians had little interest in the messy business of treating and curing patients. Asylums for them were simply a source of pathological specimens for the dissecting table and the microscope. Living patients were of no interest, and they were essentially abandoned to their fate.

There was one important exception to this generalization. Among this generation of German psychiatrists was one, Emil Kraepelin (1856–1926), whose poor eyesight essentially precluded him from pursuing a laboratory-based career. Instead, he built his fame on an examination of the fate of the thousands upon thousands of patients who thronged Germany's asylums, looking at mental illness as a natural historian might, searching for patterns in their pathology, and attempting to construct inductively a descriptive list or classification – a nosology – of different types of madness. Embodied in the successive editions of an increasingly influential textbook, the conclusions he drew from his endless note-cards was that madness could be sub-divided into two basic types: a pernicious, probably permanent condition that fol-lowed a deteriorating course with little prospect of improvement, dementia

Emil Kraepelin photographed in 1926: the 'great Pope' of psychiatry, as Freud sarcastically called him.

praecox; and a slightly more hopeful residual diagnosis – because it was a sometimes remitting form of mental illness – manic-depressive psychosis.

Complex nosologies had everywhere been a feature of much psychiatry in the nineteenth century. Seeking to differentiate their esoteric knowledge from the shared assumptions that ordinary members of society had long implicitly relied upon to distinguish the mad from the sane, alienists had invented the monomanias and such concepts as moral insanity. The latter was a condition in which someone retained the ability to reason, but exhibited 'a morbid perversion of the natural feelings, affections, inclinations, temper, habits, moral dispositions, and natural impulses'.[47] Often greeted with scepticism by both the courts and the public, doctrines like these fed a persistent disquiet that manifested itself in periodic spasms of anxiety lest the amorphous boundary between madness and sanity were to be exploited so as to equate any deviation from conventional moral and social standards with insanity. For clinicians, these verbal gymnastics raised a different set of problems: they were all but impossible to apply in practice. With characteristic asperity, the English alienist Henry Maudsley spoke scathingly of 'the numerous and elaborate classifications which, in almost distracting succession, have been formally proposed as exhaustive and tacitly condemned as useless...the many learned names...which have been invented in appalling numbers to denote simple things'.[48]

Kraepelin's version was different, or purported to be, since it claimed to be inductively derived from clinical experience. It quickly began to become more complex – dementia praecox was sub-divided into hebephrenic, catatonic and paranoid forms – and it was unstable in practice. A patient who recovered might have his or her diagnosis adjusted to manic-depressive psychosis, while one who stubbornly failed to recover might well be re-labelled a case of dementia praecox, a diagnostic label that was soon modified by the Swiss psychiatrist Eugen Bleuler (1857–1939), who in 1910 introduced the term 'schizophrenia' – literally, a splitting of the mind. Here was a disorder whose characteristic symptoms were a parade of disasters: incoherence, agitation, an inability to form relationships with others, badly disordered thought processes that extended to delusions and hallucinations, before an eventual decline into a grossly denuded mental universe, a dementia alluded to by Kraepelin in his initial name for the disorder. There was nothing here to lighten the gloom engulfing psychiatry and its patients.

The very language used to refer to those suffering from madness is indicative of the harshness with which they were viewed. A British psychiatrist lamented that degenerates were born every year 'with pedigrees that would condemn puppies to [drowning in] the horsepond'.[49] The mentally ill were referred to as 'tainted persons', 'lepers', 'moral refuse', 'ten times more vicious and noxious, and infinitely less capable of improvement, than the savages of primitive barbarism', and endowed with 'special repulsive characters'[50] – and this by the very people who claimed to be in the business of treating them. There were not-so-sotto voce comments that lamented that the softheartedness that came with increased civilization had interfered with 'the operation of those laws which weed out and exterminate the diseased and otherwise unfit in every grade of natural life'.[51] Others spoke darkly of 'purging the blood of races of living poisons'.[52]

One consequence of the vogue for this sort of thinking was the rise of eugenics, the effort to rein in the propensity of the poor and the defective to breed, and to encourage reproduction by the better sort. It was an idea that attracted leading intellectuals including Francis Galton (Darwin's cousin), George Bernard Shaw, H. G. Wells and John Maynard Keynes, as well as the distinguished American economist Irving Fisher, not to mention Winston Churchill and Woodrow Wilson. Many American states passed laws attempting to prohibit the marriage of the mentally unfit, and in some instances providing for their involuntary sterilization, to preclude the birth of yet more defectives. Eventually, in 1927, a challenge to these sterilizations, the case of *Buck v. Bell*, reached the United States Supreme Court. The majority resoundingly ruled 8-1 that there was no constitutional obstacle to the involuntary sterilization of an American citizen. Oliver Wendell Holmes, Jr, widely regarded as one of the most eminent jurists in the nation's history, was assigned the task of writing the opinion, and ringingly endorsed the state's position: 'It is better for all the world', he wrote, 'if instead of waiting to execute degenerate offspring for crime, or to let them starve for their imbecility, society can prevent those who are manifestly unfit from continuing their kind. The principle that sustains compulsory vaccination is broad enough to cover cutting Fallopian tubes.... Three generations of imbeciles are enough.'[53] Forty of the then forty-eight American states would have compulsory sterilization statutes on their books by 1940, though only a handful implemented them in any serious fashion, the progressive state of California prominent among them.

Elsewhere, the opposition of religious groups and the checks and balances of a democratic polity inhibited the enactment and enforcement of similar laws. But that was not the case in Nazi Germany. Ideas of racial 'purity' were at the heart, of course, of Nazi ideology. Notable German psychiatrists had been enthusiastic proponents of eugenics in the 1920s, and had not scrupled to draw logical conclusions from their belief that mental patients were hopeless inferior biological specimens. As early as 1920, the German psychiatrist Alfred Hoche (1863–1943) and his jurist colleague Karl Binding (1841–1920) had called for the suppression of 'lives unworthy of living'. Almost immediately after coming to power, in July 1933, Hitler secured the passage of the Law for the Prevention of Hereditarily Diseased Offspring, explicitly modelled on California and Virginia precedents.[54] With the active and enthusiastic participation of many leading German psychiatrists, 300,000

The staff at Hadamar, c. 1940–42, a psychiatric hospital used in the T-4 euthanasia programme, relaxed and happy after a hard day at work disposing of those the Nazis considered 'unworthy of living'.

to 400,000 people were sterilized between 1934 and 1939.[55] Then, in October 1939, Hitler issued a decree launching the so-called T-4 programme. Again, psychiatrists enthusiastically joined in implementing the new policy: the mentally ill –'useless eaters' in Nazi terminology – were rounded up and sent to a number of mental hospitals. There they were 'disinfected', that is exterminated, initially by means of lethal injection or shooting, and when that proved too slow and cumbersome, gas chambers were constructed, and they were herded into 'showers' to be murdered with carbon monoxide. More than 70,000 perished in a year and a half, as many as a quarter of a million by war's end – indeed, beyond the end, for even after the fall of the Nazi regime, and unbeknownst to the occupying powers, some psychiatrists continued to kill more of those they regarded as 'tainted persons'.[56] Madness in civilization indeed!

Chapter Nine

THE DEMI-FO*US*

Avoiding the Asylum

The earliest profit-making madhouses had found their primary market among the rich and well-to-do. That should scarcely occasion surprise. In the immortal if possibly apocryphal words of the American bank robber Willie Sutton, that was where the money was. Still, it was a paradoxical state of affairs, for until the close of the nineteenth century and the advances associated with the invention of aseptic surgical techniques, the rich avoided hospital treatment for physical illness like the plague. It was the poor and those reduced to poverty who were treated in general hospitals, while the rich opted for treatment at home.

That abhorrence of the institution did not disappear when it came to the management of madness. Victorian letters, diaries and autobiographies are full of evidence that their authors feared asylums and had low expectations about the kinds of care their relations would receive in such places. Money could pay for alternatives, and there was considerable temptation to resort to them: building a cottage to confine an insane relative on a secluded portion of an aristocratic estate and hiring the necessary staff; placing the disturbed in single lodgings (St John's Wood in London became a favourite place for such establishments, having the extra advantage of easy access to the advice of discreet society physicians – its reputation as a haven for such illicit confinement was exploited by Wilkie Collins in his novel, *The Woman in White*, 1859);[1] or patients could simply be sent abroad, beyond the reach of prying official eyes and to places that provided some additional protection against the possibility of gossip, scandal and stigma.[2] French and Swiss asylums, for example, advertised openly in London and Paris in an effort to attract such custom.

Perhaps the most striking example of the resort to such expedients is provided by the case of Anthony Ashley Cooper, from 1851 the 7th Earl of Shaftesbury. Shaftesbury served as chairman of the English Lunacy Commission from its founding in 1845 until his death in 1885, and in that capacity promoted the asylum as the sole appropriate response to cases of insanity. Testifying before a parliamentary enquiry in 1859 into the operation of the English lunacy laws, he observed that, were his wife or daughter to become mentally deranged, he would at once arrange for her admission to a modern asylum, which provided the best possible environment for humane care and cure. His choice of relations was perhaps deliberate, because his behaviour did not match his public proclamations. His third son, Maurice, was epileptic and mentally disturbed. Despite his lifelong and vociferous opposition to the practice, Shaftesbury had him secretly and privately confined, and when there was a prospect that this situation might become public, he sent him abroad to confinement, first in the Netherlands and latterly in Lausanne, Switzerland, where the poor young man subsequently died in 1855, aged just twenty.

Affluent families were often willing to go to extraordinary lengths before opting for the confinement of their mentally disturbed relations. Two cases drawn from the casebooks of England's most socially exclusive private asylum, Ticehurst, must suffice to make the point.[3] Mrs Anne Farquhar, described as a gentlewoman, had suffered a fall in 1844 while pregnant. Gradually, she then withdrew into the role of an invalid, finally taking to her bed on a full-time basis some time in 1854 or 1855. She now developed a morbid fear of falling out of the 'very large' bed to which she had retired. The servants were therefore ordered to pile 'tables, sofas, chairs, etc' around it to guard against the eventuality. Nor was this her only eccentricity:

> She has laid in bed for the last three years and not allowed herself
> to be properly washed or attended to – body and bed linen not
> changed for months – hands and arms begrimed with dried faeces
> – shutters and windows tightly closed – curtains drawn around
> her bed – a large fire in hot weather, none in cold – covered with
> dirty shawls and old flannel petticoats...sleeps the greater part of
> the day and keeps awake at night, takes her food, which she eats
> more like an animal than a human being at all hours night and day
> – generally chews her animal food and spits it out.

And so on. For years, 'she has either been visited by or been under the care of the most eminent medical men in England', all the while without ever being officially certified as insane. Besides their complaisance about Mrs Farquhar's mental state, the society physicians had not done much for her physical health: on admission to Ticehurst, she was filthy, covered in boils, jaundiced and constipated.[4] Even the Ticehurst staff, inured to the problem of dealing with incontinent patients, found this case a difficult one. Three days after the event, the attendants who had fetched her from her home in Blackheath, southeast of London, still complained of nausea brought on by the experience of entering her room.

Or take the case of Charles de Vere Beauclerk, an old Etonian who was descended from an illegitimate son of Charles II and Nell Gwyn. In his early twenties, Beauclerk began to manifest paranoid delusions that his parents were out to poison him. A mental specialist having pronounced him 'mentally unsound', his parents employed the usual expedient of sending him off to the colonies, where he ran up large gambling debts. When he fetched up in Australia they purchased a military commission for him, and thinking him somewhat improved, used their connections to have him transferred to serve as aide de camp to Lord Elgin, the Viceroy of India. It was a rather spectacular misjudgment because his obvious mental peculiarities threatened to cause a scandal, and the parents hastily arranged for Charles to return to England. Soon, he attracted unwanted attention when he attempted to sue his father, the 10th Duke of St Albans, for causing him to go bald. His eccentricities multiplied: he became wholly inactive and ate four or five portions at every meal; mercifully, however, he slept most of the time. Insulated by their great wealth, the family contrived to keep him at home, until the Duke's death in 1898 forced their hand. Charles, now the 11th Duke, was formally certified as insane and sent to Ticehurst Asylum, where he remained till his death in 1934, 'without issue' as *Debrett's Peerage* delicately put it.

Violence, the fear of a mad relative squandering family money, simple exhaustion brought on by trying to cope with difficult or impossible relations, or an event that threatened to expose the family secret – all these might eventually lead even the wealthiest families to embrace an institutional alternative to domestic care. As mental illness came to be explained by alienists as the product of degeneration and biological inferiority, the need to disguise the presence of the taint of insanity in the family bloodlines became more urgent, though difficult to sustain. So too did the temptation to opt for something short of an asylum: a sanatorium, a private or hydropathic clinic, a nursing home, or an inebriate asylum – anything that provided a fig-leaf against the imputation of insanity. Despite the depth of the novelist Virginia Woolf's (1882–1941) disturbance, and previous periods when she was known to be suicidal, her psychiatrist George Savage (1842–1921) sent her to Burley, a nursing home in Twickenham, rather than subject her to the stigma of commitment to an asylum. She returned there on several subsequent occasions when her disturbed state could no longer be managed at home, even with the four nurses she and her husband, Leonard, had hired to cope with her anorexia, insomnia and depression. Such establishments for the treatment of the nervous proliferated all across Europe during the nineteenth century, particularly in spa towns such as Lamalou-les-Bains in France and Baden-Baden in Germany, where 'nervous' patients could be said to be off taking the waters.[5] Queen Victoria, Kaiser Wilhelm I, Napoleon III,

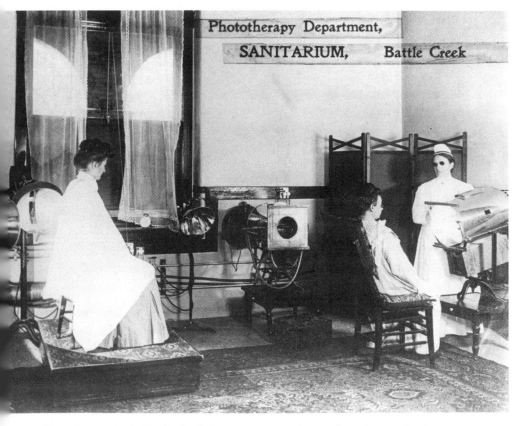

Phototherapy at the Battle Creek Sanitarium, one of many therapies on offer there.

Hector Berlioz, Fyodor Dostoevsky, Johannes Brahms and Ivan Turgenev were only the most prominent of the many celebrities who came to Baden-Baden.

Similar establishments began to appear in the United States as well. The largest and most successful of these was located in Battle Creek, Michigan. The Battle Creek Sanitarium (the changed spelling was a calculated marketing device) had begun inauspiciously. It was created as the Western Health Reform Institute by Ellen White, a founder of one of the multitude of new religions or religious denominations that sprang up in the United States during the nineteenth century, the Seventh-day Adventist Church, but struggled till it was taken over by two of her followers, the Kellogg brothers, John Harvey and William. Though the original building burned to the ground in 1902, it was rebuilt, renamed and greatly enlarged (PL. 36). The 106 patients it had attracted in 1866 were swamped by the 7,006 who patronized it in 1906. Eventually it attracted all sorts of affluent and nervous patients, who came to recharge their batteries by indulging in a cleansing, vegetarian diet, frequent enemas, hydrotherapy and electrotherapy using elaborate static electricity machines, as well as massage and extensive exercise in the open air. Along with a host of lesser luminaries, the Kelloggs attracted patients ranging from Lincoln's widow Mary Todd Lincoln to the famed flyer Amelia Earhart; Alfred Dupont to John D. Rockefeller; President Warren G. Harding to Irving Fisher, one of the leading American economists of the first half of the twentieth century; Henry Ford to Johnny Weissmuller (better known as Tarzan) – all came to benefit from the Kelloggs' ministrations and soothe their nerves. And on the side, the brothers founded a breakfast cereal empire that sought to keep their customers properly nourished and 'regular', a fabulously successful business that far outlasted the Sanitarium itself – for ill-judged expansion in the late 1920s just before the Great Depression sealed the latter's fate.

The Borderlands of Insanity

Of course, the highly agitated, the suicidal, those who no longer possessed even a semblance of self-control, or who had tendencies towards violence, were scarcely suitable for the Sanitarium, or most analogous institutions elsewhere. But there were a multitude of other candidates for these establishments, and even a burgeoning market for outpatient, office-based treatment. One of the more dramatic features of the story of madness in the nineteenth century was the explosive growth of patient numbers in asylums. It was not just the silting up of the institutions with chronic patients, but a rise in rates of admission that deeply troubled contemporaries, and has provoked scholarly controversy since. Some have been tempted to see the increased populations as symptomatic of a real rise in the numbers of the mad, perhaps even the product of a mysterious new virus loosed upon the land.[6] Others, myself among them, have pointed out that these theories rest on nothing more than idle speculation, and have adduced evidence that what was at work was a steady broadening of the criteria for calling someone mentally ill, a process of 'diagnostic creep' that George Cheyne already profited from when he persuaded his wealthy patients they were suffering from 'the English malady'. It is a process that has been equally evident, as we shall see, over the past quarter of a century and more, a period which has seen the proliferation of new official categories of mental illness, and has spawned epidemics of such illnesses as bipolar disorders and autism, as more ambiguous cases are added to the core population that once led to the identification of these conditions.[7]

The French spoke of the 'demi-fous', the half-mad, and English alienists took to referring to those who dwelt on the borderlands of insanity and inhabited the realms of Mazeland, Dazeland and Driftland.[8] Such 'incipient lunatics', the carriers of 'latent brain disease', included a whole array of neurotics, hysterics, anorexics and sufferers from a newly fashionable disorder, 'neurasthenia', or weakness of the nerves, a term made popular by the American neurologist George M. Beard (1839–83), who not only labelled the disease but proclaimed himself one of its victims. They formed the foundation on which some portions of what by now we can begin to call psychiatry ventured to break out of the gloomy and isolated 'Walpurgis night' that was the world of the asylum,[9] and to invent a new office-based form of practice, based upon a financially lucrative if therapeutically frustrating clientele suffering from milder forms of nervous disorder, those who 'hovered', as the Philadelphia gynaecologist William Goodell (1829–94) put it, 'on the narrow borderland that separates hysteria from insanity'.[10]

Those suffering from 'shattered nerves' were not simply a creation of an imperialistic group of doctors bent on expanding the parameters of their practice. To the contrary, there proved to be an eager clientele for these *Nervenarzten*, as German members of the fraternity styled themselves. The United States was no exception to the trend, and in some ways it led the way. One of the first exemplars of newly industrialized warfare was the

American Civil War (1861–65). Amid all the carnage – well over half a million soldiers died, and casualties ran to over a million – were a plethora of men who suffered injuries to their brains and nervous systems, providing ample opportunity for those treating them to learn from what they observed. The classic text describing what they saw, and its implications for medicine, was S. W. Mitchell, G. R. Morehouse and W. W. Keen's *Gunshot Wounds, and Other Injuries of Nerves*, published in 1864. After the war was over, in cities along the eastern seaboard, many army surgeons set themselves up as neurologists – specialists in the treatment of diseases of the nervous system. And they found their waiting rooms swamped. Not only were there those who had suffered dramatic physical trauma, but also soldiers complaining of more diffuse nervous complaints. And not just soldiers. The brass plates advertising Silas Weir Mitchell, neurologist, or William Alexander Hammond, neurologist, attracted large numbers of civilians as well, male and female alike. Indeed, perhaps more women than men.

Mitchell and his colleagues found these patients wearisome to deal with. More than once, Mitchell spoke of hysteria as the neurologist's 'hated charge'. The complaints of those who crowded their waiting rooms were myriad but hard to pin down, or to connect to the picture of the nervous system Mitchell and others had begun to draw up. In his frustration, Mitchell remarked that hysteria – the condition from which he concluded many of these nervous invalids were suffering – ought to be renamed 'mysteria'. But at the end of the day, neither he nor his colleagues could afford to turn such people away. These patients were too lucrative for that, and too importunate in their demands that the nerve doctors recognize the somatic reality of their diffuse complaints. Hysteria was a term with ancient historical roots, as we have seen in Chapter Two.[11] And to it, the American neurologists had now added the new disorder, neurasthenia.

American nervousness, like the English malady before it, was portrayed as the product and the price of America's more advanced civilization. The pace of modern life, with its electric telegraph, its high-speed trains, its frantic struggle for material success, even the dubious decision to allow some women to obtain higher education, all imposed extraordinary strains on the nervous system, nowhere more so than among businessmen and the professional classes. It was a disease, overwhelmingly if not quite exclusively, of the wealthy and the refined. Overtaxing one's nervous system, running down one's batteries, exhausting one's reserves, bankrupting one's mental equilibrium by overdrawing one's account – the metaphors used to describe what had happened to those crowding the waiting rooms at once flattered them, and reassured them that they were suffering from a real, physically rooted disease, one they could almost wear as a badge of honour, rather than being a source of shame. Mitchell wrote a bestselling advice book that summed up the matter in the three words of its title: the neurasthenic were the victims of *Wear and Tear* (1871). And the solution to their travails lay close at hand. As the title of its sequel informed them, they needed to pay attention to building up *Fat and Blood* (1877) to nourish and replenish their depleted reserves of mental strength and energy.

Beard's diagnosis of neurasthenia explained the fatigue, the anxiety, the headaches, the insomnia, the impotence, neuralgia and depression the nervous patients complained they suffered from. Crucially for establishing the medical status of the condition, and for appealing to prospective patients, Beard had insisted that 'nervousness is a physical not a mental state, and its phenomena do not come from emotional excess or excitability'.[12] But it was Mitchell who came up with the most practical treatment for the condition. Or practical if one were sufficiently rich: his so-called rest cure was by definition scarcely a practical solution for the working man or woman. For those who could afford it, it promised a therapy that to all appearances worked to restore the body of the exhausted businessman or professional, or his socially prominent wife.

Virginia Woolf was one of those subjected to Mitchell's treatment, albeit at the hands of a series of British psychiatrists and neurologists, for the treatment spread rapidly to Europe, along with the term neurasthenia – something that was highly unusual at the time, for the United States was (rightly) regarded as a medical backwater, and its physicians generally scorned as inferior.[13] And though Woolf's savage satire of what it involved reflects the fury provoked by her own experience, it accurately captures the treatment's central elements: 'you invoke proportion; order rest in bed; rest in solitude; silence and rest; rest without friends, without books, without messages; six months' rest; until a man who went in weighing seven stone six comes out weighing twelve'.[14] Fat and blood with a vengeance: complete social and physical isolation; massage in place of exercise; an enforced physical idleness; a high-calorie diet. Woolf was not alone in her protests,[15] but other patients seem to have had a more benign view of the process.[16] Certainly it was popular with their physicians, for whom it provided a scientific and somatically based approach, one that, perhaps not coincidentally, had more than a touch of the punitive and the disciplinary about it.[17]

Electricity was one element of Mitchell's treatment, a therapeutic intervention already widely employed by his fellow practitioners. Not electricity used to provoke convulsions; that would be a twentieth-century invention. But low-voltage or static electricity, delivered with crackles and sparks by impressive and complex machinery, replete with polished chrome and brass. If nervous impulses were electrical, what better mode of treatment could possibly be employed? The wonders of modern physics were thus mobilized to reassure the nervous patient of the physical status of their disorders, and to ward off the spectre of malingering. The undeniably somatic character of the treatment provided a telling riposte to anyone inclined to cast doubt on the moral status of the neurasthenic.

Nervousness was not an American monopoly, which is precisely why neurasthenia and the rest cure moved like lightning across the Atlantic and established themselves as indispensable in the specialized practices of nerve doctors, whether they were psychiatrists seeking surcease from the horrors of life in the madhouse, or neurologists attempting to establish a still tenuous alternative specialism laying claim to expertise in the management of nervous and mental disorders. The superintendents of asylums of the insane did not take kindly to competition from neurologists, while neurologists initially regarded their institutional brethren with contempt. 'Your ways',

Treatment with an electrical vibrator (1900): a nurse applies faradic current to a female patient.

said Mitchell sharply, 'are not our ways.' Asylum doctors had isolated themselves from their professional brethren, and lost all contact with the progress of scientific medicine.[18]

Eventually, however, a rapprochement of sorts occurred. Such public squabbling threatened the reputations of both sides, and in any event, two distinct modes of practice ultimately began to emerge. Asylums would persist as the major centres of treatment for the most severely disturbed for another half-century and more. And those neurologists who began to specialize in the treatment of the 'functional' forms of mental illness soon found themselves joined in the enterprise by alienists disenchanted with the monotony of institutional practice – many of them drawn from the psychiatric elite and anxious to gain their share of a more lucrative, less disturbed, possibly more treatable set of patients.[19]

Hysteria on the Stage

Though neurasthenia proved a popular diagnosis on both sides of the Atlantic, hysteria was the nervous disorder that achieved the most prominent place in fin-de-siècle Europe. Initially, it acquired its greatest renown in Paris, where the eminent French neurologist Jean-Martin Charcot (1825–93) produced a long-running spectacle on a peculiarly Parisian stage, his *Leçons du Mardi* at the Salpêtrière Hospital. Here he had charge of wards containing an eclectic mix of patients, ranging across the whole gamut of neurological dysfunction, though he had no contact with the mental medicine of the asylum system. (Only later would hysteria achieve still greater prominence in Vienna, where Charcot's one-time pupil, Sigmund Freud, constructed an alternative model of the aetiology of mental disorders and a novel therapeutics of a purely psychological sort via his encounter with a series of such patients – discussed below.)

Charcot's early fame as a neurologist had rested on his work on the scleroses, locomotor ataxia (one of the complications of tertiary syphilis), Parkinson's disease, and other disorders of the brain and spinal cord.[20] His turn towards hysteria occurred gradually, and largely as a fortuitous result of an internal re-organization of the Salpêtrière. Out of the vast repository of poverty-stricken pathological specimens that made up the hospital, Charcot was put in charge of a mixed ward of epileptic and what were then called hysterio-epileptic patients. Drawn from the ranks of the Parisian poor, this portion of Charcot's clientele could not have stood in starker contrast to the sorts of patients who flocked to the American neurologists' consulting rooms. (Not to worry: his extremely lucrative private practice brought him patients from all over Europe, including such figures as Baroness Anna von Lieben of Vienna, one of the richest women of the age, and an array of Russian, German and Spanish millionaires, not to mention the occasional American.)

From the outset, and all through his career, Charcot was convinced that hysteria belonged alongside the scleroses and the rest. It was a real neurological disorder, rooted in an as-yet mysterious set of lesions in the brain and the nervous system, a position he held tightly to even as his own clinical observations demonstrated that some hysterical paralyses followed pathways that were directly at odds with established knowledge about neuro-anatomy, and reflected mistaken lay notions about how bodies were put together. Three years before his death, he still insisted that: 'Its anatomical lesion still eludes our means of investigation, but it expresses itself in a way unmistakable to the attentive observer through tropic disorders analogous to those seen in organic lesions of the central nervous system.' And he voiced his conviction that 'some day the anatomo-clinical method will count another success in revealing at last the primordial cause, the anatomical cause, which is known presently by so many material effects'.[21]

Charcot, from his early engagement with hysteria, thus threw his by now considerable professional weight behind the claim that the disorder was not malingering or play-acting, but a real, somatic disturbance (albeit one with obvious psychological overtones). Hysteria returned the favour. Not immediately, perhaps, but Charcot's decision to embrace the medical legitimacy of hypnosis (that relabelled version of mesmerism that had first been proffered by the Scottish surgeon James Braid (1795–1860) some years earlier),[22] and his public demonstrations of his hysterical patients in the *Leçons du Mardi*, proved a sensation. Everyone came to view the hysterical circus, and Charcot's fame grew exponentially.

Despite hysteria's general associations with the female sex (a linkage embodied in the very name of the disorder), Charcot was convinced that, like neurasthenia, it was a disorder that attacked men and women alike. And some of his male patients were the antithesis of the sort of effeminate hysterical male portrayed in Wilkie Collins's *The Woman in White* (in which Frederick Fairlie's exquisitely fine-tuned nervous system is closely linked to his prurient interest in little boys): blacksmiths, for example, and other

Jean-Martin Charcot, the 'Napoleon of the Neuroses', cradling his pet monkey.

vigorous artisans. It was not the male hysterics who drew the audience to Charcot's clinical demonstrations, however, but the attractive, scantily clad women, who under the influence of the mesmerizing male gaze, repeatedly enacted the various stages of the hysterical fit: the seizure and the seemingly impossible bodily contortions of course, but more entertainingly still, the *attitudes passionelles*, the emotional gestures, cries and whispers that displayed unmistakably erotic overtones. One journalist reported receiving a private audience, during the course of which Charcot performed ovarian compression on 'a young and beautiful girl with a magnificent shape and abundant blonde hair'. Then the performance for the larger audience began on the stage, 'the patient's stretcher arranged so she could be seen from all parts of the room with the aid of a spotlight' and in such a fashion that 'her exclamations could be heard [by everyone]'.[23]

A few contemporary feminist critics protested at this 'sort of vivisection of women under the pretext of studying a disease for which he knows neither the cause nor the treatment'.[24] Charcot was condemned as the orchestrator of

> disgusting experiments practised on lunatics and hysterical
> patients in the Salpêtrière. The nurses drag these unfortunate
> women, notwithstanding their cries and resistance, before
> men who make them fall into catalepsy. They play on these
> organisms off their balance, on which the experiment strains
> the nervous system and aggravates the morbid conditions,
> as if it were an instrument which should give the whole gamut
> of mental aberration and of the depravity of the passions. One
> of my friends told me that she and the Duchess of P...had seen
> a doctor of great reputation make one unhappy patient pass,
> without transition, from a celestial beatitude to a condition of
> infamous sensualment. And this before a company of literary
> men, artists, and men of the world.[25]

Male literary figures including Tolstoy and Maupassant chimed in to voice their disdain. But, as is so often the case, these criticisms seem only to have increased the numbers pressing for a view of the performance.

The physician Axel Munthe (1857–1949), in his autobiographical *The Story of San Michele*, has provided us with a vivid reconstruction of the scene, one he himself observed and participated in: 'The huge amphitheatre was filled to the last place with a multicoloured audience drawn from *tout Paris*, authors, journalists, leading actors and actresses, fashionable demimondaines' – all gathered for the show. Now came the performers, the grey-coated, sombre Charcot, the master of ceremonies for the proceedings, and then the women who would do his bidding, apparently under the influence of the hypnotic trance:

> Some of them smelt with delight a bottle of ammonia when told
> it was rose water, others would eat a piece of charcoal when
> presented to them as chocolate. Another would crawl on all fours
> on the floor, barking furiously when told she was a dog, flap her
> arms as if trying to fly when turned into a pigeon, lift her skirts
> with a shriek of terror when a glove was thrown at her feet with
> a suggestion of being a snake. Another would walk with a top hat
> in her arms rocking it to and fro and kissing it tenderly when
> told it was her baby.[26]

The masculine dominance, the foolishness and frailty of the female, both were decisively on display.

The patients disporting themselves in the throes of their disorder were also recorded by the lens of the camera. The *Iconographies*, the collections of photographs of the performers who made up the circus, circulated widely and disseminated the Charcotian vision of hysteria to an audience who could only virtually witness the Parisian scene. They did much to fix the image of hysteria in the public mind, and perhaps to spread suggestively what purported to be neutral, naturalistic recordings of a neuropathic disorder. The photograph (at least before the age of digital manipulation) carried the illusion of providing the truth, a direct and unmediated portrait or even a mirror of nature, the instantaneous representation of what passed before the lens of the camera.

But the limitations of lighting, and the technical requirements of picture-taking with wet collodion plates, or even the later silver gelatino-bromide coating, made for long exposures, sometimes twenty minutes per plate. Perhaps appropriately, given that Charcot's posthumous critics (who, as we shall see, included even – no, especially – his collaborators and protégés) viewed his clinical demonstrations as fraudulent, the 'objective' photographs that recorded the pathologies were themselves necessarily staged, posed and manufactured constructions whose status as 'facts' is as slippery as the live demonstrations they purport to record.[27]

Planche XXIII.

ATTITUDES PASSIONNELLES

EXTASE (1878).

Attitudes passionelles: extase (*1878*). *The erotic overtones of Charcot's pictures of his hysterical patients at the Salpêtrière are nowhere more obvious than here.*

During Charcot's lifetime, with the important exception of Hippolyte Bernheim (1840–1919) in provincial Nancy, criticism of his work came mostly from abroad, for he was both powerful and thin-skinned, fully capable of ruining the careers of lesser men who crossed him. Not for nothing did he bathe in his reputation as the 'Napoleon of the Neuroses'. After his death, however, in 1893, it was another matter. Even his closest protégés turned on him, denying the reality of the dramas they had helped to stage. The *Leçons du Mardi* were, said Axel Munthe, 'an absurd farce, a hopeless muddle of truth and cheating'.[28]

Freud and the Birth of Psychoanalysis

But at the height of Charcot's fame, in 1885, among the swirl of foreigners seeking enlightenment and perhaps sponsorship from the great man, a young Austrian physician whose career was foundering had shown up to work under him for five months, hoping desperately to revive his fortunes back in Vienna. Sigmund Freud (1856–1939) had not initially intended to focus his attention on hysteria. He had a conventional training in neuroanatomy and neurology, and aspirations in those directions. But it was to hysteria that he was drawn, like many another. After his return to Vienna, and his reluctant abandonment of his hopes of an academic career in favour of private practice, he continued to treat conventional neurological cases, especially children with cerebral palsy. But there were too few of them to support his new wife and a rapidly growing family of children, so it was fortunate that his practice also drew in a number of patients with hysteria. Like American neurologists, he might have wished it otherwise, but the hysterics provided an indispensable source of income, and it was here that he began to concentrate his efforts.

Freud had made every effort to secure a place in Charcot's inner circle while in Paris, gaining the grand man's gratitude by volunteering to translate the third volume of his *Leçons sur les maladies du système nerveux* (*Lectures on Diseases of the Nervous System*) into German – this despite his self-admitted limitations in French. He had brought with him Charcot's emphasis on the somatic roots of hysteria, along with the use of hypnosis in its treatment. The former would remain central to his thinking till the late 1890s, when he grudgingly abandoned his grand 'Project for a Scientific Psychology', with its ambition to link the complexities of inner experience to basic neural processes. Hypnosis he had abandoned somewhat earlier. He had never mastered the technique, and his Viennese colleagues, seeing it as little more than 'mere' suggestion, followed the lead of the powerful neuropathologist Theodor Meynert (1833–92) and dismissed the whole approach as quackery.

Charcot had attempted to argue otherwise. He insisted that only those with the defective nervous systems of the hysteric were susceptible to the hypnotic trance. Taking this position allowed him to employ what to others appeared to be a psychological therapy based upon suggestion, while continuing to insist that fundamentally hysteria was a somatic disease. It was a position adopted by many of Charcot's British admirers, for whom to flirt with psychological accounts of mental disorder was to break with the discipline of medical science in favour of quackery, self-delusion and fraud. Hence, as the British nerve doctor and neurologist Horatio Donkin (1845–1927) articulated the consensus, 'it is certain from general experience that human beings are hypnotizable in direct proportion to their nervous instability'.[29]

It was this position that the work of Hippolyte Bernheim had done much to discredit, since his experiments seemed to show that even the 'psychologically normal' could be hypnotized.[30] Charcot's views likewise found little sympathy among Austrian physicians. Freud's abandonment of hypnosis may thus have been overdetermined. He had translated Bernheim into German in 1888, peppering his translation with editorial commentary signalling his dissent, but within months, he was no longer defending Charcot's position on the matter and, one suspects, beginning to reconsider how to reframe the connections between psychological processes and mental illness.

When Freud's hopes of an academic career were dashed, and he turned instead to private practice as a neurologist, he found it hard to earn a living. Into the 1890s, he was dependent to a considerable degree on referrals (and even loans) from the eminent Viennese physician Josef Breuer (1842–1945), a man almost a decade and a half older than he, who was blessed with a flourishing practice that brought him more patients than he could handle. It was a dependence that chafed, and after the two men broke with each other in the mid-1890s, Freud came to despise Breuer. But it was through Breuer that Freud first encountered patients with hysteria, and it was the volume they published jointly in 1895, *Studien über Hysterie* (*Studies on Hysteria*), that both formed the foundation of Freud's career as a psychotherapist and led, within a very short period, to the creation of psychoanalysis, at once a

Sigmund Freud in 1891, aged thirty-five.

new approach to the therapeutics of mental disorder, and a novel conceptualization of its aetiology.

'Anna O.', arguably the single most famous patient in the history of psychoanalysis, was, in fact, Breuer's patient, not Freud's. Her real name was Bertha Pappenheim (1859–1936), and, like many of Breuer's (and Freud's) patients, she came from a rich Jewish family, prominent among Vienna's haute bourgeoisie. She had come to Breuer's attention in 1880, when she first became his patient. Anna/Bertha had spent months devotedly nursing her dying father. His death led her to display some of the puzzling and daunting array of symptoms that commonly at that time led to a diagnosis of hysteria.

'Anna O.', actually Bertha Pappenheim (1882), the Ur-patient of psychoanalysis, a photograph taken at the Bellevue Sanatorium at Kreuzlingen, where she was confined as a mental patient after her allegedly successful treatment by Joseph Breuer.

She developed a persistent cough, insomnia, then spasms resembling fits, followed by a paralysis of her extremities on her right side. Her vision began to fail. The formerly well-behaved woman gave way to episodes of uncontrollable anger. Her German deteriorated, and before long, she could only speak and comprehend English. There were periods when she refused to eat or drink.

Breuer's treatment consisted of frequent and prolonged conversations with her. Over time, she began to sift back through her remarkable memory, and to recall traumatic episodes that were associated with each of her individual symptoms, and the recollection of these scenes, Breuer reported, had a cathartic effect. One by one, her dramatic pathologies disappeared. According to Breuer, it was Anna herself who dubbed his treatment 'the talking cure'.[31] A decade later, Breuer referred a string of female patients with hysterical symptoms to his young friend and protégé, and Freud claimed to have found the same thing:

> We found, to our great surprise at first, that *each individual hysterical symptom immediately and permanently disappeared when we had succeeded in bringing clearly to light the memory of the event by which it was provoked and in arousing its accompanying affect, and when the patient had described that event in the greatest possible detail and had put the affect into words.*[32]

It was these case histories – Anna O., Frau Emmy von N., Fräulein Elisabeth von R., Miss Lucy R., Katherina and Frau Cäcilie M. – that had led Freud to propose that he and Breuer should write and publish a book on hysteria, and that suggested its format: a series of psychologically charged vignettes that read like short stories, or detective tales. For the central message of *Studies on Hysteria* was that '*hysterics suffer mainly from reminiscences*',[33] memories that lingered somehow beyond conscious recollection, poisoning the mind and producing the puzzling symptoms that had proved so frustrating to the many physicians who had sought to treat such patients. Half-murdered memories needed bringing back to life, for when that was accomplished, their pathological powers disappeared, and, simultaneously, so did the patient's hysteria.

By his own account, by the early 1890s Breuer had no interest in continuing to treat cases of hysteria.[34] His successful general practice brought him a lucrative living, and besides, he was too busy for the time-consuming cathartic method. Freud, however, welcomed 'the crowds of neurotics' who now began to flock to his consulting rooms, and promptly 'abandoned the treatment of organic nervous diseases'.[35] In almost the same breath, he also abandoned hypnosis; discontinued the cathartic method as too simplistic; broke socially and intellectually with Breuer, and began to elaborate an alternative therapeutics that revolved around 'free association' on the part of the patient; forsook efforts to reduce psychological events to underlying neuropathology; and opted instead for an increasingly complex psychodynamic account of the origins of mental disorder.

Repression

It was a remarkably risky series of moves, made more so by his near-simultaneous embrace of a new account of the origins of his patients' symptoms. Their disturbances, he came to believe, had their roots in sex, more properly in sexual trauma – repressed memories of sexual molestation and incestuous assaults as a child. These episodes were, he asserted, always and everywhere at the root of hysteria. It was a claim that quickly brought ridicule even from Vienna's leading psychiatrist and sexologist, Richard von Krafft-Ebing (1840–1902). Freud's ideas, he announced, were 'a scientific fairy tale'.[36]

Within a year, Freud had moved off on a different tangent: sex was still central to his account, but rather than actual traumas and assaults, what was at work was childhood fantasies and their repression. Over a decade and more, he refined his model, arguing that the libido, the energy that was supplied by unconscious sexual drives, was the source of all manner of complex psychological discomforts and conflicts. Mental life, he argued, followed a deterministic logic every bit as susceptible to scientific study and analysis as the physiological facts that others examined in the laboratory. Painstakingly teased out from dreams, slips of the tongue and the free association he encouraged his patients to engage in, the sources of their underlying troubles could be laid bare, and in the process of making the unconscious conscious, the patient could be led to cure himself or herself.

As Freud portrayed it, the unconscious was a fearsome place. It was made (and generally marred) from the very earliest weeks and months of life by the looming presence of parental figures in the newborn's mental universe, and the picture grew darker still over infancy. The family was the arena for a host of frightful and dangerous psychodramas that populated the child's unconscious, fomented its repressions and created its psychopathologies. Forced to repress unacceptable desires, and to deny their Oedipal fantasies to possess the parent of the opposite sex and eliminate the parent of the same sex, or to drive them deeper into the unconscious, children lived in a world of hidden psychic conflict. Here was a new account of the links between the pathologies of the mind and the progress of civilization. Cravings and suppressions, a search for substitute satisfactions and ways of sublimating what could not safely be acknowledged, false forgetting, all the distorting constraints of 'civilized' morality created a minefield from which few emerged unscathed and unscarred.

The overwhelming majority of Freud's psychiatric contemporaries regarded the ravings, the disturbed perceptions, the unruly emotions that exhibited such a tenacious hold on their patients as just so much noise. Their sole significance was as symptoms of disordered brains. Otherwise, they were purely epiphenomenal and not worth attending to. For Freud and his followers, by contrast, they were crucial. Madness was at once rooted in meanings and symbols, and had to be treated at the level of meaning. Disturbed actions, cognition and emotions were of the utmost significance, and the profoundly difficult task that confronted doctor and patient was to sift through the clues they presented, exhuming what the psyche had invested immense energy in burying. Inevitably, this excavation was an intense and fraught process. It required, so it was claimed, months if not years of probing to get past internal barriers and resistance, and to force the unconscious into consciousness.

One of the great attractions of Freud's intellectual edifice was that his model of the mind and his technique for treating its disturbed manifestations were so tightly interwoven, and mutually reinforced each other. Though developed initially to diagnose and treat still (barely) functioning, if disturbed and distressed patients labelled as suffering from neurotic illnesses, it potentially could be (and in later years was) expanded to account for the psychoses. And, at the opposite end of the spectrum, it purported to provide a reading of the 'normal' personality. Emil Kraepelin (the 'great Pope' of psychiatry, as Freud scornfully called him) had erected a seemingly impenetrable barrier between the biologically degenerate and physically inferior specimens who swarmed the back wards of lunatic asylums, and the majority of sane citizens. Freud, by contrast, denied that madness was simply the problem of the Other. It lurked, it would seem, in all of us, at least to some degree. The same forces that led one to mental invalidism allowed another to produce accomplishments of surpassing cultural importance. Civilization and its discontents, Freud proclaimed, were inevitably and irretrievably locked in an indissoluble embrace.

Chapter Ten

DESPERATE
REMEDIES

The Trials of Total War

On 28 July 1914, the world went mad. Or rather, Europe went mad and soon made sure that the rest of the world shared in its insanity. The madness, so the German Kaiser assured his young troops, would be over by Christmas – and so it was, but four Christmases later. The assassination on 28 June of the feckless and deeply unpopular Archduke Franz Ferdinand, heir to the Austro-Hungarian throne, by the Bosnian Serb Gavrilo Princip had rapidly led to a declaration of war that soon consumed the continent, and eventually brought conflict across the world. It was war on a grand, or rather on an appalling scale, with the massive industrial might of the modern world turned to the task of destruction. The contending forces rapidly bogged down in the Flanders mud. Northern France was turned into a wasteland. Trenches were dug, barbed wire defences erected and a war of attrition ensued. Both sides claimed to be fighting for civilization. Tanks, artillery, machine guns and bayonets did their bloody, flesh-tearing work, and as if that were not enough, scientists provided poison gas and the guardians of civilization unleashed its horrors on the battlefield. Millions perished. Millions more suffered horrific injuries – loss of limbs, loss of sight, paralysis, disfigurement. Generals on both sides, seemingly bereft of conscience, sent junior officers and other ranks by the million into the meat grinder, destroying, physically or mentally, almost an entire generation of young men. Mutinies, the collapse of the tsarist regime in Russia, the scale of the carnage, the sheer futility of the fight, nothing seemed to sway the politicians. The madness must continue, lest civilization perish. And perish it nearly did.

For four years, men cowered in trenches as death and destruction rained down upon them. Suicidal attacks were launched. Machine guns mowed the advancing troops down, like rows of corn submitting to the attentions of a combine harvester. Gravely wounded men lay beyond reach, screaming and moaning in agony, till death stilled their cries. At vast loss of life, a hundred yards of featureless territory were periodically secured, only to be lost to the next enemy offensive. Mud and blood, blood and mud. And then came gas, with its spectacle of comrades dying of suffocation as their lungs filled with blood and water, and their guts were reduced to slime, their eyes blistered and burned, and froth issued from their mouths; a slow, agonizing death ensued. Escape from the nightmare was impossible. To desert was to be captured and shot as a coward. To remain was to experience daily trauma, to witness and participate in unspeakable acts, to hear moans, sobs and shrieks of agony from the maimed and the dying, to see bodies torn apart and then left to rot: swelling, smelling, blackened, bloated.

It was more than many could bear. Before Christmas of 1914 – by which time the glorious adventure was supposed to be over – military strategists were having to cope with an acute and wholly unanticipated problem. It ought not to have been entirely unexpected, given what might have been

German troops go gaily off to war in 1914, 'from Munich via Metz to Paris'. All the fighting would be over by Christmas, the Kaiser had assured them; it would be a walk in the park.

learned from the American Civil War, and the Boer War the British had fought
in South Africa at the turn of the century. But those warning signs had been
ignored; the problems that surfaced among the troops early in the Great War
could not be. As the English poet Wilfred Owen (1893–1914) wrote in his
poem, 'Mental Cases':

These are men whose minds the Dead have ravished.
Memory fingers in their hair of murders,
Multitudinous murders they once witnessed.
Wading sloughs of flesh these helpless wander,
Treading blood from lungs that had loved laughter.
Always they see these things and hear them,
Batter of guns and shatter of flying muscles,
Carnage incomparable, and human squander
Rucked too thick for these men's extrication.

Therefore still their eyeballs shrink tormented
Back into their brains, because on their sense
Sunlight seems a blood-smear; night comes blood-black;
Dawn breaks open like a wound that bleeds afresh.
Thus their heads wear this hilarious, hideous,
Awful falseness of set-smiling corpses.
Thus their hands are plucking at each other;
Picking at the rope-knouts of their scourging;
Snatching after us who smote them, brother,
Pawing us who dealt them war and madness.[1]

Witnessing those 'who die as cattle',[2] most of them mute so far as
posterity is concerned, some soldiers contrived in words and images to record
some semblance of the war's horrors. Their poetry and their art serve as stark
reminders of the carnage and the madness that engulfed their comrades in
arms, and often themselves. Some perished – Owen would die in the war's
last hours, a mere week before the 11 November armistice. Others, including
the German artist Max Beckmann (1884–1950), who had volunteered as a
medical orderly, joined the ranks of the conflict's mental casualties: by 1915,
he was hospitalized, unfit for further duty. *The Night* (*Die Nacht*) painted
in the immediate aftermath of the military violence, powerfully evokes the
spectre of pointless and horrific violence, rape, murder, torture (PL. 38).

In shades of brown and red, devoid of the 'civilized' conventions of representational art, the image presents a crazy distortion of reality, a shattered sense of perspective, jagged, angular, nightmarish: a vision of psychotic hell from which there is no escape. The palette of Cubism, its resort to fragmentation and its weighty geometry provided a new set of artistic resources Beckmann could draw upon, together with the 'beast-like' nature and frantic line of *les Fauves* ('fauve' is French for wild beast). The flat, chaotic panorama of the painting, violent, bereft of any intimations of depth, gives the impression that its subjects have been smashed into the canvas, as war has smashed human beings and their civilization, all have been pummelled into the same mad plane.[3] There is no exit, no conceivable avenue of escape. We are damned.

If Beckmann's vision is an allegory, his contemporary Otto Dix (1891–1969) by contrast gave us an unvarnished look at 'the work of the Devil' – the 'lice, rats, barbed wire, fleas, shells, bombs, underground caves, corpses, blood, liquor, mice, cats, gas, artillery, filth, bullets, mortars, fire, steel: that is what war is!' He had fought as a machine gunner in the Artois, Champagne and at the Battle of the Somme. He knew the experience of 'how someone beside me suddenly falls over and is dead and the bullet has hit him squarely'.[4] The memories haunted him, and a decade and more after war's end, he produced a series of etchings, *Der Krieg* (*The War*), and a monumental painted triptych, the *War Triptych* (PL. 39), that rendered in stark black and white, and then in vivid colour, what most fortunately never witness. *Gott mit uns* (*God with us!*), proclaimed the belt buckles on German uniforms. Hell on earth was more like it, visions of men 'guttering, choking, drowning…the blood/Come gargling from the froth-corrupted lungs',[5] and then their corpses riddled with worms and maggots, swarming with flies, rotting away to reveal whitened bones and grinning skulls.

The mutilated and the dead, those the generals had expected to see. But what of the others? Soldiers who were mute. Who shook uncontrollably. Who spent sleepless nights haunted by nightmares. Who declared themselves blind overnight, though they surely had not been blinded. Who complained of heart palpitations – so-called soldier's heart. Who proclaimed themselves paralysed, though no physical event seemed to have provoked the paralysis. Whose bodies were twisted, and who walked with a peculiar and unnatural gait. Who wept and screamed incessantly. Who claimed to have lost all memory. The generals knew what they thought was at work: malingering,

Otto Dix produced a series of savage portraits of the realities of trench warfare, Der Krieg (The War) *– ugly, nightmarish images forming a visual reminder of the effects of war on human beings. The title of this one, in English, is* Night-time Encounter with a Madman.

weakness of will. These men were cowards, shrinking from performing their patriotic duty. They should be shot. And some were, *pour encourager les autres.*

Shell Shock

Army medics reached a different conclusion: these men were mentally ill, they had broken down – their nerves were shot. They did not deserve to be. German doctors concluded these men were suffering from *Schreckneurose,* or terror neurosis. The British called it shell shock, a term that encapsulated the earliest medical theories about what had gone wrong: the concussive effects of high explosives had traumatized the brain and the nervous system, inflicting invisible injuries on those who appeared physically unharmed. Tears to the spinal cord, minute haemorrhages in the brain were undetectable, at least in the living body, but were the real physical cause of the protean symptoms the doctors now confronted.

Not everyone was convinced. The initial disposition of many psychiatrists was to blame their traditional foe, degeneration. Just before the war broke out, Charles Mercier (1815–1919), one of Britain's leading psychiatrists, had insisted that breakdowns did 'not occur in people who are of sound mental constitution. [Mental illness] does not, like smallpox and malaria, attack indifferently the weak and the strong. It occurs chiefly in those whose mental constitution is originally defective, and whose defect is manifested in the lack of the power of self-control and of forgoing immediate indulgence.'[6] Steeped in the teachings of Charcot, French neuropsychiatrists concurred: all these soldiers manifesting mental symptoms were defective degenerates, weak, terrified, decrepit souls, whose breakdowns were thoroughly predictable and had little to do with the exigencies of war.[7] German psychiatrists were mostly of a similar mind.

Greater experience with shell shock served to heighten doubts about claims that its symptoms were the product of concussive events shaking up the nervous system. Soldiers who had never been within miles of the front developed symptoms of the disorder. The physically ill and maimed seemed to enjoy a remarkable immunity from its depredations. And prisoners of war, removed from the risks of the front, were miraculously spared its ravages. One did not have to be a cynic, or a military officer, to doubt the earlier medical speculations about shell shock's origins.

If not damage to the brain and central nervous system, then what might account for these soldiers? If their problems were simple malingering, it was odd that even extreme pressure could not cause them to abandon their symptoms. The 'blind' soldier, for example, did not blink as a lighted candle was brought ever closer to his eyes. The 'deaf' one did not react to sudden, unexpected noise. Mutism persisted despite the application of painful stimuli. The notion that shell shock might be a form of hysteria appealed to many. And that the mental stresses of combat could be the trigger that broke down ordinary stoicism seemed increasingly likely.

Psychiatrists on all sides could, with little difficulty, combine such theorizing with a continued allegiance to the notion that the mentally ill were a biologically inferior lot. That was the view that Charcot and his school had developed in Paris, and it was a sentiment equally common among German and Austrian *Nervenarzten*. There was, however, some discomfort at labelling those who fought for *la patrie* or the Fatherland degenerates, especially as shell shock materialized among the officer class as well as the other ranks, and as soldiers who had showed great bravery over many months later succumbed to the disorder. More and more army doctors were drawn to the idea that, under sufficient stress, even the strongest minds gave way. Madness and mental trauma seemed tightly bound up with each other, and if the trauma was not of the sexual kind that Freud had emphasized, his notions of unconscious conflict and the transformation of mental troubles into bodily symptoms seemed at least partially borne out by these wartime experiences. A flight into illness in the face of hellish dangers made much good sense. Here were tens of thousands, hundreds of thousands of previously 'normal' people cursed with traumatic memories, desperately trying to repress what they had seen and done, haunted by their dreams and nightmares; and here on a mass scale was evidence of how these psychological pressures and conflicts surfaced in the form of physical symptoms.

In some instances, this move towards a heightened emphasis on the psychological roots of mental disturbance was associated with an embrace of psychologically based treatment. The charismatic German psychiatrist Max Nonne (1861–1959) utilized hypnotism with what he claimed was great success. The Cambridge neurologist W. H. R. Rivers (1864–1922), posted to the hospital for officers at Craiglockhart (a converted hydropathic institution near Edinburgh), treated his patients, who included the war poets Siegfried Sassoon (1886–1967) and Wilfred Owen, with Freudian-inflected psychotherapeutic techniques, and a great deal of sympathy.[8] Sassoon dubbed his new home 'Dottyville' (PL. 37).

But to assume that when psychiatrists accorded greater weight to psychological factors in the genesis of shell shock, they were necessarily more sympathetic would be quite wrong. On the contrary, if these men's symptoms were a product of their suggestibility – their psychological vulnerabilities – then very different conclusions could be drawn. The German psychiatrist Karl Bonhöffer (1868–1948), had no illusions about what he thought was going on:

> [The] hysterical reactions [of the shell-shocked] are the result of the more or less conscious wish for self-preservation. The difference in behaviour between the Germans who came directly from the line of fire into the hospital station and the French prisoners was striking. Among the Germans the familiar forms of hysterical reactions could be found with great frequency, while among the French, who had come from the same front circumstances, no trace of hysteria was to be seen.... 'Ma guerre est fini' was the common turn of phrase. There was, hence, no longer any reason for an illness to develop.[9]

Only a thin line separated such views from the convictions of the military brass that shell shock 'victims' were nothing of the sort, but merely shirkers and cowards who deserved no sympathy, only punishment. And the sorts of treatment meted out to many suggests that such sympathy as their psychiatrists possessed was with the views of their military superiors. The sadism, the punitive component of their practices is all too evident. The hysterical paralyses of the shell-shocked and the faked paralysis of the malingerer were both equally unanchored in any real neurological disorder, and both were manifestations of a weakened will. There was, besides, enormous pressure to return the patients to the front line, and little official concern with the long-term psychological health of the cannon fodder. Temporary abatement of symptoms would suffice. Small wonder that so many gave way to the temptation to resort to autocratic, sometimes brutal methods of treatment, and found ways to rationalize what they were doing as a form of therapy.

Separately, and apparently independently, German, Austrian, French and British psychiatrists made use of powerful electric currents to inflict great pain on their patients in an effort to force them to abandon their symptoms, to get the mute to speak, the deaf to hear, the lame to walk. Most famous among the Germans was Fritz Kaufmann (1875–1941), inventor of the Kaufmann cure, which combined intensely painful electric shocks applied to apparently paralysed limbs for hours at a time, with shouted commands to perform military drills. The aim was to get the patient to give in, abandon his attachment to his symptoms, and be ready to return to the killing fields. In the Austro-Hungarian army, Julius Wagner-Jauregg (1857–1940), the distinguished professor of psychiatry at the University of Vienna, did not deign to administer similar treatment himself, but he carefully supervised an underling, Dr Kozlowski, while he applied powerful electric shocks to men's mouths and testicles. Other shell-shocked soldiers were forced to watch while waiting their turn on the treatment table.

Who could be surprised at such barbaric treatment from those the British dismissed as Huns? Except that French and British neuropsychiatrists enthusiastically made use of exactly the same approach. In Tours, the French neurologist Clovis Vincent (1879–1947) employed a faradic electrical treatment he called *torpillage*. Electrodes carefully designed to deliver a fearsomely sharp galvanic current were attached to the patient's body, ostensibly to encourage him to move his 'paralysed' limbs, and this was accompanied by other techniques intended to heighten the patient's fright. Treatment had to be swift and merciless. Vincent stood over the patient, absolutely implacable, insisting that the pain would continue until the sick person gave up. In the words of a young and enthusiastic disciple, André Gilles, 'these pseudo-impotents of the voice, the arms, or the legs, are really only impotents of the will; it is the doctor's job to will on their behalf'.[10] On one memorable occasion, but only one, these 'therapeutic interventions' provoked an assault on Vincent by one of his patients, Baptiste Deschamps. Deschamps was court-martialled for his pains.

Lewis Yealland (1884–1954), a young Canadian neurologist, was attached to Britain's premier hospital for nervous diseases in Queen Square, London. Together with his colleague Edgar Adrian (1889–1977; who would later win a Nobel Prize), he too adopted an authoritarian approach. During treatment, the shell-shocked patient 'is not asked whether he can raise his paralysed arm or not; he is ordered to raise it and told he can do it perfectly if he tries. Rapidity and an authoritative manner are the chief factors in the re-education process.'[11] Unfortunately, they did not always suffice, so alternative measures were then called for.

A mute soldier is brought into a darkened room. He is fastened to a chair, and a tongue depressor is inserted into his mouth. He is informed in

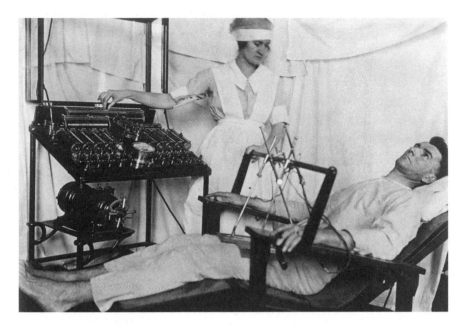

Electrical treatment of shell shock. Electrodes have been attached to the man's thighs, and electricity is about to be used to treat tremors or paralysis in his legs.

no uncertain terms that by the time he leaves the premises, his voice will be restored. Silence. Electrodes are attached to his tongue. The force of the current causes him to arc his back, a movement so forceful that it tears the electrodes from his tongue. More silence. He fails to comply with the order to speak. The process is repeated. After an hour, he utters a barely audible 'ah'. Relentlessly, Yealland presses on. Hours pass. The soldier begins to stammer and cry. More shocks. Ultimately he talks, but he must say 'thank you' to his therapist and tormentor before he is allowed to leave.[12]

Vincent and Yealland were on the winning side when the war dragged to a close. However much their patients may have hated their treatment, that was an end to the matter. In the chaos of post-war Vienna, with the collapse of the Austro-Hungarian empire and in the bitter aftermath of defeat, Julius Wagner-Jauregg faced the possibility of a very different fate. Disgruntled veterans forced his prosecution for war crimes, citing the cruelty with which he had treated his patients and the tortures he had visited upon them. Wagner-Jauregg insisted his motives had been pure. He sought only to help. He called on Sigmund Freud to testify on his behalf, and Freud did so, absolving his colleague of wrongdoing. The professional classes closed ranks. The judges acquitted. Wagner-Jauregg returned to his professorial chair in triumph.[13]

Fever

Wagner-Jauregg had long speculated that raising the body temperature of those afflicted with insanity could potentially cure their condition, and beginning in the late 1880s he had experimented with a variety of means of producing febrile conditions, including infecting patients with *Streptococcus pyogenes*, a bacterium that caused erysipelas (a very dangerous tactic in a pre-antibiotic era).[14] The dismal therapeutic outcomes did not seem to discourage him, and when, in the closing months of the war, Wagner-Jauregg encountered an Italian prisoner of war suffering from tertian malaria, he seized the opportunity to conduct a new round of experiments, this time

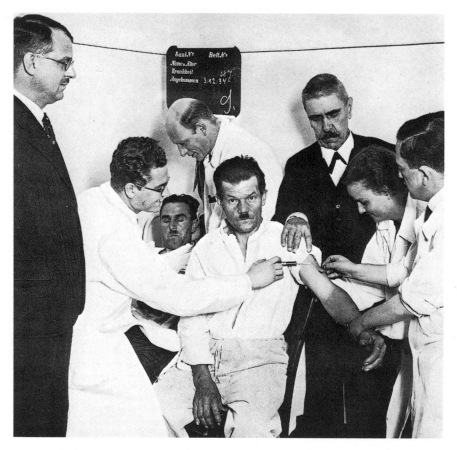

Julius Wagner-Jauregg overseeing the injection of a patient with malarial blood (1934). Blood taken from a patient with malaria (in the background) is being transfused into a patient with tertiary syphilis (centre). Wagner-Jauregg is the figure in the black jacket standing just behind the GPI patient.

confining his attentions to patients suffering from general paralysis of the insane, or GPI. Drawing blood from the malarial patient, Wagner-Jauregg then injected it into the patient with general paralysis, thus producing the high, spiking fevers he was convinced would produce a cure.

The diagnosis of GPI had been one of psychiatry's few genuine achievements in the nineteenth century, and in the years leading up to the First World War, the long-held suspicion that the appalling neurological and psychiatric consequences of this condition had their origins in a prior infection with syphilis had been decisively confirmed (see p. 263).[15] Quite apart from the singular misery such a diagnosis heralded, GPI was of major concern because it afflicted so substantial a portion of psychiatry's core patient population, perhaps as much as 15 or 20 per cent of male asylum admissions in the early twentieth century (though a considerably smaller fraction of female admissions). Symbolically and practically, anything that offered the hope of arresting the awful downward spiral of its victims would naturally be of surpassing importance.[16]

It was precisely such an outcome that Wagner-Jauregg claimed for his malarial treatment. He speculated that the method somehow broke down the blood–brain barrier that ordinarily prevented drugs from reaching the brain, thus allowing salvarsan and mercury (the treatments for early-stage syphilitic infection) to enter the central nervous system. Others pointed to the vulnerability of the syphilitic spirochete to heat in a test tube, and speculated that the fever associated with malaria destroyed the parasite.[17] The debate was never resolved, but within a few years of war's end, Wagner-Jauregg's innovation spread worldwide. Soon, hospitals were using paretics with malaria as a source of infected blood, and the precious liquid passed among them in thermos flasks sent through the post.[18] A review of 35 studies of the treatment published in 1926 suggested that a little more than a quarter of those treated, 27.5 per cent, achieved a complete remission of their symptoms,[19] and clinicians and their patients clamoured for the new 'cure'. Where previously neurosyphilitic patients had been doubly stigmatized – at once mad and suffering from a sexually-transmitted disorder – they now redefined themselves as physically sick and actively sought treatment. Their therapists responded in kind, substituting a more empathetic and positive approach for their prior dismissal of such patients as 'hopeless', 'immoral' and 'stupid' degenerates.[20] Malarial therapy brought Wagner-Jauregg a Nobel Prize in 1927, the first of only two to be awarded for psychiatric interventions.

By any measure, malarial treatment was a terrifying and physically brutal experience. The high, spiking fevers and the chills it brought on were experienced by many patients as a near-death experience. But those who emerged on the other side (and not every patient responded to the quinine that was supposed to bring the malaria under control) were convinced it had been worth it, as were their psychiatrists. We cannot be so sure. Malarial treatment was never submitted to the rigours of a controlled trial on patients, and the uncertain natural course of GPI complicates the picture. Periods when the deterioration slowed or flattened out for a time were a feature of the disease, and the mere conviction of doctors and patients that the treatment worked is suggestive, but not dispositive.[21] After all, for millennia, bleedings, purges and vomits had been advocated as sovereign remedies for all manner of diseases. Within a decade and a half, as it happens, the advent of penicillin would render such questions moot, for the new antibiotic was, indeed, a magic bullet when administered to those with syphilis.

Regardless of whether or not one accepts the verdict of 'not proven' when it comes to the malarial treatment of GPI, two vital consequences flowed from the early twentieth-century medical discoveries about the aetiology of the disease, and Wagner-Jauregg's subsequent therapeutic innovation. First, the laboratory work that uncovered an infectious cause for the illness of a significant fraction of those thronging the crowded wards of the asylums provided a considerable boost for the notion that insanity was rooted in the body, and in some quarters for the even more specific idea that just as numerous other diseases were now coming to be understood as having a bacteriological origin, madness too might prove to have a similar cause. And second, for the first time, Wagner-Jauregg's treatment seemed to suggest that this presumed biological disorder might be cured by biologically based therapeutic interventions of some sort.

A Crisis of Legitimacy

The troubles of those who ended up confined in mental hospitals seemed to many to be of a qualitatively different sort from the complaints of those who fetched up in the waiting rooms of nerve-doctors and psychoanalysts. The 'Bedlam mad' who were involuntarily committed to asylums were in many instances those who exhibited massive and lasting disturbances of behaviour, emotion and intellect – signs that signalled a complete loss of contact with the common-sense reality the rest of us share. They clung to beliefs others viewed as utterly delusional. They hallucinated, seeing and hearing things that had no external reality. They exhibited social withdrawal to an extreme degree, often accompanied by a profound loss of emotional responsiveness, and many ultimately descended into a state of dementia.

These were the people the Victorians had called lunatics or the insane. By the early twentieth century, those terms were increasingly viewed as anachronistic. Instead, those who had once themselves been referred to as mad-doctors, alienists or medico-psychologists (and increasingly preferred to answer to the title 'psychiatrist'), now referred to their charges as psychotic. Some began to adopt the nomenclature proposed by the German psychiatrist Emil Kraepelin (p. 263), and spoke of those afflicted with dementia praecox or manic-depressive illness. During the first four decades of the twentieth century, and beyond, these became the preferred terms for describing such forms of mental disturbance – though praecox patients were increasingly labelled schizophrenic once the Swiss psychiatrist Eugen Bleuler had come up with that term in 1908, not least because it seemed to suggest a less hopeless prognosis than calling someone prematurely demented. But a confusing collection of symptoms gathered under each of these two major diagnostic umbrellas, and the distinctions between the diagnoses were more readily made in theory than in practice. Nor was everyone convinced that they were two radically distinct forms of psychiatric disturbance, and manic-depressive patients who failed to get well were liable to find themselves reclassified as schizophrenic. At the very least, however, creating new names for madness appeared to lend some order to chaos, and provided a basis on which the profession could try to come to terms with the pathologies it sought to treat.

Numerically and politically, the branch of psychiatry that ministered to the needs of patients like these occupied the dominant position within the profession. For decades, that leading faction had embraced a deeply pessimistic and biologically reductionist view of mental illness. Madness, they taught, was the inevitable and irreversible expression of a morbid constitutional defect. That absolved the profession of blame for its failure to cure, and allowed psychiatry to present itself as providing a social function of inestimable value, the 'sequestration' of 'morbid varieties or degenerations of the human kind', who might even be 'extruded violently'.[22] But the redefinition of the profession's mission as one of quarantining the incurable rather than restoring the temporarily distracted to sanity left a specialism that saw itself as part of a healing profession in a distinctly uncomfortable position. To play the role of a glorified board-house keeper was scarcely commensurate with their aspirations to professional status, and the problems this situation posed grew ever more pressing, as comparisons with the state of the rest of the medical profession grew ever more pointed and invidious.

For in the last decades of the nineteenth century, and the first years of the new century, medicine had been transformed. The revolution was a slow one, hindered by the conservatism of most physicians and their commitment to models of illness that had persisted for centuries. But the discoveries of men such as Louis Pasteur (1822–95) and Robert Koch (1843–1910) had eventually forced even the most reactionary elements to embrace the germ theory of disease. Work in the laboratory at first seemed remote from the realities of the bedside, and there was fierce resistance to the new knowledge in many quarters.[23] For example, when Koch announced in 1884 that he had discovered the bacterium that causes cholera, one of the most devastating diseases in the nineteenth century, in the intestines and stools of victims of the disease in Calcutta, his findings were greeted with scepticism in Germany, and promptly repudiated by an official British scientific commission made up of thirteen eminent physicians, one of whose members denounced Koch's work as 'an unfortunate fiasco'.[24]

But scepticism gave way as vaccines were developed against such deadly diseases as rabies and diphtheria, and as a new generation of doctors learned the value of drawing on the authority of laboratory science to legitimize their practice. Joseph Lister (1827–1912) had used Pasteur's researches to justify the use of carbolic acid as an antiseptic in the operating theatre, and he too had found that his claims of decreased mortality and of the bacterial causation of wound infection were spurned by his colleagues. In the not so long run, however, the value of aseptic surgery came to be broadly acknowledged, and the upshot was a remarkable expansion in the kinds of surgery that were technically possible, as well as greatly diminished post-surgical mortality and morbidity. Indeed, by the early twentieth century, the prestige of surgery and general medicine was soaring. The prospects of their practitioners were transformed, and it was confidently expected that medical science would soon extend its dominion over still wider realms of disease and debility. The practical payoffs of the bacteriological revolution seemed limitless.

Psychiatry had no such triumphs to report, at least before Wagner-Jauregg began to boast of the breakthrough his malarial treatment represented.

The discipline's therapeutic impotence might be explained away by gestures towards defective heredity, but at the price of professional marginalization of the specialty, and a profound sense of disillusion among its more ambitious practitioners. Small wonder, then, that a number of them, while clinging tightly to the belief that mental illness was rooted in biology, sought a way out of the cul-de-sac they found themselves in. In some quarters, the search was soon on for ways to intervene, and for alternative theories of the origins of mental illness that might lead in more promising directions.

Kraepelin himself had flirted with one possible alternative aetiology for madness, and he became increasingly convinced of its importance. Might not dementia praecox and manic-depressive illness, he mused in successive editions of his authoritative textbook, prove in reality to be the result of auto-intoxication, the self-poisoning of the brain by chronic infections lurking elsewhere in the body?[25] A number of prominent figures in general medicine had begun to embrace similar ideas as they strove to bring a variety of chronic ailments – arthritis, rheumatism, heart and kidney disease – into the bacteriological paradigm that now exercised an all-encompassing influence in medicine. The confirmation of syphilitic origins of GPI seemed to many psychiatrists to point to a more general hypothesis about the roots of mental illness.

The Germ of Madness

Prominent among these psychiatrists was Henry Cotton (1876–1933), a young American with a dazzling academic resumé. Adolf Meyer (1866–1950), a Swiss-trained psychiatrist who had emigrated to the United States in 1892, had set up an extremely selective training programme at the Worcester State Hospital, Massachusetts, in 1896, designed to train a fresh generation of practitioners who could serve as the shock troops of a new, scientific psychiatry, one that would bring the tools and techniques of the laboratory to bear on the recalcitrant problem of treating madness. Cotton had worked under him and then, with Meyer's support, travelled to Germany in 1906 to train directly under the men who were widely regarded as the most important figures in the field at the time, including Alois Alzheimer (after whom Alzheimer's disease is named) and Kraepelin himself. Back in the United States, and barely thirty, Cotton then secured one of the glittering prizes of his profession, the superintendency of a state hospital.

Once established at Trenton in New Jersey in 1907, Cotton was determined to remake his asylum into a modern hospital. Within less than a decade, he had installed a new operating theatre, improved laboratories and accumulated a substantial professional library filled with the current medical literature. More importantly from his point of view, and building upon the hints Kraepelin had provided, he had become convinced that he had uncovered the aetiology of madness. All forms of mental illness, he announced, from the mildest to the most severe, were the manifestation of a single underlying disorder: 'I do not believe there is any fundamental difference in the functional psychoses. The more we study our cases, [the more] we are forced to conclude that distinct disease entities in the functional group…do not exist.'[26] The very name 'mental illness' was a misnomer, since what all mental patients were suffering from was an illness like any other, one rooted in disturbances of the body. Fortunately, the pathologies in question were not the consequence of defective heredity, as most of his psychiatric colleagues mistakenly believed, but were caused by the same germs that modern medical science had implicated in the aetiology of so many other diseases. Their presence could be demonstrated in the laboratory, and their pernicious effects removed by the practice of what he called surgical bacteriology.

Chronic infections, Cotton contended, lurked unseen in various parts of the body, creating toxins that spread through the bloodstream to poison the brain. Initially convinced that the teeth and tonsils were the primary cause of the trouble, he sought their removal on a massive scale. When that did not suffice to produce a cure, he looked elsewhere. 'Modern methods of clinical diagnosis,' he announced, 'such as the X-ray, bacteriological and serological examinations – in conjunction with a careful history and a thorough physical examination – will, in the majority of cases, bring to light these hidden infections of which the patient is usually blissfully ignorant.'[27] Stomachs, spleens, cervixes, and most especially colons, were likely sources of trouble, and all might need to be surgically excised, in whole or in part. Some might worry about the effects of this programme of surgical evisceration. Cotton hastened to put such doubts at rest: 'The stomach is for all the world like a cement mixer often used in the erection of large buildings and just about as necessary. The large bowel is, similarly, for storage and we can dispense with it just as freely as with the stomach.'[28] Aggressive treatment along these lines, he contended, cured up to 85 per cent of the mad.

Cotton was not alone in pursuing the goal of curing mental illness by eliminating chronic infections. In England, Thomas Chivers Graves (1883–1964), who was in charge of all the mental hospitals in and around Birmingham, had independently reached similar conclusions, and though he lacked the resources to perform abdominal surgery, he aggressively removed teeth and tonsils, opened up and cleansed sinuses, and washed faecal matter from the body with prolonged colonic irrigations. When Cotton visited Britain on two occasions in the 1920s, both men basked in the approval of the leading lights of the British medical establishment. On the occasion of Cotton's first visit in 1923, Sir Frederick Mott (1853–1926), a Fellow of the Royal Society and pathologist to all London's mental hospitals, extravagantly praised his work, as did the newly installed president of Britain's major psychiatric association, Edwin Goodall (1863–1944).[29] Four years later, after Cotton had addressed a joint meeting of the British Medical Association and the Medico-Psychological Association, he was lauded by the president of the Royal College of Surgeons, Sir Berkeley Moynihan (1865–1936), as the psychiatric Lister. 'No mental hospital will in the future', he predicted, 'be considered as adequately equipped unless it has an X-ray laboratory, a skilled bacteriologist, and can command the services of an enlightened surgeon.'[30]

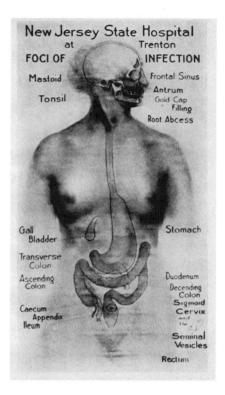

Foci of infection: a chart Henry Cotton used repeatedly, displaying all the nooks and crannies in the body where focal sepsis could lurk undetected, insidiously poisoning the body and brain.

Despite the fact that Cotton and Graves attracted some prominent admirers – in the United States these included John Harvey Kellogg, the breakfast magnate and superintendent of the famed Battle Creek Sanitarium (see Chapter Nine), Hubert Work (1860–1942), president of the American Medical Association, and Stewart Paton (1865–1942), author of the most influential American textbook of psychiatry of the early twentieth century – they also attracted vocal criticism. Curiously, none of the critics seized upon Cotton's admission that his abdominal surgery was accompanied by mortality rates that approached one-third of those he treated.[31] Psychiatrists complained of being besieged by families urging them to employ the miracle cure that Cotton's treatment promised, and voiced disquiet at the extravagance of his claims and the 'over-optimistic estimate of what can be done along surgical and bacteriological lines'.[32] But almost no one questioned the legitimacy of allowing colleagues to engage in such large-scale experimentation on captive bodies, or saw fit to make an issue of the large number of maimed or even dead patients that the operations produced. America's most powerful and prominent psychiatrist, Adolf Meyer, who had taken on the ethically dubious task of supervising an inquiry into the results of his protégé Henry Cotton's work (and had learned that the real mortality figures of the surgery approached 45 per cent), simply suppressed its findings, preferring to avoid a potential scandal rather than intervening to protect patient lives.[33]

Shock Therapy

Wagner-Jauregg's experiments with malaria, and Cotton and Graves's single-mindedpursuit of the threat of chronic sepsis proved to be the opening salvo of a wave of psychiatric experimentation on the vulnerable bodies of those confined in mental hospitals. All across Europe and North America, the 1920s and 1930s witnessed the introduction of a quite remarkable array of somatic treatments designed to root out madness and restore the lunatic to sanity. Everywhere, the desperation felt by the families of those whose minds were unhinged, the professional ambitions of psychiatrists eager to move beyond their assigned role as curators of museums of the mad, and the fiscal pressures that the burden of chronic madness visited upon the body politic, encouraged therapeutic experimentation, and no countervailing forces held it in check. Certainly, patients had little say in the matter. Morally, socially and physically removed from the ranks of humankind, locked up in institutions impervious to the gaze of outsiders, deprived of their status as moral actors, and presumed by virtue of their mental state to lack the capacity to make informed choices for themselves, patients were mostly unable to resist those who controlled their very existence, though some managed to do so.

Many of the more extravagant interventions have faded from our collective memory. Who now recalls that barbiturates were employed to produce deep, prolonged sleep as a means of disconnecting the mentally ill from their mad thoughts?[34] Or the injection of horse serum into spinal canals to produce meningitis, thus provoking high fevers and mobilizing the body's immune system, so that 'the scavenger action of these cells would rid the central nervous system of toxins that were deleterious to its proper functioning'?[35] Or the experiments by Harvard psychiatrists at the McLean Hospital, the private resort for disturbed Boston Brahmins, where body temperatures were deliberately lowered to 85 degrees Fahrenheit (29 degrees Centigrade) and below, temperatures barely consistent (and sometimes, it turned out, not consistent) with life?[36] Or the resort to injections of strychnine or colloidal calcium, or of cyanide?[37]

If these interventions enjoyed limited popularity and only a short life, others such as lobotomy and electro-convulsive therapy lasted, spread much more widely and had a dramatic impact on public perceptions of mental illness and its treatment. As we shall see below, ultimately, when some renegade psychiatrists embraced 'anti-psychiatry' in the 1960s and beyond, they would find a new reflection in popular culture. In novels and in Hollywood films psychiatrists would be vividly invoked as part of a portrait of a healing profession run amok, sadistically employing what masqueraded as treatment as weapons in the subjugation of the mad. When these new treatments emerged, however, they were almost uniformly hailed by the psychiatric profession and by the new category of science journalists as demonstrations of how progress in medical science was finally being brought to bear on the therapeutics of mental disorder.

By the late nineteenth and early twentieth centuries, the laboratory revolution in medicine was extending beyond investigation of the bacteriological origins of disease. One of the most dramatic therapeutic breakthroughs that resulted from work on the endocrine system occurred in 1922, when Frederick Banting (1891–1941) and Charles Best (1899–1978) in Canada successfully isolated insulin, and used it to bring a whole ward of comatose and dying children back to life. How else might this magic compound prove useful?

Born in Nadwórna in what was then a province of the Austro-Hungarian empire (but part of Poland between the two world wars, and now in the Ukraine), Manfred Sakel (1900–57) was practising at the Lichterfelde Hospital in Berlin in the late 1920s, a private psychiatric facility where he treated morphine and heroin addicts. Seeking to alleviate withdrawal symptoms, and to stimulate his patients' appetites, he began using the new hormone. On occasion, they lapsed into a hypoglycemic coma. Relocating to Vienna in 1933, he was assigned to a ward for schizophrenics and began experimenting with what he called insulin shock therapy. By November 1933, he was reporting the first results to the Verein für Neurologie und Psychiatrie. He was soon claiming a 70 per cent remission rate, with many other patients, on his account, improving considerably. By the time the Swiss Psychiatric Society assembled in 1937,[38] there were favourable reports from as many as twenty-two countries about the efficacy of the treatment. Facing a rising tide of Austrian anti-Semitism, however, Sakel relocated to New York, to a post at the Harlem Valley State Hospital, and remained in America till his death from a heart attack in 1957. Sakel proselytized energetically on behalf of his discovery, noting that

> it consists essentially of the production of consecutive daily
> shocks with very high doses of insulin; these occasionally provoke
> epileptic seizures, but more frequently produce somnolence or
> coma, accompanied by profuse perspiration – in any case a clinical
> picture which would ordinarily be alarming....When we consider,
> however, that the patients who come to us for treatment are
> generally looked upon as lost or very seriously ill in any case,
> I think there is very good justification for attempting a therapy,
> however dangerous, which gives some promise of success.[39]

Dangerous and dramatic the treatment most certainly was. Medical and nursing attention had to be constant and unremitting, as the patients hovered on the brink of death. Despite the most assiduous attention, between 2 and 5 per cent of those treated died. The rest were resuscitated with injections of glucose. Dozens of such treatments were administered in a single case, and the treatment was widely embraced,[40] though its demands on scarce resources ensured that only a small minority of patients received it.

Sakel himself thought that 'the mode of action of the epileptic seizure is on the one hand like a battering ram which breaks through the barriers in resistant cases, so that the "regular troops" of hypoglycaemia can march through'.[41] Controlled studies eventually demonstrated that insulin coma therapy was useless, though the initial reaction of many prominent psychiatrists to this challenge was fury,[42] and in some places it remained in use until the early 1960s. At Trenton State Hospital as late as 1961, for example, the Princeton mathematician John Nash (who in 1994 was awarded the Nobel

Prize for his contributions to game theory) received insulin coma therapy to treat his schizophrenia.[43]

If resource constraints always placed limits on the use of insulin comas, these problems did not inhibit the use of other forms of shock therapy developed in the 1930s. Just a year after Sakel announced his novel therapy, a Hungarian psychiatrist, Ladislas Meduna (1896–1964), working in Budapest, began to experiment with ways to produce convulsions in his patients. His flimsy rationale was the (false) assertion that schizophrenia and epilepsy could not co-exist. He first made use of injections of camphor in oil, but these were poorly tolerated and proved an unreliable way of provoking seizures, besides being linked with 'anxiety [that] amounts to panic and is associated with assaultive and suicidal behaviour'.[44] Undeterred, he experimented with strychnine, and when that also proved unsatisfactory, settled on injections of pentathylenetetrazol (soon known as metrazol in the United States) as his drug of choice.

Metrazol, while somewhat more predictable in its effects, had scarcely less savage consequences than camphor for those injected with it. Meduna himself spoke of using 'brute force...as with dynamite, endeavouring to blow asunder the pathological sequences and restore the diseased organism to normal functioning...a violent onslaught...because at present nothing less than such a shock to the organism is powerful enough to break the chain of noxious processes that leads to schizophrenia'.[45] One contemporary observer commented that 'outstanding among other very marked reactions are the patients' facial and verbal expressions testifying to their feelings of being excessively frightened, tortured, and overwhelmed by fear of impending death'.[46] And this existential terror was not the only, or even the most severe of the side effects. As another psychiatrist reported, 'the most serious drawback to this treatment is the occurrence of such complications as joint dislocations, fractures, heart damage, permanent brain trauma, and even an occasional death. Because of the extreme fear and apprehension shown by most patients towards the treatment and because of the violent convulsion and serious complications which result at times, a search for some satisfactory substitute is in progress.'[47]

It was discovered quite rapidly. In Rome, two Italian physicians, Ugo Cerletti (1877–1963) and Lucio Bini (1908–64), had been experimenting with passing electrical currents through dogs to observe their physiological effects. Many of the animals died, but then a chance visit to a slaughterhouse,

Ugo Cerletti witnessed pigs being stunned with electrodes like these in a slaughterhouse in Rome, providing the inspiration for administering electroshock to psychiatric patients.

where pigs were stunned by passing a current through their heads prior to having their throats slit, suggested that using a similar technique in humans (minus the butchering) might have therapeutic possibilities. In April 1938, they undertook the first human trial with what came to be called electro-convulsive therapy, or ECT, and after initially using too little current, succeeded in provoking a grand mal seizure in their patient. ECT, it transpired, was both cheaper and more reliable than metrazol, and the effects were essentially instantaneous: no long and uncertain period of terror while waiting for the convulsion, and upon recovery, so Cerletti claimed, the patient had no memory of what had just occurred. Straightforward and inexpensive to deliver, ECT was soon embraced internationally.[48] It, too, was associated with fractures, particularly of the hip socket and the spine, and as early as 1942, to avoid these problems, ECT began to be administered with a muscle relaxant, first curare and then succinylcholine, which required the use of anaesthesia and oxygenation.[49]

Controversies swirled about whether the new shock therapies worked by damaging the brain. The Harvard neurologist Stanley Cobb (1887–1968) conducted a series of animal experiments and concluded that 'the therapeutic effect of insulin and metrazol may be due to the destruction of great numbers of nerve cells in the cerebral cortex. This destruction is irreparable.... The use of these measures in the treatment of psychoses and neuroses from which recovery may occur seems to me entirely unjustifiable.'[50] Sakel drew the opposite conclusion: while conceding that cutting off the brain's supply of oxygen during insulin comas created brain damage, he speculated, completely without evidence, that the cells killed were the malignant ones

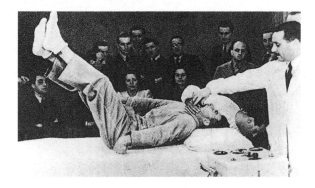

A patient seizing after receiving unmodified ECT (1948): Lucio Bini is the figure on the right checking the patient's mouthguard.

that caused psychosis.[51] The advocates of ECT exhibited no such propensity to embrace the idea that the usefulness of the treatment they employed might rest on its brain-damaging effects, and though some critics made, and continue to make, such claims, they were scorned by the procedure's proponents.[52]

Targeting Brains

No one argued, however, that the other major physical treatment developed in the second half of the 1930s didn't produce brain damage, because the very basis of this approach rested upon a direct surgical assault on the frontal lobes of the brain. Leucotomy (or lobotomy as its principal American proponents preferred to call it) was an idea developed by the Portuguese neurologist Egas Moniz (1874–1955). Portugal in the mid-1930s was a backward and impoverished country ruled over by a right-wing dictator, António Salazar, and in the ordinary course of events, a small-scale experiment conducted there might have been of little consequence. Moniz could not perform his operation himself because his hands were crippled by arthritis, so he was dependent upon a colleague, Pedro Almeida Lima (1903–86), to do the surgery. The first handful of operations involved boring holes into the skull and injecting alcohol into the frontal lobes to destroy brain tissue. The results were encouraging, to Moniz at least, though in subsequent surgery a small knife-like device was used instead to sever portions of the white matter of the frontal lobes. Between November 1935 and February 1936, the surgery was performed on twenty patients, some of whom had been 'ill' for as little as four weeks. Though follow-up was perfunctory, Moniz acknowledged that the patients frequently exhibited incontinence, apathy and disorientation. But he insisted that these effects would prove to be transitory, and that 35 per cent of those he had treated were improved substantially, and another 35 per cent were somewhat better. These claims were challenged by Sobral Cid (1877–1941), the psychiatrist who had supplied Moniz with his patients. Those operated on, he asserted, were profoundly damaged, not improved, and he refused to send any more patients to share their fate.

Yet Moniz had swiftly published a monograph in Paris asserting his claim to have secured improvement in 70 per cent of the schizophrenics he had operated upon.[53] Those claims impressed Walter Freeman (1895–1977), a neurologist in Washington, DC, and by September 1936, he and his neurosurgeon colleague James Watts (1904–94) had performed the first American operation. By the following year, the two men had modified the operation and were drilling through the skull before inserting an instrument that resembled a butter knife to make sweeping cuts through the frontal lobes, severing brain connections and, so they claimed, producing remarkable results. They dubbed the new operation the standard or 'precision' lobotomy, though there was nothing precise about inflicting random damage on patients' brains.

Freeman and Watts had difficulty deciding just how much brain tissue to destroy: too little, and the patient remained mad; too much, and the outcome was a human vegetable, or even death on the operating table. They convinced themselves that the solution was to cut until the patient exhibited signs of disorientation. That meant, of course, performing the operation under local anaesthetic. Watts cut, while Freeman asked a series of questions, and kept a transcript of the replies. The typewritten records are disturbing to read, none more so than the exchange when Freeman asked the person on the operating table what was passing through his mind and, after a pause, the patient responded, 'a knife'.

Such operations were, the surgeons pronounced, a great success, rescuing numerous patients from a lifetime of chronic illness on the back wards of a mental hospital. Many of their colleagues were unconvinced. Indeed, when Freeman first announced what they had been doing, at a meeting of the Southern Medical Society in Baltimore, he was greeted with 'sharp criticism and cries of alarm…a chorus of…hostile cross-examination' that abated only when Adolf Meyer, the eminent professor of psychiatry at nearby Johns Hopkins University, intervened to urge the audience to allow the experiment to proceed.[54] And proceed it did.

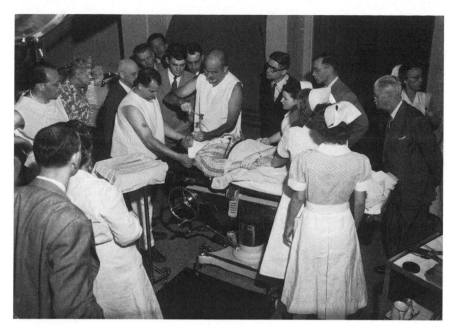

Walter Freeman performing a transorbital lobotomy at Fort Steilacoom hospital in Washington State on 8 July 1948. An ice pick is being driven into the patient's brain via the orbit over the eye.

Gradually, Freeman's insistence that the operation worked miracles bore fruit, and mental hospitals in the United States began to make use of it.[55] William Sargant (1907–88), a British psychiatrist who shared much of Freeman's evangelical zeal and his conviction that madness was rooted in the brain, and who had been awarded a Rockefeller Foundation fellowship to spend time at Harvard, came down to view the results. He subsequently departed for Britain where he performed many lobotomies himself, and encouraged his colleagues to follow suit.[56] The Second World War slowed things, and a more pressing problem was that there were, at the time, very few neurosurgeons, and the 'precision' operation took as long as two hours to perform.

Searching for a way to speed up the process, and allow the operation to make a serious dent in the nearly half a million mad folk thronging the wards of America's mental hospitals, Freeman came across an article in the Italian medical literature outlining a much simpler way to access the frontal lobes,[57] so simple, in fact, that Freeman later boasted that in twenty minutes, he could teach any damn fool to perform a lobotomy, even a psychiatrist. (Psychiatry was a profession the neurologically trained Freeman held in low regard.) Transorbital lobotomy, as Freeman christened his new approach, was something he first attempted on an outpatient basis. Two or three electroshocks were administered in rapid succession, rendering the patient unconscious. An ice-pick was introduced under the eyelid and a mallet was used to break through the eye socket and penetrate to the frontal lobes. A sweeping motion was used to sever brain tissue, the patient was supplied with sunglasses to cover up the resultant black eyes, and upon regaining consciousness was, according to Freeman, able to resume normal activities in a surprisingly short amount of time.

Transorbital lobotomy was immediately controversial. James Watts, Freeman's long-time partner, was appalled and a sharp rift developed between the two men. Watts's mentor at Yale Medical School, John Fulton (1899–1960), made his displeasure known, writing to Freeman to threaten him with physical violence if he came near New Haven. But Freeman was not in the least deterred. He insisted that his new operation was more effective and less damaging to the brain than the more elaborate procedures being developed by neurosurgeons. He barnstormed across the United States demonstrating how easily transorbital operations could be performed. Where a standard 'precision' lobotomy took two to four hours, Freeman demonstrated that he could operate on upwards of a dozen patients in a single afternoon.[58] He and Watts had together performed 625 operations between 1936 and 1948. By 1957, Freeman alone had performed another 2,400 transorbital operations, and state hospitals across the country had adopted the procedure during the late 1940s.[59]

The adoption of these various forms of physical treatment was a matter of great pride to psychiatrists, mental hospital administrators and politicians. Here were visible symbols of psychiatry's reconnection to scientific medicine and its break from early isolation and therapeutic impotence. The official journal of New York State's massive network of mental hospitals (eighteen in all) trumpeted them as a sure sign of progress:

> The physical therapies have emphasized the essential unity of
> mind and body. The fact that mental illnesses are in a degree
> amenable to procedures easily comprehended by all as 'treatment'
> goes far to establish the attitude that these are really illnesses like
> all others, and not incomprehensible reactions which split the
> victim away from the rest of mankind and from ordinary concepts
> of sickness and treatment.[60]

In the wider culture, the physical treatment of the psychoses received a similarly laudatory reception. *Time* magazine praised Sakel, 'a young Viennese psychiatrist, who cures...disoriented wits by means of insulin',[61] and some years later, the *New York Times*' science reporter, William Lawrence, dubbed him 'the Pasteur of Psychiatry'.[62] When Hollywood depicted the travails of America's mental hospitals after the war, electroshock was portrayed sympathetically to a vast audience, and presented as vital to speeding the recovery of Virginia Cunningham, the heroine of the film *The Snake Pit* (played by Olivia de Havilland). It was the talk therapy administered by her handsome psychiatrist, 'Dr Kik', that ultimately brought about her cure, but shock treatment played an indispensable role in making her accessible to analysis. The highest grossing film of 1948, *The Snake Pit*

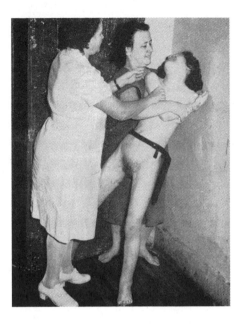

A patient futilely resisting being taken to be lobotomized. Freeman made no secret of his willingness to lobotomize patients who resisted psychosurgery – because they were mad, their preferences could be disregarded. This image is taken from the second edition of his and Watts's book, Psychosurgery.

was shown in Britain only with a disclaimer insisted upon by the Board of Censors reminding a British audience that it was an American film, and that conditions in their own mental hospitals were wonderful – far from the appalling back wards depicted on the screen.

Lobotomy and its principal protagonist, Walter Freeman, were presented in still more positive terms. Early on, the *Washington Evening Star* informed its readers that lobotomy 'probably constitutes one of the greatest surgical innovations of this generation.... It seems unbelievable that uncontrollable sorrow could be changed into normal resignation with an auger and a knife.'[63] Later on, the science reporter Waldemar Kaempffert wrote a hagiographic essay for the *Saturday Evening Post*, with pictures of Freeman and Watts operating, a piece that reached an even larger audience when it was abridged and published in *Reader's Digest*, which enjoyed a huge international circulation.[64] And an Associated Press story was similarly positive, referring to the lobotomy as 'a personality rejuvenator' that cut out the 'worry nerves' and was almost completely safe – 'only a little more dangerous than an operation to remove an infected tooth'.[65] Shortly thereafter, the operation received what was surely the most unambiguous endorsement of its merits when the Nobel Prize committee awarded the 1949 prize in medicine or physiology to Egas Moniz.[66] Moniz's award promoted an explosive increase in the number of lobotomies. In the United States alone, twice as many operations were performed in the last four months of 1949 as in the preceding eight. By 1953, 20,000 additional Americans had been lobotomized,[67] alongside thousands more around the world.

Backlash

Yet the popular and professional enthusiasm for these desperate remedies did not last. Already by the 1950s, support was steadily ebbing, and by the 1960s insulin comas, shock therapies and psychosurgery were assailed as symbols of psychiatric oppression. Renegade psychiatrists, who soon came to be lumped together as 'anti-psychiatrists', including the political opposites Thomas Szasz (1920–2012) and R. D. Laing (1927–89), made the case against them from (barely) within the profession, and on this issue, at least, many of their professional colleagues agreed with them. Even more pointed, however, was the mounting volume of criticism in literary circles and in popular culture.

Ernest Hemingway's (1899–1961) increasing depression had led to his admission to the Mayo Clinic in December 1960, where he received a series of ECTs. Discharged in mid-January 1961, his mental state remained fragile till his readmission in April, when he was once again treated with more shock therapy. Released on 30 June, he committed suicide two days later, shooting himself with a shotgun and blowing his head off. He left behind a denunciation of his treatment:

> What these shock doctors don't know is about writers…and what they do to them…. What is the sense of ruining my head and erasing my memory, which is my capital, and putting me out of business? It was a brilliant cure but we lost the patient.[68]

If the über-masculine Hemingway authored one damning assault on shock therapy, the poet and feminist icon Sylvia Plath (1932–63) provided another. Her novel, *The Bell Jar*, is a barely disguised *roman-à-clef*, and contains a vivid portrait of her own experiences with ECT, used (with insulin coma therapy) in her treatment for depression and a failed suicide attempt:

> I tried to smile, but my skin had gone stiff, like parchment. Doctor Gordon was fitting two metal plates on either side of my head. He buckled them into place with a strap that dented my forehead and gave me a wire to bite. I shut my eyes. There was a brief silence, like an indrawn breath. Then something bent down and took hold of me and shook me like the end of the world. Whee-ee-ee-ee-ee, it shrilled, through an air crackling with blue light, and with each flash a great jolt drubbed me till I thought my bones would break and the sap fly out of me like a split plant.
>
> I wondered what terrible thing it was that I had done.[69]

That Plath killed herself barely a month after her first and only novel appeared in 1963 was in all likelihood wholly unconnected to her treatment a decade earlier. Her suicide quickly became bound up with accusations others laid against her husband, Ted Hughes. But as she came to be regarded, however simplistically, as a symbol of the despair of the housewife and young mother, betrayed by a perfidious husband and unable to realize her talent, her earlier psychiatric treatment could easily be read as still another example of her oppression by patriarchal society.

Defenders of ECT (and many contemporary psychiatrists and patients continue to swear by it, though others equally passionately swear at it) would rightly complain that the cases of Hemingway and Plath are mere anecdotes, with no bearing one way or the other on the clinical value of ECT. But their testimonies both contributed to and formed part of a sea change in cultural attitudes to psychiatry, and more particularly to the physical treatments an earlier generation had been inclined to greet as evidence of scientific progress. With the exception of the flirtation in some quarters with the notion that focal sepsis poisoned the brain and thus produced mental illness (see p. 306), none of the array of physical treatments introduced in the 1920s and 1930s had any plausible rationale for why they worked. They just did. And then it turned out they didn't. And when faith was lost in insulin comas, in electrically induced convulsions, in the value of inflicting irreversible damage to the brain as a means of 'curing' mental illness, the backlash was severe.

Novels such as Ken Kesey's *One Flew Over the Cuckoo's Nest* (1962) and Janet Frame's *Faces in the Water* (1961) cast psychiatry in a devastating light.

Kesey had worked as an orderly at a mental hospital in Menlo Park, California, and portrayed an institution that cavalierly employed electroshock to discipline and subdue its patients. When such treatment failed to rein in the irrepressible hero of his novel, Randle P. McMurphy, the ultimate weapon was implemented, and he was lobotomized. The New Zealand novelist Frame had had a much closer encounter with the ministrations of a somatically orientated psychiatry. Hospitalized in a series of dehumanizing mental hospitals over a period of several years, beginning in the mid-1940s, Frame was treated with insulin comas and more than two hundred electroshocks, and was mere days away from a lobotomy at the Seacliff Mental Hospital when the surgeon's hand was stayed – by the award to her of the Hubert Church Memorial Award, one of her country's principal literary prizes. Over the years to come she developed a major international reputation, and her novels, laced with autobiographical references to her harsh treatment at the hands of incompetent and sadistic psychiatrists, were exceeded in their impact only by her three-volume autobiography, and its adaptation for the screen by the New Zealand director Jane Campion as *An Angel at My Table* (1990).

If Campion's film was a critical and an art-house success, winning a series of major prizes, Miloš Forman's adaptation of *One Flew Over the Cuckoo's Nest*, released fifteen years earlier, in 1975, was an extraordinary popular success. It won five major Oscars and it still remains, forty years after its release, an iconic and much-watched film. It is far from Hollywood's only portrayal of lobotomy as a brutal and criminal operation, carried out by sadistic and uncaring doctors. Graeme Clifford's 1982 film *Frances*, starring Jessica Lange as the Hollywood starlet Frances Farmer, is just as unsparing. Lange is tortured by being subjected to insulin comas and is given a series of electroshocks, repeatedly raped while chained to her bed and is then casually lobotomized by someone who, not coincidentally, is made up to look exactly like Walter Freeman. But Lange's performance, while powerful, pales besides Jack Nicholson's portrait of Randle P. McMurphy. Having contrived his admission to a mental hospital, assuming a 'crazy house' will be a pleasanter place to idle away his time than the prison where he is serving the last portion of a sentence for statutory rape, McMurphy creates mayhem. Wise-cracking, disobedient, defiant, he at first fruitlessly urges his fellow-inmates, their spirits crushed, to join him in rebellion, only to discover that his release date is now in the hands of his psychiatric captors. Refusing to buckle to what the film presents as unalloyed psychiatric oppression, he next is sent for electroshock treatment, the purpose of which is unambiguously punitive. It fails to effect the desired result. Only a lobotomy, an operation that reduces him to a human vegetable, can smash his spirit. So that is his fate.

These images indelibly altered public perceptions of the status of the various somatic treatments in psychiatry, and sullied the reputation of the profession itself. By the time the films were made, all but ECT had been abandoned by the profession, which now had at its disposal a variety of psycho-pharmaceutical remedies for schizophrenia and depression, not to mention a host of lesser mental ills (as discussed in Chapter Twelve). Mainstream psychiatrists might continue to protest that electroshock treatment deserved a place in their therapeutic armamentarium for malignant forms of depression that resisted chemical remedies. But in popular culture the verdict was in: ECT was a dangerous and inhumane practice, an intervention that fried people's brains and destroyed their memories. As for lobotomy, a handful of professional historians have recently tried to rehabilitate it, at least in part. Theirs has proved a hopeless endeavour. Not just among the Scientologists – for whom it is a gift that keeps on giving – but also among the public at large, the consensus is clear: lobotomy was a crime, and its chief perpetrator, Walter Freeman, nothing less than a moral monster.

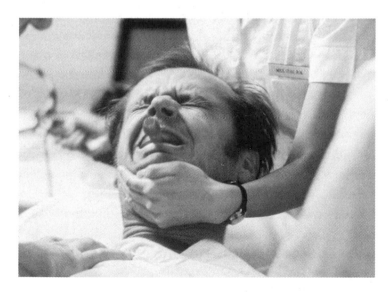

Jack Nicholson (as Randle P. McMurphy) in the 1975 film One Flew Over the Cuckoo's Nest *receives ECT to punish him for his disruption of ward routine and to force him to conform. When ECT fails, lobotomy is the last resort.*

Chapter Eleven

A MEANINGFUL
INTERLUDE

The Search for Meaning

Institutional psychiatry and its infatuation with treatments aimed at the body were responsible for the care of the overwhelming majority of mental patients in the first half of the twentieth century. Indeed, the mental hospital and the therapies its rulers advocated spread around the globe in these years. The French and the British eagerly took these emblems of Western civilization to their colonies, even if the natives sometimes appeared to be less than enamoured of these marks of progress and modernity. In India and Africa,[1] not to mention countries that had largely succeeded in eliminating or marginalizing their indigenous people – Australia, New Zealand, Argentina[2] – mental hospitals proliferated, and so did the insulin comas, electroshock, metrazol and lobotomies that were the stock-in-trade of modern, scientific psychiatry. Even China, not fully colonized by the Western powers though struggling with its semi-subordinate status, saw a handful of Western-style mental hospitals imposed on it. Establishments of this sort co-existed uneasily, however, with views and approaches to madness deeply rooted in China's own ancient medical traditions.[3]

But another, very different sort of psychiatry was now gaining influence. In the years between the two world wars, Freud's theories about mental illness and his therapeutic approach enjoyed increasing popularity, though his teachings always remained a minority taste. In a variety of ways, the experience of trench warfare, and the breakdowns it brought in its train, helped to lend plausibility to the idea that trauma and madness were closely bound up with each other. Patients who had once flocked to spa towns or

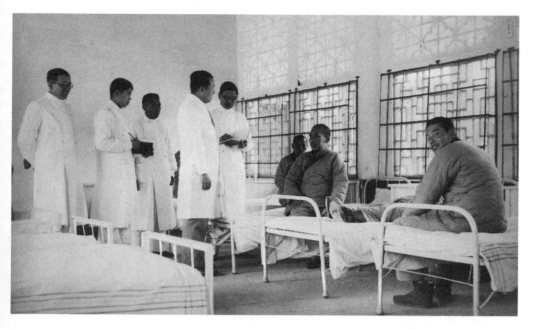

Doctors and patients in the Beijing Asylum in the 1930s. Rockefeller Foundation funds helped to bring the Western model of the asylum to China.

patronized the neurologists' rest cures and static electricity machines, by the first decades of the twentieth century seemed inclined to try psychotherapy instead. And organizationally, while psychoanalysis had its internal squabbles and schisms, it also had some distinctive strengths and sources of appeal that helped it to survive and flourish. The trajectory psychoanalysis followed over much of the twentieth century is thus worth exploring at a general level before we turn to a more detailed exploration of its fate.

The sorts of mental troubles that led increasing numbers of affluent patients to the psychoanalytic couch were as a rule profoundly distressing to those who experienced them. Many of these people seemed to outsiders to be narcissists blessed or cursed with too much money and too much time on their hands, living lives devoid of purpose and prone to forms of exaggerated self-absorption that amounted to little more than hypochondria.[4] Others, however, appeared to those who encountered them to be genuinely incapacitated: overwhelmed by a sense of hopelessness; devastated by crippling torments that arose from they knew not where; or behaving in ways that seemed baffling and almost intolerable to those they lived with. Quite how to decide who belonged in which category was, in individual cases, a matter of some dispute. What was evident, however, was that these patients' complaints did not necessarily undermine their ability to think coherently much of the time, or to exhibit some modicum of control over their actions, however precarious the rule of reason might seem to be at other times. If they possessed sufficient means, they formed a clientele which might provide the basis for a different model of psychiatric practice.

In many respects, in the two decades after the armistice in 1918 psychoanalysis flourished as never before, particularly in the German-speaking parts of Europe. These were difficult times economically. Defeat had left the Axis powers in ruins, burdened with reparations as the penalty for being on the losing side, and in the case of Austria, a mere shadow of its imperial heyday, its territories stripped away and transformed into new nation-states. The grandeur of Vienna remained, though the city was just a shrunken and shattered remnant of its former self. Ruinous hyperinflation gave way by 1929 to worldwide economic collapse. But for much of this period, Freud's intellectual enterprise grew stronger. Its appeal was limited by class and to some degree by ethnicity – its patients and practitioners remained disproportionately Jewish – and by the sectarian splits and squabbles that had begun before the outbreak of the First World War, with the departure of Freud's anointed crown prince, Carl Gustav Jung (1875–1961). Further schisms would haunt the psychoanalytic enterprise for decades.

If psychoanalytic treatment had been used but rarely and exceptionally in the treatment of shell shock, its emphasis on psychic conflict, trauma and repression as the sources of mental turmoil seemed to many to have provided the most plausible account of the mass mental breakdowns that had been so notable a feature of the conflict. Shell-shocked victims did not exactly melt away after the war, but they found themselves scorned and ignored. Promises of pensions were abrogated, except in the United States, which had entered the war late, endured fewer such casualties and since its own Civil War had developed the habit of treating its retired soldiers to an array of welfare benefits it still denies its population at large. But in general, these men, like their comrades who bore more obvious scars as reminders of what they had been through, were an embarrassment and a burden. Their courage had been exploited during the war; their health and their lives had been ruined. Now they were largely left to fend for themselves.

Freud's emphasis on symbols, on psychological conflicts and repressions, hidden meanings and the complexities of contemporary culture led artists, writers, dramatists and film-makers to make use of his ideas in a multitude of ways. Freudian notions infiltrated the advertising business, not least through the efforts of Freud's nephew, Edward Bernays (1891–1995), who founded modern public relations in New York and persuaded businesses that subliminal advertising could do wonders for sales. Psychoanalysis also came to exercise enormous influence in the modernist movement and in the rise of mass culture, not to mention its pervasive impact on child-rearing practices, at least for a time, and on our language and everyday conversations. Even now, judging from the parade of cartoons of patients on the couch, the public image of psychiatry remains in many ways tied to the talk cure and the high priests of psychoanalytic 'science'. And books on Freud and on psychoanalysis are published in astonishing numbers, few having much new to say, but most presumably making a profit for those involved.

How curious. Curious because most mental patients in the twentieth and into the twenty-first century never came near a psychoanalyst. Curious because mainstream psychiatry, except comparatively briefly in German-speaking central Europe until the rise of Hitler, in the United States for a quarter of a century after the Second World War, and more durably in Argentina, has generally viewed Freud's work with indifference, hostility or disdain. Curious because academic psychology has had no time for Freudian ideas, whose place in the modern knowledge factories we call universities has been almost exclusively confined to departments of literature, anthropology and occasionally philosophy. And curious because, outside the ranks of a small group of true believers, few people turn any longer to psychoanalysis in search of a remaking of their own mental life – as if the accountants who manage the costs of modern medical care would permit such a thing anyway. A literate audience continues to be attracted to a complex intellectual edifice that perpetually promises to lay bare the hidden workings of human psychology, while spinning fascinating tales about our unconscious selves and inner lives. In Britain and in France, as well as in a few major American cities, a small minority continues to patronize the analytic couch. But in most of the world, as a therapeutic intervention psychoanalysis is all but moribund.

The Psychoanalytic Movement

To the extent that psychoanalysis attracted a following during the first three-and-a-half decades of the twentieth century, it was largely in the German-speaking areas of Europe – in Austria-Hungary, in Zurich and parts of Switzerland, and, during the Weimar Republic that was created after the First World War, in Germany itself, especially in Berlin. Briefly, during the early years of the new century, Freud had managed to attract the attention and sympathies of Eugen Bleuler, the head of the Burghölzli hospital in Zurich (and the man who coined the term schizophrenia, see p. 265). Like most psychiatrists of his generation, Bleuler was heavily committed to a somatic account of the origins of mental illness, but more willing than most of his contemporaries to countenance a concern with the psychological dimensions of mental disorders. Having favourably reviewed *Studies on Hysteria* by Freud and Josef Breuer, he encouraged members of his staff, including the youthful Carl Jung, to explore the psychoanalytic literature. A number of them became converts to Freud's approach, even as Bleuler himself was distancing himself from psychoanalysis. It was, to his taste, far too dogmatic. In 1911, he resigned from the International Psychoanalytic Association, bluntly informing Freud that its sectarian tendencies, 'this "all or nothing" is in my opinion necessary for religious communities and useful for political parties...but for science I consider it harmful'.[5]

Bleuler's apostasy did not seem to dissuade his underlings. Men such as Karl Abraham (1877–1925), Max Eitingon (1881–1943) and Jung himself continued to proclaim the virtues of psychoanalysis. Jung's early work used word association studies to try to uncover unconscious complexes. His resort to the laboratory and his employment of quantitative techniques imparted an air of science to an enterprise that had hitherto relied upon clinical case studies, and appeared to link psychoanalysis to empirical psychology. Jung attracted considerable attention from outside the ranks of psychoanalysis itself, and his increasing prominence, together with his links to a large mental hospital treating the gravely disturbed, were a considerable asset for Freud. His ideas thus gained at least a hearing among some psychiatrists who might otherwise have simply ignored him, and Freudian notions were absorbed by foreign psychiatrists who came to study at the Burghölzli. But the converts Jung helped to attract were nonetheless a small minority. Led by Emil Kraepelin, most of the professional mainstream in Germany and Austria continued to view psychoanalysis with suspicion if not outright disdain.

French psychiatry meanwhile wanted nothing to do with Freud's theories, a position that wouldn't change in any major way until the 1960s. Nationalism seems to have played a large part in the early French rejection of psychoanalysis. The Franco-Prussian war of 1870–71 and the horrors of the First World War had created an antipathy to all things German, and ironically, given what would transpire in the 1930s, Freud was caught up in the anti-Teutonic backlash. The French claimed that all the interesting ideas he had were anticipated by (French)men including Pierre Janet (1859–1947), who had trained under Charcot. In reality, Janet's theories and approach were far less developed and elaborated than Freud's, and their attraction to a wealthy clientele was sharply undercut by Janet's insistence that susceptibility to psychotherapeutics was proof an underlying biological degeneracy. Still, Freud's ideas struggled to gain much of a hearing in French circles.

In Britain, the most prominent Freudian recruit in the early years of the twentieth century was Ernest Jones (1879–1958), who in time would become Freud's biographer and one of his closest associates. But when he and David Eder (1865–1936) attempted to address the British Medical Association in 1911 on psychoanalysis, the entire audience walked out before their papers could be discussed. To make matters worse, Jones soon had to flee England in the wake of accusations of sexual misconduct with patients.[6] Most British psychiatrists appeared to share Sir James Crichton-Browne's assessment of Freud (or Fraud, as some of them took to calling him). Freud's work, he complained, rested upon the deliberate 'ferreting out [of] verminous reminiscences' best left repressed.[7] Men such as Sir Thomas Clifford Allbutt (1836–1925) and Charles Mercier, among the most influential of Edwardian writers on nervous diseases, objected vociferously to the psychoanalytic tendency to encourage 'men and women to wallow in the very miseries that obsessed them. It either dredged up recollections that were better left buried or allowed the doctor's potent suggestions to create alleged memories that tormented patients more cruelly than their own thoughts ever did.'[8]

In essence, most British psychiatrists in the opening decades of the twentieth century believed that psychoanalysis encouraged morbid introspection when what was called for was a stiff upper lip.[9] The leading British figures in the field thus closed ranks against what they were convinced was German-Jewish nonsense, and when Hugh Crichton-Miller (1877–1959) formed the Tavistock Clinic in 1920 to provide a focus for British psychoanalysts, the head of the Institute of Psychiatry, Edward Mapother (1881–1940), used his political muscle to make sure it had no academic affiliation, no links to the University of London and no access to the public purse.[10] A further complication was that the Tavistock Clinic was too eclectic to suit the tastes of the orthodox analysts, who thus kept their distance.

Freud and the Americans

The New World was different again. Just five years before the First World War had broken out, Freud had been invited to America, as one of twenty-nine speakers at a conference put on to celebrate the twentieth anniversary of the founding of Clark University in Massachusetts. He had a low opinion of Americans, and he had initially declined the invitation. He changed his mind partly at the urging of his then-closest disciple, Carl Jung, but also when the fee he would receive was increased and the date was changed to one more convenient for him. The Doctor of Laws degree he received was to be his only academic honour in his lifetime, and the visit served to establish a small but important bridgehead for psychoanalysis in North America.

Still, it was a bitter-sweet occasion. Freud was scarcely seen as a particularly important participant in the proceedings – his fellow-speakers included two Nobel Prize-winning physicists, as well as academic psychologists and psychiatrists with a much larger profile than his.[11] And the recognition came from Americans; and America, as he would later remark, 'is gigantic – a gigantic mistake'.[12] The whole country, he informed Arnold Zweig (1887–1968) was an 'anti-Paradise' populated by 'savages' and swindlers lacking any semblance of intellectual culture. It ought to be renamed 'Dollaria', after the god it worshipped. Before his visit, he had confided to Jung that 'I...think once they discover the sexual core of our psychological theories they will drop us'.[13] And time did not modify his hatred: 'What is the use of Americans', he belligerently asked Ernest Jones in 1924, 'if they bring no money? They are not good for anything else.' It is a great historical irony, then, that it was in the United States that psychoanalysis would enjoy its greatest success, albeit a success Freud did not live to see.

Freud's visit to the United States had come at a fortuitous time. It was a country of novelties, and one of the novelties Americans invented were new religions, or new variants on old ones: Mormonism, or the Church of Jesus Christ of Latter-day Saints, as its believers prefer; Seventh-day Adventists (the group that founded the Battle Creek Sanitarium); and Jehovah's Witnesses, to name just a few. Some of these new religions, or new Protestant denominations, proclaimed themselves to be in the business of healing body and mind, none of them more insistently than the Church of Christ, Scientist, founded by Mary Baker Eddy in 1879. Opponents of her precepts dubbed Christian Scientists as members of a mind-healing cult, but many had flocked to its teachings, including those afflicted with nervous complaints. Perhaps partly in response, more mainstream Protestant churches had entered the fray. One such, led by the Reverend Elwood Worcester (1862–1940) of the socially exclusive Boston Emmanuel Church, sought to combine religious consolation and psychotherapy with a veneer of medical oversight. Initially, Worcester secured the participation of men such as the Harvard professors William James and James Jackson Putnam (see below), before they recoiled from the Frankenstein monster they belatedly realized they might have helped to create. Psychotherapy, it seemed for a moment, might slip out of medical hands and back into the realm of religion. That would never do. Freud's fierce rejection of these affronts to 'science and reason' in the course of his Clark lectures was welcome indeed to the medical men who heard him speak, and it was a message he sought to convey to a wider audience in an interview with Adelbert Albrecht that appeared in the *Boston Evening Transcript*. 'The instrument of the soul', he noted solemnly, 'is not so easy to play, and my technique is very painstaking and tedious. Any amateur attempt may have the most evil consequence.'[14]

The Clark University Conference, 10 September 1909. Freud (front row, fourth from right) posed among the other participants at the event, including G. Stanley Hall to his right and Carl Jung to his left. William James is third from the left in the front row.

Edith Rockefeller McCormick, the imperious and spendthrift daughter of John D. Rockefeller, was Carl Jung's first Dollar Tante *(aunt).*

During the course of his visit, Freud had won over James Jackson Putnam (1846–1918), who as well as being professor of neurology at Harvard was a member of a Boston Brahmin family whose prominence stretched back to before the American Revolution. It was a vital conversion, for Putnam's blessing helped both to allay some of the concerns about psychoanalysis and sexuality, and to attract some rich patients. It was Putnam, too, who founded the Boston Psychoanalytic Society in 1914. Less impressed was Putnam's colleague William James (1842–1910), brother of the novelist Henry James. James attended only one of Freud's lectures, though he did engage him in conversation on a long walk, an exchange interrupted at times by James's angina, a heart condition that would soon kill him. James pronounced himself unpersuaded, finding Freud 'a man obsessed with fixed ideas. I can make nothing in my own case with his dream theories, and obviously "symbolism" is a most dangerous method.' In a subsequent letter, he was still more scathing: 'I strongly suspect Freud…of being a regular *halluciné*.'[15]

The aftermath of Freud's visit scarcely witnessed a cascade of converts to his theories. The publication of an English-language version of his Clark lectures, which Freud himself had delivered in German, did make his basic ideas accessible to an Anglophone audience for the first time, and it was this, together with his *Three Essays on the Theory of Sexuality* (1905), that probably did more to spread his theories in American circles over the long run. The shell shock epidemic also helped to make ideas about the psychological roots of mental disturbance more plausible to some Americans, as it had done elsewhere. But mainstream American psychiatry remained hostile, seeing talk therapy as an irrelevance, or worse, when it came to treating patients who were regarded as the casualties of mental diseases firmly rooted in disorders of the body.

Some members of the rich and chattering classes, by contrast, were attracted to Freud's ideas and sought psychoanalytic treatment. To Freud's dismay, however, the two richest among them, Edith Rockefeller McCormick (1872–1932) and Mary Mellon (d. 1946), were attracted to the apostate Carl Jung, and invested substantial portions of their fortunes in an attempt – largely futile – to foster the spread of Jungian ideas.[16] Relations between Freud and Jung had festered after they returned from America, and by 1912 they had turned positively poisonous. In January 1913 the two men broke off all relations, and by the following year the schism had become irrevocable. The one-time Crown Prince of psychoanalysis severed all remaining ties with the Freudian movement, and began to develop his own brand of analytic psychology. Henceforth, Jung and the Jungians were anathema to Freud and his followers, and the Jungians responded in kind.[17]

Freud did manage to attract a few rich Americans of his own to Vienna,[18] but none with Edith Rockefeller McCormick's or Mary Mellon's vast financial resources. The invidious comparison with Jung's success in attracting *Dollar Onkels* (uncles), or rather *Dollar Tanten* (aunts), further fuelled his hatred for his former disciple. It also in all probability exacerbated his profound distaste for the United States.

Ironically, though, in America psychoanalysis was already enjoying some success. Psychiatrists who found asylum existence stifling, and longed for an office-based practice, began to embrace psychotherapy, as did some neurologists dissatisfied with a sub-specialty that married diagnostic precision about syphilis and the scleroses with therapeutic impotence. There were some new territories for this fledgling breed of psychiatrist to colonize, such as the marriage- and child-guidance clinics that had begun to emerge after the First World War. And public appetite for psychoanalytic accounts of the unconscious seems to have grown, judging by the space popular magazines gave to the subject. But mainstream medicine remained sceptical, even hostile to a practice that many regarded as a species of quackery. And then there was the question of what was meant by psychoanalysis.

Americans were never terribly enamoured of the darker side of Freud's vision. As his work in the 1920s increasingly embraced a lugubrious portrait of the fundamental tensions between civilization and the individual, and suggested that repression and perpetual feelings of discontent were perhaps the price of civilized existence, so they looked for a less unpleasant alternative. Freud's earlier proclamation, in *The Future of an Illusion* (1927), that religion was a neurosis and God the creation of a child-like longing for a father figure, did little to endear him to many in a society full of believers. That did not matter much at first, for Americans claiming to follow Freud had little trouble discounting the portions of his thinking they did not like.

No one enforced orthodoxy, so in its American guise, psychoanalysis was diluted, distorted and remade in a thoroughly eclectic fashion, recreated into a far more positive and optimistic perspective on mental troubles and the prospects for curing them. Optimism was the order of the day. One prominent example of this shift is the work of the Viennese refugee Heinz Hartmann (1894–1970; a personal favourite of Freud's), who began to develop what he called 'ego psychology' – a theoretical stance which played down psychological conflicts and the instincts, and emphasized instead the ego and its role in promoting adaptations to reality. Here was an approach many Americans found more congenial than Freud's deeply pessimistic pronouncements. More broadly, psychoanalysis in its many American guises promised relief from anxieties and mental troubles, and such promises attracted a number of disturbed, wealthy patients who would never have contemplated treatment in a mental hospital.

Hollywood, where the movie business was expanding by leaps and bounds, was visibly entranced by Freudian ideas, as we shall see later in this chapter. This was true both of those who acted in front of the cameras and those who employed them, and post-1945 the infatuation with psychoanalysis would surface quite overtly in many of the most successful films of the era.[19] On the East Coast, too, and most particularly among well-to-do members of the sizeable Jewish community in the northeast, psychoanalysts found eager consumers of their wares. It was a far smaller market than the hundreds of thousands of the severely mentally ill who thronged the wards of the increasingly crowded and decaying state mental hospitals. But it was an educated and socially prominent group, possessed of considerable social and cultural capital, not to mention the ample funds that were essential were one to afford the hour-long therapeutic encounters several times a week, stretching out over months and years, that were the precondition for classical analytic treatment. Ambulatory, affluent, articulate, and yet complaining of deep-seated anxieties and neuroses that resisted easy cures and thus required lengthy treatment, here was a far more attractive group of patients than the socially marginal, often impoverished and ill-educated people who overwhelmed the mental hospitals – delusional, hallucinating, deeply depressed and socially withdrawn, or simply demented.

The deviations and dilutions that helped to spread the gospel of psychoanalysis to a broader American audience troubled Freud's more orthodox disciples a great deal, but they lacked the power to suppress them. As early as 1921, Isador Coriat (1875–1943), who had come to listen to Freud at Clark University, joked that he had tried chanting 'there is no psychotherapy but psychoanalysis, and Freud is its prophet', but that the incantation had fallen on deaf ears.[20] Instead, an emphasis on psychological growth and possibility became the order of the day, both among indigenous American analysts such as the Menninger brothers (who were based in a family business offering psychotherapy in Topeka, Kansas), and among some of the foreign-born analysts living on the East Coast – superior beings (at least in their own eyes), who otherwise looked down on their American brethren as materialistic apostates with barely any glimmers of understanding of the grand Freudian edifice.

Into Exile

Then came Hitler. The accession of the Nazis to power soon put an end to psychoanalysis in Germany, and started what would become a flood of refugees, some to London, many more to the eastern cities of the United States, most especially New York. The Berlin institute, heavily Jewish, was the first to experience persecution, and its leadership fled to America early in the 1930s. As the decade drew to a close, they were joined by Austrians and Hungarians.[21] Vienna, indeed, reconstituted itself in Manhattan, as émigrés swiftly dominated the New York Psychoanalytic Society.[22]

The Anschluß, the annexation of Austria by Germany, took place on 12 March 1938. Freud, gravely ill with the mouth cancer that he had fought for a decade and a half, faced mortal danger, as did his family, something brought forcibly home to him when the Gestapo summoned his daughter Anna (1895–1982) to a frightening interrogation. With the help of Ernest Jones, and a subvention from his long-time financial angel Princess Marie Bonaparte (1882–1962), who paid the flight tax the Nazis demanded, the ailing Freud managed to leave for London, travelling with his wife Martha, his daughter Anna, a maid and a doctor.

In exile in Hampstead, his family recreated Freud's Vienna consulting room at his house at 20 Maresfield Gardens, and he continued to see patients (PL. 41). But his physical condition steadily worsened and the pain grew intolerable. The cancer ate into his face. The flesh stank so badly that even his pet dog shrank from him. His suffering increased, and even the stoic Freud had had enough. He reminded his long-time physician Max Schur (1897–1969) of his promise to aid him *in extremis*. 'Now is nothing but torture and makes no sense.' On 21 September 1939 Schur administered morphine to Freud for the first time. On 22 September, Schur injected him again. By the following day, Freud was dead.

Freud's death came less than a month after the opening shots of the Second World War. Many analysts had fled the continent of Europe. Those who did not mostly perished in the carnage that accompanied Nazi rule. Inevitably, the influx of refugees to the United States considerably expanded the numbers of psychoanalysts seeking to practise their trade. At the same time, however, it heightened tensions. The central Europeans had little regard for their American counterparts, even those who had conformed reasonably closely to Freudian orthodoxy. They regarded the Americans as their intellectual and cultural inferiors, and treated them accordingly. Feelings ran high, and sectarian sentiments, always present within psychoanalysis, became increasingly prominent. Splits and spats erupted, though they attracted little attention beyond the ranks of the faithful. And ironically, the war, while destroying psychoanalysis in what had long been its central European heartland, would ultimately lead to a dramatic expansion of its prospects in the United States, notwithstanding the infighting in the psychoanalytic institutes.

Freud had made his own contributions to the schisms in his lifetime. His intolerance for dissent and his immense capacity for hate were legendary, and those who disagreed with him were usually expelled from the inner circle and cast into eternal exile.[23] But such squabbles seemed to most outsiders to be of little consequence in the larger scheme of things. At Freud's death, the world once more was about to be engulfed in years of warfare, fighting that would end with the unleashing of the awful power of the atom on unsuspecting civilians. The Nazis, having done their best to exterminate German mental patients, were now in the process of transferring both personnel and equipment to camps designed to exterminate the Jews, other 'racially inferior' groups, and their political opponents. The veneer of civilization was in the process of being stripped away. Dark, destructive forces were at work once again, and in their service the powers of modern medicine and science were perverted to create a human-authored hell, or rather a multitude of hells.

Total War and Its Consequences

Even Freud, the prophet of pessimism, might have recoiled were he to have survived to see the barbarism that now befell the world. And yet it was that awful war, more than anything else, that helped to advance the psychoanalytic cause – to a limited extent in Britain, but on a far larger and more durable scale in the United States, where some version of Freud's vision came to dominate American psychiatry for a quarter of a century and more, and where psychoanalytic ideas and concepts came to pervade even popular culture. That madness was invested with meaning, indeed that meanings lay at the root of madness, explained where craziness came from and pointed the way to its cure, came to seem to many self-evident.

The new conflict that engulfed the so-called civilized world provided further proof, if proof were needed, that

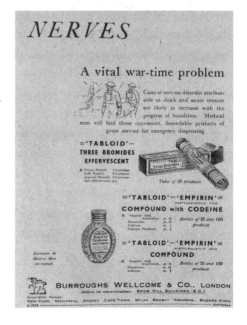

Nerves in wartime. Anticipating a spate of nervous disorders brought on by wartime pressures, the drug company Burroughs Wellcome hastened to offer a chemical remedy.

industrialized, mechanized warfare and the psychological stability of the troops were often incompatible. The lesson would be painfully relearned in the Korean War, in Vietnam, the endless series of military conflicts that marked and marred the ill-named Cold War and its aftermath, and the two Gulf Wars. After Vietnam, the political influence of the American veterans would bring about the construction of a new nosological category, Post-Traumatic Stress Disorder, or PTSD, an illness that would soon spread to embrace the victims of other forms of violence, most notably of a sexual sort. But psychiatric troubles among the troops did not wait upon the politicization of late twentieth-century psychiatry. It was an inescapable reality confronting the military during the Second World War.

The Nazis had a simple solution for the problem. Just as they had not scrupled to murder mental patients, so they did not resort to half-measures when soldiers broke down. Wehrmacht soldiers who went mad could expect to be disciplined, if not shot.[24] The consensus among German psychiatrists was that the shell shock victims of the First World War had been malingerers and cowards, and the mistake of treating them as sick men would not be repeated. It was a view the German High Command enthusiastically endorsed. Breakdowns still occurred, particularly on the Eastern Front, but officially they went unacknowledged, even as they were dealt with by savage sanctions, by impromptu firing squads and by thrusting the war neurotics back into battle.

The British were less keen on shooting their own, but equally determined to avoid a repeat of the shell shock epidemic. Official policy, worked out among leading British psychiatrists, was to eliminate 'any prospect of reward [for displaying neurotic symptoms]: nobody should get out of the Army through neurosis and no pensions should be paid'.[25] Complicated treatment was to be avoided, since that simply encouraged the soldier to view himself as sick, and instead he should be kept close to the front lines, and pushed back into his unit as soon as possible.

Throughout the war, however, psychiatric casualties accumulated. On average, across all theatres of battle, between 5 and 30 per cent of the sick and the wounded who were evacuated from the fighting were psychiatric casualties. Official statistics routinely understated the size of the problem, and wherever the fighting was fiercest, the incidence of psychiatric breakdowns was highest. 'Combat stress' officially accounted for only 10 per cent of those admitted for medical treatment during the Dunkirk retreat,[26] but this is probably a serious underestimate of the real scale of the problem, since many of the evacuees were admitted to military psychiatric wards following their return to Britain.[27] Over the course of the war, 40 per cent of the British soldiers discharged as unfit for further duty were discharged for psychiatric reasons.[28]

In Italy in 1944, one Canadian division was engaged in fierce fighting in two consecutive battles. Psychiatric casualty rates varied among the nine units making up the division: from 17.4 per cent to 30.5 per cent in the first engagement, and from 14.6 per cent to 30 per cent in the second. But even though commanders had been instructed before the second action 'to adopt a severe disciplinary attitude to psychiatric casualties in the belief they were due to laxness or weakness', the percentage of psychiatric casualties for the division as a whole actually rose, from 22.1 per cent to 23.2 per cent. Psychiatric casualties among British and Canadian troops during the Normandy invasion were at least equally high, and only a small fraction of those treated – less than 20 per cent of the total – resumed combat duty afterwards.[29] Spike Milligan (1918–2002), who would go on to become a famous British comedian, was one such casualty. Intense fighting at Monte Cassino in Italy led to a first breakdown. He was treated for three days behind the lines and sent back to his unit. But for a week he cried, stammered and cowered at the sound of battle, until his commanders had had enough. This time he was sent far away from the fighting back to base camp, where he was employed – who says armies don't have a sense of irony – as a psychiatric clerk. His war was over, and he, like many another psychiatric casualty, 'never got over that feeling [of shame]', and thought the day he was evacuated 'one of the saddest days of my life'.[30]

It was going to be different for the Americans, who stayed out of the war till the Japanese attack at Pearl Harbor on 7 December 1941 forced their hand. All save the most blinkered isolationists, however, knew that war was coming, and American psychiatry mobilized to persuade the military powers that the surest way of avoiding the problems of the First World War was to screen all potential recruits, and eliminate the psychiatrically unfit. That way, the logistical and morale problems associated with mass mental casualties could be avoided. The new policy was deemed a great success. It weeded out potential recruits numbering nearly a million and three quarters – a frightening figure, but at least the Army would surely be spared the problems associated with breakdowns at the front.

Except that it wasn't. As early as 1942, mere months after the United States had entered the war, psychiatric casualties had begun to mount among the troops, just as if the pre-screening had never taken place. The horrors of the battlefield, sometimes even the prospect of the horrors of the battlefield, created masses of new psychiatric casualties, and, of course, equivalently massive demands for psychiatrists and psychologists to respond to the looming threat to army morale and efficiency. Not shell shock, for that term had been abandoned, but 'war neurosis' or 'combat exhaustion' proliferated apace.[31] There were more than a million admissions to American hospitals in the war years for neuropsychiatric problems. Among combat units in the European theatre in 1944, admissions were as high as 250 per 1,000 men per year, an extraordinary percentage.[32] And in the Sicilian campaign in 1943, for example, American psychiatric casualties were evacuated to North Africa for treatment; only 3 per cent of them returned to the fight.[33] Meanwhile, '[o]f the casualties severe enough to require evacuation during the major US campaign in the Pacific, at Guadalcanal in summer and fall 1942, 40 per cent were psychiatric'.[34] And the surge in the ranks of the psychiatrically impaired showed no signs of diminishing in the immediate aftermath of the conflict. In 1945, 50,662 neuropsychiatric casualties crowded the wards of military hospitals, and to those institutionalized, we must add the 475,397 discharged servicemen who were receiving Veterans' Administration pensions for psychiatric disabilities by 1947.[35]

Strangely, given the marginal place of Freudians in pre-war psychiatry, both the British and the American armies had entrusted the command of their wartime psychiatric services to men sympathetic to psychoanalysis: J. R. Rees (1890–1969) of the Tavistock Clinic for the British, and William Menninger (1899–1966) of the Menninger Clinic in Topeka, Kansas, for the Americans. Perhaps it was an echo of the lessons learned in the First World War: that psychiatric casualties were the product of psychological stress. Whatever the reason, the grave shortage of psychiatric manpower (there were only 2,295 members of the American Psychiatric Association in 1940, mostly working in mental hospitals, and the army would employ at least that number by itself by 1945) meant that physicians had to be rapidly retrained and put to work, and that training, led by Menninger, was in psychotherapy, not physical therapies. Given the large numbers of casualties, individual psychotherapy was an impossibility, so group treatment came to the fore.

Psychoanalysis, American Style

Following the war, the more eclectic British psychiatrists drew from their experiences the idea of the therapeutic community, and sought to remodel civilian mental hospitals along these lines. The stress was on the social and the psychological, and on mobilizing both patients and staff to create an environment that promoted recovery; though, notwithstanding the prominent role played by a number of British psychoanalysts in developing the approach – Wilfred Bion (1897–1979), John Rickman (1891–1951), Harold Bridger (1909–2005) and S. H. Foulkes (1898–1977) – such psychotherapy as was on offer was based on group sessions, not individual analysis. The therapeutic community's more 'democratic' ethos – it purported to erase or minimize distinctions of rank and status, though this was the ideal, not the reality – fitted well with the more egalitarian culture of post-war Britain, and group psychotherapy was, of course, much cheaper than individual psychoanalysis.[36]

On the whole, the war had left British psychiatrists chastened, and the official history of the Tavistock Clinic conceded that 'we made scarcely any major new contribution to the treatment of traumatic neuroses' during the fighting.[37] It was a sober judgment, and one that their one-time military superiors fully shared. At war's end, the British officer corps dismissed the 'trick cyclists', as they disparagingly called them, as 'naïve, inexperienced, ignorant of military realities and over-dogmatic'.[38] No longer having much need or desire for psychiatric services with combat over, the military's long-standing disdain for the profession resurfaced.

British psychiatry's American counterparts, however, blessed with a more affluent and accommodating marketplace, and perhaps more skilful at marketing their accomplishments to a credulous public, set up their shingles and practised individual psychotherapy. As early as 1947, in a remarkable break from pre-war precedents, more than half of all American psychiatrists worked in private practice or at outpatient clinics; and by 1958, as few as 16 per cent practised their trade in traditional state hospitals. Moreover, this rapid shift in the profession's centre of gravity occurred in the context of an extraordinary expansion in the absolute size of the profession. From fewer than 5,000 members in 1948, the American Psychiatric Association's ranks had risen to more than 27,000 by 1976.[39] In 1948, Brigadier (as he now was) William Menninger was elected president of the APA, the first of many psychoanalysts to assume the role, and *Time* magazine celebrated the occasion by putting his portrait on its cover, with a picture of the human brain,

William Menninger, in his office at the Menninger Clinic in Topeka, Kansas.

complete with a keyhole and a key. The unlocking of the secrets of madness could now be expected to proceed apace.

By the 1960s, the chairs of the majority of the university psychiatric departments in the United States were analysts by training and persuasion,[40] and the discipline's major textbooks heavily emphasized psychoanalytic perspectives.[41] (No comparable shift had occurred in Europe.) American psychiatry attracted growing numbers of applicants for its internships and residencies, and the best of these supplemented their university training with didactic analyses at powerful analytic institutes that remained separate and at a distance from medical schools. Psychoanalytic training was the ticket, if not quite the *sine qua non*, for a successful career as an academic psychiatrist in America, and high-status practice largely consisted of office-based psychotherapy. Patients with severe and chronic forms of mental disorder were for the most part marginalized and ignored by the professional elite, who much preferred their prosperous outpatient clientele.

It took money – a great deal of money – to afford classical psychoanalytic treatment. Yet for a time, large sections of America's haute bourgeoisie persuaded themselves it was worth it, and in New York, Boston, Chicago, Los Angeles, San Francisco and elsewhere they flocked to the psychoanalytic couch in sufficient numbers to support their therapists in grand style. After a time, at least in theory, psychoanalytic treatment was seen as potentially relevant even in the treatment of psychosis, and at some ritzy private establishments – such as the Menninger Clinic, Chestnut Lodge, Austen Riggs and the McLean Hospital – efforts were made to treat schizophrenics with the talking cure.[42]

These were the golden years for psychoanalysts in the United States. Secure in their status, they looked down their noses at the 'directive-organic' psychiatrists who still lurked in the state hospitals, many of them by necessity now recruited from overseas. While the median income in 1954 of their state hospital colleagues was a mere $9,000, among analysts the comparable figure was more than twice as much – $22,000. Nor were the attractions only financial. Institutional psychiatrists, with the exception of those who worked in a handful of small institutions catering to the very rich, were trapped in a system that was overwhelmed by vast numbers of chronic, lower-class patients, in rural, isolated mental hospitals reeking, quite literally, of failure and decay. Their analytic counterparts dealt with an opulent, articulate and educated crowd, who shared their cultural background and lived in what they, perhaps smugly, saw as America's most vibrant and attractive urban centres.

Pathological Mommies

Psychoanalytic perspectives also enjoyed a widening respectability in the culture at large. Postwar geographical mobility left new mothers desperate for child-rearing advice. Into this void stepped Dr Benjamin Spock (1903–98), the first paediatrician trained in psychoanalysis. *The Common Sense Book of Baby and Child Care* appeared in 1946, and sold a half million copies in the first six months. By Spock's death in 1998 it had sold over 50 million copies and been translated into more than thirty languages. It was the bestselling book in postwar America after the Bible. Its accounts of child-rearing and maturation drew heavily on Freudian notions, presented in a folksy and friendly fashion that made them part of a common set of cultural understandings.[43]

The British didn't embrace Dr Spock quite so heartily, but two prominent psychoanalysts, John Bowlby (1907–90) and Donald Winnicott (1896–1971), were influential, so that psychoanalytic ideas had an extensive impact on British child-rearing practices, and even on ideas about the sources of juvenile delinquency. Bowlby's work centred around the concept of attachment between mother and child, and the problems that maternal deprivation appeared to cause.[44] During the war, many children had been evacuated from London and other urban centres to escape German bombings; others had been placed in group nurseries to allow their mothers to contribute to the war effort; and then there were Jewish refugee children escaping the horrors of the Final Solution.

Winnicott, who had worked with evacuated children, made much of the importance of play and affection in producing a good childhood. Classical Freudian thought pictured relations between parent and child as fraught and full of conflict, seething with unconscious and barely suppressed sexual longings and feelings. By contrast, Winnicott was reassuring: mothers (and parental figures in general) should be content to be 'ordinarily devoted' and 'good enough', rather than striving for an impossible perfection. Such parents could, he insisted, guide their children to a healthy independence and adulthood. His emphasis on giving 'young mothers... support in their reliance on their natural tendencies'[45] was understandably popular with them.

On the other hand, because he played down the erotic and the harsher elements in Freud's theories, he was not always so popular with more traditional psychoanalysts. The upshot was, however, that while adult psychoanalysis was stuck at the margins of psychiatry in Britain, in this modified (dare I say domesticated) form, child psychoanalysis was surprisingly influential, aided by the eventual willingness of the National Health Service to underwrite child therapists with an analytic orientation.[46] Perhaps, too, the continuing impact of these writings helps to explain the respect many educated lay people in Britain still accord to psychoanalytic ideas.

Not all the psychoanalytic portraits of family life were so benign, however. Freud's theories had discerned the roots of psychopathology in this setting, and his American followers laid a host of problems at the feet of the family. And more especially, the analysts indicted America's mothers, as the source, it would appear, of an ever-expanding array of illness and debility, and even a threat to the health of the nation.

Not satisfied with ministering to what had hitherto been regarded as mental illness, psychoanalysis had begun to suggest that its counsels might also be of use in understanding and treating a still broader class of disorders. Like hysteria before them, shell shock and combat neurosis had often involved the apparent transformation of mental strains into physical symptomatology. In the 1930s, the psychoanalyst Franz Alexander (1891–1964), transplanted from Berlin to Chicago, had begun to speak of psychosomatic disorders. The idea that mind and body might overlap and interpenetrate in some fashion turned out to have a great appeal to others, not least the Rockefeller Foundation, whose officers had decided in the early 1930s to make psychiatry a major focus of their medical philanthropy. For a brief time, Alexander was in receipt of their largesse, but it was cut off when they discovered that most of the proceeds of their grant had been transferred to the pockets of Herr Doktor Professor Alexander, who aspired to live the life of a German aristocrat. The Chicago Institute for Psychoanalysis survived anyway, and in the years after the Second World War, Alexander's ideas about psychosomatic illness became steadily more fashionable. The range of disorders with psychosomatic roots rapidly proliferated, and the analysts produced an ever-more elaborate model of how troubles in mind surfaced as bodily symptoms. 'Gastric neurotic symptoms', Alexander proclaimed, 'have a very different psychology from those of emotional diarrhea or constipation; cardiac cases differ in their emotional background from asthmatics.'[47]

Different perhaps, but the one constant was 'Mom'. Behind the scenes, she worked her devastation. Take asthma, for instance. Its origins, the analysts taught, lay in an 'asthmatogenic mother' – ambivalent, guilt-ridden, hostile and rejecting, though blithely denying these unconscious feelings and transforming them into a simulacrum of a protective (actually a pathologically over-protective) parent.[48] More devastating still was the role of parents, and particularly mothers, in the genesis of frank mental disorders: 'borderlines' (those who hovered on the boundary between neurotic and psychotic); schizophrenics; and autistic children (victims of a disorder first identified by Leo Kanner (1896–1961), professor of child psychiatry at Johns Hopkins University, in 1943).[49]

All these disorders were perceived to have their roots in perverse mothering, or perhaps a combination of inadequate parents: a domineering, rejecting, aggressive mother who had picked out a psychologically inadequate, passive and withdrawn male as her mate. Kanner suggested in 1949 that autistic children were trapped in a web of pathological family relationships, exposed from 'the beginning to parental coldness, obsessiveness, and a mechanical type of attention to material needs only.... They were kept neatly in refrigerators which did not defrost.'[50] It was a metaphor he would return to more than a decade later, when he proclaimed in a widely noticed interview that autistic children were the product of emotionally frozen parents unluckily 'just happening to defrost long enough to produce a child'.[51] His views were enthusiastically adopted and put into practice by the transplanted Viennese psychoanalyst Bruno Bettelheim (1903–90) at his Orthogenic School at the University of Chicago. Like his counterparts at the psychoanalytically inclined Chestnut Lodge Mental Hospital in Maryland, who were treating schizophrenics they viewed as the product of refrigerator mothers, Bettelheim sought a 'parentectomy', a complete exclusion of the parents of the children he was treating. And in bestselling books including *The Empty Fortress* (1967), he denounced mothers and fathers who he claimed had fostered a domestic environment that resembled nothing so much as a concentration camp.[52]

Peter Gay (b. 1923), the Yale historian of the Enlightenment and admirer of Freud, took to the pages of *The New Yorker* to call Bettelheim and his associates 'heroes', and to pronounce with an air of authority that 'Bettelheim's own theory of infantile autism is in all respects much superior to its rivals'.[53] Many years later, however, the Nobel Prize-winning geneticist James D. Watson (b. 1928), co-discoverer of the double helix and the father of a schizophrenic son, undoubtedly represented the views of many parents when he denounced Bettelheim as 'after Hitler, the most evil person of the twentieth century'.[54] But such anger was rarely openly expressed at the time, for Bettelheim spoke with the authority of psychoanalytic science, then at the peak of its popularity. Parents, labouring under the double stigma of having a mentally sick child and of being held responsible for the madness, were mostly shamed into silence.

Freudian Hegemony

Ernest Jones, the indispensable disciple who had helped to put in place the Praetorian guard that defended Freud in his lifetime, began to publish his three-volume biography of his master in 1953; the last volume appeared in 1957. A reliable hagiographer, Jones used his unrivalled access to Freud's letters and papers to settle a host of scores with those who had 'betrayed' him and so were serially dismissed as psychotic heretics, but it was the portrait of Freud as the lone heroic intellectual, the giant of the science of the mind who belonged in the same Pantheon as Copernicus, Galileo or Darwin, that captured the imagination of Jones's contemporaries. *The New Yorker*'s assertion that this account of Freud's life was 'the greatest biography of our time'[55] reflected an equally inflated sense of the importance of its subject, but it was an assessment that was widely shared in intellectual circles at the time.

On Freud's death, W. H. Auden (1903–73) memorialized his passing: 'to us he is no more a person/now but a whole climate of opinion/under whom we conduct our different lives'.[56] It was an apt reflection of the status Freud had acquired in certain literary and artistic circles. In *Studies on Hysteria*, the Ur-text of psychoanalysis that had appeared under both his name and Breuer's, Freud had acknowledged that the case studies he had contributed to that volume, a series of psychologically charged vignettes, read 'like short stories'. As such, he lamented, they lacked 'the serious stamp of science'.[57] It was a thought that rankled, and he immediately sought to blunt the charge with the assertion that 'the nature of the subject is evidently responsible for this, rather than any preference of my own'. But it was an insightful remark, however painful he found it. And it was perhaps the source of some of the enthusiasm with which those whose métier was telling stories – in prose, poetry or painting – came to regard his work. That and the fascination with language, symbols, memory, dreams, distortions and sex, not to mention the excesses and repressions that Freud claimed marked mental life, and the meanings with which he managed to invest behaviours, thoughts and emotions others had long dismissed as so much meaningless noise.

Auden found himself drawn quite directly into such storytelling just after the end of the Second World War, when the exiled Russian composer, Igor Stravinsky (1882–1971), chose him to write the libretto for an opera about madness and excess. Stravinsky had visited an exhibition of Hogarth's *A Rake's Progress* in Chicago in 1947. It struck the composer that the series of engravings resembled nothing so much as the storyboards that in the mid-twentieth century might have served as outlines for a Hollywood film. Stravinsky was seized by the idea of turning Tom Rakewell's tale into an opera. It would be his only full-length opera, receiving its first performance in 1951, and became one of a handful of postwar operas to be staged with some regularity – a popularity that perhaps owes more than a little to its neoclassical score, wondrously apposite for an eighteenth-century tale.[58]

But the opera's visibility and contemporary appeal surely owed a great deal as well to Stravinsky's choice of the person to write the libretto: someone widely regarded as one of the greatest writers of the twentieth century, W. H. Auden[59] (who wrote it with his faithless lover Chester Kallman); and on another front (albeit a quarter of a century later), to the association of another major figure in the arts, David Hockney (b. 1937), whose stage sets for a production of *The Rake's Progress* at Glyndebourne in 1975 seem to have achieved an iconic status almost comparable to Hogarth's originals (**PL. 40**). Hockney deliberately chose as his inspiration Hogarth's engravings, not his painted versions of Tom Rakewell's downfall, using cross-hatching and other techniques from that medium as the basis for his designs for both sets and costumes, and subtly quoting from other works by Hogarth. These choices are quite apparent in the set for the closing scene in Bedlam, with Hogarth's archetypical mad folk transmuted into a set of lunatic heads peering out at the audience from their individual boxes or cells, and above them high on the left a reworked version of Hogarth's map of Hell, which Hockney borrowed from a later Hogarth satire linking religious enthusiasm and madness (see p. 175).[60] Like Stravinsky's score, and Auden's libretto, to both of which Hockney's images subtly gesture in their linearity, the result is art that is visibly modern and also visibly in debt to its eighteenth-century inspiration.

Nor was Stravinsky's work the only opera written in the immediate postwar years to flirt with the edges of Unreason. *Peter Grimes* by Benjamin Britten (1913–76), composed during the war and first performed in London on 7 June 1945, between the end of the conflict in Europe and Japan's capitulation, was an unlikely success. Written by a pacifist and a known homosexual, in an era when to be either invited severe moral censure and legal repression, it nonetheless was instantly acclaimed as a masterpiece, and within three years had been performed in Budapest, Hamburg, Stockholm, Milan, New York, Berlin and at least eight other cities around the world.

Repression in the Freudian sense was a leitmotiv of the libretto, with its intimations of sadism and pederasty and barely disguised condemnation of the homophobia of the era. Britten himself had grown up on the Suffolk coast at Aldeburgh, and had conceived the opera while he and his partner, Peter Pears, were living in Escondido, California, nostalgic for the England they had left. The story of the Suffolk fisherman, unstable to begin with and driven to raging madness and finally death by the hostility of the villagers amidst whom he lives ('Him who despises us we'll destroy', sing the mob who set out to find and attack him in the final climactic part of the opera), assuredly drew upon Britten's own haunted sense of his otherness and marginality – his most intimate relationship, after all, was one that could at any moment cause his isolation, persecution and prosecution by those who lauded his artistry.

Late in life, his heart failing, Britten would once again engage with themes of suppressed homosexual longings, affection, obsession and death in a version of Thomas Mann's partially autobiographical 1912 novella, *Death in Venice*, which would constitute his final opera, first performed in 1973. By then, British law had partially removed the legal threat that hung over homosexual relations via the Sexual Offences Act 1967, but public condemnation of same-sex relationships remained almost as fierce as ever, a prejudice that likewise surfaced in the contemporary claim of many psychiatrists, Freudians prominent among them, that to be gay was, *ipso facto*, to be mentally ill. Full of symbolism, the score weaves together once more temptation and repression, this time linked to the agonizing fear of humiliation and the costs of concealment, and a consuming obsession with a beautiful boy that ends inevitably in disappointment and death. The echoes of Britten's longing for adolescent boys, apparently never consummated, are transparent for an informed audience, contributing perhaps to a heightened identification with the tensions and self-lacerating elements that mark the music – lyrical, agitated, agonized, savage and sinister by turns.[61] Madness may here be less overt, less insistently present than in *Peter Grimes* (or even in another Britten opera with connections to Venice, *The Turn of the Screw*, commissioned by and first performed at the city's Biennale in 1954), but it lurks there nonetheless, the shadowy counterpart of the distress and the misery that accompany the portrait of impossible love. Passion and Unreason wrestle throughout the opera with reason and intellect, and the outcome is death – an unconscious echo, perhaps, of an earlier operatic tradition, the Wagnerian concept of *Liebestod* (Love/Death),[62] and Freud's own growing emphasis in his last years on *Eros* and *Todestrieb* or *Thanatos*, the death drive or instinct.[63]

Psychoanalysis offered an enormously rich new treasure trove of concepts with which to approach life's mysteries elsewhere in the arts too. In the visual arts and literature, Freud's influence was widespread: Surrealist artists dabbled in dreams, their paintings dripping with distortions and subliminal references to sex and the unconscious;[64] experiments proliferated with 'automatic' painting and writing, undermining dominant conceptions of order and reality, blurring the boundaries between dreams and waking life; and novelists and dramatists embraced a greater emphasis on psychological introspection, with a growing frankness and directness in employing sexual themes. Not all of these developments can be directly ascribed to Freud's influence. D. H. Lawrence (1885–1930), who pushed sexual themes beyond the tolerance of British censors, had nothing but contempt for psychoanalysis, and pronounced himself repelled by the enterprise.[65] In many other writers, the Freudian influence has to be inferred, even when it is hard to miss. Not everyone was as explicit as James Joyce (1882–1941), who spoke of the master as a 'traumconductor', called incest a 'freudful mistake', and portrayed one of his characters as 'yung and easily freudened'.[66]

Tennessee Williams's (1911–83) best work in the 1940s and 1950s was shot through with autobiographical references to his childhood traumas: his father's desertion; his neurotic and hysterical mother; his mentally frail sister Rose who was eventually diagnosed as schizophrenic and (disastrously) lobotomized. His own homosexuality in an intolerant age did not help matters, and his recurrent depression, not to mention his growing dependence on drugs and alcohol, all made their mark on his writing. Emotional turmoil, the insufferable mother, family repressions, violence both physical and symbolic, sexual undercurrents of a thoroughly unconventional sort and rape are leitmotivs of his plays, from *The Glass Menagerie* (1944), through *A Streetcar Named Desire* (1947), *The Rose Tattoo* (1951) and *Cat on a Hot Tin Roof* (1955). Who can forget Blanche Dubois, for example: a creature who puts on a display of social snobbery and sexual propriety, and teases her brother-in-law Stanley as an ape. In reality, she has fled to the Kowalskis to escape the scandal of her husband's suicide after she caught him having sex with a man, her social shame exacerbated by her resort to a string of meaningless affairs that led her neighbours to label her a 'woman of loose morals'? Or her dreadful fate: raped by the drunken Stanley while her sister is off-stage giving birth, she is carted off to the asylum, struggling at first, then as she loses contact with reality, announcing, 'I have always depended on the kindness of strangers'.

However, as his new plays from *Orpheus Descending* (1957) onwards were commercial flops and his popularity plunged,[67] Williams undertook personal analysis. It was not a success, not least because he was referred to Lawrence Kubie (1896–1973), a prominent New York analyst who made

Vivien Leigh as Blanche Dubois, and Marlon Brando as Stanley Kowalski, in the film version of A Streetcar Named Desire *(1951). The film critic Pauline Kael commented that 'Vivien Leigh gives one of those rare performances that can truly be said to evoke pity and terror'.*

a fortune from his show-business clients, and who regarded homosexuality as a disease in need of a psychoanalytic cure. (Kubie had introduced two of his other show-business patients to each other: Kurt Weill and Moss Hart, and the musical the two men then wrote together, *Lady in the Dark*, introduced none other than Sigmund Freud himself to Broadway.) But in the course of his analysis, Williams wrote *Suddenly Last Summer* (1958), a play in which a fearsome New Orleans matron, Violet Venable, conspires to inflict a lobotomy on her niece who is threatening to reveal the dark secret of the older woman's life, her near-incestuous liaison with her son Sebastian, now dead, and her role as sexual bait to attract the young men with whom he had wished to sleep. The operation, Violet hopes, will serve 'to cut this hideous story out of her brain!'. The reference to his sister Rose's lobotomy is unmistakable, but psychoanalytic overtones appear throughout the play. They extend to the very name of the psychiatrist who threatens the erasure of Catherine's memories, Dr Cukrowicz, a patronymic he tells the audience is Polish for sugar. Dr Sugar/Dr Kubie: Williams is having a laugh, and his psychoanalyst is the joke.

If writers increasingly drew upon Freudian themes, literary scholars embraced them with even greater enthusiasm. Academics in search of 'theory' to justify the superiority of their own understanding of literature seized on Freud's work. Freud had anticipated them, in discussions of Hamlet and Lear, for example, not to mention his appropriation of the story of Oedipus from Sophocles, naming the complex he made the centrepiece of his later theories of human psycho-sexual development after the character in the play, with its theme of mother–son incest. Major critics including I. A. Richards (1893–1979), Kenneth Burke (1897–1993) and Edmund Wilson (1895–1972) all drew upon psychoanalytic thinking, and from the 1950s onwards, Lionel Trilling (1905–75) and Steven Marcus (b. 1928), central figures in New York literary circles, eagerly adopted Freud's ideas. Trilling was infatuated with Freud's *Civilization and Its Discontents* (1929) and with his latter-day embrace of *Todestrieb*. Marcus has provided a Freudian interpretation of much of Dickens's work,[68] and a study of Victorian pornography that owes a great deal to psychoanalytic ideas.[69] And the two men's heavy investment in psychoanalysis was reflected in their collaboration as co-editors of Ernest Jones's biography of Freud. On the other coast of America, the formidable Frederick Crews (b. 1933) once pronounced that: 'Psychoanalysis is the only psychology to have seriously altered our way of reading literature.... Literature is written from and about motives, and psychoanalysis is the only thorough-going theory of motives that mankind has devised.'[70] (He later repented, dismissing Freud as a false prophet, and psychoanalysis as a pseudo-science.)[71]

Not just literary critics, but other public intellectuals in the 1950s and 1960s also openly embraced psychoanalysis. Norman O. Brown (1913–2002) sought to psychoanalyse history, and drew eager throngs of students to Santa Cruz, where he held forth. His bestselling *Life Against Death: The Psychoanalytical Meaning of History* (1959) propounded the notion that individuals and society were imprisoned by Freudian repression, from which they had to break free by affirming life. Its sequel, *Love's Body* (1966), focused on the struggle between eroticism and society. Brown joined R. D. Laing, the Scottish anti-psychiatrist, in suggesting that schizophrenics might be saner than those without the disease. The 1960s counterculture lapped it up.[72]

From the conservative right, Philip Rieff (1922–2006) spoke of the advent of psychological man and the triumph of the therapeutic.[73] From the radical left, Herbert Marcuse (1898–1979) proffered his own peculiar amalgam of Marx and Freud.[74] Perhaps nowhere was the intellectual embrace of Freud more extensive than among anthropologists, with figures including Margaret Mead (1901–78), Ruth Benedict (1887–1948), Clyde Kluckhohn (1905–60) and Melford Spiro (1920–2014) all regarding psychoanalytic ideas as central to their work. For the moment, the criticism voiced by Karl Popper (1902–94) from his chair at the London School of Economics, that psychoanalysis was non-falsifiable and thus a pseudo-science that explained everything and nothing, found few sympathetic listeners outside the ranks of his fellow philosophers of science.

Madness and the Movies

If the growing impact of psychoanalytic ideas within American psychiatry in the post-Second World War era thus had its counterpart across a broad swathe of high culture and in the arts, there is one final arena that was of surpassing importance in introducing at least a bowdlerized version of psychoanalytic theory to the masses. One of the major cultural innovations of the twentieth century was the motion picture, and madness as a subject turned out to be tailor-made for the cinema. Immediately after the First World War, the first classic silent film that revolved around mental illness was made in Germany. *The Cabinet of Dr Caligari* (1920; directed by Robert Wiene) had a shocking premise: a mad asylum doctor employed hypnotism to create a sleepwalking patient, who then roved the community outside killing on command. The viewer's sense of disorientation was heightened by filming the action in front of painted sets that embodied sharp angles and distorted perspectives to create a nightmarish world, wherein violent and untamed

The Cabinet of Dr Caligari *(1920): Cesare is hypnotized and put back into the coffin-like cabinet where he is kept between his murderous rampages.*

madness flourished. Moral deformity and physical deformity echoed each other in surreal fashion, a visual cascade of the menacing, the misshapen and the bizarre evoking the crazed mental state of the film's protagonists. And then, at the very last moment (and it was an afterthought), the whole plot was turned upside-down: the entire tale, with its savage and conscience-less psychiatrist at its centre, was revealed to be a delusion, a cinematic representation of the mad imagination of one of the asylum's patients.

The American film industry had begun its migration to southern California in 1910, and by the 1920s, Hollywood films were grossing more money than those made anywhere else. In years to come, the American movie industry would become commercially, if not artistically, the dominant force worldwide. And from the outset, the movie moguls who made massive fortunes from entertaining the masses, the people they employed (and for decades controlled through the studio system) and many of the films they produced, were affected in one way or another by Freudian ideas. As early as the autumn of 1924, Samuel Goldwyn (1879–1974) sailed the Atlantic and fetched up in Vienna, chequebook in hand. He planned to offer Sigmund

Freud $100,000 to come to Hollywood 'to commercialize his study and write a story for the screen'. Who better than Freud to write 'a really great love story'? Goldwyn was denied an audience and sent away with a flea in his ear.[75]

The Hollywood moguls were a crass and venal lot. Prudes at least in public (in private the stories of young starlets and the casting couch were firmly grounded in a grimly exploitative reality), they knew that sex and violence sold, provided it was kept within the bounds of propriety. Then there was the talent they used and discarded like so much interchangeable human trash, valuable only so long as the box office returns were good. Acting and directing careers, with all their narcissism and uncertainties, created a hothouse culture in which neuroses and addictions proliferated. Producers, directors, screenwriters, actors, all the components of Tinsel Town, soon decided they needed shrinking. So it was that psychoanalysis established its most lucrative enclave of all. Those who ministered to the voracious appetites of the moguls and the wounded psyches that created celluloid illusions found that their incomes exceeded even the sums earned by those who had captured the *grandes dames* of New York society.

In Hollywood, it seemed, everybody had an analyst. Even the odd mogul who didn't opt for the couch himself sent neglected children and betrayed wives to pour out their troubles, and perhaps gain some measure of consolation for their gilded but troubled lives.[76] Money flowed in the film industry like water, and a large amount of it found its way into Freudian pockets, if not Freud's pockets. But much of this side of the Hollywood scene remained the province of insiders, save when gossip columnists, occasionally prodded by the studios, spilled some of it into the public arena.

David O. Selznick (1902–65), addicted to amphetamines, a compulsive gambler and womanizer, a man obsessed with controlling others, briefly entered analysis when he was prostrated by depression in the aftermath of producing *Gone with the Wind* (1939), the most financially successful film of the age. Soon, he insisted that his wife Irene (1907–90), the daughter of his former partner, fierce rival and even more powerful mogul, Louis B. Mayer (1884–1957), enter into her own analysis with the same analyst, May Romm. Selznick soon tired of the experience and stopped going. His wife did not, and perhaps as a result of gaining some perspective on her situation, dumped her husband and embarked on a new career as a theatrical impresario. He responded by marrying his latest extra-marital fling, the actress Jennifer Jones, who had first to divorce the husband she had cheated on. Ms Jones was soon taking turns with Irene on Dr Romm's couch. Irene's father, Louis B. Mayer, briefly also joined in *la ronde*, as his wife Margaret teetered on the edge of a nervous breakdown, and then was put away in a mental hospital and divorced. Armed with such powerful endorsements, Dr Romm was soon ministering to a host of leading ladies and men, including such box-office stars as Eva Gardner, Joan Crawford, Robert Taylor and Edward G. Robinson.

Romm's rivals were meanwhile tending to the psychic wounds of comparable lists of Hollywood insiders. Periodically, Karl Menninger (1893–1990; brother of William) flew in to Hollywood from Omaha to schmooze with the stars. From New York, Lawrence Kubie acquired a stable of 'creative artists'. Locally, figures such as Ernst Simmel (1882–1947), Martin Grotjahn (1904–90), Judd Marmor (1910–2003), Ralph Greenson (1911–79), and one with a distinctly Dickensian name, Frederick Hacker (1914–89), made fortunes from the glitterati and the hucksters whose puppets they were.

No wonder psychobabble soon surfaced on the screen, and the gospel according to Freud (or the Tinsel Town version thereof) entered the collective subconscious across America and wherever the increasingly globalized Hollywood film industry succeeded in extending its reach. From the 1940s to the 1960s, even into the 1970s, the image of the analyst and of the powers of the profession was generally exceedingly favourable. Freud's ideas and their clinical application were routinely dumbed down to conform to Hollywood's needs, but quite unlike the portraits of somatic psychiatrists as vicious, controlling psychopaths, shocking and mutilating their patients to keep them in line, psychoanalysts got a rather good press.

Lady in the Dark, based on Moss Hart's 1941 Broadway hit (Hart wrote the book, Ira Gershwin the lyrics and Kurt Weill the music) and released in 1944, proved to be the first of a whole string of psychoanalytically inflected films. The ubiquitous Joseph Mankiewicz (1909–93) did his best to make a self-fulfilling prophecy out of his prediction to Karl Menninger that 'the next period of years will bring psychiatry in general, and psychoanalysis in particular, into great prominence as a source of literary, dramatic, and motion picture material,'[77] but he had plenty of assistance. *Dangerous Moonlight*, a 1941 RKO potboiler, features a character whose combat fatigue is so profound that he can remember nothing at all. And a series of other contemporary films – *Blind Alley*; *Now, Voyager*; *Kings Row*; *Home of the Brave* – placed psychiatrists at the centre of the action. Fred Astaire even played a tap-dancing shrink in *Carefree* (1938).[78] David O. Selznick, having produced in

I'll Be Seeing You (1944) a sentimentalized depiction of the psychological wounds a returning veteran, Zach Morgan, has suffered in combat, hired Alfred Hitchcock, and a year later released perhaps the most overt attempt of them all to bring Freud to the masses.

Spellbound brought together Ingrid Bergman, playing a frigid Freudian analyst, Dr Constance Petersen, and Gregory Peck, who arrives at Green Manors mental hospital as Dr Anthony Edwardes, but turns out to be the amnesiac and possibly murderous veteran, John Ballantyne. As the opening credits roll, the audience learns that the mystery they are about to watch demonstrates the powers of psychoanalysis, the 'modern science' that has finally managed 'to open the locked doors' of the mind. What will be revealed is how, 'once the complexes that have been disturbing the patient are uncovered and interpreted, the illness and confusion disappear...and the devils of unreason are driven from the human soul.'

The music swells, and the melodrama commences. To lend the gloss of science to what followed, Selznick employed and credited his own analyst,

Salvador Dalí looking at a design for the dream sequence in Spellbound *(1945).*

May Romm, as a consultant. And ever-concerned to overlay schmaltz with what he took to be high art, he commissioned the Surrealist artist Salvador Dalí to construct the film's dream sequences, full of psychoanalytic symbols – scissors, eyes, curtains, playing cards, wings and a wheel (not to mention some others that were dropped when their 'meaning' was explained to Selznick, notably a close-up of pliers that stood for castration). The truth is uncovered when Peck recovers his repressed memories of a childhood trauma and the effects of combat on his psyche. The analogies between psychoanalysis and the search for hidden meanings, and detection and the unravelling of crime are a common element in the noir films that were such a feature of the Hollywood of the 1940s and 1950s,[79] and here they are given an additional characteristic touch when Constance takes off her glasses, her sexual passion bubbling to the surface (at least as far as the Production Codes of the time permitted), and the newly glamorous Ingrid Bergman abandons her previous icy persona for the embrace of her lover.

Oddly, some psychoanalysts, Karl Menninger prominent among them, protested at the film's portrait of their profession, angry at its simplifications, but also its portrait of another analyst finally unmasked as the murderous villain by the relentless Constance Petersen. It was a foolish overreaction, for the film was a smash-success at the box office and did much to spread the notion that psychoanalysis possessed the key to the secrets of madness and its cure. It was the first of a whole series of films picturing analysis and analysts in a sympathetic light. The height of the homage was meant to be John Huston's biopic, *Freud*. Huston had filmed a documentary about shell-shocked soldiers, *Let There Be Light*, in 1946. But even though the film gave the (completely false) impression of miraculous cures, the War Department decided its effect on military recruitment would be devastating, and for thirty-five years banned any showings of it.

Huston now sought to eulogize Freud,[80] and since one intellectual giant deserved another, he hired the French existential philosopher Jean-Paul Sartre to write the screenplay, and planned to cast Marilyn Monroe as Freud's patient, Frau Cäcilie. But Sartre's screenplay ran to 1,500 pages and was utterly unfilmable, while Anna Freud, who was determined that Hollywood would not demean her father's legacy, used her links to Marilyn's analyst Ralph Greenson (1911–79) to squash the proposal that Ms Monroe should act in the film. Huston made it anyway, and its earnestness ensured that when it was distributed in 1962 it was a critical and box office flop. Still,

Hollywood's worship of psychoanalysis continued, all the way down to 1977's *I Never Promised You a Rose Garden* and Robert Redford's directorial debut in 1980, *Ordinary People*.

Based on Joanne Greenberg's 1964 *roman-à-clef*, and set in a fictionalized version of Chestnut Lodge, a Maryland mental hospital for the very rich where psychoses were treated with psychoanalysis, *I Never Promised You a Rose Garden* follows the story of a suicidal, delusional, hallucinating, self-mutilating adolescent, played by Kathleen Quinlan, who is gradually brought back to reality, warts and all, by a compassionate analyst, Dr Fried (in real life the petite Frieda Fromm-Reichmann, played here by the tall Swedish actress Bibi Andersson). Though there are some searing portraits of patient abuse, the overwhelming message about the talking cure is how Dr Fried's persistence and skill enable her to discover the traumatic roots of her patient's troubles and return her to the ranks of the sane. *Ordinary People*, which features the accidental death of one son of an upper-middle-class family, the mental breakdown of his brother and the frozen response of a mother who laments that the wrong son died, again features an analyst who disentangles the underlying repressions and the sources of psychopathology, helping the boy to recover, though his mother remains a refrigerator and abandons both her ineffectual husband and the son she rejects for the cold comfort of her family of origin.

The overwhelmingly positive portrait of analysts in these and earlier films could scarcely form a more striking contrast with the image of institutional psychiatry found in *One Flew Over the Cuckoo's Nest* (1975) and *Frances* (1982), two Hollywood films dealing with what film-makers pictured as the shock 'em and mutilate 'em brigade of biological psychiatrists that we examined in the previous chapter. But it was biology not psychology that would soon triumph. The three-and-a-half-decade-long period when psychoanalysis dominated American psychiatry and culture, an era when madness was defined and treated by, and through, its alleged meanings, was about to come to a remarkably abrupt end. The romance with Freud was all but over.

Chapter Twelve

A PSYCHIATRIC REVOLUTION?

The End of Asylumdom

Visiting Venice, the well-heeled traveller has the option of escaping the crowds of tourists by taking a twenty-minute boat ride across the lagoon to the island of San Clemente (PL. 43). There, a five-star hotel awaits, complete with marble corridors and staircases, and all the accoutrements of a luxury hostelry, housed in a building that is advertised as a former monastery – as indeed it was, until Napoleon shut it and other religious institutions down in the early nineteenth century. The property's owners boast of 'the atmosphere of its ancient origins, with frescoes and an impressive Renaissance façade' and promise their guests that 'all traces of the island's history have been preserved [forming]...an inviting and peaceful oasis overlooking the city of Venice'.

Like much marketing copy, this is something less than the whole truth. The San Clemente Palace played a very different role in Venetian life between 1844 and 1992, and that period in its history is one its current owners are anxious to disguise, indeed to airbrush out of history. Nowhere in the glossy materials that promote the hotel's charms as the only structure (apart from a chapel) to grace the small island, is there any mention of the fact that it functioned in those more recent years as Venice's asylum for madwomen, the counterpart to the madhouse at San Servolo once visited by Shelley and Byron:

> As thus I spoke,
> Servants announced the gondola, and we
> Through the fast-falling rain and high-wrought sea
> Sailed to the island where the madhouse stands.

We disembarked. The clap of tortured hands,
Fierce yells and howlings and lamentings keen,
And laughter where complaint had merrier been,
Moans, shrieks, and curses, and blaspheming prayers
Accosted us. We climbed the oozy stairs
Into an old courtyard...[1]

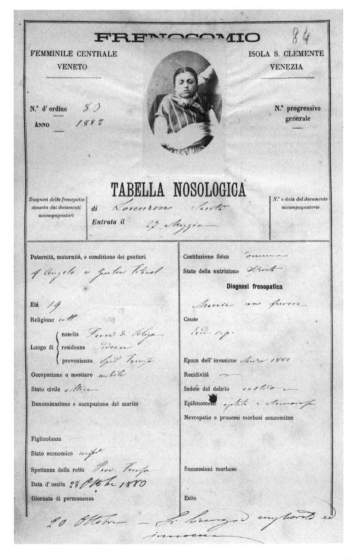

*An admissions certificate for a patient at the San Clemente asylum in Venice, for 1880.
The complex of buildings is now a luxury hotel.*

The female asylum had an equally fearsome reputation. For Venetians, 'going to San Clemente' became synonymous with going mad, and when Mussolini tired of his mistress Ida Dalser, he had the poor woman incarcerated here amid the mad folk, where she remained shut up and sequestered for the rest of her days.[2] Abandoned in 1992, the madhouse had a temporary role as a home for the stray cats of Venice, before speculators bought it up and turned it into a rival of the Cipriani Hotel on the Giudecca. Recently acquired by Turkish developers when the resort's first owners went bankrupt, it is being refurbished on a still more lavish scale. Exorcising the unlucky ghosts of the past is proving a trifle difficult, it seems.

In 2010, those in search of more permanent luxury accommodation in north London were offered the chance to purchase a flat in a new development, Princess Park Manor, named after Princess Diana. Would-be purchasers were assured that they could live in 'A Victorian masterpiece which has delighted and inspired aficionados of fine architecture for generations... a supremely elegant residence...of Italianate splendour [which] throughout its history has had an aura of grandeur about it.' It was a huge success. Besides the usual parade of rich overseas buyers who queue up to purchase trophy properties in London these days, it attracted members of the boy band, One Direction, and a goodly number of lavishly paid Premiership footballers.

The developers boasted that here was a chance to occupy a building that had been created after a contest entered by more than thirty of London's foremost architects of the mid-nineteenth century, but they were coy about what that contest had been for. Princess Park Manor is a conversion of the second county lunatic asylum for Middlesex, Colney Hatch, opened with great fanfare in 1851 by Prince Albert, and home to tens of thousands of the capital's mad through the years. At the time, it was regarded as the most modern asylum in the world. Visitors to the Great Exhibition of 1851, who had come to view that tribute to the achievements of modern industrial Britain, were provided with a guide to the wonders of the new asylum, and an invitation to visit an architectural contrivance considered nearly as spectacular as the Crystal Palace that housed the Exhibition itself. Colney Hatch soon acquired a more dismal reputation, its six miles of corridors connecting badly overcrowded wards housing hordes of the hopeless, and 'going down the Hatch' became a local slang term for going mad. All of that is elided, for it would scarcely accord with the attempt to sell the site to the *nouveaux riches* of London.

The vast expanse of Colney Hatch Asylum, the second county asylum for Middlesex.

But San Clemente Palace and Princess Park Manor are the exceptions rather than the rule. Most Victorian asylums have experienced a very different fate. Their mouldering ruins, haunting and haunted, are everywhere, scattered across Europe and North America, and even in the formerly remote corners of the world the West once colonized. On huge swathes of unoccupied land, hulking buildings collapse, bearing mute testimony to the abandonment of the enthusiasms of earlier generations. Located as many of them were in isolated rural communities – to economize on the cost of land – there is little incentive to redevelop them. As derelict, dilapidated and decayed as the handful of lost souls who still call some of these places home, the Victorian museums of madness are rapidly fading away.

'For dust thou art, and unto dust shalt thou return' we are informed in the Book of Genesis. Over the past half-century or so, the enormous investment of capital – intellectual as well as financial – that for the preceding century and more underwrote the seemingly limitless expansion of the empire of asylumdom has been written off. The distinctive moral architecture of the mental hospital is no more, or soon will be, once the ravages of weather, insects and animals have finished the job of demolition (PL. 42).

As late as the 1960s, Central State Hospital in Milledgeville, Georgia, still housed upwards of twelve thousand patients, making it the largest mental hospital in the world.[3] Now, its two hundred buildings scattered across nearly 2,000 acres stand empty, many falling in on themselves. No one in the future will ever encounter the sights and sounds that once greeted those who ventured into its hallways – or the characteristic smells that marked asylums like this: the unforgettable odour of decaying bodies and minds, of wards impregnated with decades of human waste, of the slop served up for generations as food, the unsavoury concoction clinging like some foul miasma to the physical fabric of the buildings. Outside, in the ill-tended grounds, thousands of graves lie half-hidden, numbered metal tags marking the final fate of many of those once confined for years on end.

Hundreds of miles to the north lies the old Trenton State Hospital in New Jersey, the mecca of exodontia and evisceration, where Henry Cotton once ruthlessly hunted down the focal sepsis he claimed caused mental illness. It too is now largely empty, though a small remnant still huddle in some portions of the premises. The once handsome trees that adorn its grounds are tangled, neglected and overgrown. Their sepulchral shade creates a dank and dismal atmosphere in the abandoned buildings they tower over. Mould and putrefaction are everywhere. Iron bars on the windows deposit brown rust stains on the stone and brick beneath. Emptiness and an eerie silence reign. Rotted metal screens encrusted with nameless dirt and filth partially obscure the broken panes of glass beneath, through which the trespassing visitor can peer into empty wards, bereft of furnishings, both human and inanimate. The guardhouse that once kept out the curious is unmanned. No one strives any longer to sustain the previously inviolable boundary between the worlds of the mad and the sane. Such scenes could be replicated all across what calls itself the civilized world.

In England and Wales, more than 150,000 patients were to be found locked up in mental hospitals on any given day during the 1950s; in the United States the figure was nearly four times that many. Throughout Europe, mass confinement of the mad had been the rule from the mid-nineteenth century onwards, and the pattern was replicated wherever the West made its presence felt. So too with the demise of asylumdom. It began first in Britain and North America, and it was decades before other European societies followed suit.

Almost uniquely, Japan still hasn't, or has barely begun to follow this pattern. From a very low rate of hospitalization in 1945, the population of Japanese mental hospitals grew dramatically over the next fifty years. Whereas the rate of hospitalized patients in 1945 was approximately 2 per 10,000 people, in 1995 it was more than ten times as high, and it decreased only very slightly over the next ten years, from 29 per 10,000 to 27 per 10,000.[4] In 1989, patient stays in Japanese mental hospitals averaged 496 days, or more than forty times the average length of stay in the United States. More than two decades later, Japanese patients still remained hospitalized on average for

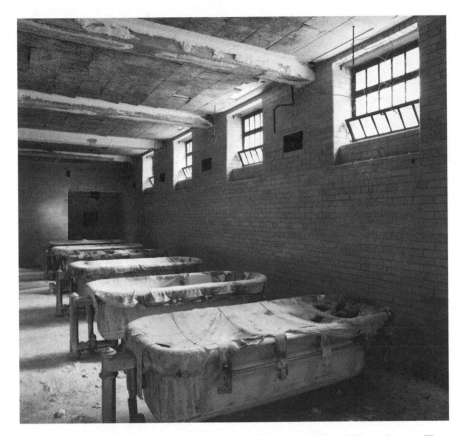

The hydrotherapy unit at the abandoned state hospital in Grafton, Massachusetts. The heavy canvas tops once kept recalcitrant patients safely immersed in water, with only their heads projecting through an opening in the unyielding fabric.

more than a year, though in 2011 the government announced controversial plans to decrease the number of inpatients by 70,000 over the following decade. With mental illness still regarded as a great stigma, it seems many continue to prefer a policy of custodial care. Japanese culture privileges public order over individual rights, and families seek confinement to conceal someone whose madness is seen as threatening the marriage prospects of their relatives, and as the source of profound shame and embarrassment. The Japanese government, however, is fearful of the mounting costs of institutionalization, particularly as unprecedented numbers of the elderly are being confined in mental hospitals.[5] How these conflicting pressures will resolve themselves remains quite uncertain, but the signs are that Japan, having adopted the asylum essentially a century after Europe and North America, is now, fifty years after them, seeing the beginnings of its decline.[6]

Almost imperceptibly initially, mental hospital censuses in the United Kingdom and the United States began to show a decrease from the mid-1950s onwards. The pace picked up dramatically from the mid-1960s, and in both countries, inpatient numbers have subsequently declined almost to vanishing point. If the United States still housed its most seriously mentally ill in 2013 at the same rate as it did in 1955, its mental hospitals would contain almost 1.1 million people on any given day. Instead, a tiny remnant, well under 50,000 patients, inhabit such institutions as remain.

By any measure, this is an extraordinary volte-face. Once the publicly supported asylum appeared on the scene in the nineteenth century, the population confined in such places increased remorselessly year on year. The handful of temporary reversals of this trend occurred in times of war. In England, for example, during the First World War, mental hospitals were stripped of many of their staff, and their already meagre budgets were cut. Predictably, the patients suffered; many starved. Figures from the English county of Buckinghamshire, for example, show that death rates increased steadily as the war dragged on, until in 1918, a third of the patients in the hospital died. Those running the hospital 'had cut the patients' rations below survival level in an attempt to save money.... As soon as the dietary [regimen] was improved (albeit at considerable cost) in 1919, the death rate dropped.'[7]

During the Second World War, in occupied France, an estimated 45,000 psychiatric inpatients died of starvation and infectious diseases, with death rates almost tripling in mental hospitals during the war years, a process some have called a programme of 'soft extermination'.[8] Inpatient numbers fell rapidly, if temporarily, from 115,00 to 65,000. The Nazis acted more directly, murdering those they referred to as 'useless eaters'.

Setting aside these extraordinary circumstances, however, the historical pattern of a remorseless increase in the size of institutional populations was an entrenched feature of the psychiatric landscape in the mid-twentieth century. Moreover, at the end of the Second World War, all the signs seemed to point to the continuation of what had become the standard response to psychosis almost everywhere. In the immediate aftermath, most American states re-labelled the 'insane' as the 'mentally ill'; English legislation of 1930 had replaced the term 'lunatic' with the more cumbersome 'person of unsound mind'; in 1948, the French Ministry of Public Health abandoned the term *aliénés* (which had been used in official documents since 1838) and replaced it with *malades mentaux*; and the Italians chose *infirmi di mente* to take the place of *alienati di menti*. Asylums, mad-houses, *établissments d'aliénés* and the like were all now to be called mental hospitals.[9] But the commitment to the proposition that those who had lost their minds should be institutionalized persisted, verbal cosmetics notwithstanding.

In the immediate postwar period, the British government argued that 'one of the biggest problems that faces the [mental health] service is the provision of more accommodation in mental hospitals'.[10] State governments across the United States reached similar conclusions. Muck-raking journalists and conscientious objectors, who had been sent to serve as attendants in state hospitals to punish them for refusing to fight, competed with one another to expose the shortcomings of existing mental health provision.[11] The most famous of these critiques was by Albert Deutsch (1905–61), a journalist who had written the first history of the treatment of mental illness in the United States and had been made an honorary member of the American Psychiatric Association as a token of the profession's gratitude. His essays on the conditions he found in American mental hospitals, accompanied by vivid photographs, appeared first in the pages of the crusading New York newspaper, *PM*, and were then republished in book form as *The Shame of the States* (1948).

Many other essays were written by people who had recently visited the German death camps, and Harold Orlansky's article, 'An American Death Camp', explicitly compared the state of the back wards of America's asylums to Dachau, Belsen and Buchenwald. Deutsch, meanwhile, described the male incontinent ward at Philadelphia's Byberry State Hospital as 'like a scene out of Dante's Inferno. Three hundred nude men stood, squatted, and sprawled in this bare room, amid shrieks, groans, and unearthly laughter.... Some lay about on the bare floor in their own excreta. The filth-covered walls were rotting away.'[12]

Yet even confronted by the devastating realities of life in many state mental hospitals, this generation of reformers did not call for the institutions' abolition. The problems they had observed, they were convinced, were the product of the ignorance of the public and the parsimony of the politicians. First-hand reports like theirs were designed to rouse a somnolent citizenry by revealing the horrors that were being perpetrated in their name, and to get voters to demand that the mental hospitals be given sufficient money to provide proper care for the mentally ill. As Alfred Maisel (1909–78) put it in the pages of *Life* magazine, the goal of bringing the truth to light was to shame the states into providing adequate funds. That would be sufficient 'to put an end to concentration camps that masquerade as hospitals and to make cure rather than incarceration the goal'.[13]

In postwar Europe, the commitment to the asylum solution seemed undimmed. Most German psychiatrists who had collaborated in Hitler's T-4 extermination programme kept their positions, and a new generation of mentally disturbed patients emerged to fill the asylums. By the 1960s, West Germany maintained 68 state mental hospitals, with an average of 1,200 beds in each. In France, mental hospitals were larger still, with some containing as many as 4,000 beds, while as late as 1982, 20 mental hospitals in Italy each housed over 1,000 patients. French authorities in the 1950s and 1960s urgently sought to relieve overcrowding in existing facilities by building more. Even late on in this period, the French government envisioned adding 20,000 extra psychiatric beds. Under Franco's fascist regime, and for a few years after his death in 1975, Spain continued to expand the mental hospital sector, doubling the number of institutions, from 54 in 1950 to 109

The male incontinent ward at Byberry State Hospital, Philadelphia, Pennsylvania. This and other images of the hospital were taken surreptitiously in 1944 by Charles Lord, a Quaker conscientious objector assigned to work as an attendant. Next door was a ward for violent men, known to Lord and his colleagues as the 'death house'.

in 1981, with the inpatient population rising from 24,586 to 61,474. At the opposite end of the political spectrum, under the social democratic regimes in Sweden and Denmark, mental hospital populations increased through the 1970s. Still, in all these countries, and in others as well, deinstitutionalization eventually came to pass. As this recital makes clear, however, the demise of the asylum was more protracted if viewed in a broad comparative perspective than simple acquaintance with the rapid progress of deinstitutionalization in Anglophone countries might lead one to believe.

A Technological Fix?

The downturn in American and British mental hospital populations began in the mid-1950s, coinciding almost precisely with the introduction of the first modern drug treatment for major mental illness. Chlorpromazine, marketed as Thorazine in the United States and Largactil (or 'large action') in Europe and elsewhere, was approved for sale by the United States Food and Drug Administration in 1954 (for more on this, see below). Thirteen months later, it was being given to two million people in that country alone. Most psychiatrists hailed the therapeutic breakthrough they claimed this represented. Instead of relying on crude empirical treatments including the various shock therapies, or the even cruder surgical intervention that was lobotomy, the profession could now prescribe and administer that classic symbolic accoutrement of the modern physician – drugs.

For British and American observers, the coincidence in the timing of the introduction of Thorazine and the reversal of the upward trend in mental hospital populations provided a simple technological explanation for the end of the asylum era. In 1961, the Joint Commission on Mental Illness and Health that had been set up by the United States Congress five years earlier reported that: 'Tranquilizing drugs have revolutionized the management of psychotic patients in American mental hospitals, and probably deserve primary credit for reversal of the upward spiral of the state hospital inpatient load.'[14] Two decades later, Sir Keith Joseph, Secretary of State for Social Services in the first government of Margaret Thatcher, was still more emphatic. Introducing the 1971 White Paper on *Hospital Services for the Mentally Ill*, he asserted that 'the treatment of psychosis, neurosis and schizophrenia have been [sic] entirely changed by the drug revolution. People go into hospital with mental disorders and they are cured.'[15] But if it were really so simple

– drugs = deinstitutionalization – then the French (who in fact actually developed chlorpromazine), the Germans, the Italians, the Dutch, the Spanish, the Swedes and the Finns would have rapidly followed down the same path. But it took a quarter of a century and more for the mental health systems of continental Europe to start to empty their mental hospitals. Drugs alone, it would seem, did not suffice to produce deinstitutionalization.

It is easy to be seduced by statistics, particularly when they appear to reinforce a conclusion one wants to reach on other grounds. The temptation to conflate correlation and cause is one every statistical neophyte is warned against, and yet it is a temptation to which many of us regularly fall prey. Though the ability of modern psychopharmacology to influence the course of mental illness has been massively oversold – Thorazine and the drugs that have followed in its wake are no psychiatric penicillin – prescription pills have indeed revolutionized the practice of psychiatry and have increasingly influenced broader cultural understandings of mental illness. Many millions of people worldwide consume psychotropic medication daily. The pharmaceutical industry makes vast profits from selling these drugs, and heavily markets their efficacy and the notion that they 'prove' the biological origins of mental illness. Small wonder then that the notion that the introduction of psychotropic drugs fuelled the discharge of psychiatric patients was so easily swallowed in Anglo-American circles.

And yet, even without the counter-examples from other societies, a more careful look at the British and American evidence would by itself have been sufficient to suggest that the contribution of the drugs revolution to hospital discharges had been grossly oversold. While it is true that at the aggregate, national level, mental hospital populations only began to trend downwards in the mid-1950s, in many places such declines are observable as early as 1947 and 1948, long before the new drugs appeared on the scene. As the British psychiatrist Aubrey Lewis (1900–75) pointed out, national figures on mental hospital populations, taken by themselves, may be a seriously misleading guide to when the deinstitutionalization process actually began.[16] They tend to mask earlier changes at the local level, and the degree to which the fall in overall numbers, when it did occur, represented a continuation of rather than a departure from existing trends. Nor can the introduction of the new drugs explain why, more than a decade later, the elderly were abruptly discharged in such large numbers in the United States, or why, five years after that, the pattern of sharp reductions in inpatient numbers spread to encompass younger age groups. Assuredly, psychotropic drugs did not suddenly become more effective ten or fifteen years after their introduction. Nor were new compounds produced in the late 1960s that had greater efficacy for the elderly, or in the early 1970s that improved outcomes for younger patients.

In the first decade after the drugs were introduced, some hospitals used them extensively, others sparingly. Patients who differed by age, gender and diagnosis were differentially likely to receive drug treatment. And yet even the New York psychiatrists Henry Brill (1906–90) and Robert E. Patton (1921–2007), whose work is usually cited to cement the connection between drugs and declining hospital populations, acknowledged in 1957 that 'no quantitative correlation could be shown between the percentage of patients receiving drug therapy at a particular hospital or a given category and the amount of improvement in releases'.[17] Five years later, a retrospective study of California state hospitals, which at first had varied widely in the degree to which they prescribed phenothiazines (of which chlorpromazine was the first), directly compared patients who received drug treatments and those who did not. It concluded that drug treatment was in fact associated with longer periods of hospital stay, and found that mental hospitals which had treated the highest percentage of their first admission schizophrenic patients with Thorazine had lower discharge rates than those whose use of the drugs was much lower.[18] Soon thereafter, prescription of the phenothiazines became so routine that further studies of this sort became difficult or impossible to pursue, but a variety of scholars who have systematically reviewed the available evidence have arrived at similar conclusions: the influence of the new drugs on deinstitutionalization was at best indirect and limited, and conscious shifts in social policy were a far more important determinant of the emptying of mental hospitals.[19]

Doomed Institutions

Speaking to the National Association for Mental Health in 1961, Enoch Powell, who was Minister of Health in the Macmillan government in Britain, was typically forthright. Mental hospitals were, he announced, 'doomed institutions'. The government planned to run them down, and in doing so, he proposed 'to err on the side of ruthlessness'. Traditional asylums had outlived their usefulness, and he pronounced himself eager 'to set the torch to the funeral pyre'.[20] A Ministry of Health circular followed, instructing regional hospital boards 'to ensure that no money is spent on upgrading or reconditioning of mental hospitals which in ten or fifteen years are not going to be required...for the large, isolated, and unsatisfactory buildings, closure will almost always be the right answer'.[21] And inevitably, curtailing expenditure on physical fabric ensured that many more mental hospitals would join the ranks of those considered 'unsatisfactory' and thus in need of closure.

The care of the mentally ill in the United States was traditionally the responsibility of individual states, rather than the federal government. The rundown of state mental hospitals thus varied widely in both timing and extent, because not all states moved at the same pace. Other features, too, of the particular shape that deinstitutionalization took in the United States were influenced by America's political structure. The ramshackle barracks-asylums that Americans had inherited from the nineteenth century were in a particularly parlous state as this process began. The Great Depression had been accompanied by the admission of more patients, while the demands of war had siphoned off what few medically qualified personnel, doctors and nurses alike, had staffed these nominally therapeutic environments.[22]

'Progressive' states such as New York, Massachusetts, Illinois and California had invested most heavily in the asylum solution, but faced the largest potential fiscal challenges when demands were made to improve the hospitals.[23] Making matters worse, the tighter postwar labour market and the unionization of state workers (much more common in northern states) were sharply increasing the costs of the institutions, as work-weeks fell from the 65 or 70 hours that had been typical of the 1930s to 45 hours a week or less. More and more convinced that the immense capital costs and necessary funding for daily operations would not be forthcoming, and that conditions in the hospitals were likely to remain dire, those in positions of authority began to explore alternatives. Milton Greenblatt (1914–94), who served as commissioner of mental health for Massachusetts between 1967 and 1972, provided a blunt assessment of the Hobson's choice he and his counterparts confronted: 'In a sense, our backs are to the wall. It's *phase out* before we go *bankrupt*.'[24]

In important ways, the movement to discharge mental patients in the United States was facilitated and encouraged by broader changes in social policy at the federal level which, perhaps inadvertently, created new incentives for states to move in this direction. The expansion of public assistance programmes and the passage of Medicare and Medicaid as part of Lyndon Johnson's Great Society programmes in the late 1960s provided some discharged mental patients with a guaranteed income for the first time. These federal subventions were, however, unavailable for those still confined to mental hospitals, who remained a drain on state budgets. As states began to realize that they could transfer costs by discharging mental patients, they moved rapidly to do so. These incentives largely explain both the increasingly sharp decline in hospital censuses that begins in the late 1960s, and the fact that the overwhelming majority of those discharged were at first geriatric patients, transferred from state hospitals to private nursing and board and care (residential) homes whose fees were paid by federal dollars. A further surge in discharge rates occurred in the mid-1970s, this time among younger patients, after the Nixon administration introduced changes to the Social Security Program, the Supplemental Security Income programme, which extended federal benefits to the disabled, including those with a mental disability.[25]

In portraying the move from the asylum to 'the community' as a revolutionary step forward – a beneficent 'reform' – the proponents of change were assisted by a barrage of scholarly and polemical criticism of traditional mental hospitals, much of it authored by social scientists, but in other cases the work of renegade psychiatrists, in particular the American Thomas Szasz and the Scottish psychiatrist R. D. Laing (see below). The tone of these studies was universally pessimistic.

Ivan Belknap (1914–84), who had studied a grossly underfunded state hospital in Texas, concluded that mental hospitals 'are probably themselves obstacles in the development of an effective program for treatment of the mentally ill'; and he urged that 'in the long run the abandonment of the state hospitals might be one of the greatest humanitarian reforms and the greatest financial economy ever achieved'.[26] H. Warren Dunham (1906–85) and S. Kirson Weinberg (1912–2001), whose field research had been at the Cleveland State Hospital in Ohio, were similarly sombre.[27] Here was an 'environment... to which any normal person would have difficulty adjusting...[an organization] characterized by conflicts in its structure, its personnel and its patient population which lead to negligence, even destruction, of the therapeutic goal.'[28] Official propaganda notwithstanding, the mental hospital was a place where 'any behavior on the part of the patient, reasonable or unreasonable, emotionally or unemotionally couched, positively or negatively oriented, tends to be regarded as evidence of mental derangement'; and one where 'control of the patient is emphasized at the expense of his improvement'.[29]

The most famous and widely read of these sociological critiques of the mental hospital was written by the Chicago-trained sociologist, Erving Goffman (1922–82). His *Asylums: Essays on the Social Situation of Mental Patients and Other Inmates* (1961) was the product in part of three years spent on the staff at the National Institute of Mental Health (NIMH) Laboratory of Socio-Environmental Studies, including a year of Institute-supported fieldwork at St Elizabeth's Hospital in Washington, DC, long considered one of the nation's finest and the only mental hospital operated directly by the federal government. *Asylums* was in many ways an idiosyncratic book – one that drew upon an eclectic variety of sources, including such things as novels and autobiographies, and studiously avoided any attempt to provide an ethnographic description of a particular mental hospital. Indeed, without consulting the acknowledgments that preface the book, few would have guessed that his sole fieldwork had taken place at St Elizabeth's, and that this was his only first-hand experience of mental hospital life. Goffman sought to produce something very different from the dense descriptions of other sociologists, attempting instead to demonstrate that mental hospitals as a class were what he called 'total institutions', places where work, sleep and play all took place in the same constricting environment. Life under such circumstances, he argued, proved massively damaging to those confined. Behaviours that looked pathological to the outsider were, on the contrary, understandable responses to the grossly deforming impact of mental hospital existence. Long-continued residence in such places tended inexorably to damage and dehumanize the inmates, who were 'crushed by the weight' of what, on close inspection, was essentially a 'self-alienating moral servitude'.[30] Muck-raking journals had viewed the mental hospitals' failings as remediable provided more money was spent, Goffman was scornful of what he saw as romantic illusions. The defects of asylums were structural and inevitable. Nothing could alter them.

A decade later, Goffman was no kinder about these places. They were, he stated:

> hopeless storage dumps trimmed in psychiatric paper. They have
> served to remove the patient from the scene of his symptomatic
> behavior...but this function has been performed by fences, not

doctors. And the price that the patient has had to pay for this service has been considerable dislocation from civil life, alienation from loved ones who arranged the commitment, mortification due to hospital regimentation and surveillance, permanent post-hospital stigmatization. This has not merely been a bad deal; it has been a grotesque one.[31]

Thomas Szasz, a Hungarian-born American psychoanalyst who taught psychiatry at the State University of New York at Syracuse, had famously announced in 1961 that mental illness was 'a myth'.[32] Real diseases were rooted in the body, and could be detected either by laboratory tests and scans, or on the autopsy table. By contrast, he claimed, mental illnesses were merely metaphorical sorts of 'disease', in reality just disparaging labels that allowed the state and its agents (psychiatrists) to employ therapeutic rhetoric to confine troublesome people without the benefit of a trial or the protections accorded to an accused criminal. Institutional psychiatry, in Szasz's eyes, was simply an instrument of oppression. Its practitioners were jailers, not healers, their protests to the contrary notwithstanding, and mental hospitals were barely disguised prisons. He campaigned steadily to abolish involuntary commitment, and to eliminate the institutions themselves, joining forces with the Church of Scientology in 1969 to form the Citizens Commission on Human Rights, which denounced psychiatry as 'an industry of death'.

If Szasz was a man of the libertarian right, railing against the tyranny of the modern state, the Scottish psychiatrist Ronald (better known as R. D.) Laing was a self-proclaimed Marxist. That was not the only stark difference between them. Laing saw mental illness as real enough, but stressed that madness was the product of society, and more particularly of family relationships. The seemingly strange behaviour and confused speech of the mental patient, interpreted by many as meaningless, were in fact rich with meaning, an expression of the distress they experienced, and the 'double-binds' those around them imposed – parents, for example, who simultaneously insisted upon and rejected emotional intimacy with their children, and refused to acknowledge what they were doing. But like Szasz, Laing objected vehemently to the mental hospital, which he saw as a destructive place. Schizophrenia, he contended, was a form of super-sanity, in the face of what he announced was a mad world.[33] Patients needed to be left in the community and coaxed to complete their therapeutic journey,[34] not institutionalized and drugged into submission.

Szasz and Laing were ostracized by their professional colleagues, lumped together as 'anti-psychiatrists' and dismissed as anti-scientific ideologues. But the fiercely critical view they and figures including Goffman had advanced of the impact of the mental hospital on its inmates found at least some sympathy among mainstream psychiatrists. The British psychiatrist Russell Barton (1924–2002), superintendent of Severalls Mental Hospital in Kent, and later head of the Rochester Psychiatric Center in New York, coined the term 'institutional neurosis' to describe the impact of confinement on the long-stay mental patient, and J. K. Wing (1923–2010) and George Brown (b. 1930) at London's Institute of Psychiatry authored a well-received monograph on *Institutionalism and Schizophrenia*.[35] North American psychiatrists joined the chorus. Fritz Redlich (1910–2004), chairman of Yale's psychiatry department, wondered aloud about whether 'the patients are infantile… because we infantilize them'.[36] The California psychiatrist Werner Mendel was more emphatic still: 'the hospital as a form of treatment for the severely ill psychiatric patient is always expensive and inefficient, frequently anti-therapeutic, and never the treatment of choice'.[37]

Belatedly, these anti-institutional sentiments were taken up by psychiatrists in continental Europe. Italy, for example, abruptly passed a law in 1978, Legge 180, which banned all future admissions to traditional mental hospitals, as well as the construction of any new institutions of this sort. The legislation was informally known as the Basaglia Law, after the charismatic left-wing Italian psychiatrist Franco Basaglia (1924–80), who was its principal author and who had been avowedly influenced by Erving Goffman and other American critics of the total institution.[38] This change drew wide attention, in part because of Basaglia's prominence in European intellectual circles, and in part because of the stark simplicity of the approach the law embodied. Basaglia died only two years after the new legislation, but its implementation continued, albeit controversially. Even prior to 1978, some decrease had occurred in inpatient numbers in Italy, but the ending of the supply of new patients brought about, as the authors of the legislation intended, a steady further drop, from 78,538 in 1978 to only 11,803 in 1996. Four years later, all remaining mental hospitals officially closed their doors.[39] Italy had joined the rest of the Western world in moving the mad out of the asylum and back into the community.

The Fate of Those with Chronic Mental Illness

But, as was also the case everywhere, the Italians had closed their mental hospitals without troubling to provide alternative structures to handle the problems posed by serious mental illness. Much of the burden was displaced on to families, and they have been vociferous about the social difficulties they are confronted with.[40] Other patients were simply moved from public mental hospitals to private residential facilities, about which the authorities profess to know little.[41] Still others find themselves in prison or on the street.

Problems of this sort had already surfaced in Britain and the United States long before the Italians had begun to deinstitutionalize. In the midst of all the excitement about the replacement of the mental hospital and the breathless proclamations about the virtues of the community, it seems that few people noticed the degree to which the new programmes remained figments of their planners' imaginations. Nor did many appear to realize, for some considerable time, that despite all the rhetoric on both sides of the Atlantic about 'better services for the mentally handicapped' (the title of an official statement of British policy now over a quarter of a century old),[42] the reality was the much darker one of retrenchment or even elimination of state-supported programmes for victims of severe and chronic forms of mental disorder. Community care was a shell game with no pea.[43]

Some of those discharged from mental hospitals have unambiguously benefited from the shift in social policy. Victims of an earlier tendency towards what many have called 'overhospitalization', they have experienced few problems obtaining employment and housing, maintaining social ties and so forth, blending all but imperceptibly into the general population. Such benign outcomes are, however, far from constituting the norm.

Among those with more noticeable continuing impairment, it comes as no surprise that ex-patients placed with their families seem on the whole to have fared best. It would be a serious mistake, though, to suppose that even here deinstitutionalization has proceeded smoothly and has proved unambiguously beneficial.[44] A good deal of the distress and misery has remained hidden because of families' reticence about complaining, a natural tendency, but one that has helped to sustain a false optimism about the effects of the shifts to community treatment.[45] Yet whatever the difficulties encountered by these ex-patients, and their families, they pale by comparison with the experiences of the greater numbers who have no families, or

The sidewalk psychotic: in the aftermath of deinstitutionalization, many of the homeless mentally ill live on the streets.

whose families simply refuse to accept responsibility for them. The sidewalk psychotic has become a familiar feature of the urban landscape: homeless, mad, abandoned.[46] Clustering for the most part in the least desirable parts of cities, where existing inhabitants are too poor and politically powerless to resist, they live among other marginal people – criminals, addicts, alcoholics, the utterly impoverished – and eke out a precarious existence. In the United States from the late-1960s onwards, as already noted, first among the elderly and then among younger people with serious mental disturbances, the availability of even small welfare payments encouraged the growth of nursing homes and board and care homes in which large numbers came to be confined. An entrepreneurial industry emerged, one which profits from this form of human misery, and is almost wholly unregulated by state authorities.

National surveys suggested that more than 50 per cent of those placed in nursing homes were in facilities with more than 100 residents, and a further 15 per cent in places housing more than 200. In New York, for example, media exposés showed massive concentrations of discharged patients in squalid, run-down hotels, and in 'homes' surrounding the now-shuttered huge mental hospitals on Long Island – Pilgrim and Central Islip. In an irony that may have been lost on the distracted souls who once haunted their halls, these profit-making facilities were often run by former employees of the old asylums. States either ignored or actually sponsored such developments. Hawaii, for example, faced a massive shortage of beds when its mental health bureaucracy opted to accelerate discharge from its mental hospitals. The problem was solved by explicitly encouraging the proliferation of unlicensed facilities. Nebraska at first shied away from such a laissez-faire approach and decided some form of state provision was required. Accordingly, in a splendidly original variation on the ancient practice of treating the mad like cattle, it placed the licensing and inspection of homes for the mentally ill in the hands of its state department of agriculture. When scandals erupted, it removed the licenses – but not the patients – from 320 of these homes, and abandoned the inmates to their fate. Still other states, for instance Maryland and Oregon, opted for perhaps the safest course of all: no follow-up of those they released and hence a blissful official ignorance about their likely fate. All too often, the mentally disturbed are left at the mercy of speculators who have every incentive to warehouse their charges as inexpensively as possible, since the volume of profit is inversely proportional to the amount expended on the inmates.

The ramshackle network of such establishments, intended as a cheap alternative to the state hospital, and the swelling presence of the seriously mentally disabled among the ranks of the homeless, stand as an indictment of contemporary American mental health policy. They constitute perhaps the most extreme example of what has become the new orthodoxy, an 'almost unanimous abdication from the task of proposing and securing any provision for a humane and continuous form of care for those mental patients who need something rather more than short-term therapy for an acute phase of their illness'.[47] Here, ecologically separated and isolated from the rest of us, the most useless and unwanted segments of our society can be left to decompose, quietly, and, save for the occasional media exposé, all but invisibly.

Britain has had its own dismal and depressing experience with community care. During 1973–74, for example, while £300 million was spent on the mentally ill still receiving institutional treatment, a mere £6.5 million was spent on residential and day-care services for those 'in the community'. A decade and a half later, an official inquiry into the state of the mental health services found the situation little changed: community care remained 'a poor relation: everybody's distant relative, but nobody's baby'.[48]

With this exception, successive British governments, like their American counterparts, have quite deliberately avoided funding any systematic study of what has happened. Indeed, they appear to have done their best methodically to impede such studies, not least by curtailing the availability of basic statistical information: a tactic justified by invoking the Rayner Review's remarkable recommendation in 1981 that 'information should not be collected primarily for publication...[but] because the Government needs it for its own business'.[49] Evidently, the Government has decided that it does not need to know (or prefers not to know) what its policies in this area have meant in practice: what has happened to those no longer confined in mental hospitals, when and how existing provision fails to meet basic needs, and so forth. After all, in the absence of systematic data, individual scandals can be dismissed as 'anecdotal'; and local authority protests that they are being handed an impossible burden and given no additional resources to address even part of the need can be met with obfuscation, or with advice about how to avoid their apparent legal obligations under the Chronically Sick and Disabled Persons Act of 1970.[50]

But some of the mentally ill behave in ways that create almost unbearable disturbances in the texture of daily life. Their infractions of rules of public decorum, their actual or potential violence, the havoc and chaos their presence portends exceed the bounds of community tolerance. Without the asylums that once functioned to move such people off the streets, an alternative must be found. And that alternative is often jail. In America, for example, the largest single concentration of the seriously mentally ill resides in the Los Angeles County Jail; nationwide, estimates published in 2006 were that '15% of State prisoners and 24% of jail inmates...[meet] the criteria for a psychotic disorder'.[51] In France estimates put the number of mentally ill in prisons at over 12,000, out of a total prison population of 63,000.[52] In Britain, too, the Director-General of the Prison Service complained that 'the proportion of the prison population who show signs of mental illness has risen seven-fold [between the late 1980s and 2002]. For them, care in the community has become care in custody...the problem is near overwhelming.'[53] The confinement of the mad in prisons shocked the consciences of nineteenth-century reformers, and helped to prompt the age of the asylumdom. The closure of these nineteenth-century establishments has, it would seem, brought us full circle.

The Drugs Revolution

If the new psychotropic drugs were not the first cause of deinstitutionalization, their advent did nonetheless transform psychiatry, and broader cultural conceptions of madness besides. The introduction of Thorazine in 1954 was scarcely the first time pharmaceuticals had been used to treat the mentally ill and alleviate psychiatric symptoms. Some nineteenth-century psychiatrists, for example, experimented with giving their patients marijuana, though most soon abandoned the practice. Opium was mobilized as a soporific in cases of mania. Later on in the nineteenth century, chloral hydrate and the bromides had their enthusiasts, and their use continued into the twentieth century.

Bromides in excess produced psychotic symptoms and their widespread use outside the asylum led to toxic reactions that landed substantial numbers of patients in mental hospitals, diagnosed as mad; and chloral, though effective as a sedative, was addicting, and with long-term use resulted in hallucinations and symptoms akin to delirium tremens. Evelyn Waugh's *The Ordeal of Gilbert Pinfold* (1957) provides a thinly fictionalized account of the hallucinations and mental disturbance that could result. Addicted to alcohol and phenobarbitol, Waugh dosed himself liberally with bromides and chloral, and, as he admitted, the novel's portrayal of a middle-aged Catholic novelist teetering on the edge of madness and then falling into the abyss mirrors what happened to him during his 'late lunacy'.

Lithium salts seemed to calm the agitation of manic patients, and some hydrotherapeutic establishments used them in the treatment of their nervous patients. But lithium could easily prove toxic, producing anorexia, depression, even cardiovascular collapse and death. Its value would later be championed by the Australian psychiatrist John Cade (1912–80) after the Second World War, and the existence of calming effects in mania would prompt some continuing clinical interest in these compounds in Europe and North America.

The 1920s saw experiments with barbiturates, including attempts to place mental patients in chemically induced periods of suspended animation in the hopes that this would produce a cure (as mentioned p. 308). But barbiturates, too, had major drawbacks: they were addicting, overdoses could easily prove fatal, and withdrawal symptoms when they were discontinued were highly unpleasant, even dangerous. Besides, like the earlier drugs prescribed by psychiatrists, their use produced mental confusion, impaired judgment and an inability to concentrate, as well as a whole spectrum of physical problems.

The new anti-psychotics were different, so their proponents claimed, and in time they would become the sheet anchor of modern psychiatry. Psychoanalytic psychotherapy occupied the commanding heights of American psychiatry in the mid-twentieth century, and an eclectic focus on a vague compound of social, psychological and biological factors constituted the orthodoxy elsewhere. Half a century later, few psychiatrists had much time for psychotherapy, and their paymasters, either governments or private insurance companies, showed little disposition to reimburse them for providing it.

Talking cures of a new sort, such as the comparatively brief interventions characteristic of cognitive-behavioural therapy (CBT), have become the province of the heavily feminized (and cheaper) professions of clinical psychology and social work. Psychiatry's very identity is now closely bound up with its monopoly over the prescribing of drugs, and in psychiatrists' hands, pills have replaced talk as the dominant response to disturbances of cognition, emotion and behaviour. Patients and their families now look to their doctors for the magic potions that will produce better living through chemistry. Those assurances may yet prove to have a solid and durable foundation, though at present they rest on faith more than science. Or perhaps they will not. More likely they may be only part of the story, and in that case, the social and the psychological dimensions of mental illness may well have received a premature burial.

It is entirely possible that madness will after all turn out to have some of its roots in meanings, not Freudian meanings perhaps, but meanings nonetheless. Above all, madness remains remarkably mysterious and hard to comprehend, though that is not what the dominant ideology in psychiatry would have the rest of us believe. Biological reductionism rules. Not coincidentally, the pharmaceutical industry grows rich.

Chlorpromazine – the first of the phenothiazines that initially revolutionized psychiatric practice – was synthesized on 11 December 1950 by the small French pharmaceutical house, Rhône-Poulenc. Its psychiatric applications were a matter of serendipity. The company initially experimented with it as a way to reduce the dosage of anaesthetic needed during surgery, as an anti-emetic and then as a treatment for skin irritations. In those days, controls over the distribution of drugs, and over therapeutic experiments with new compounds, were remarkably lax. A French naval surgeon, Henri Laborit (1914–95), given a small supply to play with, used it on some psychiatric patients, and was startled by the effects it had on them. Patients seemed to lose interest in their surroundings, and their florid symptoms abated, without much evidence of somnolence. Pierre Deniker (1917–98) and Jean Delay (1907–87), who practised psychiatry at the Hospital of Saint-Anne in Paris, heard about this work and began giving the drug to patients. Within months, it was being marketed in France as Largactil.

An early advertisement for the virtues of Thorazine, touting its value in curbing the agitated husband's inclination to beat his wife. The stress on the drug's ability to make the patient more accessible to psychotherapy is an obvious attempt to appeal to the psychoanalysts who then dominated American psychiatry, a group otherwise disinclined to prescribe chemicals to treat mental disorders.

American physicians were, however, highly sceptical of European medical research, and Rhône-Poulenc had therefore elected to sell the marketing rights to the drug to the American company, Smith, Kline & French. Relabelling the drug as Thorazine, they secured Food and Drug Administration approval to market it in 1954. On an initial investment for research and development of only $350,000, the corporation realized massive profits. Within a year of its commercial introduction, Thorazine had increased the company's sales volume by a third, and a major portion of Smith, Kline & French's subsequent growth, from net sales of $53 million in 1953 to $347 million in 1970, was directly or indirectly attributable to this enormously profitable product.

This explosive growth pattern was no accident. It reflected a huge, sustained and expensive sales drive on the part of the company. Over a

Depressed? We have the solution! An advertisement for 'mother's little helper' – a pill for the housewife trapped in a prison of domesticity.

seven-year period, both state legislatures and state hospital staffs were bombarded with a hail of sophisticated marketing materials designed to convince them of the advantages of the drug as a cheap, effective form of treatment, suitable for administration on a mass basis to mental hospital patients. It was one of the first so-called blockbuster drugs, and other pharmaceutical houses rushed to share in the bonanza, producing marginally different versions of the original drug that they could patent as their own. The psychopharmacological revolution was well and truly launched.

Thorazine and its derivatives gave psychiatry for the first time a therapeutic modality that was easy to dispense and closely resembled the approach to treating disease that increasingly underpinned the cultural authority of medicine at large. The contrast with lobotomy and shock therapy was clear, and Smith, Kline & French almost immediately advertised that one of the primary advantages of its new potion was that 'Thorazine reduces the need for electroshock therapy'.[54] For all the initial excitement surrounding their introduction, however, the new drugs were at best a treatment that reduced psychiatric symptoms. That was a considerable attraction. But they did not cure the underlying disease.

Soon enough, the pharmaceutical industry brought other classes of psychoactive drugs to market. First, there were the so-called minor tranquillizers. Miltown and Equanil (meprobamate), which made users drowsy, and later on Valium and Librium (the benzodiazepines), which allegedly didn't. With the advent of these drugs, the troubles of everyday life were effortlessly redefined as psychiatric illnesses. Here were the pills that proffered a solution to the boredom of the trapped housewife, the blues of overwhelmed mothers and of the fading middle-aged of both genders. As early as 1956, statistics suggest that as many as one American in twenty was taking tranquillizers in any given month. Anxiety, tension, unhappiness could all be smoothed away by medication it seemed. Once again, however, these advantages were secured at a price: many of those taking the drugs became physically habituated to them, until they found it difficult or impossible not to continue using them, for to abandon the pills was to court symptoms and psychic pain worse than those that had driven the decision to use them in the first place. The Rolling Stones sang ominously of the 'little yellow pill', 'mother's little helper' that 'helps [the housewife] on her way', to her 'busy dying day'. But consumers clamoured for them, and prescription pills, uppers and downers, were soon no longer a monopoly of the married and the middle-aged. Rock stars and teenagers popped them too.

Other compounds that changed people's moods were developed in the late 1950s, beginning with Iproniazid, a monoamine oxidase inhibitor, in 1957, and Tofranil and Elavil, so-called tricyclic anti-depressants, in 1958 and 1961 respectively.[55] Perhaps in part because many depressed people suffer in silence, the belief persisted that depression was comparatively rare. The success of Prozac in the 1990s changed that mind-set completely. Depression has become a disease of epidemic proportions. Alluding to Auden's famous remark about Freud (p. 345), the American psychiatrist Peter Kramer (b. 1948) commented that: 'In time, I suspect we shall come to discover that modern psychopharmacology has become, like Freud in his day, a whole climate of opinion under which we conduct our different lives.'[56] And so it has proved.

The Re-Constitution of Psychiatry

Before the Second World War, as seen in the previous chapter, most American psychiatrists, like their counterparts elsewhere, plied their trade in mental hospitals. And although the twentieth century had seen the growth of a small number of practitioners who made a living working with less disturbed patients in an office setting, in 1940 psychiatrists formed a marginal and despised specialty, mostly still trapped within the walls of custodial asylums.

All that changed rapidly during the war and in its immediate aftermath. As early as 1947, in a remarkable development, more than half of all American psychiatrists worked in private practice or at outpatient clinics; and by 1958, as few as 16 per cent practised their trade in traditional state hospitals. Moreover, this rapid shift in the profession's centre of gravity occurred in the context of an extraordinary expansion in the absolute size of the profession.[57] And many of them practised psychoanalysis, in either its orthodox or simplified forms.

The divisions between so-called dynamic psychiatrists and those the new professional elite referred to scornfully as 'directive-organic psychiatrists' (i.e. those who told their patients to shape up, and supplemented these injunctions with shock therapies and other forms of physical intervention) did not precisely mirror the division between institutional and office-based psychiatry. But it came close enough. Besides being more affluent, those of the mentally ill who sought outpatient treatment were naturally for the most part much less disturbed. But how were the Freudians and their fellow-travellers to respond to all the talk of the new drugs?

Many responded initially by ignoring the pharmaceutical remedies. Such drugs were, these practitioners asserted, merely treating psychiatric symptoms, not reaching the psychodynamic core of patients' problems. They were a band-aid, not a cure. But as the drugs proliferated in both number and kind, this tactic became harder to sustain, and many adopted an alternative approach to the pharmaceutical challenge: drugs, they admitted, were a useful adjunct, a means to render disturbed, hallucinating, delusional patients calmer, and thus accessible to psychotherapy. That was where the real therapeutic work was done. Drug companies, alert to the preferences and prejudices of those they needed to sell to, adapted their marketing copy, and drug advertisements of the period thus emphasized the use of anti-psychotics as adjuncts to psychotherapy.

To most American analysts practising in the 1960s, their hegemony over the psychiatric profession must have seemed assured. They had the most desirable, lucrative patients and earned far more than the benighted part of the profession still stuck in mental hospitals – more, even, than many of their colleagues in other medical specialisms. Their ideas were everywhere in the broader culture, eagerly embraced by artists, writers and intellectuals. Freud's own portrait of himself as an intellectual giant who had revolutionized human understanding, was widely respected. The humanistic and intellectual side of psychoanalysis was attracting talented recruits to psychiatry, and the university departments where these students trained were dominated by the psychoanalytically orientated. What could possibly go wrong, what could disturb their dominance? Something so solid surely could not melt into air. And yet it did.

The very ambition of psychoanalysis to be a general science of mind created, oddly enough, one sort of vulnerability. Where other forms of psychiatry thought categorically about mental illnesses – the worlds of the sane and the insane were discrete and radically opposed to each other – psychoanalysis approached mental illness dimensionally. Rather than sharp discontinuities between the mad and the rest of us, all of us were to some degree pathological, flawed creatures, and the sources of mental disturbances were rooted in all our psyches. The critiques of psychiatry as an instrument of social control were originally directed at the mental hospital, obviously vulnerable to claims it was a prison or concentration camp in disguise. But this tendency of psychoanalysts to medicalize human differences and to broaden the boundaries of mental pathology – to assert that the criminal, for example, were sick, not bad, and that personality flaws were a kind of mental illness – increasingly, these were propositions that raised concerns about psychiatry's role. If difference and eccentricity were redefined as medical problems and then subjected to compulsory treatment, what did that imply for human freedom?

Psychoanalysts had never taken diagnostic distinctions of the sort famously reified by Kraepelin and others terribly seriously. Hebephrenic or disorganized schizophrenia, paranoid schizophrenia, undifferentiated schizophrenia, manic-depressive psychosis and the like: these were just crude and unhelpful categories. What mattered to the analysts was the psycho-pathology of the particular individual they were treating, not some abstract set of arbitrary labels. But other people thought that labels such as schizo-phrenia and manic-depressive illness referred to real diseases, and when it became apparent that psychiatrists simply couldn't agree about diagnosis, the embarrassment and the threat to the profession's legitimacy was profound.

A succession of studies during the late 1960s and 1970s had demonstrated the extraordinary unreliability of psychiatric diagnoses.[58] Even with respect to what were regarded as the most serious forms of psychiatric disturbance, different psychiatrists only agreed upon the diagnosis about 50 per cent of the time. Many of these studies had been conducted by the profession itself, including a landmark study by the British psychiatrist John Cooper and his associates of differential diagnosis in a cross-national context.[59] That research showed that what British psychiatrists diagnosed as manic depression, their American counterparts were prone to label schizophrenia, and vice versa.

The work that drew most public attention, though, and inflicted most damage on psychiatry's public image, was an experiment using pseudo-patients conducted by the Stanford social psychologist David Rosenhan (1929–2012), the results of which appeared in 1973 in *Science*, one of the two most widely read scientific journals in the world.[60] The research subjects went to a local mental hospital claiming to be hearing voices. Having been admitted, they were instructed to behave perfectly normally. Most were diagnosed as schizophrenic, and their subsequent conduct was interpreted through that lens, so the chart of one subject who wrote down details about the ward recorded that 'patient engages in writing behavior'. Fellow patients, but not the psychiatrists, could see that the pseudo-patients were shamming; when the pseudo-patients were eventually discharged, many were classified as 'schizophrenic in remission'.

As soon as Rosenhan's paper appeared, psychiatrists protested loudly that the study was unethical and the methodology flawed. Their complaints were not completely unfounded, but 'On Being Sane in Insane Places' was widely seen as yet another black mark for the profession. Legal scholars began openly to mock psychiatry's claims to clinical competence. One prominent law review article suggested that psychiatric 'expert' testimony was nothing of the sort, but rather was akin to 'flipping coins in the courtroom' – and it marshalled an abundance of references to prove it.[61]

There was yet another, perhaps even more important reason why diagnostic imprecision created increasing problems for the profession by the early 1970s. The pharmaceutical industry had discovered that finding new treatments for mental illness offered enormous potential profits. For drug development to proceed, however, and for the regulatory authorities to grant licenses to release new drugs to the market, it was vital to have access to homogeneous groups of patients. To demonstrate that one treatment was statistically superior to another required increasingly large numbers of patients who could be assigned to the experimental and control groups that double-blind testing relied upon.[62] But unless the patients reliably shared the same diagnosis, how could comparisons be made? And once it appeared that a new compound had an effect on some patients but not others, this too prompted a heightened concern with diagnostic precision, since distinguishing between sub-populations was essential to create the necessary evidence of efficacy.

How shall we decide who is mad and who is sane? That was a question that demanded an answer. No X-rays, no MRIs, no blood tests or laboratory findings provide assistance to those who must make this most basic of distinctions. Some, following the lead of Thomas Szasz, have concluded that, without such biologically based diagnostic criteria, mental illness is but a fiction, a misleading label imposed on some who cause us trouble. But most others know better: some of our fellow creatures – deluded, distracted, depressed or demented – are so alienated from the reality the rest of us seem to share that it seems inescapable that they are mad (or, more politely, mentally ill). With respect to the most serious cases of alienation, we would probably be tempted to question the sanity of someone who dissented from the consensus. Where to draw the line, though, in less obvious cases? We may laugh when we read the courtroom testimony of John Haslam, one of the most famous (or infamous) mad-doctors practising in the early nineteenth century: 'I never saw any human being who was of sound mind.' But in truth, beyond the hard core of easily recognizable behavioural or mental disturbance, the boundary between the normal and the pathological remains extraordinarily vague and indeterminate. And yet lines are drawn, and lives lie in the balance. Crazy or merely eccentric? It matters greatly.

Taken together, the questions swirling around psychiatry's diagnostic competence prompted the American Psychiatric Association to begin efforts to standardize diagnosis. A task force was established, and given a mandate to create a more reliable nosology. Psychoanalysts yawned and ignored it. The task force was led by Robert Spitzer (b. 1932), a Columbia University psychiatrist, who swiftly recruited like-minded souls to the panel, most of them from Washington University in St Louis, Missouri.[63] The task force members were heavily biased in favour of biological models of mental illness, and liked to refer to themselves as DOPs, or 'data-oriented persons', though in reality their labours involved political horse-trading more than science.[64] They preferred pills to talk, and in their hands a wholly distinctive new approach to the diagnostic process became a decisive weapon in the battle to re-orientate the profession.

Unable to demonstrate convincing chains of causation for any major form of mental disorder, the Spitzer task force abandoned any pretence at doing so. Instead, they concentrated on maximizing inter-rater reliability to ensure that psychiatrists examining a particular patient would agree on what was wrong. This entailed developing lists of symptoms that allegedly characterized different forms of mental disturbance, and applying those to a 'tick the boxes' approach to diagnosis. Faced with a new patient, psychiatrists would record the presence or absence of a given set of symptoms, and once a threshold number of these had been reached, the person they were examining was given a particular diagnostic label, with 'co-morbidity' invoked to explain away situations where more than one 'illness' could be diagnosed. Disputes about what belonged in the manual were resolved by committee votes, as was the arbitrary decision about where to situate cut-off points: i.e., how many of the laundry list of symptoms a patient had to exhibit before he or she was declared to be suffering from a particular form of illness. Questions of validity – whether the new classificatory system of listed 'diseases' corresponded in some way with distinctions that made aetiological sense – were simply set to one side. If diagnoses could be rendered mechanical and predictable, consistent and replicable, that would suffice. The 'surface' manifestations of mental diseases that the psychoanalysts had long dismissed as merely the symptoms of the underlying psychodynamic disorders of the personality became instead scientific markers, the very elements that defined different forms of mental disorder. And the control of such symptoms, preferably by chemical means, became the new Holy Grail of the profession.

Eventually, a new edition of the *Diagnostic and Statistical Manual* (DSM) had to be put to the vote of the membership of the American Psychiatric Association. Belatedly, the psychoanalysts realized that their neglect of the process was a catastrophic error. Even the category of illness into which most of their patients fell, neurosis, was about to disappear from the profession's official system of labels, with predictable effects on their livelihoods. But their attempts to rescue their position were blocked by a clever and cynical counter-move by Robert Spitzer: as a gesture of apparent compromise, he allowed the insertion of the term 'neurotic reaction' in parentheses after certain diagnoses. The association voted in the affirmative, and in 1980 the third edition of the *Diagnostic and Statistical Manual* appeared (in reality the first substantial and significant edition), with dramatic effects on the future of psychiatry and on broader cultural conceptions of mental illness.[65] Outside North America, many psychiatrists preferred a different classificatory system, part of the larger International Classification of Diseases or ICD, issued by the World Health Organization, and some continue to do so. But the links swiftly forged by the multinational pharmaceutical industry between the DSM diagnostic categories and novel drug treatments in psychiatry helped to ensure that DSM's influence would be the more profound, and that psychiatrists everywhere would ultimately have to bow to its authority. ICD and DSM categories have increasingly converged, and by all accounts the next edition of ICD, the eleventh, will see an even closer rapprochement between the two systems.

Not long after publication of the third edition of the manual, when a revised version appeared in 1987, the fig-leaf Spitzer had offered the psychoanalysts had disappeared, just as he had planned it would when he made the original gesture.[66] By the time the fourth edition appeared in 1994, the DSM ran to over 900 pages, identified almost 300 psychiatric illnesses, and sold hundreds of thousands of copies at $85 a time. It was the indispensable item on the bookshelves of each and every American mental health professional, and ultimately proved to be the battering ram that secured the worldwide hegemony of the new American psychiatry. The very language and categories we employ to describe mental distress, the official boundaries of where mental pathology lies, even the existential experience of mental patients themselves, have all been indelibly marked by this document.

DSM III's triumph marked the advent of a classificatory system that increasingly linked diagnostic categories to specific drug treatments. It led to an acceptance on the part of both profession and public of a conceptualization of mental illnesses as specific, identifiably different diseases, each amenable to treatment with different drugs. Most importantly, since the medical insurance industry began to require a DSM diagnosis before agreeing to pay for a patient's treatment (and the preferred course and length of treatment came to be linked to individual diagnostic categories), DSM III became a document that it was impossible to ignore, and impossible not to validate. If a mental health professional wanted to be paid (and could not afford to operate outside the realms of insurance reimbursement, as most self-evidently could not), then there was no alternative but to adopt the manual.

In subsequent years, particularly once anti-depressant drugs took off in the 1990s, biological language saturated professional and public discussions of mental illness. Steven Sharfstein (b. 1942), the then president of the American Psychiatric Association, referred to the upshot of this process as the transition from 'the biopsychosocial model [of mental illness] to... the bio-bio-bio model'. Almost from the beginning of this transformation, American psychoanalysts found themselves largely bereft of patients and cast out from the commanding heights of the psychiatric profession.

It was a demise accelerated by another fateful decision analysts had made early on as they organized the training of new generations of the profession in the United States. Anxious to retain absolute control over training analyses and over who could enter the profession, they had formed institutes that lay completely outside the university system. But the rise of the modern research university, its role as the repository of pure science and its growing prestige as the factory where knowledge was produced and disseminated all added to the structural weakness of groups which lacked this form of legitimation. Psychoanalysis's exclusion from these hallowed halls – a fate it had voluntarily, even eagerly sought when it did not appear to matter – made it easier to dismiss as sect, not science.

Paradoxically, then, in the very country where it had enjoyed the greatest success – the United States – psychoanalysis came closest to professional oblivion. Once it lost its hegemony, a resurgent biological psychiatry had no time for the Freudian enterprise, and quickly sought to sideline it. If psychoanalysis survived at all in the United States, it tended to be in the halls of literature and anthropology departments, with the odd philosopher thrown in for good measure. A tiny residual market for its therapeutic wares remained, mostly Jewish and confined to a few major urban centres, but psychoanalysis as a therapeutic enterprise soon became an endangered species.[67]

Its fate elsewhere was not quite as dismal. Never dominant professionally in countries including Britain and France, psychoanalysis retained more of the limited following it had previously enjoyed, and continued to exercise a fascination for many intellectuals that shows little sign of abating. Until recently, it is true, the French Freud was something of a caricature. Parisian psychoanalysis most commonly was the idiosyncratic version derived from the work of Jacques Lacan (1901–81). Lacan had begun to attract attention in the 1960s, and he became an object of near-veneration in some quarters until his death in 1981.[68] (Lacan's version of psychoanalysis was so peculiar that he had already been ejected from the ranks of orthodox Freudian analysis. His 'analytic hour', for example, was sometimes as short as a few minutes, sometimes even less – a single *parole* (word) whispered to the patient in the waiting room counting as (and being billed as) a therapeutic session. That way, he could see (and charge) as many as ten patients in a single hour.[69]) If nothing else, though, Lacan's popularity did encourage French intellectuals to engage with Freud himself, and some of that heightened interest has persisted, even as the Lacanian legacy fades. Across the channel in Britain, despite internal divisions and sectarian squabbling that can be traced all the way back to the Second World War (and the emerging divide between the orthodox Freudians, led by Freud's daughter Anna, and the renegade faction led by Melanie Klein), psychoanalysis continues to maintain a very visible public presence. Never having enjoyed the prominence and power within the psychiatric profession of their American counterparts, British psychoanalysts are perhaps less haunted by a sense of decline and impending collapse.

Therapeutically, the marginalization of psychoanalysis may not have been a great loss, particularly when it came to the treatment of the seriously mentally ill. Though some American analysts such as Harry Stack Sullivan (1892–1949) and Frieda Fromm-Reichmann (1889–1957), and the Italian psychiatrist Silvano Arieti (1914–81) had claimed to have had some success with the treatment of psychosis,[70] and in Europe the followers of Melanie Klein (1882–1960) and Jacques Lacan had also broached the possibility of adapting psychoanalytic techniques to the treatment of profoundly disturbed patients, few outside the ranks of the true believers accorded these assertions much credibility, then or now.[71]

But the psychoanalysts' assertion that madness had meaning did promote an attention to the individual, encouraged psychiatrists to listen to and learn about the psychological meaning of mental disorder for those who suffered from it, and was associated with an insistence on the value of careful observation of their travails. In an era of swift DSM diagnoses, and prompt near-universal drug treatment, the phenomenology of psychopathology has suffered almost terminal neglect, and that most assuredly is a great loss. It has reached the point where the eminent neuroscientist and long-time editor of the *American Journal of Psychiatry*, Nancy Andreasen (b. 1938), has felt compelled to issue a warning that 'there has been a steady decline in the teaching of careful clinical evaluation that is targeted to the individual person's problems and social context.... Students are taught to memorize DSM rather than to learn complexities' about the mental illnesses confronting them. The diagnostic manual, she laments, 'has had a dehumanizing impact on the practice of psychiatry'.[72] Left unspoken, but surely even more important, has been the dehumanizing impact of these developments on the patients who are the object of professional attention.

In the drive to produce a universal and objective classification, and to provide a Procrustean bed into which every individual's psychopathology can and must be fitted, the central goals of those working within the DSM paradigm are to eliminate so far as is possible individual clinical judgment, with all the differences of opinion that inevitably flow from relying on something so mutable; and to banish human subjectivity more generally. That focus by psychiatrists makes possible rapid, routine and replicable labelling. Patients' troubles are typically diagnosed in less than half an hour – a remarkable though some might think a distinctly dubious achievement, bearing in mind the life-changing consequences that often flow from such decision-making. The very logic of the DSM approach quite deliberately precludes any serious attention to complexity and to the particular features of the individual case. That is its virtue as a device for stabilizing professional judgment – and also its vice if one questions the validity of such a crude and mechanized perspective on the vast range of human suffering that is madness.

Biology Bites Back

In the late nineteenth century, psychiatrists the world over were convinced that mental illness was a disease of disordered brains and bodies. Mental patients were an inferior species of humanity, the living embodiment of degenerative processes that accounted for their defects: emotional blunting; disturbances of thought and of speech; lack of initiative or its opposite, a startling lack of control over behaviour; delusions; hallucinations; raving mania; or deep depression. The late twentieth century witnessed a similar re-embrace of biology as the basis of mental illness and an increasing neglect of its other dimensions. The presidential proclamation issued by George H. W. Bush in 1991 on behalf of the National Institute of Mental Health, declaring that the 1990s were 'the decade of the brain', merely ratified a transformation that had already become deeply rooted in psychiatry, and not just in the United States.

Patients and their families learned to attribute mental illness to faulty brain biochemistry, defects of dopamine or a shortage of serotonin.[73]

36 ABOVE *The Battle Creek Sanitarium, Michigan, USA, for affluent and nervous patients. By 1933 it had been forced into receivership, a casualty of the Great Depression.*

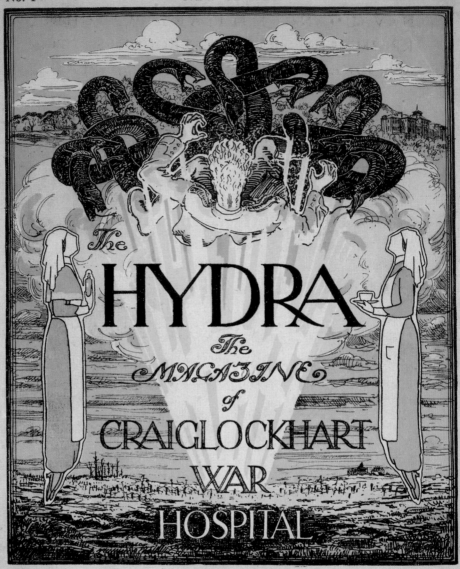

No. 1   NEW SERIES   November 1917

H. & J. Pillans & Wilson, Printers, Edinburgh

37 ABOVE The Hydra, *a magazine produced by patients at Craiglockhart war hospital, where in the First World War shell-shocked officers were treated, including Siegfried Sassoon and Wilfred Owen.*

38 OPPOSITE ABOVE Die Nacht (The Night) *(1918–19), by Max Beckmann. A dark vision of violence in a small room, with three torturers. A man is being strangled; a raped woman is tied to a post; a child is being dragged off to be tortured or murdered; all sense of order or perspective is collapsed into a world of evil and madness. Beckmann wanted, he said, to 'give mankind a picture of its fate'.*

39 PREVIOUS PAGE, BELOW
The central panel of the War
Triptych *(1929–32), by Otto
Dix: bloated German corpses
rotting in a trench, one with
his legs riddled with bullet
holes; a skeleton impaled on
a tree; a fiery sky heralding
the Apocalypse. No wonder
the Nazis dismissed Dix from
his teaching post in Dresden
because his work was 'likely to
affect the military will of the
German people'.*

40 ABOVE Bedlam *(1975),
by David Hockney: a model of
Hockney's design for the staging
of the final scene of Stravinsky's
opera* The Rake's Progress,
at Glyndebourne.

41 OPPOSITE *Freud's Study
in Hampstead. When Freud
left Austria in 1938 for exile
in London to escape Nazi
persecution, he took his couch
and personal effects with him,
and recreated his study at
Berggasse 19, Vienna, in his
house in Maresfield Gardens
in north London. The room is
preserved as part of the Freud
Museum to this day.*

42 OPPOSITE *A corridor in
the abandoned Grafton State
Hospital, Massachusetts, which
was closed in 1973. Many
such asylums that once housed
thousands now lie empty and
neglected, falling into ruin.*

43 ABOVE *Aerial view of the
island of San Clemente, Venice,
now a luxury hotel complex.
But it was not always such a
desirable destination. Between
1844 and 1992 it was the city's
asylum for madwomen.*

44 ABOVE *A spoof advertisement (2014) with a serious message, created by the Canadian artist, activist and self-described 'natural epileptic' Billiam James, who drew visual inspiration from the seventeenth-century Kama Sutra and Ragamala paintings, and verbal inspiration from Jefferson Airplane.*

It was biobabble as deeply misleading and unscientific as the psychobabble it replaced – in reality, the origins of major forms of madness remain almost as mysterious as ever – but as marketing copy it was priceless.[74] Meantime, the psychiatric profession was seduced and bought off with enormous amounts of research funding. Where once psychiatrists had existed in a twilight zone on the margins of professional respectability (their talk cures and obsessions with childhood sexuality only amplifying the scorn with which most mainstream medics viewed them), now they were the darlings of medical school deans, the millions upon millions of their grants and indirect cost recoveries helping to finance the expansion of the medical-industrial complex that has been so notable a development of the years since the Second World War.

Much of that financing has come from a pharmaceutical industry that has grown to maturity over the past three quarters of a century. Big Pharma is an international phenomenon these days. Its marketing muscle reaches across the globe. Its search for profitable new compounds ignores national boundaries, except insofar as it often retreats to the global periphery to conduct its researches, where ethical constraints are more easily evaded, and the information gleaned from multi-centred clinical trials more easily kept under company control.[75] And its profits are astounding, far exceeding those of many other segments of the economy. That the bulk of them are earned in the rich and unregulated medical free-for-all that is the United States is one of the primary reasons for the growing global hegemony of American psychiatry.[76]

For psychiatric drugs have been a central part of Big Pharma's expansion and its profits. That is not because we possess a psychiatric penicillin. Quite the contrary: for all the marketing hype surrounding psychopharmacology, its pills and potions are palliative, not curative – and often not even that. But ironically, it is precisely the relative therapeutic impotence of psychotropic drugs that has made them so valuable, and has vaulted them so regularly into the ranks of the so-called blockbuster drugs, those that amass north of a billion dollars in profits for the industry. Drugs that cure are great – for the patient. For the pharmaceutical houses, this is not always so. Antibiotics, for example, at least until their excessive use in factory farming renders them ineffective, cure bacterial infections in short order. Diseases that a century ago were major, even fatal events are now routinely cured by a single course of treatment. Not so much money there, once the initial excitement subsides, though sales volume makes for profits that are not to be sneezed at. So diseases that can be managed, but not cured, are ideal: diabetes, types 1 and 2; hypertension; the build-up of lipids in the bloodstream and the blocking of arteries by cholesterol; arthritis; asthma; acid reflux; HIV infections – these are conditions that linger for years and are the source of potentially immense windfalls. To be sure, as patents expire, profits fall, but there is always the possibility of tweaking a formula, creating a variant of a patent, perhaps a new class of drugs to prescribe. Chronic conditions are chronically profitable.

Enter psychiatry, whose disorders may be elusive and sometimes controversial, their aetiology still mysterious and poorly understood, but many are persistent, disabling and distressing. They are impossible to ignore, difficult though they may be to understand and to treat. Once new classes of drugs emerged that provided a measure of symptomatic relief (or could be claimed to do so), the potential market was enormous.

So it has proved. Anti-psychotics and anti-depressants regularly rank among the most profitable of all drugs sold on the planet. Tranquillizers are not far behind. Abilify (an anti-psychotic manufactured by Bristol-Meyers Squibb) is selling at a rate of $6 billion per year. Cymbalta (an anti-depressant and anti-anxiety pill from Eli Lilly) has projected worldwide sales of $5.2 billion. Zoloft, Effexor, Seroquel, Zyprexa and Risperdal, all drugs used to treat depression or schizophrenia, had sales between $2.3 billion and $3.1 billion in 2005, and generated huge profits over long periods. Both anti-psychotics and anti-depressants regularly rank in the top five classes of drug by sales volume in the United States.[77] In 2010, global sales of anti-psychotic drugs totalled $22 billion; anti-depressants, $20 billion; anti-anxiety drugs, $11 billion; stimulants, $5.5 billion; drugs used to treat dementia, $5.5 billion. And these numbers take no account of the fact that many prescriptions for anti-convulsant drugs are written for patients with a diagnosis of bipolar disorder.[78]

But in the immortal words often (wrongly) attributed to the economist Milton Friedman, 'there is no such thing as a free lunch', and one must remember that medical treatments of all sorts, even the most efficacious, carry a risk of side effects (PL. 44). That caveat needs to be borne in mind when assessing the psychopharmacological revolution and its impact on psychiatry. It will not do to be a Luddite, to scorn or deny such progress as has been made. And yet the problems that have surfaced in the psychiatric arena are multiple and deeply troubling. The lunch on offer has proved very expensive indeed, and for a good many consumers not worth what it costs.

Drug treatments in psychiatry are, unfortunately, not always particu-larly efficacious, and such efficacy as they do possess has regularly been overstated by psychiatrists and in the published scientific literature. The price patients may pay for such benefits as the drugs do provide has, on the other hand, often been underestimated or actively concealed. Part of the problem, particularly in the early years of psychopharmacology, was an abundance of poorly designed studies that systematically biased findings in a positive direction. In later years, the growing power of the pharmaceutical industry, and the lengths to which it has gone in its pursuit of profit, has led informed observers to worry that what appears to be 'evidence-based psychiatry' might more properly be called 'evidence-biased psychiatry'.

Though it took as long as twenty years for the psychiatric profession to acknowledge the fact,[79] the first generation of anti-psychotics, the pheno-thiazines, were often associated with profound and disabling side effects. Some patients developed symptoms that resembled Parkinson's disease. Others became constantly restless, unable to sit still. Then there were those who, conversely, remained immobile for extended periods. Most serious of all was a condition that came to be called 'tardive dyskinesia', or late-onset dyskinesia, a disorder, often masked while taking the drug, that produced sucking and smacking movements of the lips, rocking and uncontrolled movements of the extremities – and ironically, often interpreted by the laity as signs of mental disturbance. Tardive dyskinesia, in particular, afflicted a large fraction of those on long-term treatment (estimates ranged widely, from 15 to 60 per cent of such patients), and was in most cases a hard to reverse, iatrogenic (i.e., doctor-caused) condition.

In many patients, the first generation of phenothiazines did reduce florid symptomatology, making their lives more bearable and more tolerable to those around them. Others, though, and they have been a very sizeable fraction of the whole, had no therapeutic response to the drugs. For many but not all patients in the first group, the trade-off between the side effects and symptomatic relief was worthwhile. For non-responders, it clearly was not, and the side effects numerous patients in both groups experienced were serious, debilitating, stigmatizing and often permanent.

The gradual acknowledgment of these serious side effects prompted some to denounce what they called 'toxic psychiatry',[80] and Scientology (which markets its own bizarre forms of therapy) has established a museum in Hollywood that calls itself 'Psychiatry: An Industry of Death'. Few dispassionate observers accept such hyperbole. Nor should they. To argue that the new drug treatments are never advantageous, indeed always harmful, is absurd. Such contentions require us to dismiss much persuasive evidence to the contrary. That is not to say, however, that one should uncritically swallow the equally one-sided and overblown claims of the pharmaceutical industry and its allies within the psychiatric profession.

The pattern established by this first generation of psychotropic drugs has held good for all those that came after: the various anti-depressants, whose introduction sparked a massive expansion in the numbers being diagnosed with depression, making it the common cold of psychiatry; and the so-called 'atypical anti-psychotics' that entered the marketplace two decades ago, a heterogeneous array of pills that had different chemical properties, and purported to avoid many of the serious side effects that plagued the pheno-thiazines. Prozac made people 'better than well', and then it turned out that it did not. It, and related anti-depressants called SSRIs (selective serotonin re-uptake inhibitors), are anything but a panacea. Whatever positive effects these drugs have are often outweighed by the problems they create,[81] not least because a number of studies suggest that, save in severe depressions, they are barely, if at all, superior to placebo.[82] As the Harvard psychiatrist Steven E. Hyman summarizes, the situation remains bleak: even though 'many anti-depressant drugs have been developed since the 1950s...none of them has improved on the efficacy of [the first generation of such drugs], leaving many patients with modest benefits or none at all'.[83]

When SSRIs came to be used in the treatment of children, the increased risk of suicidal thoughts and suicide (a side effect long concealed and denied by the drug industry) was initially publicized not by psychiatrists but by investigative journalists working for the BBC in the UK.[84] The National Institute for Health and Care Excellence (NICE), a British government body charged with appraising the clinical value of new treatments, had been on the brink of endorsing the use of SSRIs in children. It changed its mind, and in 2004 recommended against their use. As further negative clinical trial data leaked into the public domain, they eventually prompted the American Food and Drug Administration to require a so-called 'black box warning' of the heightened danger, the most serious cautionary flag available short of remov-ing the drugs from the market, and the FDA refused to license drugs such as Paxil and Zoloft for use in young people. Later still it emerged that, while published studies suggested that SSRIs were effective in treating depression in children and adolescents, the research in question 'had been manipulated so that essentially negative studies were transformed into positive studies, hiding the fact the drugs didn't work and masking the problems of treatment'.[85] More seriously still, evidence surfaced of just how many studies of SSRIs had been suppressed – all of them negative, and none of them seeing the light of day until outside pressure was brought to bear.[86]

Atypical anti-psychotics are also often referred to as second-generation anti-psychotics. That is misleading, since arguably the most powerful of them, clozapine, was not a new drug at all. It was synthesized by the German company Wander in 1958, the subject of a series of clinical trials in the 1960s and first marketed in 1971, but withdrawn by its manufacturer four years later, because its use was occasionally associated with a dangerous, sometimes fatal decrease in white blood cells, agranulocytosis.[87] More than a decade later, in 1989, it gradually re-entered commerce as a therapy for schizophrenics who were unresponsive to other drugs, a treatment of last resort that was to be accompanied by stringent safety precautions. Its price was high. Sandoz charged $9,000 for a year's supply, while a year's supply of chlorpromazine (Thorazine) cost around $100. Yet the use of clozapine rapidly proliferated, in part because of claims that side effects like tardive dyskinesia were much less frequent than with other anti-psychotic drugs.

Soon, it spurred the development of other 'atypical' pills, such as Risperdal, Zyprexa and Seroquel, that could be patented. Though these were chemically a heterogeneous lot, it was good marketing copy to call them all second-generation anti-psychotics, and the label stuck. As a group, sold as having additional benefits and many fewer side effects, they were hugely profitable. Psychiatrists everywhere embraced them, despite their greatly increased costs. Before long, they were also being touted as a remedy for bipolar disorder as well. A decade later, however, an editorial in the *Lancet* denounced them as a 'spurious invention': 'the second-generation drugs have no special atypical characteristics that separate them from the typical, or first-generation anti-psychotics. As a group they are no more efficacious, do not improve specific symptoms, have no clearly different side-effect profiles than first-generation anti-psychotics, and are less cost effective.'[88] Only clozapine, for example, is associated with no reported cases of tardive dyskinesia, but creating the category of 'atypical' anti-psychotics allowed the pharmaceutical industry to obscure the fact that this was not true of the other drugs in this artificially created class.

Epilogue

As civilized human beings, we like to console ourselves with visions of progress, illusory as that concept often proves to be. Perhaps we have not seen progress in the realms of literature and art (though some would dispute that claim), but surely science moves forward, and medicine too, insofar as it is a science rather than an art. In the developed world, at least, we now enjoy longer, and certainly more materially abundant if not culturally richer and happier lives. Except if we are mad, that is. Modern psychiatry and its potions notwithstanding, one of the more sobering realities about serious mental illness in the twenty-first century is that its sufferers not only die at a much younger age on average than the rest of us (as much as twenty-five years sooner), but also that the incidence of serious illness and mortality in this population has accelerated in recent decades.[89] On this most basic of levels we seem to be regressing.

Psychiatry seems to be in trouble too. The neo-Kraepelinian approach it adopted when DSM III was published in 1980 at first served it well. The reliability and replicability of psychiatric diagnoses increased, and embarrassing disputes about what was wrong with a particular patient receded into the past. Freudians lost the internecine professional war decisively, and psychiatrists embraced once more a biological account of mental disorders that superficially made sense to their medical brethren, however schematic it remained. And the new approach proved extraordinarily attractive to the drug companies, who underwrote the psychiatric research enterprise, and as the years went by, increasingly influenced the very terms in which mental illness was discussed, even the categories of illness that purportedly exist in the world.

Each successive edition of the manual, the revised third edition (III R) of 1987, the fourth edition (IV of 1994) and its 'text revision' (IV TR of 2000), adhered to the fundamental approach psychiatry had adopted in 1980, though new 'illnesses' were added on each occasion, the definitions of psychopathology were tweaked and the page count mounted. But as 'illnesses' proliferated in each revision, and the criteria for assigning a particular diagnosis were loosened, the very problem that had led to the invention of the new versions of the DSM recurred, and major new threats to psychiatric legitimacy surfaced.

The loosening of diagnostic criteria led to an extraordinary expansion of the numbers of people defined as mentally ill. This has been particularly evident among, but by no means confined to, the ranks of the young. 'Juvenile bipolar disorder', for example, increased forty-fold in just a decade, between 1994 and 2004. An autism epidemic broke out, as a formerly rare condition, seen in less than one in five hundred children at the outset of the same decade, was found in one in every ninety children only ten years later. The story for hyperactivity, subsequently relabelled ADHD is similar, with 10 per cent of male American children now taking pills daily for their 'disease'. Among adults, one in every seventy-six Americans qualified for welfare payments based upon mental disability by 2007.

If psychiatrists' inability to agree among themselves on a diagnosis threatened to make them a laughing-stock in the 1970s, the relabelling of a host of ordinary life events as psychiatric pathology promised more of the same. Thus, when American psychiatry embarked on still another revision of the manual in the early twenty-first century, the resulting DSM 5 was supposed to be different from its predecessors. (The change from the previous system of Roman numerals was designed to allow for continuous updating of the manual, as with software releases: DSM 5.1, 5.2 and so on.) Those put in charge of the enterprise announced that the logic that had underpinned the two previous editions was deeply flawed, and they would fix things. Drawing on the findings of neuroscience and genetics, they would move away from the symptom-based system that they now acknowledged was inadequate, and build a manual that linked mental disorders to brain function. They would also take account of the fact that mental disorder is a dimensional, not a categorical kind of thing: a matter of being more or less sane, not a black and white world with sanity in this corner and mental illness in that. It was a grand ambition. The only problem was that it was an ambition impossible to fulfil. Having thrashed about in pursuit of this chimera, those running the project were ultimately forced to concede defeat, and by 2009 they were back to tinkering with the descriptive approach.

As the work proceeded, it appeared that social anxiety disorder, oppositional defiant disorder, school phobia, narcissistic and borderline personality disorders would be joined by such things as pathological gambling, binge eating disorder, hypersexuality disorder, temper dysregulation disorder, mixed anxiety depressive disorder, minor neurocognitive disorder and attenuated psychotic symptoms syndrome. Yet we are almost as far removed as ever from understanding the aetiological roots of major psychiatric disorders, let alone these more controversial diagnoses (which many people would argue do not belong in the medical arena in the first place). Such diagnoses do, however, provide lucrative new markets for psychopharmacology's products, which has caused some critics to question whether commercial concerns are illegitimately driving the expansion of the psychiatric universe – and these critics have had a field day by pointing to the fact that the great majority of the members of the DSM task force are recipients of drug company largesse.

Relying solely on symptoms and behaviour to construct its illnesses, and on organizational fiat to impose its negotiated categories on both the profession and the public, psychiatry almost immediately found itself facing a revolt from within its own ranks. Robert Spitzer, the principal architect of DSM III, and Allen Frances (b. 1942), the editor-in-chief of DSM IV, began attacking the scientific credibility of the newest edition years before it appeared in print.[90] They alleged that it pathologized everyday features of normal human existence, and would threaten to create new epidemics of spurious psychiatric illness. Unlike the Scientologists, critics such as these were not easily dismissed,[91] and they twice succeeded in delaying DSM 5's release.

In May 2013, DSM 5 finally materialized. It did not make an auspicious debut. Just before its publication, two enormously influential psychiatrists rendered their own verdicts. Steven E. Hyman, the former director of NIMH condemned the whole enterprise. It was, he pronounced, 'totally wrong in a way [its authors] couldn't have imagined. So in fact what they produced was an absolute scientific nightmare. Many people who get one diagnosis get five diagnoses, but they don't have five diseases – they have one underlying condition.' Thomas R. Insel (b. 1951), the current director of the National Institute of Mental Health issued a similar verdict. The manual, he proclaimed, suffered from a scientific 'lack of validity.... As long as the research community takes the D.S.M to be a bible, we'll never make progress. People think everything has to match D.S.M. criteria, but you know what? Biology never read that book.' NIMH, he said, would be 'reorienting its research away from D.S.M. categories [because] patients with mental illness deserve better'.[92]

A few months earlier, in a private conversation that he must have realized would become public, Insel had voiced an even more heretical thought. His psychiatric colleagues, he said dismissively, 'actually believe [that the diseases they diagnose using the DSM] are real. But there's no reality. These are just constructs. There is no reality to schizophrenia or depression...we might have to stop using terms like depression and schizophrenia, because they are getting in our way, confusing things.'[93] Insel is keen to replace descriptive psychiatry with a diagnostic system built upon biological foundations. But in the present state of our knowledge, that formula is an idle fantasy. Much as psychiatry (and many of those who suffer from mental disorders) might wish it otherwise, madness remains an enigma, a mystery we seemingly cannot solve. Its depredations remain something we can at best palliate. Over the past half century, the expansion of neuroscience has been remarkable, and its discoveries legion. Unfortunately, none of them have proved of much clinical use to date in the treatment of mental illness. Nor have neuroscientists as yet uncovered the aetiological roots of madness. In recent decades, new imaging technologies have flourished. Functional Magnetic Resonance Imaging (fMRI) has been employed, its digital read-outs transformed by modern electronic alchemy into pictures of the brain that light up in technicolour. Surely these marvels of modern science will at last reveal the germ of madness?

Not yet, and not likely for some time to come. Despite important advances in our understanding, we are very far indeed from being able to connect even very simple human actions to the underlying structure and functioning of people's brains. We are decades away, after all, from successfully mapping the brain of the fruit fly, let alone successfully tackling the infinitely more complex task of unravelling the billions upon billions of connections that make up our own brains.

Some enthusiasts for neuroscience make much of the fact that particular regions of the brain show heightened levels of activity on fMRIs when people, for example, are making choices, or telling lies. Even the philosophical idealist Bishop Berkeley would not be surprised by that. When I move, speak, think, experience an emotion, presumably this is correlated with physical changes in my brain, but such correlations prove nothing about the causal processes, any more than the existence of a particular sequence of events demonstrates that some early event in the sequence ineluctably caused a later event. *Post hoc ergo propter hoc* ('after this, therefore because of this') is an elementary logical fallacy. What fMRIs are crudely measuring is the flow of blood in the brain, and demonstrating heightened activity of this sort is a far cry from giving us privileged insights into the contents of people's thoughts, not to mention the instability and ambiguity of the results when experiments are replicated.

Like the poor folks waiting for Godot (who, as it happens, were quite possibly waiting for a madman), we are still waiting for those mysterious and long-rumoured neuropathological causes of mental illness to surface. It has been a long wait, and on more than one level a misguided one, I think, if the expectation is that the ultimate explanation of madness lies here and only here.

Why is that? It makes no sense to regard the brain (as biological reduc-tionists do) as an asocial or a pre-social organ, because in important respects its very structure and functioning are a product of the social environment. For the most remarkable feature of the human brain is how deeply and pro-foundly sensitive it is to psychosocial and sensory inputs. What this means, as the neuroscientist Bruce Wexler (b. 1947) puts it, is that 'our biology is social in such a fundamental and thorough manner that to speak of a rela-tion between the two suggests an unwarranted distinction'.[94]

To an extent unprecedented in any other part of the animal kingdom, humans' brains continue to develop post-natally, and the environmental elements that most powerfully affect the structure and functioning of these brains are themselves a human creation. Human beings exhibit a remarkable neuroplasticity, at least through adolescence, and we must thus bear in mind the critical importance of non-biological factors in transforming the neural structures we are born with, thereby creating the mature brain. The very shape of the brain, the neural connections that develop and that constitute the physical underpinnings of our emotions and cognition, are profoundly influenced by social stimulation, and by the cultural and especially the familial environment within which these developments take place. It is in these settings that the brain's structure and organization are fine-tuned. Quite simply, to quote Bruce Wexler again, 'human nature...allows and requires environmental input for normal development'[95] – and, one can immediately add, abnormal development. And that development continues for a very long time, with increases in connectivity and changes in brain organization, especially in the parietal and frontal lobes, taking place well into the third decade of life. Freud's speculations about how the early psychosocial envi-ronment was connected to psychopathology may no longer seem remotely plausible to most of us, but the fundamental notion that some of the roots of madness need to be sought outside our bodies is surely not misplaced.

The best modern neuroscience, in my view, stresses that rather than being localized in particular regions of the brain or being the properties of individual neurons, thinking, feeling and remembering are the product of complex networks and interconnections that form as we mature. These in turn depend upon the selective survival and growth of cells and the pruning of connections among cells – processes that are heavily dependent upon the interactional environment in which the human infant is raised, and that are particularly important for the development of the cerebral cortex, the

Detail from Dulle Griet (Mad Meg), *by Pieter Breugel the Elder (c. 1562). Mad Meg is storming the mouth of Hell itself, in a mad, monstrous world consumed by violence.*

proportionate size of which in us exceeds that of any other species. That environment is to an unprecedented extent a human-made environment, much of it taking effect through the medium of language. Human development may not always proceed smoothly and without flaws, and somewhere in that murky mix of biology and the social lie the roots of madness.

The metaphysical wager that much of Western medicine embraced centuries ago, that madness had its roots in the body, has in most respects yet to pay off. Perhaps, I have suggested, it never will entirely. It is hard to imagine, at least for the most severe forms of mental aberration, that biology will not prove to play an important role in their genesis. But will madness, that most solitary of afflictions and most social of maladies, be reducible at last to biology and nothing but biology? There one must have serious doubts. The social and the cultural dimensions of mental disorders, so indispensable a part of the story of madness in civilization over the centuries, are unlikely to melt away, or prove to be nothing more than epiphenomenal features of so universal a feature of human existence. Madness indeed has its meanings, elusive and evanescent as our attempts to capture them have been. It remains a fundamental puzzle, a reproach to reason, inescapably part and parcel of civilization itself.

NOTES

Chapter One: Confronting Madness

1. Significantly, I think, one of the definitions of 'common sense' in the *Oxford English Dictionary* reads as follows: 'The endowment of natural intelligence possessed by rational beings; ordinary, normal or average understanding; the plain wisdom that is everyone's inheritance. (This is "common sense" at its minimum, without which one is foolish or insane.)'

2. C.-K. Chang, et al., 2011; C. W. Colton and R. W. Manderscheid, 2006; J. Parks, D. Svendsen, P. Singer and M. E. Foti (eds), 2006. One study reports that rates of suicide among those diagnosed as schizophrenic have increased ten-fold. See D. Healy, et al., 2006.

Chapter Two: Madness in the Ancient World

1. Deuteronomy 25: 18. These and subsequent citations are to the King James translation of the Bible.

2. 1 Samuel 15: 2–3.

3. 1 Samuel 15: 8–9.

4. 1 Samuel 15: 23.

5. 1 Samuel 15–31.

6. 1 Samuel 18: 10–11; 19: 9–10.

7. 1 Samuel 20: 30–34.

8. Josephus, *The Antiquities of the Jews*, with an English translation by H. St J. Thackeray, Ralph Marcus and Allen Wikgren, 9 vols, Cambridge, Mass.: Harvard University Press, Vol. 5, 1968, p. 249. The reference in this passage to Saul's 'physicians' is almost certainly an anachronism. Biblical passages refer only to Saul's servants. But, as we shall see, Josephus lived in age when medical accounts of madness existed alongside older religious interpretations, and in some instances Greek-trained doctors attempted to intervene and to treat madness.

9. 1 Samuel 16: 23.

10. 1 Samuel 18: 10–11.

11. George Rosen, 1968, pp. 36, 42.

12. 1 Samuel 19: 24.

13. See, for example, Amos 7: 1–9; Jeremiah 1: 24; Isaiah 22: 14; 40, 3, 6; Ezekiel 6: 11; 8: 1–4; 21: 14–17; Jeremiah 20: 9.

14. Jeremiah 20: 1–4.

15. Jeremiah 38, 39.

16. Jeremiah 26: 20–23.

17. See, for example, Karl Jaspers' essay 'proving' that Ezekiel was a schizophrenic: 'Der Prophet Ezechiel: Eine pathographische Studie', pp. 95–106 in his *Rechenschaft und Ausblick, Reden und Aufsätze*, Munich: Piper Verlag, 1951. Earlier, Jean-Martin Charcot (see Chapter Nine) and his followers had dismissed many Christian saints as hysterics.

18. Daniel 4: 30–33.

19. Mark 16: 9.

20. Mark 5: 1–13. Compare Luke 8: 26–33; Matthew 8: 28–34.

21. Luke 8: 27, 34.

22. For a nuanced discussion of some of the issues here, see Robert Parker, 1983, Chapter 8.

23. Clark Lawlor, 2012, p. 37.

24. *Odyssey* 20, 345–49. I borrow this translation from Debra Hershkowitz, whose *The Madness of Epic: Reading Insanity from Homer to Statius*, 1998, has greatly influenced my understanding of Homer and other Classical authors on the subject of madness.

25. *Iliad* xvii, 210–12.

26. *Iliad* xxii–xxiii.

27. *Iliad* xiv, 118.

28. Euripides, *Heracles*, in *Euripides III*, translated by William Arrowsmith, Chicago: University of Chicago Press, 2013, p. 47, lines 835–37.

29. For discussions, see R. Padel, 1995; and E. R. Dodds, 1951.

30. Ruth Padel, 1992, Chapter 1, especially pp. 4–6. See also the illuminating discussion in John R. Green, 1994.

31. Paul Cartledge, 1997, p. 11.

32. Ruth Padel, 1992, p. 6.

33. On Herodotus' own complex attitudes towards questions of divine and natural causation, see G. E. R. Lloyd, 1979, pp. 30ff.

34. Herodotus, quoted and translated in G. E. R. Lloyd, 2003, pp. 131, 133. See also the discussion in G. Rosen, 1968, pp. 71–72.

35. Quoted in G. E. R. Lloyd, 2003, p. 133.

36. Herodotus, quoted and translated in G. E. R. Lloyd, 2003, pp. 133, 135; R. Parker, 1983, p. 242.

37. Quoted in G. E. R. Lloyd, 2003, p. 118.

38. L. Targa (ed.), 1831, quoted in Ilza Veith, 1970, p. 21.

39. For a broader discussion, see Andrew Scull, 2011, from which I have drawn the two preceding paragraphs.

40. I have drawn here on the excellent discussion in G. E. R. Lloyd, 2003, especially Chapter 3, 'Secularization and Sacralization'. On Asclepius and his cult, see Emma J. Edelstein and Ludwig Edelstein, 1945.

41. See the classic discussion in Oswei Temkin, 1994, Part I: Antiquity.

42. Quoted in R. Parker, 1983, p. 244.

43. Hippocrates: *The Genuine Works of Hippocrates*, Vol. 2, ed. Francis Adams, 1886, pp. 334–35.

44. *On the Sacred Disease*, translated and quoted in G. E. R. Lloyd, 2003, pp. 61, 63. Of course, it should go without saying that precisely the same set of criticisms, mutatis mutandis, could have been levelled at the humoral account provided by the Hippocratics, who were, we would now judge, just as capable – or rather incapable – of curing the disorder they purported to treat.

45. Hippocrates: *The Genuine Works of Hippocrates*, Vol. 2, ed. Francis Adams, 1886, p. 344

46. Hippocrates: *The Medical Works of Hippocrates*, trans. John Chadwick and W. N. Mann, 1950, pp. 190–91.

47. Hippocrates: *The Medical Works of Hippocrates*, trans. John Chadwick and W. N. Mann, 1950, p. 191.

48. Anti-phlogistic physicians saw disease as fundamentally a problem of inflammation and fever. Hence the use of remedies designed to counteract these states, such as bleeding, purging and making use of emetics, all designed to counteract and to deplete the over-active, over-heated body.

49. Vivian Nutton, 1992, p. 39.

50. Vivian Nutton, 1992, pp. 41–42.

51. Peter Brown, 1971, p. 60.

52. Geoffrey Lloyd and Nathan Sivin, 2002, esp. pp. 12–15, 243. I have drawn extensively in what follows on this pioneering attempt to compare these two worlds, and also on the work of Shigehisa Kuriyama cited below. I am also most grateful to two friends and historians of Chinese medicine, Miriam Gross and Emily Baum, for their generous assistance.

53. D. E. Eichholz, 1950.

54. Geoffrey Lloyd and Nathan Sivin, 2002, p. 242.

55. Geoffrey Lloyd and Nathan Sivin, 2002, p. 250.

56. For an ambitious attempt to survey this fragmentary information for late imperial China, see Fabien Simonis, 2010, Chapter 13.

57. Very useful for its discussion of these varying, competing and overlapping traditions is Paul D. Unschuld, 1985. Also useful on religion and medicine in medieval China (c. 300–900), especially the mutual influences and interpenetration of Buddhist and Taoist practices, is Michel Strickmann, 2002.

58. Shigehisa Kuriyama, 1999, p. 222.

59. Shigehisa Kuriyama, 1999, subtly explores the existence of great variation within an appearance of continuity in his discussion of Chinese ideas about the pulse, and the diagnostic practices that were founded upon claims about what inferences could be drawn from *qiemo*, the feeling of the pulse. Chinese physicians placed enormous emphasis on *mo*. Different sites on the wrist were, so it was claimed, indicative of what was going on in different regions of the body, and subtle variations in what could be felt at these sites were a key element in grasping underlying pathology. On the verbal level, the case for continuity in these practices is clear. Though there were a few later additions, they added but little to the twenty-four *mo* identified as early as two millennia ago, and 'palpation in China was practiced confidently and flourished stably for over two thousand years, and still flourishes today' (p. 71). But the terms used to describe purportedly minute but significant variations in what can be felt all blended into one another, and were closely related. Descriptions were metaphorical and allusive. Inevitably, despite claims of continuity and stability of meanings, the reality is that variability in practice was unavoidable both within and across historical periods.

60. Fabien Simonis, 2010, p. iii.

61. These terms, while all referring to forms of madness, were not used interchangeably. *Feng* was a general term, whereas *kuang* madness involved hyperactivity and rage and arose from an excess of *yang* energy; and *dian* madness approximated to what in the West tended to be called melancholia, and was the result of an excess of *yin* energy. Alternatively, the latter could mean to jolt or fall down, and in this sense could refer to epilepsy.

62. Fabien Simonis, 2010, p. 11.

63. Fabien Simonis, 2010, p. 14.

64. Fabien Simonis, 2010, Chapters 11, 12. For a different, less persuasive perspective on these developments, see Vivien Ng, 1990.

65. F. Simonis, 2010, pp. 1–2.

66. Peter Brown, 1971, pp, 176–77.

67. Hakim A. Hameed and A. Bari, 1984.

68. Dominik Wujastyk, 1993.

69. R. B. Saper, et al., 2008; Edzard Ernst, 2002.

Chapter Three: The Darkness and the Dawn

1. Steven Runciman, 1966, pp. 506–08; in his words, it was destruction 'unparalleled in history'.

2. On these developments, see htpp://www.iranicaonline.org/articles/Greece-x.

3. Peter Brown, 1971, p. 193; W. Montgomery Watt, 1972, pp. 7–8.

4. W. Montgomery Watt, 1972, Chapter 1.

5. The long and complex history of the revolt of the Spanish Netherlands is not something I can rehearse here. It had begun in the last four decades of the sixteenth century, and was fuelled by a complex mixture of religious, financial and political factors. By the time Philip III succeeded his father, Philip II, in 1598, in many ways the die had been cast. Though the new king retained a measure of control in the Catholic south, Spanish authority had disintegrated in the heavily Calvinist northern provinces. It was in all probability partly to distract attention from the twelve-year truce Spain had been reluctantly forced to sign on 9 April 1609 that Philip chose that same moment to expel Moors and Jews from Spain. (The edict expelling the Moriscos is also dated 9 April 1609.) The coincidence of timing makes it difficult to reach any other conclusion. See Antonio Feros, 2006, p. 198. War in the Low Countries restarted when the truce ended in 1621, but by then the United Provinces in the north were powerful and internationally recognized, and the conflict was subsumed in the broader conflagration that was the Thirty Years War. In the ensuing decades, Spain descended into financial chaos, and lost its status as a major European power. The Dutch meanwhile became one of the richest and most powerful European states, with a strong navy and rapidly growing wealth from their extensive overseas trading and empire.

6. I draw here directly upon the work of W. Montgomery Watt, who has provided a synthetic statement of the issues at hand. See *The Influence of Islam on Medieval Europe*, 1972, Chapter 2 and passim.

7. See on this point the discussion in htpp://www.iranicaonline.org/articles/Greece-x, on which I have drawn heavily here.

8. Manfred Ullmann, 1978, p. 4.

9. Michael W. Dols, 1992, p. 9.

10. Peter Brown, 1971, pp. 194–98.

11. Sir William Osler, himself regarded as the greatest clinician of the first half of the twentieth century, described the *Canon* as 'the most famous medical text-book ever written', one that remained 'a medical bible for a longer period than any other work': 1921, p. 98.

12. On the translation movement, see Dimitr Gutas, 1998.

13. Manfred Ullmann, 1978, p. 7.

14. Lawrence Conrad, 1993, p. 693.

15. Lawrence Conrad, 1993, p. 694. Michael Dols stresses that Christian Syriac-speaking physicians had regularly translated Greek texts before the Arab conquests,

embedding Galen's ideas firmly in Syria, Iraq and Persia: 1992, p. 38. More generally, Franz Rosenthal, 1994.

16. Here I follow very closely Lawrence Conrad's illuminating discussion of these issues. See also Manfred Ullmann, 1978, pp. 8–15.

17. Lawrence Conrad, 1993, p. 619.

18. Manfred Ullmann, 1978, p. 49.

19. See on this point the discussion in Plinio Prioreschi, 2001, pp. 425–26.

20. Ishaq ibn Imran, *Maqala fi l-Maalihuliya*, as quoted and discussed in Michael W. Dols, 1987a.

21. Manfred Ullmann, 1978, pp. 72–77.

22. Timothy S. Miller, 1985.

23. On their early history, see Michael W. Dols, 1987b.

24. Lawrence Conrad, 1993, p. 716.

25. For example, Al-Hasan ibn Muhammed al-Wazzan (also known as Leo Africanus), was an administrator at the hospital at Fez in Morocco. Captured and taken to Rome in 1517, he reported that the mad at the hospital were bound with heavy chains and confined in rooms whose walls were reinforced with heavy wooden and iron beams. See Leo Africanus, 1896, Volume 2, pp. 425ff.

26. Michael W. Dols, 1992, p. 129.

27. Peter Brown, 1971, pp. 82–108.

28. Henry A. Kelly, 1985, Chapter 4; Peter Brown, 1972, p. 136.

29. Peter Brown, 1972, p. 122.

30. Darrel W. Amundsen and Gary B. Ferngren, 'Medicine and Religion: Early Christianity through the Middle Ages', in Martin E. Marty and Kenneth L. Vaux (eds), *Health/Medicine and the Faith Traditions: An Inquiry into Religion and Medicine*, Philadelphia: Fortress Press, 1982, p. 103, discussed in Michael W. Dols, 1992, p. 191.

31. Michael W. Dols, 1992, p. 191.

32. Peter Brown, 1972, p. 131.

33. Michael W. Dols, 1992, p. 206.

34. See, for example, Cyril Elgood, 1962.

35. Michael W. Dols, 1992, p. 10.

36. Toufic Fahd, 1971.

37. Michael W. Dols, 1992, p. 214.

38. Nizami, 1966, *The Story of Layla and Majnun*, trans. by R. Gelpke.

39. Nizami, 1966, p. 38.

40. Jacques Le Goff, 1967, p. 290.

41. Paul Slack, 1985, p. 176.

42. Peter Brown, 1992.

43. Peter Brown, 1972, p. 67.

44. Richard Fletcher, 1997.

45. 'The Life of St. Martin, by Sulpicius Severus', in Frederick R. Hoare, 1954, p. 29.

46. Peter Brown, 1972, p. 131.

47. Matthew 10: 1, 8.

48. Ronald C. Finucane, 1977, p. 17.

49. Ronald C. Finucane, 1977, p. 19.

50. Edmund G. Gardner (ed.), 2010.

51. Peter Brown, 1981, p. 3.

52. Oddly, that relic now rests in the Chapel of Our Lady of the Assumption, on Enders Island off the coast of Connecticut in the United States.

53. The Abbott of Abingdon drew up an extended list of all the relics the monastery had acquired by 1116. For the general phenomenon of churches collecting relics, see Richard Southern, 1953.

54. Ronald C. Finucane, 1977, pp. 28–31.

55. Legend has it that when the bag containing her skull was searched by Roman guards it contained only rose petals, but by the time it was carried into Siena, the petals had changed back into the saint's head.

56. Andrew Marvell, 'To His Coy Mistress', *c.* 1650.

57. Ronald C. Finucane, 1977, p. 76.

58. Quoted in Ronald C. Finucane, 1977, pp. 91–92.

59. In the twentieth century, Becket's assassination inspired T. S. Eliot's *Murder in the Cathedral* (1935).

60. Alban Butler, 1799, 'Saint Genebrard, or Genebern, Martyr in Ireland', p. 217.

61. See, for example, J. P. Kirsch, 1981, 'St Dymphna', in *The Catholic Encyclopedia*, Vol. 5, New York: Appleton, 1909; William Ll. Parry-Jones, 1981.

62. Peter Brown, 1981, p. 107.

63. A surviving manuscript of the Townley cycle of what were once perhaps 32 plays performed in Wakefield, Yorkshire, is now housed in the Huntington Library, California. References to the Pope and to Catholic sacraments are slashed through, and twelve pages towards the end were ripped out and are now lost, presumably because their Catholic references were too numerous to retain them.

64. See the illuminating discussion in Penelope Doob, 1974, Chapter 3.

65. Quoted in Penelope Doob, 1974, p. 120.

66. Dante, *Inferno*, Canto 30: 20–21. The translation I have used is by Allen Mandelbaum: *The Divine Comedy of Dante Alighieri: Inferno*, New York: Random House, 1980.

67. Dante, *Inferno*, Canto 30: 22–27.

68. Penelope Doob, 1974, documents how thoroughly this and the following connections between madness and sin form a leitmotiv of much of Middle English literature. I am indebted to her analysis in what follows.

69. Dante, *Inferno*, Canto 28.

70. John Mirk, *Festial: A Collection of Homilies* (*c.* 1382), edited by Theodore Erbe, London: Early English Text Society, 1905, p. 56. Mirk's sermons were probably the most prominent English collection of sermons written in the vernacular before the Reformation, and were intended as a guide for parish priests, though they also circulated more broadly among the educated laity.

71. Rabanus Maurus Magnentius, *De universo libri*, quoted in Penelope Doob, 1974, p. 2.

72. Katherine Park, 1992, p. 66.

73. W. Montgomery Watt, 1972, p. 67.

74. Donald Lupton, *London and the Countrey Carbonadoed and Quartred into Severall Characters*, London: Nicholas Oakes, 1632, p. 75. I owe this reference to Colin Gale.

75. Ronald C. Finucane, 1977, p. 64, referring to broader clerical disdain for doctors.

Chapter Four: Melancholie and Madnesse

1. In Portugal, Hungary, Poland, Scandinavia, witch hunting and trials for witchcraft extended well into the eighteenth century.

2. George Gifford, 1587.

3. Martin Luther, quoted in H. C. Erik Midelfort, 1999, p. 97.

4. Thomas Hobbes, *Leviathan*, 1968, p. 92 (original edition, 1651).

5. Joseph Glanvill, 1681, quoted in Roy Porter, 1999, pp. 198–99.

6. Stuart Clark, 1997, p. 152.

7. Lambert Daneau, 1575, quoted in Stuart Clark, 1997, pp. 163–64.

8. Stuart Clark, 1997, pp. 188–89.

9. 'It cannot be said that the principle that devils might inhabit humans was abandoned by a substantial portion of the literate classes of Europe, including the medical profession, until beyond the end of the seventeenth century.' Stuart Clark, 1997, pp. 390–91.

10. H. C. Erik Midelfort, 1999, p. 158: 'For physicians, this was truly "the age of melancholy".'

11. Andrew Boorde, 1547, quoted in Stanley W. Jackson, 1986, pp. 82–83.

12. Andreas Laurentius, 1598, pp. 88–89, 125. The original French edition of 1594 went through more than twenty editions, and appeared in English, German and Italian, as well as Latin.

13. Andreas Laurentius, 1598, p. 87.

14. Timothie Bright, 1586, pp. xii–xiii, 90, 102. Bright's and Laurentius' views here closely resemble the discussions of melancholia in Avicenna's *Canon of Medicine*, which in their turn are derived from Galen and Rufus of Ephesus.

15. Andreas Laurentius, 1598, pp. 107–08.

16. J. Dryden, *Absolom and Achitophel*, 1681, Part I, lines 163–64.

17. Robert Burton, *The Anatomy of Melancholy*, 1948, pp. 148–49 (original edition Oxford, 1621).

18. Stanley W. Jackson, 1986, p. 97.

19. Robert Burton, *The Anatomy of Melancholy*, 1948, p. 970.

20. Robert Burton, *The Anatomy of Melancholy*, 1948, p. 384.

21. Robert Burton, *The Anatomy of Melancholy*, quoted in Richard Hunter and Ida Macalpine, 1963, p. 96.

22. Timothie Bright, 1586, pp. i, iv, 187. Bright is mostly remembered now as the inventor of shorthand.

23. Andrew Boorde, 1547.

24. Felix Platter, Abdiah Cole and Nicholas Culpeper, 1662, quoted in Stanley W. Jackson, 1986, pp. 91–94.

25. The prominent but controversial Swiss-German physician Paracelsus (1493–1541), one of the first serious critics of Galenic medicine, was likewise enamoured of both astrology and alchemy, and routinely employed both in his medical practice.

26. Quoted in Michael MacDonald, 1981, p. 213.

27. Michael MacDonald, 1981, p. 141.

28. John Cotta, 1616, quoted in Richard Hunter and Ida Macalpine, 1963, p. 87.

29. John Cotta, 1612, pp. 86, 88.

30. John Cotta, 1612, p. 51.

31. Edward Jorden, 1603, The Epistle Dedicatorie (unpaginated).

32. For further discussion of this case, see Andrew Scull, 2011, pp. 1–23. The interpretation of Jorden's intervention as religiously motivated and not the disenchanted secularism it has sometimes seemed was first advanced and documented by Michael MacDonald, 1991.

33. Samuel Harsnett, 1599.

34. Samuel Harsnett, 1603.

35. Kenneth Muir, 1951, claims to have identified over fifty separate fragments from Harsnett's polemic embedded in the text of *Lear*.

36. Tommaso Campanella (1568–1639) was the spiritual leader of a plot against the King of Spain, who then ruled the province of Calabria (to which Campanella had been exiled following earlier suspicions of heretical leanings). Many of his fellow conspirators were hanged or publicly dismembered, but by setting his cell on fire and convincingly pretending to be insane, even when subjected to torture and sleep deprivation, Campanella escaped execution. His judges hesitated to execute a madman since he was in no position to repent, making them responsible for sending him to eternal damnation. Imprisoned for more than a quarter of a century in a series of Neapolitan castles, Campanella was eventually released in 1626, but not before bravely publishing (in 1616) a defence of Galileo against the Inquisition. Some years after his release, threatened with renewed persecution, Campanella fled to Paris, where he remained under the protection of the French king until his death in 1639.

37. T. S Eliot, 1964, 'Seneca in Elizabethan Translation', pp. 51–88.

38. Ben Jonson's *Every Man in His Humour*, first performed by the Lord Chamberlain's Men in 1598 with William Shakespeare taking the role of Kno'well (the gentleman whose desire to spy on his son serves as the lynchpin of the plot), adhered very closely to the model provided by Classical comedy, not least in Jonson's depiction of barely Anglicized versions of the stock characters favoured by Plautus.

39. *Hercules Furens*, in *Seneca, Tragedies*, translated by Frank Justus Miller, Loeb Classical Library Volumes. Cambridge, MA, Harvard University Press; London, William Heinemann Ltd: 1917, lines 1006ff., 1023ff.

40. *Titus Andronicus*, Act 2, Scene 4, line 22.

41. That some Puritans, racked by guilt, corresponded to the stereotype of the melancholic, depressed and sometimes suicidal character is attested to in the copious literary remains of one Nehemiah Wallington (1598–1658), a London wood-turner. In an era when most men of his class and background were illiterate, Wallington left behind more than two thousand pages of notes, diaries and letters that recorded his battle with religious doubts, his delusions that the Devil had talked for him for an hour and more in the shape of a crow, and his repeated bouts of melancholy, all beautifully analysed in Paul S. Seaver, 1988.

42. I owe this point (and much else besides) to my friend and colleague John Marino.

43. Miguel de Cervantes, *Don Quixote*, translated by John Rutherford, London: Penguin Classics, 2003, pp. 142–43.

44. One should note, though, that one of the most important of these, the development of linear perspective from

the 1420s onwards, itself had Classical origins. It was his study of the Pantheon in Rome that led Filippo Brunelleschi (1377–1446) to create the cathedral dome in Florence and to develop a new sense of linear perspective that was quickly theorized mathematically by Leon Battista Alberti (1404–72) and almost equally quickly transformed Western art.

45. To the twenty-first century eye, there is something Dalí-esque about many of the images that crowd the landscape.

46. Sebastian Brant, *Daß Narrenschyff ad Narragoniam*, Basel, 1494.

47. Michel Foucault, 2006, pp. 8–9.

48. Erasmus, *The Praise of Folly*, edited by Clarence Miller, 1979, p. 65.

49. 'Now what shall I say about those who find great comfort in soothing self-delusions about fictitious pardons for their sins, measuring out the times in purgatory down to the droplets of a waterclock...? Or what about those who rely on certain little magical tokens and prayers thought up by some pious impostor for his own amusement or profit?', Erasmus, *The Praise of Folly*, 1979, p. 64.

50. 'And then too, isn't it pretty much the same sort of nonsense when particular regions lay claim to a certain saint, when they parcel out particular functions to particular saints, and assign to particular saints certain modes of worship: one offers relief from a toothache, another helps women in labour, another restores stolen goods; one shines a ray of hope in a shipwreck, another takes care of the flocks.... Some saints have a variety of powers, especially the virgin mother of God, to whom the ordinary run of men attribute more almost than to her son.' Erasmus, *The Praise of Folly*, 1979, p. 65.

51. Erasmus's Prefatory Letter to Thomas More, reprinted in *The Praise of Folly*, 1979, p. 4.

52. Erasmus, *The Praise of Folly*, 1979, pp. 64–65.

53. This is a paradox deeply embedded in Christianity from its earliest years. Compare, for example, some passages in Paul's first Epistle to the Corinthians (1 Corinthians Chapter 1, verses 20, 25, 27–28), where he writes at length on the subject:

> Hath not God made foolish the wisdom of this world? ... Because the foolishness of God is wiser than men; and the weakness of God is stronger than men.... But God hath chosen the foolish things of the world to confound the wise; and God hath chosen the weak things of the world to confound the things which are mighty; And base things of the world, and things which are despised, hath God chosen, yea, and things which are not, to bring to nought things that are.'

54. Erasmus, *The Praise of Folly*, 1979, pp. 129–30.

55. Erasmus, *The Praise of Folly*, 1979, p. 132.

56. Not that Plato and Socrates exhaust the Classical references to be found in *The Praise of Folly*. Virgil, Horace, Homer and Pliny are but some of the other Greek and Latin authors who surface in its pages.

57. The reference is to Plato, *The Symposium* translated by M. C. Howatson, 2008, 216c–217a.

58. Erasmus, *The Praise of Folly*, translated by Thomas Chaloner, London: Thomas Berthelet, 1549, reprinted

by the Early English Text Society, # 257, London, Oxford University Press, 1965, p. 37.

Chapter Five: Madhouses and Mad-Doctors

1. Jacques Tenon, 1778, p. 85.

2. Montpellier does not seem atypical of French provincial provision for the insane. At Dijon, for example, at the time of the French Revolution, the Bon Pasteur housed nine mentally ill women.

3. Colin Jones, 1980, p. 373. This section relies on Jones's pioneering research.

4. Colin Jones, 1980, p. 380.

5. Colin Jones, 1980, p. 380.

6. Sade was released from Charenton in 1790, when the Constituent Assembly abolished *lettres de cachet*, and subsequently became a delegate to the National Convention, conveniently disavowing his aristocratic past. By 1801 he was imprisoned once more in the Bicêtre (Napoleon having found that arbitrary detention was too valuable a weapon to give up), and then transferred back to Charenton following an intervention by his relatives, where he died a 'lunatic' in 1814. In total, he was locked up for more than a quarter of a century.

7. Jacques Tenon, 1778 lists half a dozen madhouses in the Faubourg St Jacques, nine more in the Faubourg St Antoine and three in Montmartre. The largest of these, run by a Mademoiselle Laignel on the cul-de-sac des Vignes, contained 36 female lunatics; taken together these establishments confined fewer than 300 inmates, the majority of them listed as imbecile or senile. The violent and the agitated were lodged elsewhere, many of them in municipal institutions.

8. Robert Castel, 1988, estimates that '"family prisoners" made up roughly nine-tenths of those detained under *lettres de cachet* issued by the Ancien Régime', p. 16.

9. Neil McKendrick, John Brewer and J. H. Plumb, 1982.

10. I am indebted here to Fabrizio Della Seta, 2013, and more generally, throughout my discussions of madness and opera, to my friend Amy Forrest and my brother-in-law Michael Andrews, for their suggestions and insights. Delilah Forrest, Amy's daughter, was also most helpful in drawing my attention to particular features of Handel's and Mozart's scores for *Orlando* and *Idomeneo*.

11. Michael Robinson, 2013, suggests that 'The message Handel seems to be implying here is that anyone daring to sing in five time is either delirious or wishes to be thought mad.'

12. Compare, for example, Verdi's *Macbeth* (1847), with its sleepwalking, haunted Lady Macbeth, or the French composer Ambroise Thomas's *Hamlet* (1868), with its deployment of both real and feigned madness, and the heightened place it provides for a crazed Ophelia in a radically pruned and simplified plot. Wandering further afield still from its original inspiration, there is Dmitri Shostakovich's *Lady Macbeth of the Mtsensk District*, a 1934 opera that provoked Stalin's fury and came close to causing the composer to lose his life, partly for its sympathetic portrait of a murderess and its references to Siberian exile, but even more so for its explicitly modernist musical idioms and what one American critic

called the 'pornophony' of the music that accompanied its sex scenes.

13. For an excellent discussion of *Idomeneo*, to which I am indebted here, see David Cairns, 2006, Chapter 2. Daniel Heartz, 1992 also has a very useful discussion of *Idomeneo*.

14. Daniel Heartz, quoted in Kristi Brown-Montesano, 2007, p. 225.

15. Charpentier's *Médée* [Medea] (1693) preceded *Orlando* by four decades, and perforce embraced the theme of madness, but further examples include Handel's own *Hercules* (1744); Mozart's *Idomeneo* (1781); Donizetti's *Anna Bolena* (1830), *Lucia di Lammermoor* (1835) and *Linda di Chamounix* (1842); Bellini's *Il Pirata* (1827), *I Puritani* (1835) and *La sonnambula* (1831); Thomas's *Hamlet* (1868); Mussorgsky's *Boris Godunov* (1868); Verdi's *Nabucco* (1842) and *Macbeth* (1847); and Puccini's *Tosca* (1900).

16. *European Magazine* 6, 1784, p. 424.

17. Both quoted in Christine Stevenson, 2000, p. 7.

18. Alexander Cruden, 1739.

19. Daniel Defoe, 1728.

20. William Belcher, 1796.

21. William Pargeter, 1792, p. 123.

22. Samuel Johnson, himself a Grub Street man, described the typical inhabitant of one of its garrets as 'a man without virtue who writes lies at home for his own profit. To these compositions is required neither genius nor knowledge, neither industry nor sprightliness; but contempt of shame and indifference to truth are absolutely necessary.' *The Idler*, 30, November 1758. And, of course, Aleander Pope's *Dunciad* was explicitly written as a satire of 'the Grub-street Race' of commercial writers.

23. Eliza Haywood, 1726.

24. For another late eighteenth-century English novel with a madhouse theme, see Charlotte Smith's *The Young Philosopher*, London: Cadell and Davies, 1798.

25. One might mention a historical irony here: Donizetti himself died mad, probably the victim of tertiary syphilis. See Enid Peschel and Richard Peschel, 1992.

26. For clear examples of this sort of ideological distancing, see Samuel Richardson, 1741, especially letters 153 and 160.

27. Henry Mackenzie, 1771, Chapter 20.

28. Nicholas Robinson, 1729, p. 43.

29. John Brydall, 1700, p. 53.

30. Blaise Pascal, *Pensées* (1669), reprinted in *Œuvres complètes*, Paris: Gallimard, 1954, p. 1156.

31. Andrew Snape, 1718, p. 15.

32. Thomas Willis, 1683, p. 206, emphasis in the original.

33. Cf. Molière, *Le Malade imaginaire*, Paris, 1673.

34. Nicholas Robinson, 1729, pp. 400–01.

35. Quoted in Ida Macalpine and Richard Hunter, 1969, p. 281.

36. Quoted in Ida Macalpine and Richard Hunter, 1969, p. 275.

37. Quoted in Ida Macalpine and Richard Hunter, 1969, p. 281.

38. Colonel Greville, George III's equerry, in his *The Diaries of Colonel the Hon. Robert Fulke Greville*, 1930, p. 186.

39. Joseph Guislain, 1826, pp. 43–44. Translation the author's own.

40. Benjamin Rush to John Rush, 8 June 1810, reprinted in *The Letters of Benjamin Rush*, vol. 2, 1951, p. 1052.

41. Joseph Mason Cox, 1813, pp. 159, 163, 164, 165. Besides appearing in three English editions in the space of nine years, Cox's treatise was rapidly translated into French and German, and an American edition appeared in 1811. His innovation fell on receptive ears.

42. George Man Burrows, 1828, p. 601.

43. George Man Burrows, 1828, p. 601.

44. William Saunders Hallaran, 1810, p. 60.

45. J. H. Plumb, 1975, p. 69.

46. John Locke, in *Educational Writings of John Locke*, 1968, pp. 152–53, 183.

47. John Ferriar, 1795, pp. 111–12.

48. Thomas Bakewell, 1815, pp. 55–56.

49. Samuel Tuke, 1813, p. 148.

50. Dora Weiner, 1994, p. 232. See also Gladys Swain, 1977.

51. See Jan Goldstein, 2001, Chapter 3.

Chapter Six: Nerves and Nervousness

1. Richard Blackmore, 1726, p. 96.

2. Richard Blackmore, 1726, p. 97.

3. Alexander Pope, *Epistle to Arbuthnot*.

4. Quoted in George Rousseau, 1993, p. 167.

5. Jonathan Swift, 'Verses on the Death of Dr Swift' and 'The Seventh Epistle of the First Book of Horace Imitated'.

6. George Cheyne, 1733, p. 260.

7. George Cheyne, 1733, p. 262.

8. George Cheyne, 1733, p. ii.

9. Thomas Willis, 1674, p. 124. Originally published in Latin in London in 1664 by Thomas Grigg. The translation here appeared in Thomas Willis, *The Practice of Physick*, translated by Samuel Pordage, 1684.

10. Thomas Willis, 1681.

11. Thomas Sydenham, 1742, pp. 367–75.

12. George Cheyne, 1733, p. 174.

13. George Cheyne, 1733, pp. 49–50.

14. George Cheyne, 1733, pp. i–ii.

15. George Cheyne, 1733, pp. 52, 262.

16. George Cheyne, 1733, p. 262.

17. David Hume, *A Treatise on Human Nature*, Part III 'Of the Will and Direct Passions', Section I, 'Of Liberty and Necessity', 2007; Thomas Boswell, 1951, pp. 42–43.

18. Nicholas Robinson, 1729, pp. 181–83, 407–08.

19. Nicholas Robinson, 1729, p. 102.

20. Nicholas Robinson, 1729, p. 406.

21. Thomas Willis, 1683, p. 206.

22. Hermanni Boerhaave, 1761.

23. In Victorian times, schoolboys would stick a pin through one of a cockchafer's wings and watch it spin.

24. See John Wesley, 1906, Vol. 1, pp. 190, 210, 363, 412, 551; Vol. 2, pp. 225, 461, 489.

25. William Black, 1811, pp. 18–19; John Haslam, 1809, pp. 266–67; William Pargeter, 1792, p. 134.

26. I rely a great deal in what follows on the researches of the distinguished historian of witchcraft and mental illness in Germany, H. C. Erik Midelfort, whose dissection

of the Gassner phenomenon has been published as *Exorcism and the Enlightenment*, 2005.

27. Quoted in Henri Ellenberger, 1970, p. 58. I have drawn in part on Ellenberger's account of Mesmer's career in what follows, along with Robert Darnton's *Mesmerism and the End of the Enlightenment in France*, 1968.

28. On some accounts, Mozart wrote his Piano Concerto No. 18 in B flat major (K. 456) for her.

29. Quoted in Gloria Flaherty, 1995, p. 278.

30. Historians have previously asserted that Mesmer attended the concert, which would seem a distinctly unwise move on his part. Frank Pattie, 1979, has claimed, however, that this was a myth.

31. For its afterlife in Victorian Britain, see Alison Winter, 1998.

Chapter Seven: The Great Confinement

1. William Shakespeare, *Hamlet*, Act 4, Scene 5.

2. Andrew Snape, 1718, p. 15.

3. *The World*, 7 June 1753.

4. Nicholas Robinson, 1729, p. 50; Richard Mead, 1751, p. 74; William Arnold, 1786, p. 320; Thomas Pargeter, 1792, p. 122. Compare the report of the Committee on Begging to the French Constituent Assembly in the immediate aftermath of the French Revolution, which laments 'the greatest, the most fearful of human miseries that can befall such unfortunate persons, degraded in the most noble part of themselves'. (Quoted in Robert Castel, 1988, p. 50.)

5. Fanny Burney, 1854, Vol. 4, p. 239.

6. Countess of Harcourt, 1880, Vol. 4, pp. 25–28.

7. J.-E. D. Esquirol, 1819, quoted in Dora Weiner, 1994, p. 234.

8. House of Commons, *Report of the Select Committee on Madhouses*, 1815, p. 3.

9. House of Commons, *First Report of the Select Committee on Madhouses*, 1816, pp. 7ff.; Edward Wakefield, 1814.

10. The York Asylum was founded in 1772 as a charity asylum run on traditional lines. It was quite distinct from the later Quaker asylum, the York Retreat, founded in 1796 and discussed further below. Indeed rumours about the mistreatment of patients at the York Asylum were part of William Tuke's motivation to establish a separate Quaker asylum in York.

11. House of Commons, *Report of the Select Committee on Madhouses*, 1815, pp. 1, 4–5.

12. *Report of the Metropolitan Commissioners in Lunacy to the Lord Chancellor*, London: Bradbury and Evans, 1844.

13. The text is reproduced in its entirety in Robert Castel, 1988, pp. 243–53.

14. See Jan Goldstein, 2001, Chapters 6, 8 and 9.

15. Helmut Gröger, Eberhard Gabriel and Siegfried Kasper (eds), 1997.

16. Eric J. Engstrom, 2003, pp. 17–23.

17. Percy Bysshe Shelley, 'Julian and Maddalo: A Conversation' (1818–19).

18. Carlo Livi, 'Pinel o Chiarugi? Lettera al celebre Dott. Al. Brierre de Boismont...', *La Nazione*, VI, 18, 19, 20 September 1864, quoted in Patrizia Guarnieri, 1994, p. 249.

19. Silvio Tonnini, 1892, p. 718.

20. See Julie V. Brown, 1981.

21. Dorothea Lynde Dix, 1843, p. 4. David Gollaher's compelling account (1995) of Dix's career draws attention to her direct borrowing from the British lunacy reformers. I have drawn on his exemplary biography in what follows.

22. Dorothea Lynde Dix, 1843, pp. 8–9. Surely it is not a coincidence that this description echoes the narrative of those who had exposed the state of patients hidden in the bowels of the York Asylum.

23. See the account of Dix's foray to Scotland in Andrew Scull, Charlotte MacKenzie and Nicholas Hervey, 1996, pp. 118–21.

24. Dorothea Lynde Dix, 1845, pp. 28–29.

25. George E. Paget, 1866, p. 35.

26. See, for example, Stephen Garton, 1988; Catherine Coleborne, 2001; Thomas Brown, 1980.

27. Harriet Deacon, 2003, pp. 20–53.

28. See Jonathan Sadowsky, 1999.

29. Rauvolfia continues to be used on a small scale in Western medicine for the treatment of hypertension.

30. Waltraud Ernst, 1991.

31. For the first full-length study of such an institution, see Waltraud Ernst, 2013.

32. Richard Keller, 2007; Claire Edington, 2013; and, more generally, Sloan Mahone and Megan Vaughan (eds), 2007.

33. Jonathan Ablard, 2003; E.A. Balbo, 1991.

34. For a splendid and detailed elaboration of these points, see Emily Baum, 2013.

35. Akihito Suzuki, 2003.

36. John Ferriar, 1795, pp. 111–12 (Ferriar was a physician to Manchester Lunatic Asylum). For similar sentiments from another madhouse keeper, see Thomas Bakewell, 1805, pp. 56–56, 59, 171.

37. See especially Samuel Tuke, 1813. (An American edition was published in Philadelphia within a matter of months.)

38. Samuel Tuke, 1813, pp. 133–34, 151–52.

39. Samuel Tuke, 1813, p. 156.

40. Samuel Tuke, 1813, p. 177.

41. William A. F. Browne, 1837.

42. Andrew Scull, 1981b.

43. For one of his many tributes to the work of Madame Pussin, see Philippe Pinel, 2008 [1809], pp. 83–84.

44. Philippe Pinel, 2008 [1809], p. xxiii, n. 2.

45. Philippe Pinel, 2008 [1809], pp. 101–02.

46. Philippe Pinel, 2008 [1809], p. 140.

47. J.-E. D. Esquirol, 1818, p. 84.

48. William A. F. Browne, 1837, pp. 50, 180.

49. Anonymous, 1836–1837, p. 697.

50. John Conolly, 1847, p. 143.

51. See, for example, Dorothea Lynde Dix, 1845, pp. 9–10.

52. William A. F. Browne, 1864, pp. 311–12.

53. Crichton Royal Asylum *7th Annual Report*, 1846, p. 35.

54. Crichton Royal Asylum *10th Annual Report*, 1849, p. 38.

55. Quoted in Jan Goldstein, 2001, p. 86.

56. Philippe Pinel, 1801, pp. xlv–xlvi.

57. Philippe Pinel, 2008 [1809], pp. 123–30, 136.

58. Philippe Pinel, 2008 [1809], p. 139.

59. See the discussion in Jan Goldstein, 2001, pp. 113–16.
60. Samuel Tuke, 1813, p. 110.
61. Samuel Tuke, 1813, p. 111, quoting the words of the first visiting physician to the York Retreat, Thomas Fowler.
62. William F. Bynum, 1974, p. 325.
63. Philippe Pinel, 1801, pp.158–59.
64. William Lawrence, 1819, p. 112.
65. Pierre Cabanis, 1823–25.
66. William A. F. Browne, 1837, p. 4; for an almost identical view, see Andrew Halliday, 1828, p. 4.
67. John Conolly, 1830, p. 62.
68. William A. F. Browne, 1837, p. 4.
69. William Newnham, 1829, p. 265.
70. John P. Gray, 1871.
71. Georges Lantéri-Laura, 2000, pp. 126–27.
72. Franz Gall and Johann Spurzheim, 1812, pp. 81–82.
73. Johann Spurzheim, 1813, p. 101.
74. Mark Twain, 2013, p. 336.
75. Though he had observed morbid changes in the brains of his patients, Bayle still thought that the origins of the disease might well be social. For example, he acknowledged that these symptoms were particularly common among those who had served in Napoleon's armies, but put this down to the traumas soldiers had experienced, and the disappointments they had suffered with the collapse of empire. Similarly, Esquirol observed that prostitutes seemed particularly prone to the disorder, but attributed this to the immorality of their lives.
76. *Journal of Mental Science* 2, October 1858.
77. Pinel had insisted on substituting the new term '*aliénation*' for what he proclaimed was the vulgar popular term '*folie*' (*Nosographie philosophique* Vol. 1, Paris: Crapelet, 1798) and '*aliéniste*' was its natural accompaniment. In a similar vein, Esquirol had sought to change the language his fellow-countrymen used for the place where alienists confined the mad: 'I would like these establishments to be given a specific name which presents no painful idea to the mind; I would like them to be called asylums.' J.-E. D. Esquirol, 1819, p. 26.
78. Robert Gardiner Hill, 1839, pp. 4–6.
79. Joseph Mortimer Granville, 1877, Vol. 1, p. 15.
80. Quoted in Dorothea Lynde Dix, 1850, p. 20.
81. *The Times*, 5 April 1877.
82. *The Scotsman*, 1 September 1871.
83. 'Heilungsaussichten in der Irrenstalten', 10, September 1908, p. 223.
84. James Crichton-Browne, *Annual Report of the West Riding Lunatic Asylum*, 1873.
85. 'Lunatic Asylums', *Quarterly Review* 101, 1857

Chapter Eight: Degeneration and Despair

1. Philippe Pinel, 'Aux auteurs du journal', *Journal de Paris*, 18 January 1790, p. 71.
2. Philippe Pinel, 1805, p. 1158.
3. J.-E. D. Esquirol, 1805, p. 15.
4. J.-E. D. Esquirol, 1838, Vol. 2, p. 742.
5. H. Girard, 1846, pp. 142–43.
6. Benjamin Rush, 1947, p. 168.
7. Benjamin Rush, 1947, p. 333.
8. *Tenth Annual Report of the State Lunatic Hospital at Worcester*, 1842, Boston: Dutton and Wentworth, p. 62.
9. Butler Hospital for the Insane, *Annual Report* 1854, p. 13.
10. Pliny Earle, 1868, p. 272
11. *Thirteenth Annual Report of the State Lunatic Hospital at Worcester*, 1845, Boston: Dutton and Wentworth, 1846, p. 7. See also Amariah Brigham, 1833, p. 91.
12. Thomas Beddoes, 1802, p. 40.
13. Alexander Morison, 1825, p. 73.
14. William A. F. Browne, 1837, pp. 56, 59.
15. David Uwins, 1833, p. 51.
16. Silas Weir Mitchell, 1894.
17. Crichton Royal Asylum, *9th Annual Report*, 1848, p. 5.
18. Crichton Royal Asylum, *13th Annual Report*, 1852, p. 40
19. Crichton Royal Asylum, *18th Annual Report*, 1857, pp. 24–26.
20. John C. Bucknill, 1860, p. 7.
21. Charlotte MacKenzie, 1985.
22. Ebenezer Haskell, 1869.
23. Vincent van Gogh to Theo van Gogh, May 1890.
24. When Clare wrote letters to newspapers, he signed them 'A Northamptonshire Pheasant', and he never mastered spelling or conventional orthography.
25. The text of the poems quoted here is taken from *The Poems of John Clare*, edited with an Introduction by J. W. Tibble, London: J. M. Dent & Sons Ltd and New York: E. P. Dutton & Co. Inc., 1935. With thanks to Linda Curry, Chair of the John Clare Society for her assistance.
26. Charles Reade, 1864. As Reade was well aware, Conolly had a short time previously been sued for damages in connection with the confinement of Mr Ruck, an alcoholic confined on a certificate of lunacy issued by Conolly in an asylum from which he received 'consultation fees'. The jury in the case concluded that these sums were a kick-back, and Conolly was ordered to pay swingeing damages of £500. The case drew widespread publicity given Conolly's prominence as the man who had abolished mechanical restraint in London's asylums. It was not Conolly's last brush with the law. As for Hamlet, that the Prince was mad was known to be an *idée fixe* with Dr Conolly.
27. The novel contains, of course, a memorable portrait of a character driven to obsessive madness by the endless iterations of Chancery lawyers in the person of the gentle Miss Flite.
28. John T. Perceval, 1838, 1840, pp. 175–76, 179. On the Society, see Nicholas Hervey, 1986.
29. See the discussion of Conolly and Hill in Andrew Scull, Charlotte MacKenzie, and Nicholas Hervey, 1996, pp. 70–72.
30. See Rosina Bulwer Lytton, 1880, for her polemical account of her travails, and Sarah Wise, 2012, pp. 208–51, for a more balanced assessment of the case.
31. Reported in *Annales médico-psychologiques* 5, 1865, p. 248. See Ian Dowbiggin, 1985a.
32. Daniel Hack Tuke, 1878, p. 171.
33. Henry Maudsley, 1871, pp. 323–24.
34. Henry Maudsley, 1895, p. 30.
35. W. A. F. Browne, in Crichton Royal Asylum, *18th Annual Report*, 1857, pp. 12–13.

36. S. A. K. Strahan, 1890, pp. 337, 334.
37. Max Nordau, 1893. Nordau's book appeared in English in 1895 and enjoyed an international success, most notably for its denunciation of degenerate art and artists.
38. William Greenslade, 1994, p. 5.
39. Some modern scholars have called into question Nietzsche's syphilis. Perhaps they are right, though the perils of retrospective diagnosis are clear. At the time, his asylum doctors were convinced he suffered from general paralysis of the insane, or tertiary syphilis.
40. William Booth, 1890, pp. 204–05.
41. Edward Spitzka, 1878, p. 210.
42. York Retreat, *Annual Report* 1904.
43. Quoted in Henry C. Burdett, 1891, Vol. 2, pp.186, 230.
44. Charles G. Hill, 1907, p. 6. Compare similar comments two years later by the president of the American Neurological Association, Silas Weir Mitchell, 1909, p. 1: 'Amid enormous gains in our art, we have sadly to confess the absolute standstill of the therapy of insanity and the relative failure, as concerns diagnosis, in mental maladies of even that most capable diagnostician, the post-mortem surgeon.'
45. Quoted in Edward Shorter, 1997, p. 76.
46. Hideyo Noguchi and J. W. Moore, 1913.
47. James Cowles Prichard, 1835, p. 6.
48. Henry Maudsley, 1895, p. vi.
49. S. A. K. Strahan, 1890, p. 334.
50. Henry Maudsley, 1883, pp. 241, 321.
51. S. A. K. Strahan, 1890, p. 331.
52. Reported in *Annales médico-psychologiques* 12, 1868, p. 288, quoted in Ian Dowbiggin, 1985, p. 193.
53. *Buck v. Bell*, 247 US 200, 1927.
54. For a discussion of the links between the Nazi proponents of 'racial hygiene' and the American eugenicists, see Stefan Kühl, 1994. According to Margaret Smyth, a graduate of Stanford Medical School and superintendent of the California State Hospital in Stockton, 'The leaders in the German sterilization movement state repeatedly that their legislation was formulated after careful study of the California experiment.' Margaret Smyth, 1938, p. 1234.
55. See Robert Proctor, 1988; Aly Götz, Peter Chroust, and Christian Pross, 1994.
56. See M. von Cranach, 2003; Michael Burleigh, 1994.

Chapter Nine: The Demi-Fous
1. Akihito Suzuki, 2006, p. 103.
2. See, for example, the discussion of Morison's domestic psychiatric practice in Andrew Scull, Charlotte MacKenzie, and Nicholas Hervey, 1996, Chapter 5.
3. For comparable examples from Switzerland, see the cases cited in Edward Shorter, 1990, p. 178.
4. Ticehurst Asylum Casebook 5, 2 July 1858, Contemporary Medical Archives, Wellcome Medical Library, London.
5. Edward Shorter, 1990 pp. 190–92.
6. Edward Hare, 1983; Edwin Fuller Torrey, 2002.
7. Andrew Scull, 1984; David Healy, 2008; Michael A. Taylor, 2013; Gary Greenberg, 2013.

8. Andrew Wynter, 1875; J. Mortimer Granville, in Andrew Wynter, 1877, p. 276: Granville contributed five chapters to the second edition.
9. John C. Bucknill, 1860, p. 7, where he complains that the asylum physician is forced to dwell in 'a morbid atmosphere of thought and feeling ... of lurid delusion [that leaves him at grave risk] from the seeming contagion of mental disease'. What, one wonders, of the patients? (Walpurgis night, incidentally, was traditionally the time when witches gathered together.)
10. William Goodell, 1881, p. 640.
11. Andrew Scull, 2011.
12. George M. Beard, 1881, p. 17.
13. Indeed, in 1893, Beard's disease received the ultimate contemporary accolade, the appearance *Handbuch der Neurasthenie*, edited by Franz Carl Müller.
14. Virginia Woolf, *Mrs Dalloway* (1925). Sir William Bradshaw is a brutal rendition of Sir George Savage, whose psychiatric practice centred on the chattering classes.
15. Compare Charlotte Perkins Gilman's *The Yellow Wallpaper*, a short story in which a barely disguised Mitchell (who had personally administered the rest cure to Gilman) drives his patient mad. Edith Wharton was another of Mitchell's patients, her treatment ending a year before she published her first novel.
16. Anne Stiles (webpage). Suzanne Poirier, 1983, claims that 'Former female patients flooded his mails with letters of praise and admiration', pp. 21–22.
17. Though men were given the rest cure, they were seldom so completely immobilized as were their female counterparts. Mitchell's writings on the subject use predominantly the female pronoun when speaking of nervous patients. As a Civil War surgeon, he had dealt harshly with men he suspected of malingering. His comments about neurasthenic and hysterical women suggest such sentiments lingered here too, only barely beneath the surface veneer of the caring physician. In insisting that patients be removed from their own houses, for instance, he remarked that 'for the most entire capacity to make a household wretched there is no more complete human receipt than a silly woman who is to a high degree nervous and feeble, and who craves pity and likes power'. Silas Weir Mitchell, 1888, p. 117. Freud would later coin the term 'secondary gain'. Self-evidently, Mitchell was already aware of how the sick role could be exploited as a source of power.
18. Silas Weir Mitchell, 1894.
19. For a discussion of this latter development, see Andrew Scull, Charlotte MacKenzie and Nicholas Hervey, 1996, Chapters 7–9. At least initially, 'functional' did not mean 'psychological'. Rather, it referred to physiological rather than structural changes in the nervous system. Or as George Beard, 1880, p. 114, phrased the distinction, 'What the microscope can see, we call structural – what the microscope cannot see, we call functional.' Both were somatic conditions.
20. Jean-Martin Charcot's career is surveyed in the magisterial biography by Christopher Goetz, Michel Bonduelle and Toby Gelfand, 1995.

21. Jean-Martin Charcot, 'Preface', in Alex Athanassio, 1890, p. i.

22. James Braid, 1843.

23. Quoted in Christopher Goetz, Michel Bonduelle, and Toby Gelfand, 1995, pp. 235–36.

24. Celine Renooz, 1888.

25. Anonymous, 1877 – a report of her speech at an August 1887 conference on vivisection.

26. Axel Munthe, 1930, pp. 296, 302–03.

27. With some modifications, the last two paragraphs are drawn from Andrew Scull, 2011, pp. 122–23.

28. Axel Munthe, 1930, p. 302.

29. Horatio Donkin, 1892, pp. 625–26; Charcot had articulated his own views on the matter for an English-speaking audience a little earlier in the same authoritative volume: J.-M Charcot and Gilles de la Tourette, 1892.

30. See Hippolyte Bernheim, 1886.

31. Modern scholars have shown that this account of Anna O.'s treatment is in most respects false. Not only did Breuer's cathartic method fail to cure her, but she remained disturbed for a decade and more after she left his hands, requiring several extensive periods of confinement in a sanatorium in Switzerland. When she ultimately recovered, she had nothing good to say about the talking cure. The Ur case of psychoanalysis is a myth – on a multitude of levels a series of fictions.

32. Josef Breuer and Sigmund Freud, 1957, p. 255, emphasis in the original.

33. Josef Breuer and Sigmund Freud, 1957, p. 7, emphasis in the original.

34. See the preface to the second edition of *Studies on Hysteria* published in *The Standard Edition of the Complete Psychological Works of Sigmund Freud*, Vol. 2, London: Hogarth Press, 1981.

35. Sigmund Freud, 1963, pp. 15–16.

36. Quoted in Jeffrey Masson, 1985, p. 9.

Chapter Ten: Desperate Remedies

1. Wilfred Owen, 'Mental Cases', 1918.

2. Wilfred Owen, 'Anthem for Doomed Youth', 1917.

3. I am particularly indebted here, as in a number of other places throughout my text, to the insights and prompting of my friend Amy Forrest.

4. Otto Dix, War Diary, 1915–1916, quoted in Eva Karcher, 1987, p. 14; Dix quoted in the catalogue for the exhibition *Otto Dix 1891–1969*, Tate Gallery 1992, pp. 17–18.

5. Wilfred Owen, 'Dulce et Decorum Est' (1917–18).

6. Charles Mercier, 1914, p. 17.

7. Seeking to capitalize on the greater prestige of neurology, some psychiatrists used the hybrid term neuropsychiatry, a term which reinforced at a symbolic level the perception that mental illness was unambiguously a disorder of the body.

8. For Rivers' own account, see his paper 'An Address On the Repression of War Experience', *Lancet* 96, 1918. Rivers' work at Craiglockhart is central to Pat Barker's trilogy of novels, *Regeneration* (1991), *The Eye in the Door* (1993) and *The Ghost Road* (1995), and he appears under his own name in Sassoon's semi-fictionalized memoir, *Sherston's Progress*, 1936.

9. Quoted in Paul Lerner, 2001, p. 158.

10. Quoted in Marc Roudebush, 2001, p. 269.

11. E. D. Adrian and L. R. Yealland, 1917, quoted in Ben Shephard, 2000, p. 77.

12. Quoted in Elaine Showalter, 1985, pp. 176–77.

13. When the Nazis completed the Anschluß in 1938, absorbing the vestige that was Austria into the Third Reich, the anti-semitic Wagner-Jauregg joined the ranks of the party that would soon usher Freud into exile and do all it could to exterminate psychoanalysis and psychoanalysts as adherents of a degenerate Jewish science. As president of the Austrian League for Racial Regeneration and Heredity, Wagner-Jauregg also vigorously sought the sterilization of those of 'inferior racial stock'.

14. Alongside the rapidly developing skin infection known as St Anthony's fire, this streptococcal infection was associated with pain, chills and shivering, and could cause lasting lymphatic damage or even death.

15. August von Wassermann had developed a blood test for syphilis in 1906 at the Robert Koch Institute for Infectious Diseases; and seven years later Hideyo Noguchi and J. W. Moore published their classic paper in the *Journal of Experimental Medicine*, 1913, demonstrating that the brains of those afflicted with GPI were infected with *Treponema pallidum*, the corkscrew-shaped organism that causes syphilis.

16. Frederick Mott, pathologist to the London mental hospitals, spoke of regularly encountering end-state paretics, 'wrecks of humanity sitting in a row, their heads on their breasts, grinding the teeth, saliva running out the angles of the mouth, oblivious to their surroundings, with expressionless faces and cold, livid hands'. Quoted in Hugh Pennington, 2003, p. 31.

17. See Honorio F. Delgado, 1922; Nolan D. C. Lewis, Lois D. Hubbard and Edna G. Dyar, 1924, pp. 176–21; Julius Wagner-Jauregg, 1946, pp. 577–78.

18. This practice raised serious ethical issues. The Wassermann test is not specific to syphilis. A positive reaction can occur, for example, in patients with systemic lupus erythematosus, tuberculosis and (ironically) malaria. Hence there was a non-trivial possibility that as well as contracting malaria, a misdiagnosed patient could also be given syphilis. Among the few psychiatrists disturbed by this possibility was William Alanson White, superintendent of the federal mental hospital in Washington, DC, White banned use of the treatment on these grounds, but he was almost alone in doing so.

19. J. R. Driver, J. A. Gammel and L. J. Karnosh, 1926.

20. See Joel Braslow, 1997, pp. 71–94.

21. *Treponema pallidum* is vulnerable *in vitro* to temperatures of around 106° Fahrenheit, suggesting a possible mechanism by which the treatment might have worked, but whether this is what happened *in vivo* is not clear. Wagner-Jauregg argued that the malaria infection stimulated the immune system and that this somehow explained why his treatment worked, but this was pure speculation, ungrounded in any evidence.

22. Henry Maudsley, 1879, p. 115.
23. Christopher Lawrence, 1985.
24. John B. Sanderson, 1885.
25. See, for example, Emil Kraepelin, 1896, pp. 36–37, 439; and also 6th edition, p. 154; 8th edition, Vol. 3, p. 931.
26. Henry A. Cotton, 1923, pp. 444–45.
27. Henry A. Cotton, 1919, p. 287.
28. Henry A. Cotton, 1921, p. 66.
29. In 'Notes and News', *Journal of Mental Science* 69, 1923, pp. 553–59. Goodall praised Cotton's work as an antidote to the pernicious doctrines propagated by Sigmund Freud: the American's work 'should have served to draw members from the alluring and tempting pastures of psychogenesis to the narrower, steeper, more rugged and arduous, yet straighter paths, of general medicine'.
30. Sir Berkeley Moynihan, 1927, pp. 815, 817. Moynihan was not alone in comparing Cotton's work to Lister's pioneering of antiseptic surgery, and the audience was reminded that 1927 marked the centenary of Lister's birth, and of the scepticism with which the latter's work had originally been greeted by his surgical colleagues.
31. 'Total colectomy has been done...in 133 cases, with 33 recoveries and 44 deaths. Partial resection at the right side was done in 148 cases, with 44 recoveries and 59 deaths' – results Cotton blithely claimed were 'largely due to the very poor physical condition of most of the patients'. Henry A. Cotton, 1923, pp. 454, 457.
32. See A. T. Hobbs, 1924, p. 550.
33. For a detailed account of the focal sepsis episode, see Andrew Scull, 2005.
34. Introduced by one of Eugen Bleuler's underlings in Zurich, Jakob Kläsi, *Dauernarkose* produced an artificial sleep lasting six or eight days. It had a reported mortality rate of 6 per cent.
35. Robert S. Carroll, 1923; E. S. Barr and R. G. Barry, 1926, p. 89.
36. J. H. Talbott and K. J. Tillotson, 1926. Two of their ten patients died in the course of the 'treatment'.
37. Illinois Department of Public Welfare, *Annual Report* 11, 1927–28, pp. 12, 23; 1928–29, p. 23. T. C. Graves, 1919.
38. At this meeting, attended by psychiatrists from all over the Western world, there were sixty-eight presentations on insulin treatment, made to an audience that exceeded 200. See the discussion in Edward Shorter and David Healy, 2007, Chapter 4.
39. Manfred Sakel, 1937, p. 830.
40. By 1941, for example, an American survey revealed that 72 per cent of 365 public and private mental institutions used insulin coma therapy. See US Public Health Service, 1941. Shortages of glucose in wartime Britain curtailed the use of the treatment, and forced the use of potato starch as substitute means of bringing the patients out of their comas. Many hospitals temporarily abandoned the treatment as personnel shortages made it impossible to administer.
41. Benjamin Wortis, translation of a lecture given by Manfred Sakel in Paris, 21 July 1937, St Elizabeth's Hospital Treatment File, Entry 18, National Archives, Washington, DC.
42. See Harold Bourne, 1953, and the discussion of the profession's reaction in Michael Shepherd, 1994, pp. 90–92.
43. Sylvia Nasar, 1998, pp. 288–94.
44. L. von Meduna and Emerick Friedman, 1939, p. 509.
45. L. von Meduna, 1938, p. 50. (Cardiazol was the European trade name for metrazol.)
46. Solomon Katzenelbogen, 1940, pp. 412, 419.
47. Nathaniel J. Berkwitz, 1940, p. 351.
48. On ECT's rapid international adoption, see Edward Shorter and David Healy, 2007, pp. 73–82.
49. Though sometimes confused with the electrical treatments like the Kaufmann cure used in the First World War, ECT was quite distinct from those deliberate inflictions of pain, being used to induce seizures and temporary unconsciousness, not pain, fear and aversion in the sentient patient.
50. Stanley Cobb, 1938, p. 897.
51. M. J. Sakel, 1956.
52. For a recent discussion by two proponents of ECT, see Edward Shorter and David Healy, 2007, pp. 132–35. Not everyone shares their sanguine perspective.
53. Egas Moniz, 1936.
54. *Baltimore Sun*, 21 November 1936.
55. The growing interest in lobotomy in 'progressive' state hospitals during the early 1940s is traced in Jack D. Pressman, 1998, Chapter 4.
56. His colleague Wylie McKissock performed his 500th operation by April 1946, and had done more than 1,300 by 1950.
57. A. M. Fiamberti, 1937.
58. For an eyewitness account of one of these mass lobotomy demonstrations, see Alan W. Scheflin and Edward Opton Jr, 1978, pp. 247–49. In a letter to Moniz, Freeman boasted that in West Virginia he in one day 'operated upon 22 patients in 135 minutes, about six minutes per operation'. In twelve days, he operated on some 228 patients. Walter Freeman to Egas Moniz, 9 September 1952, Psychosurgery Collection, George Washington University, Washington DC.
59. Freeman proudly reported that a Dr J. S. Walen had managed to perform almost 200 transorbital operations at the Evanston, Wyoming State Hospital based on his written instructions alone, and that at State Hospital Number 4 (a revealing name in itself), Dr Paul Schrader had 'all but solved the problems of the disturbed ward at that particular hospital' by performing in excess of 200 transorbital operations. Walter Freeman, 'Adventures in Lobotomy', unpublished manuscript, George Washington University Medical Library, Psychosurgery Collection, Chapter 6, p. 59.
60. *Mental Hygiene News*, quoted in Jack D. Pressman, 1998, pp. 182–83.
61. 'Medicine: Insulin for Insanity', *Time*, 25 January 1937. The *New York Times* also made approving noises. See the editorial published on 14 January 1937, p. 20.
62. 'Insulin Therapy', *New York Times*, 8 August 1943, E9.
63. *Washington Evening Star*, 20 November 1936.
64. Waldemar Kaempffert, 1941, pp. 18–19, 69, 71–72, 74. He repeated his encomiums for a more upscale readership

in the *New York Times*, 11 January 1942. The pictures identifying Freeman and Watts – not, it should be noted, the brain surgery – almost led to their medical licences being revoked, for it constituted a form of prohibited 'medical advertising'.

65. Stephen McDonough, 1941.

66. Together with the earlier award to Wagner-Jauregg for the malarial treatment of GPI, these remain the only Nobel Prizes awarded to date in the field of psychiatry, though the Columbia neuropsychiatrist Eric Kandel did win the 2000 Nobel Prize in Physiology or Medicine for his work on the physiology of memory.

67. Elliot Valenstein, 1985, p. 229.

68. Hemingway made this remark to his biographer. See A. E. Hotchner, *Papa Hemingway: A Personal Memoir*, New York: Random House, 1966, p. 280.

69. Sylvia Plath, 2005, p. 143.

Chapter Eleven: A Meaningful Interlude

1. See, for example, Jonathan Sadowsky, 1999; Jock McCulloch, 1995; Waltraud Ernst, 1991 and 2013.

2. Catharine Coleborne, in press; Roy Porter and David Wright (eds), 2003.

3. Emily Baum, 2013. Neil Diamant, 1993, emphasizes the limited degree to which the Chinese embraced mental hospitals, the continued reliance on the family as the primary locus for such care as the mentally ill received, and the co-operation between the police and asylums in Canton and Beijing, with the small mental hospitals mainly being used as a means to control and contain some troublesome and disruptive individuals. For broadly similar arguments, see Veronica Pearson, 1991.

4. The American neurologist Silas Weir Mitchell denounced such people as 'the pests of many households, who constitute the despair of physicians', and the British alienist James Crichton-Browne muttered darkly about the 'psychopathic or neuropathic…not certifiable, passing muster as a self-regulating human being, often as one who is injured and misunderstood, but who is more or less or from time to time abnormal, difficult, irritable, depressed, suspicious, capricious, eccentric, impulsive, unreasonable, cranky, deluded, and subject to all kinds of imaginary maladies and nervous agitations.' Both quoted in Janet Oppenheim, 1991, p. 293.

5. Quoted in Peter Gay, 1988, p. 215.

6. Jones went to Toronto, where he remained for five years before returning to England. Sexual scandal erupted again during his time in Canada: he paid hush money to a woman who accused him of sexual assault; and there was much talk of his irregular (i.e., unmarried) relationship with his former patient Loe Kann, who was addicted to morphine. These were but a few of his peccadilloes, for Jones was a serial seducer. But he was a tireless advocate for Freudian ideas during these years, and did much to attract a number of North Americans to the psychoanalytic perspective.

7. James Crichton-Browne, 1930, p. 228.

8. Janet Oppenheim, 1991, p. 307.

9. Michael Clark, 1988. Britain's first professor of psychiatry, Joseph Shaw Bolton of Leeds University,

dismissed psychoanalysis as 'insidious poison' (1926) and Charles Mercier, 1916, predicted that Freud's system would soon go 'to join pounded toads and sour milk in the limbo of discarded remedies'.

10. Mapother's successor as the head of London's Institute of Psychiatry, Aubrey Lewis, was equally determined to marginalize psychoanalysis. A masterly and ruthless academic politician, Lewis was determined to ensure that no British department of psychiatry should have a psychoanalyst as its head. None did. Cf. David Healy, 2002, p. 297.

11. In the ten-page brochure advertising the conference, Freud is almost an afterthought. His sworn enemy, William Stern, receives top billing among the foreign guests, and only at the very end is there any mention of Freud's participation, which was accorded the grand total of two lines.

12. Freud to Ferenczi, quoted in Peter Gay, 1988, p. 564. (Gay discusses Freud's vicious anti-Americanism at some length on pp. 553–70, from which I have drawn the quotations that follow.) Sándor Ferenczi, the Hungarian psychoanalyst who had also accompanied Freud on the journey to Clark was fully aware of the irony of the situation. He imagined Freud's musings on the subject ('How could I take so much pleasure in the honors the Americans have bestowed on me, when I feel such contempt for Americans?') And Ferenczi then commented: 'Not unimportant is the emotion that impressed even me, a reverent spectator, as somewhat ridiculous, when almost with tears in his eyes he thanked the president of the university for the honorary doctorate.' Sándor Ferenczi, 1985, p. 184.

13. Zweig was an internationally known German writer and pacifist, who engaged in lengthy correspondence with Freud for more than a dozen years. He emigrated to Palestine following Hitler's rise to power. He was psychoanalysed there, and for a time was the main link between the psychoanalytic community there and Freud himself. Freud to Jung, 17 January 1909, in William McGuire (ed.) 1974, p. 196.

14. *Boston Evening Transcript*, 11 September 1909.

15. Quoted in Ralph B. Perry, 1935, pp. 122, 123.

16. Edith Rockefeller McCormick, spendthrift daughter of John D. Rockefeller and wife of one of the heirs to the great combine harvester fortune, moved to Zurich to be treated by Jung, having failed to bribe him to relocate to America. She 'qualified' as a Jungian analyst, embarked on a series of affairs and endowed a Jungian training centre with a quarter of a million dollars. Mary Mellon, married to Paul Mellon, the heir to the Mellon banking fortune, converted her husband to the cause, and together they established the Bollingen Foundation, which to this day attempts to promote Jung's mystical version of psychoanalysis.

17. Chapter 7 of George Makari, 2008, provides a useful discussion of these developments.

18. Freud found the situation demeaning and unpleasant. He confided to Heinrich Meng that 'Unfortunately I am forced…to sell the rest of my sparse working time dearly. I would have to charge a German 250 Marks per hour,

and therefore I prefer Englishmen and Americans who pay the hourly rates usual in their own countries. That is, I do not prefer them, I just have to take them on.... Freud to Meng, 21 April 1921, Library of Congress, Washington, DC.

19. See, for example, Stephen Farber and Marc Green, 1993; and Krin Gabbard and Glen O. Gabbard, 1987. I shall examine this phenomenon at greater length later in this chapter.

20. Isador Coriat to Ernest Jones, 4 April 1921, Otto Rank Papers, Rare Book Room, Columbia University, New York City.

21. The tendency to concentrate in New York and a handful of other urban centres was rooted not just in the long-standing patterns common to all immigrant groups, but also in the fact that only half a dozen of the then forty-eight states permitted foreign medical practitioners to practice their profession.

22. On these developments, see George Makari, 2012.

23. In the words of one of his followers, 'daß Freud allzeit ein grimmer Hasser war. Stets hat er weitaus mächtiger hassen als lieben können'. [Freud had always been a great hater. He could hate much more powerfully than he could love.] Isidor Sadger, 2005 (originally published as *Sigmund Freud: Persönliche Erinnerungen* in 1929). Sadger was a devoted disciple who had attended Freud's lectures as early as 1895, one of the first three people to do so, and subsequently was a faithful participant in the so-called Wednesday Psychological Society. He is one of those who failed to escape the Nazi menace. He was murdered at the Theresienstadt concentration camp on 21 December 1942.

24. Only 48 German soldiers had been shot in the First World War. By contrast, 10,000 had been executed by the end of 1944, and a further 5,000 were killed as a disciplinary measure in the first four months of 1945. Ben Shephard, 2000, p. 305. Painful Kaufmann 'cures' were also once more the order of the day.

25. Ben Shephard, 2000, p. 166.

26. R. J. Phillips, 'Psychiatry at the Corps Level', Wellcome Library for the History of Medicine, London, GC/135/B1/109.

27. Edgar Jones and Simon Wessely, 2001.

28. Ben Shephard, 2000, p. 328.

29. Edgar Jones and Simon Wessely, 2001, pp. 244–45.

30. Spike Milligan, 1980, pp. 276–88, quoted in Ben Shephard, 2000, p. 220.

31. Roy S. Grinker and John P. Spiegel, 1945; Abram Kardiner and Herbert Spiegel, 1947.

32. Gerald Grob, 1990, p. 54.

33. Ben Shephard, 2000, p. 219.

34. Ellen Herman, 1995, p. 9.

35. Ben Shephard, 2000, p. 330.

36. See D. W. Millard, 1996; T. P. Rees, 1957; Edgar Jones, 2004.

37. H. V. Dicks, 1970, p. 6.

38. Ben Shephard, 2000, p. 325.

39. Nathan Hale, Jr, 1998, p. 246.

40. Psychoanalysts dominated the most prestigious positions in the field. By 1961, they held 32 of the 44 professorial positions in medical schools in the Boston area, and that formed part of a nationwide trend. Of the 91 medical schools in the country, 90 were teaching psychoanalysis; virtually all the best residents were seeking psychoanalytic training; and in 1962, of the 89 departments of psychiatry, 52 were headed by someone who belonged to a psychoanalytic institute. Nathan G. Hale, Jr, 1998, pp. 246–53.

41. The most widely used was Arthur P. Noyes and Lawrence Kolb, 1935, followed by Jack R. Ewalt, Edward A. Strecker and Franklin G. Ebaugh, 1957 – a text that before the 1950s had reflected Adolf Meyer's teachings but now adopted a Freudian stance. Silvano Arieti's edited *American Handbook of Psychiatry*, which first appeared in a two-volume version in 1959, included references to other theories and approaches, but was fundamentally another psychoanalytic text.

42. Nathan G. Hale Jr, 1998, especially Chapter 14; Joel Paris, 2005.

43. See A. Michael Sulman, 1973.

44. Bowlby wrote a widely influential report commissioned by the World Health Organization (WHO), *Maternal Care and Mental Health*, which was published in 1951.

45. Donald Winnicott, 1964, p. 11.

46. E. Rous and A. Clark, 2009.

47. Franz Alexander, 1943, p. 209; for his earliest ideas on the subject, see Franz Alexander 1933.

48. Compare Franz Alexander, 1950, pp. 134–35; Margaret Gerard, 1946, p. 331; and Harold Abramson (ed.), 1951, esp. pp. 632–54.

49. Leo Kanner, 1943.

50. Leo Kanner, 1949.

51. 'The Child is Father', *Time*, 25 July 1960. In later years Kanner would disavow these positions and claim that he had always believed that autism was in some sense an 'innate' disorder.

52. Bruno Bettelheim, 1967 and 1974. After his death in 1990, Bettelheim's reputation came under sustained attack. He was denounced as a vicious and violent child abuser, someone who had falsified his academic background and was a serial liar. The academic community that had surrounded him and supported him were accused of complicity in a reign of terror. For more than three decades, however, he had enjoyed a worldwide reputation as a great clinician and a paragon of humanity.

53. Peter Gay, 1968.

54. Quoted in Andrew Solomon, 2012, p. 22.

55. *The New Yorker* 32, 28 April 1956, p. 34.

56. W. H. Auden, 'In Memory of Sigmund Freud' (1940).

57. Josef Breuer and Sigmund Freud, 1957 [1895], p. 160.

58. It is a great favourite of James Levine and the Metropolitan Opera, who regularly stage Jonathan Miller's production of the score.

59. In the words of the *Guardian*'s theatre critic, Philip Hensher, Auden 'now clearly seems the greatest poet in English since Tennyson'. *Guardian*, 6 November 2009.

60. Hogarth, *Credulity, Superstition and Fanaticism: A Medley* (1762); see p. 175.

61. Donald Mitchell (ed.), 1987, contains an exceptional series of essays on this opera, many of them written

by those who had collaborated with Britten as he composed the score or who were involved in its first staging.

62. Madness stalks through Wagner's later operas, and it is no accident that he named his Bayreuth villa *Wahnfried* ('Freedom from Madness'). In his own words, 'Hier wo mein Wähnen Frieden fand – Wahnfried – sei dieses Haus von mir benannt.' ('Here where my delusions have found peace, let this house be called Freedom from Madness.')

63. The contrast first emerged in the 1920 essay, *Beyond the Pleasure Principle* (Freud, 1922), and was elaborated still further in 1930's *Civilization and Its Discontents* (Freud, 1961). Freud himself did not employ the term *Thanatos*. It was introduced by his disciple Wilhelm Stekel (1868–1940), and has since become the standard way Freudians draw the contrast.

64. See, for example, David Lomas, 2000.

65. See, for example, his letters of 4 December 1921 and 19 February 1924, reprinted in *The Letters of D. H. Lawrence*, 1987, Vol. 4.

66. James Joyce, *Finnegan's Wake*, 1939, pp. 378, 411.

67. *Orpheus Descending* closed on Broadway after only 68 performances.

68. Steven Marcus, 1965.

69. Steven Marcus, 1974.

70. Frederick C. Crews, 1975, p. 4.

71. Frederick C. Crews (ed.), 1998.

72. Norman O. Brown, 1959 and 1966.

73. Philip Rieff, 1959 and 1966.

74. Herbert Marcuse, 1955.

75. Ernest Jones, 1953–57, Vol. 3, p. 114. On one account, Freud's rejection of this munificent sum caused a sensation in New York. Apparently, Freud's well-documented desire for dollars had its limits, or perhaps he realized, as Goldwyn evidently did not, that he was scarcely the Hollywood screenwriter type.

76. Moguls like Samuel Goldwyn and Joseph Mankiewicz sought absolution for their multitude of sins on the analytic couch, though their behaviour seemed not to alter one whit. Directors were equally conspicuous consumers. The list of actors, from Cary Grant to Jason Robards to Montgomery Clift, Judy Garland to Jennifer Jones to Vivien Leigh (not forgetting Marilyn Monroe) seems almost endless. See Stephen Farber and Marc Green, 1993, for some of the sordid details.

77. Joseph Menninger to Karl Menninger, 13 July 1944, in Karl A. Menninger, 1988, p. 402.

78. I owe these references to Stephen Farber and Marc Green, 1993, p. 36.

79. See Edward Dimendberg, 2004.

80. The film was, Huston announced, 'an eighteen-year-old obsession, based on the firm conviction that very few of man's great adventures, not even his travels beyond the earth's horizon, can dwarf Freud's journey into the uncharted depths of the human soul'. John Huston, 'Focus on Freud', *New York Times*, 9 December 1962.

Chapter Twelve: A Psychiatric Revolution?

1. Percy Bysshe Shelley, 'Julian and Maddalo: A Conversation' (1818–19).

2. In fact, many believe they were married, and that Mussolini made a vigorous effort to destroy all evidence.

3. Pilgrim State Hospital on Long Island in New York held the record in the previous decade, with 13,875 inmates and a campus that sprawled across the boundaries of four townships. Nearby Kings Park State Hospital and Central Islip State Hospital contained a further 9,303 and 10,000 patients respectively. At the latter asylum, patients used to arrive on a special train on a spur of the Long Island Railroad, the carriages equipped with bars on the windows to prevent escapes. But New York State began emptying its hospitals earlier than Georgia, allowing the Milledgeville hospital to obtain for a time the dubious privilege of being the world's largest asylum.

4. I am grateful to Akihito Suzuki of Keio University for supplying these figures, which were compiled by Ando Michihito and Goto Motoyuki.

5. E. Landsberg, 2011. See also Hiroto Ito and Lloyd I. Sederer, 1999.

6. The hiding of patients by families in early nineteenth-century Europe was something reformers commented upon at the time, so here too Japanese twentieth-century practices had earlier historical analogues.

7. John Crammer, 1990, pp. 127–28.

8. F. Chapireau, 2009; Marc Masson and Jean-Michel Azorin, 2002.

9. Simon Goodwin, 1997, p. 8.

10. Ministry of Health 1952, p. iv.

11. For reports by the conscientious objectors, see Frank L. Wright (ed.), 1947.

12. H. Orlansky, 1948.

13. Alfred Q. Maisel, 1946.

14. Joint Commission on Mental Illness and Health, 1961, 39.

15. Department of Health and Social Security [England]. 1971.

16. Aubrey Lewis, 1959.

17. Henry Brill and Robert E. Patton, 1957. In both this and subsequent papers, Brill and Patton were never able to show more than a temporal coincidence between the introduction of drug treatment and falling numbers of inpatients.

18. Leon J. Epstein, Richard D. Morgan and Lynn Reynolds, 1962. Contemporaneous studies of data for Washington, DC and Connecticut by other scholars echoed these findings.

19. Andrew Scull, 1977; Paul Lerman, 1982; William Gronfein, 1985; Gerald Grob, 1991.

20. Enoch Powell as reported in National Association for Mental Health (now MIND), *Annual Report*, 1961.

21. Ministry of Health Circular, 1961, quoted in Kathleen Jones, 1972, p. 322.

22. The Governors' Conference, which brought together the state chief executives, commissioned a report which documented the scope of the problems. See Council of State Governments, 1950.

23. In New York State in 1951, one third of the amount spent on state operations went to underwrite the costs of its

mental hospitals, compared with a national average of 8 per cent. Gerald Grob, 1991, p. 161. Southern states spent the least, and were as a rule the slowest to deinstitutionalize.

24. Milton Greenblatt, 1974, p. 8, emphasis in the original.

25. Discharge rates increased by two and a half times in the period between 1964 and 1972 compared with 1960–64, and doubled again between 1972 and 1977.

26. Ivan Belknap, 1956, pp. xi, 212.

27. H. Warren Dunham and S. Kirson Weinberg, 1960. Curiously, the research which this monograph reported had been undertaken more than a dozen years earlier and supported, not by the NIMH, but by Ohio's State Division of Mental Diseases, presumably because of the fiscal burdens its mental hospitals represented, and the controversies then swirling about them. A complete draft of the report on this work was completed by June 1948, and appears largely unaltered as the 1960 publication. Having reported these facts (see pp. 260–61), the authors provide no explanation for the long delay before their book appeared in print.

28. H. Warren Dunham and S. Kirson Weinberg, 1960, pp. xiii, 4.

29. H. Warren Dunham and S. Kirson Weinberg, 1960, p. 248.

30. Erving Goffman, 1961. Other examples of total institutions were prisons and concentration camps, p. 386.

31. Erving Goffman, 1971, Appendix: 'The Insanity of Place', p. 336.

32. Thomas Szasz, 1961.

33. R. D. Laing, 1967, p. 107.

34. R. D. Laing and Aaron Esterson, 1964.

35. Russell Barton, 1965. John K. Wing and George W. Brown, 1970.

36. F. C. Redlich, 'Preface' to William Caudill, 1958, p. xi.

37. Werner Mendel, 1974

38. G. de Girolamo, et al., 2008, p. 968.

39. Marco Piccinelli, et al., 2002; Giovanna Russo and Francesco Carelli, 2009; G. de Girolamo, et al., 2007.

40. G. B. Palermo, 1991.

41. G. de Girolamo et al., 2007, p. 88.

42. Department of Health and Social Security [England], 1971.

43. P. Sedgwick, 1981, p. 9.

44. See the early study by Jacqueline Grad de Alarcon and Peter Sainsbury, 1963; and Clare Creer and John K. Wing, 1974.

45. G. W. Brown, et al., 1966, p. 59. For Italian complaints of this sort, see A. M. Lovell, 1986, p. 807. For the situation in Canada, see E. Lightman, 1986.

46. H. Richard Lamb (ed.), 1984; Richard C. Tessler and Deborah L. Dennis, 1992. For Denmark, see M. Nordentoft, H. Knudsen, and F. Schulsinger, 1992.

47. Peter Sedgwick, 1982, p. 213.

48. Community Care: Agenda for Action: A Report to the Secretary of State 1988. Action, needless to say, was the last thing that was forthcoming.

49. Government Statistical Services Cmnd. 8236, 1981, Annex 2, paragraph 17.

50. See the memorandum from one of Mrs Bottomley's bureaucrats, quoted and discussed in Kathleen Jones, 1993, pp. 251–52. (Virginia Bottomley was British Secretary of State for Health in John Major's Conservative cabinet in the early 1990s.)

51. Mental Health Problems of Prison and Jail Inmates, US Dept. of Justice, Bureau of Justice Statistics, 2006, p. 1.

52. The Economist, 14 May 2009.

53. HM Prison Service, The Mental Health of Prisoners, London: October 2007, p. 5.

54. Thorazine advertisement, in Diseases of the Nervous System 16, 1955, p. 227.

55. Iproniazid had been introduced in 1952 as a treatment for tuberculosis, but it was subsequently observed to stimulate the central nervous system and began to be used as a mood enhancer. It was hypothesized that its therapeutic action in treating psychiatric illness derived from its ability to raise levels of monoamines in the brain by inhibiting their re-absorption. It and related drugs were dubbed monoamine oxidase inhibitors, or MAOIs. They sometimes produced extreme rises in blood pressure and even fatal intracranial haemorrhages, something that was later traced to these drugs' interactions with diet or other medications. Tricyclics are a different class of drugs with a three ring chemical structure – hence their name. Their discovery, too, was largely serendipitous. Their mode of action was different, inhibiting the re-uptake of the neurotransmitters norepinephrine (noradrenaline) and serotonin, and they came with a different set of side effects: sweating, constipation and sometimes mental confusion. Both classes of drugs were replaced in the 1990s by selective serotonin re-uptake inhibitors (SSRIs) such as Prozac, largely on the basis of skilled marketing by the pharmaceutical industry, for the superior efficacy of SSRIs is mythical.

56. Peter Kramer, 1993.

57. Nathan G. Hale Jr, 1998, p. 246.

58. Aaron T. Beck, 1962; Aaron T. Beck, et al., 1962; R. E. Kendell, et al., 1971; R. E. Kendell, 1974.

59. John E. Cooper, Robert E. Kendell, and Barry J. Gurland, 1972. To cite one particularly striking example of their findings, British and American psychiatrists were both shown videotapes of two British patients and invited to diagnose what was wrong with them: 85 and 69 per cent of American psychiatrists diagnosed schizophrenia; 7 and 2 per cent of their British colleagues did so.

60. David Rosenhan, 1973.

61. Bruce J. Ennis and Thomas R. Litwack, 1974.

62. Statistical significance, which is all regulators require, is very different from clinical significance (i.e., the finding that a drug makes a genuine and sizeable difference to patient welfare). The weaker the actual difference produced by a particular therapy, the more necessary it is to employ a large sample size to help to generate statistical significance (i.e., a better than chance 'improvement', however that is measured). That is one reason why large, multi-site trials have become the norm.

63. Ronald Bayer and Robert L. Spitzer, 1985.

64. Stuart A. Kirk and Herb Kutchins, 1992; Herb Kutchins and Stuart A. Kirk, 1999; Allan V. Horwitz, 2002.

65. As its title indicates, DSM III had some predecessors. American psychiatrists had constructed two previous

official diagnostic systems of their own – small pamphlets that appeared successively in 1952 and 1968. Both set up a broad distinction between psychoses and neuroses (roughly speaking, between mental disorders that involved a break with reality, and those that, less seriously, involved a distorted view of reality), and they divided up many of a hundred or so varieties of mental illnesses that were recognized in accordance with their alleged psychodynamic aetiologies. In that respect, they reflected the dominance of psychoanalytic perspectives in post-Second World War American psychiatry. But diagnostic distinctions of the broad, general sort these first two editions set forth were of little significance for most analysts, focused as they were on the individual dynamics of the particular patient they were treating. The first two DSMs were therefore seldom consulted and were seen as little more than paperweights – rather insubstantial ones at that. DSM II was a small, spiral-bound pamphlet running to no more than 134 pages, and encompassing barely a hundred different diagnoses that were listed alongside the most cursory of descriptions. It sold for a mere three dollars and fifty cents, which was more than most professional psychiatrists thought it was worth.

66. Robert Spitzer, 2001, p. 558.

67. Symptomatic of this changed environment was the bankruptcy and closure of what had for decades been leading centres of psychoanalytic treatment of serious forms of mental disorder, Chestnut Lodge in Maryland and the Menninger Clinic in Kansas, once the very launching pad of the psychoanalytic dominance of American psychiatry.

68. For an uncritical view of Lacan and his machinations, authored by an adoring disciple, see Elisabeth Roudinesco, 1990; and for a savage and splendidly amusing assessment of the book and the man it describes, see Raymond Tallis, 1997. See also the final chapter of Sherry Turkle, 1992, for a discussion of the collapse of the Lacanian enterprise into sectarian squabbling.

69. Lacan in fact is reported to have seen an *average* of ten patients an hour in his clinical practice between 1970 and 1980, which means that much of the time he must have cycled through many more than that.

70. Silvano Arieti, 1955. The revised 1974 edition won a National Book Award for science.

71. See, for example, Kim T. Mueser and Howard Berenbaum, 1990. Their conclusion is clearly negative. Surveying attempts to test its effects, they find no evidence that it works, and some suggestion that it actually makes things worse, leading them to assert that 'if a drug had the "efficacy profile" of psychoanalysis it would surely not be prescribed, and no one would have the slightest qualm about relegating it to the "dust bin of history"'. For a dissenting view from a patient who insists that psychoanalysis was the key to rescuing her from madness, see Barbara Taylor, 2014.

72. Nancy Andreassen, 2007.

73. On dopamine and schizophrenia, see Solomon H. Snyder, 1982; Arvid Carlsson, 1988; for serotonin and depression, see Jeffrey R. Lacasse and Jonathan Leo, 2005.

74. See especially the work of the Anglo-Irish psychiatrist David Healy, 1997, 2002 and 2012.

75. Adriana Petryna, Andrew Lakoff and Arthur Kleinman (eds), 2006; Adriana Petryna, 2009.

76. In 2002, prescription drug sales worldwide amounted to approximately $400 billion, with sales in the United States alone accounting for more than half that total. There are ten drug companies in the Fortune 500 list of the largest corporations. That year, the profits of those ten companies ($35.7 billion), exceeded the total profits ($33.7 billion) of the other 490 corporations combined.

77. In the United States, sales of anti-depressants increased from $5.1 billion in 1997 to $12.1 billion in 2004.

78. Steven E. Hyman, 2012.

79. George Crane, 1973.

80. Peter Breggin, 1991.

81. These can include sexual dysfunction, insomnia, agitation and weight loss, among others.

82. NICE, 2010; A. John Rush, et al., 2006. J. C. Fournier, et al., 2010; Irving Kirsch, et al., 2008; J. Horder, P. Matthews and R. Waldmann, 2011; Irving Kirsch, 2010.

83. Steven E. Hyman, 2012.

84. The upshot was a series of Panorama programmes, mostly based upon research by Shelley Joffre, a journalist with no medical training, who dug into the trials and exposed something the producers of Paxil, GlaxoSmithKline, had taken pains to conceal, that this class of drugs produced no benefit to offset the risks they brought in their train. See David Healy, 2012.

85. David Healy, p. 146.

86. E. H. Turner, et al., 2008; C. J. Whittington, et al., 2004.

87. There is the potential for a series of other life-threatening side effects as well, including obstructions of the bowel, seizures, bone marrow depression, heart problems and diabetes.

88. Peter Tyrer and Tim Kendall, 2009. For similar conclusions, see J. A. Lieberman et al., 2005.

89. British estimates are that, depending upon the nature of the serious mental illness, men's lives on average are shortened by between 8 and 14.6 years; women by between 9.8 and 17.5 years. C.-K. Chang, et al., 2011. For the US, the discrepancies between the mentally ill and the general population are considerably higher. See J. Parks, et al. (eds), 2006.

90. For an account of the unfolding controversy, see Gary Greenberg, 2013.

91. Their complaints were, however, met with an *ad hominem* attack from leading American psychiatrists, who claimed Spitzer and Frances were motivated by pique at seeing their creations cast aside, or perhaps, they suggested, even by the loss of royalties the editor-in-chief of DSM IV will suffer when his version of the classificatory system is rendered obsolete. See Alan Schatzberg, et al., 2009.

92. Both quoted in Pam Belluck and Benedict Carey, 2013.

93. Interview with Gary Greenberg, quoted Garry Greenberg 2013, p. 340.

94. Bruce E. Wexler, 2006, pp. 3, 13.

95. Bruce E. Wexler, 2006, p. 16. These paragraphs draw heavily on Wexler's insights.

BIBLIOGRAPHY

Ablard, Jonathan, 2003. 'The Limits of Psychiatric Reform in Argentina, 1890–1946', in Roy Porter and David Wright (eds), *The Confinement of the Insane: International Perspectives, 1800–1965*, Cambridge: Cambridge University Press, 226–47.

Abramson, Harold (ed.), 1951. *Somatic and Psychiatric Treatment of Asthma*, Baltimore: Williams and Wilkins.

Adrian, E. D., and L. R. Yealland, 1917. 'The Treatment of Some Common War Neuroses', *Lancet*, 189, 867–72.

Africanus, Leo, 1896. *The History and Description of Africa Done Into English in the Year 1600 by John Pory, and now edited, with an introduction and notes, by Dr. Robert Brown*, 3 vols, London: Hakluyt Society.

Alexander, Franz, 1933. 'Functional Disturbances of Psychogenic Nature', *Journal of the American Medical Association*, 100, 469–73.

Alexander, Franz, 1943. 'Fundamental Concepts of Psychosomatic Research: Psychogenesis, Conversion, Specificity', *Psychosomatic Medicine*, 5, 205–10.

Alexander, Franz, 1950. *Psychosomatic Medicine*, New York: Norton.

Andreassen, Nancy, 2007. 'DSM and the Death of Phenomenology in America: An Example of Unintended Consequences', *Schizophrenia Bulletin*, 33, 108–12.

Ankarloo, Bengt, and Stuart Clark (eds), 1999. *Witchcraft and Magic in Europe: The Eighteenth and Nineteenth Centuries*, Philadelphia: University of Pennsylvania Press.

Anonymous, 1836–1837. 'Review of *What Asylums Were, Are, and Ought to Be*', *Phrenological Journal*, 10(53), 687–97.

Anonymous, 1857. 'Lunatic Asylums', *Quarterly Review*, 101, 353–93.

Anonymous, 1877. 'Madame Huot's Conference on Vivisection', *The Animal's Defender and Zoophilist*, 7, 110.

Arieti, Silvano, 1955. *The Interpretation of Schizophrenia*, New York: Brunner.

Arieti, Silvano, 1959. *American Handbook of Psychiatry*, 2 vols, New York: Basic Books.

Arnold, William, 1786. *Observations on the Nature, Kinds, Causes, and Prevention of Insanity, Lunacy, or Madness*, 2 vols, Leicester: Robinson and Caddell.

Athanassio, Alex, 1890. *Des Troubles trophiques dans l'hystérie*, Paris: Lescrosnier et Babé.

Bakewell, Thomas, 1805. *The Domestic Guide in Cases of Insanity*, Stafford: For the author.

Bakewell, Thomas, 1815. *A Letter Addressed to the Chairman of the Select Committee of the House of Commons, Appointed to Enquire into the State of Mad-houses*, Stafford: For the author.

Balbo, E. A., 1991. 'Argentine Alienism from 1852–1918', *History of Psychiatry*, 2, 181–92.

Barr, E. S., and R. G. Barry, 1926. 'The Effect of Producing Aseptic Meningitis upon Dementia Praecox', *New York State Journal of Medicine*, 26, 89–92.

Barton, Russell, 1965. *Institutional Neurosis*, 2nd ed., Bristol: J. Wright.

Baum, Emily, 2013. 'Spit, Chains, and Hospital Beds: A History of Madness in Republican Beijing, 1912–1938',

unpublished PhD thesis, University of California, San Diego.

Bayer, Ronald, and Robert L. Spitzer, 1985. 'Neurosis, Psychodynamics, and DSM III', *Archives of General Psychiatry*, 42, 187–96.

Beard, George M., 1880. *A Practical Treatise on Nervous Exhaustion*, New York: E. B. Treat.

Beard, George M., 1881. *American Nervousness; its Causes and Consequences*, New York: G. P. Putnam's Sons.

Beck, Aaron T., 1962. 'Reliability of Psychiatric Diagnoses: 1. A Critique of Systematic Studies', *American Journal of Psychiatry*, 119, 210–16.

Beck, Aaron T., Ward, C. H., Mendelson, M., Mock, J. E., and J. K. Erbaugh, 1962. 'Reliability of Psychiatric Diagnoses: 2. A Study of Consistency of Clinical Judgments and Ratings', *American Journal of Psychiatry*, 119, 351–57.

Beddoes, Thomas, 1802. *Hygeia*, vol. 2, Bristol: J. Mills.

Belcher, William, 1796. *Belcher's Address to Humanity: Containing…a receipt to make a lunatic, and seize his estate*, London: For the author.

Belknap, Ivan, 1956. *Human Problems of a State Mental Hospital*, New York: McGraw-Hill.

Belluck, Pam, and Benedict Carey, 2013. 'Psychiatry's Guide Is Out of Touch with Science, Experts Say', *New York Times*, 6 May.

Berkwitz, Nathaniel J., 1940. 'Faradic Shock in the Treatment of Functional Mental Disorders: Treatment by Excitation Followed by Intravenous Use of Barbiturates', *Archives of Neurology and Psychiatry*, 44, 760–75.

Bernheim, Hippolyte, 1886. *De la Suggestion et de ses applications à la thérapeutique*, Paris: L'Harmattan.

Bettelheim, Bruno, 1967. *The Empty Fortress: Infantile Autism and the Birth of the Self*, New York: Free Press.

Bettelheim, Bruno, 1974. *A Home for the Heart*, New York: Knopf.

Black, William, 1811. *A Dissertation on Insanity*, 2nd ed., London: D. Ridgeway.

Blackmore, Richard, 1726. *A Treatise of the Spleen and Vapours; or, Hypochondriacal and Hysterical Affections*, London: J. Pemberton.

Boerhaave, Hermanni, 1761. *Praelectiones academicae de morbis nervorum*, 2 vols, ed. Jakob Van Eems, Leiden.

Bolton, Joseph Shaw, 1926. 'The Myth of the Unconscious Mind', *Journal of Mental Science*, 72, 25–38.

Boorde, Andrew, 1547. *The Breviary of Helthe*, London: W. Middleton.

Booth, William, 1890. *In Darkest England and the Way Out*, London: Salvation Army.

Boswell, James, 1951. *Boswell's Column*, introduction and notes by Margery Bailey, London: Kimber.

Bourne, Harold, 1953. 'The Insulin Myth', *Lancet*, 262, 964–68.

Bowlby, John, 1951. *Maternal Care and Mental Health*, Geneva: World Health Organization.

Braid, James, 1843. *Neurypnology: or the Rationale of Nervous Sleep Considered in Relation with Animal Magnetism*, London: Churchill.

Brant, Sebastian, 1494. *Daß Narrenschyff ad Narragoniam*, Basel.

Braslow, Joel, 1997. *Mental Ills and Bodily Cures: Psychiatric Treatment in the First Half of the Twentieth Century*, Berkeley and London: University of California Press.

Breggin, Peter, 1991. *Toxic Psychiatry: Why Therapy, Empathy, and Love Must Replace the Drugs, Electroshock, and Biochemical Theories of the "New Psychiatry"*, New York: St Martin's Press.

Breuer, Josef, and Sigmund Freud, 1957. *Studies on Hysteria*, trans. and ed. James Strachey, New York: Basic Books; London: Hogarth Press.

Brigham, Amariah, 1833. *Remarks on the Influence of Mental Cultivation and Mental Excitement upon Health*, Boston: Marsh, Capen & Lyon.

Bright, Timothie, 1586. *A Treatise of Melancholie*, London: Vautrollier.

Brill, Henry, and Robert E. Patton, 1957. 'Analysis of 1955–56 Population Fall in New York State Mental Hospitals in First Year of Large-Scale Use of Tranquilizing Drugs', *American Journal of Psychiatry*, 114, 509–17.

Brown, George W., Bone, Margaret, Dalison, Bridget, and J. K. Wing, 1966. *Schizophrenia and Social Care*, London and New York: Oxford University Press.

Brown, Julie V., 1981. 'The Professionalization of Russian Psychiatry, 1857–1911', unpublished PhD thesis, University of Pennsylvania.

Brown, Norman O., 1959. *Life Against Death: The Psychoanalytical Meaning of History*, Middletown, Conn.: Wesleyan University Press.

Brown, Norman O., 1966. *Love's Body*, New York: Random House.

Brown, Peter, 1971. *The World of Late Antiquity*, London: Thames & Hudson; New York: Harcourt, Brace, Jovanovich.

Brown, Peter, 1972. *Religion and Society in the Age of Saint Augustine*, London: Faber and Faber; New York: Harper & Row.

Brown, Peter, 1981. *The Cult of the Saints: Its Rise and Function in Latin Christianity*, Chicago: University of Chicago Press.

Brown, Peter, 1992. *Power and Persuasion in Late Antiquity: Towards a Christian Empire*, Madison: University of Wisconsin Press.

Brown, Thomas, 1980. '"Living with God's Afflicted": A History of the Provincial Lunatic Asylum at Toronto, 1830–1911', unpublished PhD thesis, Queen's University, Kingston, Ontario.

Brown-Montesano, Kristi, 2007. *Understanding the Women of Mozart's Operas*, Berkeley: University of California Press.

Browne, William A. F., 1837. *What Asylums Were, Are, and Ought to Be*, Edinburgh: A. & C. Black.

Browne, William A. F., 1864. 'The Moral Treatment of the Insane', *Journal of Mental Science*, 10, 309–37.

Brydall, John, 1700. *Non Compos Mentis: or, the Law Relating to Natural Fools, Mad-Folks, and Lunatick Persons*, London: Isaac Cleave.

Bucknill, John C., 1860, 'The President's Address to the Association of Medical Officers of Asylums and Hospitals for the Insane', *Journal of Mental Science*, 7, 1–23.

Burdett, Henry C., 1891. *Hospitals and Asylums of the World*, vol. 2, London: J. & A. Churchill.

Burleigh, Michael, 1994. *Death and Deliverance: 'Euthanasia' in Germany, c. 1900–1945*, Cambridge and New York: Cambridge University Press.

Burney, Fanny, 1854. *Diary and Letters of Madame D'Arblay*, ed. Charlotte F. Barrett, London: Colburn, Hurst and Blackett.

Burnham, John C. (ed.), 2012. *After Freud Left: A Century of Psychoanalysis in America*, Chicago: University of Chicago Press.

Burrows, George Man, 1828. *Commentaries on the Causes, Forms, Symptoms, and Treatment, Moral and Medical, of Insanity*, London: T. & G. Underwood.

Burton, Robert, 1948 [1621]. *The Anatomy of Melancholy*, New York: Tudor.

Butler, Alban, 1799. *The Lives of the Primitive Fathers, Martyrs, and Other Principal Saints*, 12 vols, 3rd ed., Edinburgh: J. Moir.

Bynum, William F., 1974. 'Rationales for Therapy in British Psychiatry, 1780–1835', *Medical History*, 18, 317–34.

Bynum, William F., and Roy Porter (eds), 1993. *Companion Encyclopedia of the History of Medicine*, 2 vols, London: Routledge.

Bynum, William F., Porter, Roy, and Michael Shepherd (eds), 1985–88. *The Anatomy of Madness*, 3 vols, London: Routledge.

Cabanis, Pierre, 1823–25. *Rapports du physique et du moral de l'homme* (1802), reprinted in his posthumous *Oeuvres complètes*, Paris: Bossagen Frères.

Cairns, David, 2006. *Mozart and His Operas*, Berkeley: University of California Press; London: Allen Lane.

Carlsson, Arvid, 1988. 'The Current Status of the Dopamine Hypothesis of Schizophrenia', *Neuropsychopharmacology*, 1, 179–86.

Carroll, Robert S., 1923. 'Aseptic Meningitis in Combating the Dementia Praecox Problem', *New York Medical Journal*, 3 October, 407–11.

Cartledge, Paul, 1997. '"Deep Plays": Theatre as Process in Greek Civic Life', in Patricia E. Easterling (ed.), *The Cambridge Companion to Greek Tragedy*, Cambridge: Cambridge University Press, 3–35.

Castel, Robert, 1988. *The Regulation of Madness: The Origins of Incarceration in France*, Berkeley: University of California Press; Cambridge: Polity.

Caudill, William, 1958. *The Psychiatric Hospital as a Small Society*, Cambridge, Mass.: Harvard University Press.

Chang, C. K., Hayes, R. D., Perera, G., Broadbent, M. T. M., Fernandes, A. C., Lee, W. E., Hotopf, M., and R. Stewart, 2011. 'Life Expectancy at Birth for People with Serious Mental Illness and Other Disorders from a Secondary Mental Health Care Register in London', *PLoS One*, 18 May, 6 (5):e19590. Doi:10.1371/journal.pone.0019590.

Chapireau, F., 2009. 'La mortalité des malades mentaux hospitalisés en France pendant la deuxième guerre mondiale: étude démographique', *L'Encéphale*, 35, 121–28.

Charcot, J.-M., and Gilles de la Tourette, 1892. 'Hypnotism in the Hysterical', in Daniel Hack Tuke (ed.), *A Dictionary of Psychological Medicine*, 2 vols, London: J. & A. Churchill, 606–10.

Cheyne, George, 1733. *The English Malady*, London: G. Strahan.

Clark, Michael, 1988. '"Morbid Introspection", Unsoundness of Mind, and British Psychological Medicine *c*. 1830–*c*. 1900', in William F. Bynum, Roy Porter and Michael Shepherd (eds), *The Anatomy of Madness*, vol. 3, London: Routledge, 71–101.

Clark, Stuart, 1997. *Thinking with Demons: The Idea of Witchcraft in Early Modern Europe*, Oxford: Clarendon Press.

Cobb, Stanley, 1938. 'Review of Neuropsychiatry', *Archives of Internal Medicine*, 62, 883–99.

Coleborne, Catherine, 2001. 'Making "Mad" Populations in Settler Colonies: The Work of Law and Medicine in the Creation of the Colonial Asylum', in Diane Kirkby and Catharine Coleborne (eds), *Law, History, Colonialism: The Reach of Empire*, Manchester: Manchester University Press, 106–24.

Coleborne, Catharine, in press. *Insanity, Identity and Empire*, Manchester: Manchester University Press.

Colton, C. W., and R. W. Manderscheid, 2006. 'Congruencies in Increased Mortality Rates, Years of Potential Life Lost, and Causes of Death Among Public Mental Health Clients in Eight States', *Preventing Chronic Disease*, 3:26, online, PMCID: PMC1563985

Conolly, John, 1830. *An Inquiry Concerning the Indications of Insanity*, London: John Taylor.

Conolly, John, 1847. *The Construction and Government of Lunatic Asylums and Hospitals for the Insane*, London: John Churchill.

Conrad, Lawrence, 1993. 'Arabic-Islamic Medicine', in William F. Bynum and Roy Porter (eds), *Companion Encyclopedia of the History of Medicine*, vol. 1, London: Routledge, 676–727.

Cooper, John E., Kendell, Robert E., and Barry J. Gurland, 1972. *Psychiatric Diagnosis in New York and London: A Comparative Study of Mental Hospital Admissions*, London: Oxford University Press.

Cotta, John, 1612. *A Short Discoverie of the Unobserved Dangers of Several Sorts of Ignorant and Unconsiderate Practisers of Physicke in England*, London: Jones and Boyle.

Cotta, John, 1616. *The Triall of Witch-craft, Shewing the True and Right Methode of the Discovery*, London.

Cotton, Henry A., 1919. 'The Relation of Oral Infection to Mental Diseases', *Journal of Dental Research*, 1, 269–313.

Cotton, Henry A., 1921. *The Defective Delinquent and Insane*, Princeton: Princeton University Press.

Cotton, Henry A., 1923. 'The Relation of Chronic Sepsis to the So-Called Functional Mental Disorders', *Journal of Mental Science*, 69, 434–65.

Council of State Governments, 1950. *The Mental Health Programs of the Forty-Eight States*, Chicago: Council of State Governments.

Cox, Joseph Mason, 1813. *Practical Observations on Insanity*, 3rd ed., London: R. Baldwin and Thomas Underwood.

Crammer, John, 1990. *Asylum History: Buckinghamshire County Pauper Lunatic Asylum – St John's*, London: Gaskell.

Cranach, M. von, 2003. 'The Killing of Psychiatric Patients in Nazi Germany between 1939 and 1945', *The Israel Journal of Psychiatry and Related Sciences*, 40, 8–18.

Crane, George E., 1973. 'Clinical Psychopharmacology in Its Twentieth Year', *Science*, 181, 124–28.

Creer, Clare, and John K. Wing, 1974. *Schizophrenia at Home*, London: Institute of Psychiatry.

Crews, Frederick C., 1975. *Out of My System: Psychoanalysis, Ideology, and Critical Method*, New York: Oxford University Press.

Crews, Frederick C. (ed.), 1998. *Unauthorized Freud: Doubters Confront a Legend*, New York: Viking.

Crichton-Browne, James, 1930. *What the Doctor Thought*, London: E. Benn.

Cruden, Alexander, 1739. *The London-Citizen Exceedingly Injured: Or, a British Inquisition Display'd...Addressed to the Legislature, as Plainly Shewing the Absolute Necessity of Regulating Private Madhouses*, London: Cooper and Dodd.

Daneau, Lambert, 1575. *A Dialogue of Witches*, London: R. Watkins.

Dante Alighieri, 1980. *The Divine Comedy of Dante Alighieri: Inferno*, trans. Allen Mandelbaum, New York: Random House.

Darnton, Robert, 1968. *Mesmerism and the End of the Enlightenment in France*, Cambridge, Mass.: Harvard University Press.

Deacon, Harriet, 2003. 'Insanity, Institutions and Society: The Case of Robben Island Lunatic Asylum, 1846–1910', in Roy Porter and David Wright (eds), *The Confinement of the Insane: International Perspectives, 1800–1965*, Cambridge: Cambridge University Press, 20–53.

Defoe, Daniel, 1728. *Augusta Triumphans: Or, the Way to Make London the Most Flourishing City in the Universe*, London: J. Roberts.

de Girolamo, G., Barale, F., Politi, P., and P. Fusar-Poli, 2008. 'Franco Basaglia, 1924–1980', *American Journal of Psychiatry*, 165, 968.

de Girolamo, G., Bassi, M., Neri, G., Ruggeri, M., Santone, G., and A. Picardi, 2007. 'The Current State of Mental Health Care in Italy: Problems, Perspectives, and Lessons to Learn', *European Archives of Psychiatry and Clinical Neuroscience*, 257, 83–91.

Delgado, Honorio F., 1922. 'The Treatment of Paresis by Inoculation with Malaria', *Journal of Nervous and Mental Disease*, 55, 376–89.

Della Seta, Fabrizio, 2013. *Not Without Madness: Perspectives on Opera*, trans. Mark Weir, Chicago: University of Chicago Press.

Department of Health and Social Security [England], 1971. *Better Services for the Mentally Handicapped*, Cmnd 4683, London: HMSO.

Diamant, Neil, 1993. 'China's "Great Confinement"?: Missionaries, Municipal Elites and Police in the Establishment of Chinese Mental Hospitals', *Republican China*, 19:1, 3–50.

Dicks, H. V., 1970. *Fifty Years of the Tavistock Clinic*, London: Routledge & Kegan Paul.

Dimendberg, Edward, 2004. *Film Noir and the Spaces of Modernity*, Cambridge, Mass. and London: Harvard University Press.

Dix, Dorothea Lynde, 1843. *Memorial to the Legislature of Massachusetts*, Boston: Monroe and Francis.

Dix, Dorothea Lynde, 1845. *Memorial to ... New Jersey*, Trenton: n.p.

Dix, Dorothea Lynde, 1845. *Memorial Soliciting a State Hospital for the Insane, Submitted to the Legislature of Pennsylvania*, Harrisburg: J. M. G. Lescure.

Dix, Dorothea Lynde, 1850. *Memorial Soliciting Adequate Appropriations for the Construction of a State Hospital for the Insane, in the State of Mississippi*, Jackson, Miss.: Fall and Marshall.

Dodds, Eric R., 1951. *The Greeks and the Irrational*, Berkeley: University of California Press.

Dols, Michael W., 1987a. 'Insanity and its Treatment in Islamic Society', *Medical History*, 31, 1–14.

Dols, Michael W., 1987b. 'The Origins of the Islamic Hospital: Myth and Reality', *Bulletin of the History of Medicine*, 61, 367–90.

Dols, Michael W., 1992. *Majnun: The Madman in Medieval Islamic Society*, Oxford: Clarendon Press.

Donkin, Horatio B., 1892. 'Hysteria', in Daniel Hack Tuke (ed.), *A Dictionary of Psychological Medicine*, 2 vols, London: J. & A. Churchill, 618–27.

Doob, Penelope, 1974. *Nebuchadnezzar's Children: Conventions of Madness in Middle English Literature*, New Haven: Yale University Press.

Dowbiggin, Ian, 1985a. 'French Psychiatry, Hereditarianism, and Professional Legitimacy, 1840–1900', *Research in Law, Deviance and Social Control*, 7, 135–65.

Dowbiggin, Ian, 1985b. 'Degeneration and Hereditarianism in French Mental Medicine, 1840–1890 – Psychiatric Theory as Ideological Adaptation', in William F. Bynum, Roy Porter and Michael Shepherd (eds), *The Anatomy of Madness*, vol. 1, London: Tavistock, 188–232.

Driver, J. R., Gammel, J. A., and L. J. Karnosh, 1926. 'Malaria Treatment of Central Nervous System Syphilis. Preliminary Observations', *Journal of the American Medical Association*, 87, 1821–27.

Dunham, H. Warren, and S. Kirson Weinberg, 1960. *The Culture of the State Mental Hospital*, Detroit: Wayne State University Press.

Earle, Pliny, 1868. 'Psychologic Medicine: Its Importance as a Part of the Medical Curriculum', *American Journal of Insanity*, XXIV, 257–80.

Easterling, Patricia E. (ed.), 1997. *The Cambridge Companion to Greek Tragedy*, Cambridge: Cambridge University Press.

Edelstein, Emma J., and Ludwig Edelstein, 1945. *Asclepius: A Collection and Interpretation of the Testimonies*, 2 vols, Baltimore: Johns Hopkins University Press.

Edington, Claire, 2013. 'Going In and Getting Out of the Colonial Asylum: Families and Psychiatric Care in French Indochina', *Comparative Studies in Society and History*, 55, 725–55.

Eichholz, D. E., 1950. 'Galen and His Environment', *Greece and Rome*, 20(59), 60–71.

Elgood, Cyril, 1962. 'Tibb ul-Nabbi or Medicine of the Prophet, Being a Translation of Two Works of the Same Name', *Osiris*, 14, 33–192.

Eliot, T. S., 1932. *Selected Essays*, London: Faber and Faber; New York: Harcourt, Brace.

Ellenberger, Henri F., 1970. *The Discovery of the Unconscious: The History and Evolution of Dynamic Psychiatry*, New York: Basic Books.

Engstrom, Eric J., 2003. *Clinical Psychiatry in Imperial Germany: A History of Psychiatric Practice*, Ithaca: Cornell University Press.

Ennis, Bruce J., and Thomas R. Litwack, 1974. 'Psychiatry and the Presumption of Expertise: Flipping Coins in the Courtroom', *California Law Review*, 62, 693–752.

Epstein, Leon J., Morgan, Richard D., and Lynn Reynolds, 1962. 'An Approach to the Effect of Ataraxic Drugs on Hospital Release Dates', *American Journal of Psychiatry*, 119, 36–47.

Erasmus, Desiderius, 1979 [1511]. *The Praise of Folly*, ed. Clarence Miller, New Haven: Yale University Press.

Ernst, Edzard, 2002. 'Ayurvedic Medicines', *Pharmacoepidemiology and Drug Safety*, 11, 455–56.

Ernst, Waltraud, 1991. *Mad Tales from the Raj: The European Insane in British India, 1800–1858*, London: Routledge.

Ernst, Waltraud, 2013. *Colonialism and Transnational Psychiatry: The Development of an Indian Mental Hospital in British India*, c. *1925–1940*, London: Anthem Press.

Esquirol, J.-É. D., 1805. *Des Passions, considérées comme causes, symptômes et moyens curatifs de l'aliénation mentale*, Paris: Thèse de médecin.

Esquirol, J.-É. D., 1818. 'Maison d'aliénés', *Dictionnaire des sciences médicales*, vol. 30, Paris: Panckoucke, 47–95.

Esquirol, J.-É. D., 1819. *Des Établissments des aliénés en France et des moyens d'améliorer le sort de ces infortunés*, Paris: Huzard.

Esquirol, J.-É. D., 1838. *Des Maladies mentales considérées sous les rapports médical, hygiénique et médico-légal*, 2 vols, Paris: Baillière.

Ewalt, Jack R., Strecker, Edward A., and Franklin G. Ebaugh, 1957. *Practical Clinical Psychiatry*, 8th ed., New York: McGraw-Hill.

Exhibition Catalogue, 1992. *Otto Dix 1891–1969*, London: Tate Gallery.

Fahd, Toufic, 1971. 'Anges, démons et djinns en Islam', *Sources orientales*, 8, 153–214.

Farber, Stephen, and Marc Green, 1993. *Hollywood on the Couch: A Candid Look at the Overheated Love Affair Between Psychiatrists and Moviemakers*, New York: W. Morrow.

Ferenczi, Sándor, 1985. *The Clinical Diary of Sándor Ferenczi*, ed. J. Dupont, Cambridge, Mass.: Harvard University Press.

Feros, Antonio, 2006. *Kingship and Favoritism in the Spain of Philip III, 1598–1621*, Cambridge and New York: Cambridge University Press.

Ferriar, John, 1795. *Medical Histories and Reflections*, vol. 2, London: Cadell and Davies.

Fiamberti, A. M., 1937. 'Proposta di una tecnica operatoria modificata e semplificata per gli interventi alla Moniz sui lobi prefrontali in malati di mente', *Rassegna di Studi Psichiatrici*, 26, 797–805.

Finucane, Ronald C., 1977. *Miracles and Pilgrims: Popular Beliefs in Medieval England*, London: J. M. Dent.

Flaherty, Gloria, 1995. 'The Non-Normal Sciences: Survivals of Renaissance Thought in the Eighteenth Century', in Christopher Fox, Roy Porter and Robert Wokler (eds),

Inventing Human Science: Eighteenth-Century Domains, Berkeley: University of California Press, 271–91.

Fletcher, Richard, 1997. *The Barbarian Conversion: From Paganism to Christianity*, New York: Holt.

Foucault, Michel, 1964. *Madness and Civilization: A History of Insanity in the Age of Reason*, New York: Pantheon; London: Tavistock.

Foucault, Michel, 2006. *History of Madness*, ed. Jean Khalfa, trans. Jonathan Murphy. London: Routledge.

Fournier, J. C., DeRubeis, R. J., Hollon, S. D., Dimidjian, S., and J. D. Amsterdam, 2010. 'Antidepressant Drug Effects and Depression Severity', *Journal of the American Medical Association*, 303, 47–53.

Freeman, Hugh, and German E. Berrios (eds), 1996. *150 Years of British Psychiatry, Vol. 2: The Aftermath*, London: Athlone.

Freud, Sigmund, 1922. *Beyond the Pleasure Principle*, London and Vienna: The International Psycho-Analytical Press.

Freud, Sigmund, 1961. *Civilization and Its Discontents*, trans. and ed. James Strachey, New York: W. W. Norton.

Freud, Sigmund, 1963. *An Autobiographical Study*, trans. James Strachey, New York: W. W. Norton.

Gabbard, Krin, and Glen O. Gabbard, 1987. *Psychiatry and the Cinema*, Chicago: University of Chicago Press.

Gall, Franz, and Johann Spurzheim, 1812. *Anatomie et physiologie du système nerveux en general*, vol. 2, Paris: F. Schoell.

Gardner, Edmund G. (ed.), 2010. *The Dialogues of Saint Gregory the Great*, Merchantville, NJ: Evolution Publishing.

Garton, Stephen, 1988. *Medicine and Madness: A Social History of Insanity in New South Wales, 1880–1940*, Kensington NSW: New South Wales University Press.

Gay, Peter, 1968. 'Review of Bruno Bettelheim, *The Empty Fortress*', *The New Yorker*, 18 May, 160–72.

Gay, Peter, 1988. *Freud: A Life for Our Time*, New York: Norton.

Gerard, Margaret W., 1946. 'Bronchial Asthma in Children', *Nervous Child*, 5, 327–31.

Gifford, George, 1587. *A Discourse of the Subtill Practises of Devilles by Witches and Sorcerers*, London: Cooke.

Gilman, Sander L., 1982. *Seeing the Insane*, New York and London: John Wiley.

Gilman, Sander L., King, Helen, Porter, Roy, Showalter, Elaine, and G. S. Rousseau, 1993. *Hysteria Beyond Freud*, Berkeley: University of California Press.

Girard [de Cailleux], H. 1846, 'Rapports sur le service des aliénés de l'asile de Fains (Meuse), 1842, 1843 et 1844 par M. Renaudin', *Annales médico-psychologiques*, 8, 136–48.

Glanvill, Joseph, 1681. *Sadducismus triumphatus: or, a full and plain evidence concerning witches and apparitions*, London.

Goetz, Christopher G., Bonduelle, Michel, and Toby Gelfand, 1995. *Charcot: Constructing Neurology*, New York and Oxford: Oxford University Press.

Goffman, Erving, 1961. *Asylums: Essays on the Social Situation of Mental Patients and Other Inmates*, Garden City, New York: Anchor Books.

Goffman, Erving, 1971. *Relations in Public: Microstudies of the Public Order*, New York: Basic Books.

Goldstein, Jan, 2001. *Console and Classify: The French Psychiatric Profession in the Nineteenth Century*, rev. ed., Chicago: University of Chicago Press.

Gollaher, David, 1995. *Voice for the Mad: The Life of Dorothea Dix*, New York: Free Press.

Goodell, William, 1881. 'Clinical Notes on the Extirpation of the Ovaries for Insanity', *Transactions of the Medical Society of the State of Pennsylvania*, 13, 638–43.

Goodwin, Simon, 1997. *Comparative Mental Health Policy: From Institutional to Community Care*, London: Sage.

Götz, Aly, Chroust, Peter, and Christian Pross, 1994. *Cleansing the Fatherland: Nazi Medicine and Racial Hygiene*, trans. Belinda Cooper, Baltimore: Johns Hopkins University Press.

Grad de Alarcon, Jacqueline, and Peter Sainsbury, 1963. 'Mental Illness and the Family', *Lancet*, 281, 544–47.

Granville, Joseph Mortimer, 1877. *The Care and Cure of the Insane*, 2 vols, London: Hardwicke and Bogue.

Graves, Thomas C., 1919. 'A Short Note on the Use of Calcium in Excited States', *Journal of Mental Science*, 65, 109.

Gray, John P., 1871. *Insanity: Its Dependence on Physical Disease*, Utica and New York: Roberts.

Green, John R., 1994. *Theatre in Ancient Greek Society*, London: Routledge.

Greenberg, Gary, 2013. *The Book of Woe: The DSM and the Unmaking of Psychiatry*, New York: Blue Rider Press.

Greenblatt, Milton, 1974. 'Historical Factors Affecting the Closing of State Hospitals', in Paul I. Ahmed and Stanley C. Plog (eds), *State Mental Hospitals: What Happens When They Close*, New York and London: Plenum Medical Book Company, 9–20.

Greenslade, William, 1994. *Degeneration, Culture, and the Novel, 1880–1940*, Cambridge: Cambridge University Press.

Greville, Robert F., 1930. *The Diaries of Colonel the Hon. Robert Fulke Greville*, ed. Frank M. Bladon, London: John Lane.

Grinker, Roy S., and John P. Spiegel, 1945. *War Neuroses*, Philadelphia: Blakiston.

Grob, Gerald, 1990. 'World War II and American Psychiatry', *Psychohistory Review*, 19, 41–69.

Grob, Gerald, 1991. *From Asylum to Community: Mental Health Policy in Modern America*, Princeton: Princeton University Press.

Gröger, Helmut, Eberhard, Gabriel, and Siegfried Kasper (eds), 1997. *On the History of Psychiatry in Vienna*, Vienna: Verlag Christian Brandstätter.

Gronfein, William, 1985. 'Psychotropic Drugs and the Origins of Deinstitutionalization', *Social Problems*, 32, 437–54.

Guarnieri, Patrizia, 1994. 'The History of Psychiatry in Italy: A Century of Studies', in Mark S. Micale and Roy Porter (eds), *Discovering the History of Psychiatry*, New York and Oxford: Oxford University Press, 248–59.

Guislain, Joseph, 1826. *Traité sur l'aliénation mentale*, Amsterdam: J. van der Hey.

Gutas, Dimitri, 1998. *Greek Thought, Arabic Culture: The Graeco-Arabic Translation Movement in Baghdad and Early Abbasid Society*, London: Routledge.

Hale, Nathan G. Jr, 1971. *Freud and the Americans: The Beginnings of Psychoanalysis in the United States, 1876–1917*, Oxford: Oxford University Press.

Hale, Nathan G. Jr, 1998. *The Rise and Crisis of Psychoanalysis in the United States: Freud and the Americans, 1917–1985*, New York: Oxford University Press.

Hallaran, William Saunders, 1810. *An Enquiry into the Causes Producing the Extraordinary Addition to the Number of Insane*, Cork: Edwards and Savage.

Hallaran, William Saunders, 1818. *Practical Observations on the Causes and Cure of Insanity*, Cork: Hodges and M'Arthur.

Halliday, Andrew, 1828. *A General View of the Present State of Lunatics, and Lunatic Asylums in Great Britain and Ireland …*, London: Underwood.

Hameed, Hakim A., and A. Bari, 1984. 'The Impact of Ibn Sina's Medical Work in India', *Studies in the History of Medicine*, 8, 1–12.

Harcourt, Countess of, 1880. 'Memoirs of the Years 1788–1789 by Elizabeth, Countess of Harcourt', in Edward W. Harcourt (ed.), *The Harcourt Papers*, vol. 4, Oxford: Parker, 25–28.

Hare, Edward, 1983. 'Was Insanity on the Increase?', *British Journal of Psychiatry*, 142, 439–55.

Harsnett, Samuel, 1599. *A Discovery of the Fraudulent Practises of John Darrel, Bachelor of Artes, In His Proceedings Concerning the Pretended Possession and Dispossession of William Somers…Detecting In Some Sort the Deceitful Trade in These Latter Dayes of Casting Out Deuils*, London: Wolfe.

Harsnett, Samuel, 1603. *A Declaration of Egregious Popish Impostures, To Withdraw the Harts of Her Maiesties Subjects from…the Truth of the Christian Religion…Under the Pretence of Casting out Deuils*, London: Roberts.

Haskell, Ebenezer, 1869. *The Trial of Ebenezer Haskell…*, Philadelphia: For the author.

Haslam, John, 1809. *Observations on Madness and Melancholy*, London: J. Callow.

Haywood, Eliza, 1726. *The Distress'd Orphan, or Love in a Mad-house*, 2nd ed., London: Roberts.

Healy, David, 1997. *The Anti-Depressant Era*, Cambridge, Mass.: Harvard University Press.

Healy, David, 2002. *The Creation of Psychopharmacology*, Cambridge, Mass.: Harvard University Press.

Healy, David, 2008. *Mania: A Short History of Bipolar Disorder*, Baltimore: Johns Hopkins University Press.

Healy, David, 2012. *Pharmaggedon*, Berkeley: University of California Press.

Healy, D., Harris, M., Tranter, R., Gutting, P., Austin, R., Jones-Edwards, G., and A. P. Roberts, 2006. 'Lifetime Suicide Rates in Treated Schizophrenia: 1875–1924 and 1994–1998 Cohorts Compared', *British Journal of Psychiatry* 188, 223–28.

Heartz, Daniel, 1992. *Mozart's Operas*, Berkeley: University of California Press.

Herman, Ellen, 1995. *The Romance of American Psychology: Political Culture in the Age of Experts, 1940–1970*, Berkeley: University of California Press.

Hershkowitz, Debra, 1998. *The Madness of Epic: Reading Insanity from Homer to Statius*, Oxford and New York: Oxford University Press.

Hervey, Nicholas, 'Advocacy or Folly: The Alleged Lunatics' Friend Society, 1845–63', *Medical History*, 30, 1986, pp. 245–75.

Hill, Charles G., 1907. 'Presidential Address: How Can We Best Advance the Study of Psychiatry', *American Journal of Insanity*, 64, 1–8.

Hill, Robert Gardiner, 1839. *Total Abolition of Personal Restraint in the Treatment of the Insane. A Lecture on the Management of Lunatic Asylums*, London: Simpkin, Marshall.

Hippocrates, 1886. *The Genuine Works of Hippocrates*, Vol. 2, ed. Francis Adams, New York: William Wood.

Hippocrates, 1950. *The Medical Works of Hippocrates*, trans. John Chadwick and W. N. Mann, Oxford: Blackwell.

Hoare, Frederick R. (trans. and ed.), 1954. *The Western Fathers*, New York and London: Sheed and Ward.

Hobbes, Thomas, 1968. *Leviathan*, Harmondsworth: Penguin.

Hobbs, A. T., 1924. 'A Survey of American and Canadian Psychiatric Opinion as to Focal Infections (or Chronic Sepsis) as Causative Factors in Functional Psychoses', *Journal of Mental Science*, 70, 542–53.

Horder, J., Matthews, P., and R. Waldmann, 2011. 'Placebo, Prozac, and PLoS: Significant Lessons for Psychopharmacology', *Journal of Psychopharmacology*, 25, 1277–88.

Horwitz, Allan V., 2002. *Creating Mental Illness*, Chicago: University of Chicago Press.

Hume, David, 2007. *A Treatise of Human Nature*, Oxford: Clarendon.

Hunter, Richard, and Ida Macalpine, 1963. *Three Hundred Years of Psychiatry, 1535–1860*, London: Oxford University Press.

Hyman, Steven E., 2012. 'Psychiatric Drug Discovery: Revolution Stalled', *Science Translational Medicine*, 4, 155, 10 October.

Ito, Hiroto, and Lloyd I. Sederer, 1999. 'Mental Health Services Reform in Japan', *Harvard Review of Psychiatry*, 7, 208–15.

Jackson, Stanley W., 1986. *Melancholia and Depression: From Hippocratic Times to Modern Times*, New Haven: Yale University Press.

Joint Commission on Mental Illness and Health, 1961. *Action for Mental Health*, New York: Basic Books.

Jones, Colin, 1980. 'The Treatment of the Insane in Eighteenth- and Early Nineteenth-Century Montpellier', *Medical History*, 24, 371–90.

Jones, Edgar, 2004. 'War and the Practice of Psychotherapy: The UK Experience 1939–1960', *Medical History*, 48, 493–510.

Jones, Edgar, and Simon Wessely, 2001. 'Psychiatric Battle Casualties: An Intra- and Interwar Comparison', *British Journal of Psychiatry*, 178, 242–47.

Jones, Ernest, 1953–57. *The Life and Work of Sigmund Freud*, 3 vols, New York: Basic Books.

Jones, Kathleen, 1972. *A History of the Mental Health Services*, London: Routledge and Kegan Paul.

Jones, Kathleen, 1993. *Asylums and After*, London: Athlone Press.

Jorden, Edward, 1603. *A Briefe Discourse of a Disease Called the Suffocation of the Mother*, London: Windet.

Joyce, James, 1939. *Finnegan's Wake*, New York: Viking.

Kaempffert, Waldemar, 1941. 'Turning the Mind Inside Out', *Saturday Evening Post*, 213, 24 May, 18–74.

Kanner, Leo, 1943. 'Autistic Disturbances of Affective Contact', *Nervous Child*, 2, 217–50.

Kanner, Leo, 1949. 'Problems of Nosology and Psychodynamics of Early Infantile Autism', *American Journal of Orthopsychiatry*, 19, 416–26.

Karcher, Eva, 1987. *Otto Dix*. New York: Crown.

Kardiner, Abram, and Herbert Spiegel, 1947. *War Stress and Neurotic Illness*, New York: Hoeber.

Katzenelbogen, Solomon, 1940. 'A Critical Appraisal of the Shock Therapies in the Major Psychoses and Psychoneuroses, III – Convulsive Therapy', *Psychiatry*, 3, 409–20.

Keller, Richard, 2007. *Colonial Madness: Psychiatry in French North Africa*, Chicago: University of Chicago Press.

Kelly, Henry A., 1985. *The Devil at Baptism: Ritual, Theology and Drama*, Ithaca: Cornell University Press.

Kendell, R. E., 1974. 'The Stability of Psychiatric Diagnoses', *British Journal of Psychiatry*, 124, 352–56.

Kendell, R. E., Cooper, J. E., Gourlay, A. J., Copeland, J. R., Sharpe, L., and B. J. Gurland, 1971. 'Diagnostic Criteria of American and British Psychiatrists', *Archives of General Psychiatry*, 25, 123–30.

Kirk, Stuart A., and Herb Kutchins, 1992. *The Selling of DSM: The Rhetoric of Science in Psychiatry*, New York: Aldine de Gruyter.

Kirsch, Irving, 2010. *The Emperor's New Drugs: Exploding the Antidepressant Myth*, New York: Basic Books.

Kirsch, Irving, Deacon, B. J., Huedo-Medina, T. B., Scoboria, A., Moore, T. J., and B. T. Johnson, 2008. 'Initial Severity and Antidepressant Benefits: A Meta-Analysis of Data Submitted to the Food and Drug Administration', *PLoS Medicine*, 5, 260–68.

Kraepelin, Emil, 1896. *Psychiatrie: Ein Lehrbuch für Studierende und Ärzte*, 5th ed., Leipzig: Barth.

Kramer, Peter D., 1993. *Listening to Prozac*, New York: Viking.

Kühl, Stefan, 1994. *The Nazi Connection: Eugenics, American Racism, and German National Socialism*, New York: Oxford University Press.

Kuriyama, Shigehisa, 1999. *The Expressiveness of the Body and the Divergence of Greek and Chinese Medicine*, New York: Zone Books.

Kutchins, Herb, and Stuart A. Kirk, 1999. *Making Us Crazy: DSM: The Psychiatric Bible and the Creation of Mental Disorders*, New York: Free Press.

Lacasse, Jeffrey R., and Jonathan Leo, 2005. 'Serotonin and Depression: A Disconnect between the Advertisements and the Scientific Literature', *PLoS Medicine*, 2, 1211–16.

Laing, R. D., 1967. *The Politics of Experience*, New York: Ballantine.

Laing, R. D., and Aaron Esterson, 1964. *Sanity, Madness and the Family*, London: Tavistock.

Lamb, H. Richard (ed.), 1984. *The Homeless Mentally Ill*, Washington DC. American Psychiatric Press.

Landsberg, E., 2011. 'Japan's Mental Health Policy: Disaster or Reform?', *Japan Today*, 14 October.

Lantéri-Laura, Georges, 2000. *Histoire de la phrenologie*, Paris: Presses universitaires de France.

Laurentius, A., 1598. *A Discourse of the Preservation of the Sight: of Melancholike Diseases; of Rheumes, and of Old Age*, trans. Richard Surphlet, London: Theodore Samson.

Lawlor, Clark, 2012. *From Melancholia to Prozac: A History of Depression*, Oxford: Oxford University Press.

Lawrence, Christopher, 1985. 'Incommunicable Knowledge: Science, Technology and the Clinical Art in Britain 1850–1914', *Journal of Contemporary History*, 20, 503–20.

Lawrence, D. H., 1987. *The Letters of D. H. Lawrence*, Vol. 4, Warren Roberts, James T. Boulton and Elizabeth Mansfield (eds), Cambridge: Cambridge University Press.

Lawrence, William, 1819. *Lectures on Physiology, Zoology, and the Natural History of Man*, London: J. Callow.

Le Goff, Jacques, 1967. *La civilisation de l'Occident médiéval*, Paris: Arthaud.

Lerman, Paul, 1982. *Deinstitutionalization and the Welfare State*, New Brunswick, NJ: Rutgers University Press.

Lerner, Paul, 2001. 'From Traumatic Neurosis to Male Hysteria: The Decline and Fall of Hermann Oppenheim, 1889–1919', in Mark S. Micale and Paul Lerner (eds), *Traumatic Pasts: History, Psychiatry and Trauma in the Modern Age, 1870–1930*, 140–71. Cambridge: Cambridge University Press.

Lewis, Aubrey, 1959. 'The Impact of Psychotropic Drugs on the Structure, Function and Future of the Psychiatric Services', in P. Bradley, P. Deniker and C. Radouco-Thomas (eds), *Neuropsychopharmacology*, vol. 1, 207–12. Amsterdam: Elsevier.

Lewis, Nolan D. C., Hubbard, Lois D., and Edna G. Dyar, 1924. 'The Malarial Treatment of Paretic Neurosyphilis', *American Journal of Psychiatry*, 4, 175–225.

Lieberman, J. A., Stroup, T. S, McEvoy, J. P., Swartz, M. S., Rosenheck, R. A., Perkins, D. O., Keefe, R. S., Davis, S. M., Davis, C. E., Lebowitz, B. D., Severe, J., and J. K. Hsiao, 2005. 'Effectiveness of Antipsychotic Drugs in Patients with Chronic Schizophrenia', *New England Journal of Medicine*, 353, 1209–23.

Lightman, E., 1986. 'The Impact of Government Economic Restraint on Mental Health Services in Canada', *Canada's Mental Health*, 34, 24–28.

Lloyd, G. E. R., 1979. *Magic, Reason and Experience: Studies in the Origin and Development of Greek Science*, Cambridge and New York: Cambridge University Press.

Lloyd, G. E. R., 2003. *In the Grip of Disease: Studies in the Greek Imagination*, Oxford: Oxford University Press.

Lloyd, Geoffrey, and Nathan Sivin, 2002. *The Way and the Word: Science and Medicine in Early China and Greece*, New Haven: Yale University Press.

Locke, John, 1968. *Educational Writings of John Locke*, ed. James L. Axtell, Cambridge: Cambridge University Press.

Lomas, David, 2000. *The Haunted Self: Surrealism, Psychoanalysis, Subjectivity*, New Haven: Yale University Press.

Lovell, A. M., 1986. 'The Paradoxes of Reform: Re-Evaluating Italy's Mental Health Law of 1978', *Hospital and Community Psychiatry*, 37, 802–08.

Lytton, Rosina Bulwer, 1880. *A Blighted Life: A True Story*, London: London Publishing Office.

Macalpine, Ida, and Richard Hunter, 1969. *George III and the Mad-Business*, London: Allen Lane.

McCulloch, Jock, 1995. *Colonial Psychiatry and 'the African Mind'*, Cambridge: Cambridge University Press.

MacDonald, Michael, 1981. *Mystical Bedlam: Madness, Anxiety, and Healing in Seventeenth-Century England*, Cambridge and New York: Cambridge University Press.

MacDonald, Michael (ed.), 1991. *Witchcraft and Hysteria in Elizabethan London: Edward Jorden and the Mary Glover Case*, London: Routledge.

McDonough, Stephen, 1941. 'Brain Surgery Is Credited with Cure of 50 "Hopelessly" Insane Persons', *Houston Post*, 6 June.

McGuire, William (ed.), 1974. *The Freud/Jung Letters: The Correspondence between Sigmund Freud and C. G. Jung*, Princeton: Princeton University Press.

McKendrick, Neil, Brewer, John, and J. H. Plumb, 1982. *The Birth of a Consumer Society: The Commercialization of Eighteenth-Century England*, Bloomington: Indiana University Press.

MacKenzie, Charlotte, 1985. '"The Life of a Human Football"? Women and Madness in the Era of the New Woman', *The Society for the Social History of Medicine Bulletin*, 36, 37–40.

Mackenzie, Henry, 1771. *The Man of Feeling*, London: Cadell.

Mahone, Sloan, and Megan Vaughan (eds), 2007. *Psychiatry and Empire*, Basingstoke: Palgrave Macmillan.

Maisel, Alfred Q., 1946. 'Bedlam 1946', *Life*, 20, 6 May, 102–18.

Makari, George, 2008. *Revolution in Mind: The Creation of Psychoanalysis*, New York: Harper Collins; London: Duckworth.

Makari, George, 2012. 'Mitteleuropa on the Hudson: On the Struggle for American Psychoanalysis after the Anschluß', in John Burnham (ed.), *After Freud Left: A Century of Psychoanalysis in America*, Chicago: University of Chicago Press, 111–24.

Marcus, Steven, 1965. *Dickens: From Pickwick to Dombey*, New York: Basic Books; London: Chatto & Windus.

Marcus, Steven, 1974. *The Other Victorians: A Study of Sexuality and Pornography in Mid-Nineteenth Century England*, New York: Basic Books; London: Weidenfeld & Nicolson.

Marcuse, Herbert, 1955. *Eros and Civilization: A Philosophical Inquiry into Freud*, Boston: Beacon Press.

Masson, Jeffrey, 1985. *The Assault on Truth*, New York: Penguin.

Masson, Marc, and Jean-Michel Azorin, 2002. 'La surmortalité des malades mentaux à la lumière de l'Histoire', *L'Évolution Psychiatrique*, 67, 465–79.

Maudsley, Henry, 1871. 'Insanity and its Treatment', *Journal of Mental Science*, 17, 311–34.

Maudsley, Henry, 1879. *The Pathology of Mind*, London: Macmillan.

Maudsley, Henry, 1883. *Body and Will*, London: Kegan Paul and Trench.

Maudsley, Henry, 1895. *The Pathology of Mind*, new ed., London and New York: Macmillan.

Mead, Richard, 1751. *Medical Precepts and Cautions*, translated from the Latin by Thomas Stack. London: Brindley.

Meduna, L. von, 1938. 'General Discussion of the Cardiazol [Metrazol] Therapy', *American Journal of Psychiatry*, 94, 40–50.

Meduna, L. von, and Emerick Friedman, 1939. 'The Convulsive-Irritative Therapy of the Psychoses', *Journal of the American Medical Association*, 112, 501–09.

Mendel, Werner, 1974. 'Mental Hospitals', *Where Is My Home*, mimeographed, Scottsdale: NTIS.

Menninger, Karl A., 1988. *The Selected Correspondence of Karl A. Menninger, 1919–1945*, Howard J. Faulkner and Virginia D. Pruitt (eds). New Haven: Yale University Press.

Mercier, Charles, 1914. *A Text-Book of Insanity and Other Nervous Diseases*, 2nd ed., London: George Allen & Unwin.

Mercier, Charles, 1916. 'Psychoanalysis', *British Medical Journal*, 2, 897–900.

Micale, Mark S., and Paul Lerner (eds), 2001. *Traumatic Pasts: History, Psychiatry and Trauma in the Modern Age, 1870–1930*, Cambridge: Cambridge University Press.

Micale, Mark S., and Roy Porter (eds), 1994. *Discovering the History of Psychiatry*, New York and Oxford: Oxford University Press.

Midelfort, H. C. Erik, 1999. *A History of Madness in Sixteenth-Century Germany*, Stanford: Stanford University Press.

Midelfort, Hans C. Erik, 2005. *Exorcism and the Enlightenment: Johann Joseph Gassner and the Demons of Eighteenth-Century Germany*, New Haven: Yale University Press.

Millard, David W., 1996. 'Maxwell Jones and the Therapeutic Community', in Hugh Freeman and German E. Berrios (eds), *150 Years of British Psychiatry Vol. 2: The Aftermath*, London: Athlone, 581–604.

Miller, Timothy S., 1985. *The Birth of the Hospital in the Byzantine Empire*, Baltimore: Johns Hopkins University Press.

Milligan, Spike, 1980. *Mussolini: His Part in My Downfall*, Harmondsworth: Penguin.

Mitchell, Donald (ed.), 1987. *Benjamin Britten: Death in Venice*, Cambridge: Cambridge University Press.

Mitchell, Silas Weir, 1888. *Doctor and Patient*, Philadelphia: J. B. Lippincott.

Mitchell, Silas Weir, 1894. 'Address Before the Fiftieth Annual Meeting of the American Medico-Psychological Association', *Journal of Nervous and Mental Disease*, 21, 413–37.

Mitchell, Silas Weir, 1909. 'Address to the American Neurological Association', *Transactions of the American Neurological Association*, 35, 1–17.

Moniz, Egas, 1936. *Tentatives opératoires dans le traitement de certaines psychoses*, Paris: Masson.

Morison, Alexander, 1825. *Outlines of Lectures on Mental Diseases*, Edinburgh: Lizars.

Moynihan, Berkeley, 1927. 'The Relation of Aberrant Mental States to Organic Disease', *British Medical Journal*, 2, 815–17. [Collected in Addresses on Surgical Subjects, Philadelphia and London: W. B. Saunders, 1928.]

Mueser, Kim T., and Howard Berenbaum, 1990. 'Psychodynamic Treatment of Schizophrenia: Is There a Future?', *Psychological Medicine*, 20, 253–62.

Muir, Kenneth, 1951. 'Samuel Harsnett and King Lear', *Review of English Studies*, 2, 11–21.

Müller, Franz Carl (ed.), 1893. *Handbuch der Neurasthenie*, Leipzig: Vogel.

Munthe, Axel, 1930. *The Story of San Michele*, London: John Murray.

Nasar, Sylvia, 1998. *A Beautiful Mind*, New York: Simon and Schuster; London: Faber.

Newnham, William, 1829. 'Essay on Superstition', *The Christian Observer*, 29, 265–75.

Ng, Vivien W., 1990. *Madness in Late Imperial China: From Illness to Deviance*, Norman: University of Oklahoma Press.

NICE, 2010. *Depression: The NICE Guide on the Treatment and Management of Depression in Adults*, London: Royal College of Psychiatry Publications.

Nizami, 1966. *The Story of Layla and Majnun*, translated from the Persian and edited by R. Gelpke, Oxford: Bruno Cassirer.

Noguchi, Hideyo, and J. W. Moore, 1913. 'A Demonstration of *Treponema pallidum* in the Brain in Cases of General Paralysis', *Journal of Experimental Medicine*, 17, 232–38.

Nordau, Max, 1893. *Entartung*, Berlin: C. Duncker.

Nordentoft, M., Knudsen, H., and F. Schulsinger, 1992. 'Housing Conditions and Residential Needs of Psychiatric Patients in Copenhagen', *Acta Psychiatrica Scandinavica*, 85, 385–89.

Noyes, Arthur P., and Lawrence Kolb, 1935. *Modern Clinical Psychiatry*, Philadelphia: W. B. Saunders.

Nutton, Vivian, 1992. 'Healers in the Medical Marketplace: Towards a Social History of Graeco-Roman Medicine', in Andrew Wear (ed.), *Medicine in Society: Historical Essays*, Cambridge: Cambridge University Press, 15–58.

Oppenheim, Janet, 1991. *"Shattered Nerves": Doctors, Patients, and Depression in Victorian England*, New York and Oxford: Oxford University Press.

Orlansky, Harold, 1948. 'An American Death Camp', *Politics*, 5, 162–68.

Osler, William, 1921. *The Evolution of Modern Medicine: A Series of Lectures Delivered at Yale University on the Silliman Foundation in April 1913*, New Haven: Yale University Press; London: Oxford University Press.

Padel, Ruth, 1992. *In and Out of the Mind: Greek Images of the Tragic Self*, Princeton: Princeton University Press.

Padel, Ruth, 1995. *Whom Gods Destroy: Elements of Greek and Tragic Madness*, Princeton: Princeton University Press.

Paget, George E., 1866. *The Harveian Oration*, Cambridge: Deighton, Bell and Co.

Palermo, G. B., 1991. 'The Italian Mental Health Law – A Personal Evaluation: A Review', *Journal of the Royal Society of Medicine*, 84, 101.

Pargeter, William, 1792. *Observations on Maniacal Disorders*, Reading: For the author.

Paris, Joel, 2005. *The Fall of an Icon: Psychoanalysis and Academic Psychiatry*, Toronto: University of Toronto Press.

Park, Katherine, 1992. 'Medicine and Society in Medieval Europe 500–1500', in Andrew Wear (ed.), *Medicine in Society: Historical Essays*, Cambridge: Cambridge University Press, 59–90.

Parker, Robert, 1983. *Miasma: Pollution and Purification in Early Greek Religion*, Oxford: Clarendon Press.

Parks, Joe, Svendsen, Dale, Singer, Patricia, and Mary Ellen Foti (eds), 2006. *Morbidity and Mortality in People with Serious Mental Illness*, Alexandria, VA: National Association of State Mental Health Program Directors.

Parry-Jones, William Ll., 1972. *The Trade in Lunacy*, London: Routledge.

Parry-Jones, William Ll., 1981. 'The Model of the Geel Lunatic Colony and its Influence on the Nineteenth-Century Asylum System in Britain', in Andrew Scull (ed.), *Madhouses, Mad-Doctors, and Madmen*, Philadelphia: University of Pennsylvania Press, 201–17.

Pattie, Frank, 1979. 'A Mesmer-Paradis Myth Dispelled', *American Journal of Clinical Hypnosis*, 22, 29–31.

Pearson, Veronica, 1991. 'The Development of Modern Psychiatric Services in China, 1891–1949', *History of Psychiatry*, 2, 133–47

Pennington, Hugh, 2003. 'Can You Close Your Eyes Without Falling Over?', *London Review of Books*, 11 September, 30–31.

Perceval, John T., 1838, 1840. *A Narrative of the Treatment Experienced by a Gentleman During a State of Mental Derangement*, 2 vols, London: Effingham, Wilson.

Perry, Ralph B., 1935. *The Thought and Character of William James*, Boston: Little, Brown.

Peschel, Enid, and Richard Peschel, 1992. 'Donizetti and the Music of Mental Derangement: *Anna Bolena, Lucia di Lammermoor*, and the Composer's Neurobiological Illness', *Yale Journal of Biology and Medicine*, 65, 189–200.

Petryna, Adriana, 2009. *When Experiments Travel: Clinical Trials and the Global Search for Human Subjects*, Princeton: Princeton University Press.

Petryna, Adriana, Lakoff, Andrew, and Arthur Kleinman (eds), 2006. *Global Pharmaceuticals: Ethics, Markets, Practices*, Durham, NC: Duke University Press.

Piccinelli, Marco, Politi, Pierluigi, and Francesco Barale, 2002. 'Focus on Psychiatry in Italy', *British Journal of Psychiatry*, 181, 538–44.

Pinel, Philippe, 1801. *Traité médico-philosophique sur l'aliénation mentale ou La manie*, Paris: Richard, Caille et Ravier.

Pinel, Philippe, 1805. 'Recherches sur le traitement générale des femmes aliénées', *Le Moniteur universel*, 281, 30 June, 1158–60.

Pinel, Philippe, 2008 [1809]. *Medico-Philosophical Treatise on Mental Alienation. Second Edition: Entirely Reworked and Extensively Expanded (1809)*, trans. Gordon Hickish, David Healy and Louis C. Charland, Oxford: Wiley, 2008.

Plath, Sylvia, 2005. *The Bell Jar*, New York: Harper.

Plato, 2008. *The Symposium*, ed. Frisbee Sheffield, trans. M. Howatson, Cambridge: Cambridge University Press.

Platter, Felix, Cole, Abdiah, and Nicholas Culpeper, 1662. *A Golden Practice of Physick*, London: Peter Cole.

Plumb, J. H., 1975. 'The New World of Children in Eighteenth Century England', *Past and Present*, 67, 64–95.

Poirier, Suzanne, 1983. 'The Weir Mitchell Rest Cure: Doctor and Patients', *Women's Studies*, 10, 15–40.

Porter, Roy, 1999. 'Witchcraft and Magic in Enlightenment, Romantic and Liberal Thought', in Bengt Ankarloo and Stuart Clark (eds), *Witchcraft and Magic in Europe, Vol. 5: The Eighteenth and Nineteenth Centuries*, Philadelphia: University of Pennsylvania Press, 191–282.

Porter, Roy, and David Wright (eds), 2003. *The Confinement of the Insane: International Perspectives, 1800–1965*, Cambridge: Cambridge University Press.

Pressman, Jack D., 1998. *Last Resort: Psychosurgery and the Limits of Medicine*, Cambridge: Cambridge University Press.

Prichard, James Cowles, 1835. *A Treatise on Insanity, and Other Disorders Affecting the Mind*, London: Sherwood, Gilbert, and Piper.

Prioreschi, Plinio, 2001. *A History of Medicine: Byzantine and Islamic Medicine*, Omaha, Nebraska: Horatius Press.

Proctor, Robert, 1988. *Racial Hygiene: Medicine Under the Nazis*, Cambridge, Mass.: Harvard University Press.

Reade, Charles, 1864. *Hard Cash: A Matter-of-Fact Romance*, Leipzig: Tachnitz.

Rees, T. P., 1957. 'Back to Moral Treatment and Community Care', *British Journal of Psychiatry*, 103, 303–13.

Renooz, Celine, 1888. 'Charcot Dévoilé', *Revue Scientifique des Femmes*, 1, December, 241–47.

Richardson, Samuel, 1741. *Letters Written to and for Particular Friends, on the Most Important Occasions*, London: Rivington.

Rieff, Philip, 1959. *Freud: The Mind of the Moralist*, New York: Viking.

Rieff, Philip, 1966. *The Triumph of the Therapeutic: Uses of Faith After Freud*, New York: Harper and Row.

Rivers, William H. R., 1918. 'An Address On the Repression of War Experience', *Lancet*, 96, 173–77.

Robinson, Michael, 2013. *Time in Western Music*, e-Book: Acorn Independent Press.

Robinson, Nicholas, 1729. *A New System of the Spleen, Vapours, and Hypochondriack Melancholy*, London: Bettesworth, Innys, and Rivington.

Rosen, George, 1968. *Madness in Society: Chapters in the Historical Sociology of Mental Illness*, New York: Harper and Row.

Rosenhan, David, 1973. 'On Being Sane in Insane Places', *Science*, 179, 250–58.

Rosenthal, Franz, 1994. *The Classical Heritage in Islam*, trans. E. and J. Marmorstein, London and New York: Routledge.

Roudebush, Marc, 2001. 'A Battle of Nerves: Hysteria and Its Treatment in France During World War I', in Mark S. Micale and Paul Lerner (eds), *Traumatic Pasts: History, Psychiatry and Trauma in the Modern Age, 1870–1930*, Cambridge: Cambridge University Press, 253–79.

Roudinesco, Elisabeth, 1990. *Jacques Lacan and Co.: A History of Psychoanalysis in France, 1925–1985*, trans. Jeffrey Mehlman, London: Free Association Books.

Rous, E., and A. Clark, 2009. 'Child Psychoanalytic Psychotherapy in the UK National Health Service: An Historical Analysis', *History of Psychiatry*, 20, 442–56.

Rousseau, George, 1993. 'A Strange Pathology: Hysteria in the Early Modern World, 1500–1800', in Sander L. Gilman, Helen King, Roy Porter, Elaine Showalter, and G. S. Rousseau, *Hysteria Beyond Freud*, Berkeley: University of California Press, 91–223.

Runciman, Steven, 1966. *A History of the Crusades*, vol. 3, Cambridge: Cambridge University Press.

Rush, Benjamin, 1947. *The Selected Writings*, ed. Dagobert D. Runes, New York: Philosophical Library.

Rush, Benjamin, 1951. *The Letters of Benjamin Rush*, ed. Lyman H. Butterfield, vol. 2, Princeton: Princeton University Press.

Rush, A. John, Trivedi, M. H., Wisniewski, S. R., Stewart, J. W., Nierenberg, A. A., Thase, M. E., Ritz, L., Biggs, M. M., Warden, D., Luther, J. F., Shores-Wilson, K., Niederehe, G., and M. Fava, 2006. 'Bupropion-SR, Sertraline, or Venlafaxine-XR After Failure of SSRIs for Depression', *New England Journal of Medicine*, 354, 1231–42.

Russo, Giovanna, and Francesco Carelli, 2009. 'Dismantling Asylums: The Italian Job', *London Journal of Primary Care*, 2, April.

Sadger, Isidor, 2005. *Recollecting Freud*, ed. Alan Dundes and trans. Johanna Jacobsen Madison: University of Wisconsin Press. [Originally published as *Sigmund Freud: Persönliche Erinnerungen* in 1929.]

Sadowsky, Jonathan, 1999. *Imperial Bedlam: Institutions of Madness in Colonial Southwest Nigeria*, Berkeley: University of California Press.

Sakel, Manfred, 1937. 'A New Treatment of Schizophrenia', *American Journal of Psychiatry*, 93, 829–41.

Sakel, M. J., 1956. 'The Classical Sakel Shock Treatment: A Reappraisal', in Arthur M. Sackler (ed.), *The Great Physiodynamic Therapies in Psychiatry*, New York: Hoeber-Harper, 13–75.

Sanderson, John B., 1885. 'The Cholera and the Comma-Bacillus', *British Medical Journal*, 1 (1273), 1076–77.

Saper, R. B., Phillips, R. S., Sehgal, A., Khouri, N., Davis, R. B., Paquin, J., Thuppil, V., and S. N. Kales, 2008. 'Lead, Mercury, and Arsenic in US- and Indian-Manufactured Ayurvedic Medicines Sold via the Internet', *Journal of the American Medical Association*, 300, 915–23.

Sassoon, Siegfried, 1936. *Sherston's Progress*, London: Faber and Faber.

Schatzberg, Alan F., Scully, James H., Kupfer, David J., and Darrel A. Regier, 2009. 'Setting the Record Straight: A Response to Frances [sic] Commentary on DSM-V', *Psychiatric Times*, 1 July.

Scheflin, Alan W., and Edward Opton Jr, 1978. *The Mind Manipulators*, New York: Paddington.

Scull, Andrew, 1977. *Decarceration: Community Treatment and the Deviant: A Radical View*, Englewood Cliffs, NJ: Prentice-Hall.

Scull, Andrew (ed.), 1981a. *Madhouses, Mad-Doctors, and Madmen: The Social History of Psychiatry in the Victorian Era*, Philadelphia: University of Pennsylvania Press.

Scull, Andrew, 1981b. 'The Discovery of the Asylum Revisited: Lunacy Reform in the New American Republic', in Andrew Scull (ed.) *Madhouses, Mad-doctors, and Madmen: The Social History of Psychiatry in the Victorian Era*, Philadelphia: University of Pennsylvania Press, 144–65.

Scull, Andrew, 1984. 'Was Insanity Increasing? A Response to Edward Hare', *British Journal of Psychiatry*, 144, 432–36.

Scull, Andrew, 2005. *Madhouse: A Tragic Tale of Megalomania and Modern Medicine*, London and New Haven: Yale University Press.

Scull, Andrew, 2011. *Hysteria: The Disturbing History*, Oxford: Oxford University Press.

Scull, Andrew, MacKenzie, Charlotte, and Nicholas Hervey, 1996. *Masters of Bedlam: The Transformation of the Mad-Doctoring Trade*, Princeton: Princeton University Press.

Seaver, Paul S., 1988. *Wallington's World: A Puritan Artisan in Seventeenth-Century London*, Palo Alto: Stanford University Press.

Sedgwick, Peter, 1981. 'Psychiatry and Liberation', unpublished paper, Leeds University.

Sedgwick, Peter, 1982. *Psychopolitics*, London: Pluto Press.

Shephard, Ben, 2000. *A War of Nerves: Soldiers and Psychiatrists in the Twentieth Century*, London: Jonathan Cape; Cambridge, Mass.: Harvard University Press.

Shepherd, Michael, 1994. 'Neurolepsis and the Psychopharmacological Revolution: Myth and Reality', *History of Psychiatry*, 5, 89–96.

Shorter, Edward, 1990. 'Private Clinics in Central Europe, 1850–1933', *Social History of Medicine*, 3, 159–95.

Shorter, Edward, 1997. *A History of Psychiatry*, New York: Wiley.

Shorter, Edward, and David Healy, 2007. *Shock Treatment: A History of Electroconvulsive Treatment in Mental Illness*, New Brunswick: Rutgers University Press.

Showalter, Elaine, 1985. *The Female Malady*, New York: Pantheon.

Simonis, Fabien, 2010. 'Mad Acts, Mad Speech, and Mad People in Late Imperial Chinese Law and Medicine', unpublished PhD thesis, Princeton University.

Slack, Paul, 1985. *The Impact of Plague in Tudor and Stuart England*, London and Boston: Routledge & Kegan Paul.

Smyth, Margaret H., 1938. 'Psychiatric History and Development in California', *American Journal of Psychiatry*, 94, 1223–36.

Snape, Andrew, 1718. *A Sermon Preach'd before the Right Honourable the Lord-Mayor...and Gouvenors of the Several Hospitals of the City of London*, London: Bowyer.

Snyder, Solomon H., 1982. 'Schizophrenia', *Lancet*, 320, 970–74.

Solomon, Andrew, 2012. *Far From the Tree: Parents, Children and the Search for Identity*, New York: Simon & Shuster; London: Chatto and Windus.

Southern, Richard, 1953. *The Making of the Middle Ages*, New Haven: Yale University Press; London: Hutchinson.

Spitzer, Robert L., 2001. 'Values and Assumptions in the Development of DSM-III and DSM-IIIR', *Journal of Nervous and Mental Disease*, 189, 351–59.

Spitzka, Edward, 1878. 'Reform in the Scientific Study of Psychiatry', *Journal of Nervous and Mental Disease*, 5, 201–29.

Spurzheim, Johann, 1813. *Observations on the Deranged Manifestations of Mind, or Insanity*, London: Baldwin, Craddock and Joy.

Stevenson, Christine, 2000. *Medicine and Magnificence: British Hospital and Asylum Architecture, 1660–1815*, New Haven: Yale University Press.

Stiles, Anne, 'The Rest Cure, 1873–1925', *BRANCH: Britain, Representation and Nineteenth-Century History*. Ed. Dino Franco Felluga. Extension of *Romanticism and Victorianism on the Net*. 2 November 2012. Web page accessed 9 September 2013.

Strahan, S. A. K., 1890. 'The Propagation of Insanity and Allied Neuroses', *Journal of Mental Science*, 36, 325–38.

Strickmann, Michel, 2002. *Chinese Magical Medicine*, Palo Alto: Stanford University Press.

Sulman, A. Michael, 1973. 'The Humanization of the American Child: Benjamin Spock as a Popularizer of Psychoanalytic Thought', *Journal of the History of the Behavioral Sciences*, 9, 258–65.

Suzuki, Akihito, 2003. 'The State, Family, and the Insane in Japan, 1900–1945', in Roy Porter and David Wright (eds), *The Confinement of the Insane: International Perspectives, 1800-1965*, Cambridge: Cambridge University Press, 193–225.

Suzuki, Akihito, 2006. *Madness At Home: The Psychiatrist, the Patient, and the Family in England, 1820–1860*, Berkeley: University of California Press.

Swain, Gladys, 1977. *Le sujet de la folie: Naissance de la psychiatrie*, Toulouse: Privat.

Sydenham, Thomas, 1742. *The Entire Works of Dr Thomas Sydenham, Newly Made English from the Originals*, ed. John Swan, London: Cave.

Szasz, Thomas, 1961. *The Myth of Mental Illness*, New York: Harper and Row.

Talbott, J. H., and K. J. Tillotson, 1941. 'The Effects of Cold on Mental Disorders', *Diseases of the Nervous System*, 2, 116–26.

Tallis, Raymond, 1997. 'The Shrink from Hell', *Times Higher Education Supplement*, 31 October, 20.

Targa, Leonardo (ed.), 1831. *Aur. Cor. Celsus on Medicine*, trans. A. Lee, vol. 1, London: Cox.

Taylor, Barbara, 2014. *The Last Asylum: A Memoir of Madness in Our Times*, London: Hamish Hamilton.

Taylor, Michael A., 2013. *Hippocrates Cried: The Decline of American Psychiatry*, New York: Oxford University Press.

Temkin, Oswei, 1994. *The Falling Sickness: A History of Epilepsy from the Greeks to the Beginnings of Modern Neurology*, Baltimore: Johns Hopkins University Press.

Tenon, Jacques, 1778. *Mémoires sur les hôpitaux de Paris*, Paris: Pierres.

Tessler, Richard C., and Deborah L. Dennis, 1992. 'Mental Illness Among Homeless Adults', in James R. Greenley and Philip J. Leaf (eds), *Research in Community and Mental Health*, 7, Greenwich, Conn.: JAI Press, 3–53.

Tonnini, Silvio, 1892. 'Italy, Historical Notes upon the Treatment of the Insane in', in Daniel Hack Tuke (ed.), *A Dictionary of Psychological Medicine*, 2 vols, London: J. & A. Churchill, 715–20.

Torrey, Edwin Fuller, 2002. *The Invisible Plague: The Rise of Mental Illness from 1750 to the Present*, New Brunswick, NJ: Rutgers University Press.

Tuke, Daniel Hack, 1878. *Insanity in Ancient and Modern Life*, London: Macmillan.

Tuke, Daniel Hack (ed.), 1892. *A Dictionary of Psychological Medicine*, 2 vols, London: J. & A. Churchill.

Tuke, Samuel, 1813. *Description of the Retreat: An Institution near York for Insane Persons of the Society of Friends*, York: Alexander.

Turkle, Sherry, 1992. *Psychoanalytic Politics*, 2nd ed., London: Free Association Books.

Turner, E. H., Matthews, A. M., Linardatos, E., Tell, R. A., and R. Rosenthal, 2008. 'Selective Publication of Antidepressant Trials and Its Influence on Apparent Efficacy', *New England Journal of Medicine*, 358, 252–60.

Twain, Mark, 2013. *The Autobiography of Mark Twain*, vol. 2, ed. Benjamin Griffin and Harriet Elinor Smith, Berkeley: University of California Press.

Tyrer, Peter, and Tim Kendall, 2009. 'The Spurious Advance of Antipsychotic Drug Therapy', *Lancet*, 373, 4–5.

Ullmann, Manfred, 1978. *Islamic Medicine*, trans. Jean Watt, Edinburgh: Edinburgh University Press.

Unschuld, Paul D., 1985. *Medicine in China: A History of Ideas*, Berkeley: University of California Press.

US Public Health Service, 1941. *Shock Therapy Survey*, Washington, D.C.: Government Printing Office.

Uwins, David, 1833. *A Treatise on Those Disorders of the Brain and Nervous System, Which Are Usually Considered and Called Mental*, London: Renshaw and Rush.

Valenstein, Elliot, 1985. *Great and Desperate Cures: The Rise and Decline of Psychosurgery and Other Radical Treatments for Mental Illness*, New York: Basic Books.

Veith, Ilza, 1970. *Hysteria: The History of a Disease*, Chicago: University of Chicago Press.

Wagner-Jauregg, Julius, 1946. 'The History of the Malaria Treatment of General Paralysis', *American Journal of Psychiatry*, 102, 577–82.

Wakefield, Edward, 1814. 'Extracts from the Report of the Committee Employed to Visit Houses and Hospitals for the Confinement of Insane Persons. With Remarks. By Philanthropus', *The Medical and Physical Journal*, 32, 122–28.

Watt, W. Montgomery, 1972. *The Influence of Islam on Medieval Europe*, Edinburgh: Edinburgh University Press.

Wear, Andrew (ed.), 1992. *Medicine in Society: Historical Essays*, Cambridge: Cambridge University Press.

Weiner, Dora, 1994. '"Le geste de Pinel": The History of a Psychiatric Myth', in Mark S. Micale and Roy Porter (eds), *Discovering the History of Psychiatry*, New York and Oxford: Oxford University Press, 232–47.

Wesley, John, 1906. *The Journal of John Wesley*, ed. Ernest Rhys, London: Everyman.

Wexler, Bruce E., 2006. *Brain and Culture: Neurobiology, Ideology, and Social Change*, Cambridge, Mass., and London: MIT Press.

Whittington, C. J., Kendall, T., Fonagy, P., Cottrell, D., Cotgrove, A., and E. Boddington, 2004. 'Selective Serotonin Reuptake Inhibitors in Childhood Depression: Systematic Review of Published Versus Unpublished Data', *Lancet*, 363, 1341–45.

Willis, Thomas, 1674. *Cerebri anatome*, London: Jo. Martyn.

Willis, Thomas, 1681. *An Essay of the Pathology of the Brain and Nervous Stock*, trans. Samuel Pordage, London: Dring, Harper and Leigh.

Willis, Thomas, 1683. *Two Discourses Concerning the Soul of Brutes...*, trans. Samuel Pordage, London: Dring, Harper and Leigh.

Willis, Thomas, 1684. *The Practice of Physick*, trans. Samuel Pordage, London: Dring, Haper, Leigh and Martyn. [Translation of *Cerebri anatome*.]

Wing, John K., and George W. Brown, 1970. *Institutionalism and Schizophrenia; A Comparative Study of Three Mental Hospitals 1960–1968*, Cambridge: Cambridge University Press.

Winnicott, Donald, 1964. *The Child, the Family and the Outside World*, London: Penguin.

Winter, Alison, 1998. *Mesmerized: Powers of Mind in Victorian Britain*, Chicago: University of Chicago Press.

Wise, Sarah, 2012. *Inconvenient People: Lunacy, Liberty and the Mad Doctors in Victorian England*, London: Bodley Head.

Wright, Frank L. (ed.), 1947. *Out of Sight, Out of Mind*, Philadelphia: National Mental Health Foundation.

Wujastyk, Dominik, 1993. 'Indian Medicine', in William F. Bynum and Roy Porter (eds), *Companion Encyclopedia of the History of Medicine*, vol. 1, London: Routledge, 755–78.

Wynter, Andrew, 1875. *The Borderlands of Insanity*, London: Hardwicke.

Wynter, Andrew, 1877. *The Borderlands of Insanity*, 2nd ed., London: Hardwicke.

SOURCES OF ILLUSTRATIONS

INDEX

Page numbers in *italic* refer to captions to illustrations in the text; numbers in **bold** refer to colour plate numbers

Abraham, Karl 326
Achilles 21, 22
acupuncture 43, *44*
Addington: Anthony 134, 135; Henry 135
ADHD *see* hyperactivity
admissions: banning of 374; certificate of *359*; rise in 273; tertiary syphilis and 15, 218, 301; in wartime 338
Adrian, Edgar 298
aetiology: of GPI 218, 302; of mental illness 154, 167, 224, 228, 260, 263, 277, 402, 285, 305, 306, 407; bacterial origins 305, 306, 307, 319; medical or religious 80–85, 86–87, 88, 89–91, 92, 94–95, 96, 97–98, 99, 107–08; as mystery 16, 409; viral origins 273
Africa, and Western psychiatry 199, 200, 290, 322
agranulocytosis 405
Albrecht, Adelbert 329
alcoholism 246, 247, 259
Alexander, Franz 343
Alexander, Henry 191
Alexander the Great 36, 50
alienism 12, 190, 192–93, 214, 216, 217, 229; and asylums 220, 221, 222, 223; embrace of the body 211–12, 217; and GPI 218; origins of term 419n77; struggles of 208–12, 221, 223, 229, 230, 231, 238–39, 240, 242, 260, 420n44
Alleged Lunatics' Friend Society 240
Allah 68
al-Majusi 47
al-Razi *see* Rhazes
alternative medicine 47
Alzheimer, Alois 263, 305
Alzheimer's disease 263, 305
American Civil War 274, 292, 324, 420n17
American Journal of Psychiatry 220, 391
American Psychiatric Association 390; and standardization of diagnoses 387–88
American psychiatry: post-Second World War expansion of 338–39, 340, 383–84; and psychoanalysis 340, 341, 351, 379, 380, 381, 426–27n65, 427n67; worldwide hegemony of 389, 401
American Revolution 224, 226–27, 330
Am Steinhof 260
Amsterdam 120, 124, *126*, 155; **19**
anatomy 33, 153
Anatomy of Melancholy 93, 94, 95; *see also* Burton, Robert
Andreasen, Nancy 391
Angel at My Table, An 320
animal magnetism 181, 182; discrediting of 186–87; *see also* mesmerism
Anna O. *see* Pappenheim, Bertha
Anne, Queen (England) 164, 166
anorexia 273
anti-anxiety drugs 402
antibiotics 401
anti-convulsant drugs 402
anti-depressant drugs 382, 383, 402, 404; and children 404; side effects 400, 403, 404, 426n55

anti-psychotic drugs 380–84, 402, 403, 404, 405; atypical 405; marketing of 401; side effects of 402, 403, 404, 405; *see also* phenothiazines, *and* Thorazine
anti-psychiatry 309, 318, 351, 374
anti-semitism 248, 310
anxiety 383
Arab civilization 49, 50–51, 52, 54; influence on Western Europe 52, 81–84, 85; toleration of Jews and Christians 50–51, 53; *see also* Islam
Arabic medicine *see* Islamic medicine
Arabic numerals 52, 81
Aretaeus 29
Argentina 200, 322, 325
Arieti, Silvano 391
Ariosto, Ludovico 109
Arles 234; **33**
artists in asylums 233
Asclepius 31, 72
Astaire, Fred 354
asthma 343, 402
asthmatogenic mothers 343
astrology 30, 96, 415n25; **15, 25**
asylums: admission to 232; architecture of 136–38, 222; attractions of 222, 223; avoidance of 268, 269; as birthplace of psychiatry 220, 222; and civilization 198, 201; as curative 222; as death camps 365; decay of 361–62, *363*; **42**; declining reputation of 223, 229, demise of 367, 368, 369–70; developing medical control of 217; eighteenth-century 136, 137, 138, 237–38; growing size of 222, 223, 233, 259, 260, 261, 272–73; nineteenth-century embrace of 189, 190,192–99; as nurseries of madness 231, 371–72, 373–74, 420n9; overcrowding of 231; pessimism about 229, 230, 231; as quarantining the insane 244, 245, 246; in seventeenth century 122, 123; utopian expectations for 198–99, 204–05, 206–07, 230
asylum superintendents 12, 203, 206, 210, 214, 221, 222–23, 227, 276, 374; patients' views of 233
Athens 22, 23, 26, 37
attendants, asylum 231, 239–40
Auden, W. H. 345, 346, 383
Austin Riggs Mental Hospital 341
Australia 199, 270, 322
Austria 137, 174, 176, 180, 190, 193, 194, 248, 260, 283, 284, 296, 297, 310, 324, 325, 326, 334, 421n13
autism 273, 343, 344, 407, 424n51
Avicenna 47, 54, 65, 66, 82, *83*, 84, 91, 415n14; **7**
Ayurvedic medicine 45, 46, 47
Awl, William 206–07

bacteriological revolution 304, 309
Baden 195, 271, 272
Baghdad 51, 52, 54
Bakewell, Thomas 160
Balzac, Honoré de 246
baquet (Mesmer's tub) *184*, 185, 222
barbiturates 308, 379
barred windows 130, 138, 203, 238, 425n3
Barton, Russell 374
Basaglia, Franco 374; Basaglia Law, the 374
Battie, Sir William 134

Battle Creek Sanatarium *271*, 272, 307, 328; **36**
Baudelaire, Charles 258
Bayle, Antoine 217, 218
Beard, George M. 273, 275
Beauclerk, Charles de Vere 270
Becket, Thomas à 74, 414n59; **9**
Beckmann, Max 292, 293, 395; **37**
Bedlam 84, 85, 106, 113, 114, 121, 154, 171, 172, 210, 211, 346; **1**, *32*; and criminal insane 234; in fiction 144; and Hogarth 130, *131*; at Moorfields 122, 136, **22**; nineteenth-century scandals at 192; photography at 233; on the stage 106, 346; **40**
Bejing asylum 202, *323*
Belcher, William 139
Belknap, Ivan 371
Bell, Luther 222
Bell Jar, The 318–19
benzodiazapines 383
Berlin 248, 309, 343; Charité hospital 159; psychiatric clinics 262; psychoanalytic institute 333
Bernays, Edward 325
Bernheim, Hippolyte 283, 284
Bête humaine, La 247–48
Bethlehem/Bethlem Hospital *see* Bedlam
Bettelheim, Bruno 344, 424n52
Bicêtre, Paris 161, 204, 416n6
Bielefeld asylum 260
Binding, Karl 266
Bini, Lucio 311–12, *313*
biobabble 410
biological basis of mental illness 210, 211, 260, 263, 302, 305, 306, 307, 387, 392, 406, 411
biological reductionism 211, 246, 247, 303, 380, 387, 390, 406, 410–11
bipolar disorder 15, 273, 402; juvenile 407
black bile 56, 65, 91, 94, 114
Black Death 70
Blackmore, Sir Richard 164, 171, 172, 179
Bleak House 239, 419n27
Bleuler, Eugen 265, 303, 326
blindness 74, 177, 182–83, 184; hysterical 293, 296, 297
blood-letting 28, *30*, 66, 68, 74, 92, 94, 96, 171, 208, 302, 412n48
Bloomingdale Asylum 204, 209, 210
board and care homes 375, 376, 377
Boerhaave, Hermann 155, 173
Boer War 292
Bonaparte, Napoleon 136, 195, 196, 258, 416n6, 419n75
Bonhöffer, Karl 297
Boorde, Andrew 91, 95
Booth, William 259
Bosch, Hieronymus 121, 149; **20**
Boston 196, 204, 329, 330
Boswell, James 170
Bowlby, John 342
Braid, James 278
brain: diseases of 277, *307*; injuries to 274; localization of functions 213; **30**; and mental illness 33–34, 91, 92, 95,166, 167, 168, 171, 188, 189, 211, 212, 216, 217, 218, 245, 262, 263, 392, 401, 407, 409; as organ of mind 212; plasticity of 410; research on physiology of 216, 263, 409
Breugel, Pieter (the Elder) 113, *411*

Breuer, Josef 284, 285, 286, 287, 326, 345, 421n31
Brigham, Amariah 214, 220
Bright, Timothie 92, 95, 415n14, 415n22
Brill, Henry 369
Brislington House 161, 239
Bristol-Meyers Squibb 402
Britain 144, 159, 190, 199, 201, 211, 214, 220, 295, 298, 307, 315, 317, 335, 337, 339, 342, 360, 369, 386; and deinstitutionalization 362, 369, 375, 377–78; and psychoanalysis 325, 327, 390–91; *see also* England, Scotland
British Medical Association 307, 327
Britten, Benamin 346, 347
bromides 379
Brontë, Charlotte 142
Brown, George 374
Brown, Norman O. 350–51
Brown, Peter 46
Browne, William Alexander Francis 204, 207, 208, 212, 214, 230
Brydall, John 153
Bucknill, John Charles 13, 231
Buck v Bell 266
Bulwer Lytton *see* Lytton
Burghölzli hospital 326
Burroughs Wellcome 335
Burton, Robert 92, 93, 94, 95
Byberry State Hospital 365, 366
Byron, Lord George Gordon 194, 258
Byzantium 48–49, 50, 65, 67

Cabanis, Pierre 211
Cabinet of Dr Caligari, The 351, 352
Cade, John 379
Cairo 51, 65
California: and involuntary sterilization 266; and mental hospitals 370
Caligula (Roman emperor) 102
Callot, Jacques 90
Calvinists 120, 139, 198; 19
Cambyses II (King of Persia) 24–25
Campanella, Tommaso 101, 415n36
camphor 311
Campion, Jane 320
Canada 199, 337
Canon of Medicine (Avicenna) 54–55, 83, 415n14; 7
Canterbury Cathedral 74; 12–14
Cape Colony 199
Carpenter, William 216
Carefree 354
case notes 232, 233
cathartic cure 286, 287
Catholic Church 70, 72, 86, 116, 117, 177, 179; and exorcism 100; and witches 87, 88, 89
Celsus 29
Central Islip State Hospital 260, 376, 425n3
Central State Hospital, Milledgeville 260, 361–62, 425n3
cerebral palsy 283
Cerletti, Ugo 311–12, 312
certification of insanity 232, 237–38
Cervantes 36, 110
cervix, as site of infection 306
chains 20, 65, 93, 97, 113, 114, 128, 130, 138, 191, 205, 414n25; abolition of 202, 205–06
Changeling, The 106

Charcot, Jean-Martin 279, 295, 327, 412n17; 30; criticisms of 280, 283; and hypnosis 278, 280, 281, 284; and hysteria 277, 278, 280, 281, 283, 284
Charenton 128, 209, 217, 218, 416n6
Chateau de Vincennes 128
Chestnut Lodge Mental Hospital 341, 344, 347; bankruptcy of 427n67
Cheyne, George 162, 163, 166, 168, 169, 169, 170, 171, 179, 273
Chiarugi, Vincenzo 194
child-rearing, changes in 160; and Dr Spock 341, 342; and psychoanalysis 342
child psychiatry 342, 343
chilling, artificial 309
China 36–37, 38, 45–46, 52, 173; and asylums 201, 322, 323, 423n3
Chinese medicine 38–39, 40–42, 43, 46, 322, 413n59; and madness 413n61, chloral hydrate 379
chlorpromazine 367, 369, 380, 405; *see also* anti-psychotic drugs; Thorazine
cholera 304
Christianity 21, 36, 67, 89, 123, 174, 212; early spread of 67, 71, 100; evangelical 239; and healing 53; and hospitals 65; and intolerance 71, 81; persecution of 70–71, 73, 75; and positive views of madness 36, 115, 116; and Roman empire 70–71; sin and illness 82–83
Christian Science 328–29
chronic patients 223, 229, 232, 273
Church of Jesus Christ of Latter-day Saints *see* Mormons
Cibber, Caius Gabriel 122, 124
Cid, Sobral 314
civilization: and madness 168–70, 224, 226–27, 228, 244, 245, 265, 288–89; and neurasthenia 274–75; and psychoanalysis 288–89, 332, 333
Clare, John 236–37, 419n24
Clark University 328, 329, 330–31, 333, 423n11
Claybury County Asylum 260, 261
Cleomenes (King of Sparta) 24–25, 26
clinical trials 386–87, 401, 404, 405, 426n62
clozapine 405
Cobb, Stanley 312
cognitive-behavioural therapy (CBT) 380
colectomies 308, 422n31
Colijns, David 120; 19
Collins, Wilkie 187, 268, 278
Colney Hatch Asylum 259, 260, 360, 361
colons, and mental illness 306, 307
combat exhaustion 336, 337, 338
commitment laws 240
common sense 412,n1
community care, failings of 375, 376–78
Conolly, John 206, 212, 214, 238, 242, 419n26
Conques, abbey of 73; 10
conscientious objectors, and mental hospitals 365, 366
Constantinople 46, 48, 49, 51, 53, 54; sack of 49–50, 73
consumer society, birth of 129, 130
Cooper, John 386
Coriat, Isador 333
costs of institutionalization 363, 425–26n23
Cotta, John 98

Cotton, Henry 305–08, 307, 362, 422n29; and Lister, 422n30
Coulmier, François Simonet de 209
Counter-Reformation 86, 116, 119, 120; 18
Cox, Joseph Mason 134, 156–57, 158, 159, 417n41
Craiglockhart military hospital 296; 37
Credulity, Superstition and Fanaticism 175, 176–77
Crews, Frederick 350
crime, and degeneracy 245
Crichton Royal Asylum 230, 231
Crichton-Browne, Sir James 233, 327, 423n4
Crichton-Miller, Hugh 327
Cruden, Alexander 139
cupping 74, 92, 94
cure rates, claimed 206–07, 306; decline of 223
cutting for stone 121; 20
cyanide, as treatment 309

Dadd, Richard 234, 235; 1, 32
Daily Telegraph 239, 242, 258
Dalí, Salvador 355, 356 415–16n44
Dalser, Ida 260
Daneau, Lambert 89
Dante Alighieri 79, 365
Darwin, Charles 156, 233, 243, 245, 266, 345
Darwin, Erasmus 156
Daumier, Honoré 112; 16
David (King of Israel) 16, 18, 120
deafness, hysterical 296
Death in Venice 347
decade of the brain 392
Defoe, Daniel 139
Degenerate art 248, 258, 259
degeneration: and mental illness 243, 244–48, 257, 258–59, 265, 266, 270, 301, 392; and shell shock 295
deinstitutionalization 367, 370–71, 374, 375–76, 376; and drugs 367, 368, 369, 378, 425n17
Dekker, Thomas 107
Delay, Jean 380
delinquency 245
delirium 33
delusions 11, 92, 97, 112, 233, 265, 270, 384, 387, 392, 415n41, 416n49
dementia 211, 218, 244, 265, 303, 387, 402
dementia praecox 263, 264, 265, 303, 305; *see also* schizophrenia
demons 52, 53, 67, 68, 72, 77, 87, 90, 91, 177, 178, 181; 11
Deniker, Pierre 380
Denmark 367
depression 15, 34, 94, 188, 236, 271, 275, 318, 319, 348, 383, 387, 392, 402, 404, 408; *see also* melancholia
Descartes, René 167
Deutsch, Albert 365
Deutscher Verein für Psychiatrie (German Society for Psychiatry) 221
Devil, the *see* Satan
devils and madness 20, 24, 40, 72, 88, 95, 415n8; 18; Chinese views 42; *see also* demons
Diagnostic and Statistical Manual of the American Psychiatric Association (DSM) 14, 391–92, 426–27n65; decreasing legitimacy of 406, 407, 408, 409; editions of 388–89, 406, 407, 408, 427n91;

expansion of 389, 406; and insurance payments 389; links to drug treatments 389; and pharmaceutical industry 389, 406, 408; professional importance of 389; psychoanalytic contempt for 388–89, 426–27n65; task forces on 387, 388, 389

diagnosis: cross-national 386, 426n59; growing importance of 386–87, 389, 390; reliability of 388, 389, 392, 406; retrospective 15; routinization of 391–92; uncertainties of 239, 260, 264–65, 303, 385, 386, 387, 407, 408; unreliability of 385–86; see also nosology

diagnostic creep 273, 406–07

Diamond, Hugh W. 245

Dickens, Charles 187, 239, 350

diet and mental illness 92, 94

dissection 33; of brains 209, 213, 217, 218

Distress'd Orphan, The 140–42, 141

disturbances of affect 92, 94, 95, 392

Dix, Dorothea 196–98, 197, 204, 418n21, 22

Dix, Otto 234, 293, 294, 395; 34, 39

Dolhuis see madhouse

Donizetti, Gaetano 142–43, 143, 417n25

Donkin, Horatio 284

Don Quixote 110–12; 16

dopamine 392

doshas 46

Dostoevsky, Fyodor 36, 272

drama and madness 258; Classical Greece 21, 23, 24, 130; as comic relief 106, 107; Elizabethan and Jacobean 101, 102, 103–07, 108, 109; and psychological introspection 348; Roman 102

Dryden, John 92, 94

Dublin 165

Dulle Griet (Mad Meg) 113, 411

Dunham, H. Warren 371

Dunkirk 336

Dürer, Albrecht 94, 114, 115; 25

dynamic psychiatry see psychoanalysis

Earle, Pliny 227

Eder, David 327

ego psychology 332

Egypt 49; plagues of 17

Eitingon, Max 326

Elavil 383

elderly, release from mental hospitals 368–69, 371

electro-convulsive therapy (ECT) 309, 311–13, 312, 318, 319, 321, 382, 422n49; claims of brain damage 312, 313; and Hollywood 317, 321; and lobotomy 316; and loss of legitimacy 319, 320, 321; origins 311–12

electroshock see electro-convulsive therapy

electrotherapy 272, 276, 323; for shell shock 298–99, 299

Eli Lilly 402

Eliot, T. S. 414n59

enemas 272

England 72, 74, 78, 87, 100, 102, 103, 116, 129, 155, 156, 162, 170, 176, 196, 202, 210, 214, 230, 237, 269, 270, 307, 327, 346, 362, 364, 423n6; nineteenth-century asylums 193

English Civil War see English Revolution

English malady, the 162, 168–69, 179, 273

English Revolution 150, 176; 22

Enlightenment, the 10, 86, 160, 177, 181, 344

Entartung (Degeneration) 246

enthusiastic religion 179–80; and madness 174, 175, 176, 346

epilepsy 26, 29, 31–32, 35, 56, 70, 177, 182, 245, 247, 259, 269, 277, 310, 311; 44

Equanil 383

Erasmus, Desiderius 36, 115, 116–19, 117

Eros 347

erysipelas 300, 421n14

Esquirol, Jean-Étienne Dominique 190, 192, 205, 214, 223, 225, 226, 262, 419n75, 419n77

eugenics 266, 267, 420n54

Euripides 21, 22, 102

evil spirits 18, 20, 39, 177, 180

exorcism 43, 53, 67, 71, 76, 77, 88–89, 90, 91, 99, 100, 119, 177, 179, 180, 181, 360; 11; criticisms of 119

Expressionist art 259

extermination of mental patients 266–67, 267, 364, 366

Ezekiel 18, 412n17

Faces in the Water 319

Falret, Jules 242

family: and biological accounts of mental illness 392; and care of the mentally ill 77, 85, 121, 123, 127, 128, 133–34, 136, 192, 196, 197, 198, 199, 201, 202, 238, 268–70, 271, 375–76; in China 423n3; criticism of 205; in Japan 201, 363, 425n6; and mad business 134, 135, 333; as source of pathology 205, 288, 342, 343, 344, 348, 357, 373

Fanon, Frantz 200

faradic electricity 276, 298, 299

Farmer, Frances 320

fear, in treatment 153–55, 156–57, 159, 160

feeble-mindedness 245

feigned madness 100, 101, 103–04, 108–09, 415n36, 416n12; see also malingering

female hysterics 280, 281, 282, 283

Ferranese, Luigi 214

Ferriar, John 160, 161

Ferrier, David 261

fever 33, 412n48

fever therapy 300–02, 309; see also malaria treatment

fiction and madness 112, 140–41, 144, 238, 244–46, 247, 248, 257, 309, 318–20

films and madness 15, 309, 317, 318–21, 324, 332, 348, 349, 351–57; see also Hollywood and individual films

First World War 290–98, 300, 324, 326, 327, 328, 331, 336, 337, 351, 424n24; 37

Fletcher, John 106

Florence: asylum 194; 28; cathedral 415–16n44; and origins of opera 130

Flourens, Jean Pierre 216

focal sepsis 305, 306–07, 307, 319

folk beliefs 31, 40, 53, 67, 74, 78, 86–87, 167, 177, 178, 179, 189, 202; 10, 20

folk remedies 74, 199, 202; 26, 27

Food and Drug Administration (FDA) 367, 381, 404

Fools, Holy 115

Forman, Miloš 320

Forster, John 242

Foucault, Michel 115, 127, 207

Fowler, Lorenzo N. 215, 217

Fox, Edward Long 161, 239

Frame, Janet 319, 320

France 51, 73, 77, 78, 102, 124, 126, 128, 159, 179, 186, 190, 214, 227, 242–43, 271, 290, 364, 366, 378, 380; clerical asylums in 208, 210; and colonial asylums 200; construction of asylums 192–93; and psychoanalysis 325, 326–27, 390; and sense of national decay 246; see also French Revolution

Frances 320

Frances, Allen 408, 427n91

Frank, Johann Peter 137

Frankford Retreat 204, 209

Franklin, Benjamin 182, 186

Frau Cäcilie M. 287, 356

free association 287, 288

Freeman, Walter 314–16, 315, 317, 320, 321, 422n58, 422n59

French Revolution 125, 129, 211, 224, 226, 418n4

frenzy 70, 106, 132

Freud, Anna 334, 356 391

Freud, Sigmund 21, 264, 285, 296, 344, 345, 349, 351, 383, 385, 391, 410, 422n29; and America 328–30, 329, 331, 332, 333, 423n10, 423n11; and Bernheim 284; and Bleuler 326; couch of 397; 41; death 334; exile 334–35, 421n13; as 'Fraud' 327; growing influence of 322, 347; as hater 434n23; and Hollywood 352–53, 354, 355, 356, 425n75, 425n76, 425n80; and hypnosis 283, 284, 287; and hysteria 283, 284, 285, 286, 287; and William James 329, 329, 330; and Jung 324, 330, 33; and literature 350; as neurologist 283, 284; in Paris 277, 283; and psychoanalysis 284–85, 287, 288, 289; and religion 332; and sexual trauma 288; and Vienna 423–24n18; and Wagner-Jauregg 299, 421n13

Freud Museum 41

Fromm-Reichmann, Frieda 357, 391

Fulton, John 316,

Functional Magnetic Resonance Imaging (fMRI) 409

Gaderene swine 20

Galen 28, 29, 33, 36, 37–38, 50, 54, 55, 56, 65, 91, 154, 166, 413n15, 415n14; dissecting a pig 35; re-importation of work into Western Europe 82, 84, 85

Galenic medicine see Hippocratic medicine

Galileo 96, 167, 415n36

Gall, Franz Joseph 213, 214; 30, 31

Gassner, Johann Joseph 177–80, 178, 181

Gay, Peter 344

gender: and madness 28–29, 97; segregation by 207

General Paralysis of the Insane (GPI) 217, 218, 219, 300, 301, 302, 419n75, 420n39, 421n16; proportion of asylum admissions for 218, 301; syphilitic origins of 263, 301, 421n15

genetics and mental disorders 14, 407

George III, madness of 154–55, 189

Germany 12, 52, 77, 78, 80, 177, 179, 242–43, 246, 260, 262–63, 271, 304, 305, 326, 334, 351; Nazi 266–67, 267, 334; political fragmentation and

asylums 195–96, *195*, 220, 366; and psychoanalysis 326, 333, 334
germ theory of disease 260; *see also* bacteriological revolution
Gheel 75, 76, 77
ghosts 40, 88, 89; *Ghosts* 258
Gifford, George 88
Gilman, Charlotte Perkins 420n15
Giotto di Bondone 77
Girard de Cailleux, Henri 226
Glanvill, Joseph 89
Glover, Mary 98–99
Glyndebourne 346; **40**
Goffman, Erving 372, 374; *Asylums* 372
Goldwyn, Samuel 352, 353, 425n75, 425n76
Goodall, Edwin 307
Goodell, William 273
gothic novels 140–42, 238–39
Goya, Francisco 29
Grafton State Hospital *363*; **42**
Granada 51, 81; hospital at 65, *66*
Graves, Thomas Chivers 306, 308
Gray, John 212
Great Confinement 127, 161, 190, 199, 202, 239
Great Depression 272; **36**
Greek medicine *see* Hippocratic medicine, *and* temple medicine
Greeks and madness 20–21, 22, 23, 24, 25, 26, 27, 28, 34, 35, 36, 412n8
Greenberg, Joanne 357
Greenblatt, Milton 370
Greene, Robert 110
Greenson, Ralph 354, 356
Griesinger, Wilhelm 262
Grotjahn, Martin 354
Grub Street 129, 130, 417n22
Guillotin, Joseph 186
Guislain, Joseph 155, 156

Haarlem 124
Hacker, Frederick 354
Hadamar *267*
hadith 68
Hallaran, William Saunders 159
hallucinations 11, 18, 23, 33, 70, 92, 97, 110, 246, 265, 379, 384, 392
Hamlet 103, 107, 108–09, 350, 419n26
Hammond, William Alexander 274
Handel 132, 133, 416n11
Hanwell County Lunatic Asylum 259
Hard Cash 238
Hardy, Thomas 248, 257
Harlem Valley State Hospital 310
Harsnett, Samuel 100, 415n35
Hartford Retreat 204
Hartmann, Heinz 332
Harvard University 246, 309, 312, 315, 329, 330, 404
Haskell, Ebenezer *232*, 233
Haslam, John 210, 387
Hauptmann, Gerhart 248,
Hawaii 276–77
Haydn, Joseph 181,
Haywood, Eliza 140–42, *141*
Heartz, Daniel 133
hebephrenic schizophrenia 265 385; *see also* schizophrenia
Hector 21, 22
hellebore 66, 173; **26**

Hemingway, Ernest 318
Henry VIII (King of England) 74, 78, 115
Heracles 22, 109; **4**
herbal remedies 66, 173; **26, 27**
Hercules *see* Heracles
Hercules Furens 102, 103
Herod (King of Judea) 78–79
Herodotus 24, 25, 26
Hill, Charles 262
Hill, Robert Gardiner 242
Hippocrates 27, 27, 31, 55, 154, 166, 173
Hippocratic medicine 27–29, 31, 32, 33, 34, 39, 40, 41, 46, 50, 53, 55–56, 70, 154; **6**; re-entry into Western Europe 74, 81–84, 85; *see also* humoral theory of disease
Hitchcock, Alfred 355
Hoche, Alfred 266
Hockney, David 346; **40**
Hogarth, William 129, 130, *131*, 165, *175*, 176, 177, 345, 346
Holbein, Hans (the Younger) 115–16, *117*
Hollywood 309, 316, 317, 320–21, 345, 352, 403; and Freud 332, 352, 353, 354, 425n75, 425n76, 425n80; *see also* films and madness
Holmes Jr, Oliver Wendell 266
holy fool 36, 115–19, 416n53
Homer 21, 22, 416n56,
homophobia 346, 347
homosexuality 346, 347, 348, 349; regarded as a disease 349
Hooke, Robert 122
hospitals, in medieval and early modern Europe 84, 85
House of Correction 123, 125
Hughes, Ted 319
Hume, David 88, 170,
humoral theory of disease 28, 29–30, 33, 34, 40–41, 56, 85, 166, 167; **6**; and madness 89–90, 92, 94, 121, 154, 174, 263, 412n44
Hunayn ibn Ishtaq 55, 84
Huston, John 356, 425n80
Huys, Pieter 121
hydrotherapy 272, *363*
Hyman, Steven 404, 408
hyperactivity (ADHD) 407
hypnosis 234, 278; **34**; and Charcot 278, 280–81, 283, 284; and Freud 283, 284, 287; as quackery 284; in wartime 296
hypochondria 91, 163, 164, 165, 166, 170; in modern sense 323
hysteria 12, 29, 35, 56, 98, 99, 163, 166, 167, 177, 245, 246, 273, 274, 348, 420n17; and psychoanalysis 283–87; as somatic illness 170–71, 274, 275, 276, 277, 278, 283, 284, 285, 286, 287

Ibn Sina *see* Avicenna
Ibsen, Henrik 258; *Ghosts* 258
idiocy 243, 247
Idomeneo (Mozart) 132–33
Illenau asylum 194, *195*
Illinois, and mental hospitals 370
illness, as divine punishment 80, 81, 180; and medical marketplace 82
incest 80, 246, 350
India 36, 50, 68, 199, 200, 322
I Never Promised You a Rose Garden 357
infection and mental illness *see* focal sepsis
Inferno 79, 365; *see also* Dante Aligheri

inquisitions in lunacy 239
insanity: as social death 236, 237; types of *13*; *see also* madness, *and* mental illness
Insel, Thomas 408
Institute of Psychiatry, (London) 327, 374
institutionalism 374
institutional neurosis 374
insulin 309; coma therapy 310, 311, 317, 320, 322, 422n38, 422n40; loss of legitimacy as treatment 310, 318
International Classification of Diseases (ICD) 389
Iproniazid 303, 426n55
Iran *see* Persia
iron, used in treatment 68, 182, *184*, 185
Ishaq ibn Imran 56, 65
Islam 46, 50, 53; in India 47; influence on West 51; and madness 53, 65–66, 68–69, 85, 414n25
Islamic medicine 29, 50, 53, 54, 55, 56; and hospitals 65, *66*, 84–85; and lunatics 85
Italian psychiatry 222
Italy: and birth of opera 130; and decline of the asylum 374, 375; political fragmentation and asylums 194–95

Jackson, Elizabeth 98, 99
jails and mentally ill 128
James, Billiam **44**
James, William 246, 329, *329*, 330
Jane Eyre 142
Janet, Pierre 327
Japan 336, 346; and asylums 201, 362–63; and home confinement *201*, 425n6
Jehovah's Witnesses 328
Jeremiah 18, 19
Jesus 68, 73; casting out demons and devils 20, 67, 71, 89, 120; **11**
juvenile delinquency, and psychoanalysis 342
Jews: and Nazis 259; persecution of 333, 335, 342; and psychoanalysis 285, 324, 332
jinn 52, 53, 68, 69
Johnson, Samuel 417n22
Jones, Ernest 327, 328, 423n6; as Freud biographer 344–45, 350
Jorden, Edward 98, 99, 415n32
Joseph, Sir Keith 367
Josephus 18, 412n8
Journal of Mental Science 220, 231, 243
journals, psychiatric 218, 220, 221
Joyce, James 348
Jung, Carl Gustav 324, 328, *329*, *330*, 331

Kanner, Leo 343, 344
Kaufmann, Fritz 297, 298
Kaufmann cure 298, 422n49, 424n24
Keen, W. W. 274
Kellogg, John Harvey 272, 307
Kellogg, William 272
Kerr, John C. 201
Kesey, Ken 319–20
King Lear 100, 101, 350
Kings Park State Hospital 260, 425n3
Klein, Melanie 391
kleptomania 244
Koch, Robert 304
Kraepelin, Emil 263, *264*, 265, 289, 303, 305, 306, 384, 406; and psychoanalysis 326, 385

INDEX

Krafft-Ebing, Richard von 288
Kramer, Peter 383
Kubie, Lawrence 348, 349, 349, 350, 354
Kyd, Thomas 103

laboratory and medicine 304; and
psychiatry 306, 307
Laborit, Henri 380
Lacan, Jacques 390–91, 427n68, 427n69
Lady in the Dark 349, 354
Laing, R. D. 36, 318, 351, 371, 373, 374
Lancet 405
Lange, Jessica 320
Largactil *see* Thorazine
Laurentius, Andrea 91, 92, 415n14
Lavoisier, Antoine 186
Lawrence, D. H. 348
Lawrence, Sir William 211
Leçons du Mardi 277, 283
leeches 94
Leiden 124, 173
Leigh, Vivien 349, 425n76
leprosy 70, 72, 74, 79, 81, 199, 265
lettre de cachet 128, 209, 416n8; abolition
of 129, 416n6
leucotomy *see* lobotomy
Lewis, Sir Aubrey 368, 423n10
Librium 383
Lichterfelde Hospital, Berlin 309
Liebestod (Love/Death) 347
Life 365–66
life expectancy 70; and mental illness 14,
427n89
Lima, Pedro Almeida 313
Lister, Joseph 304, 307
lithium 379
lobotomy 309, 313–16, 318, 315, 321, 322,
348, 350, 367, 382; loss of legitimacy
318; side effects 313, 314; patient
resistance to 317; precision 314, 316;
transorbital 315–16, 315, 422n58,
422n59
Locke, John 160
locomotor ataxia 277
London 74, 84, 98, 106, 122, 129, 130, 132,
153, 216, 270, 298, 334, 342, 346, 360,
374; and asylums 258, 307, 333; and
madhouses 135, 136, 139, 191, 200,
268; 22; and medicine 165; and theatre
109, 110
Lord, Charles 366
Los Angeles County jail 378
Louis XVI (King of France) 129, 186
Lucia di Lammermoor 142–43, 143
Lunacy Commissioners: England 193, 198,
242, 269; Scotland 230
lunatic balls 207
Luther, Martin 88, 116
Lytton, Sir Edward Bulwer 240–42
Lytton, Lady Rosina Bulwer 240–42, 241

Macbeth 108,
McCormick, Edith Rockefeller 330, 331,
423n16
MacDonald, Michael 96
Mackenzie, Henry 144
McLean Asylum 204, 309
mad-doctors 12, 66, 139, 142, 175, 176, 239,
387; term abandoned 210, 303
madhouses 126, 142, 359; emergence of
121, 122, 123, 125, 134–36, 220, 221;

fears of false confinement in 129, 139–
40; harsh treatment in 154, 190–92;
lotteries for 123–24; reputation of 144;
for the rich 220; on the stage 106, 107;
see also trade in lunacy
madness: as alternative way of seeing 36;
and animality 16, 19, 20, 69, 80, 153,
246, 247, 248; 2; and beating 153–54;
and the body 85, 302, 305, 421n7;
changing labels for 364–65, 406, 407;
and dependency 122, 123; as divine
punishment 16, 17–18, 19, 20, 78–79,
90, 91, 107; 2; as incurable 244, 303,
304; and infection 302; and literature
15, 69; losing respectability as a term
210; and meaning 289, 324, 357, 380,
391, 411; and murder 45, 127, 142, 246,
247, 248, 257; naturalistic accounts
of 26–27, 32, 33, 35, 85, 89–90, 95, 96,
107, 121; and possession 31, 40, 42, 85,
88, 89, 90, 91, 95, 176; 18; and religion
20, 21, 22, 24–25, 31, 35, 39, 75–77, 85,
88, 89, 95, 96, 174, 175, 176, 328–29;
and sin 80, 131, 243, 414n68; and
social change 226, 227, 228; and the
supernatural 24, 27, 31, 32, 33, 35, 55,
89–90, 95, 96, 121; and syphilis 258,
259, 300–02, 300; and violence 79, 80,
142–43, 202, 247, 248, 272
Magendie, François 216
magic 71, 96, 107, 176
Maisel, Alfred 365–66
Majnun: as literary character 69; 8; as term
for madness 68–69
Malade imaginaire, Le 164, 165, 188
malaria therapy 300–01, 300, 302, 304,
308, 421n18
male hysterics 278, 280
malingering 99, 166, 188, 195, 276, 278,
295, 296, 297, 336, 420n17; and Nazi
response 424n24; *see also* feigned
madness
Mandeville, Bernard de 171
mania 12, 26, 31, 34, 35, 56, 93, 94, 97, 102,
113, 122, 133, 190, 202, 210, 216, 229,
244, 379, 392; and lithium 379
manic-depressive psychosis 264, 303, 305,
385, 386
Mankiewicz, Joseph 354, 425n76
Man of Feeling, The 144
Mansuri hospital, Cairo 65
Mapother, Edward 327, 423n10
Marcus, Steven, 350
Marcuse, Herbert 351
Maria Theresa (Empress) 180, 184
marijuana 379
Marmor, Judd 354
Marston, John 107, 114
martyrs 70–71, 72, 74, 75
Maryland 377
Mason, Joseph 134
Massachusetts 196, 370
materialism 211, 213
Maudsley, Henry 243–44, 265
Maupassant, Guy de 258, 280
Mayer, Louis B.: 353, 354; Margaret 354
mechanical restraint 202, 242, 419n26; *see
also* chains, *and* straitjackets
Medea 22–23, 102, 417n15
Medicaid and Medicare 371
medical schools and psychiatry 260

Medico-Psychological Association 220, 307
Meduna, Ladislas 311
melancholia 26, 31, 34, 35, 56, 114, 167, 190,
229, 415n41; as fashionable disorder 91,
92; and genius 92, 94; in Renaissance
91, 94, 95
Mellon, Mary 331, 423n16
memory: creation of 327; loss of 293; and
madness 286, 287, 296
Meprobate 383
Mendell, Werner 374
meningitis, deliberate induction of 309
Menninger, Karl 333, 354, 356
Menninger, William 333, 338, 340, 354
Menninger Clinic 333, 338, 340, 341, 427n67
mental hospital: census of 362, 363,
364, 366–67, 368, 369, 371, 374; late
twentieth-century critiques of 369–71,
372–73, 385
mental illness: aetiology of 14, 385, 388,
401; categorical views of 389, 407;
diagnosis of 14, 385–88; dimensional
views of 385, 389, 407; as disease
of civilization 160–70, 228–29, 243;
increase of 222, 223, 273, 406; as myth
11, 99, 373, 387; phenomenology of 391
Mercier, Charles 237, 295, 423n9
mercury 173, 301
Mesmer, Franz Anton 181, 182, 184, 184,
185, 186, 222
mesmerism 182, 183, 186, 187; clinics
dispensing 186; investigation of 186–
87; ridicule of 182, 183; *see also* animal
magnetism
Methodism 174, 175, 176, 179
metrazol 311, 312, 322
Meyer, Adolf 305, 308
Meynert, Theodore 284
microscopy and mental illness 244, 263
Middleton, Thomas 106
Miles, Sir Jonathan 136
Milledgeville State Asylum (Georgia) *see*
Central State Hospital
Milligan, Spike 337
Miltown 383
mind: and body 81, 95, 211–12, 316; and
soul 211–12, 214
miracle plays 78–79, 415n63
miraculous cures 31, 67, 68, 71, 73, 74, 78,
100, 179; 10, 12–14; Erasmus's critique
of 118
Mitchell, Silas Weir 229, 274, 275, 276, 277,
420n15, 420n17, 423n4
Molière (Jean-Baptiste Poquelin) 164, 165
'Mom', as toxic figure 343, 344; *see also*
refrigerator mothers
monasteries 70, 82, 84, 89, 194, 195
Moniz, Egas 313, 314, 318
monoamine oxidase inhibitors 383, 426n55
monomania 216, 264
Monro, Thomas 139
Monroe, Marilyn 356, 425n76
Montpellier 82, 91, 127–28, 416n2
Moore, J. W. 263, 421n15
Moorfields 122, 136, 137
moral insanity 264
moral treatment: debates about 207,
208; and medical treatment 208–09,
210, 213, 217, 229; origins of 160–61,
202–05; and phrenology 214, 216; role
of superintendent 205, 206

445

morbid introspection 327
More, Thomas 116
Morehouse, G. R. 274
Morel, Bénédict-Augustin 243, 246, 247
Morison, Sir Alexander 228, *229*, 234; **34**
mortality, and mental illness 406; *see also*
   life expectancy
Moscow 196
Moses 17
mother's little helper *382*, 383
Mott, Sir Frederick 307, 421n16
Moynihan, Sir Berkeley 307
Mozart, Wolfgang Amadeus 132, 181
Muhammad 50, 68
Munthe, Axel 280, 283
museums of madness 223, 259, 361
music and madness 18, 120, 121, 132,
   142–43, 182, *184*, 185; **19**; *see also* opera
   and madness
mutism 296, 297, 298–99
mystery plays *see* miracle plays
mysticism and madness 36
myths: Greek 32, and madness 23, 113

nakedness and madness 20, 69, 80, 113,
   114, *114*, 116, 130, 190, 192, 365, *366*;
   18
Napier, Richard 96, 97; **15**
Naples 82; and syphilis 162
Napoleon *see* Bonaparte, Napoleon
narcissism 323, 407
Nash, John 310–11
National Institute for Health and Care
   Excellence (NICE) 404
National Institute of Mental Health, (NIHM)
   372, 392, 408
Nazis: and arts 259; **39**; and degeneration
   246, 266; extermination of Jews 335;
   extermination of mental patients
   335; and psychoanalysis 333–34, 334,
   421n13; **41**
Nebraska 377
Nebuchadnezzar 16, 19, 20, 78; **2**
Nero (Roman Emperor) 71, 102
nerves: and mental illness 154, 164, 166,
   167, 168, 169–70, 171, 172, 173, 188–89,
   212, 216, 217, 224, 245, 262, 271–72,
   273, 274, 275, 420n17; **34**; Mesmer's
   treatment of 182, 184–85, 186, 187, 188;
   nature of nervous system 174; in war
   295, 298, *335*
Netherlands 51, 78,120, 123, 125, 413n5
neurasthenia 273, 274, 275, 276, 277, 420n17
neurology 153, 229, 261, 273, 274, 275,
   277, 284, 296, 297, 323, 330, 421n7; and
   psychoanalysis 331
neuropathology 284, 287
neuropsychiatry 295, 298, 421n7
neuroscience 391, 407, 409, 410
neuroses 279, 283, 312, 333, 339, 353, 388,
   426n65
neurosis 348, 426–27n65; and the military
   336
neurosurgery 315, 316
neurotransmitters and mental illness 14
Newnham, William 212
Newton, Isaac 96, 167, 174, 181
New York 204, 209, 260, 310; mental
   hospitals 316, 370
New York State Asylum for Lunatics, Utica
   220

New Yorker, The 344, 345
New Zealand 199, 320, 322
Nicholson, Jack 320, *321*
Nietzsche, Friedrich 258, 420n39
Nigeria 199
Night, The (*Die Nacht*) 292, 395; **38**
Nixon, Richard 371
Nizami 69; **8**
Noguchi, Hideyo 263, 421n15
Nonne, Max 296
Nordau, Max 246, 258, 420n37
nosology 263, 264–65, 336, 385, 387, 388,
   389
nursing homes 375, 376, 377
Nutton, Vivian 36
nymphomania 244

Odysseus 21
Oedipal conflicts 288
Oedipus 21, 23, 102, 350
'On Being Sane in Insane Places' 386
One Flew Over the Cuckoo's Nest (novel and
   film) 319, 320, *321*, 357
opera and madness 130, 131, 132, 133,
   142–43, *143*, 345, 346, 347, 416n11,
   416n12, 417n15, 425n62; **40**
Ophelia 108, 416n12; **17**
opium 379
Ordeal of Gilbert Pinfold, The 379
Ordinary People 357
Oregon 377
Orlando (Handel) 132, 133
Orlando furioso 109, 110, *111*
Orlansky, Harold 365
Osler, Sir William 413n11
Ottomans 49, 50, 51, 53–54
outpatient treatment 272, 316, 339, 341
Owen, Wilfred 292, 296; **37**
Oxford University 82, 239

Paget, Sir James 198
Pappenheim, Bertha 285–87, *286*, 421n31
Paracelsus 415n25
Paradis, Maria Theresia 182–84, 187
paranoid schizophrenia 265, 385
parentectomy 344
Pargeter, William 139
Paris 82, 84, 116, 125, 127, 128, 129, 160,
   190, 228, 234, 258, 314, 380, 415n36;
   and Charcot 278–81, 296; hospital
   medicine 126, 136, 217, 263; and
   hysteria 277, 278–79; madhouses 209,
   268, 416n7; and medieval medicine
   82; and mesmerism 184–86, 186–87,
   190; and moral treatment 204, 205; and
   phrenology 214; and psychoanalysis 390
Parkinson's disease 277, 403
Pascal, Blaise 153
passions and madness 80, 92, 94, 108, 153,
   225, 226, 246, 248, 347
Pasteur, Louis 304, 317
pathological anatomy and medicine 216,
   263; and psychiatry 217
patients: admission 232; dehumanization
   of 391, 392; mistreatment of 232–33,
   232; murder of, in Nazi Germany
   266–67, 364; neglect of 263; nervous
   274; psychiatric contempt for 265, 266,
   392; and psychoanalysis 332–33, 339,
   341, 384, 427n71; resistance of 231,
   232–33, 239–41, 308, *317*; starvation

of, in France and Britain 364; views of
   the asylum 232, 233, 234, 235, 236, 237;
   vulnerability of 308
Paton, Stewart 307
Patroclus 21, 22
Patton, Robert E. 369
penicillin 302
Perceval, John 239–40
Persia 36, 48, 50, 54, 68; 7, **8**
pessimism: Freud's 332, 335; therapeutic
   229, 230, 231, 263, 265, 303–04
Peter Grimes 346–47
pharmaceutical industry 382, 383, 384,
   386–87, 401; and concealment of
   evidence 403, 404, 405; profits of 401,
   402, 404, 405, 427n76
phenothiazines 380; marketing of 302,
   side effects of 403, 404; *see also* anti-
   psychotic drugs, *and* Thorazine
Philadelphia 204, 209, 365, *366*
photography and mental illness *219*, 233,
   235, 244, *245*, 281, *282*
phototherapy *271*
phrenitis 35, 56
phrenological busts *215*, 217; **30**
phrenology 213–17, 233; **31**; loss of
   respectability 216, 217
physiognomy and mental illness *13*, 229,
   233, 243, 244, *245*
Pierce, Bedford 261
Pilgrim, The 106
pilgrims 52, 72, 74, 75, 84, 180; **12–14**
Pilgrim State Hospital 260, 376, 425n3
Pinel, Philippe 161, 190, 204, 205, 208, 209,
   226, 227, 419n77; **24**
Plath, Sylvia 318–19
Plato 35, 46, 50, 118, 119; **3**
Platter, Felix 95
Plautus 102, 415n38
poetry and mental illness 236, 237, 258,
   292, 258–59
poison gas 290, 291
Pontigny, abbey of 73
Pope, Alexander 165, 176, 417n22
Pope: Alexander II 81; as Antichrist 88;
   Gregory I 72; Paul IV 116; Pius VI 180;
   Urban II 81
Popper, Karl 351
pornography, Victorian 350
Portugal 313
possession 67, 68, 69, 72, 87, *90*, 91, 95, 99,
   111, 119, 177, *178*, 180
Post-Traumatic Stress Disorder (PTSD) 336
Powell, Enoch 369
Praise of Folly, The 36, 115, 116–19
'primitive' people as exempt from madness
   168, 224, 227
print, and culture 86, 121; and medical
   culture 82–84
prisons and the mentally ill 378
prophets, Jewish 18, 19, 36
prostitutes 124, 127, 128, 245, 246, 248, 259,
   419n75; **23**
Protestantism 86–87, 88, 100, 116, 119, 120,
   179, 328–29
Prozac 383, 404, 426n55
pseudo-patients 386
psychiatric legitimacy, threats to 242,
   406–07
psychiatric screening, in Second World War
   337, 338

psychiatry 11, 12, 14, 199, 401; American, expansion of 338, 339; colonial 199, 200, 201, 202, 322–23; directive-organic 341, 384; and drugs 379, 380, 381–83, 384, 385, 401; and general medicine 316; in Germany 262–65; an industry of death 373, 403; legal criticisms of 386; military 295, 296, 297, 336, 337, 338, 339; move beyond the asylum 273, 276, 322–24, 331–32, 383–84; neurological criticisms of 261, 276–77; as oppression 321, 373–74; origins of term 221–22; and physical treatments 318; precarious state of 260, 303–04, 305, 384, 386, 387, 391–92; recruitment to 260, 261; and social control 385, training 338, 385; use of term in Anglophone culture 303
psychoanalysis: and advertising 325, *381*; Americanization of 332, 333, 339–40, 385; and anthropology 351; appeal of 289, 323, 325, 384–85, 390–91; and the arts 324–25, 345, 347, 348; beginnings of 287, 288, 289, 322–23; in Britain 390, 391, 423n9, 423n10; cultural influence of 325, 335, 341 350, 384–85; decline of 325, 388–89, 390, 391, 406, 426–27n67; and diagnosis 385, 387–88, 406; and drug treatments 384; expansion of 324, 335, 384–85, 424 n40, 424n41; in France 390; as general science of mind 385; in German-speaking Europe 325–26, 333–34; and Hollywood 353–57; hostility towards 325, 326–27, 331, 332; institutes 333, 343, 380; and literary criticism 350; patients of 285–87, 302; as pseudo-science 351; and psychosis 341, 391, 427n71; schisms of 324, 331, 334–35, 391; and Second World War 335, 338, 339; and the United States 328, 329, 330, 331, 332, 334, 335, 339, 340, 341, 379, 381, 384–85, 390, 423n6; and universities 390, 424n40
psychological accounts of mental illness 296–97; as quackery, 284, 332, 422n29
psychology: academic 325; clinical 380
psychopharmacology 14, 368, 380–82, 401, 402, 403, 408; and perceptions of mental illness 368, 378, 379
psychoses 14, 289, 306, 312, 318, 357, 426–27n65
psychosomatic illness 343
psychotherapeutics 287, 288, 289, 296–97, 328–29, 331, 333, 338, 339, 379
psychotropic drugs *see* anti-depressants, *and* anti-psychotics
purges 28, 66, 74, 92, 94, 96, 171, 172, 302, 412n48
Puritans 98, 99, 100, 107, 415n41
Pussin, Jean-Baptiste and Marguerite 161, 204
Putnam, James Jackson 329, 330

Quakers 196, 202, *366*
qi 40, 43
Qu'ran 53, 68

racial domination, psychological consequences of 200
Radcliffe, John 164
Rake's Progress: Hogarth 130, *131*, 345; Stravinsky 345–46; **40**

rape 257, 292, 348, 395; **38**; of patients 191, 192, 320
rates of institutionalization 201, 202
Rauvolfia serpentina 199, 418n29; **27**
Ray, Isaac 227
Reade, Charles 238, 419n26
Reconquista, Christian 51, 81
Redlich, Fritz 374
Rees, T. P. 338
Reformation 70, 77, 78, 86, 100, 119–20, 414n70,
refrigerator mothers 344, 357
Reil, Johann Christian 221
relics 414n 52, 414n53; power of 72, 73
religion as neurosis 332
religious cures for madness 20, 31–32, 72–74, 75, 85, 95, 174, 176, 177, *178*, 202, 328–29
repression 287, 288, 289, 324, 327, 346, 348, 357
Reserpine *see Rauvolfia*
rest cure 275, 276, 323, 420n15, 420n16
Rey, Dr Félix 234; **33**, **35**
Rhazes (al-Rhazi) 47, 84
Rhône-Poulenc 380, 381
Richardson, Samuel 170, 189
Rieff, Philip 351
Risperdal 402, 405
Rivers, W. H. R. 296, 421n8
Robben Island 199
Robinson, Nicholas 154, 171, 172
Rockefeller, John D. 272, *330*, 423n16
Rockefeller Foundation 201, 315, *323*, 343
Rogers, John 191
Rolling Stones 383
Roman empire 21, 27, 36, 37, 38, 45–46, 48; and Christianity 21, 67, 69, 70–71, 73; collapse of 46, 49, 70, 82; drama 101–02, 103; and Greek physicians 36; and hospitals 65; and madness 31–35, 121
Roman Empire (Eastern) *see* Byzantium
Rome 194, 311, *312*
Romm, May 353, 354, 356
Ronde, La (Reigen) 248
Rosen, George 18
Rosenhan, David 386
Rowlandson, Thomas *138*
Royer-Collard, Antoine-Athanase 218
Rubens, Peter Paul 27, 114, 119, 120; **18**
Rufus of Ephesus 56, 91, 415n14
Rush, Benjamin 156–57, *157*, 226, 227
Russia: asylums 173, 195–96; collapse of tsarist regime 290, psychiatry in 196

Sade, Marquis de 128, 209, 416n6
St: Catherine of Siena 73, 414n55; Dymphna 75–77; Foy 73–74; **10**; Ignatius 120; **18**; Martin of Tours 71; Zeno, bishop of Verona 76, 77
St Elizabeth's Hospital 372, 421n18
St Luke's Hospital for Lunatics 136, 137, *137*, *138*
saints, Christian 72, 73, *75*, 416n50; graves as sites of pilgrimage 73, 74
St Vitus's dance 177
Sakel, Manfred 309, 310, 311, 312, 317
Salpêtrière 125, 126, 127; **23**, **24**; hysteria at 277, 278, *282*, 283; insane in 125, 161, 190
Salvarsan 301
Samuel 17, 18

San Bonifacio Hospital, (Florence) 194; **28**
San Clemente asylum 194, 358, *359*; **43**
San Clemente Palace Hotel 358, *359*, 360, 361; **43**
Sandoz 405
San Servolo asylum 194, 358
Sargant, William 315
Sartre, Jean-Paul 356
Sassoon, Siegfried 296, 297; **37**
Satan 20, 71, 78, 87, 88, 89, 95, 96, 98, 99, 100, 120, 177, 180, 181, 415n41
Saul 16, 17–18, 78, 120, 412n8; **19**
Savage, Sir George 271, 420n14
scarification 92
schizophrenia 15, 265, 310, 311, 321, 326, 343, 348, 367, 369, 385, 386, 402, 408, 426n59; and second-generation anti-psychotics 405; as super-sanity 351, 373–74; and talking cure 341; *see also* dementia praecox
Schnitzler, Arthur 248
Schröder, Paul 222
Schur, Max 334
Science 386
Scientific Revolution 86, 174
Scientology 321, 373, 403, 408
scleroses 277, 278, 331
Scotland 198, 230, 231
Scotsman, The 222
Scott, Sir Walter 142
sculpture and madness 113
Second World War 325, 334, 335, 343, 364, 379, 391, 401; and psychiatric casualties 336–38, 424n24
selective serotonin re-uptake inhibitors (SSRIs) 404, 405, 426n55
self-mutilation 259
Selznick, David O. 353, 354, 355, 356
Selznick, Irene 353, 354, 355
Seneca 102
Seroquel 402, 405
serotonin 392
Seventh Day Adventist Church 272, 328
sex and madness 246, 247, 258, 259, 288–89, 347, 401
Shaftesbury, Lord, and son Maurice 269
Shakespeare, William 36, 100, 101, 103, 104, 106, 415n38; and madness 101, 103, 107, 188–89
Sharfstein, Steven 390
shell shock 295–99, *299*, 336, 338, 356; early symptoms of 293–94; early theories of 293; as hysteria 296–97; post-war fate of victims 324; and psychoanalysis 324
Shelley, Percy Bysshe 194, 258–59
's-Hertogenbosch asylum, 122, *123*, 125
Ship of Fools: Bosch 59, 114; **3**; Brant 115
Shirley, James 107
shock therapies 155–59, 173, 309–10, 311–13, 316, 317, 318–19, 320, 321, 322, 354, 357, 366, 382, 384; *see also* electro-convulsive therapy; insulin coma therapy; Metrazol
shrines: and cures in Christianity 67, 74, 77, 180; **12–14**; in Greece 31
Sicily 52, 195, 338
sidewalk psychotics 376, *376*
slavery 198
Simmel, Ernst 354
Smith, Kline & French 381, 382

Smollett, Tobias 140
Snake Pit, The 317
Snape, Andrew 153, 189
social class and mental illness 92, 96, 97, 135–36, 168–70, 172, 179, 185, 188, 224, 226, 227, 228–29, 234–35, 258, 268–69, 278; and psychoanalysis 323, 324, 341
sociology and mental health 371, 372, 373
social work, psychiatric 380
Socrates 35, 118, 416n56
Sophocles 21, 46, 114, 350
Soranus 29
South Africa 199, 290
Spain 23, 50, 51, 52, 65, 78, 102, 200, 415n36; early asylums 66, 85; expulsion of Moors and Jews 51, 81–82, 413n5; and Netherlands 120, 413n5
Spanish Tragedy, The 103, 106
Spellbound 355, 355, 356
spiritual healing 67, 95, 96, 97, 100
Spitzer, Robert 387, 388, 389, 408, 427n91
Spitzka, Edward 261
spleen 91, 163, 164, 165, 166, 171
Spock, Benjamin 341, 342
Spurzheim, Johann 213, 214; 30
Stadelmann, Dr Heinrich 234; 34
statistics and insanity 232, 426n62
Stekel, William 425n63
sterilization, compulsory 26, 266, 267, 420n54
stigma 11, 14, 129, 220, 260, 265, 266, 268, 270–71, 344, 363
straitjacket 139, 155, 206, 225
Stravinsky, Igor 345, 346; 40
Streetcar Named Desire, A (play and film) 348, 349
Streptoccocus pyogenes 300, 421n14
strychnine, as cure 309, 311
Studien über Hysterie (Studies on Hysteria) 284, 286, 326, 345
Suddenly Last Summer 350
suicide 245, 247, 248, 259, 272, 318, 319, 348; and anti-depressants 404
Sullivan, Harry Stack 391
Supreme Court (United States) 266
Surrealist art 347
Sweden 367
Swift, Jonathan 114, 114, 165, 176
swinging chair 156–57, 158–59, 158
Swiss Psychiatric Society 310
Sydenham, Thomas 166, 168
symbols and madness 113, 132, 289, 324, 330, 345, 347, 356
syphilis 168, 173, 219, 258, 259, 331, 417n25; 25; origins of 162; tertiary 15, 263, 277, 300, 301, 302, 420n39; treatments for 163, 300, 301, 302, 421n18
symptoms, as diagnostic markers 388, 407, 408
Syria 48, 49, 54; 5
Szasz, Thomas 11, 318, 371, 373, 374, 387; and Scientology 373

tardive dyskinesia 403, 405
Tavistock Clinic 327, 338, 339
Tenon, Jacques 126, 416n7
Tess of the D'Urbervilles 248, 257
Texas 371
Thanatos (death drive) 347, 350, 425n63
Thérèse Raquin 246–47

Thorazine 367, 368, 369, 378, 380, 381, 381, 382, 405; see also phenothiazines
Three Essays on the Theory of Sexuality 331
Ticehurst Asylum 233, 239, 240, 269, 270
Time 317, 339–40
Times, The 222, 239, 242
Titus Andronicus 103–06
Todestrieb see Thanatos
Tofranil 383
Tolstoy, Leo 36, 280
torpillage 298
torture 200, 298–99
Toulouse-Lautrec, Henri de 258
toxic psychiatry 403
trade in lunacy 129, 134–36, 176, 237–38, 268; reputation of 139–40, 144, 220, 221, 237–39
Tranquillizer, the 156–57, 157
tranquillizers 383, 402
translation: of Arabic and Syriac texts 82; of Greek and Latin texts 55
trauma, and madness 85, 91, 286, 288, 293, 295, 296–97, 298, 322, 323, 324, 348, 357; physical 274; see also shell shock
travel, as remedy for mental illness 173
Treatise on Cold Damage Disorders 42
Trenton State Hospital 306, 310, 362
trepanation 121
Treponema pallidum 421n21
Très riches heures du duc de Berry 77; 11
trick cyclists 339
tricyclic anti-depressants 383, 426n55
Trilling, Lionel 350
tuberculosis 165, 190, 210, 421n18, 426n55
Tuke, Daniel Hack 13, 243
Tuke, Samuel 202, 209
Tuke, William 161, 202, 203, 208, 209, 223, 418n10
Twain, Mark 216, 217

unconscious, Freudian 288, 289, 325, 326, 331–22, 347
United States 262, 273, 305, 307, 311, 365, 367; and asylums 190, 196–98, 201, 209, 210, 220, 260, 362, 365, 370–71; and commitment laws 260; and deinstitutionalization 364, 367, 368, 370, 375, 376, 376; and drug company profits 401–02, 427n76, 427n77; and lobotomy 315, 316, 317, 318; as medical backwater 275; and phrenology 214; and psychoanalysis 325, 328, 333, 334, 335, 340, 341, 390; and sanitariums 272; and veterans 324; and Second World War 338

validity, psychiatric diagnosis 388–89, 392
Valium 383
van Gogh, Vincent 234, 258–59; 33, 35
Vapours, the 163, 164, 166, 171, 176
Venice 35, 55, 82, 83, 130, 258, 347; asylums 194, 358, 359, 360
Victoria (Queen of England) 198, 211, 241, 271
Vienna 181, 182, 184, 187, 193, 194, 195, 248, 260, 299, 310, 326; and Freud 277, 278, 283, 285, 288, 324, 331, 333, 334, 352, 397
Vietnam War 336
Vincent, Clovis 298, 299
Virgil 79, 416n56

Virgin Mary 78, 89, 90
visual arts and madness 15, 112–14, 119–20, 121, 129–30, 259
Voltaire (François-Marie Arouet) 87
vomits 28, 66, 74, 92, 96, 171, 302, 412n48

Wagner, Richard 347, 425n62
Wagner-Jauregg, Julius 298, 299, 300–02, 300, 305, 308, 421n13, 421n21
Walpole, Horace 176
war and psychiatric illness 336–38; see also combat exhaustion, and shell shock
war crimes 299
Warburton, Thomas 135, 136, 191, 192
warm baths as remedy 92
Warren, Richard 189
War Triptych (Der Krieg) 293, 395; 39
Washington, DC 372
Wasserman test 421n15, 421n18
water cures 271
Watson, James D. 344
Watts, James 314, 316, 317
Waugh, Evelyn 379
Weill, Kurt 349, 354
Weinberg, S. Kirson 371
Wesley, John 174, 176
Western imperialism 56; and asylums 199–201, 202, 322, 323
West Riding Lunatic Asylum 219, 233, 261
Wexler, Bruce 410
Wharton, Edith, and rest cure 420n15
White, Ellen 272
Whitefield, George 174, 175, 176, 177
Wilhelm II, Kaiser 290, 291
Williams, Tennessee 348, 350
Willis, Reverend Francis 154, 155
Willis, Thomas 153, 154, 166, 167, 168, 172, 173
Wing, John K. 374
Winnicott, Donald 342
Winslow, Forbes 220
witches 86, 87, 87, 88, 89, 91, 94, 96, 98, 99, 167, 179–80
witch hunts, European 86–87, 88, 414n1
Wollstonecraft, Mary 142
Woman in White, The 268, 278
women and madness 28–29, 30, 66, 97, 138, 164, 176, 194, 240–42, 274, 280, 281, 318, 358, 420n17; 43
Woodward, Samuel 214, 227
Woolf, Virginia 271, 275, 420n14
Work, Hubert 307
workhouses 191, 196
wrongful confinement, claims of 129, 139, 140, 141, 142, 232

Yahweh 16, 17, 19; 5
Yale Medical School 316, 374
Yealland, Lewis 298, 299
yellow bile 65, 91
Yellow Emperor's Inner Canon 41, 42
yin-yang theory 40–41
York Asylum 192, 418n10
York Retreat 161, 196, 202, 203, 203, 209, 243, 418n10
Yunani medicine 47

Zola, Émile 246–48, 258
Zurich 325, 326
Zweig, Arnold 328, 423n13
Zyprexa 402, 405